GOSPEL WRITING

GOSPEL WRITING

A Canonical Perspective

Francis Watson

WILLIAM B. EERDMANS PUBLISHING COMPANY
GRAND RAPIDS, MICHIGAN / CAMBRIDGE, U.K.

Published 2013 by
Wm. B. Eerdmans Publishing Co.
2140 Oak Industrial Drive N.E., Grand Rapids, Michigan 49505 /
P.O. Box 163, Cambridge CB3 9PU U.K.

Printed in the United States of America

18 17 16 15 14 13   7 6 5 4 3 2 1

Library of Congress Cataloging-in-Publication Data

Watson, Francis, 1956-
Gospel writing: a canonical perspective / Francis Watson.
      pages   cm
Includes bibliographical references and index.
ISBN 978-0-8028-4054-7 (pbk.: alk. paper)
1. Bible. N.T. Gospels — Criticism, interpretation, etc.
2. Bible. N.T. Gospels — Canon.   I. Title.

BS2555.52.W38   2013
226'.066 — dc23

2012046193

www.eerdmans.com

Contents

Contents

Abbreviations

AB	Anchor Bible
ABR	*Australian Biblical Review*
ACT	Ancient Christian Texts
AJA	*American Journal of Archaeology*
Aland	K. Aland, *Synopsis Quattuor Evangeliorum*
ANF	Ante-Nicene Fathers
ArtB	*Art Bulletin*
AYB	Anchor Yale Bible
BEThL	Bibliotheca Ephemeridum Theologicarum Lovaniensium
BHT	Beiträge zur historischen Theologie
Bib	*Biblica*
BZ	*Biblische Zeitschrift*
BZNW	Beihefte zur Zeitschrift für die Neutestamentliche Wissenschaft
CBQ	*Catholic Biblical Quarterly*
CCSA	Corpus Christianorum Series Apocryphorum
CCSL	Corpus Christianorum Series Latinorum
CSCO	Corpus Scriptorum Christianorum Orientalium
CSEL	Corpus Scriptorum Ecclesiasticorum Latinorum
DBI	*Dictionary of Biblical Interpretation*
EKKNT	Evangelisch-Katholischer Kommentar zum Neuen Testament
ETL	*Ephemerides Theologicae Lovanienses*
EvTh	*Evangelische Theologie*
EVV	English Versions
FC	Fathers of the Church

FRLANT	Forschungen zur Religion und Literatur des Alten und Neuen Testaments
GCS	Die Griechischen Christlichen Schriftsteller der ersten drei Jahrhunderte
HE	*Historia Ecclesiastica*
HNT	Handbuch zum Neuen Testament
HTR	*Harvard Theological Review*
ICC	International Critical Commentary
JAAR	*Journal of the American Academy of Religion*
JBL	*Journal of Biblical Literature*
JECS	*Journal of Early Christian Studies*
JR	*Journal of Religion*
JSHJ	*Journal for the Study of the Historical Jesus*
JSNT	*Journal for the Study of the New Testament*
JSNTSupp	Journal for the Study of the New Testament Supplements
JTI	*Journal of Theological Interpretation*
JTISupp	Journal of Theological Interpretation Supplements
JTS	*Journal of Theological Studies*
LCL	Loeb Classical Library
LW	*Gotthold Ephraim Lessing, Werke*
LWB	*Gotthold Ephraim Lessing, Werke und Briefe*
MT	Masoretic Text
Nestle-Aland[27]	Nestle-Aland, *Novum Testamentum Graece,* 27th edition
NHC	Nag Hammadi Codex
NHMS	Nag Hammadi and Manichean Studies
NHL	*Nag Hammadi Library*
NHS	Nag Hammadi Studies
NIGTC	New International Greek Testament Commentary
NovT	*Novum Testamentum*
NovTSupp	Novum Testamentum Supplements
NPNF	Nicene and Post-Nicene Fathers
NTS	*New Testament Studies*
PG	Patrologia Graeca
PL	Patrologia Latina
PNTC	Pelican New Testament Commentaries
SBLSS	Society of Biblical Literature Seminar Series
SBT	Studies in Biblical Theology
SC	Sources Chrétiennes

SecC	*Second Century*
SJT	*Scottish Journal of Theology*
SNTSMS	Studiorum Novi Testamenti Societas Monograph Series
SNTW	Studies of the New Testament and Its World
ThHKNT	Theologischer Handkommentar zum Neuen Testament
ThZ	*Theologische Zeitschrift*
TU	Texte und Untersuchungen zur Geschichte der altchristlichen Literatur
VC	*Vigiliae Christianae*
VCSupp	Vigiliae Christianae Supplements
WMANT	Wissenschaftliche Monographien zum Alten und Neuen Testament
WUNT	Wissenschaftliche Untersuchungen zum Neuen Testament
ZNW	*Zeitschrift für die neutestamentliche Wissenschaft und die Kunde der älteren Kirche*

Ancient Texts

1 Apol.	*1 Apologia*
1 Clem.	*1 Clement*
2 Apol.	*2 Apologia*
2 Clem.	*2 Clement*
ActsTh	*Acts of Thomas*
Adv. Haer.	*Adversus Haereses*
AH	*Arabic Harmony (Diatessaron)*
Ant.	*Jewish Antiquities*
ApJn	*Apocryphon of John*
BJ	*Bellum Judaicum*
CF	*Codex Fuldensis*
C. Iovin.	*Contra Iovinianum*
Comm. in Matth.	*Commentariorum in Matthaeum*
Conf.	*Confessiones*
De Civ. Dei	*De Civitate Dei*
De Cons. Evang.	*De Consensu Evangelistarum*
De Doct. Chr.	*De Doctrina Christiana*
De Mens.	*De Mensuris et Ponderibus*
De Praescr.	*De Praescriptione Haereticorum*
De Vir. Ill.	*De Viris Illustribus*

Dial.	*Dialogus cum Tryphone*
Did.	*Didache*
Eph.	Ignatius, *To the Ephesians*
GEger	*Egerton Gospel* (= "*Unknown Gospel*")
GEgy	*Gospel according to the Egyptians*
GHeb	*Gospel according to the Hebrews*
GMary	*Gospel of Mary*
GPet	*Gospel of Peter*
GTh	*Gospel of Thomas*
HE	*Historia Ecclesiastica*
Hist. Rom.	*Historia Romana*
Hom. in Luc.	*Homiliae in Lucam*
Hom. in Matt.	*Homiliae in Mattheum*
Hom. in Num.	*Homiliae in Numeros*
HypAr	*Hypostasis of the Archons*
IGMt	*Infancy Gospel of Matthew*
In Apoc.	*Commentarii in Apocalypsim Iohannis*
In Ioan.	*In Ioannem*
In Luc.	*Expositio Evangelii secundum Lucam*
mMenah.	Mishnah, *Menahot*
mNed.	Mishnah, *Nedarim*
mNeg.	Mishnah, *Nega'im*
mPes.	Mishnah, *Pesaḥim*
mSanh.	Mishnah, *Sanhedrin*
mShab.	Mishnah, *Shabbat*
Paed.	*Paedagogus*
Pan.	*Panarion*
Pasch.	*Peri Pascha*
PJas	*Protevangelium of James*
P. Oxy.	*Oxyrhynchus Papyri*
Rom.	Ignatius, *To the Romans*
Smyrn.	Ignatius, *To the Smyrnaeans*
Strom.	*Stromateis*
ThCont	*Book of Thomas the Contender*
Trall.	Ignatius, *To the Trallians*

Acknowledgements

I am grateful to members of the New Testament Seminars at Aberdeen and, more recently, Durham for their willingness to engage with the material and ideas developed in this book. Discussions with my former Aberdeen colleagues Simon Gathercole and Peter Williams — about the "Q" hypothesis, the *Gospel of Thomas,* the Coptic language, miscellaneous papyrus fragments, and much else — were particularly helpful during the early stages of this project. Equally formative was my participation in the three-year project on "The Identity of Jesus" held under the auspices of the Center for Theological Inquiry at Princeton. I am grateful to the group as a whole for the extraordinary quality of theological, hermeneutical, and exegetical debate that it sustained; my particular thanks to the co-chairs, Richard Hays and Beverly Gaventa, and to Dale Allison for many fruitful conversations. To Mark Goodacre I am indebted for unbelief in Q and for helpful comments on drafts of chapters 3 and 4 of this book. In working alongside Jens Schroeter, Jörg Frey, and Clare Rothschild as editors of *Early Christianity,* my conviction has been strengthened that New Testament scholarship needs to be concerned with the second century no less than the first. Conversations with John Barclay, Judith Lieu, Lewis Ayres, Walter Moberly, Jane Heath, and Paul Foster have helped to sharpen my thinking at a number of points. Jeff Spivak, for three years my Research Assistant, performed invaluable service especially in obtaining out-of-the-way secondary literature and new images of relevant papyri. Todd Brewer and Matthew Crawford have also provided much-valued assistance in the later stages of the project, especially in developing the website that accompanies Chapter 11. Michael Thomson of Eerdmans has been supportive and patient throughout this work's lengthy gestation. I must also express my warmest thanks to the Leverhulme Trust for awarding me a generous three-year Research Grant, and to the Arts and Humanities Research Council for a Research Grant to fund a follow-up project on "The Fourfold Gospel and Its Rivals."

Prologue

Initially an announcement communicated in person by specially commissioned messengers, "the gospel" is subsequently reduced to writing and issues in the collection generally known as "the four gospels" or simply "the gospels." Although these texts were traditionally ascribed to four named and independent authors, three of them are closely interrelated, with the anonymous text known for convenience as "Mark" forming the basis on which the later synoptic evangelists "Matthew" and "Luke" built their own more extensive structures. These later evangelists are also widely believed to have drawn from a second text, "Q," which can — perhaps — be reconstructed with more or less accuracy by careful analysis of the double tradition (that is, the non-Markan material common to Matthew and Luke). As for "John," indications of a high degree of independence from the other gospels must be balanced by the many points of contact. A number of similar stories or sayings suggest either an indirect acquaintance with one or more of the synoptics or access to synoptic-like traditions. And so "the four gospels" come into being, one after another, during the period between *c.* 65 and 100 CE: first Mark, shortly before or after the fall of Jerusalem, followed by Matthew and Luke, in that order but in quick succession, and finally John, "the fourth gospel," composed at the very end of a period later defined as "the first century" and bringing the canonical collection to completion.

The standard modern account of gospel origins ends at that point, but a couple of clarifications may be added in order to justify the decision to proceed no further. First, it is true that gospels or gospel-like texts continued to be composed during the second and subsequent centuries, and that several of these — or significant fragments of them — have in recent times been recovered from virtual oblivion. Yet the scholarly consensus is that this mate-

1

rial should be consigned to the category of the "apocryphal," later in origin than the canonical counterparts on which it is often dependent, and historically worthless if our concern is with Jesus himself. Second, it is also true that the four gospel collection was not explicitly recognized as such until relatively late in the second century. Yet, it may be argued, the gap between the completion of the four gospel collection and its explicit recognition may be filled by noting the numerous indications that early ecclesiastical writers were already aware of it. Later second-century writers did not invent the four gospel collection themselves but spoke of it as established long before their own time. And so we are pointed back to the late first century. It seems that the formation of the collection coincides with the process of composition.

This account of gospel origins, or something very like it, has changed little during the past century and a half. It is the rock on which other scholarly projects are founded, whether the object of enquiry is the historical Jesus, the development of tradition, or the individual evangelist's theology, narrative technique, communal context, or political stance. This is the account that initiates the beginning student into the world of New Testament scholarship, and that must be mastered if he or she is ever to feel at home in it. It is communicated in introductory lectures and is deeply embedded in textbooks, commentaries, and monographs.

Individual elements in the standard account have not gone without challenge. Mark may be placed after rather than before Matthew and Luke. The *Gospel of Thomas* may be set alongside the hypothetical Q as an independent though parallel development within the earliest sayings tradition. Provocatively early datings may be proposed for dialogue gospels from the Nag Hammadi collection, under the influence of once-popular speculations about a "pre-Christian Gnosticism." In more contemporary idiom, a concern may be expressed to recover lost voices speaking through texts marginalized by the canon. These challenges are heterogeneous and sometimes idiosyncratic. It is doubtful whether any of them has significantly reshaped the world into which the student is initiated, and it is also doubtful how far they *deserve* to do so. The standard account has remained in place for a century and a half not through institutional inertia alone but because it represents a major intellectual achievement. Many of its results are still compelling, and the perspectives it opens up retain their transformative potential in countering misperceptions that flourish among the pious and the irreligious alike. One can only benefit from the reading strategies that this scholarly tradition promotes, and from the habits of attention to nuance and difference that it inculcates. If, in spite of this, a *paradigm shift* is needed, the new paradigm will not seek merely to subvert and destroy but will propose a more comprehensive framework within which older results, insights, and perspectives may still have their place.

The fundamental problem with the standard account of gospel origins arises not from its individual results but from its limitation to the first century. As we have already seen, it justifies this self-limitation by assuming that the composition history of the individual gospels is coextensive with the formation of the canonical collection. To do so, it must play down *both* the evidence that many more than four gospels were in circulation during the first two centuries *and,* conversely, the lack of unambiguous evidence that four texts were differentiated from the others from the outset. To put the point in theoretical terms, the standard account fails to grasp that canon formation presupposes a process of *reception.* No religious, philosophical, or literary text enters the world with the label "canonical" already attached. Canonical status is a matter not for authors but for readers; it arises not from composition but from usage. As a rule, it is only after the death of the author that a work either consolidates its initial impact by establishing a quasi-permanent position within a particular reading community, or, more commonly, fails to do so and consequently fades from view. Many texts are produced and consumed, but few are selected for classic or canonical status. Selection is subsequent to production: authors and editors produce, but it is *later* readers who select by continuing to engage with a limited number of texts while allowing others to fall by the wayside.

It is possible that it was otherwise in the case of "the" four gospels. Production and selection may have been telescoped into a single event; readers may have immediately acknowledged a self-evident normative claim inherent in each of these four texts. Yet historical process does not normally act out the requirements of naively formulated dogma quite so conveniently. Like other readers before and since, early Christian readers will have *decided,* individually and collectively, which texts to read and reread, with a view to forming a broad communal consensus. If so, it is no longer possible to view four gospels as preselected for canonicity from the very beginning, and all other gospels as preselected for apocryphal redundancy. It is later readers who make these decisions, not texts, authors, or editors. While these readers may have excellent reasons for preferring one text to another, or for electing to coordinate texts rather than choosing one at the expense of another, their decisions are inevitably *contingent* in the sense that they might have been otherwise.

In the light of this, it might seem tempting to conclude that the standard

3

account of gospel origins displays an apologetically motivated bias in favour of the canonical collection. The temptation should be resisted, however. The standard account derives from mid-nineteenth-century German scholarship and predates the manuscript discoveries of the late nineteenth and twentieth centuries which have greatly extended our knowledge of early gospel literature: most notably the extensive excerpt from the *Gospel of Peter* (first published in 1892); the Oxyrhynchus fragments (1897, 1904), subsequently attributed to the *Gospel of Thomas* (1956); and the fragments of the Egerton gospel (1935, 1987). The new material was often fragmentary and difficult to reconstruct. It appeared to have little relevance to the ongoing discussion of synoptic or Johannine origins; in particular, the "synoptic problem" seemed capable of solution without it. Since the category of the "apocryphal gospel" lay ready to hand, it was easy to assume that the new material could be straightforwardly accommodated within it, and to leave more searching questions about the canonical/noncanonical divide unasked. It would be heavy-handed to allege "apologetic bias" in this connection.

More significantly, the standard account of gospel origins is itself deeply ambivalent about the four gospel collection. It is concerned with the four individual texts that constitute the collection, with their differences and their interrelatedness, but it rejects the theological claim that the canonical gospel bears witness to Jesus in and through its irreducible plurality. Plurality means difference, and difference is here construed as contradiction or tension: the large-scale contradiction between Johannine and synoptic christologies that fundamentally challenges the integrity and coherence of the canonical collection, together with the almost limitless small-scale contradictions that come to light wherever the same material is presented by more than one evangelist. These differences are "contradictions" in the sense that they cannot be reconciled at the level of empirical historical reality. This preoccupation with contradictions reflects the modern discipline's foundational decision to reject the age-old harmonizing project derived from Tatian and Augustine, which only began to lose ground in the eighteenth century as the Gospel "Harmony" gave way to the Gospel "Synopsis." The Harmony had attempted to show that the gospels provide a single consistent account of the historical life of Jesus in spite of their plurality and the "apparent contradictions" to which this gives rise. In the new scholarly regime signified by the Synopsis, the tenuous link between plurality and singularity is finally severed. The plurality of the individual evangelists is absolutized: there is a Markan Jesus, a Matthean Jesus, a Lukan Jesus, and a Johannine Jesus, coexisting disharmoniously. Singularity is now to be attained by a new critical procedure: not the harmonizing of differences but the application of the criterion of "authenticity." The singularity is now that of a historical Jesus constructed exclusively from gospel material deemed authentic, carefully differentiated from the larger body of material held to reflect only the later concerns of church or evangelist. If the gospels are valuable primarily for their authentic recollections of the historical Jesus, their plurality can only be construed negatively; accounts of Jesus diversify precisely as they deviate from their singular historical object. In this perspective, the canonical plurality is a negative rather than a positive factor, a minus rather than a plus.

Whatever the merits or otherwise of this account, it cannot be said to betray a bias in favour of the canon. On the contrary: in opposing canonical plurality as obstructing the way back to Jesus, it is opposed to the canonical gospel itself. The Jesus that is sought is other than the Jesus of Matthew, Mark, Luke, or John, though significant traces of him are no doubt to be found in at least three of these four. It is the perceived defectiveness of the canonical plurality that generates the "quest" for the infinitely precious object hidden somewhere behind the texts.

A picture begins to emerge of a research paradigm in which the construction of the object of investigation — the gospel testimony to Jesus — is determined by three fundamental decisions. The first is the decision to establish a *terminus ad quem* at the end of the first century, the date assigned to "the fourth gospel" which completes the canonical collection. In contrast, the second century is designated as the period of the earliest "apocryphal" gospels, the most important of which — the *Gospel of Thomas* — is conventionally dated to *c.* 110-40 to prevent any confusion with the canonical four. On this account, the ecclesial distinction between canonical and noncanonical gospels is a straightforward extrapolation from their period of origin; the year 100 *CE* is projected back onto early Christian history so as to establish a boundary between the two epochs of gospel writing. Against this, we should recognize that the canonical/noncanonical distinction is not given with the texts themselves but arises out of their reception. Gospel writing proceeds unabated before and after the moment *we* refer to as "the end of the first century," and it is this ongoing process that is presupposed in the retrospective differentiation of the canonical few from the noncanonical many.

The second fundamental decision responds to the failure of the older project of gospel harmonization by understanding plurality as disharmony. The four gospels are found to be in conflict with one another in matters small and great, and, in the absence of any concept of canonical coherence or integrity, that conflict must remain eternally unresolved. Yet difference can only be identified with disharmony on the basis of a naive account of truth as correspondence. On this account, Statement A may be held to be true if and only if it corresponds to Event A as that event would have been perceived by an ideally situated onlooker. Insofar as Statements $A+$ or B lack an empirically observable basis in Event A, they must be held to be false. Gospel differences show that the gospels are full of such noncorrespondences and thus that they undermine one another's truth-claims and their readers' confidence in them. Lacking here is any positive appreciation of the active or constructive moment in the reception process. The reception of the figure of Jesus that issues in the gospel narratives is understood negatively as deviation from an original truth.

The third fundamental decision follows directly from the second. If reception is deviation, investigators must proceed against the flow of the reception process in order to recover and reconstruct whatever vestiges of original truth are preserved intact. (Assuming that few if any such vestiges are to be found in later gospel literature or even in the "fourth gospel" itself, what lies beyond the canonical terminus can safely be left out of account.) Authentic fragments preserved within the synoptic gospels must therefore be differentiated from the mass of inauthentic material in which they are now embedded, in the hope that a coherent and cogent picture of the "historical Jesus" will emerge as they are pieced together. This hope must be regarded as illusory, however. The uninterpreted Jesus is a chimera, a mythical entity that supposedly existed in and for itself prior to its becoming something else for others.

At each of these three points — the marginalizing of the second century, the problematizing of plurality, the quest for a truth preceding interpretation — the conventional account of gospel origins overlooks or undervalues the phenomenon of reception. In opposition to this account, I shall argue that a single yet diverse reception process unites initial responses to Jesus by his first followers with the articulation of the fourfold canonical gospel, by way of a transmission of tradition in which gospel writing plays a central role. This *canonical perspective* can accommodate many of the standard account's individual findings, while relocating them within a fundamentally different and more comprehensive framework.

A canonical perspective on early Christian gospels would begin by discarding the end-of-first-century terminus, a concept that systematically distorts the object of enquiry. As a result, the story of gospel origins may be extended into the second century and beyond, with the aim of showing how the dynamic of the Jesus tradition issues in a proliferation of gospel writing and culminates in the construction of a fourfold canonical gospel out of the mass of available literature. To view the fourfold gospel retrospectively as the *goal* of gospel writing is not to deny that it is also the product of contingency. Quite different responses to the plurality of gospel literature were available; those who first claimed that the gospel is fourfold in form did not present this as a statement of the obvious, requiring no defence. In the abstract, the rationale for a fourfold gospel consisting of Matthew, Mark, Luke, and John is anything but obvious, a point tacitly acknowledged when appeal is made to the four living creatures of Revelation and Ezekiel in order to justify it: the surreal symbolism mirrors the oddity of the fourfold construct itself. Yet it is precisely because this composite textual object is so counterintuitive that it is worthy of investigation in its own right, over and above the ongoing study of its individual components.

The investigation requires sensitivity to issues of history, hermeneutics, and theology, and will therefore ignore the outworn essentialist demand for a "purely historical" discourse uncontaminated by theology or hermeneutics, or for a "theological interpretation" from which historical concerns are rigorously excluded. Given a sufficiently flexible account of each of the three orientations, there is no reason why they should not coexist and cooperate.

Historically, the aim is to account for the genesis of the canonical gospel within the context of early Christian gospel production as a whole. In order to do so, it will be necessary to reconstruct a precanonical situation in which gospel writing constitutes a single dynamic field as yet undivided by the canonical decision. Only subsequently, from a canonical standpoint, can one speak of "the" gospels or "the four" gospels; the definite article and the enumeration are appropriate as and when the individual texts emerge out of the broader field of early gospel literature, but they have no place in discussion of the earlier period. It is therefore to be expected that gospels later deemed canonical were at first intimately related to gospels later passed over, and that all kinds of intertextual connections may still be discerned in spite of the canonical boundary. Against this background, the fourfold gospel may itself be seen as an act of gospel production, marking the defining moment in the reception-history of the individual texts it contains while also establishing a new, composite text which generates a more comprehensive reception-history of its own. The reception of the fourfold gospel will from now on form the context in which the ongoing reception of the individual gospel takes place. Where one gospel is to the fore — in preaching, liturgy, commentary, art, or other communicative media — the remaining three will never be far away. This focus on the fourfold canonical gospel will serve to embed the individual texts *more* firmly within their overarching historical context, rather than less.

Hermeneutically, the primary concern here is with the implications of the fourfold canonical form for interpretative practice. In setting an individual text in a new intertextual context, all canons have the potential to shape the practice of interpretation, and that hermeneutical potential is especially significant when the texts in question are so similar and yet so different. In this similarity and difference they are also a singular entity: not only "the four gospels" but also "the gospel, according to . . ." or simply "the gospel." The fine dialectical balance between oneness and plurality has often succumbed to various kinds of undialectical uniformity, both ancient and modern, "precritical" and "critical." It must therefore be shown that the canonical gospel does actually exist, and in a form that has shaped — and that might continue to shape — the interpretation of its individual components. All canons serve not only to include, however, but also to exclude; gospels deemed noncanonical are hermeneutically relevant for the light they shed on this single process of inclusion-exclusion. While some of these texts have a limited available reception history, stemming mainly from the decades since their modern rediscovery, it is important to consider how the prior category of the "apocryphal" has shaped this modern reception and how its relation to the corresponding "canonical" category has been construed. These categories arise not from inherent differences of genre but from a communal decision no more or less "arbitrary" than the decision of any other community about the texts it chooses to engage with or to pass over.

Theologically, the position developed here serves to underline the mediated character of all knowledge of Jesus — over against the claim that we can have access to an uninterpreted "historical" figure by abstracting him from his own reception. The question who Jesus was or is in himself cannot be differentiated from the question who he was or is for others, whether disciples or opponents. The issue of his identity and significance is inherently controversial, and there is no neutral ground available on which it could be settled once for all. As Jesus himself says, he comes to bring not peace but the sword of division; whoever is not with him is against him. Indeed, early Christians are forced to confront the reality of division and dissent even within their own ranks. As Luke indicates to Theophilus, each attempt to write the gospel represents a new answer to the question who Jesus is, on the assumption that the answers embodied in earlier gospels are either inadequate or misleading; and every gospel seeks its readers' endorsement of the answer it proposes, in preference to the alternative answers proposed by its competitors. In the composite canonical gospel, the reading-and-hearing community that is the catholic church stipulates that four of these answers are to be regarded as complementary statements of gospel truth, whereas the threat of falsification hangs over all other gospel literature. The canonical decision establishes a boundary that both defines and constructs the truth and falsehood it demarcates.

The lines between historical, hermeneutical, and theological dimensions of the present argument are only lightly drawn, however. All three are at least tacitly present at every point, and the term "canonical" is intended to embrace them all. If the book is to be characterized as a whole, it might be seen as an exercise in *historically informed theological hermeneutics.* Yet such a label intends no clear, tidy demarcation from the discourses of so-called "historical-critical" or "secular" scholarship, or of "patristics" or "historical" or "systematic" theology. The point is rather to acknowledge the multidimensional nature of the object in question, resisting the will to dominate it evident in every attempt to reduce it to safe and manageable proportions.

PART ONE

The Eclipse of the Fourfold Gospel

CHAPTER 1

Augustine's Ambiguous Legacy

If there are to be four gospels at all, they must differ from one another. Without differences they would simply be four copies of a single gospel. But if they together constitute the one canonical gospel, they must also be similar, variations on a common theme rather than disparate and unrelated. Difference and similarity belong together. Where there is difference there will also be similarity, if the canonical gospel is indeed singular. Where there is similarity there will also be difference, given that the canonical gospel is also plural. In its fourfold form, the canonical gospel actually *prescribes* difference. It represents the recognition that no single telling of Jesus' story can be final and definitive, and that the same story must be told and retold in variant forms. If the canonical gospel is to come into view as a textual object in its own right, then both difference and similarity, plurality and singularity, must be given their due. Where this delicate balance is lost, the gospels will be viewed either as heterogeneous or as uniform, and each of these undialectical extremes will represent a reaction against the other. Either way, the integrity of the canonical form will be compromised.

Historically, gospel differences have often been viewed not as integral to the truth of the gospel but as potentially subversive of it. A difference that might be seen as enhancing the gospel testimony is understood instead as a *contradiction,* real or apparent. The criterion by which a contradiction is identified has to do with the texts' relationship not only to one another but also to prior historical reality. A contradiction arises when one factual assertion is exclusive of another. Jesus is said to have bestowed sight on a blind man both as he approached the city of Jericho (Lk. 18.35) and as he left it (Mk. 10.46). Since one cannot approach and leave the same location simultaneously, this is an apparent or real contradiction. The contradiction is only *apparent* if, in reality, Jesus performed two very similar miracles, one on the way into Jericho and the other on the way out. The contradiction is *real* if the same miracle is in view and if, in consequence, at least one of the two mutually exclusive assertions about its setting must be judged to be false. A contradiction between texts entails a noncorrespondence with factual occurrence.

It follows, however, that the possibility of contradiction only arises on the assumption that correspondence with factual occurrence is the appropriate criterion for assessing gospel truth — an assumption that may be held both by the critic and by the apologist. The critic appeals to gospel contradictions in order to demonstrate that the canonical gospel is an unstable construct that must be dismantled if the truth about the real or historical Jesus is to be brought to light. The apologist aims to show that the alleged contradictions are more apparent than real, and, beyond that, that the full historical truth will come to light only when the discrete narratives of the individual evangelists are reassembled into a single composite whole. In both cases, gospel differences are construed negatively, as entailing *prima facie* contradictions and potential disjunction from actual historical occurrence. In both cases, canonical pluriformity is sacrificed in the quest for a singular historical truth, whether minimal or maximal. And in both cases, the criterion of correspondence to factual occurrence proves destructive of the form of the canonical gospel.

The problem cannot be resolved by observing that the alleged contradictions are trivial and that it is of no consequence whether Jesus bestowed sight on a blind man as he approached Jericho or as he left it. The alleged contradictions are far from trivial. For one thing, there are very many of them, and they often relate to issues at the heart of Christian faith and life. More importantly, to trivialize the alleged contradictions is also to trivialize the differences that constitute the individual gospels in their discrete identities. The problem of alleged contradictions can only be resolved by recognizing that the criterion of correspondence to factual occurrence is already rejected in the canonical form itself. As Origen recognized but Augustine did not, the apparent contradiction demonstrates the inadequacy of this criterion and compels the reader to seek the truth on a different plane to that of sheer factuality.[1]

---

1. The contrasting approaches of Origen and Augustine are noted by Brevard Childs, who also remarks that "[u]nfortunately, the exegetical and theological potential offered by Origen of seeing in the Gospels a literary genre different from that of historical reporting was not pursued" (*The New Testament as Canon: An Introduction* [London: SCM Press, 1984], p. 146).

It was Augustine rather than Origen who shaped the subsequent Western understanding of gospel relationships, above all in his work on the agreement of the evangelists, *De Consensu Evangelistarum.*[2] Augustine here laid down principles of gospel harmonization that remained influential even as they were rejected in post-Enlightenment scholarship; the Enlightenment's dismantling of the canonical gospel is founded on Augustinian premises. Precisely in seeking to vindicate the canonical gospel, Augustine prepares the way for its dissolution.

Unlike post-Enlightenment scholarship, however, Augustine does believe in the fourfold canonical gospel. He has valuable if rudimentary insights to offer about gospel origins, and his development of the traditional Irenaean symbolism remains theologically suggestive. Where he is *not* trying to force plural narratives into singularity, he has much to offer. Even where he assumes a purely negative view of plurality as a potential threat to gospel truth, his sustained attention both to general principle and to textual detail compels respect and admiration. Here as elsewhere, one finds oneself instructed by Augustine even in dissenting from him.

Perspectives Historical and Theological

Augustine proposes a literary solution to the problem of the similarities and differences between the synoptic gospels. Mark, he claims, wrote his gospel in dependence either on Matthew alone or (more probably) on Matthew together with Luke.[3] Neither hypothesis is highly regarded in most current

---

2. Latin text, CSEL 43, ed. F. Weihrich (Vienna: Österreichische Akademie der Wissenschaften, 1904); Eng. trans. in NPNF, first series, vol. 6 (repr. Grand Rapids: Eerdmans, 1991), pp. 65-236. Throughout the present work, translations are my own unless otherwise indicated.

3. The view that Mark is an abbreviated version of Matthew is commonly known as the "Augustinian hypothesis," whereas the view that Mark is dependent on both Matthew and Luke is known as the "Griesbach hypothesis" after Johann Jakob Griesbach (1745-1812), on whom see further below. The distinction between the two hypotheses goes back to Griesbach himself, who states: "Fallitur etiam *Augustinus* de Consens. Evang. L.1. C. 2. Matthaei breviatorem et pedissequum Marcum esse contendens" (J. J. Griesbach, *Commentatio qua Marci Evangelium totum e Matthaei et Lucae commentariis decerptum esse monstratur* [1789-90[1], 1794[2]], repr. in *J. J. Griesbach: Synoptic and Text-Critical Studies, 1776-1976*, ed. Bernard Orchard and Thomas R. W. Longstaff, SNTSMS [Cambridge: Cambridge University Press, 1978], pp. 74-102 [Latin], pp. 103-35 [Eng. tr.]; p. 101). Neither Griesbach nor most of his recent followers have noticed that Augustine himself came to regard Mark's use of both Matthew and Luke as more probable than his earlier theory (cf. *De Cons. Evang.* iv.10.11).

scholarship, rightly committed to the priority of Mark. But what is significant is that Augustine should propose this type of literary hypothesis at all. His proposal is in tension with his commitment to gospel harmonization, which normally assumes that all four gospels have direct access to apostolic tradition, from which their points of both similarity and difference are derived. It is also in tension with the ancient tradition that Mark's gospel is dependent not on any written text but on the preaching of Peter in Rome. In spite of these potential difficulties, Augustine presents his hypotheses without any sign of anxiety or consciousness of innovation.

At the start of his work Augustine briefly sets out his views on the individual gospels.[4] These four evangelists "are said to have written in the following order: first Matthew, then Mark, then Luke, then John."[5] Matthew and John, the two apostolic authors, enclose and support the two nonapostolic ones, Mark and Luke.[6] The first gospel was originally written in the language of the first Christians: Matthew "is said to have been written in the Hebrew language."[7] A long-established tradition is here passed on without further comment.[8] Tradition also presupposes that the four gospels are independent works deriving directly or indirectly from individual apostles: Matthew and John, but also Peter and Paul in the case of Mark and Luke.[9] This assumed independence could be exploited for apologetic purposes. For Chrysostom, independence is a precondition for the evangelists' trustworthiness, and is demonstrated by their differences and discrepancies:

4. This work may be dated to *c.* 399-400: so F. Weihrich, *De Consensu Evangelistarum,* pp. I-VI; H. J. Vogels, *St Augustins Schrift De Consensu Evangelistarum unter vornehmlicher Berücksichtigung ihrer harmonistischen Anschauungen* (Freiburg i.B.: Herdersche Verlagshandlung, 1908), pp. 15-18; A. Penna, "Il 'De Consensu Evangelistarum' ed i 'canoni eusebiani,'" *Bib* 36 (1955), pp. 1-19; p. 3. For its purpose and context, see Vogels, pp. 1-15; H. Merkel, *Die Widersprüche zwischen den Evangelien: Ihre polemische und apologetische Behandlung in der Alten Kirche bis zu Augustin,* WUNT (Tübingen: Mohr Siebeck, 1971), pp. 224-27.

5. Augustine, *De Cons. Evang.* i.2.3.

6. Augustine, *De Cons. Evang.* i.2.3.

7. Augustine, *De Cons. Evang.* i.2.4.

8. According to Papias, "Matthew compiled the sayings [τὰ λόγια] in the Hebrew language, and each person translated them as he was able" (Eusebius, *HE* iii.39.16). Papias's claim about an original Hebrew or Aramaic Matthew was accepted by Irenaeus, Origen, Ephrem, Epiphanius, Chrysostom, and Jerome, and was often linked with corresponding traditions about the origins of the other three gospels.

9. Texts in K. Aland (ed.), *Synopsis Quattuor Evangeliorum* (Stuttgart: Württembergische Bibelanstalt Stuttgart, 1967[4]), pp. 531-48. For discussion of traditions relating to Mark, see C. Clifton Black, *Mark: Images of an Apostolic Interpreter* (Edinburgh: T. & T. Clark, 2001).

For if they had agreed in all things exactly, with regard to time and place and in their very words, our opponents would be convinced that they had colluded together and wrote as they did by mutual agreement. . . . But as things stand, their disagreement in minor matters frees them from all suspicion and testifies clearly in favour of the writers' integrity.[10]

Although this apologetic argument remains in circulation to this day, it is incompatible with the type of source-critical hypothesis introduced by Augustine. Having repeated the tradition about Matthew, Augustine now ventures into uncharted territory. The evangelists, he argues, are *not* independent of each other, in spite of appearances to the contrary:

Although each of them may seem to keep to his own order of narration, we do not find [*non reperitur*] that each of them decided to write without awareness of his predecessor, or to omit in ignorance matters recorded by another; but as each was inspired, he added his own distinctive contribution [*non superfluam cooperationem sui laboris adiunxit*].[11]

The inspiration of the later evangelists occurs in and through their engagement with their predecessors. Augustine has learned this not from the tradition — which took the opposite view, as Chrysostom illustrates — but from his own study of the texts.[12] Reading carefully and critically, we find that Mark did not write independently of his predecessor, Matthew, even though he did not precisely follow the Matthean order of narration. The traditional sequence — first Matthew, then Mark — is here reinterpreted as a literary relationship, and evidence for this claim is provided in the form of a succinct survey of the five possible relationships to other gospels in which given Markan passages may stand:

Mark, following [Matthew], appears to be his footman, as it were, and his summarizer [*tamquam pedissequus et breviator*]. While Mark has (1) nothing shared only with John, (2) only a few items unique to himself, and (3) still fewer shared with Luke alone, (4) with Matthew he has a great deal in common, much of it virtually identical and expressed in the same

10. Chrysostom, *Hom. in Matt.* i.6 (translation adapted from NPNF, first series, vol. 10 [repr. Grand Rapids: Eerdmans, 1991], p. 3).

11. Augustine, *De Cons. Evang.* i.2.4.

12. It is not the case that the tradition of Matthean priority "included the view that Mark was the abbreviator of Matthew" (B. Reicke, "Synoptic Problem," in *Dictionary of Biblical Interpretation*, ed. John Hayes [Nashville: Abingdon Press, 1999], vol. 2, pp. 517-24; p. 518). The concept of literary dependence appears to be Augustine's innovation.

words [*multa paene totidem adque ipsis verbis*], whether shared with him alone or (5) together with the others.[13]

Mark shares so much material with Matthew because he wrote in full knowledge of the earlier gospel. The relationship is so close that Mark may be seen as an attendant, accompanying Matthew wherever he goes, and as his abbreviator. Augustine's evidence for this claim is probably derived from the "Eusebian Canons," or tables of gospel parallels arranged in ten categories, mediated through Jerome's new gospel translation.[14] All five of the possible relationships Augustine specifies are covered by the Canons, and the lists of enumerated passages that follow each of them:

(1) [*Mk+Jn*]: cf. Canons VII, *Mt+Jn;* IX, *Lk+Jn.*
(2) *Mk alone:* Canon X, 19 items.
(3) *Mk+Lk:* Canon VIII, 14 items, thus "fewer" than the preceding category.
(4) *Mk+Mt:* Canon VI, 47 items.
(5) *Mk+Mt+(Lk and/or Jn):* Canons I-II, IV, 211 items.

It is hard to see how Augustine could have stated so confidently that passages common to Luke and Mark only are "still fewer" than passages unique to Mark if he had not had access to the Canons.[15] Seeming to con-

---

13. Augustine, *De Cons. Evang.* i.2.4; enumeration added.

14. For the text of the Eusebian Canons and the prefatory letter to Carpianus, see Nestle-Aland[27], pp. 82*-89*; for the Latin version, with Jerome's prefatory letter to Pope Damasus, see *Biblia Sacra iuxta Vulgatam Versionem,* ed. R. Gryson (Stuttgart: Deutsche Bibelgesellschaft, 1994[4]), pp. 1515-26. In *De Cons. Evang.,* Augustine seems to have used Jerome's translation of the gospels: see F. C. Burkitt, *The Old Latin and the Itala* (Cambridge: Cambridge University Press, 1896), pp. 59-78. Burkitt's apparent demonstration of Augustine's use here of the Vulgate led Theodor Zahn to suggest his knowledge of the Eusebian Canons (*Einleitung in das Neue Testament,* vol. 2 [Leipzig: Deichert, 1899], p. 195). Both claims were criticized, however, by H. J. Vogels, who argued that Augustine's text was assimilated to the Vulgate in the later manuscript tradition (*St Augustins Schrift,* pp. 19-48).

15. A. Penna attempts to demonstrate that Augustine was not dependent on the Canons by identifying cases where he fails to exploit the range of parallels Eusebius provided ("Il 'De Consensu Evangelistarum' ed i 'canoni eusebiani,'" pp. 7-19). For example: "Le parole attribuite a Giovanni Battista (*Mt.* 3, 1-12) non sono integrate con *Giov.* 3, 28, che costituirebbe una breva sezione del canone I, parallela a *Mt.* 3, 11" (p. 13). In fact, Augustine's treatment of Mt. 3.1-12 and parallels (*De Cons. Evang.* ii.12.25-29) carefully registers most of the information the Canons make available about which parts of this passage are present or absent in which of the other gospels. At Mt. 3.11 (section 11, canon I: all four gospels), Augustine chooses not to present the complex Johannine material in full (sections 6, 12, 14, 28 = Jn. 1.15, 26-27, 30-31; 3.28) but refers only to Jn. 1.15. Penna's method does not allow Augustine to be selective in his presentations of parallels.

firm a special relationship between Mark and Matthew, the evidence of the Canons leads Augustine to the conclusion that Mark is Matthew's *breviator*.

In the work as a whole the main preoccupation is with detailed comparisons between the gospel texts as they stand. Priority is given to Matthew, and Markan and Lukan versions of common material are discussed in relation to the fundamental Matthean version. In this Augustine follows the canonical order, and his attempt to demonstrate the "consensus of the evangelists" does not require a hypothesis of literary dependence. Yet it seems clear that he holds such a hypothesis. It is important for him that a later evangelist writes in full awareness of his predecessor or predecessors. When, for example, Mark passes over the entire Sermon on the Mount, that does not mean he is ignorant of it. It is as material present in Matthew is *knowingly* omitted or supplemented that Mark's "cooperation" in the work of gospel-writing is seen to be "not superfluous." Mark can hardly be Matthew's *breviator* if he writes his gospel independently of Matthew, for the task of the *breviator* is precisely to produce an abridgement or summary of a prior text.

Augustine's view of Mark as "following" Matthew is a striking deviation from the consensus that the apostle whom Mark followed was Peter. According to Papias, Mark was Peter's "interpreter" (ἑρμηνευτής), one who "followed" (παρηκολούθησεν) not the Lord but Peter.[16] Later writers repeat and supplement each of Papias's key terms. Mark was Peter's "disciple and interpreter" (Irenaeus),[17] who "long followed and remembered" what Peter said (Clement).[18] Mark was instructed by Peter, who acknowledged him as his "son" (Origen, citing 1 Peter 5.13),[19] since Mark had been baptized by him.[20] Ephrem, Eusebius, Epiphanius, and Jerome all know that Mark was the follower, interpreter, or disciple of Peter. For good measure, the tradition variously adds that Mark was urged to compose his gospel by Peter's hearers in Rome;[21] that the apostle himself either expressed no opinion about his work[22] or (on the contrary) was pleased with it;[23] that Mark took his gospel with him to Alexandria, where he proclaimed it and founded

---

16. Eusebius, *HE* iii.39.15; Aland, *Synopsis,* p. 531.

17. Irenaeus, *Adv. Haer.* iii.1.3; Aland, *Synopsis,* p. 533.

18. Eusebius, *HE* vi.14.6; Aland, *Synopsis,* p. 539.

19. Eusebius, *HE* vi.25.5; Aland, *Synopsis,* p. 540.

20. "Monarchian Prologues," cf. Epiphanius, *Pan.* li.3.6.10; Aland, *Synopsis,* pp. 539, 545.

21. Eusebius, *HE* ii.15.1; vi.14.6 (= Clement of Alexandria, *Hypotyposeis*); Ephrem, *Comm. in Diatess. Tatiani;* Aland, *Synopsis,* pp. 539, 544.

22. Eusebius, *HE* vi.14.7 (= Clement of Alexandria, *Hypotyposeis*); Aland, *Synopsis,* p. 539.

23. Eusebius, *HE* ii.15.2 (cf. Jerome, *De Vir. Ill.* 8); Aland, *Synopsis,* pp. 539, 546.

churches;[24] and that he was known as *colobodactylus* owing to his dispro-portionately short fingers.[25] Such traditions are incompatible with Augus-tine's view that Mark is dependent not on Peter but on Matthew. For the tradition, Mark is Peter's son; for Augustine, he is Matthew's. The nonapostolic Mark and Luke are "like beloved sons" to Matthew and John, the apostolic evangelists, and are placed between them so as to be sup-ported on either side.[26]

Near the close of his work, Augustine returns to the questions of synop-tic relationships, having discovered in the course of writing it that the agree-ments of Mark and Luke against Matthew are more significant than he had previously supposed. Either Mark follows Matthew (Augustine's earlier opinion), or,

> as seems more probable [*quod probabilius intelligitur*], he accompanies both of them [*cum ambobus incedit*]. For although he agrees with Mat-thew at many points, at not a few others he agrees rather with Luke.[27]

Mark "accompanies" Matthew or, as now seems more likely, both Mat-thew and Luke. He writes in full awareness of his precedessors,[28] and he de-liberately conforms his work to theirs, each of them in turn. That embryonic source-critical hypotheses are in view is clear, since alternative explanations for empirical data are here proposed of which one can be judged "more probable" than the other. The new hypothesis is research-based, arising out of the detailed comparisons between synoptic parallels to which the main body of Augustine's work is devoted. It also represents a further deviation from tradition, according to which the sequence Matthew-Mark-Luke-John corresponds to the order of composition.

The original source-critical theory — Mark's use of Matthew — is mod-ified as a result of the comparison between Mark and Luke with which Book 4 opens, after the Matthean parallels have been exhaustively discussed in Books 2 and 3. Augustine notes that, from the opening Isaianic citation to

---

24. Eusebius, *HE* ii.16.1; cf. Ephrem, *Comm. in Diatess. Tatiani;* Jerome, *De Vir. Ill.* 8; Aland, *Synopsis,* pp. 543, 544, 546.

25. "Evv. Prologi Vetustissimi" (= "Anti-Marcionite Prologues"); Hippolytus, *Refutatio Om-nium Haeresium* vii.30.1; Aland, *Synopsis,* pp. 532, 541.

26. Augustine, *De Cons. Evang.* i.2.3: "tamquam filii amplectendi ac per hoc in loco medio constituti utroque ab eis latere munirentur."

27. Augustine, *De Cons. Evang.* iv.10.11.

28. Augustine, *De Cons. Evang.* i.2.4: ". . . non tamen unusquisque eorum velut alterius praecedentis ignarus voluisse scribere repperitur."

the call of the first disciples, Mark 1.1-20 follows the order of Matthew 3.1–4.22.[29] Mark's role as *breviator* of Matthew is evident in the respective accounts both of the ministry of John the Baptist (Mt. 3.1-12; Mk. 1.2-8) and of the temptations (Mt. 4.1-11; Mk. 1.12-13). But Augustine also notes that in the following sequence Mark corresponds to Luke's order rather than to Matthew's: the exorcism in the synagogue at Capernaum (Mk. 1.21-28; Lk. 4.31-37) and the cleansing of the leper (Mk. 1.40-45; Lk. 5.12-16) are briefly discussed, although the primary concern is with apparent discrepancies rather than sequence.[30] Reading on into Mark and Luke, Augustine claims — not quite accurately — that Mark and Luke narrate in parallel throughout the section from the cure of the haemorrhaging woman and the raising of Jairus's daughter (Mk. 5.21-43; Lk. 8.40-56) through to the healing of a deaf mute (Mk. 7.31-37).[31] It is such literary observations as these that lead to the conclusion that Mark's secondariness in relation to Matthew is to be extended to his relationship to Luke.[32]

Augustine's source-critical hypotheses represent a preference for scholarly research over the traditional assumption that the four gospels have independent apostolic origins. While he does not engage fully with that tradition, it is his own comparative study of the gospel texts that has led him to reject it. If, as Irenaeus claimed, Matthew wrote his gospel for the "Hebrews" while Peter and Paul were still preaching in Rome, and if, after their demise, Mark wrote an account of what he had heard from Peter and Luke of what he had heard from Paul,[33] then the agreements not just in general content but also in precise sequence and wording would be inexplicable. To nonspecialist readers of the gospels, the tradition of independent apostolic origins (direct or indirect) might seem to provide a plausible and attractive explanation of gospel similarities and differences. An explanation along these lines is already presupposed in the traditional attributions to Matthew, Mark, Luke, and John. It is only where the gospels are systematically studied alongside

29. Augustine, *De Cons. Evang.* iv.1.2.

30. Augustine, *De Cons. Evang.* iv.2.3–3.4.

31. Augustine, *De Cons. Evang.* iv.4.5. In reality, the parallel extends only as far as the feeding of the five thousand (Mk. 6.30-44; Lk. 9.10-17).

32. See the detailed analysis of the relevant passages in Books 1 and 4 of Augustine's work in D. Dungan, "Augustine and the Augustinian Hypothesis," in *New Synoptic Studies: The Cambridge Gospel Conference and Beyond,* ed. W. R. Farmer (Macon, GA: Mercer University Press, 1983), pp. 37-64. Dungan rightly points out that Augustine's change of mind on synoptic relationships has been generally overlooked (pp. 62-63).

33. Irenaeus, *Adv. Haer.* iii.1.1.

one another that their independence comes to seem impossible. While Augustine undertakes his comparisons in order to discover the principles of gospel harmonization, his study also suggests source-critical possibilities that might have led in a quite different direction. His willingness to modify his own initial view indicates that this, for him, is in principle a legitimate and promising topic for ongoing scholarly discussion.[34]

There is no sense here that, as a *merely* scholarly project, the study of gospel origins lies outside the concerns of the Christian community. Augustine knows of no such dichotomy between scholarship and the church. Elsewhere, in his great hermeneutical treatise *De Doctrina Christiana*, he develops a comprehensive biblical hermeneutic in which the texts' theological rationale — which is to promote the love of God and neighbour — is given pride of place, but in which scholarly procedures such as textual criticism and exegesis of the Greek and Hebrew texts are also eloquently advocated.[35] An ongoing investigation of gospel origins would be entirely at home within the ethos of this generously inclusive hermeneutics.

Augustine's remarks on the "synoptic problem" are brief and rudimentary, but they show some awareness that the problem exists and that it requires a primarily literary solution. Though probably incorrect, his proposed solutions do not deserve the contempt with which they are often dismissed. Thus B. H. Streeter comments as follows on Augustine's view of Mark as *breviator* of Matthew:

> Augustine did not possess a Synopsis of the Greek text conveniently printed in parallel columns. Otherwise a person of his intelligence could

---

34. The four major pieces of evidence that Augustine does on occasion envisage source-critical theories are: (1) the claim that the later evangelist was not ignorant of the earlier one (Augustine, *De Cons. Evang.* i.2.4); (2) the reference to Mark as *breviator* of Matthew (i.2.4); (3) the apparent substitution of a Matthew-Mark link for the traditional Peter-Mark one (i.2.4); (4) the decision that Mark's relationship to both Matthew and Luke is, on empirical grounds, "more probable" than the theory of a relationship to Matthew alone (iv.10.11). These points are either played down or passed over by H. J. de Jonge, who denies all source-critical interests to Augustine, noting that for him all four evangelists have access to the apostolic tradition in its entirety ("Augustine on the Interrelations of the Gospels," in *The Four Gospels (FS Frans Neirynck)*, vol. 3, ed. F. Van Segbroeck [Louvain: Louvain University Press/Peeters, 1992], pp. 2409-17). It is true that the brief source-critical remarks near the beginning and end of Augustine's work exercise little or no influence on its central argument.

35. Book 1 of this work is devoted to the theological rationale of the biblical texts, which Augustine finds in the double love commandment. An account of the range of specialized knowledge required of the biblical interpreter is given in Book 2 (especially ii.11.15–18.28, 25.38–42.63).

not have failed to perceive that, where the two Gospels are parallel, it is usually Matthew, and not Mark, who does the abbreviation. . . . [O]nly a lunatic would leave out Matthew's account of the Infancy, the Sermon on the Mount, and practically all the parables, in order to get room for purely verbal expansion of what was retained.[36]

If the hypothetical post-Matthean Mark had done as Streeter recommends, retaining Matthew's account of the Infancy, the Sermon on the Mount, and the parables while abstaining from purely verbal expansion, he would have been a copyist and not an evangelist in his own right. The possibility of a later gospel lacking precisely the items specified by Streeter is demonstrated by the Gospel of John, whose author Streeter views not as a lunatic but as a "mystic and prophet."[37] The solution to the synoptic problem cannot be straightforwardly read out of a modern Greek synopsis. Those who disagree with Streeter do not necessarily hold "eccentric views of what constitutes evidence," like those "highly cultivated people who think Bacon wrote Shakespeare."[38]

Streeter is probably right on Markan priority and Augustine probably wrong.[39] If he is wrong, however, it is not because he has allowed his theological convictions to cloud his critical judgement. His two alternative hypotheses stem from ongoing study of the texts, and he prefers the second to the first because it reflects his own more thorough investigation of the relationship between Mark and Luke. The first hypothesis replaces the personal link between Mark and Peter with a literary link between Mark and Matthew, the second substitutes the order Matthew-Luke-Mark for the traditional chronological sequence. Augustine might reasonably have chosen to regard the ancient traditions he rejects as "historical evidence," just as Eusebius did. Instead, he gives priority to the internal evidence of the texts, which makes it impossible to imagine that Matthew and Mark both had independent apostolic origins. His proposed literary explanation of their relationship is ven-

---

36. B. H. Streeter, *The Four Gospels: A Study of Origins* (London: Macmillan, 1930[4]), pp. 157-58.

37. Streeter, *Four Gospels*, p. 363.

38. Streeter, *Four Gospels*, p. 164.

39. See Christopher Tuckett, *The Revival of the Griesbach Hypothesis: An Analysis and Appraisal*, SNTSMS (Cambridge: Cambridge University Press, 1983); Peter M. Head, *Christology and the Synoptic Problem: An Argument for Markan Priority*, SNTSMS (Cambridge: Cambridge University Press, 1997); Mark Goodacre, *The Case against Q: Studies in Markan Priority and the Synoptic Problem* (Harrisburg, PA: TPI, 2002), pp. 19-45.

tured not for the sake of any immediate theological advantage, but because any light that scholarly investigation can shed on the scriptural texts is to be welcomed. Scholarly investigation is not to be confused with the final end of scripture, which is to promote the love of God and of neighbour, but neither is it to be neglected or disparaged. For Augustine, the study of scripture calls for the full range of available intellectual resources.

Augustine's literary-critical hypotheses have their broader context within a theological construal of the church's fourfold gospel. Here the key role is played by the Gospel of John, and the necessary conceptual tools are provided by the traditional identification of the fourfold gospel with the "four living creatures" of Revelation 4.6-7, one like a lion, the second like a calf, the third with a human face, the fourth like a flying eagle. While the four living creatures prove nothing, they do provide Irenaeus, Augustine, and others with conceptual resources for theological reflection on the phenomenon of the fourfold gospel. Augustine is familiar with two versions of this tradition. In Irenaeus, the human figure is associated with Matthew, the eagle with Mark, the calf with Luke, and the lion with John.[40] In a second version of the scheme, which Augustine prefers, Matthew is connected with the lion, Mark with the human figure, Luke with the calf, and John with the eagle.[41] Augustine criticizes the first version on the grounds that its advocates "based their conjecture only on the beginnings of the books, not on the evangelists' entire scope [*non de tota intentione evangelistarum*], which is what really needed to be investigated."[42] This is a valid criticism of Irenaeus, whose equations are all based on the openings of the respective gospels: the lion-like confidence of "In the beginning was the Word . . ." (John); the figure of Zacharias the priest, potentially associated with a sacrificial calf (Luke); the humanity emphasized by Jesus' genealogy (Matthew); and the introductory Isaiah citation that evokes "the winged aspect of the gospel"

---

40. On Augustine's knowledge of Irenaeus, see Bertold Altaner, "Augustinus und Irenäus," in his *Kleine patristische Schriften*, ed. G. Glockmann (Berlin: Academie Verlag, 1967), pp. 194-203. A more direct influence may have been Ambrose, who provides his own statement of the Irenaean scheme in the prologue to his Luke commentary (*In Luc.*, prol. 8). Possible echoes of Ambrose's work in *De Consensu* are listed in Vogels, *St Augustins Schrift*, pp. 54-56.

41. Although it is not mentioned, Jerome's version of the scheme may represent an intermediate stage between Irenaeus and Augustine (Jerome, *C. Iovin.* i.26; *Comm. in Matth.* [Preface], both of which might have been available to Augustine). A single transposition is required to convert Irenaeus's version (Mt = human, Mk = eagle, Lk = calf, Jn = lion) into Jerome's (Mk = lion, Jn = eagle). Similarly, a single transposition converts Jerome's version (Mt = human, Mk = lion) into Augustine's (Mt = lion, Mk = human).

42. Augustine, *De Cons. Evang.* i.6.9.

(Mark).[43] Augustine argues that the symbolic connections should seek to account for the *whole* of each gospel — although in practice he does not fully develop this point. Careful investigation is said to reveal a priestly orientation in a number of passages in the Gospel of Luke; but he does not specify what these are. The leonine, kingly orientation of Matthew is asserted purely on the basis of the magi's quest for "the king of the Jews" (Mt. 2.2). It is in connection with John that the symbolism proves its worth in illuminating the fourfold canonical gospel as a whole.

Augustine's reflections on the Johannine eagle bring to light a basic difference within the company of the four living creatures:

> These three creatures — the lion, the human and the calf — are all earthbound [*in terra gradiuntur*]. It follows that the three corresponding evangelists are primarily concerned with the things Christ did in the flesh, and with his instructions for the conduct of this mortal life, addressed to those who still bear the burden of the flesh. John, on the other hand, flies like an eagle above the clouds of human weakness, and gazes on the light of unchangeable truth [*lucem incommutabilis veritatis*] with the sharpest and steadiest eyes, those of the heart.[44]

> The first three evangelists present their diverse accounts of what Christ did in human flesh during his historical life [*quas Christus per humanam carnem temporaliter gessit*], whereas John had in view above all the Lord's divinity, in which he is equal to the Father, and strove to emphasize this in his gospel so far as he thought it necessary for his readers. He is therefore borne up high above the other three, so that you may consider these as remaining on this earth below in order to engage with the human Christ [*cum Christo homine conversari*], but John as ascending above the clouds covering the whole earth and attaining that pure heaven where, with sharpest and steadiest intellectual vision [*acie mentis acutissima atque firmissima*], he sees the Word of God who was in the beginning with God, through whom all things were made, and knows him as made flesh to dwell among us. . . .[45]

Three of the living creatures are associated with the earth and the fourth with the sky, and this creates a fundamental distinction within the fourfold

---

43. Irenaeus, *Adv. Haer.* iii.11.8.
44. Augustine, *De Cons. Evang.* i.6.9.
45. Augustine, *De Cons. Evang.* i.4.7.

canonical gospel which transcends the differences among the earthbound creatures themselves. The synoptic gospels have to do with Jesus' humanity, but also with our own; for they offer instruction for our journey through this earthly life. The fourth gospel has to do with Jesus' divinity, but also with our own participation in the divine; for it enables us to share in its own vision of ultimate reality, the eternal life of the undivided trinity. This eagle is characterized not only by its soaring flight but also by the keenness of its vision. It can gaze straight into the sun. In applying the image of the eagle to John rather than to Mark, Augustine has used the traditional symbolism as he says it should be used: to characterize an entire gospel in its differentiation from the others.[46]

While the Johannine Jesus remains a human, earthbound figure, his humanity is the flesh assumed by the divine Word; and it is this divine and enfleshed Word who speaks when Jesus proclaims that "I and the Father are one" (Jn. 10.30). That is the unchangeable truth this gospel enables us to contemplate. In the fourth gospel, on Augustine's reading of it, we rise above — or penetrate behind — the this-worldly, historical phenomena of Jesus' life to the transcendent heavenly reality that is its basis and context. Canonical structure corresponds here to christological dogma. If the fundamental distinction within the fourfold gospel is the one that demarcates Christ's humanity (the synoptics) from his divinity (John), then the "two natures doctrine" finds its basis and rationale precisely in this canonical structuring. Augustine's differentiation of John from the synoptics is therefore to be distinguished from the approach characteristic of modern scholarship. For Augustine the respective emphases on humanity and divinity represent divergent yet complementary orientations within a fourfold canonical gospel rather than incommensurable expressions of early Christian doctrinal diversity.[47]

46. Augustine's use of the Johannine eagle is theologically more substantial than two earlier attempts to justify this equation. According to Epiphanius, the living creature with the face of an eagle corresponds to John, who "proclaims the Word who came from heaven and was made flesh and flew to heaven like an eagle after the resurrection with the Godhead" (*De Mens.* 35, translation from *Epiphanius' Treatise on Weights and Measures: The Syriac Version,* ed. James Elmer Dean [Chicago: University of Chicago Press, 1935]). According to Jerome, John, "like an eagle soars aloft and reaches the Father himself, saying, 'In the beginning was the Word, and the Word was with God, and the Word was God,' and so on" (*C. Iovin.* i.26, translation from NPNF 6).

47. The distinctiveness of the fourth gospel in relation to the others is already noted by Clement of Alexandria, for whom this is a πνευματικὸν εὐαγγέλιον written to complement the synoptic emphasis on τὰ σωματικά (cited in Eusebius, *HE* vi.14.7). While Clement's terminology evokes the hermeneutical distinction between literal and allegorical, Augustine's reflects the developed christological dogma.

In the distinction between the first three gospels and the fourth, the canonical gospel corresponds not only to the two natures doctrine but also to
the structure of the human soul. According to Augustine, there are

> two faculties [*virtutes*] assigned to the human soul, one active, the other
> contemplative; one by which one journeys [*illa qua itur*], the other by
> which one arrives [*ista qua pervenitur*]; one by which one labours for
> purity of heart in hope of seeing God; the other by which one is at rest
> and sees God; one concerned with directions for the conduct of this tem-
> poral life [*in praeceptis exercendae vitae huius temporalis*], the other, with
> instruction in that life which is eternal [*in doctrina vitae illius
> sempiternae*].[48]

In this account of the human condition, the present life is a journey towards a vision of God that belongs to the life to come but that can be anticipated here and now. The *virtus contemplativa* belongs to the soul as pres-
ently constituted, and not just to its postmortem or postresurrection state;
it is related to the *virtus activa* as the Sabbath to the rest of the week. In its
relation to the divine, it is the fixed point that gives the active life its true
orientation, making it a journey towards a goal rather than an aimless wandering. Yet it is not a substitute for the active life. One cannot and should
not live by contemplation alone, abstaining from action, seeking to love
God without the love of neighbour. Nor are the faculties of action and contemplation simply given along with existence itself. They require to be directed, in relation both to the journey and to its goal. The whole of scripture is concerned with this double-sided direction, but it is especially
evident in the fourfold gospel:

> Three evangelists give a fuller account of the Lord's historical acts
> [*temporalia facta Domini*] and of the sayings which serve to guide our
> conduct in the present life — thereby concerning themselves with the
> active faculty. John, on the other hand, narrates far fewer of the historical
> acts but records the sayings with care and in great detail, especially those
> that deal with the unity of the Trinity and the blessedness of eternal life
> — thereby fulfilling his intention of commending the contemplative
> faculty.[49]

---

48. Augustine, *De Cons. Evang.* i.5.8. This distinction is closely related to Augustine's extended meditation on the double love commandment in *De Doct. Chr.* i.22.20–40.44.

49. Augustine, *De Cons. Evang.* i.5.8.

The "historical acts" narrated by the synoptics but not by John include most of the incidents of the Galilean ministry. The teaching about conduct is contained above all in the Sermon on the Mount (named as such by Augustine himself), which he elsewhere describes as "the perfect model of the Christian life" and as "perfect in all the precepts by which the Christian life is moulded."[50] In the case of John, Augustine is impressed especially by the focus on Jesus' own identity in relation to the Father, the central theme of the Johannine debates and discourses. This Johannine rendering of Jesus' relation to God mediates and shapes the practices of contemplation that seek the vision of God as the goal of the human journey. Augustine's reflection on the fourfold gospel proposes a christology, an ethic, and a spirituality that correspond to its bipartite structure.

The Illusions of Harmony

While the first three living creatures are all characterized as earthbound, each has a distinct identity of its own. The lion is almost as different from the human or the calf as it is from the eagle. It is unfortunate, then, that in the main body of his work on the consensus of the evangelists Augustine seeks to minimize difference. Difference is seen as a threat to be negotiated, and techniques of harmonization are developed in order to ensure that multiple perspectives will always be reduced to singularity. "Even where there is difference in wording [*varium . . . in verbis*]," he argues, "there is no departure from the same sense [*ab eadem . . . sententia*]."[51]

It is true that Augustine is acutely conscious of differences of wording, and trains his reader to notice them and to take them seriously. He never complains that critics of the gospels are forcing him to attend to minutiae that are really beneath his notice, distracting him from his great work on the doctrine of the trinity.[52] Gospel differences are not minutiae noted only by the malicious. On the contrary, they are objective features of the sacred texts, indeed they constitute the individuality of these texts, and they are therefore

---

50. Augustine, *De Sermone Domini in Monte secundum Matthaeum* i.i.i.

51. Augustine, *De Cons. Evang.* i.12.26.

52. Augustine tells how, "during the years in which I was gradually composing the books, *On the Trinity,* by unceasing labour, I also wrote others, temporarily interposing the latter into periods meant for the former. Among these, there are four books, *On the Harmony of the Evangelists,* composed because of those who falsely accuse the evangelists of lacking agreement" (*Retractations* ii.42; Eng. trans. in *FC* [Washington, D.C.: Catholic University of America Press, 1968]).

worthy of attention. While some of the differences Augustine discusses are well-known problems treated by earlier Christian writers, in most cases they seem to reflect his own independent research.[53] Gospel differences are far from trivial; but that is in large part because they represent for Augustine a far from trivial *problem*.[54]

Gospel plurality introduces the unwelcome possibility that error may come to light. In seeking to emulate Matthew, telling the same story but differently, Mark embarks on a dangerous undertaking (at least on Augustine's initial source-critical premises). Mark chooses to omit much and to add rather less, but the danger is especially acute where the second evangelist provides his own rendering of material shared with the first.

According to Matthew, Jesus taught crowds and disciples a series of parables as he sat by the seashore, and then proceeded to Nazareth, his hometown, where he provoked astonishment and offence (Mt. 13.1-58). Mark records the same parabolic teaching in abbreviated form, but then has Jesus setting out to cross the lake and stilling the storm that arose during the crossing (Mk. 4.1-41). Matthew's account is not improbable in itself, yet, for Augustine, Mark is more likely to have provided the true historical sequence.[55] Mark clearly deviates from Matthew here, but does he "contradict" him, in which case the first evangelist may have fallen into error? Given that both evangelists were inspired to write by the Holy Spirit, contradiction and consequent error are in principle impossible. Yet even "apparent" contradic-

53. Problems that Augustine inherits from earlier writers include the divergent genealogies (Julius Africanus, *Letter to Aristides*); the flight to Egypt or the return to Nazareth (Eusebius, *Quaestiones ac Solutiones circa Euangelia ad Stephanum*, q. 16); the instruction to the disciples to carry a staff or no staff at all (Apollinaris of Laodicea, *Commentarius in Matthaeum*, fr. 46); and Christ's crucifixion at the third or sixth hour (Ambrosiaster, *Liber Quaestionum Veteris et Novi Testamenti*, q. 65). For texts and translations, see H. Merkel, *Die Pluralität der Evangelien als theologisches und exegetisches Problem in der Alten Kirche* (Bern: Lang, 1978), pp. 50-57 (Africanus), 72-76 (Eusebius), 96-99 (Ambrosiaster), 98-99 (Apollinaris); for analysis, see the same author's *Widersprüche zwischen den Evangelien*. A general familiarity with traditional problems and solutions is likely even if H. J. Vogels is right to argue that Augustine's knowledge of earlier harmonization literature was minimal (*St Augustins Schrift*, pp. 48-61).

54. In *De Cons. Evang.* i.7.10, Augustine states his intention not only of refuting the gospels' critics but also of addressing fellow Christians who take an interest in the problem of harmonization. His own personal stake in the issue may stem in part from his relationship to Manicheanism, as H. Merkel argues (*Widersprüche*, pp. 224-27). Manichean views on the gospels are preserved and refuted in Augustine's *Contra Faustum* (on which see Merkel, pp. 23-31). Pagan critics such as Celsus, Porphyry, and Julian are more concerned with absurd or otherwise objectionable elements in the gospels than with contradictions per se.

55. Augustine, *De Cons. Evang.* ii.42.89.

tions can appear all too real. Inconsequential though they may seem in isolation, they may occur at any point where two or more evangelists are telling the same story, and their cumulative effect on the Christian reader may be such as to undermine faith. Thus gospel differences must be investigated with an eye to apparent contradictions, and apparent contradictions must be shown to be no more than apparent, resolvable into the singularity of a composite narrative. The plurality of the gospels is a threat to their credibility. Evangelists subsequent to Matthew open up the possibility of error manifested as contradiction, and it is Augustine's task to close off that possibility. The difference between the four living creatures loses its theological significance as it is converted into a problem for apologetics. And so Augustine undertakes a systematic investigation of the principles of gospel harmonization, developing a range of explanatory devices in order to demonstrate noncontradiction or "consensus."[56]

The problem of divergent sequence is addressed by postulating *displacement*. This is straightforward where an evangelist provides only a vague indication of sequence ("After these things . . . ," for example, or "In those days . . ."). In the case of the sequel to Matthew's parable collection, the evangelist reports that "when Jesus had finished these parables, he went away from there, and coming to his own country he taught them in their synagogue . . ." (Mt. 13.53-54). In the light of Mark, we need not suppose that Jesus proceeded directly from the lakeside to Nazareth. The account of the visit to Nazareth has become displaced from the true historical sequence, but an evangelist is not obliged to follow that sequence and there is no need to suppose error or contradiction in such cases.

> What does it matter where any of [the evangelists] locates a particular story? What difference does it make whether he includes the material in its proper sequence, or inserts at a later point what was previously omitted, or mentions at an earlier stage what really happened at a later — so long as he contradicts neither himself nor a second writer in narrating the same facts or others?[57]

---

56. See Vogels, *St Augustins Schrift*, pp. 93-130, for analysis of Augustine's harmonistic practice under the headings of "Worte und Reden" (pp. 96-106), "Geschichten" (pp. 106-17), and "Chronologie" (pp. 117-30); also Merkel, *Widersprüche*, pp. 227-50.

57. Augustine, *De Cons. Evang.* ii.21.51 (reading *adversetur* rather than *adversentur*). Augustine is here discussing Matthew's account of the healing of Peter's mother-in-law (Mt. 8.14-17), which occurs *after* the cleansing of a leper (Mt. 8.1-4), in contrast to the Markan sequence (Mk. 1.29-45).

Augustine here *stipulates* that differences in sequence are not to be regarded as "contradictions," while acknowledging that they entail a degree of noncorrespondence to historical occurrence. Only if both divergent texts were intended to represent an actual historical sequence might it be said that one is correct and the other in error. These differences in sequence are explicable along psychological lines:

> However excellent and trustworthy the knowledge one has acquired of the facts, it is not in one's own power to determine the order in which one will recall them to memory; for the way in which one thing comes to mind before or after another is something which proceeds not as we will but simply as it is given to us. It is therefore reasonable to suppose that each of the evangelists believed it his duty to narrate what was to be narrated in the order in which it pleased God to suggest to his recollection the matters he was engaged in recording.[58]

If it was the Holy Spirit who governed the processes of recollection that underlie the different sequences, it might be possible to investigate *why* one evangelist was led to narrate events in one sequence and another in another. In other words, one might expect to find a theological rationale for a nonhistorical sequence. This promising suggestion remains undeveloped, however, for it falls outside "the scope of the work we are undertaking at present," which is "simply to demonstrate that none of the evangelists contradicts either himself or the others."[59] Yet Augustine does here accept in principle that canonical plurality discloses a degree of noncorrespondence to prior historical reality, and that this can be adequately explained not only psychologically but also theologically.

The limits of the noncorrespondence Augustine is prepared to tolerate are evident in his exceptionally cautious appeal to *variation*. According to Matthew, the divine voice at Jesus' baptism announced that "*This is* my beloved Son, in *whom* I am well-pleased"; according to Mark and Luke, "*You are* my beloved Son, in *you* I am well-pleased" (Mt. 3.17; Mk. 1.11; Lk. 3.22). On this occasion, Augustine remains unconcerned about the difference and is even prepared to assess it positively:

> If you ask which of these different utterances represents what was actually said by the voice, you may select whichever you wish, provided you un-

58. Augustine, *De Cons. Evang.* ii.21.51.
59. Augustine, *De Cons. Evang.* ii.21.52.

derstand that those writers who have not reproduced exactly the same words have still reproduced the same sense. Indeed these variations in the manner of expression are also useful, since what is said in one way only may be inadequately understood or interpreted in something other than its true sense. . . .[60]

Variations between gospels may be regarded either negatively (as a problem to be contained), or neutrally (as different renderings of the same sense), or positively (as enabling fuller understanding). But positive assessments such as this one are all too rare in Augustine's work, since they entail a degree of noncorrespondence to historical reality that he is normally reluctant to concede.

According to Matthew, John the Baptist said of the Coming One that he, John, was unworthy to *carry* his shoes (Mt. 3.11). According to Mark and Luke, what he said was that he was unworthy to *unloose* his shoes, preceded in Mark alone by "to stoop down and . . ." (Mk. 1.7; Lk. 3.16). In view of Augustine's attitude to the divine voice at Jesus' baptism, one might have expected him to allow these variants to stand. The two versions refer to very similar forms of menial service, and they make exactly the same point about the Baptist's inferiority to the Coming One. Yet Augustine chooses to emphasize the factual issue: "It is reasonable to pose the question what it was that John declared himself unworthy to do — whether to bear the shoes or to unloose the shoe's latchet."[61] If John uttered just one of these statements, then we might suppose that an evangelist who reports the other has suffered a memory-slip. John certainly referred to his own unworthiness in relation to the Coming One's sandals, but did he speak of "unloosing" them or of "carrying" them? Augustine considers it inappropriate to imagine an evangelist afflicted with forgetfulness, and concludes instead that the Baptist either said similar things on different occasions or both things on the same occasion. In the latter case, he may have said something like, ". . . whose shoe's latchet I am unworthy to unloose, and whose shoes I am unworthy to carry." If so, then "one of the evangelists may have reproduced one part of the saying, and the rest of them the other."[62] Thus, the complete original saying is

---

60. Augustine, *De Cons. Evang.* ii.14.31. This passage recalls others where Augustine affirms plurality rather than being threatened by it: e.g. *Conf.* xii.16.23–32.43 (multiple interpretations of Gn. 1.1-2); *De Civ. Dei* xviii.43 (the complementarity of the Hebrew scriptures and the Septuagint). Unfortunately even the limited flexibility here conceded to the evangelists is atypical.

61. Augustine, *De Cons. Evang.* ii.12.29.

62. Augustine, *De Cons. Evang.* ii.12.29.

recovered by incorporating the variants into a singular utterance. This might be described as *conflation,* and it is highly characteristic of Augustine's harmonistic procedure as a whole. Equally characteristic is the alternative solution, which is to envisage two very similar sayings as uttered on different occasions: this may be described as *duplication.* Conflation makes one saying or story out of two; duplication, two out of one.[63]

Duplication is the preferred explanation in the event of intractable difference between two otherwise similar passages. Luke's Sermon on the Plain is so closely related to Matthew's Sermon on the Mount that one is inclined to see it as the same discourse but with certain passages omitted — until one notices that "Matthew tells us that this discourse was delivered on a mountain by the Lord while seated, whereas Luke states that it was spoken on a plain by the Lord while standing."[64] Augustine might have regarded this as a variation that enhances the sense of the texts, as in the case of the divine voice at Jesus' baptism. But he would then have to relax his demand for precise correspondence between the texts and historical facts, and that he is rarely willing to do. Rather than admit noncorrespondence, Augustine prefers to conclude that the Lord delivered similar teaching on more than one occasion, and that Matthew records one version of this teaching, Luke another.

Duplication may also be found within Jesus' actions. In Mark Jesus bestows sight on a blind man, Bartimaeus, as he *leaves* Jericho (Mk. 10.46; cf. Mt. 20.29). In Luke, where the blind man is not named, Jesus performs a similar action as he *approaches* Jericho (Lk. 18.35). The action is so similar that the two evangelists might seem to speak of one and the same event. Yet Augustine is resolutely opposed to any such suggestion:

> The idea that the evangelists really contradict each other here, in that one says, "As he approached Jericho . . . ," while the others say, "As he left Jericho . . . ," is one that no-one will be persuaded to accept, except those who would rather have the gospel regarded as untrustworthy than conclude that [Christ] accomplished two similar miracles in similar circumstances.[65]

63. In appealing to conflation and duplication to explain gospel variants, Augustine departs from his own principle that the same sense may be communicated — perhaps more effectively — in the use of different words. As Vogels notes, "in der Anwendung der eigenen Grundsätze zeigt er sich sehr zurückhaltend und vorsichtig" (*St Augustins Schrift,* p. 98).

64. Augustine, *De Cons. Evang.* ii.19.45, referring to Mt. 5.1; Lk. 6.17.

65. Augustine, *De Cons. Evang.* ii.65.126.

To tolerate even a single apparently harmless "discrepancy," for which a rationale might be found within the Lukan context, is to open the door to the disastrous view that the canonical gospel is untrustworthy — a view to which its own plural form makes it vulnerable. If the evangelists refer to the same miracle, one or other statement about its setting would lack the all-important correspondence to factual occurrence; the possibility of a positive nonfactual significance is not recognized. For Augustine it is more important to protect the gospel from its own plurality than to celebrate its diversity. Like his other harmonistic techniques, his appeal to duplication is problematic not only because it leads to counterintuitive conclusions, but also because it can find no positive significance in the canonical plurality. Claiming to vindicate the canonical gospel against its detractors, it undermines it by reducing it to unharmonious monotony.

The appeal to duplication is a last resort. Jesus cannot simultaneously be seated on a mountain and standing on a plain; he cannot simultaneously approach Jericho and leave it. It is only the most obdurate differences that compel the conclusion that two versions of closely similar material represent two distinct events. Most differences are more amenable: out of two or more versions, a single composite version may be created in which each of the differences has its place. When Jesus asked his disciples who people believed him to be, Luke states that he was praying (Lk. 9.18), Mark that he was on the road (Mk. 8.27). There is no difficulty in taking these statements to be true simultaneously. This case "will only disturb one who has never prayed while on the road."[66]

Augustine finds support within the gospel texts themselves for this practice of conflation. At the feeding of the five thousand, according to Mark 6.40, the crowds sat down in groups, "by hundreds and by fifties." The parallel passage in Luke 9.14 speaks only of groups of fifty.[67] For Augustine, it is clear that Luke has recounted part of the truth, Mark the whole. If Mark too had recounted only part of the truth, speaking only of the groups of a hundred, the result would have been an apparent contradiction which critics of the gospels would no doubt have exploited. Yet Mark's reference to groups of fifty as well as a hundred eliminates the appearance of a contradiction, and, more importantly, shows how divergent statements may both be true even where explicit common ground is lacking. None of the extant gospels actually tells us that Jesus asked who people believed him to be "while he was

66. Augustine, *De Cons. Evang.* ii.53.108.
67. Augustine, *De Cons. Evang.* ii.46.98.

praying on the road"; but the full text may be reconstructed along these lines, since cases where one evangelist asserts *A* and another *B* are to be understood as equivalent to cases where one evangelist asserts *A* and another *AB*.[68] The common ground must be assumed even where it is not actually visible.

Conflation may be practised on a small scale, but it also holds out the prospect of reducing the four gospels to a single composite text in the manner of Tatian's *Diatessaron*.[69] Unlike Tatian more than two centuries earlier, Augustine does not actually produce his single, harmonized gospel narrative in full, but reconstructs only fragments of the complete text. Yet his is a more ambitious project than Tatian's. In its focus on specific details and methodological principles, *De Consensu Evangelistarum* may be understood as prolegomena to a harmonized gospel, intended to show how such a gospel *might* be constructed on the basis of responsible and defensible scholarly procedures. Ostensibly concerned merely to prove a negative, that the gospels do not contradict one another, it does so by postulating a single comprehensive text that might be reconstructed out of the fourfold canonical

68. This rule is later restated in connection with the two animals on which, according to Mt. 21.1-7, Jesus rode into Jerusalem (Augustine, *De Cons. Evang.* ii.66.127). On this see Merkel, *Widersprüche*, pp. 239-41.

69. In spite of the well-known difficulties in establishing the text of the *Diatessaron* from the extant Arabic, Latin, and Syriac witnesses, these witnesses do allow a study of Tatian's harmonistic technique where they attest a common sequence. This makes a comparison with Augustine possible; see below for examples of this. There are three major resources for the study of the *Diatessaron*. (1) The *Arabic Harmony* (henceforth *AH*) translated from Syriac in the eleventh century and extant in six manuscripts. Two of these were edited by A. Ciasca in 1888, in a publication in which the Arabic text is given in volume 1 and a Latin translation in volume 2 (*Tatiani Evangeliorum Harmoniae Arabice* [Rome: Bibliographia Polyglotta, 1888]). The Arabic was translated into English by H. Hogg (ANF 10, ed. A. Menzies [repr. Grand Rapids: Eerdmans, 1974], pp. 35-129). An edition based on a newly discovered manuscript was published in 1935 by A.-S. Marmardji (*Diatessaron de Tatien* [Beirut: Imprimerie Catholique, 1935]). (2) *Codex Fuldensis* (henceforth *CF*). This sixth-century manuscript contains a Latin harmony, which its first editor (Victor of Capua, 546 CE) identified with Tatian's *Diatessaron*. See E. Ranke (ed.), *Codex Fuldensis* (Marburg & Leipzig: N. G. Elwert, 1868). (3) Ephrem's commentary on the *Diatessaron*, which survives in the original Syriac and in an Armenian translation. See L. Leloir, *Saint Éphrem, Commentaire de l'Évangile concordant, version arménienne* (Louvain: Peeters, 1953-54); L. Leloir, *Saint Éphrem, Commentaire de l'Évangile concordant, texte syriaque* (Dublin: Hoddaes Figgis, 1963); L. Leloir, *Éphrem de Nisibe, Commentaire de l'Évangile concordant ou Diatessaron: traduit du syriaque et de l'arménien* (Paris: du Cerf, 1966). For full discussion of these and other primary sources, see William L. Petersen, *Tatian's Diatessaron: Its Creation, Dissemination, Significance, and History in Scholarship*, VCSupp (Leiden: Brill, 1994).

gospel. While the realized composite text is a goal yet to be attained, Augustine can also envisage it as *predating* the canonical gospels, since it represents the full scope of the collective apostolic memory from which the individual evangelists selectively drew.

Augustine explains the logic of large-scale conflation as he discusses the Matthean and Lukan sequels to Jesus' birth in Bethlehem. In Matthew the child is under threat, and the holy family is warned by an angel to take refuge in Egypt. After Herod's death, the move to Nazareth in Galilee is occasioned by fear of his successor Archelaus, ruler of Judea. In Luke, the journey to Nazareth occurs "when they had performed everything according to the law of the Lord" (Lk. 2.39). Here, Nazareth is "their own city" to which they return as a matter of course, rather than a place of refuge from the threat of persecution. There seems no room in the Lukan narrative for the lengthy detour via Egypt. Augustine's explanation is that the later evangelist has chosen to omit the Egyptian episode and create a purely literary connection between events that were in reality disconnected. As Matthew demonstrates, a long interval separated Jesus' birth from the move to Nazareth, whereas Luke speaks of the one event as leading directly to the other. According to Augustine, a crucial methodological point comes to light in this difference:

> Here, indeed, we must recognize a principle that will also apply in other similar cases, so that these may not agitate or disturb our minds: the principle that each evangelist composes his narrative [*contexere narrationem suam*] in such a way that it seems an orderly sequence [*series digesta videatur*], with nothing omitted. For, silently passing over what he does not wish to narrate, he connects what he does wish to narrate to what he has already narrated, so that these matters might seem to follow immediately [*ut ipsa continuo sequi videantur*].[70]

In stating that "when they had performed everything according to the law of the Lord, they returned to Galilee . . ." (Lk. 2.39), Luke creates the impression that the return to Galilee followed immediately after the completion of the law's ritual requirements. Yet for Augustine the connection is a literary device intended to impose continuity on the disparate, diverse events selected for narration.

Opening up the narrative space concealed behind the Lukan connection, we discover that the real narrative sequence — that is, the harmonized, conflated one that also corresponds most closely to historical events — runs

---

70. Augustine, *De Cons. Evang.* ii.5.16.

as follows.[71] At the time of his birth, Jesus is acclaimed by the shepherds, and circumcised on the eighth day (Lk. 2.1-21). Shortly afterwards, the magi arrive in Jerusalem and are led by the star to the child's residence in Bethlehem; warned in a dream, they return to their homeland without reporting back to Herod (Mt. 2.1-12). After that, the child Jesus is presented in the temple, and is acclaimed by Simeon and Anna (Lk. 2.22-38). The seam that follows is particularly noteworthy (*L* = Luke, *M* = Matthew):

> *L* And when they had performed all things according to the law of the Lord — *M* behold, the angel of the Lord appeared to Joseph in a dream, saying, "Arise, and take the young child and his mother, and flee into Egypt. . . ." (Lk. 2.39; Mt. 2.13)

Here is conflation in action: Luke introduces a sentence which Matthew completes. This, we recall, is for Augustine the *true* sequence concealed by Luke's fictive connection between the completion of prescribed rites in Jerusalem and the return to Nazareth.[72] Augustine intends this example to illustrate a procedure that can also be applied elsewhere, with far-reaching results. Wherever in the gospels one thing is narrated *as if* it led directly to another, the passage in question will have to be compared with parallel material in other gospels, so as to investigate whether narrative sequence corresponds to reality, or whether it conceals an interval during which something else occurred that is recounted in another gospel. The individual gospels each represent no more than a fragment of the larger narrative which corresponds to the full historical reality. Only when the fragments are reassembled will text and reality be in harmony with one another. The "consensus of the evangelists" requires the sacrifice of their individual integrity, in order to attain a degree of correspondence to historical fact which their fourfold canonical form precludes.

It is Augustine's discussion of the Easter story that represents his most

71. Augustine, *De Cons. Evang.* ii.5.17.

72. In contrast, the *Diatessaron* leaves Lk. 1.5–2.39 intact, with the exception of the Matthean annunciation to Joseph inserted at the end of Lk. 1 (*AH* [= *Arabic Harmony*] i.6–ii.47 [ii.1-8]; *CF* [= *Codex Fuldensis*] ii.5–vii.39 [v.18-25]; cf. Ephrem, *Commentary* ii.1). The visit of the magi and the flight to Egypt (Mt. 2) occur *after* the Lukan return to Nazareth; in consequence, a second visit to Bethlehem is required (*AH* iii.1-18; *CF* viii.1–x.18; cf. Ephrem, *Commentary* ii.18). Tatian has taken his cue from Mt. 2.16, which permits the possibility of a two-year interval. For a similar reconstruction, see Eusebius, *Quaestiones ac Solutiones circa Euangelia ad Stephanum*, q. 16; Epiphanius, *Pan.* li.9.1-13. Texts and translations in Merkel, *Pluralität*, pp. 72-77 (Eusebius), 116-21 (Epiphanius).

ambitious exercise in conflation.[73] It is, he discovers, no easy task to piece together the fragments in order to reconstruct the actual course of events on Easter morning.

According to Matthew, the women who visit the tomb early encounter a glorious angel seated on the stone he has rolled away from the tomb (Mt. 28.2-3). In Mark, they see that the stone has been rolled away, they enter the tomb, and there encounter a young man in white (Mk. 16.4-5). The harmonizer must decide whether these two figures are to be differentiated or identified. The first option is represented by Tatian's *Diatessaron*, which tells how the women

> *L* came and found the stone removed from the tomb, *M and the angel sitting* upon the stone. And his appearance was as lightning, and his raiment white as snow; and for fear of him the guards were troubled, and became as dead men. *And when he departed*, *L* the women entered the tomb, and did not find the body of Jesus. *Mk* And they saw there a young man sitting on the right, wearing a white garment; and they were amazed. And the angel answered and said to the women, "Fear not, for I know that you seek Jesus the Nazarene. . . ."[74]

73. Augustine attempts a comprehensive harmonization of the resurrection narratives, in contrast to the focus on specific issues in earlier discussions. Eusebius's *Quaestiones Euangelicae ad Marinum* discusses the timing of the resurrection (q. 1) and the contrasting Matthean and Johannine presentation of Mary's visit(s) to the tomb (q. 2). In his letter to Basilides, Dionysius of Alexandria also discusses the timing issue, although he is concerned with the practical question of when to end the pre-Easter fast. Texts and translations in Merkel, *Pluralität*, pp. 56-63 (Dionysius), 77-89 (Eusebius). It is striking that almost all the material cited by Merkel is derived either from commentaries or from work in the question-and-answer genre (Eusebius, Ambrosiaster). Both genres encourage a focus on individual points. As Merkel notes, "Augustin ist der Erste, der das Problem [der Harmonisierung] nicht nur grundsätzlich erfasst, sondern auch eigens und in voller Breite bewältigt hat" (*Pluralität*, p. xxiv).

74. *AH* lii.49-54, cf. *CF* clxxiv.4-6; Lk. 24.2; Mt. 28.2-4; Lk. 24.3; Mk. 16.5b-6a. Italics indicate an alteration or addition occasioned by the harmonizing process: the angel is now *perceived* as seated by the women *(AH, CF)*, and his departure is specified. In *CF*, the angel's speech is given in its Matthean form (*CF* clxxiv.5-6 = Mt. 28.5-6); there is therefore no need for the Markan "young man," who is eliminated. In *AH*, the Matthean angel is silent, leaving it to his Markan counterpart to address the women. *CF*'s substitution of Matthean for Markan material is in keeping with the "Vulgatizing" tendency of this manuscript (Petersen, *Tatian's Diatessaron*, p. 129). Assimilation to the Vulgate is often also assimilation to Matthew. Conversely, nonassimilation of Mark to Matthew is more likely to represent the *Diatessaron* in its second-century form; cf. *GPet* 11.44, 13.55-56 for another second-century rendering of the Markan "young man."

Here, the Matthean angel has the task of removing the stone and terrifying the guards, and his departure is the signal for the women to enter the tomb. Within it, they meet the Markan angel, whose task is to communicate the Easter message. But Tatian can only differentiate the two angels by suppressing the fact that Matthew's angel also has a message for the women, outside the tomb, virtually identical to the one Mark assigns to his young man in white within it.

Impressed by the near-identical messages, Augustine takes the other option and identifies the two figures.[75] The difficulty is that one angel is outside the tomb and the other inside, and the solution is to suppose that the word "tomb" is used in different senses. It may refer either to the rock-hewn cavity in which Jesus' body was placed, or to a larger enclosed area around this cavity. If so, then Mark's "Entering the tomb, they saw a young man sitting on the right side" is entirely compatible with Matthew's angel seated on the stone: Mark is thinking of the larger enclosure.[76] The identification has one initial disadvantage, however. If the Matthean and Markan angels are two rather than one, it is tempting to connect them to Luke's "two men standing by them in dazzling apparel" (Lk. 24.4), who also serve as messengers. Matthew and Mark would each present a half-truth preserved entire in Luke. Yet Augustine decides against this tempting possibility, which would have been fully in line with his principles.[77] The problem is not just that Luke's angels stand whereas Matthew's and Mark's are seated: for the two angels might each in turn have risen from their seated posture as they delivered their near-identical messages to the women. The problem is rather that Luke's angels are clearly located within the tomb in the narrower sense, the rock-hewn cavity rather than the larger enclosed area: for Luke has noted that "when they went in they did not find the body" (Lk. 24.3). This encounter with angels is to be identified with the one that John appears to ascribe to Mary alone, when, on her return to the tomb, "she stooped to look into the tomb, and saw two angels in white sitting where the body of Jesus had lain, one at the head and one at the feet" (Jn. 20.11-12).[78]

---

75. Augustine, *De Cons. Evang.* iii.24.63, 67, 69. Augustine discusses both possibilities, but finally opts for the identification of the Matthean angel with the Markan one.

76. Augustine, *De Cons. Evang.* iii.24.63.

77. Augustine, *De Cons. Evang.* iii.24.67.

78. Augustine, *De Cons. Evang.* iii.24.68-69. Augustine notes that Luke's angels stand whereas John's are seated, which he sees as an indication that Lk. 24.4-8 describes the third and final element in a complex angelic encounter, of which the first is provided by Mt. 28.2-7 (= Mk. 16.5-7)

So Augustine's reconstruction of the true historical sequence is as follows. The women arrive at the tomb (i.e. the enclosure), within which they encounter the angel, who delivers his message. Rather than running away immediately (as Matthew and Mark appear to state), they enter the tomb (i.e. the cavity: so Luke and John), where they encounter two more seated angels, who engage Mary in a short dialogue (John) before standing to address a further message to the group as a whole (Luke). There is a symmetry to this composite narrative. Matthew's singular angel is identified with Mark's; Luke's pair of angels are identified with John's; and the solitary Johannine Mary is provided with Lukan companions.

This conflation of Luke and John has further important consequences, for in John 20 Mary visits the tomb *twice*. On the first occasion, she discovers it to be empty but meets no angel and returns to the male disciples with the news that the Lord's body has been removed (vv. 1-2). Peter and John the beloved disciple run to the tomb, investigate its interior, and depart (vv. 3-10). But Mary has meanwhile returned to the tomb, and, looking in, experiences her vision of angels (vv. 11-13). At this point she still knows nothing of the resurrection, and believes that the body has been removed by human agency. Only through the encounter with Jesus himself does she learn the truth and return to announce it to the disciples (vv. 14-18).

For the harmonizer, the question is which of the Johannine Mary's visits to the tomb corresponds to the single visit reported by the synoptics. In the *Diatessaron*, it is assumed that the fourth evangelist opens his Easter narrative with a summary account of the visit more fully narrated by the others, and that the rest of the story tells of events that they omit.[79] For Augustine, the problem with this is that the Johannine account of the first visit (Jn. 20.1-2) leaves no possibility of an encounter with angels or of a joyful announcement of the resurrection to the male disciples (cf. Mt. 28.8; Lk. 24.8-9). There

---

and the second by Jn. 20.11-13. Following the initial question and answer ("Woman, why are you weeping?" etc.), the seated Johannine angels arise and deliver the Lukan message ("Why do you [*pl.*] seek the living among the dead?" etc.).

79. *AH* lii.48–53.24. On their first visit to the tomb, the women encounter (1) the Matthean angel outside the tomb (*AH* lii.48-52 = Mt. 28.2-4), (2) the Markan young man, inside the tomb (*AH* lii.53-55 = Mk. 16.5-6), (3) Luke's two men in shining garments (*AH* liii.1-8 = Lk. 24.4-9). There follow the Johannine account of Mary's report to Peter and the beloved disciple, their visit to the tomb, and Mary's (fourth) encounter with angels on her return to the tomb (*AH* liii.9-21 = Jn. 20.2-14). *CF* assimilates (2) to (1), as noted above, but is otherwise similarly arranged (*CF* clxxiv.4-10).

is no option but to connect the synoptic encounter with the angel(s) with the *second* visit to the tomb.[80]

In Luke, the sequence of events is narrated as follows:

> On the first day of the week, at early dawn, they went to the tomb, taking the spices which they had prepared. And they found the stone rolled away from the tomb, but when they went in they did not find the body. While they were perplexed about this, behold, two men stood by them in dazzling apparel. . . . (Lk. 24.1-4)

The angelic announcement of the resurrection follows at this point. This account is to be coordinated with the Johannine one, according to which:

> On the first day of the week Mary Magdalene came to the tomb early, while it was still dark, and saw that the stone had been taken away from the tomb. So she ran and went to Simon Peter and the other disciple, the one whom Jesus loved, and said to them, "They have taken the Lord out of the tomb, and we do not know where they have laid him." (Jn. 20.1-2)

If the Johannine story is to be accommodated, space will have to be found for it within the Lukan one. "And they found the stone rolled away from the tomb" (Luke) corresponds closely enough to ". . . saw that the stone had been taken away from the tomb" (John). At this point, Luke and John are both speaking of the first visit to the tomb. But when Luke proceeds to tell how "when they went in they did not find the body," he is actually speaking of the *second* visit, when the weeping Mary "stooped to look into the tomb" (John): for it is then that she encounters the two angels, seated (John) and then standing (Luke). We recall that, according to Augustine, the evangelists conceal their own omissions by creating the appearance of a continuous narrative, and this is a case in point. What Luke wrote is: "And they found the stone rolled away from the tomb, but when they went in they did not find the body." As we now know, the apparent sequence conceals a series of additional events occurring between the ones referred to in the first and second half of this statement: the Johannine supplement, but also the encounter with the Matthean and Markan angel seated on the stone on the right side of the tomb (i.e. the enclosure). Nothing that Luke tells us is untrue, however. It is true both that "they found the stone rolled away from the tomb" and that "when they went in they did not find the body." While it is not true that the

---

80. Augustine, *De Cons. Evang.* iii.24.69.

one event followed directly from the other, Luke does not explicitly affirm this sequence (for example, by adding the word "immediately"). Rather, he creates an *appearance* of sequence in order to connect the fragments he has selected from the prior comprehensive story.

It is that larger story, predating the gospels, that Augustine believes he has reconstructed out of the individual evangelists' diverse and fragmentary accounts. The aim of his exegetical labours has been to arrange

> all those events which, according to the evangelists' combined testimonies, occurred around the time of the Lord's resurrection into a single narrative [*in una quadam narratione*] . . . , as these events may actually have taken place [*quemadmodum geri potuerint*].[81]

Initially intending simply to vindicate the consensus of the evangelists, Augustine has in reality achieved far more than that — if his argument is judged to be successful. He has restored the apostolic recollection of the events of Easter morning in its authentic, original, and comprehensive form. Yet there is a price to pay. The consensus of the evangelists is vindicated, but the individual evangelists are not. Their individual assertions are all true, but the sequence in which they are set is misleading and unreliable. Luke reports the women's discovery that the stone had been rolled away and that the tomb was empty *as if* this was a single event, but in reality it was not. He and John both speak of the second angelic encounter *as if* it were the first, and they each narrate part of that second encounter *as if* it were the whole. Each evangelist recounts a half-truth that is also a quarter-truth.[82]

In consequence, the truth of the gospel is detached from the gospel's plural form. Indeed, the plural form is actually a hindrance to a clear grasp of the truth. For Augustine, the truth of the gospel is located in its corre-

---

81. Augustine, *De Cons. Evang.* iii.24.69.

82. As H. J. de Jonge notes, the presupposition here and elsewhere is that each of the four evangelists drew, selectively and under the guidance of the Holy Spirit, from a "common reservoir of information" to which they all had full and equal access ("Augustine on the Interrelations of the Gospels," p. 2416). "Since in principle each evangelist could dispose of precisely the same information as any other evangelist, it was meaningful for Augustine to state that an evangelist had 'left out' something which another evangelist had included, even if the former had not used the latter's Gospel as his source" (p. 2416). Yet for Augustine the later evangelist has access not only to the common reservoir of apostolic tradition but also to its partial written embodiment in the earlier gospel: he writes not in ignorance of his predecessor (*De Cons. Evang.* i.2.4), but — we should assume — in response to his work, which, if not exactly a "source" in a narrow sense, is at least a decisive influence.

spondence with empirical historical reality, and that correspondence is only attained where the individual narratives are incorporated into a greater whole, *una narratio*. The narratives must be harmonized with one another and thereby harmonized with reality itself. In their individual, plural form they do not represent an adequate window onto reality, since each is based only on fragmentary information which it presents as though it were the whole story, leading inevitably to the appearance of serious contradiction. Thus the form of the gospel must be sacrificed for the sake of its truth. Augustine betrays no consciousness that this procedure is in any way problematic. He is untroubled by the fact that there are *four* living creatures around the divine throne, that they are very different in appearance, and that there is no divine mandate for any attempt to reduce them to singularity. It does not occur to him that the canonical plurality might pose a question to his own assumption that — at least in this apologetically sensitive domain — truth can only occur in the one-to-one correspondence of assertion to fact.

The Old and the New

The dissolution of the gospel's canonical form is already far advanced in Augustine's work. Ostensibly, of course, it remains intact. It has been vindicated against its critics. Matthew, Mark, Luke, and John have been shown not to contradict one another, but rather to complement one another. But it has also been conceded that, if a contradiction *were* to be established, the credibility of the gospel would be undermined. In other words, the authority and integrity of the fourfold canonical gospel may now be *tested* by way of simple procedures that can be applied by any attentive reader. At least since the eighteenth century, there have been very many readers of the gospels who are entirely unpersuaded by the type of argument set forth by Augustine. Such readers do not accept that the empirical facts were parcelled out between the four evangelists, and that Mark and Matthew refer (in different ways) to just one part of a complex encounter with angels on Easter morning, while Luke and John refer (again, in different ways) to another. They note that each gospel describes a single angelic encounter as though it were the whole, and that the differences between them are nonnegotiable. On Augustine's premises, this straightforward literary observation amounts to the allegation of a "contradiction" — both between texts in themselves and between texts and historical reality — which, if established, would endanger the entire canonical structure. But it is Augustine himself who endangers the canonical structure by exposing it to this kind of empirical testing. As we shall see in the following chapter, Reimarus is unthinkable without Augustine. Augustine not only makes it *possible* for Reimarus to argue that his ten contradictions within the gospel Easter narratives are destructive of Christian faith; he also makes it *easy* for him to do so.

Reimarus, Lessing, and other critics of gospel harmonization do not engage directly with Augustine. *De Consensu Evangelistarum* establishes the ground rules for the science of harmonization, but it is not itself a gospel harmony. Its primary purpose is negative and defensive: to demonstrate through a large number of worked examples that the canonical gospels are noncontradictory, and to discover principles of harmonization that can be applied in other cases as and when necessary. Only occasionally — most notably in the case of the Easter stories — does Augustine show positive enthusiasm for the task of reconstructing the true historical sequence from the canonical witnesses. In contrast, actual gospel harmonies seek not so much to refute critics as to provide a fuller and more accurate account of the life of Christ in its sequential unfolding. It is the gospel harmonies of the early modern period that are the true precursors of the so-called "quest of the historical Jesus."

Published in Amsterdam in 1699, Jean Leclerc's work offers its readers a *Harmonia Evangelica, cui subjecta est Historia Christi ex Quatuor Evangeliis concinnata* — an Evangelical Harmony, to which is subjoined the History of Christ assembled from the four gospels.[83] In this work the Greek and Latin texts of the gospels are presented in parallel columns, as in a Synopsis, with the Greek on the left-hand page and the Latin on the right.[84] Unlike a Synopsis, however, this *Harmonia Evangelica* offers to guide its readers through the labyrinth of the composite text. Everywhere on its pages a hand-symbol

---

83. Jean Leclerc (1657-1736) was born in Geneva and taught from 1684 at the Remonstrant College in Amsterdam, an Arminian seminary. Other published works include an *Ars Critica* (1696) and commentaries on the Pentateuch (1699), the historical books (1708), and other Old Testament literature (1731). On Leclerc see Maria Cristina Pitassi, *Entre croire et savoir: Le problème de la méthode critique chez Jean Le Clerc* (Leiden: Brill, 1987); Cecilia Asso, "Erasmus redivivus. Alcune osservazioni sulla filologia neotestamentaria di Jean Le Clerc," in *Vico nella storia della filologia*, ed. Silvia Caianiello and Amadeu Viana (Naples: Guida, 2004), pp. 79-115. Leclerc's Harmony is briefly discussed by Heinrich Greeven, "The Gospel Synopsis from 1776 to the Present Day," in *J. J. Griesbach*, pp. 22-49; pp. 24-26.

84. Leclerc tells his reader that the addition of Latin — almost doubling the size of the volume — was an afterthought suggested by his publisher (*Harmonia Evangelica, cui subjecta est Historia Christi ex Quatuor Evangeliis concinnata* [Amsterdam, 1699], preface ["Lectori S. P. D. Joannes Leclericus"], p. 2).

is to be found, pointing from left to right or from right to left, directing the reader from one column to another so as to follow the thread of the composite narrative as reconstructed by the harmonizer. This is a reading strategy in which the vertical movement down the column of the individual evangelist is constantly interrupted by a horizontal movement across to a different column and a different evangelist; the vertical movement is completed only by way of repeated horizontal detours in either direction. Thus there is no attempt to construct a single harmonized text: the harmony is rather to be found in the formatting of the individual gospel texts. Leclerc claims to have avoided the error of earlier Harmonies, in which the display of gospel parallels resulted only in the dismembering of the gospels themselves:

> As for both chronological order and the order of the evangelists [*ordinis temporum et Evangelistarum*], there was little method in them; for scholars thought it sufficient to arrange similar sayings and events in separate columns, while, for that purpose and in an extraordinary manner, the individual parts of the gospels were torn asunder [*divulsis . . . Evangeliorum membris*].[85]

In these earlier works, the harmony of the evangelists is achieved only through extreme violence to their texts, without arriving at any plausible chronology of the life of Jesus. Their authors seem to assume that "the evangelists themselves had absolutely no regard" for matters of chronology and sequence.[86] Leclerc's Harmony claims to treat the sequence of the gospel narratives with greater respect. In reality, however, the dismemberment of the gospels is integral to the gospel harmony genre. It is inevitable that the thread of the individual narrative will be repeatedly broken by Leclerc's hand-symbol, directing the reader to a different column and a different evangelist, in order to recover the actual sequence of events in the life of Jesus.

In the case of the empty tomb story, for example, a purely vertical reading of the Matthean column would lead us to suppose that the women's fearful and joyful departure from the tomb was followed immediately by an appearance of the risen Jesus, who greets them and repeats the message they have already received from the angel at the tomb (Mt. 28.8-10). "And departing from the tomb with fear and great joy, they ran to tell his disciples. And behold, Jesus met them, saying, Hail. . . ." On the basis of Matthew alone, we

85. Leclerc, *Harmonia Evangelica*, preface, p. 1.
86. Leclerc, *Harmonia Evangelica*, preface, p. 1.

suppose that it was *as* "they ran to tell his disciples" that "Jesus met them." Yet Matthew is not alone. Early on Easter morning, the risen Jesus appeared not once but twice — as we learn when Matthew is supplemented with John and Mark. For the Harmony, the two appearances must be coordinated with one another. One appearance was to the group of women (Matthew), the other to Mary Magdalene alone (John, Mark). In addition, as John tells us, Mary visited the tomb twice and so left it twice (Jn. 20.2, 18). The Matthean departure from the tomb with fear and great joy corresponds to the *first* Johannine departure. So Leclerc's Hand directs us from Matthew's departing women via Luke to the Johannine column. According to Luke, the women passed on the angelic message to the male disciples, but were disbelieved (Lk. 24.9-11). According to John, Mary complained to Peter and John (the Beloved Disciple) that "they have taken the Lord out of the tomb, and we do not know where they have laid him" (Jn. 20.2). In neither gospel do the women encounter Jesus himself as they return from the tomb, as Matthew appears to suggest. The Matthean appearance must therefore have taken place at a later point in the unfolding events of Easter morning.

In the Johannine account, Peter and John visit the tomb; Mary herself returns and encounters one who is not the gardener but the risen Lord, whom she recognizes as he addresses her by name (Jn. 20.3-18).[87] Having previously directed us from Matthew to Luke to John, the Hand now points back to the Markan column, where the priority of the Johannine appearance to Mary is confirmed. In Mark 16.9 we read: "Now when he rose early on the first day of the week, he appeared *first* to Mary Magdalene. . . ." Only now do we return to our Matthean starting point to learn how Jesus appeared *a second time,* to the larger group of women: *Jesus secundum cernitur a pluribus mulieribus* (Mt. 28.9-10). We must read from v. 8 (the departure from the tomb) to v. 9 (the encounter with Jesus) only by way of a long detour through each of the other three evangelists. Guided by the Hand, we retrace the actual course of events on Easter morning: the full historical reality which is not contained in any one gospel but which is distributed among the four — in such a way that each gospel *appears* to tell the full story but in reality does not.[88]

The successive indications of Leclerc's Hand are the thread that guides

---

87. Leclerc, *Harmonia Evangelica*, pp. 482, 484 (Greek); pp. 483, 485 (Latin).

88. Most of Leclerc's sequence derives ultimately from Augustine (*De Cons. Evang.* iii.24.69). The main difference is that for Leclerc, the Matthean and Markan encounter with an angel occurs in connection with the first Johannine visit to the tomb, not the second.

us through the labyrinth of the fourfold gospel. Yet there are gaps remaining even in the composite narrative. If the women do *not* encounter the risen Jesus on their first return from the tomb, but only after he has appeared to Mary, a clear sense of how the appearances relate to one another is still lacking. Also lacking is any reference to Mary's companions revisiting the tomb as she does, in order to encounter Jesus on their way back from it. These and other deficiencies are remedied by Leclerc's own historical reconstruction (the *Historia Christi ex Quatuor Evangeliis concinnata*), which unfolds below the four columns of the *Harmonia Evangelica*. This reconstruction takes the form of a "paraphrase," a popular interpretative genre of the period.[89]

The women report the angelic message to the male disciples, but are disbelieved (cf. Lk. 24.9-11). Then Mary Magdalene

> told Peter and John that she had certainly examined the tomb and seen it to be empty, and that (if he had not risen) Jesus' corpse must have been removed from there and placed she knew not where.[90]

Here, the parenthesis bridges the gap between Luke, for whom the women communicated the angelic announcement of Jesus' resurrection (Lk. 24.9), and John, for whom Mary communicated only the disappearance of the body (Jn. 20.2). The male disciples' disbelief of the first, joyful message causes Mary to doubt its truth and to suggest a prosaic explanation for the empty tomb. The harmonizing of Luke and John here accords with one of the principles of gospel harmonization later summarized in an appendix.[91] Leclerc's "Canon III" states that no individual evangelist narrates all the relevant details of an event, even where a more extensive account is given — as, here, in the case of John.[92] No evangelist has more than a fragment of the true story.

Leclerc's paraphrastic account of the *historia Christi* retells the Johannine story of Jesus' appearance to Mary at the tomb (Jn. 20.11-18), "to which she had returned following Peter and John."[93] Another gap in the narrative is

89. Leclerc, *Harmonia Evangelica*, preface, p. 2.

90. Leclerc, *Harmonia Evangelica*, p. 483.

91. "Dissertatio Secunda, in qua traduntur Canones Harmonici, quos in concinnanda Harmonia sequuti sumus" (Leclerc, *Harmonia Evangelica*, pp. 516-29).

92. Leclerc, *Harmonia Evangelica*, p. 518. Canon III reads in full: "Neque unus Evangelista, neque omnes simul omnia habent facta & dicta Christi, imo nec omnes circumstantias eorum quae copiosius narrant."

93. Leclerc, *Harmonia Evangelica*, p. 551.

thereby filled: Mary's return is not mentioned in John 20.11. More importantly, all the other women must also have returned to the tomb so that they may encounter the risen Jesus on what will now be their *second* return journey to the disciples. The gap between Matthew 28.8 (the initial return from the tomb) and 28.9 (Jesus' appearance) is created by the need to accommodate Lukan and Johannine material that knows nothing of any such appearance, but also by supplementary material provided by the harmonist himself:

> Just as Mary Magdalene, after telling the apostles that she had seen Jesus' tomb empty and had learned from angels that he had risen, returned to the tomb, where Jesus condescended to reveal himself to her; so too the other above-mentioned women returned there as Mary went to the apostles, and once again saw the tomb empty. When they were again going to the apostles, to confirm that Jesus' corpse was nowhere to be seen, the living Jesus met them, whom after he had greeted them they immediately recognized.[94]

The harmonist deduces that the other women *must* have returned to the tomb as Mary did because (1) they are said to have met Jesus on their way back from the tomb (Mt. 28.9), and (2) because the other three gospels show that this encounter *cannot* have taken place as the women returned with the angelic message, as Matthew appears to suggest. This evangelist's individual statements are all true components of the one *historia Christi*, but that is not the case with their sequence. It is true that, "departing from the tomb with fear and great joy, they ran to tell his disciples," and it is also true that "Jesus met them, saying, Hail . . . ," but it is not true that the second occurrence took place in the course of the first. Matthew has conflated two events that were actually quite separate. To harmonize the gospels is to supplement a narrative with material drawn from the parallel narratives, but also with material provided by the harmonist himself in order to resolve the problems generated by his own harmonistic method. The "dismemberment" of the gospel narrative that Leclerc wished to avoid is, in fact, inescapable. Where the harmony of the gospels is supposed to lie in the noncontradiction and interconnectedness of all their fact-like statements, textual violence is an absolute necessity. In this case it is the Matthean narrative that is its main victim.

This unacknowledged violence is not simply arbitrary, but occurs in conformity to a series of rules and principles that Leclerc takes care to specify.

94. Leclerc, *Harmonia Evangelica*, p. 486.

Canon I expresses a preference for the Lukan, Johannine, and Markan sequences over the Matthean one: Luke claims to have written in order (Lk. 1.3), whereas Matthew deviates from the others especially in his first thirteen or so chapters.[95] We have already noted Leclerc's Canon III, the "rule of incompletion," according to which any gospel narrative is actually a fragment of a greater whole even where it appears to be complete in itself. According to Canon V, gaps in a narrative *(circumstantiae omissae)* can be made good from the logic of the situation alone, even without explicit textual warrant, where this is necessary for comprehending a narrative sequence.[96] It is this rule that produces the women's second visit to the tomb. According to Canon XV, a gospel narrative can present separate events as though one followed directly from the other, where intervening events are omitted.[97] That is supposedly the case in Matthew's account of events on Easter morning. As Leclerc notes and as we have already seen, this rule goes back to Augustine, who derives it from the Lukan infancy story: the return to Nazareth is presented *as if* it followed directly from the presentation in the temple, owing to the omission of the (Matthean) flight to Egypt.[98] Similarly in the Matthean Easter story, Jesus' appearance to the women is presented *as if* it occurred directly after the encounter with angels at the tomb, since intervening circumstances narrated by Luke and John have been omitted. The crucial supplementary event is Mary's second visit to the tomb, to which the harmonist adds a second visit by the other women as well. The absence of this Johannine supplement from the synoptic gospels is not to be seen as a contradiction, for, according to Canon XII, narratives which recount the same event in more or less detail are to be regarded as in harmony with one another.[99] This rule too is attributed to Augustine,[100] as is Canon XI, where it is stated that differences in minor details are not to be regarded as potential contradictions and can be allowed to stand.[101] This rule is

---

95. Leclerc, *Harmonia Evangelica*, pp. 516, 517.

96. "Ex re ipsa colligendae circumstantiae omissae, quae necessariae sunt, ad intelligendam seriem narrationis" (Leclerc, *Harmonia Evangelica*, p. 519).

97. "Facta temporibus remota, transitione connectuntur, quemadmodum proxima, cum quae inter ea contigerunt omittuntur" (Leclerc, *Harmonia Evangelica*, p. 526).

98. Augustine, *De Cons. Evang.* ii.5.16.

99. "Qui pauciora habet non negat plura dicta aut facta, modo ne ulla sit exclusionis nota; nec qui plura habet eum, qui pauciora narrat, malae fidei arguit" (Leclerc, *Harmonia Evangelica*, p. 524).

100. Leclerc here cites Augustine, *De Cons. Evang.* ii.24.56; ii.65.125, dealing with passages where Matthew refers to two people (Gadarene demoniacs, blind men at Jericho) where Mark has only one (Mt. 8.28-34; 20.29-34; Mk. 5.1-20; 10.46-52).

101. "Exigua varietas circumstantiarum, aut ordinis, in narratione unius ejusdemque

particularly important for Leclerc's harmonizing procedure, as it exempts him from having to produce a single conflated narrative in which even trivial gospel differences must all be accommodated.

Each of these rules seeks to regulate and legitimate the practice of harmonization, which consists here in a strategy for reading the fourfold narrative as though it were singular. What they fail to acknowledge is the violent dismemberment of the individual gospel narrative which is integral to the harmonization project. Seeking to protect the gospel's fourfold canonical form from the difference that constitutes it, harmonization promotes the dissolution of the canonical gospel.

Leclerc achieves his harmonization by guiding his reader between gospel texts and by paraphrasing the resultant composite narrative. In another Harmony of 1699, published in Paris and compiled by Bernard Lamy,[102] the texts themselves are conflated — a technique developed by sixteenth-century harmonizers to ensure that nothing in the canonical gospels should be lost. This Harmony is not merely a strategy for negotiating the fourfold text, as in Leclerc's less rigorous presentation, but the production of a new text out of the very words of the old ones. Lamy describes his work as a *Commentarius in Concordiam Evangelicam et Apparatus Chronologicus et Geographicus cum Praefatione in qua demonstratur veritas Evangelii* — a commentary on the Evangelical Concord, with chronological and geographical apparatus, and (for good measure) a preface in which the truth of the gospel is demonstrated. Its intention is to reconstruct "the life of Jesus Christ our Lord, that is, the evangelical history of what he did and what he taught."[103] As in later forms of "life-of-Jesus research," the object of the inquiry must be sought by way of a critical reading of problematic sources:

> The history of Jesus Christ our Lord can only reliably be composed in the very words of the evangelists — in which, however, its parts are as it were scattered and torn asunder [*sua membra quasi sparsa et divulsa*], so that its body cannot be reassembled unless these are gathered and restored to a single form [*uni formae reddantur*], that is, to their respective times and

---

circumstantiae, non est repugnantia" (Leclerc, *Harmonia Evangelica*, p. 523). Cf. Augustine, *De Cons. Evang.* ii.14.31, where the different accounts of the divine utterance at Jesus' baptism are in view.

102. Bernard Lamy (1640-1715) was a French mathematician and philosopher, a friend of Malebranche and a follower of Descartes.

103. Bernard Lamy, *Commentarius in Concordiam Evangelicam et Apparatus Chronologicus et Geographicus cum Praefatione in qua demonstratur veritas Evangelii* (Paris, 1699), *Praefatio*, p. i.

places. This has been achieved when they are narrated in the order in which they actually occurred. Those who intend to write that history should therefore inquire into the true sequence of the acts and utterances of the Lord [*in veram seriem actuum et sermonum domini*], in which the evangelists concur — that is, into the harmony or concord of the evangelists. From this, much light is shed on the gospel: when we come to know the time, place, and circumstances of the actions or utterances narrated in the gospel, then their meaning, and the wisdom by which things are ordered in them, becomes absolutely clear.[104]

Gospel harmony is again linked to violent dismemberment; again the irony is not noted. In this case, however, the evangelists are the perpetrators of dismemberment rather than its victims. In the gospels the integrity of the historical life of Jesus is shattered, and its fragments are parcelled out between four separate narratives. The gospels are valuable in that they preserve the possibility of reconstructing the life of Jesus, yet they are misleading insofar as they do not clearly acknowledge their own fragmentary nature. Each gospel seems to represent the whole while in reality it contains only parts; thus it can seem that the gospels contradict one another. Only a gospel harmony can demonstrate that the evangelists spoke nothing but the truth — against those who, in every age, make light of their authority and claim that they are discordant. The problem with the canonical arrangement lies not only with apparent discord, however, but with the sheer inconvenience it causes the student of the life of Jesus. It is only with the aid of a harmony that the events of which the individual gospels speak may be viewed in their integrity.[105]

Lamy's composite narrative is entitled the *Harmonia,* and stands in large print in the left-hand column of each page; to the right of it are placed those gospel passages from which it is drawn, in the Vulgate translation alone. The *Harmonia* is divided into short chapters, each devoted to a particular occurrence in the life of Jesus and subdivided into verses which may or may not correspond to the verse enumeration of the equivalent gospel passages. Thus chapter 41 is mainly devoted to Jesus' appearance to the women on Easter morning and to the corrupting of the guards. The relevant text here is Matthew 28.9-15, which becomes *Harmonia,* xli.1-7. To this are appended passages from Mark and John that tell of Mary Magdalene's return

---

104. Lamy, *Commentarius, Praefatio,* p. i.
105. Lamy, *Commentarius, Praefatio,* p. ii.

to the disciples following her vision of the Lord (Mk. 16.10-11; Jn. 20.18). Since there is more than one passage to accommodate, the *Harmonia* text (xli.8-9) draws on both, with *J* designating the Johannine contribution to the composite narrative and *Mk* the Markan one. Following the Matthean account of the women's encounter with Jesus and the conduct of the guards,

> *J* Mary Magdalene came announcing to the disciples, *Mk* who had been with him, as they mourned and wept, *J* "I have seen the Lord, and he said these things to me!" *Mk* And they, hearing that he was alive and had been seen by her, did not believe.[106]

This is precisely the dismemberment of individual gospel accounts of which Leclerc complains — to which Lamy's response is that the individual accounts themselves represent the dismemberment of the life of Jesus. This Harmony asserts its superiority to the individual texts out of which it is composed, by its prominent positioning and by its new system of chapter and verse divisions. For Leclerc, the texts retain their priority. The harmonizer intervenes only by inserting the hand-signals that guide the movement behind the columns; his own paraphrase remains discreetly at the foot of the page. For Lamy, the harmonizer is the creator of a superior text out of inferior ones in which the components of the evangelical history lie "torn apart and scattered." If the harmonizer has really re-created the "true sequence of the Lord's deeds and words," there is no call for false modesty.

While it may seem questionable to regard the chronologies of the individual gospels as partially false, that is unavoidable given the differences between them. In addition, disregard for chronology is sanctioned by Augustine himself. If the sequence of each gospel is to be strictly preserved, then similar or identical incidents will be multiplied where these occur at different points in different gospels. Gadarene swine will plunge repeatedly into the sea; large-scale feeding miracles will become a matter of routine. Lamy refers to the Harmony of the Lutheran theologian Andreas Osiander (1537), "in which the evangelical history is assembled out of the four gospels in such a way that no single word is omitted, nothing alien is included, no sequence is disturbed, nothing is found outside its proper place."[107] The apparently

---

106. Lamy, *Commentarius*, p. 614 (*Harmonia*, xli.8.9).

107. The full title of Osiander's work, cited by Lamy (*Commentarius*, p. ii-iii), is: *Harmoniae Evangelicae libri quatuor, in quibus Evangelica historia ex quatuor Evangelistis ita in unum est contexta, ut nullius verbum ullum omissum, nihil alienum immixtum, nullius ordo turbatus, nihil*

reasonable premise is that, *pace* Augustine, scriptural indications of sequence *(ordo)* are no less true and reliable than anything else in scripture.[108]
The majority of harmonizers did not take this line, however, and were therefore necessarily engaged in *correcting* the received texts just as contemporary
textual critics were learning to do. Lamy criticizes an early-seventeenth-
century harmonist because he

> persuaded himself to believe that the sequence followed by each evange-
> list was given by the Holy Spirit [*a Spiritu sancto*]. A rash claim, in my
> view: for it is clear both from the texts themselves and from the authority
> of the ancient writers that a reliable chronology [*temporis rationem*] is not
> to be found in all the evangelists. When this is accepted, one is obliged *not*
> to preserve the sequence in which each evangelist writes.[109]

For Lamy it is the two apostolic eyewitnesses among the evangelists
whose sequence corresponds to the actual order of events: that is the methodological decision that differentiates this Harmony from its predecessors,
which failed to explain "why Matthew and John as eyewitnesses would wish
to produce a disordered history of the Lord rather than one arranged in
chronological sequence."[110] That Mark was not an eyewitness and did not
write in the correct sequence is confirmed by Papias's testimony as preserved
by Eusebius.[111] Luke differentiates himself from the eyewitnesses in the
opening of his gospel.[112] When he refers to the "many" who have "attempted
to draw up an account," and to the orderliness of his own work, he is not laying claim to a chronological order neglected by Matthew and Mark, his

---

*non suo loco positum: omnia vero litteris et notis ita distincta sunt, ut quid cujusque Evangelistae
proprium, quid cum aliis, et cum quibus commune sit, primo aspectu deprehendere queas.*

108. Osiander's rigorous version of the harmonization project survives into the eighteenth
and early nineteenth centuries in works such as James MacKnight's popular *Harmony of the Four
Gospels, in Which the Natural Order of Each Is Preserved* (2 vols., London, 1756[1]; 1809[4]). According
to this overoptimistic harmonist, "the best method of producing a perfect Harmony is to preserve
the thread of [the gospels'] several narrations entire, because seeming contradictions will thus be
removed, the whole will be rendered consistent, the credit of the evangelists as historians will be
better secured, and our faith built upon the most solid foundation" (i.1). To transpose the evangelists' material "in any instance where they affirmed their order, would manifestly injure their authority" (i.1).

109. Lamy, *Commentarius*, p. iv, referring to Jacobus d'Auzoles à la Peyre, *Sancta D. N. J. C.
Evangelia secundum Evangelistas* (1610).

110. Lamy, *Commentarius*, p. vi.

111. Lamy, *Commentarius*, p. vii.

112. Lamy, *Commentarius*, p. vii.

precedessors.[113] It is not Luke who corrects the Matthean and Markan sequences, but Matthew and John who correct the Markan and Lukan ones. That, Lamy claims, is what the fathers believed: in consequence, his own achievement is "not so much to construct a new Harmony as to restore an old one that has more recently been forgotten."[114]

The priority of Matthew and John is visually represented in the image that stands at the head of page 1 of Lamy's Harmony. In the centre a dove presides over the four evangelists as they write, identifiable through the conventional symbols as Matthew and John to the left, Luke and Mark to the right. The whole scene is irradiated by the glory of the sun, which shines full on John's upturned face. Matthew too faces the sun as he receives instruction from an angelic figure.[115] Mark and Luke turn away from the sun, however, preoccupied with their writing. Directly below the dove stands the legend, *Unus atque idem Spiritus,* proceeding from the cloud-like billows that suggest the divine presence. Thus the harmony of the gospels is grounded in their divine inspiration. One and the same Spirit distributes to each as he wills (cf. 1 Cor. 12.11), but the motto emphasizes the gospels' singular supernatural origin rather than the plurality of the distribution.

In Leclerc's Frontispiece the dove is replaced by Jesus himself, who stands on a pedestal with the sun's rays emanating from him and touching the heads of each of the evangelists seated around him. The architecture suggests a Roman setting, in contrast to Lamy's bare stage. The order is the conventional one; the symbols are barely visible. The evangelists have books and pens in hand, and have evidently completed their work. They have written on the basis of their proximity to Jesus, a fully human figure like themselves whose right hand gestures toward them, commending them to the reader. The pedestal bears the legend: Ταῦτα γέγραπται ἵνα πιστεύσητε (Jn. 20.31). A further inscription on the step below indicates that "these things," written "that you may believe," refers not to an individual gospel but to the ΑΡΜΟΝΙΑ ΕΥΑΓΓΕΛΙΚΗ deriving from the one Christ. It is his singular figure that dominates the picture, and the plurality of the evangelists serves no other function than to demonstrate their own unity.

These images encapsulate the Augustinian harmonization project, viewed not simply as an exercise in apologetics but as critical reconstruction

---

113. Lamy, *Commentarius*, p. 2.

114. Lamy, *Commentarius*, p. vi.

115. This angel is also the human figure who symbolizes this evangelist and who plays a direct part in the proceedings — unlike the eagle, calf, and lion.

of the life of Jesus — a venture whose potential significance Augustine himself glimpsed as he pieced together the true course of events on Easter morning. There are, however, notable absences in these images. Neither shows Mark as the epitomizer of Matthew and Luke, a radical Augustinian innovation that would not be taken up until the latter part of the eighteenth century. These evangelists look variously towards Jesus, the descending dove, their own writing tablets, or the viewer, but they hold no communication with one another. Equally, these images do not and cannot depict the "dismemberment" of the true course of Jesus' life, the fragmentation into four distinct texts that creates the need for harmonization in the first place. These images conceal the double violence that the harmonization project ironically entails: the violence to which the texts must be subjected in order to undo their own violent treatment of the life of Jesus in its integrity. Yet, if plurality and difference are fundamental to the gospel in its canonical form, the violence of harmonization misunderstands and distorts precisely the object it is so anxious to defend.[116]

Three-quarters of a century after the harmonies of Leclerc and Lamy, Johann Jakob Griesbach published his *Synopsis Evangeliorum Matthei, Marci et Lucae* (1776).[117] The parallel columns are still in place, but there is no guiding hand, no *Harmonia* or composite account of the *historia Christi*, and no Gospel of John. Nor is there any trace of the harmonist's preoccupation with the "true sequence of the Lord's acts and sayings," the *vera series actuum et sermonum Domini*.[118] In keeping with this new minimalism, the image that introduces the synopsis has only the sun in common with the earlier images. There is no Holy Spirit and no Christ; nor are there even any evangelists.[119] The personified sun here represents enlightenment rather than divine glory or inspiration. It shines into a border of

116. "The basic error of the traditional harmony was the assumption that the canonical process had been deficient in leaving the Gospels in their plural form rather than completing the process by fusing them into a fixed, authoritative interpretation. Because this development did not take place within the canonical process, but in fact was flatly rejected, the plural form remains constitutive of the canonical shape" (Childs, *New Testament as Canon*, p. 156).

117. On Griesbach (1745-1812), see G. Delling, "Johann Jakob Griesbach. Seine Zeit, sein Leben, sein Werk," *ThZ* 33 (1977), pp. 81-99, which includes a comprehensive bibliography of Griesbach's publications (pp. 96-99); Eng. trans. in *J. J. Griesbach*, pp. 5-21. The 1776 Synopsis was a separate reprint of the first part of Griesbach's Greek New Testament (1774).

118. Lamy, *Commentarius*, p. vi.

119. J. J. Griesbach, *Synopsis Evangeliorum Matthaei, Marci et Lucae: Textum Graecum ad fidem codicum versionum et patrum emendavit et lectionis varietatem adiecit . . .* (Halae: apud Io. Iac. Curt., 1776[1]), p. 3 (henceforth *Synopsis*[1]).

stylized foliage, a purely natural scene from which everything supernatural has been banished.

Griesbach initially conceives his synopsis as a teaching aid that enables the lecturer to avoid the repetitions that would occur if the synoptic gospels were studied one by one. Yet, he suggests, it has other advantages too:

> A kind of synopsis made up [*concinnanda*] of these three gospels seemed appropriate, in which passages common to three or two of them would be located opposite one another, so that the interpretation of the one would suffice for understanding the others, or just a few additional things in them would need to be explained. Indeed, one may also be permitted to hope for several further uses for such a synopsis. Not only is the interpreter greatly assisted by a comparison of synonymous phraseology employed by the evangelists, which our synopsis makes it easy to establish; but, in addition, the true character [*verum ingenium*] of each individual gospel, the quite different aim [*consilium*] that the authors had in view, and the method that each held to in writing, all of which contribute greatly to the just assessment of these writings — all of these, I thought, would be more succinctly and clearly set forth in such a synopsis than in the usual editions.[120]

The Synopsis presents itself as an aid to the study of divergent yet closely related texts. The same could also be said of many traditional Harmonies. The difference lies not in the format as such but in its rationale. The texts are aligned so that readers may *compare* them in order to gain a better understanding of each of them individually — in contrast to an arrangement designed either to facilitate the reading of a single narrative across the four columns (Leclerc), or to give precedence to a composite narrative over the individual ones (Lamy). The earlier scholars are concerned with a "Harmony" of the texts that will coincide with the authentic history of Christ, the true sequence of his deeds and words. In contrast, the term "Synopsis" speaks of a viewing-together, without reference to any purpose beyond that of comparison.[121] The focus has shifted from the history of Christ to the

---

120. Griesbach, *Synopsis*[1], pp. iv-v.

121. The shift in Griesbach's Synopsis from historical reconstruction to comparison is rightly emphasized by Thomas Hieke, "Methoden und Möglichkeiten griechischer Synopsen zu den ersten drei Evangelien," in *"Wenn drei das gleiche sagen": Studien zu den ersten drei Evangelien*, ed. Stefan H. Brandenburger and Thomas Hieke (Münster, Hamburg, and London: LIT Verlag, 1998), pp. 1-36; p. 5.

texts as such. In the Harmony, the texts lose their identity as they are blended into one another and become transparent to the life of Jesus. In the Synopsis, they recover an identity and an individuality of their own. The difference between the Synopsis and the Harmony lies mainly in what the Synopsis *lacks:* the orientation towards the composite narrative which destabilizes the individual texts and threatens them with dissolution. Although the Johannine passion and resurrection narratives were included in Griesbach's second edition (1797), and other Johannine parallels in the third (1809), the Synopsis is primarily concerned with three gospels, not four.[122] Griesbach has no interest in reconstructing a *harmonia evangelica* that is at the same time a *historia Christi ex quatuor evangeliis concinnata.*

Griesbach is quite clear that his Synopsis is not a Harmony:

> The reader of this *Synopsis of the Gospels* must be advised at the outset not to expect from this book of ours any kind of "harmony," to use the customary expression. For while I am well aware how much labour scholars have devoted to arranging a harmony, I myself can not only see in their extreme diligence very little utility, indeed virtually none at all, that our Synopsis does not surpass; but I also very much doubt if it is even possible to compose a harmonious narrative from the books of the Evangelists, one that is sufficiently agreeable to the truth and built upon firm foundations. What if *none* of the Evangelists gave a consistently accurate account of the sequence of events? Or if there is insufficient evidence to establish in particular cases who deviated from whom with regard to actual chronological order? Here I confess to this heresy![123]

Harmonizers too can acknowledge the difference between chronological order and narrative order. As we have seen, Leclerc believes that many incidents in the first half of Matthew are narrated out of chronological sequence, and that Luke is a more reliable guide in this respect. In contrast, Lamy gives priority to Matthew and John as sources for a sequential life of Jesus, and extends Papias's critique of the Markan order to include Luke. Both harmonizers assume that the correct chronological sequence is at least recoverable, however; the harmonization project itself depends on this as-

---

122. The second edition (1797) supplements the synoptic gospels *cum iis Joannis pericopis quae historiam passionis et resurrectionis Jesu Christi complectuntur* (henceforth *Synopsis*²); the third (1809), *cum iis Joannis pericopis quae omnino cum caeterorum evangelistarum narrationibus conferendae sunt.*

123. Griesbach, *Synopsis*¹, pp. vii-viii.

sumption, and it is this that Griesbach challenges.[124] If the quest for the single chronological order is abandoned, then the order followed by the respective evangelists can be preserved. Although their divergences will necessitate many repetitions and transpositions, the formatting of the synopsis enables a reader to work through Matthew, Mark, or Luke consecutively, unconcerned with historical reconstruction but using the possibility of comparison to shed light on the distinctive character of each narrative.[125] The view inherited from Augustine, that the canonical gospels are potentially undermined by their differences, is set aside, and it becomes possible to evaluate the canonical plurality positively rather than negatively. Far from participating in an "eclipse" of gospel narrative, the Synopsis represents the recovery of the plural form distorted and suppressed by the harmony.

Griesbach's Synopsis was not initially intended to help resolve what would later be called "the synoptic problem." The issue of gospel origins is not mentioned in his first edition. By the time of the second edition, however, he has seen that the new research tool is highly relevant to this question. In the interim he has published two editions of an essay arguing that Mark derives his gospel from Matthew and Luke, alternating between the two of them as he writes.[126] As we have seen, this was also Augustine's revised view, although Griesbach is unaware of that fact. Returning to his Synopsis in 1797, he rewrites the original preface, adding among other things the claim that it enables the reader to identify "the sources [*fontes*] from which each narrative seems to have drawn."[127] This applies particularly to Mark, who

> draws the whole of his narrative from Matthew and Luke, with a few insignificant exceptions; and so, where he follows Matthew's lead, he retains his order unchanged; but where Matthew and Luke diverge, he becomes the companion of Luke, and follows so closely in his footsteps that he preserves the same sequence of narratives intact.[128]

---

124. In the preface to his second edition, Griesbach concedes that "Luke seems to diverge from the chronological order less than the others," but adds: "There is however no reason to suppose that he scrupulously preserves it everywhere" (*Synopsis*[2], p. iii).

125. For Griesbach's explanation of the formatting, see *Synopsis*[1], pp. viii-x.

126. Griesbach, *Commentatio qua Marci Evangelium totum e Matthaei et Lucae commentariis decerptum esse monstratur* (1789-90[1], 1794[2]; repr. with Eng. trans. in J. J. Griesbach, pp. 74-135; see also B. Reicke, "Griesbach's Answer to the Synoptic Question," in the same volume, pp. 50-67).

127. Griesbach, *Synopsis*[2], p. v.

128. Griesbach, *Synopsis*[2], p. v.

Griesbach has evidently developed this theory through the experience of preparing his synopsis. There is no indication that he constructs his synopsis in order to demonstrate the theory; rather the theory grows out of his own formatting decisions. Crucially, in cases of disagreement over sequence, he gives priority to two gospels where they agree against a third, rather than, say, adopting the Matthean or Lukan sequence as a default position or basing his own sequence on judgements of historical probability. By prioritizing a sequence followed by two evangelists against one, he discovers in practice *(1)* that two-way divergences of this kind are common whereas three-way divergences are hardly to be found; and *(2)* that, in such cases, one of the two parties who agree against a third is always Mark (see the references in bold print in Figure 1.1, below). It seems that Mark has some kind of stake in the other two synoptic gospels.

Figure 1.1. Griesbach, the Synopsis, and the Synoptic Problem

Synopsis Evangeliorum Matthaei, Marci et Lucae	*Matthew*	*Mark*	*Luke*
Section XIV: Ministry of John the Baptist	3.1-12	1.1-8	3.1-20
Section XV: Baptism of Jesus	3.13-17	1.9-11	3.21-23
Section XVI: Temptations of Jesus	4.1-11	1.12-13	4.1-13
Section XVII: Initial Preaching	4.12	1.14	4.14-15
Section XVIII: In the Synagogue in Nazareth	—	—	4.16-30
Section XIX: Call of the Disciples	**4.13-22**	**1.15-20**	—
Section XX: Exorcism in Capernaum	—	**1.21-28**	**4.31-37**
Section XXI: Healing of Peter's Mother-in-law	[8.14-17]	**1.29-34**	**4.38-41**
Section XXII: Preaching Tour in Galilee	—	**1.35-39**	**4.42-44**
Section XXIII: Call of Disciples	—	—	5.1-11
Section XXIV: Sermon on Mount	4.23–7.29	—	[6.20-23, etc.]
Section XXV: Healing of Leper	8.1-4	1.40-45	5.12-14

Bold = agreement in sequence of two gospels (one always Mark) against a third.

Sections I-XIII of the synopsis cover the Matthean and Lukan infancy narratives, and it is only from the ministry of John the Baptist onwards that accounts are provided by three evangelists. Initially, there is no disagreement over the placement of the various units, although there may be some diversity of scale or sequence within each unit (Sections XIV-XVII). After the temptation narrative, however, Luke has Jesus return to Nazareth to speak in the synagogue (Section XVIII), whereas in Matthew and Mark he calls his first disciples as he walks along the shore of the Sea of Galilee (Section XIX). This, then, is the first divergence of two against one, and it is immediately followed by another — indeed, by a succession of narratives in which Mark agrees with Luke against Matthew (Sections XX-XXII). In both cases, Mark is the common factor, siding first with Matthew, then with Luke. It is a short step (though probably a mistaken one) from the literary observation that Mark *agrees* first with Matthew and then with Luke to the source-critical hypothesis that Mark *follows* first Matthew and then Luke. Thus indisputable literary parallels are converted into editorial decisions. Having followed Matthew and Luke to the beginning of Jesus' public preaching (Section XVII), Mark finds that his two exemplars part company and decides to omit the story that follows in Luke (Section XVIII) but to include the one that follows in Matthew (Section XIX).

It is, then, the formatting of the synopsis that underlies Griesbach's source-critical theory. Yet the formatting is also compatible with alternative accounts. Perhaps Mark followed Matthew (as Augustine initially thought), after which Luke used Mark. Or perhaps Matthew and Luke both used Mark, independently of one another. All three theories can account for the common ground between Mark and each of the other two in turn. Griesbach's appeal to the phenomena of sequence in support of a specific source-critical theory is premature: literary observations based on sequence limit the source-critical options, but they do not resolve the question of priority.[129] Arguably, it is the text-critical principle of the priority of the *lectio difficilior* that underlies the widespread though not universal rejection of Griesbach's claim that Mark was the third to write, and the acceptance of the hypothesis that he was the first. The consensus on this point rests on the judgement that there is a preponderance of cases where it is easier to suppose that Matthew and/or Luke have emended Mark than that Mark has emended Matthew and/or Luke.

Far more important than the failure of a particular hypothesis are the recovery and development of Augustine's tentative suggestion that the synoptic gospels must somehow be *interdependent*. If the main purpose of the synopsis is *comparison*, leading one to appreciate the distinctiveness of each individual gospel, that appreciation will be further enhanced if we can learn

---

129. Griesbach's synopsis does not support the claim that gospel synopses reflect the source-critical assumptions of their producers. On this issue see Bernard Orchard, "Are All Gospel Synopses Biased?" *ThZ* 34 (1978), pp. 149-62; D. L. Dungan, "Theory of Synopsis Construction," *Bib* 61 (1980), pp. 305-29; Guy Lasserre, *Les synopses: élaboration et usage* (Rome: Pontifical Biblical Institute, 1996), pp. 22-25; Hieke, "Methoden und Möglichkeiten griechischer Synopsen," pp. 6-8.

how it was that their convergences and divergences came about in the first place. There is of course a considerable risk here. If a gospel is interpreted in the light of a source-critical hypothesis that turns out to be erroneous, the whole interpretation will be undermined. If Griesbach is wrong (as he probably is), then the Mark who follows first Matthew and then Luke is a fictitious figure who will seriously distort the reading of the canonical text. The same is true in principle of any other source-critical hypothesis: Markan priority (which is presupposed throughout the present work), Q (rejected in Chapter 3, below), or Luke's selective use of Matthew as well as Mark (proposed in Chapters 3 and 4), not to mention the potential relevance of early gospels later deemed noncanonical (Chapters 5–7). The interpretation of a gospel is far more than source or redaction criticism, but that is no reason to disparage or reject these methods.

The source criticism of the modern era remains part of Augustine's legacy. Along with other modes of interpretation, it is dependent on the gospel synopsis which — in spite of Griesbach's justified strictures — remains closely related to the gospel harmony, in format if not in rationale. Both harmony and synopsis facilitate the study of one text in the light of others, an essentially Augustinian reading strategy even if deployed to un-Augustinian ends. If the synopsis encourages its users to appreciate difference rather than imposing an artificial unanimity, that need not be celebrated or deplored as a victory for Enlightenment rationalism over ecclesial tradition. It might instead be seen as a modern endorsement of the canonical decision to embrace a limited though irreducible diversity — a decision that Augustine fundamentally misunderstood when he construed difference as a threat to be overcome. At this point at least, no facile distinctions should be ventured between "premodern" and "historical-critical" exegesis.

There is a further twist to the complex story that is unfolding here. As we have seen, Augustine held *(1)* that real contradictions between canonical gospels on matters of empirical fact would seriously undermine their authority, but *(2)* that no such contradictions can be established. The modern scholarly consensus that *(2)* is false is fully justified — as is all too evident from the harmonizers' inability to make coherent sense of the events of Easter morning. Given that *(2)* is false, however, the crucial issue is whether one rejects or accepts *(1)*. A significant strand in modern gospel scholarship has assumed that the canonical gospels are indeed devalued by the countless empirical inconsistencies that shape their individual distinctiveness and thus their plurality. The genesis of this assumption in its modern form will be the theme of the following chapter.

CHAPTER 2

Dismantling the Canon: Lessing/Reimarus

Augustine's account of the fourfold canonical gospel contains three main elements. First, there are brief and rudimentary attempts to develop literary
hypotheses to account for the origins of the synoptic gospels. Notable
though this is given the earlier tradition of independent authorship, Augustine's remarks are tentative and exercise little discernible influence on the
main body of his work. Second, there is theological reflection on the construction of the fourfold gospel, inspired by the traditional symbolism and
focusing on the relationship between John and the synoptics. Third, and at
much the greatest length, there is detailed comparison between the gospel
texts which aims both to expose differences and to develop ways of negotiating them. Here the fourfold canonical gospel is subjected to empirical testing, and it is acknowledged in principle that a single demonstrable "contradiction" — between the texts themselves and so between the texts and
historical reality — would subvert the entire structure. The plurality of the
canonical gospel is viewed negatively as a source of potential weakness
which can only be contained by reducing plurality to the harmony of the
single composite narrative.

With the Enlightenment, these same issues — gospel differences, the
role of the fourth gospel, synoptic origins — are radically rethought. Gospel
harmonization is gradually abandoned, along with the doctrine of verbal inspiration required to sustain it. The irreducible difference between the gospels is now acknowledged, and competing theories of gospel origins attempt
to account for it. In principle, this emphasis on difference might have led to a
renewed appreciation of the canonical plurality as opening up theological
possibilities precisely by complicating the relationship to empirical history.
If it has proved impossible to reconstruct a *historia Christi ex quatuor*

evangeliis concinnata, that might be taken to indicate that the accurate recording of biographical details plays only a limited role within the comprehensive truth-claim the gospels seek to articulate. The crucial question is whether the concept of the "contradiction" will continue to play the role assigned to it by Augustine, which is to determine the credibility or otherwise of the canonical gospel. Enlightened critics of the harmonization project agreed with Augustine that demonstrable contradictions would seriously compromise the integrity of the gospels themselves. Contradictions were detected at the level not only of the individual narratives but also of fundamental structure, as the relationship between John and the synoptics was increasingly seen as conflictual rather than complementary. The human Jesus of the synoptics was held to be incompatible with the divine Christ of John, so that the truth about Jesus would have to be sought in the synoptics only. As if in compensation for the loss of the fourth gospel, a new gospel was proposed, an *Urevangelium* or *Quelle* which predates the first three and which (being earlier) preserves the original truth in a purer form than they do.[1]

These concerns come into sharp focus in the event known as the *Fragmentenstreit,* or "Fragments Controversy."[2] This occurred in the years 1777-79, and was directed and stage-managed by the distinguished playwright and literary critic Gotthold Ephraim Lessing, who since 1770 had been in the employ of the Duke of Brunswick as librarian of the Herzog August Bibliothek in Wolfenbüttel. The "fragments" or extracts in question

---

1. In this account of the "eclipse of the fourfold gospel," I am in broad agreement with Brevard Childs, according to whom "modern New Testament scholarship has moved in a wrong direction when it has allowed its genuine insights into the history of the formation of the New Testament literature . . . to destroy the significance of the canonical collection of the four Gospels" (*The New Testament as Canon: An Introduction* [London: SCM Press, 1984], pp. 151-52). According to Childs, "it is a basic misconstrual of the New Testament material when one seeks to reconstruct from the Gospels a life of Jesus, either by the addition of the parts into a complete harmony, or the critical sifting of the evidence in order to discover the real Jesus behind the levels of accretion" (p. 154).

2. See Hugh Barr Nisbet, *Lessing: Eine Biographie* (Munich: C. H. Beck, 2008), pp. 664-744; Martin Bollacher, *Lessing, Vernunft und Geschichte: Untersuchungen zum Problem religiöser Aufklärung in den Spätschriften* (Tübingen: Niemeyer, 1978); W. Kröger, *Das Publikum als Richter: Lessing und die "kleineren Respondenten" im Fragmentenstreit,* Wolfenbütteler Forschungen 5 (Nendeln/Liechtenstein: KTO Press, 1979); Lothar Steiger, "Die 'gymnastische' Wahrheitfrage: Lessing und Goeze," *EvTh* 43 (1983), pp. 430-45; Toshimasa Yashikata, *Lessing's Philosophy of Religion and the German Enlightenment* (Oxford: Oxford University Press, 2002), pp. 41-55. For a bibliography of the literature of the *Fragmentenstreit,* see W. Schmidt-Biggemann, *Hermann Samuel Reimarus: Handschriften Verzeichnis und Bibliographie* (Göttingen: Vandenhoeck & Ruprecht, 1979), pp. 89-137 (henceforth Schmidt-Biggemann).

were taken from an early draft of an unpublished work by Hermann Samuel Reimarus, professor of Oriental languages at the Academic Gymnasium in Hamburg, who died in 1768 and whose son and daughter Lessing had come to know during his theatrical career in that city (1766-69). Lessing is a significant figure in the development of Enlightenment gospel scholarship, both in his own right and as editor of Reimarus. The fifth of the collection of "fragments" he published in 1777 is crucially important in this respect. In its original context in Reimarus's work, this discussion of ten "contradictions" within the gospel resurrection narratives is intended to demonstrate the fictitious and fraudulent nature of fundamental Christian truth-claims. In publishing it separately, Lessing presents it instead as a challenge to the project of gospel harmonization.

In addition to editing and publishing selections from Reimarus's work, Lessing himself contributed a number of short polemical works to the *Fragmentenstreit*. Five of these are concerned specifically with the gospels.

The first is entitled *On the Proof of the Spirit and of Power,* and responds to a work by Johann Daniel Schumann, *On the Evidence of Proofs for the Truth of the Christian Religion.*[3] Schumann maintains, and Lessing criticizes, the view that the truth of the Christian religion is demonstrated by a combination of fulfilled prophecy and miracles.

The second text is entitled *The Testament of John: A Dialogue.* Like the first, with which it is closely connected, it was published in December 1777.[4] The dialogue is based on an apocryphal story in which the dying apostle confines his teaching to the injunction to "love one another." This ethically oriented "Testament of John" is tacitly contrasted with the Gospel of John, with its focus on an incarnational christology that Lessing finds himself unable to accept.

---

3. The German titles of these works are: *Über den Beweis des Geistes und der Kraft* and *Über die Evidenz der Beweise für die Wahrheit der Christlichen Religion.* For the German text of Lessing's pamphlet, see *Gotthold Ephraim Lessing, Werke,* vol. 8: *Theologiekritische Schriften III/Philosophische Schriften,* ed. H. Göbel (Munich: Carl Hanser Verlag, 1979), pp. 9-14; Eng. trans. in H. Chadwick (ed.), *Lessing's Theological Writings* (London: A. & C. Black, 1957), pp. 51-56; H. B. Nisbet (ed.), *Lessing: Philosophical and Theological Writings* (Cambridge: Cambridge University Press, 2005), pp. 83-88. Schumann's work is reprinted in *Gotthold Ephraim Lessing Werke und Briefe,* vol. 8, ed. Arno Schilson (Frankfurt am Main: Deutscher Klassiker Verlag, 1989), pp. 355-435 (henceforth *LWB*). On J. D. Schumann (1714-87), director of the Altstädter Gymnasium in Hanover since 1774, see Kröger, *Das Publikum als Richter,* pp. 31-36.

4. *Das Testament Johannis: Ein Gespräch,* in *Lessings Werke* (henceforth *LW*), 8.15-20; Eng. trans. Chadwick, *Lessing's Theological Writings,* pp. 57-61; Nisbet, *Lessing: Philosophical and Theological Writings,* pp. 89-94. Here and elsewhere, translations are my own unless otherwise specified.

The third text, the longest of the series, is entitled *Eine Duplik*. This was published in January 1778 and responds to a critique of the resurrection fragment by Johann Heinrich Ress, a leading Wolfenbüttel churchman.[5] Ress tries to show that traditional harmonizing techniques can resolve the alleged contradictions between the gospel narratives. Lessing responds with a devastating criticism of gospel harmonies, their methods and their presuppositions.

The fourth text is entitled *A Parable*, published along with *A Small Request, and a Provisional Letter of Renunciation to Herr Pastor Goeze of Hamburg*, in March 1778.[6] Unlike other contributors to the controversy, Johann Melchior Goeze directed his criticisms primarily at Lessing himself rather than the anonymous fragments per se. His first intervention dates from December 1777, and is entitled *Preliminary Thoughts on Herr Hofrath Lessing's Direct and Indirect Attacks on Our Most Holy Religion and Its Sole Foundation, Holy Scripture*.[7] While the main topic of Lessing's controversy with Goeze is his own understanding of scripture as a whole, the *Parable* also sheds light on his view of the gospels and gospel harmonies.

The fifth text is the *New Hypothesis on the Evangelists Considered as Purely Human Historians*, which remained incomplete and was published posthumously in 1784.[8] Here it is argued that the extant gospels all derive

---

5. *LW*, 8.30-101. Ress's work is entitled *Die Auferstehungsgeschichte Jesu Christi gegen einige im vierten Beitrage zur Geschichte und Literatur aus den Schätzen der Herzoglichen Bibliothek zu Wolfenbüttel gemachte neuere Einwendungen verteidiget*. Parts of it are reprinted in *LWB*, 8.475-503. See also Kröger, *Das Publikum als Richter*, pp. 53-70. The introductory section of the *Duplik* is available in English in Nisbet, *Lessing: Philosophical and Theological Writings*, pp. 95-119, under the title "A Rejoinder."

6. German title: *Eine Parabel, nebst einer kleinen Bitte, und einem eventualen Absagungsschreiben an den Herrn Pastor Goeze, in Hamburg* (*LW*, 8.117-27; Eng. trans. in Nisbet, *Lessing: Philosophical and Theological Writings*, pp. 110-19).

7. German title: *Etwas Vorläufiges gegen des Herrn Hofrath Lessings mittelbare und unmittelbare feindselige Angriffe auf unsre allerheiligste Religion, und auf den einigen Lehrgrund derselben, die heilige Schrift* (*LW*, 8.21-29). Succeeding publications by Goeze retain the title: *Etwas Vorläufiges* II was published in January 1778 (*LW*, 8.102-16), III-VIII in April (*LW*, 8.167-92). There followed a further series, entitled *Lessings Schwächen* I (May 1778; *LW*, 8.199-218), II (June 1778; *LW*, 8.257-90) and III (August 1778; *LW*, 8.314-34). Lessing responded in kind. In addition to the *Parabel* (etc.), there are the *Axiomata* (March 1778; *LW*, 8.128-59), the eleven pamphlets of the *Anti-Goeze* series (April-July 1778; *LW*, 8.160-66, 193-98, 218-56, 291-308), and *Gotth. Ephr. Lessings Nötige Antwort auf eine sehr unnötige Frage des Hrn. Hauptpastor Göze in Hamburg* and its sequel (August/October 1778; *LW*, 8.309-13, 334-41). Original publication details are in Schmidt-Biggemann, pp. 96-101.

8. German title: *Neue Hypothese über die Evangelisten als bloss menschliche Geschichtsschreiber betrachtet* (in *Gotthold Ephraim Lessing, Werke*, vol. 7: *Theologiekritische Schriften I-II*, ed. H. Göbel

from a lost original, the Hebrew gospel referred to by Papias and other patristic writers. Lessing's theory of gospel origins is significant as a precursor of the "Q" hypothesis.

All these texts stem directly or indirectly from Lessing's engagement with Reimarus — a figure whose fame or notoriety is entirely due to the patronage first of Lessing, then of D. F. Strauss,[9] and finally of Albert Schweitzer.[10] As a necessary preliminary for understanding Lessing, Reimarus must first be extracted from the grasp of the third great promoter of his work.

Since Schweitzer's classic survey of earlier life-of-Jesus scholarship, Reimarus has been generally credited with initiating what came to be known as the "quest of the historical Jesus." His significance for Schweitzer is already highlighted in the original German title of his work *(Von Reimarus zu Wrede)*. For Schweitzer, Reimarus and Wrede represent not only the beginning and end of the story he tells but also the two major options between which a choice must be made: either for the Jesus of Reimarus, whose career is determined by eschatological beliefs he shares with his contemporaries, or the Jesus of Wrede, the essentially noneschatological figure overlaid by the eschatological doctrines of the early church.[11] Indeed, Reimarus's true narrative function is to prefigure Schweitzer himself. The quest of the historical Jesus is the story of a truth glimpsed from afar by a solitary individual, lost again for many years, and then finally recovered in a moment of visionary clarity. The story proceeds from Reimarus not to Wrede but to Schweitzer, in whom the crucial original insight into Jesus' person and activity at last comes to fruition:

[Munich: Carl Hanser Verlag, 1976], pp. 614-36; Eng. trans. Chadwick, *Lessing's Theological Writings*, pp. 65-81; Nisbet, *Lessing: Philosophical and Theological Writings*, pp. 148-71).

9. See David Friedrich Strauss, *Hermann Samuel Reimarus und seine Schutzschrift für die vernünftigen Verehrer Gottes* (1862; repr. Hildesheim: Georg Olms Verlag, 1991).

10. Albert Schweitzer, *The Quest of the Historical Jesus: A Critical Study of Its Progress from Reimarus to Wrede*, trans. W. Montgomery (London: A. & C. Black, 1910); German original, *Von Reimarus zu Wrede: Eine Geschichte der Leben-Jesu-Forschung* (Tübingen: J. C. B. Mohr [Paul Siebeck], 1906[1]). The popular "quest" metaphor derives from the English title; on this see my article, "Eschatology and the Twentieth Century: On the Reception of Schweitzer in English," in *Eschatologie/Eschatology: The Sixth Durham-Tübingen Research Symposium: Eschatology in Old Testament, Ancient Judaism, and Early Christianity*, ed. H.-J. Eckstein, C. Landmesser, and H. Lichtenberger (Tübingen: Mohr-Siebeck, 2011), pp. 331-47; pp. 331-33. Citations here are from the first English edition.

11. For this view of the Reimarus/Wrede pairing, see A. Schweitzer, *Aus meinem Leben und Denken* (Leipzig: Felix Meiner, 1931), pp. 39-40.

Even so the traveller on the plain sees from afar the distant range of mountains. Then he loses sight of them again. His way winds slowly up-wards through the valleys, drawing ever nearer to the peaks, until at last, at a turn in the path, they stand before him, not in the shapes which they had seemed to take from the distant plain, but in their actual forms. Reimarus was the first, after eighteen centuries of misconception, to know what eschatology really was. Then theology lost sight of it again, and it was not until a lapse of more than a hundred years that it came in view of eschatology once more, now in its true form. . . .[12]

Reimarus was the first to take a truly historical view of the life of Jesus.[13] He is one of those rare historians who "from their mother's womb have an instinctive feeling for the real."[14] His work on the aims of Jesus and his disci-ples is "not only one of the greatest events in the history of criticism, it is also a masterpiece of general literature."[15] Reimarus "had no predecessors, nei-ther had he any disciples," and yet he has the satisfaction of having authored "one of those supremely great works which pass and leave no trace, because they are before their time."[16] There is strategy in Schweitzer's superlatives. Reimarus is cast in the role of the precursor to Schweitzer himself. There is an affinity between the two; they are kindred spirits, recognizing each other from afar yet holding themselves aloof from mere scholarly erudition and normal academic theology.[17] In his presentation of Reimarus, Schweitzer is already shaping his own self-image, preparing the way for his own entry onto the scene in his book's final chapters.[18]

Schweitzer is entirely dependent on the section of Reimarus's work that Lessing published in 1778 under the title *Vom Zwecke Jesu und seiner Jünger* ("On the Aim of Jesus and of His Disciples").[19] Here, a sharp distinction is drawn between Jesus' aim, which was to found a this-worldly messianic the-

---

12. Schweitzer, *Quest*, p. 23. Johannes Weiss is given some credit for the recovery of Reimarus's insight (*Quest*, pp. 23, 237-40), but Schweitzer has no intention of allowing Weiss to steal his thunder.

13. Schweitzer, *Quest*, p. 13.

14. Schweitzer, *Quest*, p. 25.

15. Schweitzer, *Quest*, p. 15.

16. Schweitzer, *Quest*, p. 26.

17. Schweitzer, *Quest*, pp. 25-26.

18. Schweitzer, *Quest*, pp. 328-401.

19. At the start of the Reimarus chapter (*Quest*, p. 13), Schweitzer lists only the 1778 publica-tion and the detailed rebuttal by J. S. Semler (*Beantwortung der Fragmente eines Ungenrannten insbesondere vom Zwecke Jesu und seiner Jünger* [Halle: Verlag des Erziehungsinstituts, 1779]).

ocracy, and his disciples' *later* aim, which was to promote a new spiritual religion of miracle, mystery, and ritual following the collapse of the theocratic hope shared with Jesus himself. Schweitzer has little interest in any such disjunction. He insists that Reimarus's text is primarily concerned with *eschatology*, a reading significantly influenced by the peculiarities of Lessing's original publication. At the heart of Reimarus's original text lies an extensive critique of the resurrection narratives, the fabrication of which is supposed to have laid the foundation of the new religious system now known as "Christianity." Lessing had published most of this material separately in 1777, and he did not restore it to its original context in the 1778 publication but merely indicated where it belonged.[20] In the absence of this crucial discussion, the eschatologies of Jesus and his disciples assume greater prominence in the truncated text than in its original form.[21]

In reality, Reimarus shows little or no knowledge of Jewish eschatology at the time of Jesus, and is largely dependent on a conventional characterization of Jewish messianic belief as concerned with "worldly deliverance."[22] Far from being an original and forward-looking thinker, he is at every point dependent on English deistic literature and is thoroughly ill-suited to his assigned role as founder of modern critical gospels scholarship.[23]

Lessing's response to Reimarus is no less engaged than Schweitzer's. It is a more poised performance, however — nuanced, open-ended, and exploratory. Unlike Schweitzer, Lessing does not remake Reimarus in his own self-

---

20. *LW*, 7.557.

21. For the eschatology of Jesus, see part 1, §§28-30 (*LW*, 7.537-41; Eng. trans., *Reimarus Fragments*, ed. Charles H. Talbert [London: SCM Press, 1971], pp. 122-29; henceforth, *Fragments*). For the disciples' eschatology, see part 2, §§36-45 (*LW*, 7.565-77; *Fragments*, pp. 211-29).

22. As A. C. Lundsteen noted, eschatology "ist . . . in Reimarus' Darstellung kein Hauptpunkt, sondern nur als ein nebengeordnetes Glied zusammen mit andern ebenso bedeutenden Gliedern . . . dargestellt" (*Hermann Samuel Reimarus und die Anfänge der Leben-Jesu-Forschung* [Copenhagen: O. C. Olsen, 1939], p. 10).

23. Reimarus's dependence on English deistic sources is such "dass es ein vollständiges Missverständnis ist, Reimarus als den Urheber der später bekannten Jesusforschung aufzustellen, wie es Schweitzer . . . tat" (Lundsteen, *Hermann Samuel Reimarus*, p. 135). Lundsteen's judgement is confirmed by H. Graf von Reventlow, who notes that "Reimarus ist in fast alle Einzelheiten des reichhaltigen kritischen Materials, das er in den beiden Bänden seiner 'Apologie' zum Alten und Neuen Testament zusammengeträgt, der Erbe einer umfangreichen Tradition . . ." ("Das Arsenal der Bibelkritik des Reimarus: Die Auslegung der Bibel, insbesondere des Alten Testaments, bei den englischen Deisten," in *Hermann Samuel Reimarus (1694-1768): Ein "bekannter Unbekannter" der Aufklärung in Hamburg*, Joachim Jungius Gesellschaft der Wissenschaften [Hamburg; Göttingen: Vandenhoeck & Ruprecht, 1973], pp. 44-65; p. 44). The orthodox Schweitzerian position is still maintained by Martin Bollacher (*Lessing*, p. 25).

image but remains at a critical distance from him. Yet he too *interprets* Reimarus, both in his selection of material for publication and in his editorial comments. Our main focus will be on the resurrection fragment of 1777 as the catalyst for Lessing's own independent work on the gospels.

A Controversy in the Making

Two fortuitous events provided the catalyst for Lessing's venture into the realms of theological scholarship, both involving unpublished and unknown manuscripts. One of these dated from the eleventh century; the other was recent, dating from the year 1744.

Lessing took up his appointment as librarian of the Herzog August Bibliothek, Wolfenbüttel, in May 1770. On his journey there from Hamburg he met the theologian Konrad Arnold Schmid, who had recently discovered and published a letter from a certain Adelmann to Berengar of Tours, well known for his insistence that the material elements of the Eucharist remain intact even as they are transformed into the body and blood of Christ. The letter had been discovered in the Wolfenbüttel library, and Lessing immediately began searching for further material relating to the eleventh-century eucharistic controversy. Within a few weeks, he had found a copy of Berengar's lost *De Sacra Coena,* in which the possibility of a material change to the elements was rejected, in opposition to Lanfranc's *De Corpore et Sanguine Domini.* In July Lessing announced his discovery in a letter to his father, a Lutheran minister who was no doubt gratified to learn that "Berengar held exactly the same doctrine of the Eucharist as Luther later did, and shows no trace at all of the interpretation attributed to him by the Reformed."[24] A few months later Lessing completed a book about Berengar, including substantial citations from his newly discovered text, and commented wryly to his future wife, Eva König, "You would hardly believe the excellent reputation for orthodoxy I now hold among our Lutheran theologians."[25] Since the work had to do with the rehabilitation of a supposed heretic, it was also favourably reviewed in the liberal *Allgemeine Deutsche Bibliothek.*[26]

24. Letter dated 27 July 1770 (K. Lachmann and F. Muncker [eds.], *Gotthold Ephraim Lessings Sämtliche Schriften* [Leipzig: G. V. Göschen'sche Verlagshandlung, 1886-1924] [henceforth Lachmann-Muncker], 17.266: p. 330, ll. 13-15).

25. Letter dated 25 October 1770 (Lachmann-Muncker, 17.274: p. 343, ll. 28-30).

26. At a council in Rome in 1059, Berengar of Tours (*c.* 999-1088) was compelled to deny that, after consecration, the bread and wine are "only the sacrament and not the true body and blood of

Following this initial success, Lessing planned a series of publications of further material from the library.[27] At his request, the series was granted exemption from censorship, on condition that "nothing detrimental to religion or good morals" would be published.[28] In the first two volumes, published in 1773, the main items of theological interest were Lessing's studies of Leibniz's defence of the orthodox Christian doctrines of eternal punishment and the trinity, in opposition to Socinian critics. (Leibniz had been one of Lessing's predecessors at the Wolfenbüttel library.) The Leibniz studies in the first two volumes represent items VII and XII in a system of enumeration that runs continuously through the series. In both cases Lessing is sympathetic to traditional beliefs, without expressly committing himself to them. In a letter to his more consistently freethinking brother Karl, he explains that, in his view, there is real intellectual substance in the older orthodox theology even if it is false, and that his real quarrel is with the modern "rational" theology which seeks to reconcile the claims of reason and faith but fails to satisfy either. It is best not to throw out the old dirty water before we know where fresh pure water is to be found.[29]

In the third volume of his series, published in 1774, Lessing seeks to rehabilitate a sixteenth-century Socinian or deist theologian, Adam Neuser, who fled from Europe to Constantinople where he converted to Islam and died in 1576. Lessing's discussion of this figure is based on a long letter from Neuser to his friends Casper and Landsmann, an early copy of which is held in "our library."[30] This contribution to the volume (XVII in the continuous

---

the Lord," and that these are not truly and *sensualiter* broken, crushed, or consumed. In the text discovered by Lessing, it is clear that Berengar had never intended the purely symbolic understanding of the sacrament attributed to him by his opponents — for which he was later admired by Protestant theologians such as Zwingli, Calvin, Peter Martyr, and John Jewel. Using the analogy of the incarnation, Berengar's point was that the bread and wine remained bread and wine even after their sacramental union with the Lord's body and blood. On Berengar, see H. Chadwick, "Ego Berengarius," *JTS*, n.s., 40 (1989), pp. 414-45; on Lessing and Berengar, see Volker Leppin, "Ein mittelalterlicher Fund für das aktuelle Gespräch. Lessings *Berengarius Turonensis*," in *Lessings Religionsphilosophie im Kontext: Hamburger Fragmente und Wolfenbütteler Axiomata*, ed. Christoph Bultmann and Friedrich Vollhardt (Berlin & New York: De Gruyter, 2011), pp. 88-103.

27. Under the title *Zur Geschichte und Literatur: Aus den Schätzen der Herzoglichen Bibliothek zu Wolfenbüttel*.

28. *LW*, 7.799: resolution dated 13 February 1772.

29. Letter dated 2 February 1774 (Lachmann-Muncker, 17.404: p. 101, ll. 19-21). He and his brother are agreed "dass unser altes Religionssystem falsch ist" — and yet, "Ich weiss kein Ding in der Welt, an welchem sich der menschliche Scharfsinn mehr gezeigt und geübt hätte, als an ihm" (pp. 101-2).

30. *LW*, 7.226.

system of enumeration) is immediately followed by a *Fragment eines Ungennanten* or "Anonymous Fragment" (XVIII), which Lessing entitles *Von Duldung der Deisten* ("On Toleration of Deists").[31] The connection between the two pieces is clear, and it is emphasized by Lessing both in his introduction and in his subsequent comments on the "Fragment."[32] Neuser, he claims, was not convinced of the truth of Islam as a revealed religion but accepted it on account of its broad agreement with his deist beliefs — not least in its rejection of the Christian dogmas of trinity and incarnation. He would not have taken the drastic step of conversion had diverse views been tolerated within Christendom. In a further short extract from his anonymous author, it is argued that natural religion conforms more closely to Islamic than to Christian beliefs.[33]

Like Neuser's letter, the anonymous work is said to have been discovered in the Wolfenbüttel library. Lessing reports that it is in a disordered state; it is not clear whether its various components are really parts of a single coherent work. Nor is it clear how it got into the library in the first place. A likely conjecture is that it is the work of Johann Lorenz Schmidt (1702-49), author of a rationalistic translation of the Pentateuch, who in his last years found in Wolfenbüttel a safe haven from his orthodox opponents.[34] The manuscript appears to be about thirty years old.[35]

With the exception of the date, none of these plausible-sounding claims about the anonymous work is actually true. The work was not by Schmidt but by Hermann Samuel Reimarus (1694-1768). It was not in fragmentary form. Later, acquiescing in the surrender of the manuscript, Lessing referred to it as a single work in 335 quarto sheets.[36] Lessing did not come across it in

---

31. *LW,* 7.313-30; publication details in Schmidt-Biggemann, pp. 68-69.

32. *LW,* 7.313, 326-39.

33. *LW,* 7.327-38.

34. Schmidt's 1735 translation was entitled *Die göttlichen Schriften vor den Zeiten des Messie Jesu . . . , nach einer freien Übersetzung, welche durch und durch mit Anmerkungen erläutert und bestätigt wird.* Elsewhere Lessing recounts how Schmidt came to Wolfenbüttel towards the end of his life, receiving a small pension from the duke and completing his Old Testament translation; the manuscript, together with the corrections of the earlier published work, was still in the duke's possession (*LW,* 8.407-8). On Schmidt as translator of the English deist Matthew Tindal, see Christopher Voigt, *Der englische Deismus in Deutschland. Eine Studie zur Rezeption english-deistischer Literatur in deutschen Zeitschriften und Kompendien des 18. Jahrhundert* (Tübingen: Mohr-Siebeck, 2003), pp. 102-11.

35. For Lessing's announcement of this work, see *LW,* 7.313-14.

36. Letter from Lessing to the Duke of Brunswick, dated 20 July 1778 (Lachmann-Muncker, 18.601).

the Wolfenbüttel library but evidently acquired it in Hamburg from Reimarus's son and daughter (Johann Albert Heinrich and Elise), and brought it with him to Wolfenbüttel.[37] An exchange of letters between Lessing and Moses Mendelssohn, dating from 1770-71, indicates that he had lent the manuscript to his friend.[38] At this point, nothing was said about publication. Reimarus himself had advised against this. In the introduction to the final version of his work (1768), he wrote:

> This work should be preserved for the private use of discriminating friends. It is not my intention that it be published, before the dawning of more enlightened times. It is better for the people to err a while longer than that I — even without any guilt on my part — should offend it with the truth and incite it to furious religious zealotry [*in einen wütenden Religionseifer*].[39]

Lessing thought otherwise. On a visit to Hamburg in September 1771, he may have sought and obtained permission from Reimarus's son and daughter to publish the work, on condition of strict anonymity. Proceeding to Berlin, and ignoring the advice of his friends Christoph Friedrich Nicolai and Moses Mendelssohn, he entered into negotiations with a potential publisher, which came to nothing.[40] Three years later, after publishing the first fragment in the Wolfenbüttel library series, he promises his brother "a little comedy with the theologians," if his Berlin publisher can now be persuaded to publish a second fragment.[41] This was to be entitled *Eine noch freiere Untersuchung des Canons des alten und neuen Testaments* — with "even more free . . ." alluding to J. S. Semler's four-volume *Abhandlung von freier Unter-*

---

37. Indications of the circumstances in which Lessing acquired the Reimarus material are to be found in his correspondence — especially in letters to J. A. H. Reimarus (10 April 1770; July 1776; Lachmann-Muncker, 17.318-19; 18.487), from J. A. H. Reimarus to Lessing (19 March 1778; 15-16 June 1778; 21.743, 751), and from Elise Reimarus (December 1780; 21.873). Passages in these letters imply the family's involvement in Lessing's initial publications (18.487: pp. 180-81; 21.751: p. 207, ll. 32-35; 21.873: p. 314, ll. 6-11), Lessing's promise to maintain the author's anonymity (21.743: p. 196, ll. 26-28), and his failure to consult about the publication of the final, most controversial "fragment" (21.751: p. 206, ll. 12-17; p. 210, ll. 31-35; p. 212, ll. 10-16).

38. Letters dated 29 November 1770 (Mendelssohn to Lessing), 9 January 1771 (Lessing to Mendelssohn); Lachmann-Muncker, 19.344; 17.291.

39. Gerhard Alexander (ed.), *Hermann Samuel Reimarus: Apologie oder Schutzschrift für die vernünftigen Verehrer Gottes*, 2 vols. (Frankfurt am Main: Insel Verlag, 1971), vol. 1, p. 41.

40. *LW*, 7.881, 882.

41. Letter dated 11 November 1774 (Lachmann-Muncker, 18.416: p. 117, ll. 12-15).

suchung des Canon (Halle, 1771-75). The "comedy" in question was the controversy that would surely ensue, with Lessing and Semler as the protagonists. After that plan too came to nothing, Lessing must finally have decided to persist with the fiction that the anonymous work belonged to the Wolfenbüttel library, and to publish further excerpts within his own series, unhindered by censorship.

The fourth volume of the Wolfenbüttel library series was published in January 1777, and contained five substantial items from the anonymous work which together make up item XX in the consecutive enumeration. Lessing presented the extracts as a critique of the concept of revelation, publishing them under the title *Ein Mehreres aus den Papieren des Ungenannten, die Offenbarung betreffend* ("Further Selections from the Anonymous Papers, concerning Revelation").[42] In the reference here to "papers" rather than a unified work, the original fictive description is maintained. The term "fragment" is used to similar effect. In 1774 Lessing claimed to have found "fragments of a most remarkable work among the most recent manuscripts of our library," and repeatedly emphasized that what he possessed were fragments rather than a complete work.[43] Thus, the 1774 excerpt was provided with a title and presented as an "Anonymous Fragment." Lessing repeats this format in the more important 1777 publication. The excerpts are enumerated (*Erstes Fragment*, etc.), and a title follows. Thus Lessing continues to describe as *fragments* what are actually *extracts* selected by himself.

According to Lessing, his readers have responded favourably to the fragment on the toleration of deists, and one of them has urged him to publish more of the unpublished material, lest those of little faith should suppose that it contains unanswerable objections to the Christian religion. Confident as he is in his cause, Lessing does not hesitate to oblige.[44] The first of the five new fragments criticizes the tendency of preachers and theologians to decry "mere" reason, its scope and its possibilities, in order to maximize the role of revelation.[45] The second argues that no revelation other than the universal natural one has any prospect of reaching more than a tiny minority of the human race, whose salvation it is supposed to ensure.[46] One of the argu-

---

42. Together with Lessing's comments, the fragments occupy pp. 261-544 of this substantial volume (Schmidt-Biggemann, p. 69).

43. *LW*, 7.313.

44. *LW*, 7.331.

45. "Von Verschreiung der Vernunft auf den Kanzeln" (*LW*, 7.332-44).

46. "Unmöglichkeit einer Offenbarung, die alle Menschen auf eine gegründete Art glauben könnten" (*LW*, 7.344-88).

ments here is that at least as many people must have lived in the (supposed) 4000-year history of the world before Christ as in the 1744 years since Christ.[47] This date suggests that Lessing's claim that the anonymous work is around 30 years old is correct.[48] The third fragment, the shortest of the series, concerns the exodus event.[49] At this point the anonymous work has moved beyond the theoretical issues dealt with in the first two fragments, and is now concerned with the biblical history — specifically, in this case, with its implausibility in view of the sheer numbers involved. The fourth fragment is concerned with a broader Old Testament issue, arguing that the writings of the Old Testament were not written in order to reveal a religion.[50] The anonymous author believes that the true, natural religion teaches the immortality of the soul and the reality of rewards and punishments in the future life; the lack of any such beliefs in the Old Testament is proof that it contains no genuine divine revelation. Both Old Testament fragments refer back to their immediate context in the larger work.[51]

The fifth and final fragment is concerned with the gospel resurrection narratives.[52] This was excerpted from an extensive account of the aims of Jesus and his disciples, which Lessing subsequently published in 1778, and which Schweitzer was later to see as the starting point of a "quest" that attained its goal in his own work. Within its original context in the 1778 material, the treatment of the resurrection narratives has a quite specific rationale, which disappears when it is relocated alongside the other 1777 fragments. Yet it is in this relatively self-contained 1777 form that Reimarus's discussion of the gospel resurrection narratives made its greatest impact,

---

47. *LW,* 7.355-56.

48. *LW,* 7.313, 331.

49. "Durchgang der Israeliten durchs rote Meer" (*LW,* 7.388-98). On this see Ulrich Groetsch, "The Miraculous Crossing of the Red Sea: What Lessing and His Opponents during the Fragmentenstreit Did Not See," in *Lessings Religionsphilosophie im Kontext,* pp. 181-99.

50. "Dass die Bücher A.T. nicht geschrieben worden, eine Religion zu offenbaren" (*LW,* 7.398-426).

51. In the third fragment, the exodus event is introduced as "das andere Wunder" (*LW,* 7.388), suggesting that this may have followed a discussion of an event such as the slaughter of the firstborn in the original manuscript. (In the final, greatly expanded form of the *Apologie,* first published only in 1971, the chapter on the crossing of the Red Sea [G. Alexander, vol. 1, pp. 299-326] follows a chapter "von den Handlungen Mosis in Egypten" [pp. 269-98].) The fourth fragment includes an explicit reference back to the previous chapter, where it was shown that the intention of the Old Testament authors was merely to bring the Israelites to the service of Jehovah, away from other gods — and that, prior to the Babylonian captivity, they laboured in vain (*LW,* 7.399-400).

52. "Über die Auferstehungsgeschichte" (*LW,* 7.426-57).

and the debate it generated represents a turning point in the study of the gospels. Reimarus argues that the gospel narratives cannot be harmonized and are therefore false. His opponents argue that harmonization remains possible. Lessing agrees with Reimarus that the gospel narratives cannot be harmonized, but attributes this not to deliberate fraud but to the passage of time, which allowed inaccuracies and additions to accumulate that detract from the gospels' veracity. In his remarkable critique of gospel harmonization, Lessing develops a position which acknowledges the individual integrity of the gospels while seeing them as deviating from the original truth embodied in Jesus.[53]

The 1777 resurrection fragment comprises two chapters from Reimarus's full text. The first is devoted to Matthew's story of the guards (Mt. 27.62–28.15). According to the guards' testimony, Jesus' body was stolen by his disciples; Matthew seeks to rebut this allegation by tracing it back to a bribe from the chief priests, who wished to suppress the truth about the resurrection. Reimarus argues that this story is a later invention, full of contradictions and implausibilities, but it is still of great value to him in unwittingly preserving the origin of the resurrection belief. It is probable, he thinks, that the disciples really did steal Jesus' body. Matthew acknowledges that "the Jews" now believe this to have been the case, and for Reimarus their view is all too plausible. In aligning himself with Jewish critics of Christian resurrection faith, Reimarus follows in the steps of the English deist Thomas Woolston, who is in turn dependent here on Celsus, and who also shows a special interest in the guard story.[54]

---

53. Lessing's literary contributions to the Fragments Controversy predate his publication of the final and most extensive fragment, on the aims of Jesus and his disciples. Only where this is overlooked can it appear that Lessing evades the fragments' essential point, the untruth of Christianity (as argued by Emanuel Hirsch, *Geschichte der neuern evangelischen Theologie im Zusammenhang mit den allgemeinen Bewegungen des europäischen Denkens*, 5 vols. [Gütersloh: G. Mohn, 1949-54], vol. 4, pp. 153-54). In his chapter on the Fragments Controversy as a whole (pp. 120-65), Hirsch tries to show that the basic insights of both Reimarus and Lessing remain normative, at least within the sphere of *German* Protestant theology and culture.

54. Thomas Woolston, *Six Discourses on the Miracles of Our Saviour, And Defences of His Discourses* (London, 1727-30; repr. New York & London: Garland, 1979); *Sixth Discourse*, pp. 3-28. According to Reventlow, Reimarus was aware of Woolston's work (along with that of other English deists such as Toland, Shaftesbury, Collins, Tindal, Middleton, and Morgan), although he appears not to have known Peter Annet's 1744 work, *The Resurrection of Jesus Considered*, where it was argued that Jesus did not really die (Reventlow, "Das Arsenal der Bibelkritik des Reimarus," p. 59n). An extant catalogue of Reimarus's personal library indicates that he possessed copies of most major deistic works (Reventlow, p. 60n).

Far more important is the second resurrection chapter, where an acute analysis is given of differences and contradictions between the various evangelists. Ten differences *(Verschiedenheiten)* are specified,[55] followed by a fuller discussion of ten contradictions *(Widersprüche)*. The gospels differ as to who went to the tomb,[56] and why,[57] and how many times.[58] Matthean, Lukan, and Johannine angels say quite different things.[59] John and Matthew give different accounts of the risen Lord's first appearance, to Mary alone or to Mary and to another Mary.[60] Further appearances either take place in or around Jerusalem or in Galilee, depending on which account one follows.[61] The evangelists Matthew and John remain strangely silent about the ascension, an event that in principle they ought to have witnessed.[62]

In a number of cases such differences turn out on closer inspection to be actual contradictions. The first two contradictions concern the spices, bought early on Easter morning (Mark) or on Friday evening (Luke), or perhaps provided by Joseph of Arimathea and Nicodemus at the time of Jesus' burial (John).[63] Next, there is a series of contradictions that have to do with events at the tomb. Was the stone rolled away *as* the women arrived at the tomb (Matthew), or *before* (the other evangelists)?[64] Did one or two angels appear,[65] and what did he or they look like?[66] Where did Jesus appear to Mary,[67]

---

55. Gospel differences are treated in §§20-21 (*LW*, 7.440-42; *Fragments*, pp. 174-77).

56. Mary Magdalene and the other Mary (Mt. 28.1); Mary Magdalene, Mary the mother of James, Salome (Mk. 16.1); Mary Magdalene, Joanna, Mary the mother of James, and others (Lk. 24.10); initially Mary only, then Peter and John (Jn. 20.1, 3-9).

57. To see the tomb (Mt. 28.1); to embalm the corpse (Mk. 16.1); no reason given (Jn. 20.1).

58. Twice (Jn. 20.1, 11); once in the synoptics.

59. Arrangements for the reunion in Galilee (Mt. 28.7; Mk. 16.7); a reminder of Jesus' prediction of his passion (Lk. 24.6-7); a query about Mary's weeping (Jn. 20.13).

60. Jn. 20.14-18; Mt. 28.9-10.

61. A single appearance in Jerusalem (Lk. 24.33-49); two appearances in Jerusalem (Jn. 20.19-29); an appearance on the road to Emmaus (Lk. 24.13-32; Mk. 16.12); different accounts of appearances in Galilee (Mt. 28.16-20; Jn. 21.1-22).

62. Cf. Acts 1.2, 6, 13.

63. Mk. 16.1; Lk. 23.56; Jn. 19.39-40.

64. Mt. 28.1-2; Mk. 16.4; Lk. 24.2; Jn. 20.1.

65. One (Mt. 28.2; Mk. 16.5), or two (Lk. 24.4; Jn. 20.12).

66. An angel whose appearance was like lightning, sitting on the stone after rolling it away (Mt. 28.3); a young man in white, seated within the tomb on the right (Mk. 16.5); two men in dazzling clothing, standing within the tomb (Lk. 24.4); two angels in white, seated where Jesus' body had lain, one at the head, the other at the feet (Jn. 20.12).

67. At the tomb (Jn. 20.14-18), on the way back to Jerusalem (Mt. 28.9-10), unspecified (Mk. 16.9-11).

and was she permitted to touch him or not?[68] The remaining contradictions relate to resurrection appearances elsewhere, and have already been noted under the heading of "differences." Where did Jesus appear to his male disciples, in Galilee (Matthew) or in Jerusalem (Luke)? Why is it not possible to coordinate the Matthean Galilee appearance with the Johannine one? Reimarus takes it for granted that the arts of the harmonizer will be of no avail in the face of clear contradictions such as these. The chapter concludes with an earnest appeal to the reader:

> Tell me before God, conscientious and honest reader: could you regard this testimony, about so vital a matter, as unanimous and sincere, while it contradicts itself so often and obviously in relation to persons, time, place, manner, intention, utterance, narration?[69]

The frame of reference is that of a court of law. This is what Reimarus has in mind when he speaks of "testimony" or "witnesses."[70] He himself is the prosecuting counsel, his readers are the jury. Christianity itself stands accused in the dock, but does not speak in its own defence. This courtroom drama consists entirely in the hostile interrogation of witnesses on whose credibility the case stands or falls. Did they *really* see and hear what they claim to have seen and heard? The court is concerned exclusively with factual accuracy. It cannot regard the witnesses as interpreters who have subsumed the facts into an overarching story that seeks to articulate their true meaning. The *only* question is whether they are telling the truth or whether they are lying or mistaken. If their testimony can be shown to be implausible or contradictory when judged by ordinary criteria of factual accuracy, they will have been exposed as "false witnesses" and the case against Christianity and the gospels will have been upheld.

Although Augustine would have been outraged by Reimarus's conclusions, he could have had no objection to the assumption on which they are based: that the veracity of the gospel narratives depends on the possibility of harmonizing them with one another and with prior historical reality. In his role as counsel for the defence, Augustine operates within the same law-court setting as Reimarus.

The question is whether we must regard this legalistic hermeneutic as given and inescapable. Here we simply note that, if Augustine and Reimarus

---

68. Mary forbidden to touch (Jn. 20.17); she and the other Mary clasp Jesus' feet (Mt. 28.9).
69. *LW,* 7.455 (*Fragments,* p. 197).
70. See *LW,* 7.442 (*Fragments,* pp. 21-22).

are correct in their negative assessment of gospel differences, there would be no *fourfold* story of Easter Day and its aftermath. The plurality is *integral* to this story in its canonical form, and it would be fatally undermined if all four evangelists had precisely the same women visiting Jesus' tomb for precisely the same reason, experiencing precisely the same events when they arrived. The differences are real enough, but they are already enshrined in the canonical form. They have long since been taken into account.

A Parable and a Proposal

Of Lessing's various contributions to the controversy that followed his publication of the 1777 fragments, two are directly related to his anonymous author's critique of the gospel resurrection narratives. One of these takes the form of a parable,[71] the other is a critique of gospel harmonization.[72]

The parable runs as follows. Once upon a time, there was a King who ruled his extensive domains from a Palace that was both large and irregularly constructed. The Palace had remained unaltered for many years, and to many this venerable building had its own distinctive charm. But connoisseurs of architecture thought otherwise. The Palace had insufficient windows, and those it did have were of varying shapes and sizes — as were its gates and doors. Judged from the outside, it was hard to see how the windows could admit enough light. And it would surely be more convenient to locate a single matching gateway on each of the four sides of the building. Yet the connoisseurs disagree with each other about exactly what should be done; most of them know the building only from the outside. They typify the eighteenth-century concern to "improve" ancient buildings that are out of step with modern sensibilities — updating and upgrading them, equipping them with modern amenities, toning down their idiosyncrasies. The Improvers are in a minority, however. Most people have no particular stake in current architectural fashion, and they like the Palace the way it is.

This Palace is simply Christianity. The Improvers or Modernizers are the contemporary theologians who emphasize "the reasonableness of Christianity" and who remove or conceal features inherited from less enlightened times, when the principles of sound reason were only imperfectly grasped.

---

71. *Eine Parabel, nebst einer kleinen Bitte, und einem eventualen Absagungsschreiben an den Herrn Pastor Goeze, in Hamburg* (LW, 8.117-59).

72. *Eine Duplik; LW* 8.30-101.

Lessing is aware of the possibility of reducing Christianity to an "essence" that is supposed to secure its viability within an enlightened future, but for the most part he rejects it. The only interesting and worthwhile Christianity is the religion defined in the catholic creeds, trinity and all: that is Lessing's answer to the demand that he should state his own understanding of the Christian religion.[73] This credal Christianity may not be true, and is certainly not true in the absolute, exclusive, and demonstrable sense normally assumed — and yet it has *endured*. Like the Palace, it remains an intransigent social fact which is as it is irrespective of subjective opinions about whether it ought to be otherwise. In his own way, Lessing proposes a "cultural-linguistic" answer to the question about the nature of the Christian religion.[74] Perhaps, as the fragments suggest, the Palace has been built on shaky foundations. But in that case, how is it still standing, many centuries after it was built?

> What fool rummages around in the basement of his house, simply to reassure himself that the foundations are sound? Obviously the house had to be built in one place or another. But, in the very fact that it still remains standing, I have more convincing evidence that the foundations are sound than those who saw them being laid. . . . I am only interested in what stands above the ground, not in what lies concealed beneath the ground.[75]

In the Parable of the Palace, the connoisseurs of architecture are concerned with the Palace's external appearance, and not with its foundations. The imagery varies, but Lessing's concern is the same in both cases: to assert not so much the ontological truth of Christianity as its encompassing social reality. (Of course, religions other than Christianity also possess a social reality of their own. That will later be the theme of the celebrated Parable of the Three Rings.)[76]

At this point in the Parable of the Palace, the Modernizers give way to a group of Antiquarians. These people are in possession of documents said to

---

73. *Gotth. Ephr. Lessings Nötige Antwort auf eine sehr unnötige Frage des Hrn. Hauptpastor Goeze in Hamburg* (*LW*, 8.309-13).

74. See George A. Lindbeck, *The Nature of Doctrine: Religion and Theology in a Postliberal Age* (London: SPCK, 1984).

75. *LW*, 8.39-40. This image from the *Duplik* may be one of the sources for the more elaborate Parable of the Palace.

76. This forms the centrepiece for Lessing's last and greatest play, *Nathan der Weise* (1779).

be the ground plans drawn up by the original builders. Unfortunately, their words and symbols are hard to interpret. As a result,

> Everyone interpreted these words and symbols as seemed good to them. Everyone assembled out of these old ground-plans whatever new version they favoured [*einen beliebigen Neuen*] — often to such an extent that they not only swore by it themselves but also persuaded or compelled others to take the same view.[77]

Here, the old, hard-to-interpret plans or outlines *(Grundrisse)* are the biblical texts, especially the gospels. The Antiquarians are those interpreters who insist that these texts are foundational to Christianity, yet impose on them and on others their own arbitrary interpretations. Lessing claims elsewhere that, in the writings of the evangelists, "there is hardly a single passage on whose interpretation two people have ever agreed, in the entire history of the world."[78] This exaggerated claim recalls the Antiquarians of the parable, with their undecipherable ground plans and their boundless confidence in their own ability to understand them. The Antiquarians' interpretative activity is quite precisely described. Out of the confused plurality of old ground plans or outlines, they each construct a new text of their own; in other words, they put together a gospel Harmony. In his *Duplik,* published shortly before he composed his parable, Lessing speaks in very similar terms about the substitution of a new text for the old ones:

> O that most excellent Harmony, which can only reconcile two contradictory reports, both stemming from the evangelists, by inventing a third report, not a syllable of which is to be found in any individual evangelist![79]

One gospel states that Jesus' corpse was anointed by Joseph of Arimathea and Nicodemus at the time of his burial; others report that the anointing was to have been carried out by Mary and other women on Easter morning.[80] "The burial rites are complete, and they are incomplete: is that not a contradiction?"[81] And so the harmonizer invents a double anointing. Perhaps the first anointing reflects burial customs in Jerusalem, the second in Galilee. Or perhaps the two anointings had different functions, one in-

77. *LW,* 8.119.
78. *LW,* 7.712; *Lessing's Theological Writings,* p. 106.
79. *LW,* 8.51-52.
80. Jn. 19.38-40; Mk. 16.1; Lk. 23.49–24.1.
81. *LW,* 8.50.

tended to retard the process of decomposition, the other being for the sake of the fragrance. But such suggestions are pure fabrication: "Alles das ist bloss gefabelt. . . ."[82] No evangelist knows of a double anointing; the Harmony contradicts John, correcting his claim that Jesus' burial was duly carried out immediately after his death by insisting that the burial rites had yet to be completed. The harmonizers *replace* the inspired texts with an uninspired one put together by themselves. The Antiquarians in the parable are guilty of similar interpretative misconduct.

Having been introduced to the Modernizers and the Antiquarians, we now meet a third group, fewer in number, who dare to question whether the ground plans are of any real significance at all. "It is enough," they say, "for us to experience every moment that the most benevolent wisdom fills the whole Palace, and that from it nothing but beauty, order and well-being are spread across the whole land."[83] These Questioners interpret the ground plans more successfully than do the Antiquarians, precisely because they are not committed to their absolute truth and validity; and they are promptly denounced as arsonists conspiring to burn down the Palace.

The Questioners include Lessing himself, with his insistence that the truth of Christianity is not determined by the veracity or otherwise of the gospels. They also include the anonymous Fragmentist (Reimarus), for whom the Palace would have to represent the pure original religion of nature still subsisting within the degenerate religion we know as Christianity. Although he otherwise differentiates himself from the Fragmentist, Lessing sees in him a single-minded pursuit of truth that is worthy of admiration and imitation, whether or not it attains its goal. It is with Reimarus in mind that he writes in the *Duplik:*

> Someone who seeks to establish what is actually untruth, convinced that it is the truth, in a manner that is well-intentioned, acute, and self-effacing, is of infinitely greater worth than someone who defends the best and noblest truth in the usual way [*auf alltägliche Weise*], from mere prejudice and with loud denunciations of his opponents. . . . It is not the truth that a person possesses, or thinks he possesses, but the sincere striving after truth that establishes his worth. For it is not through possession, but through enquiry into the truth, that those mental powers are extended which constitute one's progress towards perfection. Possession makes one

82. *LW,* 8.51.
83. *LW,* 8.119.

placid, lazy, and proud. If God held all truth in his right hand, and in his left the single, ever-active drive towards truth [*den einzigen immer regen Trieb nach Wahrheit*], with the stipulation that I would remain eternally in error, and said to me: Choose! — I would humbly grasp him by his left hand and say: Father, give! Pure truth is for yourself alone.[84]

This pursuit of a truth that can never be possessed aligns Lessing with Reimarus among the Questioners.

The Questioners are clearly differentiated from the Modernizers. The Modernizers are concerned with improvements to the Palace, that is, with updating Christianity. The Questioners are concerned to criticize the ground plans and their interpreters. The parable dramatizes Lessing's desire to differentiate himself and his anonymous author both from the orthodox Lutheran view of scripture represented by the Antiquarians, and from the rationalistic theology of the Modernizers.

Having introduced its theme and main characters at some length, the Parable of the Palace turns more briefly to an event in which the Questioners are vindicated and the Antiquarians put to shame.

One night, the voice of the Watchmen was heard: Fire in the Palace! Rising from their beds, the Antiquarians were concerned only to save their ground plans, as though the fire were in their own homes. They all thought, "Only let me save my ground-plan! The Palace over there cannot burn more truly than the one I have here!"[85] And so they all ran out into the street with the precious documents and began to argue about where the fire was and how it was to be put out. So far as they were concerned, the actual Palace might just as well have been burnt to the ground. In fact, however, there was no fire. What the Watchmen had mistaken for fire in the Palace was actually *ein Nordlicht* — the aurora borealis, or northern lights. Here the Parable ends.

The light from the north represents the publication of the fragments, a venture originating (as Lessing knows, though other readers do not) in the north German city of Hamburg. There Reimarus lived, wrote, and died, there Lessing made the acquaintance of his son and daughter, and there it

---

84. *LW*, 8.32-33. This passage gives rise to the fourth of Kierkegaard's "Theses possibly or actually attributable to Lessing" (S. Kierkegaard, *Concluding Unscientific Postscript* [1846], Eng. trans. [Princeton: Princeton University Press, 1941], pp. 97-113). Kierkegaard uses the passage to subvert the Hegelian system's spurious claim to finality, where the fact that the philosopher too is an "existing individual" is forgotten in an act of "world-historical absent-mindedness" (p. 109).

85. *LW*, 8.119.

was decided to publish in order to bring enlightenment and truth into the world *(zur Aufklärung der Wahrheit für diese Welt).*[86] The Parable tells of a double confusion, between destructive fire and true enlightenment (the error of the Watchmen), and between the ancient Palace and the dubious ground plans (the error of the Antiquarians). The first confusion serves to elicit and expose the second, but it has its own antecedent in the Antiquarians' earlier quarrel with the Questioners, whom they denounced as arsonists intent on burning down the Palace. Where it is already believed that there are arsonists at large whose target is the Palace, it will more readily be believed that the Palace is actually on fire. A false apprehension produces a false credulity. Confronted with the reality of enlightenment, people only perceive a threat to their precious documents.

Lessing's Parable of the Palace serves his own polemical agenda, which is to oppose those who maintain the foundational status of the Bible in general and the gospels in particular. Such people mistake an enlightening criticism of the gospel texts for an attack on the Christian religion. They fail to realize that, as Lessing had written in his initial response to the fragments,

> The Letter is not the Spirit, and the Bible is not Religion. Consequently, objections against the Letter, and against the Bible, are not objections against the Spirit and against Religion. For the Bible clearly contains more than what belongs to Religion; and it is purely hypothetical that it must be infallible even in this surplus. Also: Religion existed before there was a Bible. Christianity existed before evangelists and apostles wrote.[87]

This passage is the key both to the parable and to Lessing's entire contribution to the controversy over the fragments.[88]

---

86. As Elise Reimarus put it in a letter to Lessing dating from December 1780 (Lachmann-Muncker, 21.873: p. 314, ll. 9-11). On Elise Reimarus, see Almut Spalding, *Elise Reimarus (1735-1805), the Muse of Hamburg: A Woman of the German Enlightenment* (Würzburg: Königshausen & Neumann, 2005).

87. *LW*, 7.458. This important programmatic passage occurs near the beginning of the "Gegensätze des Herausgebers," Lessing's editorial response to the five fragments of 1777, within the fourth volume of his Wolfenbüttel library series that initiated the controversy (*LW*, 7.457-92; Eng. trans. in Nisbet, *Lessing: Philosophical and Theological Writings*, pp. 61-82; original publication details in Schmidt-Biggemann, p. 69).

88. Lessing provides his own commentary on it in his *Axiomata* (*LW*, 8.128-59; Eng. trans. Nisbet, *Lessing: Philosophical and Theological Writings*, pp. 120-47). This work was published in March 1778, alongside the briefer *Parabel, Bitte* and *Absagungschreiben;* both are directed against J. M. Goeze.

"The Letter is not the Spirit, and the Bible is not Religion." The two disjunctive statements are parallel, suggesting equations between Letter and Bible, Spirit and Religion, and thus a single disjunction between Christian faith and its textual attestation, the Palace and the ground plans. The disjunction is directed against the assumption that the biblical "letter" or text is *foundational* to the Christian religion, the view maintained by J. M. Goeze when he finds in Lessing's editorial work an attack "on our most Holy Religion and its Sole Foundation, Holy Scripture."[89] Far from being foundational to the Christian religion, scripture is essentially superfluous. The Palace exists independently of the ground plans. If fire broke out in the Antiquarians' homes and destroyed all the ground plans, the Palace would in no way be affected. If everything the apostles and evangelists wrote were to perish, then the religion they taught would continue as before.[90] The assumption that the plans are somehow identical to the Palace is absurd — at least within the framework of a parable constructed precisely to demonstrate that absurdity.

"Consequently, objections against the Letter and against the Bible are not objections against the Spirit and against Religion. For the Bible clearly contains more than what belongs to Religion; and it is purely hypothetical that it must be infallible even in this surplus." Religion and the Spirit are in some sense "contained" within the Bible, but Lessing is more concerned with what he regards as the religiously inessential element within scripture, exposed as it is to "objections" such as Reimarus's. At the heart of the resurrection fragment stands the analysis of ten contradictions within the gospel Easter stories, and Lessing evidently regards these as a test case for biblical infallibility: for if some of the contradictions turn out to be not "apparent" but real, the doctrine of infallibility will have to be abandoned. More than that, Lessing uses the contradictions to call into question the Bible's foundational status within Christian faith. In the parable, the Questioners show not only that the ground plans are fallible but also and above all that they are *superfluous*. The reason why objections like Reimarus's are essentially irrelevant to Christian faith is that they concern only the Bible, which is to be distinguished from Religion and the Spirit.

"Also: Religion existed before there was a Bible. Christianity existed before evangelists and apostles wrote." That explains why the parable has so little sympathy with those who revere the ground plans. The plans are second-

89. See note 7, above.
90. *LW,* 7.458.

84

ary rather than original, the flawed work perhaps of some early visitors to the Palace and not the architect's blueprint. The Palace predates them and has no need of them. As a historical claim, Lessing's point is unanswerable: Christianity did indeed exist before the evangelists wrote. In consequence, the problems raised by Reimarus can be simply resolved. The contradictions he analyzes occur only within later narratives that cannot be identified with the original testimony. They are "not contradictions between witnesses, but only between the history-writers [i.e. the evangelists]."[91] Since the scriptural histories are secondary and belated productions, the contradictions do not matter. They do not signify a fundamental untruth at the very origin of Christian faith, as the Fragmentist mistakenly assumed. Rather, they signify that for Christian faith textuality is secondary and scripture superfluous. That is what we are intended to learn from the Parable of the Palace.

All this sets the scene for Lessing's *Duplik,* a brilliantly executed work which proposes that the old project of gospel harmonization should be abandoned — this in response to an attempt to refute the resurrection fragment by traditional harmonistic techniques.[92] (Lessing also knows these methods from the harmonies of Leclerc and Lamy.)[93] Throughout the *Duplik,* a fault line is perceptible.

On the one hand, the integrity of the individual gospel narratives is defended against harmonizers who substitute a composite narrative of their own devising. In doing so, they give priority to the *historia Christi* or life of Jesus which (so they believe) their harmonizing methods enable them to reconstruct. In contrast, Lessing gives priority to the *textuality* of the gospels, the internal organization that gives each of them its own narrative coherence and integrity, and that represents an active reception and reconfiguring of prior historical reality.

On the other hand, gospel differences are construed negatively. There is no recognition that differences *constitute* the canonical gospel in its plural form. Instead, it is assumed that the more significant differences represent mere errors, imperfections, and oversights. The gospel-writers are *fully human,* in the sense that their compositional activity is not taken over by the Holy Spirit. As such, however, they are *only human,* liable to lapses of one kind

---

91. *LW,* 7.490.

92. This important work is still not available in English. It is entirely absent from Chadwick's collection, while Nisbet chooses to omit the crucial analysis of contradiction and harmony that takes up three-quarters of the work (*Lessing: Philosophical and Theological Writings,* pp. 95-109).

93. "Mit den Harmonien des Clericus und Lamy, welche beide in dem nämlichen Jahre 1699 herauskamen, schliesst sich meine Belesenheit in dieser Art Schriften" (*LW,* 8.68).

or another. Gospel differences mark the degeneration of an original truth, its slide into a confused textual embodiment in which truth and falsehood are no longer clearly distinguishable. Naturally, Lessing emphasizes, the Christian religion itself remains unaffected by these disharmonious and belated attempts to reduce it to textual form. In that we are meant to find reassurance.

On one side of the fault line there is an essentially literary argument about the impossibility of fusing discrete texts into a composite whole; on the other, a polemical argument about the secondary and superfluous character of textuality.

The *Duplik* opens with a succinct statement of three opposing positions:

> My Anonymous Author asserts: the resurrection of Christ is not to be believed *for this reason*, that the evangelists' reports of it contradict one another. I reply: the resurrection of Christ can remain valid, *even though* the evangelists' reports contradict one another. Now there comes a third, who says: the resurrection of Christ is absolutely to be believed, *because* the evangelists' reports of it do not contradict one another. We should attend carefully to that *for this reason*, that *even though*, and that *because*. We will find that just about everything hangs on these expressions.[94]

The "third" is one Johann Heinrich Ress, who has ventured an anonymous response to the resurrection fragment.[95] Unlike Lessing, Ress accepts the Fragmentist's premise that actual contradictions would fatally undermine the resurrection faith — and proceeds to argue in the usual way that the alleged contradictions are only "apparent" and that the four narratives are each fragments of a larger and harmonious whole. Yet, Lessing argues, the appearance of harmony is deceptive. Gospel differences are like aggressive goats, which continue to butt one another when shut up in the same narrow pen. That is the reality of the typical harmonizing paraphrase of the gospels: an enclosure containing at least as many butting goats as placid sheep.[96] Open-minded readers will not be disturbed by this, and will say to themselves:

> Were [the evangelists] not all human? At any given point, one or other of them may have had less good sources than a third. One of them may per-

---

94. *LW*, 8.30-31 (paragraph divisions removed; italics original).
95. See note 5, above.
96. *LW*, 8.34-35.

haps have written something for which he had no guarantor. . . . A particular circumstance may have been necessary purely for the sake of a transition, or to round off a section.[97]

Indeed, all historians weave fictions into their history writing. By admitting that the evangelists did likewise, we restore the integrity of their individual texts and rid ourselves of unnecessary anxieties. The butting goats are best kept apart, in separate pens.

For the Fragmentist, significant gospel differences are all goats. For his harmonizing opponent, these goats must be reclassified as sheep. It will be instructive to observe Lessing adjudicating between the two, taking an example from the Matthean Easter story. According to Matthew:

> After the Sabbath, towards the dawning of the first day of the week, Mary Magdalene came with the other Mary to see the tomb. And behold, there was a great earthquake; for the angel of the Lord descended from heaven and came and rolled away the stone, and sat upon it. And his appearance was like lightning and his raiment white as snow. . . . And the angel answered and said to the women, Fear not, for I know that you seek Jesus who was crucified. . . . (Mt. 28.1-5)

Here the Fragmentist found the third of his ten contradictions. (The first two are concerned with the timing of the preparation or purchase of spices and with the double anointing.) This third contradiction

> is between Matthew and the other evangelists. For according to their narrative Mary Magdalene goes to the tomb with the other women, and while still at a distance "they look up and see that the stone has been rolled away" [Mk. 16.4], they "find the stone rolled away from the tomb" [Lk. 24.2], they "see that the stone is removed from the tomb" [Jn. 20.1]. But according to Matthew, Mary Magdalene and the other Mary came to see the tomb: and behold, an angel descended from heaven, arrived on the scene, rolled the stone from the tomb, and sat upon it. . . . Accordingly, this all took place in the presence of the women: this cannot be denied by any false evasion.[98]

One evangelist describes the removal of the stone as occurring in the presence of the women, whereas the others regard this as already having

97. *LW,* 8.35.
98. *LW,* 7.446 (*Fragments,* pp. 182-83).

taken place when they arrive at the tomb. Both accounts are internally coherent. The Fragmentist points out that they cannot both be true.

For his opponent, J. H. Ress, the solution is to be found at the very beginning of Matthew's story. Literally translated, "After the Sabbath" should be "On the *evening* of the Sabbath."[99] But how can the evening be simultaneous with the dawning of a new day? The solution is to take "evening" literally and to understand the new day to begin at sunset — in traditional Jewish fashion. As a result, Matthew 28.1 refers to a visit to the tomb on Saturday evening, not Sunday morning. That is why nothing is said here about the spices, which (as Mark and Luke inform us) were brought the following morning on a *second* visit to the tomb. In Matthew, this prior visit is followed by an earthquake that heralds the descent of the angel, the removal of the stone, and so on (vv. 2-4). It is not said that the women actually witnessed all this; the evangelist would seem to refer to a discrete sequence of events occurring during the night. Later, at daybreak, the women are again present at the tomb and are addressed by the angel. The removal of the stone has *already* taken place, before their arrival on Easter morning, just as the other evangelists say. There is (Ress claims) no contradiction here; only an "apparent" contradiction which disappears when we recognize that the passage actually refers to discrete events occurring respectively in the evening, the night, and the morning.[100]

Lessing invites his reader to study the Matthean passage carefully, and then presents a dialogue in which an *I*-character (Lessing himself) catechizes a *You*-character (the reader).[101]

How many things do we read of in this passage? If we follow the principles of sound human understanding, we read here of a *single* event, with a beginning, a continuation, and a conclusion. But what if we read it according to the principles of the Harmonist? In that case, there are *three* events: first, an evening visit with no outcome; second, an angelic manifestation to no one; third, a morning visit with no beginning. How then does the Harmonist envisage the unnarrated conclusion of the evening visit? The women did indeed set out for the tomb, he says, "but either the city gate was already shut, or they were warned by the gatekeepers not to go too far if they wished to re-enter the city before the gate was shut."[102] In what sense was the angelic

---

99. For the exegetical issue here, see W. D. Davies and D. C. Allison, *A Critical and Exegetical Commentary on the Gospel according to St. Matthew*, 3 vols., ICC (Edinburgh: T. & T. Clark, 1988-97), 3.663-64.

100. *LWB*, 8.481-83, 495-96.

101. *LW*, 8.55-60.

102. *LW*, 8.56.

manifestation to no one? Because, according to the Harmonist, the women were not present at the time and the guards were too terrified to take in everything that took place. How does the morning visit lack a beginning? Because we find the women being addressed by an angel as already present, without any account of their return to the tomb. Thus three events are told as though they were one. If this seems a strangely compressed way to tell a story, and if we now incline towards the Fragmentist's view that the contradiction must be allowed to stand, have we not ignored the simple fact that (as the Harmonist explains) "one has to be brief if one wishes to narrate important events in few words"?[103] That is pure tautology: if one wishes to be brief, clearly one must be brief. Such an argument does nothing to rescue the evangelist's reputation as a competent narrator. Is it not true that any historian is free "to select from a series of events, which he does not feel it necessary to recount in full, those that he finds most appropriate to his particular intention"?[104] But it is one thing to select only the most important events, quite another to create a single event out of several — something that no historian would do, whether or not inspired by the Holy Spirit. Thinking to defend the evangelist's reputation as a historian, the Harmonist has unwittingly destroyed it. His work is more an indictment of the evangelists than a vindication.[105] We should consider "whether it is not better, and more respectful to the New Testament texts, to abandon every attempt at harmonization in such matters, rather than accept one that leaves an evangelist so disgracefully covered in mud."[106]

Respect for the integrity of an individual gospel was not at all what the Fragmentist had in mind in his exposure of the ten contradictions. Nevertheless, that is what Lessing learned from the resurrection fragment, together with the corresponding recognition that the act of reception that constitutes the individual gospel is indeed an *act*, a construal or interpretation of what took place in Jesus. And yet this respect and this recognition lead nowhere. Matthew's narrative has been defended against the violence perpetrated by the harmonizers. The fictive elements it shares with other historical narratives have been acknowledged, and it will no longer be seen as a mere passive record of empirical historical occurrence. To that extent, Lessing's antiharmonistic argument begins to recover the dynamic of the

---

103. *LW*, 8.57; *LWB* 8.495 for Ress's original statement.
104. *LW*, 8.58; *LWB* 8.496 for Ress's original statement.
105. *LW*, 8.100.
106. *LW*, 8.60.

plural canonical collection, in which texts are set alongside one another in their difference while retaining their individual integrity. Yet nothing further can be done with the newly restored gospels. They are just old ground plans of the Palace, of dubious authenticity and limited worth. Those who value them are derided. Those who succeed in shedding critical light on them deny their value. Were they to disappear from the scene, nothing of importance would be lost. Gospel contradictions are outward and visible signs of the inward reality that gospels are no longer needed. They will continue to exist, of course, but they have lost their former rationale, which was to announce and embody good news in its simplicity, profundity, and richness. For Lessing too they are disabled by their contradictions.

These so-called "contradictions" are in the first instance simply *differences*. In Mark's Easter story, the women arrive at the tomb *after* the stone has been rolled away; in Matthew's, they arrive *as* it is rolled away. This is clearly a "difference," and it is the sum of these differences that makes one evangelist Mark and not Matthew and the other evangelist Matthew and not Mark. To redescribe a difference as a "contradiction" is only possible if the texts are subjected to alien interpretative criteria. The fourfold canonical gospel embodies difference, and thereby precludes any simple relation to empirical reality. In the empirical realm, it is indeed true that one event cannot both precede another and occur simultaneously with it. If one person asserts the one and another person the other, then they may be said to "contradict" each other and a decision may be ventured as to which version of events comes closer to the truth. In principle, it might have been decided that Matthew was to be preferred to Mark, or Mark to Matthew. In reality, it was decided that Matthew and Mark were to coexist within a single canonical collection, and that questions about whose account corresponded most closely to empirical truth were irrelevant. Within this canonical framework, no gospel story can be a straightforward transcript of an occurrence. It is always recounted "according to" — through the interpretative mediation of — Matthew or Mark or Luke or John. To speak of "contradictions" is to use the wrong interpretative category.

Did one evangelist perhaps *intend* to contradict another? Matthew may have read Mark's Easter story and concluded, for whatever reason, that his predecessor was in error about the removal of the stone. He may have sought to "correct" his fellow evangelist; and the subjective intention to "correct" results objectively in a "contradiction." Lessing is rightly aware of this possibility. It is, he claims, one of the harmonizers' many false assumptions that no evangelist ever meant to correct or contradict another.

How does one know whether the historian, whom I have taken such trouble to reconcile with other historians, actually *wanted* to be reconciled with them? May he not rather have *disagreed* with these others, and decided silently to contradict them?[107]

We recall the fighting goats, who presumably do not *want* to be reclassified as placid sheep.

Whatever the individual evangelists may have intended, they did not envisage their incorporation into the fourfold collection. The only explicit reference to other extant gospels speaks of "many" such, and seeks to persuade its readers that only the present work is fully reliable (Lk. 1.1-4). Yet even Luke does not write in the consciousness that he is the third in a sequence, with one more to come. This arrangement comes later, and it is no less significant an element in the process of reception than the composition of individual gospels. Since the gospels' canonical form functions as a hermeneutic, it can *override* whatever may have been the intentions or expectations of individual evangelists. If Matthew thought he was "correcting" or "contradicting" Mark on the removal of the stone, the canonical collection that incorporates both texts represents a decision against him. Here there is difference without contradiction. In their canonical form, the gospels do not and cannot contradict each another.

Against the Fourth Gospel

Lessing offers an evaluation of the Gospel of John in two short pamphlets dating from late 1777: *On the Proof of the Spirit and Power* and *The Testament of John: A Dialogue*.[108] Although published separately, the two are closely connected. At the close of the first of them, Lessing expresses the wish that "the Testament of John may unite all whom the Gospel of John divides," adding that "it is indeed apocryphal, this Testament, but no less divine for that."[109] This cryptic conclusion prepares the way for the second writing, a dialogue which takes its inspiration from Jerome, citations from whom stand at the beginning and end of this text. The first citation follows on di-

107. *LW*, 8.71.

108. These works responded to Johann Daniel Schumann's *Über die Evidenz der Beweise für die Wahrheit der christlichen Religion* (September/October 1777), which in turn responded to the resurrection fragment (see note 3, above).

109. *LW*, 8.14.

rectly from the title: *Das Testament Johannis — qui in pectus Domini recubuit et de purissimo fonte hausit rivulum doctrinarum* ("The Testament of John — who reclined at the Lord's breast and drew a stream of teaching from the purest fount"). In the second citation, Jerome recounts the anecdote on which Lessing has based his dialogue:

> The blessed evangelist John remained in Ephesus until extreme old age, when he could scarcely be carried to church any more in his disciples' arms. When he was no longer able to utter many words, he used to say no more than "Children, love one another," at each of their assemblies. In the end the assembled disciples and brethren became bored [*affecti taedio*] with always hearing the same things, and they said: "Master, why do you always say that?" John replied with the worthy statement: "Because it is the Lord's commandment [*praeceptum Domini*], and if that alone is done, it suffices."[110]

Lessing indicates the source of this second citation but not of the first, derived in fact from the Preface to Jerome's commentary on Matthew. This proceeds to recount how the Fourth Evangelist was urged to write his gospel to testify to the Lord's divinity, in response to heresies which denied the coming of Christ in the flesh. After a general fast, the evangelist was inspired with his "heaven-sent Preface" and wrote: "In the beginning was the Word. . . ."[111] For Jerome, it is the fourth gospel together with the Johannine epistles which embodies the stream of teaching that the apostle John drew from the purest fount, Jesus' maternal breast. In contrast, Lessing connects the statement about the origin of the apostle's teaching with a legend about the very end of the apostle's long life. Ironically, it is Jerome himself who makes it possible to substitute the "Testament of John" (Lessing's own title for this story) for the Gospel. Jerome retells the story to illustrate Paul's injunction, "Do good to all, especially to those who are of the household of faith" (Gal. 6.10). The story itself echoes the language of 1 John, where the readers are addressed as "Little children" (1 Jn. 2.1, 12, 28, etc.) and exhorted to "love one another" (4.7, 11). The story also traces back the apostle's preaching to "the Lord's commandment," a reference to the "new command-

110. Jerome, *In Epistulam ad Galatas,* on Gal. 6.10 (Latin text cited by Lessing, *LW,* 8.20; PL 26.433C; *Hieronymus, Commentarii in epistulam Pauli apostoli ad Galatas,* ed. F. Bucchi, CCSL 77A [Turnhout: Brepols, 2006]).

111. PL 26.18B; *Hieronymus, Commentariorum in Matheum libri IV,* ed. D. Hurst and M. Adriaen, CCSL 77 (Turnhout: Brepols, 1969), pp. 2-3; Eng. trans. in NPNF, second series, 6.495.

ment . . . that you should love one another" (Jn. 13.34). Here the apostle's message is finally *reduced* to the mutual love commandment, in apparent abstraction from the Johannine emphasis on the prior divine agency to which it responds: "We love because he first loved us" (1 Jn. 4.19). It is this reduction that Lessing exploits in order to set the Testament of John in opposition to the Gospel of John.

In the Testament of John, the dialogue partners consist of a freethinking *I*-character (identified as Lessing himself, or at least as the anonymous author of *On the Proof of the Spirit and of Power*), together with an orthodox *He*-character. The story is completely unknown to the interlocutor, and is therefore retold in Lessing's own words. Every day, the aged apostle's sermons became simpler and briefer, until finally they were reduced to the single saying, "Little children, love one another!" His hearers had always regarded his sermons as more important even than daily bread. But now their daily bread has become more than a little stale:

> People so quickly tire of the Good, and even of the Best, when it begins to seem commonplace! At the first meeting in which John was *unable* to say more than "Little children, love one another!", this "Little children, love one another!" won general approval. It was also approved at the second, third, and fourth meeting; for it was thought that the weak old man *could* not say any more. But when the old man from time to time had good and cheerful days, and *still* said nothing else, and concluded the daily assembly with nothing more than a "Little children, love one another!"; and when it was realized that the old man was not just *unable* to say more but that he did not *wish* to say more, then that "Little children, love one another!" came to seem so insipid, so bare, so meaningless! Brethren and disciples could hardly listen to it any more without annoyance; and in the end they were bold enough to ask the good old man, "Master, why do you always say the same thing?" . . . John answered, "Because the Lord commanded it! Because, this alone — yes, *this alone!* —, if it is carried out, is really and truly sufficient!"[112]

The retelling of Jerome's story leads to a discussion about whether the story is essentially true — that is, whether love for the other is indeed sufficient to make one a Christian, irrespective of one's attitude towards Christian doctrines *(Glaubenslehren)*. The *I*-character is sympathetic to that view, although it is ascribed to "certain people" and is not directly attributable to

---

112. *LW*, 8.17.

Lessing himself. The orthodox *He*-character makes clear his disapproval of the apocryphal story, and is subjected to a series of Socratic questions in which Lessing exposes unattractive consequences of the view that orthodox belief is necessary for salvation. On that view, those who practise Christian love while dissenting from Christian beliefs derive no benefit from their efforts, but succeed only in making the road to hell harder for themselves. The dialogue ends in stalemate, with the *I*-character citing the Markan saying, "He who is not against us is for us," and the *He*-character countering with the Matthean "He who is not with me is against me."[113]

For Lessing, the choice between the "liberal" and the "orthodox" points of view is a choice between the Testament and the Gospel of John. The Testament reunites those whom the Gospel divides.[114] The Gospel promotes difficult and contentious doctrines about the trinity and the incarnation of a divine Christ; the Testament promotes mutual love. As the case for the Testament is derived from Jerome, so the case for the Gospel is derived from Augustine:

> *I.* Augustine tells how a certain Platonist once said that the beginning of the Gospel of John, "In the beginning was the Word" and so on, should be inscribed in letters of gold in every church, and in the most prominent place.

> *He.* Yes, indeed! That Platonist was quite right! Oh, those Platonists! It's certainly true that Plato himself could not have written anything more sublime than this opening of the Gospel of John.

> *I.* Perhaps so. But, as I can never make very much of the sublime writings of a philosopher, I consider that it would be far more appropriate for there to be inscribed — in letters of gold, in every church and in the most prominent place — the Testament of John![115]

The "sublime writings of a philosopher" refers to John as well as to Plato. The beginning of the Gospel may indeed excite the admiration of the Platonist. But what if one is not a Platonist? Why should we not regard the apocryphal Testament as more truly divine than the canonical Gospel?

Lessing uses Augustine to support his proposal to downgrade the fourth

---

113. Mk. 9.40 (= Lk. 9.50); Mt. 12.30 (= Lk. 11.23).
114. *LW,* 8.14.
115. *LW,* 8.18.

gospel just as he uses Jerome. The reference is to a passage in Book Ten of the *City of God,* where Augustine too is critical of the Platonist:

> Perhaps it seems shameful to those learned men to cease to be disciples of Plato and to become the disciples of Christ, who by his Spirit taught a fisherman to be wise and to say: "In the beginning was the Word, and the Word was with God and the Word was God. He was in the beginning with God. All things were made through him, and without him was nothing made that was made. In him was life, and the life was the light of human-kind. The light shines in the darkness, and the darkness did not overcome it." It was about this beginning of the holy Gospel named "according to John" that — as we used to hear from Simplicianus, that holy old man who was afterward bishop of the church at Milan — a certain Platonist once said that it ought to be inscribed in letters of gold and set in the most prominent position in every church. But God our Master became of no account to the proud, for "the Word became flesh and dwelt among us": so that it is not enough for these miserable people that they are sick, but they must also extol their own sickness and disdain to take that medicine by which they might be made well.[116]

For Augustine, the consensus between Platonists and Christians over the Johannine prologue breaks down with the evangelist's announcement that the Word has become flesh. That is what ought to be inscribed in letters of gold in every church. Yet the fragile consensus still stands; before they diverge, John and Plato do indeed coincide. And that is the point at which Lessing launches his attack on Christian-Platonizing metaphysics in general and the fourth gospel in particular.

The stark choice between the Testament and the Gospel is introduced at the conclusion of Lessing's previous pamphlet, *On the Proof of the Spirit and of Power,* thereby introducing its companion piece. This Johannine preoccupation also sheds light on two celebrated passages from the previous text, often quoted yet not always well understood:

> Accidental truths of history can never become the proof of necessary truths of reason.[117]

---

116. Augustine, *De Civ. Dei* x.29 (PL 41.309; *De Civitate Dei Libri I-X,* ed. B. Dombart and A. Kalb, CCSL 47 [Turnhout: Brepols, 1955], pp. 306-7).

117. *LW,* 8.12 ("zufällige Geschichtswahrheiten können der Beweis von notwendigen Vernunftswahrheiten nie werden").

This is the broad ugly ditch [*der garstige breite Graben*] over which I cannot cross, no matter how often and how earnestly I have attempted the leap [*den Sprung*]. If anyone can help me over, let him do so, I beg, I implore him! He would deserve from me a heavenly reward.[118]

Are these statements concerned with the relationship between "history" and "faith," as is often assumed?[119] If so, why does Lessing speak not of faith but of "necessary truths of reason"? And why is it so important to *deny* that these are proved by "accidental truths of history"? Who *affirms* what is here denied, and why?

These statements must be understood in the context of this short work as a whole, whose main argument is composed out of two distinct strands. The first is already indicated in the title, derived from a Pauline phrase as interpreted by Origen (cf. 1 Cor. 2.4). The "proof" or "demonstration" of the Spirit and of power refers to the vindication of Christian truth-claims by means of fulfilled prophecy ("the Spirit") and miracles ("power").[120] Lessing's counterargument is succinctly stated at the outset:

Fulfilled prophecies which I experience myself are one thing; fulfilled prophecies of which I only know from history that others claim to have experienced them are another. Miracles which I see with my eyes, and which I have opportunity to verify for myself, are one thing; miracles of which I only know from history that others claim to have seen and verified them are another.[121]

---

118. *LW*, 8.13.

119. See for example Gerd Theissen, "Historical Scepticism and the Criteria of Jesus Research, or, My Attempt to Leap Across Lessing's Yawning Gulf," *SJT* 49 (1996), pp. 147-76. For discussion of what Lessing meant, see G. E. Michalson, "Lessing, Kierkegaard, and the 'Ugly Ditch': A Reexamination," *JR* 59 (1979), pp. 324-34, and *Lessing's "Ugly Ditch": A Study of Theology and History* (University Park: Pennsylvania State University Press, 1986); T. Yashikata, *Lessing's Philosophy of Religion*, pp. 56-71.

120. Origen, *Contra Celsum* i.2. The passage was cited by the opponent against whom Lessing directed this text, J. D. Schumann (*LWB*, 8.357-58). As summarized by Schumann, Origen writes: "The doctrine of Jesus has a special type of proof of its own, which is far too lofty and noble to be compared with the Greek art of concluding and proving. The Apostle calls this diviner proof, 'the demonstration of the Spirit and of power.' He speaks of a proof 'of the Spirit' on account of the prophecies, which are so clear and lucid that everyone must be convinced by them. He speaks of a proof 'of power' on account of the astounding miracles which occurred to confirm the doctrine of Christ."

121. *LW*, 8.10.

It is no longer possible to argue from fulfilled prophecy and miracles to the truth of Christian faith, since such an argument must rely on the second-hand evidence of other people's testimony rather than on firsthand experience. In reality, of course, we constantly rely on the testimony of others rather than our own experience. But Lessing's counterargument implies that there are *particular* problems associated with appeals to fulfilled prophecy and miracles. When an evangelist tells us that a miracle occurred in which a man dead for four days was restored to his family and friends, we cannot regard his report as an adequate substitute for the firsthand experience of the event from which we are excluded.

Quite unlike Reimarus, however, Lessing passes lightly over the special problems posed by fulfilled prophecies or miracles, and proceeds to class them with all other historical facts — which are supposed to be all equally uncertain. Since "no historical truth can be demonstrated, then nothing else can be demonstrated *through* historical truths."[122] This unexpected move from the particular to the general marks the entry of the second strand into the argument. Scepticism about a specific type of alleged event is replaced by a generalized scepticism about historical knowledge per se. No accidental truth of history could prove a necessary truth of reason, *whether or not* it is an alleged miracle, *even if* it consists in something as unquestionable as the historical existence of Alexander the Great or Jesus of Nazareth. Lessing's unexplained shift from the particular to the general is puzzling. That accidental truths of history do not prove necessary truths of reason is no doubt true, but only trivially so. It is not clear why Lessing finds his situation on the near side of his "ditch" so distressing, or why he longs to cross it. What would it mean if one *could* use a contingent fact of history to prove a necessary truth of reason? Why would it be *desirable* to do so, even if it turns out to be impossible?

Lessing's famous and baffling statement is best interpreted by way of a passage that makes the same point in less abstract form:

> If I have no objection on historical grounds to the claim that Christ revived a dead person, must I therefore hold it to be true that God has a Son who is of the same essence as himself? What is the connection between my inability to raise any serious objection to the witnesses and my obligation to believe something against which my reason rebels?[123]

122. *LW*, 8.10.
123. *LW*, 8.12-13.

The contingent truths of history include the truth that Christ revived a dead person, which Lessing is prepared to treat as if wholly unobjectionable. He is also prepared to accept, hypothetically, that the necessary truths of reason might include the truth that God has a coessential Son — although in reality this is "something against which my reason rebels."[124] Even the resurrection of a dead person would not demonstrate a fundamental and inconceivable truth about God.

If that is what Lessing means, then his argument is directed against the Johannine signs-theology: "These [signs] are written that you may believe that Jesus is the Christ, the Son of God . . ." (Jn. 20.31). The Gospel reports signs such as the raising of Lazarus and speaks of Jesus as the divine Son of God, of one being with the Father — and the phrase "that you may believe . . ." seeks to connect the one with the other. This gospel marks the exact site of Lessing's broad ugly ditch. His argument is implicitly directed against the Fourth Evangelist, whose gospel proposes an entirely imaginary way from earthly occurrence to the realm of ultimacy. Whether the image is a soaring eagle or a bridge over a ravine, it is for Lessing the product of pure fantasy.

That is why the inscription from the Johannine gospel, with its magnificent gold lettering and its prominent position in every church, should be *replaced* with an inscription from the Testament of John. For Lessing, the command to "love one another" is all that can be salvaged from the collapse of Johannine theology and the dogmatic edifice it sustained.

Discredited in this way, the Johannine gospel will no longer be able to fulfil its earlier role as the key to the structure of the fourfold canonical gospel. Indeed, that fourfold canonical gospel will have effectively ceased to exist. Elsewhere, Lessing argues that the synoptic gospels find their rationale in their relation not to a later extant "spiritual gospel" but to an earlier hypothetical *Urevangelium* — a theory that will transmute in due course into the "Q" hypothesis. As they gravitate away from John, the synoptists find themselves drawn towards their long-lost primal source or *Quelle*.

---

124. Elsewhere Lessing suggests that the doctrine of the trinity *is* open to a rational interpretation (*The Education of the Human Race*, §73, *LW*, 8.505-6; Eng. trans. in *Lessing's Theological Writings*, pp. 82-96).

The Lost Original

On 25 February 1778, Lessing wrote to his brother Karl thanking him for his appreciative comments on the *Duplik* and promising to send his reply to his opponent Goeze as soon as it was available.[125] Yet, he added,

> all that is just the skirmishing of the light infantry of my main army. The main army advances slowly, and its first engagement consists in my *New Hypothesis on the Evangelists considered as purely human Historians.*[126]

Lessing went on to say that the idea for the work came from some notes he found he had made, he did not remember when or why. The finished work was intended for the Berlin publisher, Voss, and difficulties with the local censor were not anticipated. It could have been completed within the next three weeks if unexpected hindrances had not occurred.[127]

In fact, work on the *New Hypothesis* was never completed, and it was published posthumously by Karl Lessing in 1784 on the basis of four unfinished manuscripts.[128] If writings relating to the gospels mark the first phase of the *Fragmentenstreit*, the second phase consists in the bitter controversy with Goeze, where the main point of contention is Lessing's view of the Bible as a whole rather than the gospels specifically. Karl's brotherly advice to ignore Goeze and to continue work on the *New Hypothesis* went unheeded.[129]

Lessing's "new hypothesis" is that the three synoptic gospels all derive from a single original gospel or *Urevangelium*, identified with the lost Hebrew or Aramaic *Gospel according to the Hebrews* to which a number of early Christian authors refer.[130] The fullest information is provided by Jerome, who speaks of it as

---

125. A promise fulfilled on 16 March, when Lessing sent his brother "meine doppelte Antwort gegen Götzen" — that is, the *Parabel, nebst einer kleinen Bitte, und einem eventualen Absagungsschreiben* and the *Axiomata* (Lachmann-Muncker, 18.595: p. 266, l. 28).

126. Lachmann-Muncker, 18.594: p. 265, ll. 22-28.

127. Lachmann-Muncker, 18.594: p. 265, l. 28–p. 266, l. 5.

128. Details in *LW*, 7.919-23. See also the preliminary outline of Lessing's hypothesis on gospel origins, entitled "Theses aus der Kirchengeschichte," *LW*, 7.606-13.

129. Letters from Karl Lessing dated 7 February and 14 March 1778 (Lachmann-Muncker, 21.739: p. 189, ll. 18-20; 21.741: p. 191, ll. 21-22).

130. For this work of Lessing's and its later significance, see also Dieter Lührmann, *Die apokryph gewordenen Evangelien: Studien zu neuen Texten und zu neuen Fragen* (Leiden & Boston: Brill, 2004), pp. 259-83. Lührmann rightly notes that the *New Hypothesis* "entfalteten gerade in ihrer Skizzenhaftigkeit eine gar nicht gross genug einzuschätzende Wirkung" (p. 264).

the Gospel "according to the Hebrews" [*Evangelium iuxta Hebraeos*], written in the Chaldean or Syriac speech but in Hebrew letters, which the Nazarenes use to this day (also known as "according to the Apostles," or, as many claim, "according to Matthew"), and which is to be found in the library at Caesarea. . . .[131]

When people speak of the Aramaic *Gospel according to the Hebrews* as "according to Matthew," they mean that they consider it to be the original and authentic Gospel of Matthew, *Evangelium Matthei authenticum*.[132] This identification is also implied in Epiphanius.[133] Yet earlier writers who know of this *Gospel according to the Hebrews* (Clement, Origen, Eusebius) do not identify it with Matthew. Lessing wants this gospel to be other than and more than a Hebrew Matthew, since he regards it as the source not only of the Greek Matthew but also of Mark and Luke. It must therefore have been more comprehensive than any of the extant gospels extracted from it — which is why Epiphanius referred to it as the "complete" Matthew.[134] The question is whether the Nazarene gospel can still be regarded as ancient, indeed as predating the canonical gospels, if the link with the Greek Matthew is loosened.

For Lessing, the testimony of Papias provides the decisive clue. As cited by Eusebius, Papias states cryptically that "Matthew wrote the sayings in the Hebrew language, and everyone translated them as he was able."[135] Thus,

---

131. Jerome, *Dialogus adversus Pelagianos* iii.2 (PL 23.270B; *Hieronymus, Dialogus adversus Pelagianos*, ed. C. Moreschini, CCSL 80 [Turnhout: Brepols, 1990], p. 99). Passages relating to this work and the *Gospel of the Ebionites* are collected in M. R. James, *The Apocryphal New Testament* (Oxford: Clarendon Press, 1924), pp. 1-10; W. Schneemelcher (ed.), *New Testament Apocrypha*, 2 vols., Eng. trans. [Cambridge: James Clarke; Louisville: WJK, 1991-92], 1.166-72; J. K. Elliott (ed.), *The Apocryphal New Testament* (Oxford: Clarendon Press, 1999²), pp. 9-16. Lessing may have known these texts through the *Codex Apocryphus Novi Testamenti* (1719) of J. A. Fabricius, Reimarus's father-in-law.

132. Jerome, *Commentariorum in Evangelium Matthaei Libri IV* on Mt. 12.13 (PL 26.78A; CCSL 77, p. 90).

133. Epiphanius reports that the Nazarenes possess "the Gospel according to Matthew complete in Hebrew [πληρέστατον Ἑβραϊστι]," preserved "as it was written from the beginning in Hebrew letters [καθὼς ἐξ ἀρχῆς ἐγράφη Ἑβραϊκοῖς γράμμασιν]" (*Pan.* xxix.9.4; *Epiphanius, Ancoratus und Panarion*, ed. K. Holl and H. Lietzmann, 3 vols., GCS [Hinrichs: Leipzig, 1915-33], 1.332; Eng. tr., Frank Williams, *The Panarion of Epiphanius of Salamis, Books I-III*, 2 vols. [Leiden: Brill, 1987-94]).

134. *LW*, 7.625 (§35).

135. Eusebius, *HE* iii.39.16, as cited by Lessing. A majority of manuscripts read συνετάξετο rather than συνεγράψατο.

Lessing argues, Papias believed that an original Hebrew gospel was specifically a Hebrew *Matthew* — a view later echoed by Epiphanius. For Lessing, Papias was wrong about this. Church history shows no trace of multiple divergent Greek Matthews. Yet Papias might still be right about the existence of an original Hebrew gospel. In that case, our Greek Matthew would be a translation based on that Hebrew document, so successful that the translator's name was mistakenly transferred back to the original. If we correct Papias's report in this way, his otherwise puzzling remark about divergent translations may be taken to refer primarily to the extant synoptic gospels:

> Matthew, Mark, Luke are nothing other than differing and not differing translations of the supposed Hebrew original of Matthew, which each one carried out as well as he was able; ὡς ἠδύνατο ἕκαστος.[136]

Indeed, Papias's testimony points us back to

> the source [*Quelle*] from which both the better gospels that are still extant, and the less good that fell into disuse and finally disappeared, have flowed forth.[137]

What of the Gospel of John? The synoptic evangelists now find their unity not in the fourth gospel but in an original Hebrew gospel that comprehends them all. The Gospel of John becomes an anomaly. Although this evangelist made use of the original Hebrew gospel, his divine Christ has nothing whatever in common with the purely human Christ of that original and the later gospels that flowed out of it. If we doubt this, we should

> remind ourselves how the Gospel of the Nazarenes originated: from sincere people who had had personal dealings with Christ, and who were therefore completely convinced of Christ as human. . . . [T]hey could recount nothing about him that could not be true of a purely human figure, though one endowed with power from on high.[138]

Given this early authentic testimony to a purely human Jesus, the Johannine Christ would seem to be divine in proportion to his lack of basis in historical reality. Yet the Johannine Christ is nevertheless the basis for Gentile Christianity as an independent religion; had the Fourth Evangelist not writ-

136. *LW*, 7.632 (§50).
137. *LW*, 7.628 (§43).
138. *LW*, 7.633 (§55).

ten as he did, Christianity would have remained a Jewish sect.[139] The line that Reimarus drew between original Jewish messianism and the invention of the Christian religion is here redrawn within the fourfold canonical gospel. Separated now from John by another broad ugly ditch, the three synoptic gospels are assimilated to the "Ebionite" theology that Lessing attributes to the original Hebrew gospel.[140] A distinction between a "gospel of the flesh" and a "gospel of the Spirit" is still invoked,[141] but without any possibility of dialectical unity or a common object. For Lessing the synoptic "gospel of the flesh" has the human Jesus as its object, whereas the "gospel of the Spirit" projects a fantasy about a deity manifested in human form. Matthew, Mark, and Luke gravitate *away from* John as they gravitate *towards* the original Nazarene gospel.

The key to the whole construction is to be found in Papias's statement about the original Hebrew Matthew; this alone secures the early dating of the *Gospel according to the Hebrews* and its consequent transformation into the source from which all other gospels (except John) flow. This source or *Quelle* is reconstructed in a variety of ways in the period after Lessing. Only gradually does it settle into its normative form as the source of the non-Markan material common to Matthew and Luke — a more modest role than the one Lessing assigned to his *Quelle* or *Urevangelium*. Yet one significant characteristic of the various later "Q" theories is already evident in Lessing's *New Hypothesis,* the combination of specificity with broad explanatory scope. On the one hand, "Q" represents a scholarly hypothesis — or family of such hypotheses — about gospel origins. As such, it can appeal both to patristic evidence (especially to Papias) and to common ground between the gospels for which it purports to account. On the other hand, "Q" also typically represents a far-reaching reconstruction of the history of earliest Christianity. For Lessing, it represents an original milieu of Jewish messianism quite distinct in character from the later Gentile Christianity based on the Johannine divine redeemer mythology. For later scholars, Q hypotheses continue to serve various historical reconstructions of Christian origins, each with its own theological or ideological tendency. Q is never *just* Q. Above all, Q in its various forms has to do with the movement *behind* problematic canonical gospels that seeks a more secure point of access to the life of Jesus. Q represents a movement against the diachronic

139. *LW,* 7.635 (§§62-63).
140. *LW,* 7.634-35 (§§59-61).
141. *LW,* 7.635 (§64).

flow of the early Christian tradition in which the life of Jesus is interpreted, in quest of an *uninterpreted* Jesus.

(1) A theory similar to Lessing's, though more fully elaborated, is presented by Johann Gottfried Eichhorn in the first of the five volumes of his New Testament introduction (1804¹).¹⁴² Eichhorn devotes the first part of this volume to a discussion of "the oldest Gospels" (including the *Gospel according to the Hebrews* and Marcion's gospel),¹⁴³ before turning his attention to "the three catholic gospels."¹⁴⁴ Matthew, Mark, and Luke are "catholic" in that they only came into widespread use in the late second century, in contrast to the *Gospel according to the Hebrews*, which (according to Eichhorn) was already used by Papias, Hegesippus, and Ignatius.¹⁴⁵ The content of this work was highly fluid, however. It began life as an outline of the main events of Jesus' ministry, to be used in the context of missionary work, but it rapidly grew to encompass much else:

> It was initially brief, but from time to time its scope was widened by way of additions. . . . In the course of time, curiosity increased and was extended to parts of Jesus' life which had originally been regarded as unnecessary for instruction in Christianity.¹⁴⁶

Thus, patristic evidence confirms that an original *Gospel according to the Hebrews* existed, but it cannot provide definite information about its content, which varied from time to time. The *Urevangelium* must be reconstructed, and separated out from later additions, on the basis of the three synoptic or "catholic" gospels alone. Material found in all three goes back to

---

142. I have consulted the second edition of this work, which does not appear to differ significantly from the first in the points at issue: J. G. Eichhorn, *Einleitung in das Neue Testament*, vol. 1 (Leipzig: Weidmann, 1820²). A contemporary English critique of Eichhorn occurs in Connop Thirlwall's extensive introduction to his translation of Schleiermacher's *A Critical Study on the Gospel of Luke* (1817, Eng. trans. 1825; repr. Lewiston, Queenston, & Lampeter: Edwin Mellen, 1993), pp. v-cliv; pp. xliii-lxxxvi. Thirlwall's introduction represented an early (and unsuccessful) attempt to persuade an English-speaking theological readership to take an interest in German debate on gospel origins.

143. Eichhorn, *Einleitung*, 1.1-160.

144. Eichhorn, *Einleitung*, 1.161-455.

145. Eichhorn, *Einleitung*, 1.7. According to Eusebius, Papias knows a story "about a woman accused of many sins before the Lord, which the Gospel according to the Hebrews also contains" (*HE* iii.39.17); Hegesippus "made use in his *Memoirs* of the Gospel according to the Hebrews" (iv.22.8). Jerome claims that Ignatius drew from this gospel an account of a postresurrection appearance (Ignatius, *Smyrn.* 3.1; Jerome, *De Vir. Ill.* 16).

146. Eichhorn, *Einleitung*, 1,29.

the *Urevangelium* in its earliest attainable form;[147] material found in two or one represents later additions.[148] Thus, only two gospels are interested in the circumstances of Jesus' birth, which was not part of the earliest Christian preaching. Like Mark (which it must have resembled closely), the *Urevangelium* therefore originally lacked an infancy narrative. Eichhorn is dismissive of the theory that one evangelist made use of another, or that their similarities derive from firsthand experience or oral tradition; the only possible explanation of their similarities and differences is "the hypothesis of a common source [*von einer gemeinschaftlichen Quelle*] from which all three of them must have been created."[149]

We must be grateful to the early church for preserving the three "catholic" gospels — together with John, although this is historically far less valuable than the others. And yet,

> posterity would indeed be obliged to be still more grateful to her if, together with the Gospel of John, she had accorded public authority to that first simple outline of the Life of Jesus [*den ersten rohen Entwurf des Lebens Jesus*] which was imparted to the earliest missionaries for the confirmation of their teaching on their journeys — having first eliminated all additions and expansions. . . .[150]

That critical restoration of the earliest gospel was beyond the church's capabilities, however, and the task is left to us to perform, so far as it is still possible. We are helped in this by the church's decision to preserve not one but three of the accounts derived from the *Urevangelium*:

> In that way she made it possible for us, even after so many centuries, to separate the earlier account of the Life of Jesus from all later additions, and on this basis to restore a Life of Jesus purified from all later tradition [*ein von aller spätern Tradition gereinigtes Leben Jesu*].[151]

Only the three "catholic" gospels are of value for the most important task of all, which is the critical reconstruction of the life of Jesus. This

147. Eichhorn, *Einleitung*, 1.161-321.

148. Eichhorn, *Einleitung*, 1.321-93. Here material common to Matthew and Mark, Mark and Luke, and Matthew and Luke is discussed, together with material unique to each, under the heading of *Vermehrungen*, i.e. later additions.

149. Eichhorn, *Einleitung*, 1.175.

150. Eichhorn, *Einleitung*, 1.158.

151. Eichhorn, *Einleitung*, 1.158.

Urevangelium hypothesis serves that larger project. Like most such hypotheses, this one too claims to have vindicated Papias, "so often derided and despised," but now acknowledged as patron saint of the scholarly quest for the lost source.[152]

(2) Schleiermacher too feels a personal identification with Papias. His study of "the Testimonies of Papias to the two first Evangelists" (1832) opens with the confession: "It has always caused me pain, whenever I have found these two testimonies treated with a certain disparagement."[153] This study is widely credited with introducing the Q hypothesis in something approaching its modern form, that is, as a lost source that accounts for *a specific strand* of the synoptic material but not for *all* of it — as in Lessing and Eichhorn. On Schleiermacher's reading, Papias's statement on Matthew refers not to a Hebrew *Urevangelium* and to derivative gospels in Greek, but to a sayings collection of more limited scope. Matthew "wrote τὰ λόγια," and Schleiermacher argues that this cannot mean that "he collected the narratives about events in the life of Christ," that is, wrote a gospel, and that it can only mean that he "wrote a collection of Christ's sayings, whether in the form of individual utterances or longer discourses or both."[154] The reference to multiple "translations" that follows has been misunderstood; Papias refers instead to the *interpretation* of the Matthean sayings collection, its homiletical exposition and application. His own work consisted in "interpretations" (ἑρμηνείαι) of the Lord's words, and our present Gospel of Matthew may be understood similarly. The uninterpreted sayings of the authentically Matthean collection are here interpreted as they are set within a narrative framework. The gospel

> incorporates this collection into itself, and adds references to time and place where needed, on the basis of the oral tradition going back to the original and authentic evangelists; but often in a form indicating the editor's uncertainty.[155]

Our gospel is "according to Matthew" not because Matthew was himself its author but because it incorporates the sayings collection that he com-

---

152. Eichhorn, *Einleitung*, 1.502.

153. F. D. E. Schleiermacher, "Ueber die Zeugnisse des Papias von unsern beiden ersten Evangelien," *Theologische Studien und Kritiken* (1832), pp. 735-68.

154. Schleiermacher, "Über die Zeugnisse," pp. 736, 738.

155. Schleiermacher, "Über die Zeugnisse," p. 745.

piled.[156] The collection can be tentatively reconstructed by noting those points in the present text where the evangelist marks the shift from sayings material to narrative with the statement, "And it came to pass, when Jesus had finished these words [τοὺς λόγους τούτους] . . ." Wherever this formula or its equivalents are used, "this also indicates the conclusion of a section of the apostolic collection."[157] Thus the Sermon on the Mount, the missionary instructions, and the parable chapter (Mt. 5–7; 10; 13), together with later discourses, must all go back to that collection. Here Jesus' sayings have truly been *collected*, assembled into a whole by an editor; we are not to suppose that the Sermon on the Mount was an actual sermon preached by Jesus.[158]

According to Schleiermacher, family resemblances between Matthew and Jewish Christian texts such as the *Gospel according to the Hebrews* may reflect a common dependence on the authentically Matthean sayings collection.[159] Luke, however, obviously did *not* use this. Where he has similar sayings to Matthew, these tend to occur in different contexts. Indeed, in Matthew's Sermon on the Mount, sayings have been removed from their original contexts of utterance and grouped together, whereas in Luke those original contexts are often preserved.[160] Neither does Mark use the Matthean sayings collection. As in the case of his testimony to the Hebrew Matthew, Papias's testimony to the origins of Mark actually refers not to the extant gospel but to a further collection — drawn up in a disconnected fashion by Mark on the basis of Peter's preaching, and subsequently incorporated into a connected work just as the sayings collection had been.

At this point, the outlines of Schleiermacher's overall theory of synoptic origins come to light. It is entirely comprehensible, he argues, that the older independent collections underlying Mark as well as Matthew

should have preceded the collections both of speeches or sayings and of sequences of events and actions, as these occur within connected gospel-composition along synoptic lines [*der zusammenhängenden Evangelien-schreibung nach Art unserer synoptischen*]; for at a time when oral proclamation was predominant, there was only very limited scope for written presentations — except in special cases of need. . . . If, as is probable, Mark did indeed write as the interpreter of Peter, he could only have done so as

156. Schleiermacher, "Über die Zeugnisse," p. 746.
157. Schleiermacher, "Über die Zeugnisse," p. 749.
158. Schleiermacher, "Über die Zeugnisse," p. 746.
159. Schleiermacher, "Über die Zeugnisse," p. 757.
160. Schleiermacher, "Über die Zeugnisse," p. 758.

it were in his spare time [*als die Zeit dazu sich gleichsam abstehlen*]. It is highly improbable that, out of the material he drew from Peter, he would have composed a writing such as our gospel. . . .[161]

On this account, our extant gospels mark the completion of a fateful transition from oral to written transmission of the Christian message, anticipated in informal collections lacking any very clear rationale, which came into being alongside the apostolic proclamation. The gospels derive, however, not only from written sources but also from an ongoing tradition of oral narration, both of which they seek to systematize. Schleiermacher uses his hypothetical earlier written collections to *retard* and thereby to *problematize* the transition from proclamation to textuality. If Mark wrote the present gospel on the basis of Peter's proclamation, the transition is made far too easily; as interpreter of Peter, Mark can only write anything at all on his own initiative, not as part of his formal duties. By analogy with that remarkable claim, we might suppose that Matthew's compilation of his sayings collection had nothing to do with his genuinely apostolic activity.[162]

Schleiermacher confines his study to two passages from Papias and does not mention a third, where this author remarks: "I did not consider what was found in books [τὰ ἐκ τῶν βιβλίων] to be as valuable for me as what proceeded from a living and abiding voice [τὰ παρὰ ζώσης φωνῆς καὶ μενούσης]."[163] Consistently with this, there is no indication in the statements on Matthew and Mark that Papias found any real value in these gospels. Textuality is drastically subordinated to ongoing oral transmission; and Schleiermacher seems to share Papias's ambivalence towards it. To refer the two statements to ad hoc compositions, significantly different in character from the later narratives in which they were incorporated, is to extend the scope of an oral proclamation that mediates — as writing cannot — the living voice of Christ.

(3) Schleiermacher's hypothesis reflects contemporary interest in the oral factor in gospel origins, in reaction against the exclusively literary theories of Griesbach on the one hand and Eichhorn on the other. His interpretation of Papias's statement about Matthew and the λόγια is taken up by Christian Hermann Weisse in 1838 and extended into a "two-source theory" according

---

161. Schleiermacher, "Über die Zeugnisse," p. 762.

162. On Schleiermacher's attitude towards textuality, see my *Text and Truth: Redefining Biblical Theology* (Edinburgh: T. & T. Clark; Grand Rapids: Eerdmans, 1997), pp. 127-41.

163. Eusebius, *HE* iii.39.4.

to which Matthew and Luke both used Mark on the one hand and Q on the other in the composition of their gospels — "Q" now representing not an exclusively Matthean sayings collection but the non-Markan material common to both Matthew and Luke.[164] Weisse, however, turned this source-critical hypothesis *against* the oral hypothesis, or *Traditionshypothese* as he called it. For him, this hypothesis had reached its logical conclusion in the "mythical" theory of D. F. Strauss, whose formidable two-volume *Life of Jesus Critically Examined* had recently been published (1835), followed rapidly by second and third editions (1836, 1838).[165] "The mythical view," Weisse claims,

> necessarily presupposes this [tradition-]hypothesis, and could not have emerged without it, while conversely the tradition-hypothesis, pursued consistently, leads directly to the mythical view.[166]

Reaching its apotheosis in Strauss, this hypothesis originated in Lessing, who, in spite of his *Urevangelium* theory, was insistent that the essential content of Christianity was independent of written texts.[167] Lessing wished to define the essence of Christianity as "derived not from external historical occurrence but from its pure spirituality, so as to relieve it of the demand for a historical foundation or a proof from historical facts."[168] Exactly the same might be said about Strauss. For Weisse, however, the history matters, and it can be secured by way of an appropriate source-critical theory.

Papias once again provides the essential starting point. For Weisse, Schleiermacher was right to identify the Matthean *logia* with a prior sayings-collection and not with a gospel. But Weisse rejects Schleiermacher's attempt to interpret Papias's statement on Mark along similar lines. When Papias explains why Mark did not write in the proper order (οὐ μέντοι τάξει), he reports a general consensus about Mark which may originate in the deviations

164. Christian Hermann Weisse, *Die evangelische Geschichte kritisch und philosophisch bearbeitet*, 2 vols. (Leipzig: Breitkopf und Härtel, 1838). The discussion here is based on the section entitled "Von den Quellen der evangelischen Geschichte," vol. 1, pp. 1-138.

165. German title: *Das Leben Jesu, kritisch bearbeitet*. Weisse's title (see previous note) indicates that he views his own two-volume work as a response to Strauss's.

166. Weisse, *Evangelische Geschichte*, vol. 1, p. 10.

167. Weisse perceptively notes that there is no self-contradiction in Lessing here, in spite of appearances. The essence of Christianity as originally proclaimed is independent of written gospels, including the lost original one. See Lessing's posthumous "Theses über die Kirchengeschichte" (*LW*, 7.606-13), for a statement combining the two themes.

168. Weisse, *Evangelische Geschichte*, vol. 1, p. 17.

from his order of subsequent evangelists (especially Matthew). From the standpoint of a later sequence, Mark's might seem to be incorrect even if it was in reality earlier and more authentic.[169] Unlike Schleiermacher, Weisse argues for the closest possible relationship between Peter and the extant Gospel of Mark: Markan priority and the Petrine origin are here intimately related, and Papias is once more vindicated.

More important for our purposes is Papias's statement on Matthew, as interpreted by Schleiermacher. Weisse extends Schleiermacher's *logia* hypothesis at two main points, and thereby gives birth to the classical two-source theory of synoptic origins.

First, Weisse argues that we must look more closely than Schleiermacher did at the narrative framework within which the Matthean evangelist has incorporated the earlier sayings collection. If we remove the material most clearly derived from the sayings collection, the resulting narrative closely resembles Mark's. The obvious explanation is that the evangelist is dependent on the *logia* for his discourses and on Mark for his narrative:

> The same evidence that has led us to conclude that [Matthew's] gospel has the *logia* as one of its original independent components also convinces us that the narrative, through which the *logia* are there completed, is derived in all its main features from Mark, the very same Mark that we still possess as an independent Gospel.

The alternative sequence, *logia*-Matthew-Mark, would mean that Mark originated in the elimination of the *logia* from a narrative framework constructed expressly to accommodate them; an obviously unsatisfactory hypothesis. For Weisse, Markan priority follows necessarily from the *logia* hypothesis.

Second, the *logia* source is redefined so that it no longer comprises Matthew's discourses in their entirety but the non-Markan material common to Matthew and Luke. These two gospels have much in common: "Not only is Mark the common source of both, but, as we are firmly convinced, so also is Matthew's sayings collection."[170] Schleiermacher had failed to note quite how much of this material Matthew shares with Luke, just as he failed to note how much of his narrative material he shares with Mark. But it is still Schleiermacher's single observation about the term *logia* that has generated both strands of the two-source theory.

---

169. Weisse, *Evangelische Geschichte*, p. 44.
170. Weisse, *Evangelische Geschichte*, p. 83.

Armed with this theory, we may be confident that we possess

in the three synoptic gospels a circle of reports about the life and the individual teaching of Jesus, which, as regards the origin of its essential components, bears unmistakably the stamp not of the poetic or mythical, but of the historical. . . .[171]

Once again, the Q hypothesis demonstrates its flexibility and its fertility.

(4) Schleiermacher's interpretation of Papias on Matthew is probably wrong. The reference is most likely to the Gospel of Matthew, not to an earlier sayings collection. If it seems strange that Papias should have so emphasized Jesus' words at the expense of his deeds, he does something very similar in the passage about Mark, where, having previously spoken about "the things said or done by the Lord" (τὰ ὑπὸ τοῦ κυρίου λεχθέντα οὐ πραχθέντα), he explains why Mark did not write an orderly account "of the Lord's words" (τῶν κυριακῶν λογίων).[172] Papias's remarks indicate that he has a special interest in Jesus' utterances, not that the texts he refers to contain nothing else.

While Papias's confused statement about Matthew played a critical role in the development of quite different Q or *Urevangelium* hypotheses, the hypothesis in its established form is in principle independent of Papias.[173] Thus Papias plays only a minor role in Adolf von Harnack's analysis of Q, which, after over a century, still has far more in common with contemporary debate in this area than it does with the pioneering work of Wilcke, let alone with Schleiermacher, Eichhorn, or Lessing.[174] The main point of difference is that Harnack has the confidence to reconstruct the text of Q out of the relevant Matthean and Lukan passages, treating it as an extant document and not just as a hypothesis.

Given that there are two sources, Mark and Q, the one every bit as real as

---

171. Weisse, *Evangelische Geschichte*, p. 94.

172. Eusebius, *HE* iii.39.15.

173. Hence the shift from the older designation, Λ (= Papias's Λόγια), to Q, apparently introduced by Johannes Weiss (so Lührmann, *Die apokryph gewordenen Evangelien*, pp. 273-74, 277).

174. Adolf von Harnack, *Sprüche und Reden Jesu: Die zweite Quelle des Matthäus und Lukas* (Leipzig: J. C. Hinrichs, 1907); Eng. trans. *The Sayings of Jesus: The Second Source of St. Matthew and St. Luke* (London: Williams & Norgate; New York: Putnam, 1908). References here are to the English translation. For a useful account of twentieth-century Q scholarship, see James M. Robinson, "History of Q Research," in *The Critical Edition of Q*, ed. James M. Robinson, Paul Hoffmann, John S. Kloppenborg (Minneapolis: Fortress, 2000), pp. xx-lxxi.

the other, we are bound to ask which of them brings us closer to the figure of the so-called "historical," uninterpreted Jesus, assumed to be the goal of all our questing. Harnack, in constant dialogue with Wellhausen, who takes the opposite view, prefers Q.[175] Its formal structure, or lack of it, proves it to be the earlier of the two. Q

> occupies the mean position between an amorphous collection of sayings of Jesus and the definite literary form of the written gospels, and so prepared the way for the latter. Q could not have first come into existence after the time that the gospel-type — sayings, miracles and Passion, proof of Messiahship — had been created by Mark; for Q cannot possibly be regarded as a completion of Mark's gospel, and the gospel-type, after it had once arisen, established itself with sovereign authority. . . .[176]

If Q is earlier, that does not in itself make it historically more reliable than Mark. It abounds in primitive features, however. It shows no concern for church organization, and there is no sense here that "Christianity" confronts "Judaism" as a separate religious system.[177] If we set aside the baptism and temptation stories as later additions to this document, there is no explicit christology, although a sense of the personality of the Lord as the authoritative messenger of the will of God is pervasive.[178] At each point, Q shows itself to be more primitive, and less shaped by the concerns of later generations, than Mark. Above all,

> the influence of "Paulinism" which is so strong in Mark is entirely wanting, and accordingly the main theme of Mark — that Jesus, his death

175. Wellhausen discusses the relationship between Mark and Q in his *Einleitung in die ersten drei Evangelien* (Berlin: Georg Reimer, 1911²), pp. 64-79 (repr. in J. Wellhausen, *Evangelienkommentare* [Berlin: De Gruyter, 1987], pp. 1-176). Wellhausen's argument is that Matthew and Luke represent a later stage in early Christian development than Mark, that this is evident largely in the Q material, and that Q is therefore later than Mark. In Matthew and Luke, in contrast to Mark, Jesus discloses himself to his disciples "nicht erst im Hinblick auf die Passion als den durch den Tod zur Herrlichkeit bestimmten Messias, sondern er tritt von Anfang an als Messias auf, indem er schon bei Lebzeiten durch seine eben auf diesen Zweck gerichtete Predigt seine Gemeinde gründet und damit zugleich die Grundlage des Reiches Gottes auf Erden legt. Für die Vergleichung ist am wichtigsten der scheinbar nur äusserliche Unterschied, dass die Quelle, die bei Markus eng eingefasst ist, bei Matthäus und Lukas nach allen Seiten durchsickert. Er genügt zum Beweis der Priorität des Markus, auch vor Q" (p. 75).
176. Harnack, *Sayings of Jesus*, p. 229.
177. Harnack, *Sayings of Jesus*, p. 229.
178. Harnack, *Sayings of Jesus*, p. 235.

and resurrection, form the content of his own gospel — is not to be found in Q.[179]

Where these two sources agree, they are invulnerable to all critical assault. Yet we are more struck by the differences than by the similarities, and in the end Q is decidedly the more valuable of the two:

> The sayings-collection and Mark must both retain their authority, but the former must take precedence. Above all, the tendency to exaggerate the apocalyptic and eschatological element in Jesus' message, and to subordinate to this the purely religious and ethical elements, will ever find its refutation in Q. This source is the authority for that which formed the central theme of Jesus' message — that is, the revelation of the knowledge of God, and the moral call to repent and to believe, to renounce the world and to gain heaven — this and nothing else.[180]

Q, one of two sources shared by the gospels of Matthew and Luke, is also, far more importantly, one of two main sources for the historical figure of Jesus of Nazareth. If it tells us less than Mark about the outward circumstances of Jesus' life, it speaks instead of the central theme of his message. It takes us to the heart of the matter. This *Urevangelium* is not only the most primitive gospel but also the purest, unsullied still by that muddying of the waters evident almost everywhere even in the New Testament itself. The close agreement between Harnack's Q and his essence of Christianity is no coincidence.[181] Almost everything found in the one is also found in the other.

Intimately related though this Q may be to Jesus of Nazareth and the essence of Christianity, its relationship to the extant canonical gospels, both individually and as a collection, is more distant. Indeed, the relationship is one of essential antagonism.

The *Urevangelium* began by drawing Matthew, Mark, and Luke into its orbit, leaving John as an anomaly and thereby dissolving the gospel's fourfold canonical form. It then postulated a gulf of a century and a half between itself as the "original" gospel and the three "catholic" gospels with their many regrettable expansions and corruptions. Next, in ostensibly more

---

179. Harnack, *Sayings of Jesus*, p. 248 (italics removed).

180. Harnack, *Sayings of Jesus*, pp. 250-51.

181. See Harnack's classic work, *Das Wesen des Christentums* (Eng. trans. *What Is Christianity?* [London: Williams & Norgate; New York: Putnam, 1904³], esp. pp. 39-76).

modest and plausible form, it came to represent a first intrusion of textuality in a primitive paradise of oral communication. Changing course once again, it addressed itself to the anxieties of those who missed in the gospels a certain kind of history. Finally, entering into direct competition with the oldest of the canonical gospels, its collected sayings afforded unique insight into the inwardness of Jesus' person and ministry, more valuable by far than a mere external narrative oriented towards death and resurrection. Q rather than John is now the "spiritual gospel."

The question is whether an alternative account of gospel origins can be envisaged, in which the unfolding processes of reception and interpretation, normatively articulated in the fourfold canonical collection, are construed as something other than a decline into untruth and illusion.

PART TWO

Reframing Gospel Origins

CHAPTER 3

The Coincidences of Q

In one sense, the Q of Weisse and Harnack is not the *Urevangelium* of Lessing and Eichhorn. It is more modest in scope. Assuming Markan priority, it purports to explain only the non-Markan material shared by Matthew and Luke, not the origins of the synoptic tradition in its entirety.

In another sense, Q is indeed *Urevangelium*. For Harnack and others it is pure primal gospel as proclaimed by Jesus himself, rather than the gospel *about* Jesus proclaimed by the early church. On this view, the church's proclamation subordinates Jesus' own gospel — enshrined in Q — to the Pauline kerygma of the incarnate, crucified, and risen Lord. This tendency reaches its logical conclusion in the Gospel of John, where all trace of Q has disappeared; but it is already far advanced in Mark. The Matthean and Lukan fusion of Q and Mark does at least preserve Q for its modern rediscovery, but only at the cost of its own distinctive identity. The pure original gospel of Jesus is annexed by a secondary Pauline construct with which it has almost nothing in common, to which, indeed, it is opposed. And, on this view, it is Jesus himself who is lost and distorted in the process. He can be recovered from his entombment in an alien gospel only by the painstaking scholarly procedures that reestablish Q. In that way, he is brought back to life. While the quest of the historical Jesus is not identical to the quest for Q, for many it is Q that marks out the way along which the quest must proceed if it is to attain its goal.[1]

---

1. See James M. Robinson, "The Critical Edition of Q and the Study of Jesus," in *The Sayings Source Q and the Historical Jesus*, ed. A. Lindemann (Leuven: Leuven University Press, 2001), pp. 27-52. Robinson contrasts Q's appeal to Jesus' own language with "the kerygmatic development" that runs from Mark's passion narrative to the infancy narratives and resurrection appearances of Matthew and Luke (p. 33). These "Narrative Gospels" give us "a story but not history" (p. 31). We

Q, then, is two-faced, Janus-like. On the one hand, it is a modest and potentially useful hypothesis about the origin of sayings and other materials shared by Matthew and Luke. As such, it is simply an adjunct of the hypothesis of Markan priority. It helps bridge the gap between Jesus' ministry and gospels written some decades later, on the correct assumption that this bridge must have been textual in form and that oral tradition on its own is insufficient. On the other hand, Q entails a radical reconstruction of Christian origins in which the real, historical Jesus is set *in opposition to* the canonical gospels, Paul, and the mainstream church. In conjunction with the quest it enables, Q is the definitive expression of liberal Protestant ambivalence towards catholic Christianity. From this standpoint, the entire reception process that creates the fourfold canonical gospel must be evaluated negatively as distortion and degeneration. When this has been set aside by one means or another, most of the residue is found in Q.

Three initial methodological points suggest themselves in response to this. First, Q cannot be refuted on theological or hermeneutical grounds. A theological critique of Q would do little or nothing to undermine its credibility as a historical hypothesis. Q must be engaged on its own primary terrain, the texts of Matthew and Luke. Second, the negative evaluation of reception can best be countered by demonstrating in exegetical detail the logic and dynamic of the reception process, understood as ongoing interpretation of the original datum of Jesus and his ministry. Third, we should envisage this reception process as both a literary and an oral phenomenon: for the texts are scripts to be read or performed, and the communal memory of Jesus is decisively impacted by their repeated performance. A literary relationship between texts is an *expression* of the dynamic of tradition, and is in no sense in tension with it.

In the present chapter and the one following these points will be worked out in detail, in the context of an attempt to show that the phenomena of the synoptic gospels make best sense on the theory that Luke had both Mark and Matthew at his disposal as he composed his own gospel. After a chequered earlier history, this hypothesis has recently been compellingly restated by Mark Goodacre;[2] for convenience, it will be designated the *L/M (= Luke/*

---

must seek the historical Jesus not here but within Q, and specifically within the "archaic collections" it contains, beneath the later redactional layer that reflects the tensions of the revolt against Rome (pp. 36-47). The archaic collections are to be found in passages such as Q 6.20-48; 11.2b-4, 9-13; 12.22b-31 (pp. 44-45). At points like these, we find not "the trappings but the substance . . . of the kerygma" (p. 34).

2. Mark Goodacre, *The Case against Q: Studies in Markan Priority and the Synoptic Tradition*

Matthew) theory.[3] Luke will emerge as a creative interpreter of the tradition inherited from earlier evangelists, and this creativity is an expression of the tradition's own dynamic. The tradition is not an inert object to be passed on without comment from one generation to another. Ongoing interpretation is of its essence, bringing new possibilities to the fore and redressing old imbalances. In that sense Luke does not undertake his work purely on his own initiative, as "it seemed good to me also . . ." might suggest (Lk. 1.3). Rather, his interpretative freedom is the gift and demand of the tradition itself — a tradition viewed by its tradents as the self-communication of the risen Jesus through his Spirit.

To establish the likelihood that Luke is the interpreter of Matthew means establishing the unlikelihood of the Q theory. These tasks, hard enough in themselves, are further complicated by the history of scholarship in this area. Until recently, the *L/M* theory has rarely if ever been advocated in a form in which it deserved to succeed.[4] That Q still represents a default position for New Testament scholarship is not just the result of institutional inertia or methodological conservatism. Simply, Q has had better and more compelling advocacy than the rival theories.[5] But that is not a reason to acquiesce in it.

(Harrisburg, PA: TPI, 2002); *Goulder and the Gospels: An Examination of a New Paradigm,* JSNTSupp (Sheffield: Sheffield Academic Press, 1996); "Fatigue in the Synoptics," *NTS* 44 (1998), pp. 45-58; *"Beyond the Q Impasse* or Down a Blind Alley?" *JSNT* 76 (1999), pp. 33-52; "A Monopoly on Markan Priority? Fallacies at the Heart of Q," SBL Seminar Papers 2000 (Atlanta: SBL, 2000, pp. 538-622); "On Choosing and Using Appropriate Analogies: A Response to F. Gerald Downing," *JSNT* 26 (2003), pp. 237-40; "When Is a Text Not a Text? The Quasi-Text-Critical Approach of the International Q Project" and "A World without Q," in *Questioning Q,* ed. M. Goodacre and N. Perrin (London: SPCK, 2004; Downers Grove, IL: IVP, 2005), pp. 115-26 and 174-79, respectively.

3. Goodacre rightly objects to use of "the Goulder theory" to characterize this hypothesis, on the grounds that it is thereby tied to the idiosyncrasies of a particular scholar (*Case against Q,* pp. 13-14). Instead, he proposes "the Farrer theory," a reference to A. M. Farrer's celebrated article, "On Dispensing with Q" (in *Studies in the Gospels: Essays in Memory of R. H. Lightfoot,* ed. D. E. Nineham [Oxford: Blackwell, 1955], pp. 55-88). Yet idiosyncrasy obtrudes here too: Farrer forfeits the reader's sympathy and interest with his bizarre claim that the Lukan journey narrative was intended as a Christian Deuteronomy (pp. 73-86). Arguably, the limitations of this brilliant yet flawed article are reproduced in the Farrer-inspired Luke scholarship of the later twentieth century. The hypothesis in question is best described simply as the *"L/M* theory." For further remarks on the terminological issue, see my article "Q as Hypothesis: A Study in Methodology," *NTS* 55 (2009), pp. 397-415; pp. 398-99n.

4. Goodacre's *Case against Q* represents a turning point in this respect, as John S. Kloppenborg rightly acknowledges ("On Dispensing with Q? Goodacre on the Relation of Luke to Matthew," *NTS* 48 [2003], pp. 210-36; p. 212).

5. No serious threat to Q is posed by the neo-Griesbachian claim that Luke was primarily de-

Q's existence can only be sustained if Matthew and Luke write independently of each other.[6] Any item that Luke takes from Matthew is taken away
from Q; and if Luke can be shown to take even a single item from Matthew,
he may also have taken others from the same source. The Q theory is based
on the premise of Luke's total independence from Matthew. If, for example,
Matthew derived a particular beatitude from an earlier sayings collection
and Luke derived the same beatitude from Matthew, the pre-Matthean sayings collection would not be Q. As we shall argue in Chapter 5, it is highly
plausible that the synoptic evangelists may have had written sayings collections at their disposal; the *Gospel of Thomas* is a later example of a work in
this genre. In its most significant modern form, however, Q is not just a
vaguely defined sayings collection but a (hypothetical) text with clearly defined contours and a quite specific relation to Matthew and Luke.

Given the independence of Matthew and Luke and their common dependence on Mark and Q, it is remarkable how often the later evangelists
proceed in parallel with one another as they compose their respective gospels. The Q theory is based on a long series of coincidences, which extend far
beyond the "minor agreements" as normally defined.[7] These coincidences

---

pendent on Matthew alone, rather than on Mark and Matthew. On this see Allan J. McNicol with
David L. Dungan and David B. Peabody (eds.), *Beyond the Q Impasse — Luke's Use of Matthew: A
Demonstration by the Research Team of the International Institute for Gospel Studies* (Valley Forge,
PA: Trinity Press International, 1996). Here it is argued that Luke "created his narrative by moving
forward through Matthew to a certain point and then . . . *went back* to an earlier part of Matthew
and proceeded to work his way forward in Matthew again. He repeated this procedure a number
of times until he used most of the material in Matthew down to Mt 18" (p. 14, italics original).
Luke's editorial practice is thus presented in a series of five columns in which Matthean items
(numbered *1-41*) are incorporated in a set of sequences: items *1 2 3 4 10 19* (column 1), *8 14 15 23 24
25* (column 2), *6 7 9 20 28* (column 3), and so on (pp. 16-17, simplified). The claim that this editorial
procedure is "systematic, intelligible, and respectful" (p. 14) is without foundation, as the analysis
would work equally well for any randomized sequence. If *Gospel A* contains items *1-6* and *Gospel B*
contains the same items in the order *1 4 5 3 6 2*, then the "demonstration" that *Evangelist B* has incorporated them in the sequences *1 4 5* (column 1), *3 6* (column 2) and *2* (column 3) hardly
amounts to a "systematic, intelligible, and respectful" editorial policy.

6. As E. P. Sanders and Margaret Davies note, "The worst problems for the two-source hypothesis are caused by evidence which counts against the independence of Matthew and Luke"
(*Studying the Synoptic Gospels* [London: SCM Press, 1989], p. 67).

7. See Sir John Hawkins, *Horae Synopticae: Contributions to the Study of the Synoptic Problem*
(Oxford: Clarendon Press, 1909²), pp. 208-12; G. Strecker (ed.), *Minor Agreements: Symposion
Göttingen 1991* (Göttingen: Vandenhoeck & Ruprecht, 1993); A. Ennulat, *Die "Minor Agreements":
Untersuchung zu einer offenen Frage des synoptischen Problems,* WUNT (Tübingen: Mohr-Siebeck,
1994); Goodacre, *Case against Q,* pp. 152-69.

are foundational for Q, although they are rarely acknowledged by Q theorists. The question raised by the present chapter is whether the coincidences are too many and too striking for Luke's independence of Matthew to remain plausible.[8]

First, however, we turn to Luke's prologue and to Papias, to consider whether the earliest explicit statements about gospel origins can give initial plausibility to the hypothesis of a linear relationship between the synoptic gospels: from Mark to Matthew to Luke, who draws from both. These brief early statements are hard to interpret, but any account of gospel origins must reckon with them and make sense of them.

Luke, Papias, and Gospel Origins

As we have seen, Papias's statement on Matthew played a pivotal role in the development of the "Q" hypothesis. In contrast, the issue that has dominated discussion of Luke's prologue and Papias's statement on Mark has been the relationship between written texts and eyewitness testimony. Luke's reference to αὐτόπται is at the heart of modern scholarly debate on the role of the "eyewitnesses" (Lk. 1.2).[9] A similarly close relationship between apostolic testimony and gospel text is asserted by Papias, who claims that Mark's gospel is based on Peter's preaching and that it is the work of the apostle's interpreter.[10]

---

8. Compare Goodacre's remarks on the "*prima facie* case" for contact between Matthew and Luke (*Case against Q*, pp. 47-48). The problem posed by these independent parallel moves is noted by A. Lindemann, who writes: "Wie war es möglich, daß Q und Mk ungefähr zur selben Zeit sowohl von Mt als auch von Lk rezipiert wurden? Warum kamen beide Evangelisten, unabhängig voneinander, auf den Gedanken, diese beiden Texte . . . miteinander zu kombinieren?" ("Die Logienquelle Q: Fragen an eine gut begründete Hypothese," in *Sayings Source Q*, pp. 3-26; p. 11). The problem cannot be solved by postulating contact between Mark and Q, while insisting that "die Annahme der wechselseitigen literarischen Unabhängigkeit von Mt und Lk von den Texten her tatsächlich überaus plausibel ist" (p. 9).

9. See Samuel Byrskog, *Story as History — History as Story: The Gospel Tradition in the Context of Ancient Oral History*, WUNT (Tübingen: Mohr-Siebeck, 2000[1]; repr. Leiden: Brill, 2002); Richard Bauckham, *Jesus and the Eyewitnesses: The Gospels as Eyewitness Testimony* (Grand Rapids: Eerdmans, 2006).

10. For a characteristic appeal to this passage, see Martin Hengel, *The Four Gospels and the One Gospel of Jesus Christ*, Eng. trans. (London: SCM Press, 2000), pp. 78-89. According to Hengel, only an apologetically motivated rejection of the miracle stories can account for "the persistent refusal of the majority of New Testament scholars, despite all the historical arguments for the link between Mark and Peter in the early church, to accept any historical connection" (p. 88). Papias is

It is less usual to try to correlate these passages with a specific source-critical theory, which is my aim here. With some help from Papias, I shall show how Luke's prologue may be read on the assumption of this evangelist's dependence on both Mark and Matthew.[11] Naturally, the passage does not *require* any such theory. Luke's statement about his predecessors and his own relation to them is deliberately vague, and he can hardly be said to encourage the source-critical investigation of his own work. Yet his prologue may still be indirectly suggestive of a particular relationship to earlier gospels.

"Many," Luke tells us, "have attempted to compose an account of the events that have taken place in our midst" (1.1).[12] This information is provided in order to explain why Luke is here presenting his own account: inasmuch as (ἐπειδήπερ) many have already written, it seemed good to him to do likewise (1.1, 3). As is well known, the reference to predecessors is a standard feature of the literary prefaces to historiographical or scientific texts in the Greco-Roman world.[13] It can serve a twofold function, both positive and negative, although the emphasis may fall on one side or the other. Positively, the reference to predecessors establishes that there is an existing discourse on the topic in question, whose significance as an object of enquiry is thereby established. Negatively, the reference to predecessors points to the deficiency or lack in their work that provides the occasion for the new work. In the preface to his work on the Jewish War, Josephus refers to earlier historians of the war who were dependent on the accounts of others or who wrote to flatter the Romans and to disparage the Jews: these inadequacies were the occasion for his own work in its Greek form — the work of a participant who at one time had fought on the Jewish side.[14] Thus, the new work is oc-

---

invoked here to oppose the form-critical conviction that the synoptic gospels are based on anonymous community tradition.

11. Compare Michael Goulder's claim that "Luke is writing a reconciliation of Mark and Matthew to reassure Theophilus that the apparently dissonant Gospel tradition is trustworthy" (*Luke: A New Paradigm*, 2 vols., JSNTSupp [Sheffield: Sheffield Academic Press, 1989], 1.200; henceforth, *Luke*).

12. Since what have been "accomplished" or "fulfilled" among us are πράγματα, "things" or "events," I do not see here a reference to the fulfilment of scripture — the view of Luke Timothy Johnson (*The Gospel of Luke*, Sacra Pagina [Collegeville, MN: Liturgical Press, 1991], p. 27), and others.

13. According to Loveday Alexander, the affinities of Luke's prologue lie rather with ancient scientific texts than with historiographical ones (*The Preface to Luke's Gospel*, SNTSMS [Cambridge: Cambridge University Press, 1993]); but see the criticisms of Byrskog (*Story as History*, pp. 48-49) and Bauckham (*Jesus and the Eyewitnesses*, pp. 116-24).

14. *BJ* i.1-3.

casioned by the inadequacies of the earlier ones. Yet these earlier works also have a positive role in confirming the importance of the topic. Positive and negative roles together constitute the occasion for the new work:

> Since [ἐπειδή] the war of the Jews with the Romans was the greatest not only of the wars of our own time but also of those known to us from earlier reports (whether fought between one city and another or one nation and another), there are some who, having taken no part in events [τοῖς πράγμασιν] and gathered together worthless and contradictory accounts from hearsay, write of it in a thoroughly unreliable way [σοφιστικῶς ἀναγράφουσιν]. . . .[15]

These inadequate predecessors establish the need for Josephus's contribution, but they also confirm the significance of the subject matter.

For Luke too, the reference to earlier writings serves rhetorically to establish the significance of "the events that have taken place in our midst." In contrast to Josephus, there is no overt criticism. Yet Luke cannot only mean that his writing follows a precedent set by others. The reference to predecessors serves to establish the significance of one's own work, and it cannot do so if the earlier work leaves nothing further to be said. According to Luke, "many have *attempted* to compose an account of the events that have taken place in our midst." The verb (ἐπεχείρησαν) is used elsewhere for *unsuccessful* attempts. In Jerusalem the Hellenists "attempted" but failed to kill the newly converted Saul (Acts 9.29). In Ephesus Jewish exorcists "attempted" to invoke the name of Jesus, but with unfortunate results (Acts 19.13-16). According to Luke's prologue, earlier evangelists "attempted" to compose an adequate narrative whereas *he* writes on the basis of prolonged and careful study, so that Theophilus may place full confidence in *his* version of the story (Lk. 1.3-4).

The question is why Luke thinks that earlier gospels are less than fully successful, while acknowledging that they derive from the authoritative testimony of apostolic eyewitnesses (Lk. 1.2). The answer may be that apostolic testimony reported individual events or sayings but provided no systematic, ordered account of Jesus' ministry in its entirety.[16] That is Papias's problem with Mark:

> And this the Elder used to say: Mark, Peter's translator, wrote accurately [ἀκριβῶς] what he remembered of the things said or done by the Lord,

---

15. *BJ* i.1.
16. So Johnson, *Luke,* pp. 29-30, also referring to Papias.

but not in order [οὐ μέντοι τάξει]. For he neither heard nor followed the Lord, but later, as I said, Peter — who adapted his teachings as required, rather than providing an ordered account [σύνταξιν] of the dominical sayings. So Mark was not at fault [οὐδὲν ἥμαρτεν] in writing as he remembered, for he had just one concern: to omit nothing of the things he had heard and to falsify nothing in them.[17]

Here it is emphasized that Mark did indeed write accurately what he remembered, and that it was his overriding concern to do just that. There was a perfect conformity between what Mark wrote and what Peter taught. Mark was one of the "many" who sought to write an account of the events that had taken place, "*just as* [καθώς] they were delivered to us by those who from the beginning were eyewitnesses and ministers of the word." Precisely *because* his work conformed to Peter's preaching, however, it lacked order. Mark did not write in order because Peter himself drew in an ad hoc manner from his recollections of the words and deeds of the Lord, and did not recite an account of the entire ministry in sequence.[18]

In this passage, Papias — speaking through his Elder, apparently "the Elder John"[19] — is concerned primarily to *defend* Mark from his critics by explaining why he recorded the words and deeds of the Lord in such a disordered way. The Elder accepts the criticism of Mark. His narrative is indeed disordered. But that was not his fault. On the contrary, it is an indication of his fidelity to Peter's preaching; and it goes without saying that Peter himself was not at fault in drawing from his recollections what was appropriate to the occasion. While no one is to blame, the fact remains that Mark's gospel is disordered. Papias or his Elder assumes general agreement on this point. The only question is whether Mark "*attempted* to compose an account of the events that took place in our midst" but failed (the critics' view), or whether he *intended* to present individual sayings or actions out of true sequence as Peter did (the view of his defenders). About the inadequate sequence itself there is no dispute.

Given that Mark is Luke's primary source, he must belong among the "many" who attempted to compose an account, and whose work provides the occasion for Luke's both in confirming the significance of the theme and

---

17. Cited by Eusebius, *HE* iii.39.15.

18. In stating that Peter taught πρὸς τὰς χρείας, Papias may refer not to "needs" but to the *chreia* as a rhetorical form (so Bauckham, *Jesus and the Eyewitnesses*, pp. 214-17). The πρός is a problem for this view, however.

19. Eusebius, *HE* iii.39.14.

in perceived inadequacies in their treatment of it. Many *attempted* something that Luke claims to have *achieved,* by dint of long and careful investigation: an ordered account of Jesus' ministry in which individual incidents are presented in connected form and in true sequence. That is evidently what is claimed when Luke announces his intention to write "in an ordered manner" (καθεξῆς); just as, in Acts, he portrays Peter as giving an orderly, connected, sequential account of his encounter with Cornelius (Acts 11.4: καθεξῆς again).[20] While the "orderedness" of a discourse cannot be reduced to chronological sequence, the latter is fundamental where the discourse takes narrative form.[21] If so, the lack of order that Luke finds in his predecessors (including Mark) corresponds closely to the critical consensus among Mark's early readers presupposed by Papias and his Elder. It seems that Luke already shares in that critical consensus — although the deficiency he identifies in his predecessors, and which he seeks to address in his own work, is not here specific to Mark.

Why do Luke, the Elder, Papias, and public opinion as a whole believe that Mark's gospel is disordered? Why are Mark's early readers so much more critical of his achievement than those modern ones who emphasize the skill with which he has assembled a single coherent narrative out of his diverse material?[22] Papias again suggests an answer.

In its context in Eusebius, Papias's statement about Matthew follows immediately after his longer statement about Mark. They are separated only by Eusebius's comment: "That is what Papias has to say about Mark. About Matthew he speaks as follows . . ."[23] The two statements seem to have been closely connected in Papias's own text. Mark "wrote accurately what he remembered of the things said or done by the Lord [τὰ ὑπὸ τοῦ κυρίου ἢ λεχθέντα ἢ πραχθέντα], but not in order [οὐ μέντοι τάξει]. . . ." Why did he not write in order? Because Peter in his preaching did not provide "an ordered account of the dominical sayings" (σύνταξιν τῶν κυριακῶν λογίων). Yet, Papias continues, this problem was addressed by a second evangelist:

20. "Clearly the 'order' of Luke's work is its distinguishing characteristic in contrast to those who 'tried to arrange . . .'" (Johnson, *Luke*, p. 30).

21. The claim that καθεξῆς in Lk. 1.3 does *not* refer to chronological order (C. F. Evans, *Saint Luke* [London: SCM Press; Philadelphia: Trinity Press International, 1990], pp. 132-33) reflects the assumption that a claim to superiority in this regard would be unfounded.

22. So David Rhoads and Donald Michie, *Mark as Story: An Introduction to the Narrative of a Gospel* (Philadelphia: Fortress, 1982), pp. 1-5, and most subsequent Markan scholarship.

23. Eusebius, *HE* iii.39.16.

So Matthew set the sayings in order [τὰ λόγια συνετάξατο][24] in the Hebrew language, and each person translated them as far as he was able.

"So" (οὖν) suggests that Matthew wrote *after* Mark and *in response* to the perceived deficiency in Mark. As the verb indicates, Matthew did what Mark and Peter did not do. The required σύνταξις τῶν κυριακῶν λογίων, lacking in Mark, was provided by Matthew, who set the sayings in order (τὰ λόγια συνετάξατο). Mark was defective, through no fault of his own; Matthew wrote his gospel to make good his predecessor's deficiency. Papias and his Elder consider Matthew's gospel superior to Mark's. They also presuppose Markan priority.[25]

In accordance with his own interests, Papias privileges Jesus' sayings over his actions: the initial reference to "the things said and done by the Lord" is reduced to "the dominical sayings," and then, in the Matthew statement, to "the sayings."[26] There is no reason to suppose that Papias is referring to a Matthean sayings collection rather than to the Matthean gospel. Matthew is said to have written "in the Hebrew language," thereby preserving Jesus' *ipsissima verba*. This (unfounded) claim is surely intended as a guarantee of this gospel's authenticity and reliability.[27] Like Peter's sermons,

24. συνετάξατο rather than συνεγράψατο is read by most manuscripts, and may qualify as the "harder reading."

25. According to Richard Bauckham, Papias's problem with Mark's order stems from his preference for the Gospel of John (*Jesus and the Eyewitnesses*, pp. 222-30). This claim rests on three questionable interpretations of Papias's statements. (1) The οὖν at the start of the Matthew passage is said to refer back not to the Mark passage but to material omitted by Eusebius, "perhaps to the effect that Matthew, unlike Mark, was a personal disciple of Jesus" (p. 222). This is pure speculation, and ignores the thematic continuity between the two passages. (2) While the Hebrew or Aramaic Matthew maintained correct sequence, its various translations failed to preserve this (pp. 224-25); thus the perceived problem of Markan order is not resolved by Matthew. Yet Papias does not imply that Matthew's translators confused his sequence, only that they translated to the best of their abilities. (3) Papias included a statement about the Gospel of John as he did in the case of Mark and Matthew, but Eusebius omitted it (p. 226). Given that the history of the canon is one of Eusebius's fundamental concerns, this seems unlikely (cf. *HE* iii.39.17, on Papias's citations from 1 John, 1 Peter, and a story found in the *Gospel according to the Hebrews*). The link Bauckham suggests between the disciples named in Papias's preface and Jn. 1.40, 43; 21.2 (pp. 20-21, 225-26) is tenuous.

26. A special interest in Jesus' sayings is indicated in the title of Papias's five-volume work (Λογίων κυριακῶν ἐξηγήσεις, according to Eusebius, *HE*, iii.39.1). On this title see A. D. Baum, "Papias als Kommentator evangelischer Aussprüche Jesu: Erwägungen zur Art seines Werkes," *NovT* 38 (1996), pp. 257-76.

27. As R. Cameron argues, Papias's statement intends to emphasize "the earliness of the tradition and the reliability of its testimony" (*Sayings Traditions in the Apocryphon of James* [Philadelphia: Fortress, 1984], p. 111). W. D. Davies and D. C. Allison suggest that an original Aramaic sayings

then, Matthew's text needed to be translated. As Peter's sermons were translated by Mark, so Matthew's account of the dominical sayings found willing translators to make the text to some degree accessible — before (we may add, as Papias did not) it was made fully available in its familiar Greek form. The analogy with Peter and Mark suggests that Papias is not referring to multiple Greek renderings of an original Hebrew Matthew, but to a practice of oral translation similar to the one attributed to Mark.

So Papias appears to have believed that Matthew was written in response to an evident deficiency in Mark, and he therefore refers to Mark first and Matthew second — in contrast to later patristic statements on gospel origins, which invariably give priority to Matthew. Papias's unique testimony to Markan priority has gone largely unnoticed, owing to a failure to recognize the connection between his two statements.[28] In their connected form, these statements establish the summary account of gospel origins as a new form or genre, subsequent examples of which cover four gospels rather than just two.[29] Thus Irenaeus states that

> Matthew produced a written gospel [γραφὴν εὐαγγελίου] among the Hebrews in their own language [ἐν τοῖς Ἑβραίοις τῇ ἰδίᾳ αὐτῶν διαλέκτῳ], while Peter and Paul were in Rome preaching and founding the church. After their departure Mark, the disciple and translator of Peter, likewise handed down to us the things preached by Peter, in written form

---

collection was attributed to Matthew, that the sayings collection was incorporated into a Greek gospel, and that Papias attests an early and erroneous transference of the apostle's name from the earlier text to the later one (*A Critical and Exegetical Commentary on the Gospel according to St. Matthew*, 3 vols. [Edinburgh: T. & T. Clark, 1988-97], 1.17). It is hard to see how the same passage from Papias can attest *both* an early Matthean sayings collection *and* a pseudo-Matthean gospel.

28. The connection is noted by J. Kürzinger ("Das Papiaszeugnis und die Erstgestalt des Matthäusevangeliums," *BZ* 4 [1960], pp. 19-38). In consequence, the λόγια of Matthew are rightly identified with the words and deeds referred to in the Mark statement, indicating that the reference is to the Gospel of Matthew and not to a sayings source. Kürzinger is followed by Wayne Meeks, who argues similarly that "the Papias quotation does not present an independent statement about Matthew, but rather contrasts Mark, who did not make a literary composition, with Matthew, who did" ("Hypomnemata from an Untamed Sceptic: A Response to George Kennedy," in *The Relationships between the Gospels: An Interdisciplinary Dialogue*, ed. William O. Walker [San Antonio: Trinity University Press, 1978], pp. 157-72; p. 165).

29. Texts of these summary accounts are conveniently assembled (along with related material) in K. Aland, *Synopsis Quattuor Evangeliorum*, Württembergische Bibelanstalt Stuttgart (1967[4]), pp. 531-48. For analysis, see H. Merkel, "Die Überlieferung der Alten Kirche über das Verhältnis der Evangelien," in *The Interrelations of the Gospels*, ed. David L. Dungan (Leuven: Leuven University Press, 1990), pp. 566-90.

[ἐγγράφως]. And Luke, who followed Paul, set down the gospel preached by him in a book. Then John, the disciple of the Lord, who reclined upon his breast, likewise produced a gospel while living in Ephesus in Asia.[30]

Irenaeus is here dependent on Papias. Papias speaks of the Elder John along with Aristion as "disciples of the Lord," and Irenaeus identifies this "disciple of the Lord" with the "disciple whom Jesus loved," the putative author of the fourth gospel (cf. Jn. 13.23; 21.24). Papias, however, shows no knowledge of this text.[31] Irenaeus's claim that Matthew was written "among the Hebrews in their own language" echoes Papias's claim that Matthew "set the sayings in order in the Hebrew language." The only difference is that Irenaeus uses the term "gospel" to refer to a written text whereas Papias does not. For Irenaeus, Mark is "the disciple and translator of Peter." The second term derives directly from Papias; the first echoes his reference to Mark as "following" Peter. Irenaeus not only takes over Papias's view of Mark as based on Peter's preaching, he also asserts a similar relationship between Luke and Paul.

In view of Irenaeus's dependence on Papias, the differences between them are striking. According to Papias, Mark wrote first and Matthew wrote to remedy his defects. According to Irenaeus, Matthew wrote first. His gospel may be dated during the ministry of Peter and Paul in Rome, about which Papias has nothing to say, and it was only "after their departure" that gospels were written by followers of Peter and Paul who recollected their preaching. Papias's defence of Mark against his critics has disappeared. Luke and John have been added to Matthew and Mark — or, on Papias's order, to Mark and Matthew. The choice of this order may acknowledge that the two gospels known to Papias are likely to have been the earliest. There is no indication in either Papias or Irenaeus that Matthew and Luke were written at much the same time, as the Q theory must suppose. Papias testifies directly to Markan priority and indirectly, in conjunction with Irenaeus, to the priority of Mark and Matthew over Luke.

Luke considers that his predecessors provide an insufficiently ordered account of the events of Jesus' life, and he writes to rectify this inadequacy. Papias associates the inadequacy specifically with Mark, and considers that it

---

30. Irenaeus, *Adv. Haer.* iii.1.1; Greek cited in Eusebius, *HE* v.8.1-5.

31. So U. H. J. Körtner, *Papias von Hierapolis*, FRLANT (Göttingen: Vandenhoeck & Ruprecht, 1983), p. 197. For the contrary view, see Martin Hengel, *The Johannine Question*, Eng. trans. (London: SCM Press, 1989), pp. 16-23; Charles E. Hill, *The Johannine Corpus in the Early Church* (Oxford: Oxford University Press, 2004), pp. 385-94; Bauckham, *Jesus and the Eyewitnesses*, pp. 412-37.

was rectified by Matthew. In both cases, the perceived problem of order seems to derive from the existence of more than one gospel. Luke speaks of "many," Papias of Mark and Matthew. If, as Papias believes, the Markan disorder is rectified by Matthew, it is presumably the Matthean order that creates the impression of Markan disorder.[32] This impression, together with the elaborate defence it occasions, stems not from the Markan narrative as such but from its juxtaposition with Matthew. It seems that early readers of the two gospels were puzzled especially by differences of sequence. Mark was written first, and Matthew has reproduced much of the same material but in a significantly different order.

A possible conclusion is that one gospel is reliable in this respect while the other is not. That is actually the consensus position presupposed in Papias's qualified defence of Mark. Indeed, Papias's claim that Markan order is unreliable, but that this defect was corrected by Matthew, assumes that it was Matthew who exposed the unreliability of Markan order in the first place.[33] This assumption reflects a period when Matthew had begun to establish a dominant position in the life of some churches. A few years earlier, however, it may not have been so clear that Matthew's order was correct whereas Mark's was not. Perhaps neither gospel was reliable in this respect, necessitating a third gospel, based on prolonged and painstaking investigation, in order to adjudicate between the earlier two and provide an entirely trustworthy account. It is some such view that underlies the Lukan prologue.

Of course, Luke does not name either Mark or Matthew. Instead, he speaks of "many." There are a number of possible explanations for this.

(i) "Many" may imply that, while Luke is dependent primarily on Mark, he also knows a large number of other similar or related texts. From these he may have drawn the material he shares with Matthew (Q) and the material unique to himself. In that case, most of the pre-Lukan gospels have been lost. If a number of gospels were available, it is perhaps coincidental that Matthew, like Luke, is primarily dependent on Mark.

(ii) "Many" may imply that, while Luke is familiar only with a limited range

---

32. So already C. H. Weisse, *Die evangelische Geschichte kritisch und philosophisch bearbeitet*, 2 vols. (Leipzig: Breitkopf und Härtel, 1838), vol. 1, p. 44.

33. "The most probable explanation for the elder's apologia on Mark's behalf is not that in itself Mark gave the impression of an incomplete and disorganized account, but that when compared *with another gospel* which had both a different arrangement and more material, Mark appeared deficient" (John S. Kloppenborg, *The Formation of Q: Trajectories in Ancient Wisdom Traditions* [Philadelphia: Fortress, 1987], p. 53; italics original).

of texts (notably Mark; Q or Matthew), he nevertheless *believes,* rightly or wrongly, that many other such texts have been written.

(iii) As a variant of the second option, Luke may believe that gospels with which he is familiar are based on earlier, briefer written records. In that case, a gospel such as Mark would incorporate the work not only of the final evangelist but of "many" predecessors, responsible perhaps for written collections of parables or eschatological teachings.[34]

(iv) "Many" may be a rhetorically motivated hyperbole, suggesting the significance of the topic while conveying only a vague impression of the nature and extent of earlier writing about Jesus, and of Luke's own relation to it. In particular, the reference to "many" conceals Luke's indebtedness to Mark and Q or Matthew.[35]

Under the influence of source-critical theories that postulate a limited number of sources for Luke, recent scholars have tended to take the fourth position. This is probably correct, although the third view may also contain an element of truth. The fact that earlier written texts are referred to as *precedents* but not explicitly as *sources* reflects the traditional historiographical preference for dependence on eyewitness testimony rather than written sources.[36] If so, the reference to "many" is compatible with a primary dependence on Mark and Q or Matthew. In favour of the Matthean possibility is the fact that Luke attributes to his predecessors accounts of *events,* rather than collections of sayings. That would seem to describe Matthew more accurately than Q.

Luke's prologue does, however, tend to support the theory that this evangelist was dependent on both Mark and Matthew. The perceived problem of disorder in earlier gospels, to which Luke alludes, reflects the fact that different gospels can present the same events in different sequence. Such a view makes excellent sense of the Papias statements once their original connection is restored; and here the problem of sequence is specific to the relationship between Mark and Matthew. That was probably also the issue for

---

34. "This word ['many'] . . . should not be taken too literally," and must have referred to "Mark and the collections of sayings of Jesus and other material" (I. H. Marshall, *The Gospel of Luke: A Commentary on the Greek Text,* NIGTC [Exeter: Paternoster, 1978], p. 41).

35. The use of this word, "alone and in compounds, in prologues and epilogues, is a known rhetorical device, and its meaning is perhaps not to be pressed for this reason" (Joseph A. Fitzmyer, *The Gospel according to Luke: A New Translation with Introduction and Commentary,* 2 vols., AB [New York: Doubleday, 1981-85], 1.91).

36. On this see Byrskog, *Story as History,* pp. 48-65.

Luke. The fact that the two earliest statements on gospel origins *both* address the problem of sequence suggests an affinity between them. Luke's intention would then be to adjudicate differences of sequence between Mark and Matthew. Lacking Papias's confidence that the problem of sequence has already been solved by Matthew, he presents this problem as the occasion for his own gospel.

Two Annunciations

Following a genealogy and a prologue, respectively, Matthew and Luke both present extended accounts of the circumstances of Jesus' birth. This is one of a number of striking coincidences generated by the standard account of synoptic origins, according to which both evangelists wrote without knowledge of the other. Yet Matthew and Luke still have a great deal in common. *Ex hypothesi,* they compose their gospels at about the same time (for otherwise the earlier of the two will be known to the later and independence will be compromised). They both know Mark and choose to base their own gospels on his. They also know Q and use it to fill out Mark's narrative, supplementing it with material unique to each of them. They add infancy narratives and genealogies to the beginning of Mark's account and appearance stories to the end. Independently, they both venture an expanded second edition of Mark, and most of their expansions are based on the same or closely analogous material. If these parallels are anything other than coincidental, there is no Q. The Q edifice is built on the foundation of the Matthean and Lukan coincidences.[37]

These coincidences extend into the detail of the supposedly indepen-

---

37. A representative sample of recent Q research: John S. Kloppenborg, *Q Parallels Synopsis, Critical Notes and Concordance* (Sonoma, CA: Polebridge, 1988); Frans Neirynck, *Q-Synopsis: The Double Tradition Passages in Greek* (Leuven: Leuven University Press, 1995²); Athanasius Polag, *Fragmente Q: Textheft zur Logienquelle* (Neukirchen-Vluyn: Neukirchener Verlag, 1979); James M. Robinson, Paul Hoffmann, and John S. Kloppenborg (eds.), *The Critical Edition of Q* (Minneapolis: Fortress, 2000; henceforth *Critical Edition*); James M. Robinson (ed.), *The Sayings of Jesus: The Sayings Gospel Q in English* (Minneapolis: Fortress, 2002); W. Schenck, *Synopse zur Redenquelle der Evangelien* (Düsseldorf: Patmos, 1978). Contrasting Q-based studies of Christian origins are found in John Dominic Crossan, *The Birth of Christianity* (New York: HarperCollins, 1998), and Christopher M. Tuckett, *Q and the History of Early Christianity* (Edinburgh: T. & T. Clark, 1996). The account of Q's literary evolution developed by John S. Kloppenborg has been particularly influential: see his *The Formation of Q: Trajectories in Ancient Wisdom Traditions* (Philadelphia: Fortress, 1987) and *Excavating Q: The History and Setting of the Sayings Gospel* (Minneapolis: Fortress, 2000).

dent infancy narratives. Both narratives speak of Jesus' mother Mary as engaged to Joseph (a descendant of David), but as conceiving her child through the agency of the Holy Spirit. Both narratives tell of angelic announcements in which the significance of the forthcoming birth is communicated, with an instruction about the child's name. Both explain why the child was born in Bethlehem although he grew up in Nazareth. Both tell of supernaturally guided visitors to the newborn child. At most of these points, the narratives also differ from each other very markedly. Annunciations are to Joseph or to Mary; Bethlehem is either their actual home or just an ancestral home; the visitors come from far away or from near at hand. Yet many of the well-known differences between the narratives arise from motifs that the two evangelists share with each another.

These similarities are noted by Raymond Brown, who explains them as follows:

> Since it is generally agreed among scholars that Matthew and Luke wrote independently of each other, without knowing the other's work, agreement between the two infancy narratives would suggest the existence of a common infancy tradition earlier than either evangelist's work — a tradition that would have a claim to greater antiquity and thus weigh on the plus side of the historical scale.[38]

This explanation is unsatisfactory for several reasons. First, any consideration of alternative possibilities is ruled out by appeal to scholarly consensus. There is nothing inherently improbable in the suggestion that Luke's narrative may be, in a certain sense and to some degree, inspired by Matthew's and reactive to it. On that hypothesis, Luke would consciously supplement or counter Matthew's angelic announcement to Joseph with an angelic announcement to Mary — the beginning of a process of accretion that continues into the *Protevangelium of James* and beyond. Yet Brown will not entertain such a possibility. In view of the consensus that Luke had no knowledge of Matthew's work, possible indications to the contrary remain unrecognized.

Second, Brown deploys this consensus to generate "a tradition that would have a claim to greater antiquity and thus weigh on the plus side of the historical scale." The implication is that empirical historicity is the measure of value. While the Matthean and Lukan stories are largely legendary as

---

38. Raymond E. Brown, *The Birth of the Messiah: A Commentary on the Infancy Narratives in the Gospels of Matthew and Luke* (New York: Doubleday, 1993[2]), p. 34.

they stand, and are as such "a prime target for rationalistic scoffing,"[39] we can at least have recourse to more ancient and reliable traditions underlying them. In the interests of a dubious apologetic strategy, the enduring theological value of early Christian testimony to Jesus, even and especially in legendary form, is overlooked. Once again, the constructive moment of reception is viewed negatively as a problem that threatens to diminish the value of the texts.

Third, it is true that the evangelists are likely to have drawn on earlier tradition, and that some similarities between them may be explained in this way. Luke did not need to learn the names of Jesus' parents from Matthew (cf. Mk. 6.3; Jn. 1.45; 6.42). An old tradition about Jesus' Davidic descent certainly existed (cf. Rom. 1.3); an old tradition about a miraculous conception is a possibility (cf. Gal. 4.4). The association with scriptural texts may suggest that traditions about a miraculous conception (Mt. 1.22-23; Is. 7.14) and a birth at Bethlehem (Mt. 2.5-6; Mic. 5.2) existed prior to their incorporation into a full infancy narrative. Yet the similarities noted by Brown are not of a piece, and several cannot plausibly be traced back to a shared tradition. In particular, an annunciation tradition would require a context within an early connected narrative, of which there is no trace. While old traditions may have existed to the effect that Jesus was descended from David, miraculously conceived, and born in Bethlehem, such traditions could exist without narrative.[40] That is not the case with the annunciation.[41]

39. Brown, *Birth*, p. 25.

40. In Ignatius, Jesus' Davidic descent, his mother, and his virginal conception represent a complex of motifs without any need for narrative expansion: see *Eph.* 7.2 (Mary); 18.2 (Mary, David, the Holy Spirit); 19.1-2 (Mary's virginity, the star); 20.2 (David); *Trall.* 9.1 (David, Mary); *Rom.* 7.3 (David); *Smyrn.* 1.1 (David, virginity). Admittedly Ignatius is evidently acquainted with Matthew (see Paul Foster, "The Epistles of Ignatius of Antioch and the Writings That Later Formed the New Testament," in *The Reception of the New Testament in the Apostolic Fathers,* ed. Andrew Gregory and Christopher Tuckett [Oxford: Oxford University Press, 2006], pp. 159-86, where the dependence of *Smyrn.* 1.1 on the Matthean account of Jesus' baptism is demonstrated [pp. 173-81]). Yet these passages still confirm that certain motifs relating to Jesus' birth can function independently of narrative. On this point see M. Dibelius, "Jungfrauensohn und Krippenkind. Untersuchungen zur Geburtsgeschichte Jesu im Lukas-Evangelium" (1932), in his *Botschaft und Geschichte: Gesammelte Aufsätze I* (Tübingen: Mohr-Siebeck, 1953), pp. 1-78; pp. 35-39.

41. Brown does not specifically discuss the relationship of the annunciation stories. Using a similar methodology to his, Jane Schaberg concludes that "[t]he fact that both evangelists make use of an angelic annunciation indicates that the early tradition took such a form" (*The Illegitimacy of Jesus: A Feminist Theological Interpretation of the Infancy Narratives* [Sheffield: Sheffield Academic Press, 1995], p. 148). This tradition told of an angelic revelation about the pregnancy as originating from the Holy Spirit and about the birth and naming of the child (p. 151). As Luke

Matthew tells of an angelic announcement to Joseph. Mary, his be-trothed, is pregnant, and he knows he is not the father. Mary is "found to be with child of the Holy Spirit" (Mt. 1.18);[42] but the reference to the Holy Spirit seems intended for the reader, for Joseph takes it for granted that illicit sex-ual intercourse has occurred. How Mary herself might have reacted to her situation is passed over in silence. Throughout Matthew's infancy narrative she is entirely passive; she neither acts nor speaks. Joseph is minded to di-vorce her. At night, an unnamed angel appears to him in a dream and dis-closes that conception has occurred through the agency of the Holy Spirit, and that the child is to be called "Jesus" by virtue of his role as saviour. In obedience to the vision, Joseph takes Mary as his wife and accepts her son as his own, thereby incorporating him into the Davidic lineage so that Jesus is the "son of David" just as Joseph is (cf. Mt. 1.1, 20).

If Luke's annunciation story was composed in reaction to Matthew's, then his intention was to complement or correct Matthew by envisaging a quite different annunciation. Here, Mary is subject rather than object. She is addressed, by a named angel; indeed, she is praised (Lk. 1.28, 30). In contrast, Joseph is absent. Only once in this entire narrative is he the subject of a verb: "And Joseph also went up from Galilee . . ." (Lk. 2.4). Mary's actions are quite independent of Joseph, as she visits Elizabeth and sings the Magnificat (1.39-56). It is she who is mentioned before her husband and son on the occasion of the shepherds' visit (2.16), who meditates on the meaning of events (2.19, 51), and who is addressed by Simeon (2.34). The active and passive roles as-signed to Joseph and Mary in Matthew are reversed by Luke. It is, however, Matthew who provides the occasion for Luke's annunciation story in his la-conic claim that Mary "was found to be with child of the Holy Spirit." For Luke, this pregnancy must be *preceded* by an angelic announcement that se-cures Mary's active participation in her own destiny.

If Luke's annunciation story was *not* composed in reaction to Mat-

---

shows, and *contra* Matthew, it did not include a dream (p. 148), and Mary rather than Joseph was probably the recipient (p. 149). More strikingly, this tradition conveyed the fact of Jesus' illegiti-macy: for "the doctrine of the virginal conception is a distortion and a mask" behind which "lies the illegitimacy tradition" still perceptible in Matthew and, to a lesser extent, in Luke (p. 197). For Schaberg, "[t]he virgin betrothed and seduced or raped is, in the great Matthean paradox, the vir-gin who conceives and bears the child they will call Emmanuel" (pp. 72-73).

42. As Davies and Allison note, the double Matthean ἐκ πνεύματος ἁγίου (Mt. 1.18, 20) even-tually finds its way into the creeds (*Matthew*, 1.200): *qui natus est de Spiritu Sancto* = τὸν γεννηθέντα ἐκ πνεύματος ἁγίου; cf. Mt. 1.20, τὸ γὰρ ἐν αὐτῇ γεννηθὲν ἐκ πνεύματος ἐστιν ἁγίου (texts in Philip Schaff, *Creeds of Christendom*, 3 vols. [repr. Grand Rapids: Baker, 1977], 3.47-60).

thew's, we have another coincidence to add to the series required to ensure these evangelists' independence. But Luke's narrative works so well as the obverse of Matthew's that it is hard not to conclude that it was intended as such — in spite of the scholarly consensus that "Matthew and Luke wrote independently of each other, without knowing the other's work."

If Luke's story is secondary to Matthew's, there are a number of points where Matthew's wording is either echoed or adjusted for greater clarity.

(i) Following the genealogy, Matthew introduces Mary with the statement that "his *mother* [was] betrothed [μνηστευθείσης] to Joseph . . ." (Mt. 1.18; cf. 1.16). Her virginity is only later and indirectly mentioned in the citation of Isaiah 7.14 (Mt. 1.23). In Luke, Mary is introduced as "a *virgin* betrothed [ἐμνηστευμένην] to a man called Joseph . . ." (Lk. 1.27).
(ii) In Matthew, Joseph is addressed as "Joseph son of David" (Mt. 1.20). In Luke, he is more accurately said to be "of the house of David" (Lk. 1.27; cf. 2.4).
(iii) In Matthew, the miraculous conception occurs "by the Holy Spirit." In response to Mary's question, Luke's angel provides a more precise explanation of what this means: "The Holy Spirit will come upon you, and the power of the Most High will overshadow you" (Lk. 1.35).
(iv) Matthew uses a neuter participle to speak of Mary's child (τὸ γὰρ ἐν αὐτῇ γεννηθέν, Mt. 1.20). So too does Luke (τὸ γεννώμενον, Lk. 1.35).
(v) Matthew's angel instructs Joseph about the naming of the child: "She will bear a son, and you shall call his name Jesus" (Mt. 1.21). In Luke, it is Mary who is told: "*You* will bear a son, and you shall call his name Jesus" (Lk. 1.31).

At these five points, Luke's text makes excellent sense as a creative response to Matthew's. As we have seen, the two evangelists' dependence on a common annunciation tradition is unlikely, given the lack of evidence for a pre-Matthean infancy narrative. If Matthew and Luke are independent here, the coincidences continue to multiply.[43]

In Matthew's annunciation story, Mary is a silent and passive object. In Luke's, her subjecthood is restored, and it is Joseph who is silent and indeed

---

43. A similar argument could be drawn from the "visitation" motif (the magi, Mt. 2.1-11; the shepherds, Lk. 2.8-20). In both stories, a group of people is directed to Jesus' birthplace by celestial phenomena. The phrase "great joy" is common to both (Mt. 2.10; Lk. 2.10). A common underlying tradition is again unlikely.

invisible. This should not be taken to mean that Matthew's account merely reproduces patriarchal assumptions, whereas Luke's is the work of a proto-feminist.[44] Rather, the difference reflects the sombre, indeed tragic, character of the Matthean narrative in contrast to the celebratory Lukan one. Theologically, Matthew here anticipates the cross; Luke, the resurrection. The two perspectives cannot be harmonized, any more than the cross can be conflated with the resurrection. Yet, in the one case as in the other, they belong together. Their canonical belonging-together apparently originated in Luke's decision to compose a story in which Jesus' coming is heralded in a way radically different from Matthew's version.[45] Yet Luke drew fundamental motifs and language from the earlier evangelist, and remains indebted to him even as he goes his own way.[46]

Q's Uncertain Start

With their infancy stories completed, both Matthew and Luke must now make contact with the Gospel of Mark, beginning as it does with the ministry of John the Baptist and Jesus' encounter with him. In Matthew, the transition is abrupt. Immediately after learning that Joseph took up residence in Nazareth, we read that "in those days came John the Baptist . . ." (Mt. 2.23;

44. For an egregious example of a reading along these lines, see Goulder, *Luke*, 1.221.

45. Compare the argument for Luke's knowledge of Matthew's birth narrative in Goodacre, *Case against Q*, pp. 56-58.

46. While Luke may also have drawn here on non-Matthean traditions, it is not clear what these would have been or how and in what form they might have reached him. For a classic attempt to identify originally independent traditions underlying Lk. 1.5–2.20, see Dibelius, "Jungfrauensohn und Krippenkind," pp. 1-78. Dibelius argues that the text incorporates traditional accounts of (1) the birth of John the Baptist, originating in circles of his followers (Lk. 1.5-25, 57-66 [pp. 2-9]); (2) the annunciation to Mary (1.26-35, 38 [pp. 9-12]); (3) the shepherds' visit to the child in the manger (2.4-20 [pp. 53-64]). To unify this diverse material Luke has added *(i)* references to Mary's betrothal to Joseph at 1.27 and 2.5, although Mary has no husband in prospect at the annunciation and is already married in the birth story (pp. 53-55); *(ii)* passages linking the traditions about John and Jesus (1.24 ["for five months"], 36-37, 39-45 [pp. 11-15]); *(iii)* historical information about the census (2.1-3 [pp. 55-57]). Dibelius assumes, questionably, that "was zuerst in der Tradition lebt, ist die Legende, nicht der Legendenkranz" (p. 2). His quest for "kleine Einheiten" (p. 2) leads him to overlook features common to *(a)* the two annunciations: the angel Gabriel (1.19, 26), fear and reassurance (1.12-13a, 29-30), instruction about names (1.13, 31), the child's future greatness (1.15a, 32a), the role of the Holy Spirit from the moment of conception (1.15b, 35), scriptural types (1.17, 32-33); and *(b)* the accounts of Mary's annunciation and Jesus' birth: the Davidic emphasis (1.32-33; 2.4, 11), the focus on Mary rather than Joseph (1.26-38; 2.4-7, 16, 19).

3.1). In Luke, the transition is softened by the addition of the story of the twelve-year-old Jesus in the temple (Lk. 2.41-50) and by general statements about the child's development into an adult (2.40, 51, 52). Is Luke here addressing a perceived deficiency in his predecessor's presentation? Is his incorporation of John the Baptist into his infancy narrative already a response to the Matthean hiatus? In any case, both evangelists move rapidly on to the ministry of John the Baptist, which serves here as a supplementary (Mark-derived) context within which to introduce the figure of Jesus, in addition to the primary one in the respective accounts of his birth.

The question is whether Matthew and Luke turn here to both Mark and Q, or whether Luke here has recourse to both Mark and Matthew. If Luke uses Matthew as well as Mark, we may expect to find indications that he is aware of Matthean editing of Mark as well as non-Markan passages. If Luke and Matthew edit Mark independently, as the Q theory must assume, points of contact in this material will represent either coincidences or a common dependence on a Q passage that overlapped with Mark.

Both theories must be investigated in turn, in order to determine which makes the better and clearer sense of the material. It goes without saying that other theories are also possible in principle — Matthean dependence on Luke, perhaps, or (more plausibly) a "complexity hypothesis" according to which synoptic origins were in reality too complex for us to be able to reconstruct. But it is impossible to investigate every possibility at once. The onus is on those who take another view to show that their preferred hypothesis yields more plausible results than its rivals.

Luke 3.1-14

Mark's Gospel opens with *(a)* a scriptural quotation supposedly from Isaiah but actually a composite of material from Exodus 23.20, Malachi 3.1(?), and Isaiah 40.3. John the Baptizer is introduced as the fulfilment of scriptural prophecy; brief characterizations are given of *(b)* his preaching, *(c)* his impact, and *(d)* his lifestyle (Mk. 1.1-6). Matthew includes the same four elements but transposes them: *(b)* here precedes *(a)*, and *(d)* precedes *(c)* (Mt. 3.1-6). Both transpositions produce a more orderly presentation. In Luke, *(b)* again precedes *(a)*, although it is itself preceded by a long chronological note; *(c)* and *(d)* are omitted (Lk. 3.1-6). In introducing the Baptist before the Isaiah citation, Luke agrees with Matthew against Mark: that is, the texts as they stand agree with one another, irrespective of the hypotheses that might account for this. They also agree in including a time reference (simple in Matthew, elaborate in Luke),[47] and in eliminating the non-Isaianic elements from Mark's composite citation. In the case of Luke, further Isaianic material is added as if in compensation for the rejected material (Lk. 3.5-6). There is further agreement over a non-Markan expression, "all the region of the Jordan," which Matthew locates within *(c)* and Luke within *(b)* (Mt. 3.5; Lk. 3.3).

Reading on, we encounter in both Matthew and Luke a non-Markan speech of John the Baptist, in which his hearers are addressed as a "brood of vipers" and warned to bear the fruit of repentance and not to rely on their descent from Abraham (Mt. 3.7-10; Lk. 3.7-9). Matthew's version of this speech contains sixty-three words, Luke's sixty-four; a καί has been added (Lk. 3.9). Other differences are equally minimal. "Fruit worthy" becomes "fruits worthy," and "Do not presume to say . . ." becomes "Do not begin to say . . ." (Mt. 3.8-9; Lk. 3.8). This virtual agreement over more than sixty words strongly suggests a literary explanation.[48] This is therefore the point at which one may seek to establish the text of Q.[49] The brood-of-vipers speech must have needed a context in Q, and a Q account of the Baptist's ministry parallel to the Markan one might account for the Matthean and Lukan agreements against Mark. Indeed, it is precisely the function of theories of Mark/Q overlap to safeguard the Q hypothesis at points such as this. If so, the two independent evangelists' handling of their two closely related sources is remarkably similar. The parallels and coincidences necessary to sustain Q's existence continue to multiply.

On the *L/M* theory, Matthew adds the brood-of-vipers speech in order to elaborate the repentance motif he has taken over from Mark (Mk. 1.4; Mt. 3.2). Luke in turn takes this over from Matthew, and proceeds to add mate-

---

47. "In those days came John the Baptist . . ." (Mt. 3.1; cf. Mk. 1.9). "In the fifteenth year of the reign of Tiberius Caesar . . . the word of God came to John son of Zechariah . . ." (Lk. 3.1-2).

48. Compare Kloppenborg's critique of the view that Q was partially or wholly oral rather than written (*Formation of Q*, pp. 42-51; "Variation in the Reproduction of the Double Tradition and an Oral Q?" *ETL* 83 [2007], pp. 49-79).

49. Robinson, Hoffmann, and Kloppenborg, *Critical Edition*, pp. 8-13. The value of this monumental work lies in its painstaking analysis of the wording of the so-called Q material, that is, non-Markan material where Matthew and Luke overlap. At no point does it advance the case for Q's existence, however. As Robinson notes: "The IQP [International Q Project] has indeed refrained from entering into the never-ending discussion over the existence of Q, and has preferred to concentrate its energy . . . on seeking to reconstruct the text of Q, on the assumption that this may in the end be a more compelling and useful argument for its existence" (*Critical Edition*, p. lxvii).

rial of his own in which John answers questions from the crowd or groups within it arising from his demand for "fruits worthy of repentance" (Lk. 3.10-14). In making this addition, Luke follows what he recognizes as Matthean precedent.

Luke 3.15-18

Following the brood-of-vipers speech (Matthew, Luke) and the passage of dialogue (Luke only), the later evangelists revert to Mark in presenting John's messianic proclamation. Yet Matthew and Luke share an expanded version of this material, which is supposed to represent a conflation of Mark and Q. As formatted below, underlining represents words or phrases unique to a single evangelist, italics points where the wording of Matthew and Luke agrees against Mark; [a] and [b[1,2]] identify the transposition that occurs in Matthew and Luke.

> [a] There comes one stronger than me after me, and I am not worthy to stoop and undo the strap of his sandals. [b[1]] I baptize you with water, [b[2]] but he will baptize you with the Holy Spirit. (Mk. 1.7-8)

> [b[1]] I *indeed* baptize you in water for repentance; [a] but the one who comes after me is stronger than me, and I am not worthy to carry his sandals. [b[2]] He will baptize you *in the Holy Spirit and fire. His winnowing-fork is in his hand.* . . . (Mt. 3.11-12)

> [b[1]] I *indeed* baptize you with water; [a] but there comes one stronger than me, and I am not worthy to undo the strap of his sandals. [b[2]] He will baptize you *in the Holy Spirit and fire. His winnowing-fork is in his hand.* . . . (Lk. 3.16-17)[50]

There are three main points at which Matthew and Luke agree here against Mark. First, the two halves of Mark's double baptism saying (Mk. 1.8) are separated so as to enclose the coming-one saying (Mk. 1.7). The transposition of [b[1]] creates a transition from the brood-of-vipers speech that precedes. In contrast, Mark gives this material its own introduction: "And he proclaimed, saying . . ." (Mk. 1.7).

---

50. In these translations, I have replaced the conventional "whose sandals" with a simple connective in order to preserve the Greek word order.

Second, the wording of the second half of the double baptism saying is emended and expanded: the coming one will baptize *in* the Holy Spirit *and fire.* The addition of "fire" creates a connection with the non-Markan saying that follows.

Third, a metaphorical depiction of the judgement is added, and the wording of the two versions is almost identical.[51] As with the brood-of-vipers speech, a literary relationship is more likely than shared oral tradition. The question is again which of the two literary relationships under consideration can offer the more plausible explanation.

On the Q theory, all three points where Matthew and Luke diverge from Mark are ascribed to a Q version of this material most evident in Matthew. Independently and coincidentally, Matthew and Luke reject the Markan structuring of the coming-one material [a $b^{1,2}$] and prefer the Q structure [b^1a b^2].[52] Once again, each of the later evangelists unknowingly takes the same compositional decision as the other.[53]

Yet the interrelation of the texts can be explained without recourse to Q. Matthew transposes [b^1] and adds "with fire" to [b^2] in order to connect with the preceding sermon on repentance (connections italicized):

". . . Bear fruit worthy of *repentance.* . . . Every tree that does not bear good fruit is cut down and cast into the *fire.* [b^1] I indeed baptize you with water *for repentance;* [a] but the one who comes after me is stronger. . . . [b^2] He will baptize you in the Holy Spirit and *fire.* . . ." (Mt. 3.8, 10-11)

Matthew's addition of "and fire" to [b^2] also connects this with the typically Matthean judgement-saying that now follows, concluding as it does with a reference to "unquenchable fire" (cf. Mt. 13.30; 25.41). There is, then, nothing in Matthew's version of this material to suggest that he has drawn from a second source overlapping with Mark. The points at which he differs from Mark may simply represent his own redactional deci-

---

51. Matthew has two future verbs (καὶ διακαθαριεῖ, συνάξει) which have become infinitives in Luke (διακαθᾶραι, συναγαγεῖν). Luke adds a possessive: "*his* barn."

52. The coincidence is unaffected by the possibility that Mark may himself here be dependent on Q (see J. Lambrecht, "John the Baptist and Jesus in Mark 1.1-15: Markan Redaction of Q?" *NTS* 38 [1992], pp. 357-84; pp. 364-66, 373-74; D. Catchpole, *The Quest for Q* [Edinburgh: T. & T. Clark, 1993], pp. 70-76). For critique of the appeal made to Mark-Q overlaps to shore up the Q hypothesis, see Sanders and Davies, *Synoptic Gospels,* pp. 78-82.

53. For an attempt to reconstruct the precise text of Q here, see H. T. Fleddermann, *Q: A Reconstruction and Commentary* (Leuven: Peeters, 2005), pp. 217-23.

sions.[54] Luke would then follow Matthew in a number of these decisions while retaining Mark's wording at other points. There is no need to suppose that Matthew and Luke are unknowingly working in parallel to one another.

Luke 3.21-22

In the accounts of Jesus' baptism and the descent of the Spirit, agreements of Matthew and Luke against Mark are slight but not negligible. Mark states that "immediately, coming up out of the water, he saw the heavens rent [σχιζομένους]. . . ." At this point, Matthew and Luke both insert a participle (βαπτισθείς/-έντος), subordinating the baptism to its sequel; they report that the heavens or heaven "were opened" (ἠνεῴχθησαν, ἀνεῳχθῆναι), objectively and not just for Jesus; and they state that the Spirit of God or Holy Spirit came "upon him" rather than "into him" (Mt. 3.16; Lk. 3.21-22; Mk. 1.10).

On the Q theory, Matthew and Luke would again be independently following Mark while blending in some elements from the parallel Q account.[55] On the *L/M* theory, Luke follows Mark but draws some minor elements from the Matthean redaction.

Luke 3.22-38

Luke's genealogy, which follows at this point, deviates from Matthew's in tracing Jesus' Davidic descent not through the royal house of Judah, from Solomon to Jechoniah and beyond (Mt. 1.6-12), but through David's son Nathan, mentioned in 1 Chronicles 3.5 as an elder brother of Solomon (Lk. 3.31).[56] This chapter of 1 Chronicles gives an account of David's children

---

54. For detailed discussion of Matthean features of this alleged Q passage, see Goulder, *Luke,* 1.13-15.

55. Not all Q theorists hold that there was such an account. For A. Lindemann, no coherent opening for Q can be extracted from Mt. 3–4 = Lk. 3–4; Q opened instead with the beatitudes ("Die Logienquelle Q," pp. 4-9). While this may give a more coherent Q, it exacerbates the problem of coincidence in relation to Matthew and Luke. Both evangelists would independently have incorporated the same traditional fragments (the generation-of-vipers speech, the temptation narrative) at the same points in the Markan outline.

56. In Lk. 3.31 there is good manuscript evidence for Νάθαμ rather than Νάθαν, the majority

(1 Chr. 3.1-9) and of Solomon's descendants (1 Chr. 3.10-24); Matthew's gene-alogy is dependent on the second part of this chapter, which represents the obvious scriptural route for the Davidic descent. Luke's alternative version derives from the same scriptural context as Matthew's, but the decision to start from Nathan rather than Solomon means that the names that follow — of which there are forty in Luke, twenty-five in Matthew — do not refer to identifiable scriptural figures. The only possible exception occurs where there is a brief overlap with Matthew ("Zorobabel of Salathiel," Lk. 3.27; cf. Mt. 1.12). Yet Luke's genealogy elsewhere tends to reuse scriptural names without reference to the scriptural figures associated with them. Thus we read of an Amos and a Nahum (Lk. 3.25), and of a post-Davidic Joshua, Eleazar, Levi, Simeon, Judah, and Joseph (Lk. 3.29-30). In addition, at least thirteen less familiar names are also derived from scripture, extracted appar-ently at random from the Chronicler's genealogies.[57] If Matthew's genealogi-cal route via the Davidic monarchy is the obvious and scriptural one, Luke's is evidently an *alternative,* although he too draws on the resources of the Chronicles genealogies. It is Luke's *choice* not to travel on the main highway, the most direct route between the two points he wishes to connect, but to take a more circuitous route.[58] This genealogy is most plausibly understood as a reaction against one that passes through the royal house of Judah; Luke seeks to dissociate Jesus from the Solomonic line of descent, most conve-niently accessible in 1 Chronicles 3 but deliberately rejected by Luke even as he draws material for his own genealogy from the same scriptural context.[59]

---

reading. The spelling variation does not put the identification into question; Νάθαμ rather than Νάθαν is attested in the manuscript tradition at Ps. 50.2, where the reference is to "Nathan the prophet." Luke's Νάθαμ/Νάθαν is the son of David mentioned by the Chronicler — and also in 2 Sm. 5.14, probably the source for the Chronicler's expanded list of sons born to David in Jerusa-lem (1 Chr. 3.5-9).

57. 1 Chr. 3 has provided Luke not only with "Nathan" (1 Chr. 3.5; Lk. 3.31) and "Zorobabel of Salathiel" (1 Chr. 3.17, 19; Lk. 3.27), but also with "Naggai" (1 Chr. 3.7; Lk. 3.25) and "Ioanan" (1 Chr. 3.24; Lk. 3.27). Luke is indebted to the Chronicler for "Er" (1 Chr. 2.3; Lk. 3.28), "Ionam" (1 Chr. 4.19; Lk. 3.30), "Semein" (1 Chr. 5.4; Lk. 3.26), "Iorim" (1 Chr. 5.13; Lk. 3.29), "Addi" (1 Chr. 6.6; Lk. 3.28), "Maath" (1 Chr. 6.20 A; Lk. 3.26), "Melchi" (1 Chr. 6.25; Lk. 3.24, 28), "Eliezer" (1 Chr. 7.8; Lk. 3.29), "Iesous" (1 Chr. 7.27; Lk. 3.29), "Neri" (1 Chr. 8.33; Lk. 3.27), and "Mattathias" (1 Chr. 9.31; Lk. 3.25).

58. For conventional explanations for the difference between the two genealogies, on the as-sumption of their independence, see Brown, *Birth*, pp. 84-94.

59. According to Fitzmyer, Luke "avoided the royal line from Solomon to Jeconiah either be-cause of the OT strictures on the reigns of some of these kings or, more likely, because of the ora-cles in Jer 22:28-30 and 36:30-31 about the coming extinction of the Davidic dynasty" (*Luke,* I, p. 501).

If Luke's genealogy rejects the Solomonic lineage, and if that lineage is fundamental for Matthew, then the most economical explanation is that Luke presupposes and reacts against the Matthean genealogy.[60] On the Q hypothesis, another coincidence is required: independent evangelists, unknowingly moving in parallel, incorporate genealogies into their narratives which demonstrate Jesus' Davidic descent by alternative scriptural routes.[61]

Luke 4.1-13

According to the Q theory, overlaps between Q and Mark may have occurred in the material relating to the Baptist's ministry, his messianic preaching, and the baptism of Jesus.[62] In the case of the temptation accounts, Matthew and Luke are initially dependent on the brief Markan version (Mk. 1.12-13) but proceed to give a more extended account that rejoins Mark only at the conclusion (Matthew) or not at all (Luke). The Markan narrative is as follows:

60. Contrast Hengel's claim that "Matthew replaced the special Lukan genealogy with a more scriptural one," just as he had previously composed his infancy narrative as "a deliberate counterpart to Luke's account, which Matthew finds offensive" (*The Four Gospels and the One Gospel of Jesus Christ*, pp. 201, 200).

61. Commentators barely recognize the problem of coincidence that Q raises. Thus François Bovon uses the conflicting genealogies to highlight the impossibility of biblical inerrancy but does not ask about possible negative implications for Q, the existence of which he takes for granted (*Luke 1: A Commentary on the Gospel of Luke 1.1–9.50*, Eng. trans., Hermeneia [Minneapolis: Fortress, 2002], pp. 133-37). "Despite recent dissenting hypotheses, I advocate, now as ever, the priority of Mark and the existence of the sayings source, Q" (p. 6). A reasoned conclusion, or a confession of faith?

62. According to the *Critical Edition*, the following items may be assigned to Q from the first and last of these: Q 3.1a ἐν δέ (?), 3.2b {Ἰωάννη}, {ἐν τῇ ἐρήμῳ} (?) (p. 4); Q 3.3a πᾶσα . . . η . . . περί{χωρ}ο . . . τοῦ Ἰορδάνου, 3.3b {κηρύσσων} (?), 3.4 the Isaiah citation (?) (p. 6). Q 3.[[21]] {Ἰησοῦ}, {βαπτισθε}, νεῳχθη, {ο}, {οὐρανο} (p. 18). Q 3.[[22]] {καὶ}, {καταβ . . . ν} (?),{τὸ πνεῦμα}, το (?), {ὡς περιστεράν} (?), {ἐπ᾽ αὐτόν}, {καὶ φωνή} (?), [(οὐραν)] (?), {ὁ υἱός μου ὁ ἀγαπητός, ἐν} (?), {εὐδόκησα} (?). These items are deemed sufficient to ensure a Q narrative context for the brood-of-vipers speech (Q 3.7-9), the messianic preaching (Q 3.16b-17), and the temptations (Q 4.1-13). Of the sigla used here, { } = wording or lettering also found in Mark, [[ ]] = references of verses probably but not certainly in Q (pp. lxxx-lxxxii). In its nuances and gradations of certainty, the impressive complexity of the presentation — greatly simplified above — serves to distract the user from the question whether a "critical edition" ought to begin by demonstrating that the text in question actually existed.

And immediately the Spirit casts him out into the desert. And he was in the desert forty days tempted by Satan. And he was with the wild beasts. And the angels were serving him.

Is this narrative a summary of Q's fuller narrative, preserved by Matthew and Luke? In that case, do Mark-Q overlaps imply Mark's own knowledge of Q?[63] If the Markan version of a narrative is clearly secondary to one preserved by later evangelists, then the Q theory provides a ready explanation of this whereas the *L/M* theory does not. Yet Mark's temptation account does *not* summarize the supposed Q one. For Mark, Jesus is tempted throughout a forty-day period; for Q, a series of just three temptations begins when the forty days are over. There is therefore some confusion when Luke conflates the Q presentation with the Markan claim that Jesus was "in the desert forty days being tested by Satan [the devil]" (Mk. 1.13; Lk. 4.1-2). For Mark, Jesus' temptations all occur in the desert; for Q, the three temptations are located respectively in the desert, on a high mountain, and in Jerusalem. For Mark, the desert is a crowded place, populated not only by the two named individuals (Jesus and Satan) but also by wild beasts and angels. For Q, there are no wild beasts, and the angels are no more than a diabolical hypothesis. Mark may or may not be summarizing an earlier narrative, but if so it is not the Q one.

Q theorists generally agree that Matthew here preserves more of the Q wording than Luke.[64] Cases where Luke's version seems secondary to Q or Matthew include the transposition of the Jerusalem temptation to third place; the substitution of the visionary moment for Matthew's high mountain; and the devil's claim that his offer of all the kingdoms of the world is legitimate.[65]

---

63. On this possibility see B. H. Streeter, "St. Mark's Knowledge and Use of Q," in *Oxford Studies in the Synoptic Problem*, ed. W. Sanday (Oxford: Clarendon Press, 1911), pp. 165-83; Lambrecht, "John the Baptist and Jesus in Mark 1.1-15: Markan Redaction of Q?" Lambrecht (p. 381) cites Streeter's claim that Mk. 1.1-13 "read[s] like a summary of a longer and fuller account" (p. 169).

64. *Critical Edition*, pp. 22-41. Here, the only Q elements preserved by Luke alone are as follows: δέ (Q 4.1); διάβολος (Q 4.3); καί, ἀπεκρίθη, αὐτῷ, Ἰησοῦς, ὅτι (Q 4.4); καί (Q 4.5), καί, ἀποκριθείς, εἶπεν (Q 4.8); Ἰερουσαλήμ, εἶπεν (Q 4.9).

65. So Fleddermann, Q, p. 252. On the other hand, Fleddermann argues that Q contained the short, Lukan form of the scriptural citation, "Man shall not live by bread alone . . ." (Lk. 4.4): "Luke probably preserves the original text as it is unlikely that he would have dropped the words had he found them in his source" (p. 61; so also Catchpole, *Quest for Q*, pp. 12-13). But arguments to the effect that an evangelist would have been unlikely to omit something are rarely persuasive. Luke may have been uncertain how ". . . but by every word proceeding from the mouth of God" would apply to Jesus.

Luke's dependence on a Q narrative best attested in Matthew will be hard to differentiate from simple dependence on Matthew.

On the *L/M* theory, Luke has changed the order he finds in Matthew, not Q. Noting that, according to Mark, Jesus' temptations all take place in the desert, he relocates the Jerusalem temptation to the end of the story and removes the reference to the high mountain. The devil merely "led him up," in order to show him the kingdoms of the world (Lk. 4.5), and this presumably took place within the Markan desert location.[66] In harmonizing Matthew and Mark in this way, Luke fulfils his promise to provide Theophilus with an ordered sequential account, in contrast to predecessors whom he believes to be deficient in this respect.

Luke 4.14-32

Following the temptations and the arrest of John, Matthew tells how Jesus withdrew into Galilee (Mt. 4.12; cf. Mk. 1.14a). Indeed, Jesus must have returned to Nazareth or Nazara, where he had been brought up (cf. Mt. 2.23), for we now read that,

> leaving Nazara, he went and dwelt in Capernaum beside the Sea, in the regions of Zaboulon and Nephthalim, so that what was said through Isaiah the prophet might be fulfilled: "Land of Zaboulon and land of Nephthalim, the way of the sea, beyond the Jordan, Galilee of the Gentiles: the people who sat in darkness saw a great light, and for those seated in the region and shadow of death, light has dawned upon them." (Mt. 4.13-16)

Matthew has inserted this passage into a Markan context which tells of Jesus' response to the arrest of John (Mk. 1.14a = Mt. 4.12) and of his first public preaching (Mk. 1.14b-15 = Mt. 4.17). The insertion speaks of a departure from Nazara to Capernaum, and of its correspondence to the Isaianic prophecy that light would dawn in a part of Galilee associated with the sea.[67] If we now follow the *L/M* theory, which so far seems to be functioning more

66. The shorter reading καὶ ἀναγαγὼν αὐτόν (B ℵ* L) is more likely to be original than καὶ ἀναγαγὼν αὐτὸν [ὁ διάβολος] εἰς ὄρος ὑψηλὸν [λίαν] (ℵ^c 𝔐), which assimilates to Matthew.

67. In Mt. 4.13 Ναζαρά is read in B* ℵ^c 33. Other manuscripts show a range of spelling variants: -ετ B^c L, -εθ ℵ* D W Θ, -αθ Δ C P. For the textual evidence, see Reuben Swanson (ed.), *New Testament Greek Manuscripts: Variant Readings Arranged in Horizontal Lines against Codex Vaticanus: Matthew* (Sheffield: Sheffield Academic Press; Pasadena, CA: William Carey International University Press, 1995), p. 28.

smoothly than its rival, we may conjecture that the Matthean insertion was a puzzle for the later evangelist — who, we recall, has been following his predecessor's account of the three temptations while adjusting their order. Luke finds three problems with this insertion. First, Matthew has Jesus leaving Nazara without having first returned there. Second, he gives no reasonable explanation for the move from Nazara to Capernaum, merely appealing to prophecy. Third, the first half of the Isaiah citation is opaque, in spite of the appropriateness of the second half, already echoed in the Song of Zechariah (Lk. 1.79).

Luke finds a Markan solution to the first two difficulties, Jesus' unmentioned return and unexplained departure. In Mark 6.1-6, we learn that Jesus

   (i) returned to his unnamed hometown with his disciples (v. 1);

  (ii) taught in the synagogue on the Sabbath (v. 2a);

 (iii) created astonishment and offence among his hearers, who knew him not as a preacher but as a carpenter, son of Mary and brother to James and others (vv. 2b-3);

  (iv) remarked on the negative response prophets encounter in their own home contexts (v. 4);

   (v) was unable to perform many miracles on account of the townspeople's unbelief (vv. 5-6a);

  (vi) pursued his teaching ministry elsewhere (v. 6b).

It is widely recognized that Luke is dependent on Mark for his much fuller version of this story (Lk. 4.16-30). Here, we are told how Jesus

   (i) came to Nazara, where he had been brought up (v. 16a);

  (ii) attended the synagogue as usual on the Sabbath, where he read a passage from Isaiah and applied it to himself (vv. 16b-21);

 (iii) created astonishment — but not yet offence — in a congregation that knew him as the son of Joseph (v. 22);

  (iv) remarked on the expectation that he would heal in Nazareth as he had in Capernaum, and on the negative response prophets encounter in their own home contexts (vv. 23, 24);

   (v) evoked offence, unbelief, and violent hostility by speaking of two prophetic figures who encountered positive responses away from home, among Gentiles (vv. 23-29);

  (vi) walked straight through the hostile crowd and "went down to Capernaum, a city of Galilee" (vv. 30-31).

Luke's expansion of Mark's story generates difficulties of its own, especially at *(iv)*.[68] What is generally overlooked is that it also resolves difficulties posed by the Matthean insertion (Mt. 4.13-16), which occupies precisely the place in Matthew's narrative that the rejection-at-Nazareth story occupies in Luke's. Jesus, we read in Matthew, "left Nazara." We are not told that he has previously returned there, and we are not told why he departed. Luke's expansion of Mark addresses both points, significantly retaining Matthew's anomalous "Nazara."[69] Having left Nazara, Jesus "went and dwelt in Capernaum" (Mt. 4.13). In Luke too, Jesus arrives at Capernaum following his departure from Nazara — the reason for which we now understand (Lk. 4.31). Matthew appeals to a passage from Isaiah which speaks obscurely of the setting of Jesus' ministry, interpreted as the coming of a great light into a dark place (Mt. 4.15-16). Luke provides an alternative Isaiah citation, no less eloquent but considerably less obscure, which speaks concretely of Jesus' Spirit-empowered messianic vocation and which is appropriately placed on Jesus' own lips (Is. 61.1-2a; Lk. 4.18-19). The rejection-at-Nazara story is Luke's Mark-inspired solution to problems he finds with Matthew.[70]

If this reconstruction is incorrect, and if Luke had no knowledge of Matthew, then we must envisage the two evangelists as composing independent explanations as to why Jesus left Nazara for Capernaum, inserting them at virtually identical points in their narratives. Did something in Q suggest

---

68. Does v. 23 stem from an alternative, non-Markan tradition which Luke has failed to assimilate adequately into his own narrative? The identification of independent tradition in vv. 26-27 (R. Bultmann, *History of the Synoptic Tradition*, Eng. trans. [Oxford: Blackwell, 1963], p. 32) is questionable, however: the cases of Elijah and Elisha probably stem from reflection on the statement of v. 24 (cf. Mk. 6.4), that "no prophet is acceptable in his own country."

69. In Lk. 4.16 Ναζαρά is read by B* ℵ 33. Variants include -ετ Bᶜ F K, -εθ G Y W Λ, -εδ D, -ατ A Θ, -αθ Δ (R. Swanson [ed.], *New Testament Greek Manuscripts: Variant Readings Arranged in Horizontal Lines against Codex Vaticanus: Luke* [Sheffield: Sheffield Academic Press; Pasadena, CA: William Carey International University Press, 1995], p. 41). In the twelve occurrences of "Nazareth" in the NT (Mt. 2.23; 4.13; 21.11; Mk. 1.9; Lk. 1.26; 2.4, 39, 51; 4.16; Jn. 1.45, 46; Acts 10.38), -ετ and -εθ are the most common spellings in the manuscript tradition, with -ατ less frequent (only in mss. of Lk. 2.39, 51; 4.16; Jn. 1.45, 46) and -αθ represented largely by Δ (-εδ in Lk. 4.16 D is an anomaly). Outside Mt. 4.13 and Lk. 4.16, Ναζαρά occurs only in Mt. 2.23 (𝔓⁷⁰[vid] Eus Or?); on this see M. Goulder, "Two Significant Minor Agreements (Mat. 4:13 Par.; Mat. 26:67-68 Par.)," *NovT* 45 (2003), pp. 365-73; pp. 366-68. For the mss. evidence for all twelve passages, see the relevant volumes of *New Testament Greek Manuscripts* (ed. R. Swanson), listed in Bibliography (Swanson does not collate 𝔓⁷⁰, however).

70. The connection between the Matthean and Lukan passages is also noted by Goulder (*Luke*, 1.299). According to Goulder, the problem to which Luke here responds is the divergent Markan and Matthean sequence.

this theme to each of them independently? If so, it is impossible to know what that something might have been.[71]

It is more likely that, here too, Luke seeks to bring order to the confusions he finds in his predecessors — Matthew as well as Mark. Matthew's disordered account of a move from Nazareth to Capernaum is replaced by an orderly one. Following the indication from Matthew, Mark's Nazareth story is restored to its chronologically appropriate setting at the very beginning of Jesus' ministry.

Mark, the Mount, and the Plain

Throughout Matthew 3–4 the evangelist keeps close to the outline provided by Mark, although with a number of expansions. Thus, where Mark speaks of the arrest of John as the occasion for Jesus' withdrawal to Galilee and his early preaching (Mk. 1.14-15), Matthew inserts the passage about the departure to Capernaum and its scriptural basis (Mt. 4.13-16). Although divided by the insertion, the Mark passage remains basically intact. Matthew proceeds to follow Mark closely in his account of the call of the first disciples (Mt. 4.18-22; Mk. 1.16-20). At this point, the reader already familiar with Mark will expect a new account of Jesus' healing activity in Capernaum (cf. Mk. 1.21-34), all the more so as Matthew has already underlined the significance of Capernaum as the place where the great light promised in scripture will dawn on those who sit in darkness (Mt. 4.13-16).

In fact, Matthew here parts company with the Markan order, and, after a summary account of Jesus' healing activity (Mt. 4.23-25), presents his "Sermon on the Mount" (5.1–7.29). As we shall see, the setting for the Sermon is Markan and is virtually the same as the setting Luke selects for his "Sermon on the Plain" (Lk. 6.20-49). This is perhaps the most striking of all the coincidental parallels on which the Q theory rests. First, however, some brief comments on Matthew's later editing of Mark are necessary.

It is widely assumed that, for much of the first half of his gospel, Mat-

---

71. The *Critical Edition* (p. 42) finds the required Q connection in the single word Ναζαρά (Mt. 4.13; Lk. 4.16). The original context of this solitary Q fragment would seem to have disappeared; Matthew and Luke would coincidentally have attached Nazareth-related passages inspired by Q to the same Markan context (Mk. 1.14-15 = Mt. 4.12, 17 = Lk. 4.14-15). Q scholars do not agree about the occurrence of Ναζαρά at Q 4.16 (see Frans Neirynck, "The Reconstruction of Q," in *Sayings Source Q*, pp. 53-147; pp. 73-76; Fleddermann, *Q*, pp. 267-75). If it was absent (so Fleddermann), the coincidence is further escalated. Once again, debate about the text of Q pays little regard to the parallel redactional procedures the theory generates.

thew presents material derived from Mark out of its Markan sequence.[72] If there is an earlier sequence underlying Matthew 5–12, it is that of Q. From Q Matthew draws much of his Sermon on the Mount, the story of the centurion's servant (Mt. 8.5-13), the sayings about discipleship (8.18-22), much of the discourse on mission (10.1-40), the discussion of John the Baptist and the woes and thanksgiving that follow (11.1-27), and the fuller version of the Beelzebul controversy with associated sayings material (12.22-45). A similar order may be seen in Luke — with a few exceptions, of which the bringing forward of the John the Baptist material is the most significant (Lk. 7.18-35). It seems that the framework for these Matthean chapters is provided by Q.

In contrast, the Markan framework seems almost to have disappeared. Following the Sermon, Matthew 8.1-4 draws the story of the healing of a leper from Mark 1.40-45, from where (after the centurion's servant) the later evangelist moves back to Mark 1.29-31 (Peter's mother-in-law [Mt. 8.14-17]) and then (after the discipleship sayings) forward to Mark 4.35–5.20 (the stilling of the storm, the Gerasene demoniac[s] [Mt. 8.23-34]). There then follows a series of controversy stories from Mark 2 (the paralytic, the call of Levi/Matthew, eating with sinners, fasting [Mt. 9.1-17; Mk. 2.1-22]), after which Matthew deviates again from Mark as he inserts the composite story of the ruler's daughter and the haemorrhaging woman (Mt. 9.18-25), in Mark the sequel to the story of the Gerasene demoniac (Mk. 5.1-20). Only in Matthew 12–13 does the Markan order begin to reassert itself, and from chapter 14 onward the Markan outline is preserved intact.

In reality, the appearance of disorder in the editing of Mark in Matthew 8–9 is illusory, as Figure 3.1 indicates. The logic of Matthew's editing becomes clear once we subtract the non-Markan passages (indicated with square brackets),[73] and recognize that the evangelist is presenting material from Mark 1–5 in two overlapping sequences (the secondary one italicized). Only a single passage (marked with an asterisk) is out of place.

---

72. "It is . . . a matter of empirical observation that Matthew transposed Marcan passages" (Kloppenborg, *Formation of Q,* p. 72). Whereas "Matthew has rearranged and recombined Markan passages," Luke "has in general preserved Mark's order" (Kloppenborg, *Excavating Q,* p. 89). Similarly, J. M. Robinson argues that in Mt. 3–11 the framework is provided not by Mark but by Q, "into which Markan material . . . is embedded when useful to carry forward Q's agenda" ("The Sequence of Q: The Lament over Jerusalem," in *The Sayings Gospel Q: Collected Essays* [Leuven: Leuven University Press, 2005], pp. 559-98; p. 561). For a critique of the assumption that Luke keeps closer to Markan sequence than Matthew, see Goodacre, *Case against Q,* pp. 86-90.

73. The third and most extensive of these passages includes the Mission Discourse of Mt. 10, since it depends on diverse Markan and non-Markan materials.

Figure 3.1

	Matthean Sequence	Markan Sequence (1)	Markan Sequence (2)
John the Baptist	Mt. 3.1-12	Mk. 1.1-8	
Jesus' baptism	Mt. 3.13-17	Mk. 1.9-11	
The temptations	Mt. 4.1-11	Mk. 1.12-13	
First preaching	Mt. 4.12-17	Mk. 1.14-15	
Call of disciples	Mt. 4.18-22	Mk. 1.16-20	
[ ]			
The leper	Mt. 8.1-4	*Mk. 1.40-45	
[ ]			
Peter's mother-in-law, etc.	Mt. 8.14-17	Mk. 1.29-34	
[ ]			
Stilling the storm	Mt. 8.23-27		Mk. 4.35-41
Gerasene demoniac(s)	Mt. 8.28-34		Mk. 5.1-20
Paralytic	Mt. 9.1-8	Mk. 2.1-12	
Call of Levi/Matthew	Mt. 9.9	Mk. 2.13-14	
Eating with sinners	Mt. 9.10-13	Mk. 2.15-17	
Fasting	Mt. 9.14-17	Mk. 2.18-22	
Ruler's daughter, haemorrhaging woman	Mt. 9.18-26		Mk. 5.21-43
[ ]			
Grain on sabbath	Mt. 12.1-8	Mk. 2.23-28	
Sabbath healing	Mt. 12.9-14	Mk. 3.1-6	
[ ]			
Jesus' true family	Mt. 12.46-50	Mk. 3.31-35	
Parables	Mt. 13.1-52	Mk. 4.1-34	
Rejection at Nazareth	Mt. 13.53-58		Mk. 6.1-6

The apparent disorder in Matthew's editing of Mark stems from the fact that a secondary sequence overlaps with the primary one. The two sequences merge at the point where the gap between Mark 1.45 and 4.35, opened up by the beginning of the second sequence, has been closed.[74]

74. Compare the analysis of Davies and Allison, *Matthew*, 1.100-103, where it is argued that the reordering serves to create a repeated pattern of three miracle stories followed by sayings in Mt. 8–9. On this view, "sayings" covers the diverse material in 8.18-22; 9.9-17; 9.35-38. This analysis also fails to note Matthew's use of a double Markan sequence extending to chapters 12–13. The

So Matthew adheres to the Markan sequence more closely and more consistently than is often thought. As we shall now see, even the two most significant insertions into that sequence — the Sermon on the Mount (Mt. 5–7) and the missionary discourse and its sequel (Mt. 10–11) — take their starting point from Mark.

In Mark, a Sabbath healing story (Mk. 3.1-6) is separated from the Beelzebul incident (3.22-30) by a passage which speaks of Jesus' withdrawal to the sea, the gathering of crowds from a wide geographical area, the preparation of a boat as a possible means of escape, healing and exorcistic activity, the silencing of demons, the ascent of a mountain, and the selection of the Twelve (Mk. 3.7-19). This passage has major structural significance for Matthew. At the equivalent point in his own narrative, between the Sabbath healing story (Mt. 12.9-14) and the Beelzebul controversy (12.22-32), the later evangelist draws on this passage to introduce an extended quotation from Isaiah 42 (Mt. 12.15-21). Italics indicate common material:

> But *Jesus* together with his disciples *withdrew* to the sea, and a great multitude from Galilee *followed*. . . . For *he healed* many, so that those who had diseases pressed upon him to touch him. And the unclean spirits, when they saw him, fell down before him and cried out, saying, "You are the Son of God!" *And he warned them* much *not to make him known.* (Mk. 3.7a, 10-12)

> And *Jesus*, aware of this, *withdrew* from there, and many *followed* him, and *he healed* them all, *and he warned them not to make him known,* so that what was said through Isaiah the prophet might be fulfilled: "Behold, my servant whom I chose, my beloved with whom my soul is well pleased. . . ." (Mt. 12.15-18)

Matthew clearly depends here on the Mark passage, but he omits references to the geographical range of the crowds (Mk. 3.7b-8), the preparation of the boat and the reason why it was needed (Mk. 3.9, 10b), and the exorcisms (Mk. 3.11). As a result, the injunction to secrecy now applies not to the demonic confession of Jesus' identity as Son of God but to Jesus' healings; Matthew connects this secrecy motif especially with the Isaianic prophecy that "he will not strive or cry aloud, nor will anyone hear his voice in the streets" (Mt. 12.19 = Is. 42.2). He also omits here the sequel to

---

double sequence is correctly identified by F. Neirynck, who distinguishes here between "Mk (A)" and "Mk (B)" ("Matthew 4:23–5:2 and the Matthean Composition of 4:23–11:1," in *The Interrelations of the Gospels*, pp. 23-46; pp. 40-41).

Mark's account of extensive healing activity by the lake, according to which Jesus proceeded to ascend a mountain in order to choose the Twelve (Mk. 3.13-19).

It is Markan material here omitted by Matthew that has already provided him with the settings both of the Sermon on the Mount and of the Missionary Discourse. In the latter case, the relationship is as follows:

> And he goes up into the mountain, *and* he *calls* those whom he wished, and they came to him. And he appointed twelve so that they might be with him, and so that he might send them to preach and to have *authority to cast out* the demons. And he appointed *the twelve*, and named *Simon* "*Peter*," *and James the son of Zebedee and John* the *brother* of James, whom he named "Boanerges," that is, "sons of thunder"; and *Andrew* and *Philip and Bartholomew* and *Matthew and Thomas* and *James the son of Alphaeus and Thaddaeus* and *Simon the Canaanite and Judas Iscariot, who also betrayed him.* (Mk. 3.13-19)

> *And call*ing his twelve disciples he gave them *authority* over unclean spirits *to cast* them *out,* and to heal every disease and every infirmity. And these are the names of *the twelve* apostles: first, *Simon* called *"Peter"* and *Andrew* his brother, *and James the son of Zebedee and John* his *brother, Philip and Bartholomew, Thomas and Matthew* the tax-collector, *James the son of Alphaeus and Thaddaeus, Simon the Canaanite and Judas Iscariot,* the one *who also betrayed him.* (Mt. 10.1-4)

The Matthean version of the call of the Twelve does not belong to either of the two distinct Markan sequences that run through Matthew 8–13. While there is no doubt that it derives from Mark, it is used to introduce a discourse composed of largely non-Markan material.

Unlike Mark, Matthew does not locate the call of the disciples on a mountain. The reason is that he has already used Mark's reference to Jesus climbing a mountain in order to introduce the Sermon on the Mount. Matthew has also drawn from the same Markan context a characterization of the crowds that Jesus ascends the mountain to escape:

> And a great multitude *from Galilee followed,* and from Idumea and from *Jerusalem and beyond the Jordan* and around Tyre and Sidon a great multitude, hearing what he did, came to him. . . . And *he goes up into the mountain,* and he calls those whom he wished, *and* they *came to him.* (Mk. 3.7-8, 13)

And there *followed* him great crowds *from Galilee* and the Decapolis and *Jerusalem* and Judea and *beyond the Jordan*. And seeing the crowds *he went up into the mountain,* and when he was seated, his disciples *came to him.* And opening his mouth he taught them, saying, "Blessed are the poor in spirit. . . ." (Mt. 4.25–5.3)

So Matthew puts the miscellaneous material he finds in Mark 3.7-19 to three distinct uses. From it he draws, first, the setting and occasion of the Sermon on the Mount; second, the choice of the Twelve as the occasion of the missionary discourse; and third, the injunction to secrecy, which he explains as the fulfilment of scriptural prophecy. This Markan passage is of fundamental importance for the structure of Matthew's gospel. It provides the non-Q context for supposed Q material.[75]

Coincidentally or otherwise, this same non-Q context for supposed Q material is also selected by Luke, who finds a location for his Sermon on the Plain in the same Markan material while preserving its original sequence.[76]

Following the extended account of the rejection at Nazareth, Luke keeps close to Mark's sequence from the account of healings in Capernaum (Mk. 1.21-34 = Lk. 4.31-41) through to the collection of controversy stories (Mk. 2.1–3.6 = Lk. 5.17–6.11).[77] There follows Luke's version of the passages on the choice of the Twelve (Lk. 6.12-16 = Mk. 3.13-19) and the geographical origin of the crowds (Lk. 6.17-19 = Mk. 3.7-8), where Mark's order is reversed in order that the latter passage should provide the setting for the Sermon on the Plain. Italics represent verbal links with Mark, underlining with Matthew:

And it came to pass in those days that he went out *into the mountain* to pray. . . . And when it was day he called <u>his disciples</u> and chose from them *twelve.* . . . And going down with them he stood at a level place, with a great crowd of his disciples and *a great multitude* of people from all <u>Judea</u> and *Jerusalem* and the seacoast of *Tyre and Sidon,* who *came* to hear him and to be healed of their diseases. And those troubled with *unclean spirits* were healed, and the whole crowd was seeking to *touch him,* for power was going forth from him and he healed everyone. And he lifted up his eyes on

---

75. In Mt. 4.23–5.2, the summary material drawn from Mk. 3 (= Mt. 4.25–5.2) is annexed to summary material drawn mainly from Mk. 1.21, 32-34 (= Mt. 4.23-24): so Neirynck, "Matthew 4:23–5:2," p. 24.

76. The point is noted by Goulder (*Luke*, 1.340-45), and, from the standpoint of the Q hypothesis, by T. L. Donaldson (*Jesus on the Mountain: A Study in Matthean Theology,* JSNTSupp [Sheffield: JSOT Press, 1985], pp. 105-21).

77. The distinctive Lukan account of the call of Simon Peter is an exception (Lk. 5.1-11).

his disciples, and said: "Blessed are the poor, for yours is the kingdom of God. . . ." (Lk. 6.12-20)

The crucial point here is that the same Markan passage provides the setting both for Matthew's Sermon on the Mount and for Luke's Sermon on the Plain. There is no reference to teaching in Mark 3.7-19, which is concerned solely with healing activity and the choice of the Twelve. Yet both the later evangelists have selected this Markan context for their parallel Sermons, with Matthew choosing to locate it on the mountain whereas Luke brings it down to the plain. In Matthew, Jesus' teaching is introduced with a reference to his "opening his mouth," in Luke to his "lifting up his eyes" (Mt. 5.2; Lk. 6.20).

If Matthew and Luke independently found the occasion for the same Q sermon in the same passage in Mark, then this is perhaps the most striking of the many coincidences required by the Q theory.[78] That later evangelists should unknowingly and coincidentally make similar decisions at point after point seems unlikely. But if Luke has Matthew as well as Mark at his disposal and is able to follow Matthean precedent, then the coincidences disappear — and so does Q.

The Q hypothesis is said to be the only satisfactory explanation "both for Matthew's and Luke's basic agreement in the relative sequence of the double tradition (independent of Mark) and for their nearly complete disagreement in the way in which these materials are combined with the Markan framework."[79] In reality, there is far-reaching agreement in the incorporation of additional material into the Markan framework from the preaching of John the Baptist and the temptation narrative to the Inaugural

78. As in cases already discussed, the coincidence occurs at a juncture between Markan and Q material and is regularly overlooked by those concerned only with the reconstruction — not with the existence — of Q. The *Critical Edition* suggests that a version of the Q introduction to the Sermon may be preserved in Mt. 5.1 (pp. 44-45). Frans Neirynck's *Q-Synopsis* highlights the common Matthean and Lukan reference to "his disciples" as addressees of the Sermon, which may go back to Q (*Q-Synopsis*, pp. 10-11). According to Fleddermann, "Q probably introduced the Sermon with a simple καὶ εἶπεν ὁ Ἰησοῦς" (*Q*, p. 276). The common Markan setting is ignored simply because it is Markan.

79. Kloppenborg, *Excavating Q*, p. 30. The point was already made by Paul Wernle (*Die Synoptische Frage* [Tübingen: J. C. B. Mohr, 1899]): "Die Reihenfolge der Reden unter sich, wie ihre Stellung innerhalb der Mr erzählung ist bei Mt und Lc verschieden. Mt hat die Reden in den Mr zusammenhang an passender Stelle eingefügt, Lc hat sie in zwei grossen Einschaltungen untergebracht. Das verschiedene Verfahren beider Evangelisten erklärt sich am besten, wenn beiden die Reden noch von Mr getrennt vorlagen" (p. 64).

Sermon. In this material, the only relevant "disagreement" stems from Matthew's decision to insert the Markan setting for his Sermon on the Mount out of its original Markan sequence, a decision that Luke reverses while retaining the same Markan setting for his Sermon on the Plain.

Coincidences do sometimes occur. By definition, they are always surprising but never impossible. Perhaps Matthew and Luke really did make a lengthy series of parallel editorial moves as they worked on the texts of Mark and Q, beginning with their independent decisions to supplement them with infancy narratives. In that case, we may imagine the following scenario. In later years, when their more-or-less simultaneous and wholly independent gospels were already circulating widely, the aging Matthew and Luke at last encountered each other's work. Each evangelist would surely have been astonished to find that the basic conception underlying his own gospel had also been developed — quite independently — by the other. An infancy narrative with added genealogy at the beginning, appearance stories at the end, and, in between, most of Mark and most of Q dovetailed in some remarkably similar ways: everything included in the one was also present in the other. Would each evangelist have been disconcerted to discover his alter ego? Or would they have found in the coincidences and parallels a proof of common inspiration by the Holy Spirit?

CHAPTER 4

Luke the Interpreter

In all probability, Luke "used" or "was dependent on" Matthew. We must clarify what that use or dependence entails.

The hypothesis of dependence makes it possible to describe a *difference* between two evangelists as a *modification,* thereby explaining the difference as an intentional act with potential significance for interpretation. The modification may affect wording, sequence, or content; it may involve rephrasing, restructuring, expanding, contracting, inserting, or omitting. "Dependence" is the premise on the basis of which such intentional acts may be identified. It is crucially important that the premise be well founded. An interpretation based on an incorrect dependence hypothesis might well produce plausible reasons why evangelist *A* may have modified what he finds in gospel *B*, even if in reality *B* was dependent on *A* or both were dependent on *C*. Those who argue that Mark is dependent on Matthew, or on Matthew and Luke, can find phenomena within the texts which can be plausibly accommodated within either hypothesis. If, however, Matthew and Luke were really dependent on Mark, every intentional act postulated on the basis of the alternative hypotheses becomes a pure fiction. A Markan omission becomes a Matthean addition; Markan expansion becomes Matthean abbreviation. If one interprets a gospel on the basis of a source-critical hypothesis, one does so at one's own risk.

It is tempting to conclude that source-critical hypotheses should *not* be employed as a basis for interpretation. On that view, differences between gospels should be noted and carefully described, but we should not seek to convert them into intentional acts on the basis of a particular theory of dependence. In that case, source-critical discussion would be of strictly limited significance. One would engage in it only so far as was necessary to show that interpretation can and should dispense with it. That is in fact the position represented by current "narrative-critical" approaches to the gospels, which, unlike the older "redaction criticism," do not depend on any particular source hypothesis. Indeed, narrative-critical insights are achieved precisely by setting aside the conventional diachronic questions which bind textual meaning to origination, focusing instead on synchronic questions about relationships immanent within the text itself. It is arguable, and indeed plausible, that the narrative-critical perspective represents a long overdue liberation of the gospels from captivity to source-critical hypotheses.[1]

The limitation of the synchronic, narrative-critical perspective is that the Jesus of whom it speaks is no more than the protagonist in a narrative. Were someone to succeed in showing that no "historical Jesus" ever existed, narrative criticism could continue regardless. Nothing would have to be changed. The presumed flesh-and-blood individual known as "Jesus of Nazareth" might prove to be a figment of the early Christian imagination, but he would remain the protagonist of the gospel narrative. This reduction of Jesus to a figure immanent within the text is integral to narrative-critical method, and it helps to establish the point that the "real," historically- and theologically-significant Jesus cannot be detached from the process of reception that reaches its *telos* in the canonical gospel narratives. By restoring the integrity of these narratives, a narrative-critical perspective *helps* to make that point. But it cannot make that point on its own, insofar as it is confined within a synchronic frame of reference. The process of event and reception is inescapably diachronic. For that reason, a diachronic account of the reception process (so far as this is accessible to us) may serve to clarify the relationship between the flesh-and-blood Jesus of Nazareth and the figure embodied in the texts, providing a way out of the conventional and fatal dichotomy between a "Jesus of history" and a "Christ of faith." Reception occurs in large part through the active shaping of what is received in the work of interpretation. The present chapter seeks to show how, in all his rewording and rearranging, the evangelist Luke *interprets* the work of his predecessors — and especially the Gospel of Matthew.

That Luke is indeed the interpreter of Matthew, and that the Q theory is therefore false, has already been shown to be probable. The present chapter will continue to develop the case for the *L/M* theory.[2] If the plausibility of Q

---

1. That I am sympathetic to such a view will be evident from my *Text, Church, and World: Biblical Interpretation in Theological Perspective* (Edinburgh: T. & T. Clark; Grand Rapids: Eerdmans, 1994), and a number of other publications.

2. For this terminology see Chapter 3, n. 3. John Kloppenborg has recently proposed the abbreviations 2DH (Two Document Hypothesis, i.e. Markan priority plus Q), 2GH (Two Gospel

can survive the coincidences identified in the previous chapter, it may yet succumb to the analysis of Lukan compositional procedure that will be presented here. But the emphasis will not lie merely on the refutation of Q. To replace one source-critical theory with another would achieve nothing of significance if the negative account of tradition or reception as deviation from an original datum were left intact. Rather, tradition must be understood as an ongoing process of interpretation, generated by the original datum which it subsumes into itself. To dispense with Q is also to abandon the fruitless quest for an original uninterpreted object and to attend instead to the dynamic of tradition.

The literary relationship between Matthew and Luke is an expression of that dynamic — contrary to the widespread view that textuality is a static phenomenon fundamentally opposed to the dynamism of oral tradition. Where texts are written primarily to be read and performed within communal worship, they articulate the tradition in new ways and decisively shape its ongoing development. No one in the early church worries that written texts impair the freedom of the spoken word.[3] Equally groundless is the assumption that later evangelists are merely "editors" of "sources," pursuing their literary endeavours in abstraction from a worshipping community in which proto-canonical texts are already read, heard, and interpreted. Yet access to the process of tradition is largely confined to its textual traces. We can best recapture its movement by attending to the points at which the reading of one text gives rise to another, as a reader becomes an evangelist in his own right.

Rewriting Matthew

Beyond the more distant relationship evident in his infancy narratives, Luke responds to the Gospel of Matthew in three main ways. He may *adapt* or *re-*

Hypothesis, the Griesbachian claim that Mark is dependent on Matthew and Luke), and MwQH (Mark-without-Q Hypothesis, Luke's use of Matthew as well as Mark): see his *Q the Earliest Gospel: An Introduction to the Original Stories and Sayings of Jesus* (Louisville: WJK, 2008), pp. 20-31. "MwQH" displays a Q bias in substituting a reference to its absence ("wQ") for the positive relationship *(L/M)* proposed by the theory in question.

3. Papias comes closest to this, in expressing a preference for the "living and abiding voice" of individual apostolic testimonies, as communicated by "elders" and their "followers," to "what came from books" (Eusebius, *HE* iii.39.5). Papias's disparaging attitude towards books reflects a philosophical commonplace derived from Plato's *Phaedrus,* and misrepresents the fundamental role of literary production in early Christian history.

ject or *reserve* the material he finds there. The Matthean material that survives in Luke's "Sermon on the Plain" is *adapted* — selected, reworded, elaborated, subjected to minor transpositions, as appropriate. All of these procedures are evident in the Lukan beatitudes and their new sequel (Lk. 6.20-26). Other material is simply *rejected*. Nowhere do we find a Lukan version of "Blessed are the pure in heart . . ." (Mt. 5.8). Luke's "rejection" of this saying does not mean that he disliked it, and no special explanation is required as to why that might have been the case. "Rejected" means simply "chose not to include." If Luke had never omitted anything from his sources, he would have been a copyist and not an evangelist in his own right. Still other material is *reserved* — set aside for use at a later point in Luke's narrative. Thus there is no equivalent in the Sermon on the Plain to the Matthean passage on anxiety (Mt. 6.25-33, "Do not be anxious about your life . . ."). Yet Luke does include this passage in another context (Lk. 12.22-31). Finding it in Matthew's Sermon on the Mount, he sets it aside for future use, extracting it from its original context in order to relocate it in a new context of his own creation. It is this "reserved" material that provides the main key to reconstructing Luke's compositional procedure, which becomes transparent and intelligible once its guiding principles are identified.

It is widely assumed that a Luke who used Matthew as well as Mark would have to have proceeded in an irrational and counterintuitive manner. On the *L/M* hypothesis, it is said, Luke perversely creates chaos out of order. Werner Georg Kümmel for one is utterly dismissive:

> [T]hat Lk took his common material over directly from Mt is championed again and again. This position is completely inconceivable, however. What could possibly have motivated Lk, for example, to shatter Mt's Sermon on the Mount, placing part of it in his Sermon on the Plain, dividing up other parts among various chapters of his Gospel, and letting the rest drop out of sight? How could anyone explain the fact that not once does Lk place material that he has in common with Mt at the same point in the Markan framework . . . , if he took that material from Mt and was therefore dependent on the Markan order that is likewise encountered in Mt? Is it conceivable that Lk would have taken over none of Mt's additions to the text of Mk?[4]

---

4. W. G. Kümmel, *Introduction to the New Testament*, Eng. trans. (London: SCM Press, 1973), p. 64. As we have seen in the previous chapter, the claim that "not once" do Matthew and Luke agree in their placement of double tradition material is simply wrong.

Kümmel's rhetorical questions are intended not to further the debate but to insist that no such debate is necessary.[5] Nevertheless, a response to these often-repeated and poorly formulated points is not only possible but even straightforward. Initially, we simply note the oddity of the assumption that a post-Matthean evangelist *ought* to reproduce the Sermon on the Mount in its entirety. It is anachronistic to assume that Luke would have shared the modern reverence for the inaugural sermon in its Matthean form (and with its Augustinian title). Given that a new gospel is being written at all, it will have to contain new material and/or new presentations of old material; and some old material may be omitted. Why is it so "completely inconceivable" that Matthew's Sermon should be reorganized along with other Matthean (and Markan) material?

Like the Sermon on the Mount, Luke's Sermon on the Plain opens with beatitudes. Luke's versions of these have often been viewed as proof texts for the Q theory, on the grounds that they represent earlier forms of this material than the Matthean equivalents:

Blessed are the poor, for yours is the kingdom of God. Blessed are those who hunger now, for you shall be satisfied. (Lk. 6.20b-21)[6]

5. The tendency to pile up interrogatives, thereby seeming to impose an enormous explanatory burden on Q sceptics, is noted by Mark Goodacre (*The Case against Q: Studies in Markan Priority and the Synoptic Problem* [Harrisburg, PA: TPI, 2002], pp. 77-80). Goodacre himself becomes the target of this traditional interrogatory rhetoric in John Kloppenborg's critique of the "MwQH," or "Mark-without-Q Hypothesis" (*Q the Earliest Gospel*, pp. 28-31). "Why did not Luke sometimes agree with Matthew's rearrangement of Mark?" (p. 29). "Did Luke have such reverence for Markan stories that he would not take over Matthew's additions? . . . Is this a credible belief? . . . Surely it was *possible* for Luke to dismantle Matthaean pericopae, but *why* would he do it?" (p. 30; italics original). To respond in kind: How are we to explain the fact that almost all the "Q" material occurs *later* in Luke, relative to Mark, than in Matthew? Given that at Mk. 4.1 (= Mt. 13.1; Lk. 8.4) Matthew has already incorporated 69 percent of his "Q" material, Luke only 27 percent, how can it credibly be *denied* that Luke prioritizes Markan material over material shared with Matthew? (The calculations are based on the lists of Q passages in Lukan and Matthean sequence in F. Neirynck, *Q-Synopsis: The Double Tradition Passages in Greek* [Leuven: Leuven University Press, 1995²], pp. 3-5: 180 out of 262 "Q" verses in Matthew, 74 out of 271 in the case of Luke. The difference between the two totals is probably due to the verse divisions.)

6. Luke's μακάριοι οἱ πτωχοί ὅτι ὑμετέρα . . . should not be translated, "Blessed are *you* poor, for yours . . . ," as in EVV (my thanks to Mark Goodacre for alerting me to this point). The awkward shift from ostensibly third-person to second-person discourse is a sign of secondariness vis-à-vis Matthew, as is the fact that ὑμέτερος occurs only in Luke among the synoptists (Lk. 6.20; 16.12; cf. Acts 27.34). Cf. *GTh* 54 as correctly translated by T. O. Lambdin: "Jesus said, 'Blessed are the poor, for yours is the kingdom of heaven'" (*NHL*, p. 124). The awkwardness is registered by scribes who substitute third plurals for Luke's second plurals: μακάριοι οἱ πτωχοί ὅτι αὐτῶν ἡ

Blessed are the poor in spirit, for theirs is the kingdom of heaven. . . .
Blessed are those who hunger and thirst for righteousness, for they shall
be satisfied. (Mt. 5.3, 6)

Matthew, so it is said, has "spiritualized" sayings that must originally
have referred to the literally poor and hungry.[7] But Luke's version conforms
not just to what the historical Jesus might actually have said but also to this
evangelist's distinctive concerns. According to Luke, Jesus was anointed by
the Holy Spirit in order to "preach good news to the poor" (Lk. 4.18). The
God disclosed in Jesus is the God who "filled the hungry with good things,
and the rich he sent empty away" (1.53). The pairing of beatitudes addressed
to the poor and hungry with woes addressed to the rich and satisfied (6.20,
24) is closely analogous to the passage from the Magnificat, as it is to the
later Parable of the Rich Man and Lazarus (16.19-31).[8] Here and elsewhere,
Luke's editorial decisions reflect his own critical judgement as to how the
traditional sayings material can most clearly articulate Jesus' intentions as he
understands them. He is engaged in his own "quest of the historical Jesus."
Like his modern admirers, he too is influenced by ideological factors in preferring to think that Jesus blessed the (actually) poor rather than the
(merely) poor in spirit.[9]

As this case illustrates, identification of "earlier," "more original" Lukan
versions of sayings shared with Matthew is fraught with difficulty. Only tentatively, at best, might one conclude that Jesus is more likely to have said "Blessed
are the poor . . ." than "Blessed are the poor in spirit. . . ." We do not know
enough about Jesus' characteristic speech-patterns to make such judgements
with confidence, especially where the version in question seems characteristic
of the evangelist himself. Yet, even if we do regard the shorter beatitude as the
more original and find here a point in favour of the Q hypothesis, our judge-

---

βασιλεία τοῦ θεοῦ (Lk. 6.20 W), μακάριοι οἱ πεινῶντες νῦν ὅτι χορτασθήσονται (Lk. 6.21a ℵ*),
μακάριοι οἱ κλαίοντες νῦν ὅτι γελάσουσιν (Lk. 6.21b W).

7. So U. Luz, *Matthew 1–7: A Commentary*, Hermeneia (Minneapolis: Augsburg Fortress,
1989), pp. 232-35; W. D. Davies and D. C. Allison, *A Critical and Exegetical Commentary on the Gospel according to St. Matthew*, 3 vols., ICC (Edinburgh: T. & T. Clark, 1988-97), 1.442-45; H. T.
Fleddermann, *Q: A Reconstruction and Commentary* (Leuven: Peeters, 2005), p. 277.

8. On this point, see Goodacre, *Case against Q*, pp. 133-51.

9. That the Lukan beatitudes cohere with Luke's theology as a whole is obvious as soon as a
narrative-critical perspective is adopted; see Charles H. Talbert, *Reading Luke: A Literary and
Theological Commentary on the Third Gospel* (New York: Crossroad, 1982), pp. 70-71; Robert C.
Tannehill, *The Narrative Unity of Luke-Acts: A Literary Interpretation*. Volume 1: *The Gospel according to Luke* (Philadelphia: Fortress, 1986), pp. 128-32.

ment may simply derive from Luke himself. Luke clearly believes that the beatitude in its short form is appropriate to its context within Jesus' ministry as he understands it. If we find ourselves in agreement with Luke on this point, what has come to light is not Lukan priority but Lukan verisimilitude. The evangelist has succeeded in persuading us of the history-likeness of his own account; our conviction that Luke has "preserved" the authentic words of Jesus merely demonstrates the effectiveness of Luke's own rhetoric. While reliable differentiation between earlier and later versions of a saying may be possible elsewhere, no criteria for such a differentiation are available here.[10]

Those who use the Q hypothesis for the purpose of historical Jesus research like to avail themselves of the concept of "alternating primitivity" that it generates.[11] Q makes it possible for the more primitive version of a saying to occur in either Matthew or in Luke; the *L/M* hypothesis must claim that the Matthean form is normally earlier — although the possibility that in some cases Luke may have *restored* the earlier form (perhaps influenced by alternative traditions) is not ruled out in principle. If the concern is to recover Jesus' *ipsissima verba* from their subsequent interpretations, then Q may seem indispensable. But it is doubtful whether this quest for an uninterpreted Jesus is viable or coherent at all; certainly, the "primitivity" criterion is of limited use in connection with the synoptic problem. Each of the competing hypotheses can produce plausible examples of apparent "primitivity" or "secondariness," as required; Matthean priority, or Mark's dependence on Matthew and Luke, may be defended on that basis.[12] The synoptic problem will not be

10. Perhaps other passages might be selected where Lukan priority is almost inescapable? According to J. S. Kloppenborg, Lk. 11.20 = Mt. 12.28 is one such passage ("On Dispensing with Q? Goodacre on the Relation of Luke to Matthew," *NTS* 48 [2003], pp. 210-36; pp. 224-25). In Matthew Jesus casts out demons "by the Spirit of God," in Luke "by the finger of God" — clearly the *lectio difficilior,* according to Kloppenborg, and therefore the more primitive version. According to David Catchpole, however, Luke's substitution of scriptural phraseology (cf. Ex. 8.15; 31.18) for the reference to the Spirit would cohere with "the LukeR removal of a 'Spirit' reference . . . in Luke 20:42; 21:15" (*The Quest for Q* [Edinburgh: T. & T. Clark, 1993], p. 12n). The disagreement suggests that the argument from "alternating primitivity" does *not* produce the "almost unavoidable" conclusions alleged by Q theorists (Kloppenborg, p. 224).

11. For further discussion of the role played by this concept, see Goodacre, *Case against Q,* pp. 61-66. Fleddermann's "priority discrepancy" means the same thing (*Q,* pp. 60-65).

12. Advocates of the Griesbach hypothesis can claim that Mk. 1.12-13 is manifestly a summary of the Matthean and Lukan temptations narratives, and that Mk. 14.51-52 is obviously a secondary addition to the earlier evangelists' Gethsemane narratives. For an important discussion of the difficulty of establishing criteria in this area, see E. P. Sanders, *The Tendencies of the Synoptic Tradition,* SNTSMS (Cambridge: Cambridge University Press, 1969).

solved by ad hoc appeal to favoured proof texts. Insofar as the Q hypothesis is dependent on the implausibility of Luke's use of Matthew, it can be refuted not by arguing that Luke's versions of common sayings are all demonstrably secondary but by attending to the compositional procedure required for a text such as Luke's to emerge from this evangelist's engagement with Mark and Matthew.[13] If such an experiment brings to light a simple and intelligible compositional procedure, then it may be said to have succeeded. If it becomes entangled in endless complexities and speculations, it will have failed.[14]

On the *L/M* hypothesis, Luke selects five main passages from Matthew 5–7 and expands each of them with analogous material from elsewhere or of his own composition. These passages are as follows:

(i) a selection of four Matthean beatitudes, expanded by the addition of four corresponding woes (Mt. 5.3, 6, 4, 11-12; Lk. 6.20-26);[15]

(ii) the last of the six Matthean antitheses, enjoining love of the enemy, together with material from the preceding antithesis on not resisting evil, the Golden Rule, and Lukan expansions (Mt. 5.44-48 + 39b-42; 7.12; Lk. 6.27-36);

(iii) the warning against judging, with the corresponding Parable of the Mote and the Beam, with Lukan expansions and Matthean sayings about the relationship of teacher to disciple (Mt. 7.1-5 + 15.14, 10.24a, 25a; Lk. 6.37-42);

13. As Kloppenborg states, "The real point of disagreement among Synoptic Problem specialists is not what is logically possible, but which hypotheses imply *plausible editorial procedures on the part of the evangelists*" (*Excavating Q* [Minneapolis: Fortress, 2000], p. 43; italics original). The present argument attempts to show that the hypothetical *L/M* editorial procedure has been deemed implausible only because it has not been understood. For further discussion of the methodological point, see my "Q as Hypothesis: A Study in Methodology," *NTS* 55 (2009), pp. 397-415.

14. Michael Goulder's monumental *Luke: A New Paradigm*, 2 vols., JSNTSupp (Sheffield: Sheffield Academic Press, 1989) seems to me to represent a failed experiment along these lines — in spite of its many penetrating individual observations. See the criticisms of Christopher Tuckett (*Q and the History of Early Christianity* [Edinburgh: T. & T. Clark, 1996], pp. 16-31), but also Goulder's response ("Is Q a Juggernaut?" *JBL* 115 [1996], pp. 667-81), and the more positive assessment of Mark Goodacre (*Goulder and the Gospels: An Examination of a New Paradigm*, JSNTSupp [Sheffield: Sheffield Academic Press, 1996]).

15. That the Lukan beatitudes are "paradoxical" whereas purely Matthean ones are "conventional" is doubtful, given the conventional (scriptural) character of the paradoxes themselves (see Dale C. Allison, *Constructing Jesus: Memory, Imagination, and History* [Grand Rapids: Baker, 2010], p. 310). Even if Luke's beatitudes are arguably more coherent than Matthew's, that need not be an indication of priority. The same is true of the central core of the Lukan sermon (Lk. 6.27-42), whose coherence Allison rightly emphasizes (pp. 309-23).

(iv) the passage on good and bad trees and their fruits, with expansions drawn from an analogous passage elsewhere (Mt. 7.16-20 + 12.34-35; Lk. 6.43-45);

(v) the Parable of the Two Houses, introduced by a saying — "Why do you call me, 'Lord, Lord'?" — loosely based on a Matthean equivalent (Mt. 7.21, 24-27; Lk. 6.46-49).

Luke's editorial procedure is not to be seen merely as selection and re-arrangement supplemented by pieces of free composition. It is all that, but the selection, rearrangement, and composition are motivated by the intention to *interpret* the sayings material rather than simply reproducing it in mechanical fashion.

Thus woes are added to beatitudes in order to clarify what they mean. A beatitude on its own is not exclusive. In itself, a blessing of the poor may or may not entail a corresponding criticism of those who are not poor; it implies a question about them that remains unanswered. Luke's woes interpret the blessings in an exclusive sense: in his view, when Jesus addresses his disciples as "the poor" or "those who hunger now," he also intends the exact converse of his blessings in the form of woes against those of his hearers who are rich and satisfied.[16] We later learn that, in Luke's opinion, Pharisees in particular are "lovers of money" (Lk. 16.14). When Luke inserts second-person plural address into the latter part of the first three beatitudes, in contrast to Matthew's third plural, this is also a creative interpretative act, the effect of which is to localize the blessings and woes within the context of Jesus' ministry in contrast to the timeless universality of the Matthean rendering.[17] Both versions represent moments in the development of the tradition that Jesus pronounced blessings on certain classes of people, and both of them represent interpretations of that tradition — together with a third version found in the *Gospel of Thomas*.[18] The question which version approximates

---

16. Note the possible Matthean echoes in the first two woes: ἀπέχετε τὴν παράκλησιν ὑμῶν (Lk. 6.24), cf. παρακληθήσονται (Mt. 5.4b); ὅτι πενθήσετε καὶ κλαύσετε (Lk. 6.25), cf. οἱ πενθοῦντες (Mt. 5.4a). Cf. Goulder, *Luke*, 1.354-55.

17. While engaging with Matthean material, Luke partially retains the earlier evangelist's third-person plural address (μακάριοι οἱ πτωχοί/οἱ πεινῶντες νῦν/οἱ κλαίοντες νῦν, cf. Matthew's μακάριοι οἱ πτωχοί.../οἱ πεινῶντες.../οἱ πενθοῦντες). When free from Matthew's influence, second plural address is used consistently (οὐαὶ ὑμῖν τοῖς πλουσίοις/ὑμῖν οἱ ἐμπεπλησμένοι), with the sole exception of 6.25b.

18. "Jesus said: Blessed are the poor, for yours is the kingdom of heaven" (*GTh* 54). "Jesus said: Blessed are you when you are hated and persecuted. Wherever you have been persecuted they

most closely to words actually uttered by Jesus is relevant only insofar as it is also a concern of Luke's.

In Luke 6.27, the evangelist has detached the saying about love of enemies from the Matthean contrast with the law's teaching, thereby presenting it as a freestanding instruction whose relation to the law is not decisive for its meaning. Phraseology shared by the two evangelists is italicized:

> You have heard that it was said, "You shall love your neighbour and hate your enemy." But I *say to you* [ἐγὼ δὲ λέγω ὑμῖν], *Love your enemies* and *pray for those who* persecute *you*. . . . (Mt. 5.43-44)

> But I *say to you* who hear [ἀλλὰ ὑμῖν λέγω τοῖς ἀκούουσιν], *Love your enemies,* do good to those who hate you, bless those who curse you, *pray for those who* abuse *you*. . . . (Lk. 6.27-28)[19]

Luke has noted that the Matthean saying consists of a general principle (love your enemies) exemplified in a specific practice (praying for persecutors). His additions consist in alternative formulations of the principle ("do good . . ." in addition to "love . . .") and of the practice ("bless . . ." in addition to "pray . . ."). Luke may well have composed these additions himself, yet he has done so not to obtrude his own ideas into the teaching of Jesus but as an interpretative paraphrase of what Jesus is reported by Matthew to have said.

In vv. 29-31 Luke introduces material from the preceding Matthean antithesis, concerned mainly with nonresistance. The relevant items in Matthew are: (1) do not resist; (2) the other cheek; (3) the cloak as well as the coat; (4) two miles not one; (5) giving to beggars; (6) not refusing borrowers (Mt. 5.39-42). In addition to stylistic changes with minimal impact on the sense, Luke has chosen to omit (1), thereby assimilating this section to the prevailing theme of love for enemies, and (4). In (6), taking is substituted for borrowing, in keeping with the theme of response to hostile acts. Nonresistance and love for enemies are closely related themes; they can be distinguished from one another (so Matthew), but they can also be identified with one another (so Luke). Luke also finds a place here for the Golden Rule (Lk. 6.31), now presented as the comprehensive principle for action even in a hos-

---

will find no place" (*GTh* 68). "Jesus said: Blessed are they who have been persecuted within themselves. It is they who have truly come to know the Father. Blessed are the hungry, for the belly of him who desires will be filled" (*GTh* 69; cf. 79).

19. The Lukan introductory formula may preserve a vestige of the Matthean antithesis; Luke's ἀλλά is actually more sharply antithetical than Matthew's δέ.

tile environment, and not as a freestanding summary of the law and the prophets (Mt. 7.12). This is interpretation, not mere rearrangement.[20]

Having inserted Matthew's nonresistance material and Golden Rule into the teaching on love for enemies (Lk. 6.29-31), Luke returns to his primary Matthean context for the supporting argument that love for enemies is a necessary extension of love beyond the confines of reciprocity. "If you love those who love you, what credit is that to you?" answers to "Love your enemies" (6.32, 27a). "If you do good to those who do good to you . . ." answers to "Do good to those who hate you" (6.33, 27b). This second pairing of injunction and rationale is tighter than the Matthean equivalent, where "If you greet only your kin . . ." does not correspond to "Pray for those who persecute you" (Mt. 5.44b, 46a). The pairing is Luke's own composition, constructed, however, on the model of the first Matthean one. Also Lukan is a third pairing, in which "If you lend to those from whom you hope to receive . . ." corresponds to "Give to everyone who begs from you" (Lk. 6.30, 34), thereby repeating the shift in v. 30 from the dominant theme of love for enemies to the subordinate theme of giving. The two themes both exemplify the principle of nonreciprocal action for the well-being of the other, contrasted with the norms of reciprocity that "even sinners" observe (6.32-34 [3x]).

Since the rationale for nonreciprocal action is presented only indirectly, by identifying the limitations of normal reciprocity, Luke feels it necessary to return to the opening injunctions as his expansion of the Matthean passage draws towards its close.

> But love your enemies, and do good, and lend expecting nothing back, and your reward will be great, and you will be sons of the Most High, for he is kind to the ungrateful and wicked. . . . (Lk. 6.35)

Here, Luke's abbreviation of "do good to those who hate you" (v. 27) to "do good" indicates that the initial injunction is taken to mean, "do good *even* to those who hate you," and that love is to be extended *even* to enemies. Thus the focus is not on behaviour towards enemies per se, but on the *un-*

---

20. Lukan redaction of a sequence better preserved in Matthew may also be proposed under the Q theory (see J. M. Robinson, "The Sequence of Q," in his *The Sayings Gospel Q: Collected Essays* [Leuven: Leuven University Press, 2005], pp. 563-64). Robinson claims, however, that Matthew's antithetical structuring of this material is secondary (p. 563) — failing to note that a vestige of Matthew's ἐγὼ δὲ λέγω ὑμῖν (Mt. 5.44) is preserved in Luke's ἀλλὰ ὑμῖν λέγω τοῖς ἀκούουσιν (Lk. 6.27); so Goulder, *Luke*, 1.361.

limited extension of love or well-doing beyond the normal sphere of reciprocity. Repetition of the opening injunctions also prepares for the deferred statement about the nonreciprocal divine generosity, which in Matthew provides an initial rationale for love of enemies (Mt. 5.44-45). Nonreciprocal acts for the well-being of others correspond to God's own action towards the world precisely as they deviate from the all-but-universal norms of reciprocity. Behaviours that appear idiosyncratic and inexplicable from the standpoint of those human norms find their logic within the sphere of the divine-human relationship.

Luke's expansions to Matthew's final antithesis are partly his own and partly derived from analogous Matthean material. The later evangelist seeks to extend the scope and to probe the logic of material drawn from the earlier. It would be futile to ask which of the two versions is the more successful, or which approximates more closely to what was once said by a "historical" Jesus. Where such questions predominate, the error is perpetuated that interpretation is something that can be subtracted from the Jesus tradition, leaving one to reconstruct the historical figure out of an uninterpreted residue.[21] In reality, Jesus' teaching is nowhere available in uninterpreted form. One interpretation provokes and generates another — as in the case of Matthew and Luke.[22] Jesus' sayings are not handed down as inert objects that can either be preserved in pristine authenticity or reshaped at will. These sayings possess their own dynamic, and the interpretative activity brought to bear on them and inseparable from them is the response they themselves evoke. Jesus' sayings are handed down by tradents who have found them to be "the words of eternal life" (Jn. 6.68), and whose reception of them has left its mark on what they pass on. This reception process becomes visible in Matthew and Luke, but also in the present form of the *Didache,* where the teach-

21. For a theoretically sophisticated critique of the quest for an uninterpreted Jesus, see Jens Schröter, "Die Frage nach dem historischen Jesus und der Charakter historischer Erkenntnis," in *The Sayings Source Q and the Historical Jesus,* ed. A. Lindemann (Leuven: Leuven University Press, 2001), pp. 207-54. According to Schröter: "[D]ie Quellen der Vergangenheit enthalten nicht die Tatsachen und Ereignisse, sondern Deutungen von diesen . . . Die Vorstellung, es könne einen Zugang zu einer *hinter* diesen Interpretationen liegenden Wirklichkeit geben, wird damit grundsätzlich obsolet" (p. 229). Thus, "[d]ie Vorstellung des 'wirklichen' Jesus *hinter* den Quellen erweist sich dabei als obsolet, die Jesusfrage ist mithin umzuformulieren in diejenige nach einem an die Quellen gebundenen Entwurf des *erinnerten* Jesus als Inhalt des sozialen Gedächtnisses des Urchristentums" (p. 233; italics original).

22. If Matthean redactional features are absent from Luke's sermon (so Allison, *Constructing Jesus,* p. 310), it is because they are replaced by Lukan redactional features, not because Jesus' teaching is here preserved in some preredactional neutrality.

ing on love for enemies is fundamental to the "way of life" that is contrasted with the "way of death" (*Did.* 1.3-5a). We must assume that the same active engagement with the tradition has occurred in the earlier stages of the reception process extending from Matthew back to Jesus himself.

In the remainder of his Sermon on the Plain, Luke continues to use the same compositional techniques. Matthew's "Judge not, that you be not judged" (Mt. 7.1a) elicits from Luke a set of three variations (condemn not/forgive/give), which extend the scope of the Matthean principle that "the measure you give will be the measure you get" (Mt. 7.2b; Lk. 6.37-38). Sayings found elsewhere in Matthew are relocated to this context (blind leading blind: Mt. 15.14; Lk. 6.39; disciple like teacher: Mt. 10.24-25; Lk. 6.40). The juxtaposition of these sayings invites reflection on the relationship between them. Since Luke introduces the first as a "parable" (Lk. 6.39), he may see the second as its interpretation. If disciples become like their teacher, they must beware of being led into disaster by one who purports to be a reliable guide but is as blind as they are. Luke also appears to connect the "parable" of the blind leading the blind with the passage on the mote and beam, in which one person with impaired vision vainly offers to help another (Lk. 6.41-42). In its earlier Matthean context, this passage illustrates the warning to "judge not that you be not judged" (Mt. 7.1-5). As we have seen, this warning is elaborated quite differently by Luke, and the mote-and-beam passage is now re-applied to the blind or visually impaired teacher who, if he is to avoid leading his disciple into a ditch, must first recover his own sight (καὶ τότε διαβλέψεις, Lk. 6.42). In both cases, the evangelists suggest an interpretation of the mote-and-beam passage by juxtaposing it with other sayings. Jesus' sayings interpret each other, but they do so on account of juxtapositions and connections created by his first interpreters.

Juxtaposition also provides the key to passages from Matthew 5–7 that Luke omits from his Sermon on the Plain yet *reserves* or sets aside for future use. To these we now turn, retracing so far as possible the compositional procedure that produces the new juxtapositions.

A New Sayings Collection

On the *L/M* hypothesis, Luke selects five main sections of Matthew 5–7 for development in his Sermon on the Plain: four beatitudes, the final antithesis (with additional material from elsewhere), the warning against judging together with the mote-and-beam passage, the section on fruitbearing, and the Parable of the Two Houses. These are respectively drawn from Matthew 5.3-12, 38-48; 7.1-6, 16-20, 24-27; that is, from about a quarter of the available material. At each of these points, and especially the first three, Luke undertakes serious editorial work amounting to a reinterpretation of the sayings material in question — a further moment in a process of reception extending from Jesus through unknown intermediary stages to Matthew, to Luke, and beyond.

In addition to the five passages extracted from Matthew 5–7 for immediate use, Luke sets aside a further thirteen passages for use at a later point. If it be asked *why* he did so, the best answer is the one he himself gives: it seemed good to him to compose his own gospel in his own way, so as to address problems of order bequeathed by his precedessors (cf. Lk. 1.1-4). Beyond that we cannot go.[23] But we can at least show that the compositional procedure entailed in the *L/M* theory is intelligible.[24]

Along with other Matthean material and material unique to Luke, the passages extracted from the Sermon on the Mount provide building blocks for the long central section where Luke parts company with the Markan framework. Luke keeps close to that framework in his account of Jesus' Galilean ministry (Lk. 3.1–9.50 = Mk. 1.1–9.41).[25] Later, he will revert to Mark at the point where Jesus blesses the children (Lk. 18.15-17 = Mk. 10.13-16), and he will avail himself of the Markan framework up to and including the Easter narrative (Lk. 24.1-12 = Mk. 16.1-8). Between the two essentially Markan sections of his gospel, however, Luke has inserted a substantial selection of sayings material set against the background of Jesus' journey to Jerusalem (Lk. 9.51–18.14).

23. We do not need to suppose that "Luke does not like long teaching units," and that for him "Matthew's Sermon is far too long" and "covers far too much disparate ground," including matters "which might be very germane to a Jewish-Christian community, but which Luke could easily think less relevant to his own church" (Goulder, *Luke*, 1.346-47). We may note, however, that Luke's Sermon (6.20-49 [30 verses]) is around 27.5 percent of the length of Matthew's (5.1–7.27 [109 verses]), a figure broadly comparable to his parable discourse in Lk. 8.4-18, 44 percent of the length of Mk. 4.1-34, allowing for (1) Luke's more conservative attitude to Mark, and (2) the brevity of the Markan discourse in relation to the Matthean one. In the case of the Mission Discourse (Lk. 10.1-16; Mt. 9.37–10.42 [44 verses]), the equivalent figure is 36 percent.

24. Compare Mark A. Matson's analysis, "Luke's Rewriting of the Sermon on the Mount," in *Questioning Q*, ed. M. Goodacre and N. Perrin (London: SPCK, 2004; Downers Grove, IL: IVP, 2005), pp. 43-70; pp. 50-61.

25. The major exceptions are the insertion of a largely Matthew-derived section at Lk. 6.20–7.50, and the corresponding omission of an extensive section of Mark (Mk. 6.45–8.26) after Lk. 9.17.

Thirteen passages drawn from Matthew's Sermon on the Mount are incorporated into this non-Markan central section. In terms of compositional procedure, we may imagine the evangelist copying into a notebook the passages he wishes to reserve for future use; the passages are then readily available to him and may be incorporated in any order.[26] The thirteen passages are all relocated to Luke 11–16, and they are as follows:

[ ] (= passage already utilized in Lk. 6)

1 salt	Mt. 5.13	→	Lk. 14.34-35
2 lighting lamp	Mt. 5.15	→	Lk. 11.33
3 not an iota	Mt. 5.17	→	Lk. 16.17
4 adversary	Mt. 5.25-26	→	Lk. 12.58-59
5 divorce	Mt. 5.32	→	Lk. 16.18
[ ]			
6 Lord's Prayer	Mt. 6.9-13	→	Lk. 11.2-4
7 treasure in heaven	Mt. 6.19-21	→	Lk. 12.33-34
8 eye as lamp	Mt. 6.22-23	→	Lk. 11.34-36
9 two masters	Mt. 6.24	→	Lk. 16.13
10 do not be anxious	Mt. 6.25-32	→	Lk. 12.22-31
[ ]			
11 ask, seek	Mt. 7.7-11	→	Lk. 11.9-13
12 narrow gate	Mt. 7.13-14	→	Lk. 13.23-24
[ ]			
13 rejection	Mt. 7.21-23	→	Lk. 13.25-27
[ ]			

The secondary Lukan sequence is quite different from the original Matthean one and might appear to be purely random — confirming the prejudice that, if dependent on Matthew, Luke has reduced his predecessor's orderly structures to chaos. Yet the logic of Luke's editorial work comes to light if we now rearrange the Lukan passages in their own proper sequence:

A1	Lk. 11.2-4	6 Lord's Prayer
A2	Lk. 11.9-13	11 ask, seek

---

26. For the ancient use of notebooks (codices) and wax tablets for preparatory work, see Loveday Alexander, "Ancient Book Production," in *The Gospels for All Christians,* ed. R. Bauckham (Grand Rapids: Eerdmans, 1998), pp. 71-105; pp. 82-84.

B1	Lk. 11.33	*2 lighting lamp*
B2	Lk. 11.34-36	*8 eye as lamp*
C1	Lk. 12.22-31	*10 do not be anxious*
C2	Lk. 12.33-34	*7 treasure in heaven*
D	Lk. 12.57-59	*4 accuser*
E1	Lk. 13.23-24	*12 narrow gate*
E2	Lk. 13.25-27	*13 rejection*
F	Lk. 14.34-35	*1 salt*
G1	Lk. 16.13	*9 two masters*
G2	Lk. 16.17	*3 not an iota*
G3	Lk. 16.18	*5 divorce*

In sequence, Luke's use of his reserved passages ceases to seem so chaotic. The Matthean order has been largely abandoned, but new organizing principles come to light. In four cases *(A B C E)* Luke has arranged the Matthean passages in pairs, the second member of which is inserted more or less directly after the first. In the first three cases *(A B C)*, an entirely new juxtaposition is created, as the dispersal of our original Matthean enumeration indicates *(A1/2* Lk. = *6 11* Mt., and so on). In *A* and *B*, a thematic link between the paired passages is readily apparent even from the outline above, and closer investigation shows that this is also the case with *C, E*, and *G2/3*. Also in *E* and *G2/3*, traces of the original Matthean order are preserved. The notebook hypothesis represents a possible mechanism enabling the evangelist to organize his selected material and create new juxtapositions.[27]

These new juxtapositions profoundly affect the way the Matthean sayings are read and understood. The passages designated *A1/2* may serve as an example.[28]

The Sermon on the Mount includes two passages on prayer. In the first,

27. If Luke has "reserved" or preselected Matthean passages for later inclusion, this greatly simplifies the compositional procedure that must be attributed to him on the *L/M* hypothesis. In contrast, Goulder imagines Luke as finding the Matthean passages he requires during the act of composition, necessitating a complex to-and-fro movement within the Matthean text (*Luke*, 2.498, 553, 557, 558, 572, etc.).

28. Compare the discussion of this passage in Goodacre, *Case against Q*, pp. 110-13.

the Lord's Prayer occurs in the context of a double contrast between the practice of prayer enjoined upon the disciples and that of the "hypocrites" or "Gentiles" (Mt. 6.5-6, 7-15). This passage on prayer is the longest of three linked sections contrasting hypocritical with true piety, the other two being concerned with almsgiving (6.2-4) and fasting (6.16-18). Luke makes less use of this material than of any other passage of equivalent length in the Sermon on the Mount — although the mere fact of omission does not oblige us to invent reasons why he might have disliked it. He does, however, extract the Lord's Prayer from this passage, presenting it in abbreviated and simplified form (Lk. 11.2b-4). For Luke the Matthean Lord's Prayer is evidently no more sacrosanct than the Sermon on the Mount.[29] The new setting for the prayer is Jesus' own practice of prayer, which leads a disciple to request, "Lord, teach us to pray, as John taught his disciples" (Lk. 11.1). The reference to an existing practice of prayer (i.e. that of John's disciples), and to the corresponding need for a new one, may echo the harsher Matthean contrasts. Similarly, Luke's "When you pray, say . . ." may echo Matthew's "Pray then like this" (Lk. 11.2a; Mt. 6.9a). Luke's version of the prayer omits ". . . which art in heaven," ". . . thy will be done on earth as in heaven," and "deliver us from evil." It replaces "today" with "each day," and "debts" with "sins" (while retaining "everyone indebted to us").[30] Luke's version of the Lord's Prayer is not earlier than Matthew's. It is simply shorter. The evangelist may have felt free to abbreviate because he was not familiar with the liturgical use of this prayer. But even regular liturgical use does not necessarily produce fixed and stable forms.

The second passage on prayer from the Sermon on the Mount opens with the exhortation "Ask, and it will be given you. . . ." The supporting argument appeals to the effectiveness of the ordinary human practice of *requesting:* the child who asks for bread or fish will be given what he asks for,

29. While Luke's version of the Lord's Prayer *may* be dependent here on oral tradition, there is no reason to prefer such a solution to a literary one — as J. D. G. Dunn does, complaining that "the curse of the literary paradigm lies heavy on discussion at this point" (*Jesus Remembered* [Grand Rapids: Eerdmans, 2003], p. 227).

30. Several of these differences are attributed to Lukan redaction by Catchpole (*Quest for Q*, p. 29). For Catchpole, it is the address to God as "Father" that identifies the shorter Lukan prayer as earlier than the Matthean one: "There is no reason to suppose that Luke would have shortened Matt 6:9, had he known it, and every reason to suppose that Matthew is responsible for lengthening an earlier short version" (p. 30). This is a remarkably weak argument. In an earlier Lukan prayer Jesus addresses God both as "Father, Lord of heaven and earth" and simply as "Father" (Lk. 10.21). In Gethsemane and on the cross, Jesus addresses God as "Father" (Lk. 22.42; 23.34, 46). The simple vocative address (also found in 15.21) is thoroughly characteristic of Luke's Jesus.

and not some useless or dangerous object (stone or snake) that mocks his request (Mt. 7.7-11). Luke connects this to the Lord's Prayer as a continuation of Jesus' response to the request, "Lord, teach us to pray." Emendations to the wording are limited: "What father among you . . ." for "what man among you . . ."; fish/snake, egg/scorpion for bread/stone, fish/snake; those who ask will receive the "Holy Spirit" rather than "good things" (Lk. 11.9-13).

Between the two Matthean passages and linking them, Luke has inserted his "parable of the friend at midnight" (11.5-8). This may derive from some independent source, but it is more likely to be Luke's own composition, inspired by the Matthean saying about the child's request. Both passages open with an extended question, introduced by "Which of you . . . ?" (τίς ἐξ ὑμῶν [11.5]; τίνα δὲ ἐξ ὑμῶν τὸν πατέρα, [11.11]). The child requesting a fish or egg is replaced by a friend who calls inconveniently late to request "three loaves" for an unexpected visitor (11.5-6). That is no doubt why Luke replaces Matthew's "bread or fish" with "fish or egg" in the subsequent passage. Unlike the father, the householder in the parable has some reason to be reluctant: the door is locked, the children are asleep (11.7). Even so, he will accede to the request if his friend persists (11.8). The point is not to compare God to the reluctant householder but to inculcate persistence in prayer and to introduce a note of realism that qualifies the apparently limitless scope of "ask and it will be given you . . ." (11.9). The logic of Luke's parable of the friend at midnight is similar to that of his later parable of the unjust judge (18.2-7). The lesson of the earlier parable, like the later, is that disciples "ought always to pray and not lose heart" (18.1).

Luke's teaching on prayer (11.1-13) again illustrates the generative, dynamic nature of the sayings tradition. The cautionary parable of the friend at midnight is inspired by the Matthean image of the child's request, yet is intended to redress its perceived one-sidedness. Prayer is as simple as a child asking a parent to meet its needs; yet it also calls for persistence and patience, a refusal to be discouraged even if the door which was supposed to be opened remains firmly locked (11.7, 9c). In Luke's dialectical presentation, traditional material derived from the Sermon on the Mount is not simply rearranged and rephrased but creatively refashioned, so as to articulate Jesus' teaching on prayer as clearly as possible and to promote the corresponding practice.

As this analysis indicates, it is mistaken to assume that a Luke dependent on Matthew would simply have reduced the great Matthean Sermon to rubble. No single evangelist has a monopoly on the sayings tradition, since this tradition calls for an interpretative practice in which freedom and faithfulness, conservation and creativity, are more like synonyms than opposites.

Luke's Matthean Sequence

It is now possible to address more directly the "argument from order" which, for Q theorists, makes the *L/M* hypothesis so implausible. This argument is repeated again and again, normally without reconsideration of the evidence. It was given classic formulation by B. H. Streeter in a well-known passage, to which enumeration has been added by myself:

> *(1)* [S]ubsequent to the Temptation story, there is not a single case in which Matthew and Luke agree in inserting the same saying at the same point in the Marcan outline. *(2)* If then Luke derived this material from Matthew, he must have gone through both Matthew and Mark so as to discriminate with meticulous precision between Marcan and non-Marcan material; *(3)* he must then have proceeded with the utmost care to tear every little piece of non-Marcan material he desired to use from the context of Mark in which it appeared in Matthew — *(4)* in spite of the fact that contexts in Matthew are always exceedingly appropriate — *(5)* in order to re-insert it into a different context of Mark having no special appropriateness. *(6)* A theory which would make an author capable of such a proceeding would only be tenable if, on other grounds, we had reason to believe he was a crank.[31]

These six points call for further comment:

(1) It is said that the later evangelists do not "agree in inserting the same [non-Markan] saying at the same point in the Marcan outline." While it is true that Luke places blocks of sayings at different Mark-derived locations from Matthew's, that does not mean that Luke is independent of Matthew. As we have seen in the previous chapter, the same Markan passage (Mk. 3.7-19) provides the contexts for both Matthew's Sermon on the Mount and Luke's Sermon on the Plain. Luke derives the link from Matthew but restores it to the appropriate setting within the Markan outline. We know from Luke's prologue that he is concerned to correct his predecessors' account of the sequence of events, and that is just what he does here. Matthew's order is corrected, Mark's is restored. This prioritizing of the original Markan sequence over the Matthean rendering of it accounts for the absence from Luke of some (by no means all) of the Matthean accretions.[32]

31. B. H. Streeter, *The Four Gospels* (New York: Macmillan, 1925), p. 183.
32. According to J. S. Kloppenborg, an explanation is required of Luke's omission of

(2) Luke would have to "discriminate with meticulous precision between Marcan and non-Marcan material." In his prologue, Luke indicates that he is concerned with questions of sequence, and claims to have investigated his subject matter carefully. There is no reason to doubt his ability to discriminate between Markan and Matthean material. It does not take "meticulous precision" to follow Mark in the first instance but to note the supplementary Matthean material and to find ways to reincorporate much of it at a later point relative to Mark.

(3) A Luke dependent on Matthew would have to "tear every little piece of non-Marcan material he desired to use from the context of Mark in which it appeared in Matthew." While Luke does prioritize the Markan sequence, he also preserves major elements of Matthean sequence. Some Matthean sayings are extracted from their original Matthean contexts (without any recourse to violence), and set aside for use at a later point; other material is left intact. As we shall see, Luke leaves in place not only the framework of the Matthean Sermon but also the sequence of non-Markan material included in Matthew 8–12. His gospel is built on a framework that is partly Mark's, partly Matthew's, and partly his own.

(4) Luke finds new contexts for Matthean material even though "contexts in Matthew are always exceedingly appropriate." This is a version of the spurious argument that Luke *ought* to have reproduced the Sermon on the Mount in more or less its Matthean form, and that he *would have* done so as a matter of course if he had been familiar with it.[33] This argument rests on an anachronistic evaluation of a piece of text not yet dig-

---

"Matthean additions to Markan pericopae in Mt. 3.15; 12.5-7; 13.14-17; 14.28-31; 16.16-19; 19.9, 19b; 27.19, 24" ("On Dispensing with Q?" p. 219). This is an ill-assorted collection of passages. Luke's omission of Mt. 3.15 is offset by his inclusion and supplementation of 3.7-12. His omission of Mt. 12.5-7 (priests and Sabbath) contrasts with his use of Matthean additions in 12.11 (Sabbath emergency) and 12.22-32 (Beelzebul controversy). While Luke passes over Mt. 13.14-17 (the extended quotation from Is. 6), he does extract other items from Matthew's expanded parable chapter so as to incorporate them elsewhere (Mt. 13.16-17 = Lk. 10.23-24; Mt. 13.31-33 = Lk. 13.18-21). Mt. 14.28-31 (Peter walks on water) and 16.16-19 (blessing of Peter) cannot easily be detached from their contexts, and are omitted in consequence of Luke's prioritizing the Markan sequence. Like Streeter before him, Kloppenborg seems to assume that an evangelist will incorporate *all* available source material unless there are specifiable reasons for omitting it. But supporters of the *L/M* theory are no more obliged to explain every Lukan omission of Matthean material than Kloppenborg himself is obliged (as a believer in Markan priority) to explain Luke's objections to the items he omits from Mk. 6.44–8.26. Luke's "it seemed good to me . . ." should be good enough for us too.

33. The same assumption underlies Kloppenborg's criticisms of Goodacre on this point ("On Dispensing with Q?" pp. 227-30).

nified with the title "Sermon on the Mount" or elevated to canonical status as such.

(5) Having rudely "torn" a Matthean passage out of its "exceedingly appropriate" context, Luke would have reinstated it "in a different context of Mark having no special appropriateness." In contrast to the exaggerated reverence for Matthew, sympathetic consideration of the Lukan presentation of the sayings is singularly lacking. Once again, the suggestion of an exclusively Markan framework is inaccurate and misleading. Luke not only takes Matthean material into a new framework of his own, he also avails himself of a non-Markan Matthean framework — that is, a sequence of purely Matthean material extracted from the Markan contexts in which it occurs in Matthew.

(6) "A theory which would make an author capable of such a proceeding" merely projects the irrationality or incompetence of the theorist onto the unfortunate evangelist. But if Luke *(a)* follows Matthew's precedent in undertaking *his own* editorial work on Mark, restoring its original sequence, and *(b)* separates out supplementary Matthean material into self-contained blocks, within which vestiges of Matthean sequence may or may not be retained, his compositional procedure is coherent and intelligible. It is also flexible enough to allow for exceptions.

It is to Luke's retention of Matthean order that we now turn. In Luke's Sermon on the Plain, the Matthean sequence is preserved in the five passages that remain from Matthew's Sermon on the Mount: selected beatitudes, the final antithesis, the warning against judging together with the mote-and-beam passage, the image of trees and their fruits, the Parable of the Two Houses. The beginning and end of Matthew's Sermon remain intact, and the three intervening items retain their original sequence. Minor dislocations of sequence do occur, however. Material from the fifth antithesis (nonresistance) is inserted into Luke's version of the sixth (love of enemies). The sayings on the blind leading the blind and on disciples and teachers are inserted between the (expanded) warning against judging and the mote-and-beam passage, significantly altering the meaning of the latter.

These dislocations are not such as to eradicate the basic Matthean sequence. They are of a different order to the modifications that occur when Luke finally presents his thirteen extracts from the Sermon on the Mount in new combinations of his own. In the one case, the underlying Matthean sequence is still clearly visible; in the other, it has disappeared. Luke seems to value his extracted passages no less highly than those he leaves in place. The new context assigned to the Lord's Prayer indicates that it is at least as significant for Luke as the beatitudes, which retain their old context. In his use of the Sermon on the Mount, it seems that Luke is concerned *both* to maintain the Matthean sequence *and* to use Matthean material extracted from that sequence to create a new sequence of his own. As he works through Matthew 5–7, he assigns one of two roles to items he decides to retain. Matthean material may serve either Luke's own rendering of the Matthean sequence (the L/M sequence = L/M*seq*) or his use of Matthean material extracted from its original contexts and reserved for use in contexts created by himself (his L sequence = L*seq*). This distinction can be applied more widely to Luke's use of Matthew as a whole.

The Sermon on the Plain is located in a Markan context. It is the Markan sequence that underlies Luke's entire account of Jesus' Galilean ministry (Lk. 3.1–9.50), in spite of the mainly Matthean insertion in 6.20–7.50. If an L/M sequence is to be uncovered, its subordination to the L/Mk sequence will have to be taken into account. The L/M sequence will also be affected by material that Luke extracts from it for later use within his L sequence, continuing the practice he began when working on the Sermon on the Mount. We may expect there to be omissions and dislocations. Yet, if Luke persists with the compositional procedure employed in the Sermon on the Plain, it will be possible to assign all items derived from Matthew to a place either in the L/M or the L sequences.

If Luke is to avail himself of the supplementary Matthean material, he must first differentiate it from the Matthean redaction of Mark *(M/Mk)*, which — given his prioritizing of Markan sequence — will be of less interest to him. As we saw in the previous chapter, two Markan sequences run in parallel through Matthew 3–13, as the primary sequence (Matthew's rendering of Mark 1.1–4.34 = M/Mk*1*) is interrupted at Matthew 8.23 by a secondary one (Matthew's rendering of Mark 4.35–6.6 = M/Mk*2*). Non-Markan material is also interspersed throughout Matthew 3–13, and our main concern here is to retrace Luke's engagement with this.

Following the close of his Sermon on the Mount, Matthew reverts to Mark for his story of the healing of a leper (Mt. 8.1-4 = Mk. 1.40-45). This is followed by the non-Markan story of the centurion's child or servant (Mt. 8.5-13), and by the healing of Peter's mother-in-law, which temporarily breaks the M/Mk*1* sequence (Mt. 8.14-17 = Mk. 1.29-31). The two Markan stories have simply been transposed. Like the centurion's servant, Peter's mother-in-law is healed in Capernaum (cf. Mt. 8.5), and the leper is evidently healed as Jesus makes his way there from the mountain. Following the two Capernaum healings, Jesus responds to each of two would-be disciples in a second non-Markan passage (Mt. 8.18-22). Thereafter, the evangelist inaugurates his M/Mk^2 sequence with accounts of the stilling of the storm and the Gerasene demoniac(s) (Mt. 8.23-34 = Mk. 4.35–5.20). The M/Mk^1 sequence is resumed in Matthew 9.1-17, which reproduces the first three controversy stories from the five collected in Mark 2.1–3.6 (the paralytic; the call of Levi/Matthew + eating with sinners; fasting). Next, the M/Mk^2 sequence is resumed with the dual acount of the raising of the ruler's daughter and the healing of the haemorrhaging woman (Mt. 9.18-26 = Mk. 5.21-43). After two further stories which seem to represent alternative versions of Markan material that Matthew also reproduces elsewhere (Mt. 9.27-35), we arrive at the mainly non-Markan Mission Discourse (Mt. 9.35–10.42) and material relating to John the Baptist (11.1-19), woes against Chorazin and Bethsaida (11.20-24), and Jesus' thanksgiving and invitation (11.25-30). The M/Mk^1 sequence resumes with Sabbath controversy stories (Mt. 12.1-8, 9-14 = Mk. 2.23-28; 3.1-6) and the Beelzebul controversy (Mt. 12.22-32 = Mk. 3.22-30). Between the M/Mk version of this last story and the next resumption of the M/Mk^1 sequence at Matthew 12.46-50 = Mark 3.31-35 (Jesus' true family), the evangelist has inserted non-Markan passages relating to fruit bearing (Mt. 12.33-37), the sign of Jonah (12.38-42), and the return of the unclean spirit (12.43-45).

The fruit-bearing passage is a doublet of Matthew 7.16-20, and its wording may already have affected the parallel in Luke 6.43-45. Leaving this passage aside, there are nine non-Markan items in Matthew 5–12 with which Luke might engage. If he does so, retaining approximately their original sequence, then an M sequence will have been subsumed into an L/M sequence. Setting aside the Markan framework, the M sequence is as follows:

i.	Inaugural sermon	Mt. 5.1–7.29
ii.	Centurion's servant	Mt. 8.5-13
iii.	Discipleship sayings	Mt. 8.18-22
iv.	Mission Discourse	Mt. 9.35–10.42
v.	Jesus and John the Baptist	Mt. 11.1-19
vi.	Woes against towns	Mt. 11.20-24
vii.	Jesus' thanksgiving	Mt. 11.25-27
viii.	Sign of Jonah	Mt. 12.38-42
ix.	Return of unclean spirit	Mt. 12.43-45

Items iv-vii occur consecutively in Matthew, while ii-iii and viii-ix occur within contexts determined by the M/Mk^1 sequence (= Mk. 1.40–4.34).

As Luke embarks on his version of the inaugural sermon, he has already incorporated most of the Markan material interspersed within these Matthean passages into his own preceding *L/Mk* sequence.[34] Since the close of the temptation narrative, he has been following Mark and has barely needed to consult Matthew. Now, however, he begins to incorporate the supplementary Matthean material he has identified within the Markan material he has been editing. In addition to the nine listed items, he takes over from *M/Mk¹* two episodes he finds in Matthew 12: *Beelzebul controversy* and *Jesus' true family* (Mt. 12.22-32, 46-50 = Lk. 11.14-23, 27-28). Thus Luke creates *L/M/Mk* versions of these episodes, which in the case of Jesus' true family complements an existing *L/Mk* version. Adding these two *M/Mk* items to the nine *M* ones, Luke has a total of eleven items at his disposal.

In Luke 6–11, the *L/M* sequence includes all eleven items with two small-scale transpositions. In the following analysis, * indicates a deviation from the *M* order; { } *L/M/Mk*; [ ] *M* material extracted from the Sermon on the Mount:

i.	*Inaugural sermon*	Lk. 6.17-49	=	Mt. 5.1–7.29
ii.	*Centurion's servant*	Lk. 7.1-10	=	Mt. 8.5-13
iii.	**Jesus and John the Baptist*	Lk. 7.18-35	=	Mt. 11.1-19
iv.	*Discipleship sayings*	Lk. 9.57-62	=	Mt. 8.18-22
v.	*Mission Discourse*	Lk. 10.1-12, 16	=	Mt. 9.35–10.42
vi.	*Woes against towns*	Lk. 10.13-15	=	Mt. 11.20-24
vii.	*Jesus' thanksgiving*	Lk. 10.21-22	=	Mt. 11.25-27
	[*Lord's Prayer, Ask, seek*]			
viii.	{*Beelzebul controversy*}	Lk. 11.14-23	=	Mt. 12.22-32/Mk. 3.22-30
ix.	*Return of unclean spirit*	Lk. 11.24-26	=	Mt. 12.43-45
x.	{*Jesus' true family*}	Lk. 11.27-28	cf.	Mt. 12.46-50/Mk. 3.31-35
xi.	**Sign of Jonah*	Lk. 11.29-32	=	Mt. 12.38-42

In *iii*, material on Jesus and John the Baptist is brought forward into the block of *L/M* material in Luke 6.20–7.35. In *xi*, the sign of Jonah material is

34. *Peter's mother-in-law* (Lk. 4.38-39 = Mk. 1.29-31 = Mt. 8.14-17); *healing of leper* (Lk. 5.12-16 = Mk. 1.40-45 = Mt. 8.1-4); *paralytic* (Lk. 5.17-26 = Mk. 2.1-12 = Mt. 9.1-8); *call of Levi, eating with sinners* (Lk. 5.27-32 = Mk. 2.13-17 = Mt. 9.9-13); *fasting* (Lk. 5.33-39 = Mk. 2.18-22 = Mt. 9.14-17); *plucking on Sabbath* (Lk. 6.1-5 = Mk. 2.23-28 = Mt. 12.1-8); *Sabbath healing* (Lk. 6.6-11 = Mk. 3.1-6 = Mt. 12.9-14). *M/Mk²* material in Mt. 8–9 *(stilling of storm; Gerasene demoniac[s]; ruler's daughter/haemorrhaging woman)* is incorporated into the continuation of the *L/Mk* sequence in Lk. 8.1–9.50.

deferred to enable Luke to connect the passage on the return of the unclean spirit to the *L/M/Mk* account of the Beelzebul controversy. With
these exceptions, the *M* sequence identified in Matthew 5–12 remains essentially intact in *L/M* form. Luke allows the *Mk* sequence a dominant role
in the construction of his narrative, but the *M* sequence remains highly
significant, half-concealed though it is by the presence of *M/Mk*, *L/Mk*,
and *L* material.

Three of these *M* passages provide Luke with a total of seven further
items for his collection of reserved passages, set aside for later use together
with items *1-13* from the Sermon on the Mount, as listed above (p. 170):

14. *east and west*	Mt. 8.11-12	→	Lk. 13.28-30
15. *men of violence*	Mt. 11.12-13	→	Lk. 16.16[35]
16. *testimony of Spirit*	Mt. 10.19-20	→	Lk. 12.11-12
17. *nothing hidden*	Mt. 10.26-33	→	Lk. 12.2-9
18. *division*	Mt. 10.34-35	→	Lk. 12.51-53
19. *discipleship*	Mt. 10.37-38	→	Lk. 14.26-27
20. *finding, losing*	Mt. 10.39	→	Lk. 17.33

With the exception of *14 east and west* and *15 men of violence*, Luke's reserved
passages have so far been drawn entirely from the Matthean sayings collections (Mt. 5–7; 10).

The compositional procedure for the *L/M* version of the Mission Discourse is essentially the same as for the Sermon on the Mount. In both cases,
some material is omitted altogether ([ ] below), while other items are reserved for future use (< >). In both cases, the Matthean sequence is preserved
in outline (**bold**), although it is supplemented by *M* material from the immediate context (*) or by *L* additions (¶).

¶Lk. 10.1 *mission of Seventy*
Lk. 10.2 *harvest, labourers* = **Mt. 9.37-38**
*Lk. 10.3 *lambs among wolves* = Mt. 10.16a
[ ]
Lk. 10.4 *no purse or bag* = **Mt. 10.9-10**
Lk. 10.5-6 *peace to this house* = **Mt. 10.12-13**
¶Lk. 10.7-8 *eat what is set before you*

---

35. This passage is excerpted from Mt. 11.2-19, brought forward to Lk. 7.18-35. If the hypothesis of Luke's Matthean sayings collection is correct, it would have formed item no. 15.

*Lk. 10.9 heal, preach	= Mt. 10.8, 7
Lk. 10.10-12 rejection	= **Mt. 10.14-15**
<16 testimony of Spirit Mt. 10.19-20>	
<17 nothing hidden Mt. 10.26-33>	
<18 division Mt. 10.34-35>	
<19 discipleship Mt. 10.37-38>	
<20 finding, losing Mt. 10.39>	
*Lk. 10.13-15 woes against towns	= Mt. 11.21-23
Lk. 10.16 hearing you	= **Mt. 10.40**
[ ]	
¶Lk. 10.17-20 return of Seventy	

As in the case of the Sermon on the Plain, the *L/M* theory yields an intelligible and plausible account of Luke's compositional process. Material derived from Matthew is either accommodated within the framework of its Matthean sequence or reserved for incorporation into a new context. Indeed, all *L/M* material falls into one or other of these categories. The first may be designated L/M^{seq}, referring to material Luke draws from Matthew but accommodates within his own version of Matthew's sequence. The second may be designated L/M^{res}, referring to material Luke extracts from its Matthean context and reserves for incorporation elsewhere.

A Matthean framework is perceptible, alongside the more obvious Markan one, throughout Luke 3.1–11.32. Once Luke's compositional procedure has been understood, with the L/M^{seq} and L/M^{res} categories differentiated, the *L/M* order corresponds closely to the *M* one. That is the case even when *L/M* takes over elements from *M/Mk* (see Figure 4.1).

The consistency with which Luke follows the Matthean order is remarkable. Of course, the common order might be traced back to Q rather than to Luke's use of Matthew. An explanation along these lines remains possible. But there is no need for it, and it generates unnecessary complications.

One such complication relates to the Beelzebul story. This originally Markan story (Mk. 3.22-30) occurs at the appropriate point in M/Mk^1 (Mt. 12.22-32), but with significant additions:

(i) The healing of a blind and dumb demoniac as the context of the accusation (Mt. 12.22-23).

(ii) "If I cast out demons by Beelzebul, by whom do your sons cast them out? Therefore they shall be your judges. But if it is by the Spirit of God

Figure 4.1

M/Mk	M	L/M^{seq}
Mt. 3.1-6 = Mk. 1.1-6		
	Mt. 3.7-10 *Sermon on judgment*	→ Lk. 3.7-9
	Mt. 3.11-12 *{Double baptism}*	→ Lk. 3.15-17
Mt. 3.13-17 = Mk. 1.9-11		
	Mt. 4.1-11 *{Temptation narrative}*	→ Lk. 4.1-13
	Mt. 4.12-16 *(Nazareth/Capernaum)*	→ Lk. 4.16-30
Mt. 4.17-25 = Mk. 1.14-20, 3.7-8, 13	Mt. 5.1-7.29 *Sermon on the Mount* < *1-13* >	→ Lk. 6.20-49
Mt. 8.1-4 = Mk. 1.40-45		
	Mt. 8.5-13 *Centurion's servant* < *14* >	→ Lk. 7.1-10
Mt. 8.14-17 = Mk. 1.29-31		
	Mt. 8.18-22 *Discipleship*	→ Lk. 9.57-62+
Mt. 8.23-9.34 = Mk. 2.1-5.43, 3.14-19	Mt. 9.35-10.42 *Mission Discourse* < *16-19* >	→ Lk. 10.1-20
	Mt. 11.1-19 *John and Jesus* < *15* >	↑ Lk. 7.18-35
	Mt. 11.20-24 *Woes against towns*	→ Lk. 10.13-15
	Mt. 11.25-30 *Thanksgiving*	→ Lk. 10.21-22
Mt. 12.1-14 = Mk. 2.23-3.6		
	Mt. 12.22-32 *{Beelzebul}* < *20* >	→ Lk. 11.14-23
	Mt. 12.38-42 *Sign of Jonah*	↓ Lk. 11.29-32
	Mt. 12.43-45 *Return of unclean spirit*	→ Lk. 11.24-26
	Mt. 12.46-50 *{Jesus' family}*	→ Lk. 11.27-28

{ } includes Markan material
< > reserved material (*L/M^{res}*)
→ M order retained in *L/M*
↑ M passage located earlier in *L/M*
↓ M passage located later in *L/M*

that I cast out demons, then the kingdom of God has come upon you!" (Mt. 12.27-28).

(iii) "The one who is not with me is against me, and the one who does not gather with me scatters" (Mt. 12.30).

(iv) "Whoever says a word against the Son of man will be forgiven; but whoever speaks against the Holy Spirit will not be forgiven, either in this age or in the age to come" (Mt. 12.32).

The fourth of these additional items is a variant of the similar Markan saying (". . . all sins will be forgiven the sons of men . . ." [Mk. 3.28-29]), a version of which Matthew also includes here (Mt. 12.31). The third also has a Markan connection (cf. Mk. 9.40)

Luke's account of the Beelzebul controversy occurs in *L/M^seq* (or *L/Q*) and not in *L/Mk*. In consequence, he includes three of the additional passages (the fourth being reserved for use elsewhere), and gives other indications of familiarity with the Matthean version or its Q precursor. On the Q theory, this is a point where Mark and Q overlap; as ever in such cases, Matthew and Luke independently draw from both Mark and Q in surprisingly similar ways.[36] The overlap must consist in more than the individual story, however. On the Q theory, it must mark the point of intersection between two distinct narrative sequences. Matthew has incorporated the Beelzebul story at the right point in his primary Markan sequence *(M/Mk¹)*; and yet, as we learn from Luke, he has simultaneously incorporated it at the right point in the Q sequence (i.e. the *L/M* sequence as reconstructed above). Somehow and for some reason, Matthew contrives to be faithful both to Markan and Q sequence at one and the same time. Matthew's redaction of his Markan and Q sequences up to this point must have been determined by this intended conjunction. That is why, in contrast to Luke, almost all Q material has been incorporated by the time Matthew reaches the end of Mark 3.

The editorial procedure that designed such a structure, and then partially concealed it, would certainly be ingenious. But it would serve no obvious purpose. Why would Matthew have allowed a specific overlap between Mark and Q to determine the construction of the entire first half of his gos-

---

36. On this view, the most important question is whether this "doublet" is derived independently from oral tradition or whether Mark drew it from Q (so H. T. Fleddermann, "Mark's Use of Q: The Beelzebul Controversy and the Cross Saying," in *Jesus, Mark, and Q: The Teaching of Jesus and Its Earliest Records*, ed. Michael Labahn and Andreas Schmidt, JSNTSupp [Sheffield: Sheffield Academic Press, 2001], pp. 17-33; pp. 17-27). Fleddermann fails to note that this "doublet" is not actually visible as such in Matthew but is the product of the Q theory itself.

pel? As has been remarked in another connection: "A theory which would make an author capable of such a proceeding would only be tenable if, on other grounds, we had reason to believe he was a crank."[37] In contrast, the alternative explanation of the three forms of the Beelzebul controversy is characterized by simplicity and plausibility: $Mk \rightarrow M/Mk \rightarrow L/M/Mk$. In its Lukan form, the story belongs to L/M^{seq}, an important component in the orderly, reordered gospel Luke promised his readers at the outset.

Luke, then, is clearly engaged with M/Mk in his version of the Beelzebub controversy. This is no "minor agreement" that could be explained away as coincidental or the product of scribal assimilation. This engagement with M/Mk is confirmed by Luke's free rewriting of the passage on Jesus' true family, item xi in the L/M sequence (Lk. 11.27-28; cf. Mt. 12.46-50/Mk. 3.31-35), and by two further reserved passages extracted from Matthean additions to Markan controversy stories:

21.	*Sabbath emergency*	Mt. 12.11	$\rightarrow$	Lk. 14.5
22.	*blasphemy*	Mt. 12.31-32	$\rightarrow$	Lk. 12.10

In spite of inevitable complexities, the L/M hypothesis can offer a clear and compelling account of Luke's editorial procedure. Luke (1) prioritizes the Markan order, which he normally reproduces without reference to Matthew; (2) retains the order of much of the extensive supplementary material within the equivalent M/Mk sequence, which is reincorporated at a later point relative to Mark than in Matthew; (3) reserves other supplementary items from Matthew for use in his own L sequence.[38]

---

37. Streeter, *Four Gospels*, p. 183.

38. At this point it is worth noting the implications of this analysis for the Griesbach hypothesis. In the modern version of the theory, it is accepted that Luke is dependent on Matthew (see Allan J. McNicol with David L. Dungan and David B. Peabody [eds.], *Beyond the Q Impasse — Luke's Use of Matthew: A Demonstration by the Research Team of the International Institute for Gospel Studies* [Valley Forge, PA: Trinity Press International, 1996]). If so, then the conventional differentiation of Markan and Q material in Matthew must be abandoned: it is in fact Luke who creates a distinction between mainly narrative material *(Matthew A)* and mainly sayings material *(Matthew B)*, some of which is kept in its original sequence (but relocated in relation to the A-sequence), and some of which is more radically reordered. Mark would then simply eliminate the B-sequence, having first identified it as such by painstaking comparison of Luke with Matthew. He would also eliminate much of the material found only in Matthew or Luke. Sayings material within the A-sequence would be retained, however. Thus Mark's alternation between Matthean and Lukan order combines with a disregard for Matthean sayings material displaced from its Matthean order by Luke: only sayings material common to Matthew and Luke *and* retained by

From Sayings Collection to Text

We return now to Luke's collection of Matthean sayings, extracted from their Matthean framework and reserved for later use in contexts constructed by Luke himself. Q theorists insist that such a procedure is inconceivable. The Q theory relies on that inconceivability. In the spirit of the Lukan Jesus, Austin Farrer addresses the issue by way of a parable:

> We are not bound to show that what St. Luke did to St. Matthew turned out to be a literary improvement on St. Matthew. All we have to show is that St. Luke's plan was capable of attracting St. Luke. You do not like what I have done to the garden my predecessor left me. You are welcome to your opinion, but I did what I did because I thought I should prefer the new arrangement. And if you want to enjoy whatever special merit my gardening has, you must forget my predecessor's ideas and try to appreciate mine.[39]

Apt though this otherwise is, we should *not* forget Matthew's arrangement as we try to appreciate Luke's. The special merit of the new arrangement only becomes clear when we see how it relates to the old one.

The task, then, is to complete the inventory of Luke's Matthean sayings collection and to account for the relocation of most of its individual components to contexts within Luke 11.33–18.14, the section where Luke has no Markan or Matthean framework to follow and has sole responsibility for organizing his material. Almost all L/M^{res} items are incorporated into this section, together with items unique to Luke.

Luke draws from Matthew 5–12 a total of twenty-two L/M^{res} sayings (or more extended passages). Since these items need to be differentiated from L ones (items distinctive to Luke), the Matthean derivation will from now on be indicated by adding M to the enumeration:

| M1 | salt | Mt. 5.13 | → | Lk. 14.34-35 |
| M2 | *lighting lamp* | Mt. 5.15 | → | Lk. 11.33 |

Luke in approximately its Matthean sequence is included in Mark. If these complex and apparently pointless redactional procedures are judged implausible, the Griesbach hypothesis will have been refuted. The possibility of refutation is indeed entailed in W. R. Farmer's claim that "the 'Two-Gospel Hypothesis' is scientifically testable" ("The Two-Gospel Hypothesis: The Statement of the Hypothesis," in *The Interrelations of the Gospels*, ed. David L. Dungan [Leuven: Leuven University Press, 1990], pp. 125-56; p. 144).

39. A. M. Farrer, "On Dispensing with Q," in *Studies in the Gospels: Essays in Memory of R. H. Lightfoot*, ed. D. E. Nineham (Oxford: Blackwell, 1955), pp. 55-88; p. 65.

M3	not an iota	Mt. 5.18 →	Lk. 16.17
M4	accuser	Mt. 5.25-26 →	Lk. 12.57-59
M5	divorce	Mt. 5.32 →	Lk. 16.18
M6	Lord's prayer	Mt. 6.9-13 →	Lk. 11.2-4
M7	treasure in heaven	Mt. 6.19-21 →	Lk. 12.33-34
M8	eye as lamp	Mt. 6.22-23 →	Lk. 11.34-36
M9	two masters	Mt. 6.24 →	Lk. 16.13
M10	do not be anxious	Mt. 6.25-33 →	Lk. 12.22-32
M11	ask, seek	Mt. 7.7-12 →	Lk. 11.9-13
M12	narrow gate	Mt. 7.13-14 →	Lk. 13.23-24
M13	depart	Mt. 7.22-23 →	Lk. 13.26-27
M14	east and west	Mt. 8.11-12 →	Lk. 13.28-30
M15	men of violence	Mt. 11.12-13 →	Lk. 16.16
M16	testimony of Spirit	Mt. 10.19-20 →	Lk. 12.11-12
M17	nothing hidden	Mt. 10.26-33 →	Lk. 12.2-9
M18	division	Mt. 10.34-35 →	Lk. 12.51-53
M19	discipleship	Mt. 10.37-38 →	Lk. 14.26-27
M20	finding, losing	Mt. 10.39 →	Lk. 17.33
M21	Sabbath emergency	Mt. 12.11 →	Lk. 14.5
M22	blasphemy	Mt. 12.31-32 →	Lk. 12.10

With the exception of the passages on prayer *(M6+M11)*, these passages are all relocated within the Lukan framework section (Lk. 11.33–18.14), that is, the major part of the "journey narrative" that begins so impressively with the announcement of the journey to Jerusalem in Luke 9.51-53. These passages therefore occur in a context later than their original Matthean one. There are very few examples of Matthean sayings extracted from their original Matthean sequence and brought forward to an earlier point in the Lukan sequence.[40]

After completing his work on M^{seq} with his free rendering of Matthew 12.46-50 *{Jesus' true family}*, Luke is in a position to engage fully with his M^{res} material. Matthew 13–18 presents Markan narrative material that Luke has already incorporated.[41] Luke shows little further interest in *M/Mk*, but what he does find in the later chapters of Matthew is individual non-Markan sayings (or more extended passages), embedded in Markan contexts from which they can easily be extracted.[42]

---

40. But note Mt. 15.14 + 10.24-25 = Lk. 6.39, 40; Mt. 12.34-35 = Lk. 6.45.

41. Mt. 13.1–19.12 = Mk. 4.1–10.12 = Lk. 8.4–9.50, with omissions and variations.

42. This compositional procedure — giving priority to the Markan narrative but incorporat-

Luke's engagement with this material produces a further selection of reserved items to add to the ones listed above. With these, Luke's Matthean sayings collection is complete:

M23	*blessed the eyes*	Mt. 13.16-17	→	Lk. 10.23-24
M24	*mustard seed, leaven*	Mt. 13.31-33	→	Lk. 13.18-21
M25	*signs of the times*	Mt. 16.2-3	→	Lk. 12.54-56
M26	*leaven of Pharisees*	Mt. 16.6	→	Lk. 12.1
M27	*little faith*	Mt. 17.19-20	→	Lk. 17.5-6
M28	*millstone*	Mt. 18.6	→	Lk. 17.2
M29	*temptations to sin*	Mt. 18.7	→	Lk. 17.1
M30	*lost sheep*	Mt. 18.12-14	→	Lk. 15.3-7
M31	*brother who sins*	Mt. 18.15	→	Lk. 17.3
M32	*forgive repeatedly*	Mt. 18.21-22	→	Lk. 17.4
M33	*twelve thrones*	Mt. 19.28	→	Lk. 22.29
M34	*last first*	Mt. 20.16	→	Lk. 13.30
M35	*two sons*	Mt. 21.28-32	→	Lk. 15.11-32
M36	*great feast*	Mt. 22.1-10	→	Lk. 14.16-24
M37	*exalt/humble*	Mt. 23.12	→	Lk. 14.11; 18.14
M38	*woe to Pharisees*	Mt. 23.23-36	→	Lk. 11.39-52
M39	*Jerusalem*	Mt. 23.37-39	→	Lk. 13.34-35
M40	*no return*	Mt. 24.17-18	→	Lk. 17.31
M41	*kingdom in midst*	Mt. 24.23-25	→	Lk. 17.20-21
M42	*lightning*	Mt. 24.26-27	→	Lk. 17.23-24
M43	*body, eagles*	Mt. 24.28	→	Lk. 17.37
M44	*days of Noah*	Mt. 24.37-39	→	Lk. 17.26-27
M45	*one taken*	Mt. 24.40-41	→	Lk. 17.34-35
M46	*thief/servant*	Mt. 24.43-51	→	Lk. 12.35-48
M47	*exclusion*	Mt. 25.1-13	→	Lk. 13.25
M48	*talents/pounds*	Mt. 25.14-30	→	Lk. 19.11-27

Of these *L/M^res* items, three are incorporated within *L/M^seq*: *M23 blessed the eyes*, *M6 Lord's prayer*, and *M11 ask, seek*. Two are incorporated within *L/Mk*: *M33 twelve thrones* and *M48 talents/pounds*. Otherwise, this material is all lo-

---

ing supplementary Matthean material in non-Markan contexts — explains the lack of a Lukan parallel to Mt. 16.17-19, which is too closely bound to its Markan context for reuse elsewhere. There is no need to speculate (with Farrer and Goulder) about "Luke-pleasing" elements in Matthew and to argue that the blessing of Peter "is exactly the kind of Matthean addition to Mark that we would expect Luke to omit" (Goodacre, *Case against Q*, p. 51).

cated within L^{seq} (Lk. 11.33–18.14), and it is with this that we are now concerned.

With Luke's Matthean sayings collection complete, we turn now to the material unique to Luke. Some of this material has already been incorporated within L/M:

L1	*fire from heaven*	Lk. 9.52-56
L2	*return of Seventy*	Lk. 10.17-20
L3	*Good Samaritan*	Lk. 10.25-37
L4	*Martha and Mary*	Lk. 10.38-42
L5	*friend at midnight*	Lk. 11.5-8

The majority of the distinctive L items are incorporated within Luke 11.33–18.14, however, along with the majority of L/M^{res} items. Together, these two categories of material constitute the inventory necessary to account for this section of Luke in its entirety. (Luke's editorial introductions and conclusions to L/M^{res} material are not specified separately.)

L6	*against covetousness*	Lk. 12.13-15
L7	*rich fool*	Lk. 12.16-21
L8	*blessed the servants*	Lk. 12.35-38
L9	*fire on earth*	Lk. 12.49-50
L10	*fate of Galileans*	Lk. 13.1-5
L11	*fig tree*	Lk. 13.6-9
L12	*daughter of Abraham*	Lk. 13.10-17
L13	*Herod the fox*	Lk. 13.31-33
L14	*Sabbath healing*	Lk. 14.1-6
L15	*guests and host*	Lk. 14.7-14
L16	*counting cost*	Lk. 14.28-33
L17	*lost coin*	Lk. 15.8-10
L18	*unjust steward*	Lk. 16.1-12
L19	*hostile Pharisees*	Lk. 16.14-15
L20	*rich man*	Lk. 16.19-31
L21	*unworthy servants*	Lk. 17.7-10
L22	*ten lepers*	Lk. 17.11-19
L23	*suffering Son of man*	Lk. 17.25
L24	*days of Lot*	Lk. 17.28-33
L25	*unjust judge*	Lk. 18.1-8
L26	*two men in temple*	Lk. 18.9-14

With the inventory complete, we are now in a position to describe how this section of Luke is constructed, and, more importantly, how the evangelist interprets the sayings tradition in his juxtapositions and supplementations.

11.33   *M2 lighting lamp* (Mt. 5.15 →)
11.34-36 *M8 eye as lamp* (Mt. 6.22-23 →)

Luke detaches *M2* from Matthew's "You are the light of the world . . ." (Mt. 5.14), just as he will later detach *M1 salt* from "You are the salt of the earth . . ." (Mt. 5.13; Lk. 14.34-35). *M2* is familiar to him as a detached saying from Mark 4.21, an *L/Mk* version of which has already been included at Luke 8.16. Luke 11.33 is therefore an *L/M/Mk* version of the saying.[43] In the earlier *L/Mk* version, the saying has to do with Jesus' parables. In adopting this indirect method of instruction, it is not Jesus' intention to conceal the light of revelation but rather to allow it to shine forth. In the *L/M/Mk* version, the saying (itself parabolic) is connected to a passage that suggests an interpretation, *M8 eye as lamp*. The "lamp" which is to shed its light and is not to be hidden is "the lamp of the body," that is, "*your* eye" (11.34; italics = Lukan alteration). The "sound" and the "evil" eyes correspond to the lamp placed either on a lampstand or, perversely, "*in a cellar or* under a bushel."[44] Luke's intention to connect the two passages is confirmed by the warning to take heed lest "the light in you be darkness" (11.35): the concealed light is the same as the darkened light. The connection is once more underlined in the concluding comparison between the light-filled body and "the lamp" which "enlightens you with its rays" (v. 36), recalling the opening image of the lamp set on a lampstand (v. 33).[45]

---

43. Other *L/M/Mk* passages in addition to *M2 lighting lamp* are: *M1 salt; M5 divorce; M16 testimony of Spirit;* the confessing/denying saying from *M17 nothing hidden;* the cross-bearing saying from *M19 discipleship; M20 finding/losing; M22 blasphemy; M24 mustard seed; M26 leaven of Pharisees; M27 little faith;* the criticism of love of honour in *M38 woe to Pharisees; M40 no return; M41 kingdom in midst.* In the case of *M5, M17, M19,* and *M20,* these represent Matthean doublets, that is, passages where Matthew has "used a convenient Marcan saying a second time" (Goulder, *Luke,* 1.34-35). Luke includes equivalents of both the original Markan and the secondary Matthean versions in the case of *M17, M19, M20, M38,* together with *M16* (where there is only one Matthean version). In a significant number of cases (*M1, M2, M22, M24, M26, M27, M40*), Luke has preferred a Matthean version of a saying to a Markan one (as in the earlier case of the Beelzebul controversy).

44. Contrast F. Bovon's claim that Lk. 11.34-36 should be interpreted independently of v. 33 (*Das Evangelium nach Lukas [Lk. 9,51–14,35],* EKKNT III/2 [Neukirchen-Vluyn: Benziger Verlag, 1996], pp. 211-12); Luke here preserves the disconnected Q sequence (pp. 206-7).

45. According to D. C. Allison, the passage presupposes a view of the eye as a light source, not

The parabolic image and its interpretation follow without a break from Jesus' condemnation of "this generation" for demanding "a sign" (Lk. 11.29-32). If the lamp set on a stand is the "sound" or "simple" eye, then the passage may have to do with the perception or misperception of that "something greater" than Solomon or Jonah that is "here," visibly present in Jesus (vv. 31, 32). On this perception or misperception depends the illumination or otherwise of bodily life in its entirety. By juxtaposing the two light-passages and connecting them to the preceding passage, Luke has Jesus speak both of the objective reality of his ministry and of the subjective reality of its reception.[46] The passage would then represent a further comment on Luke 10.23: "Blessed are the eyes that see what you see!"

11.37-54	*M38 woe to Pharisees* (Mt. 23.23-36 [*4, 6, 7, 13*] →)
12.1	*M26 leaven of Pharisees* (Mt. 16.6 →)
12.2-9	*M17 nothing hidden* (Mt. 10.26-33 →)
12.10	*M22 blasphemy* (Mt. 12.31-32 →)
12.11-12	*M16 testimony of Spirit* (Mt. 10.19-20 →)

Luke provides material drawn from Matthew 23 with a setting at a dinner party; he distributes the "woes" between Pharisees and lawyers; and he reports the hostility provoked by Jesus' criticisms (Lk. 11.37-38, 45, 53-54). Luke's editing of Matthew is along similar lines to his rendering of the final Matthean antithesis (love for enemies), which he expanded with material drawn from the previous antithesis (nonresistance), and the Mission Discourse. In each case a main sequence is perceptible, interspersed with material from the immediate context (< >) and with occasional transpositions (*). In these passages, the Matthean verse numbers (italicized; from Mt 5; 10; 23, respectively) occur in the following sequences:

Lk. 6.27-36: *44 <39 40 41 42> 46 47 45* 48*

---

as a window-like receiver of light ("The Eye Is the Lamp of the Body (Matthew 6.22-23 = Luke 11.33-36)," *NTS* 33 [1987], pp. 61-83; pp. 73-78).

46. Compare J. Fitzmyer's interpretation: "These sayings explain further the nature of the 'something greater' than Solomon or Jonah that is here. In Jesus a light has been given, which needs no further sign from heaven to authenticate it" (*The Gospel according to Luke: A New Translation with Introduction and Commentary*, 2 vols., AB [New York: Doubleday, 1981-85], 2.939). In view of the identification of the lamp with the eye, however, the lamp image should not be interpreted christologically (cf. Lk. 7.22; 10.23-24).

Lk. 10.3-12:   <16a> 9 10a 11 12 13 <10b 8 7> 14 15
Lk. 11.39-52:   25 26 23* <6 7> 27 <4> 29 30 31 32 34 35 36 <13>

These similarly constructed sequences confirm once more that the hypothesis of Lukan editing of Matthew makes good sense of the phenomena of the texts.[47] As we shall see, however, the rearranging and the rewriting of the Matthean text is a less significant indicator of Luke's interpretative activity than the juxtaposition with other texts.[48]

M26 leaven of Pharisees is a further *L/M/Mk* passage, but with no *L/Mk* equivalent since the Markan original (Mk. 8.15) is located within Luke's "Great Omission."[49] Following the dinner party with the Pharisees and the outbreak of mutual hostility, Jesus now turns to his disciples, ignoring the surging crowds, and warns them: "Beware of the leaven — *that is, hypocrisy* — of the Pharisees" (Lk. 12.1).[50] The emphatic reference to hypocrisy serves a double function. First, it summarizes the various accusations in the preceding woes, where Pharisees are accused of cleaning only the outside of the vessel, tithing herbs while neglecting more important matters, and seeking high status, while the lawyers are accused of imposing heavy burdens, participating in the murder of the prophets, and removing the key of knowledge. The supplementation of *M38 woes* with *M26 leaven* brings these accusations together under the heading of hypocrisy, the discrepancy between appearance and reality. Second, *M26* interprets the preceding woes as a warning to disciples. Rather than merely echoing the harsh verdict on Pharisees and lawyers, the disciples themselves are warned: "Beware . . . ," that is, "Look to

47. According to Fleddermann (*Q*, p. 550), the Q sequence corresponded to the Lukan one in the third passage, with the exceptions of Lk. 11.42 (located before 11.39 in Q) and 11.45 (omitted in Q). If the same Q sequence is edited in Mt. 23, the sequence vis-à-vis Q (= Luke) is as follows: <46 43* 52> 42* 39 40 41 44 47 48 49 50 51. The Q material is interspersed throughout Mt. 23, however (vv. 4, 6-7, 13, 23, 25-27, 29-30, 34-36), requiring a more complex editorial process than the simple one postulated by the *L/M* hypothesis.

48. The most interesting emendation of Matthew is the ascription of "I will send them prophets . . ." to "the Wisdom of God" rather than to Jesus himself. Presumably Luke does not consider that Jesus sent the prophets and assumes that the passage is a citation from a source unknown to him. He therefore introduces it with a citation formula of his own devising. There is no reason to suppose that the Lukan version is earlier than the Matthean one, as C. Tuckett does (*Q and the History of Early Christianity*, pp. 24-25).

49. Mk. 6.44–8.26 is passed over at Lk. 9.17, 18, which correspond to Mk. 6.43; 8.27 respectively.

50. προσέχετε in Lk. 12.1 is derived from Mt. 16.6 (ὁρᾶτε καὶ προσέχετε) rather than Mk. 8.15 (ὁρᾶτε, βλέπετε).

yourselves. . . ." Luke has reinterpreted this saying not only by rewording it but also by detaching it from its Matthean and Markan context — the aftermath of the two feeding miracles — and juxtaposing it with the woes against the Pharisees, with the result that these too must be reinterpreted as a warning to the disciples.

M17 nothing hidden now amplifies the warning against hypocrisy by announcing the eschatological exposure of everything that is now hidden. In Matthew this passage belongs to the Mission Discourse. Jesus here exhorts the disciples to proclaim from the rooftops what he teaches them in secret:

> So do not fear them. For there is nothing hidden that will not be revealed, or secret that will not be made known. What I tell you in the dark, speak in the light, and what you hear whispered, proclaim from the roofs. (Mt. 10.26-27)

Luke interprets the saying quite differently, as a reference to the final exposure of the "hypocrisy" against which *M26 leaven of Pharisees* has warned.[51] It is the juxtaposition of the two passages that has generated the new interpretation:

> [ ] There is nothing hidden that will not be revealed, or secret that will not be made known. *Therefore* what *you say* in the dark *will be heard* in the light, and what *you [ ]* whisper *in private will be* proclaim*ed* from the roofs. (Lk. 12.2-3)

In v. 3, Matthew's imperatives are replaced by future passives not because Luke is editing Q but because he is reinterpreting the saying in its Matthean form. As a result, there is now a potentially awkward transition to the sequel, "Do not fear those who kill the body . . . ," which relates more directly to confession than to hypocrisy. Luke therefore inserts, "*And I say to you, my friends,* do not fear those who kill the body . . . ," detaching this saying from the previous one (Lk. 12.4 = Mt. 10.28).

M17 nothing hidden concludes with sayings about confessing and being confessed, denying and being denied (Lk. 12.8-9 = Mt. 10.32-33). *M22 blasphemy* is inserted here because, like the conclusion of *M17*, it speaks of a double assignment of destiny and includes a reference to "the Son of man." Luke highlights the connection by introducing both passages with πᾶς ὅς

---

51. Contra Fitzmyer, Lk. 12.2-3 is not part of an "Exhortation to Fearless Confession" (*Luke,* 2.955) — a heading borrowed from the Huck Synopsis (p. 123).

(12.8, 10). The reference to the Holy Spirit leads in turn to the insertion of *M16 testimony of Spirit,* which, in conjunction with *M22 blasphemy,* creates a contrast between speaking *against* and speaking *from* the Holy Spirit. All three sayings — on confessing/denying, blasphemy, and testimony — are *L/M/Mk* with *L/Mk* equivalents.[52]

12.13-15	*L6 against covetousness*
12.16-21	*L7 rich fool*
12.22-31	*M10 do not be anxious* (Mt. 6.25-33 →)
12.32-34	*M7 treasure in heaven* (Mt. 6.19-21 →)

L7 follows directly from *L6,* a warning against "covetousness" (πλεονεξία, Lk. 12.15) occasioned by a request to intervene in a dispute about inheritance. The parable derives ultimately from *Sirach* 11.18-19:

> There is one who gets rich through graft and grasping, and this is his al-
> lotted reward: when he says, "I have found rest, and now I can enjoy the
> fruits of my labours," he does not know how long it is till he leaves these
> things to others — and dies.

In its Lukan context, *L7 rich fool* serves as a foil for *M10 do not be anxious* and *M7 treasure in heaven.*[53] The protagonist's godless self-sufficiency con-trasts with the reliance on God enjoined on the disciples. Anxiety about food, drink, and clothing is, however, more the prerogative of the poor than of the rich. The rich man is anxious only about how to store his abundant produce, whereas the disciples opt for poverty in following Jesus' injunction to "sell your possessions" (Lk. 12.33), and are thereby exposed to anxiety about their basic needs. Thus Luke's presentation of this material recalls his blessings and woes:

> Blessed are the poor, for yours is the kingdom of God.
> Blessed are those who hunger now, for you shall be satisfied. . . .
>
> But woe to you rich, for you have received your consolation.
> Woe to you that are full now, for you shall hunger. (Lk. 6.20b-21, 24-25)

---

52. Confessing/denying: cf. Mk. 8.38 = Lk. 9.26 (being ashamed); Mt. 10.32-33 = Lk. 12.8-9. Blasphemy: Mk. 3.28-29 = Mt. 12.31 = Lk. 9.26; Mt. 12.32 = Lk. 12.10. Testimony: Mk. 13.11 = Mt. 10.19-20 = Lk. 21.14-15; Mt. 10.19-20 = Lk. 12.11-12.

53. Compare the discussion in Goodacre, *Case against Q,* pp. 113-16.

Luke's emendations to *M10 do not be anxious* are limited in scope, and the Matthean sequence is preserved.[54] In contrast, *M7 treasure in heaven* is initially almost unrecognizable with its reference to "purses that do not grow old," although from that point on it corresponds more closely to the Matthean prototype. In Luke 12.31-34a, the link between *M10* and *M7* is probably Luke's own composition:

> . . . *Rather,* seek *[ ]* his kingdom *[ ]*, and all these things shall be added to you. *Fear not, little flock, for your Father is pleased to give you the kingdom. Sell your possessions and give alms, make for yourself purses that do not grow old, unfailing* treasure in heaven, where no thief *approaches* or moth *destroys.* For where your treasure is, there too your heart shall be.

Here, *M7 treasure in heaven* is presented as commentary on "seek his kingdom," so that the whole passage becomes the positive counterpart to the preceding warning against anxiety.[55] The link with *L7 rich fool* is made explicit in the contrast between "your treasure," that is, the "unfailing treasure in heaven," and the one who "stores up treasure for himself and is not rich towards God" (12.21, 33, 34).[56]

12.35-38	*L8 blessed the servants*
12.39-48	*M46 thief/servant* (Mt. 24.43-51 →)

54. Most significant perhaps is the abbreviation of Mt. 6.33, where "seek *first*" becomes simply "seek"; ". . . and his righteousness" is also omitted (Lk. 12.31). According to Catchpole, Matthew's "first" is intended to "blunt the sharp edge of eschatological radicalism. . . . [W]e can understand the realism which brings about the insertion of that word, but we can scarcely understand a Lucan move to remove it" (*Quest for Q,* p. 37). But Luke may simply have regarded "first" and ". . . and his righteousness" as redundant. Minor abbreviations need not be ideologically motivated.

55. Q 12.33-34 (= *M7 treasure in heaven*) is supposed to approximate to Matthew's wording, and may have preceded Q 12.22-31 (James M. Robinson, Paul Hoffmann, and John S. Kloppenborg [eds.], *The Critical Edition of Q* [Minneapolis: Fortress, 2000; henceforth *Critical Edition*], pp. 328-33; cf. Mt. 6.19-21, 25-33) or followed it (Fleddermann, *Q,* p. 616; cf. Lk. 12.22-31, 33-34). In each case, neither evangelist has preserved the original connection.

56. According to Goulder (*Luke,* 2.539), Lk. 12.1-40 as a whole is based on themes drawn from Mt. 16: (1) "Beware of the leaven . . ." (Mt. 16.6; Lk. 12.1); (2) "Let him deny himself . . ." (Mt. 16.24), corresponding to "fearless confession" (Lk. 12.1-12); (3) "What will it profit . . . ?" (Mt. 16.26), which inspired the Parable of the Rich Fool (Lk. 12.13-21); (4) "The Son of man is to come . . ." (Mt. 16.27) to "detachment before the coming of the Son of man" (Lk. 12.22-40). Here, as elsewhere, Goulder's claims to know exactly how and why Luke wrote as he did on the basis of Matthew are speculative and involve unnecessarily complex redactional procedures.

Matthew's eschatological discourse concludes with a passage in which the coming of the Son of man is compared, first, to a thief breaking into a house by night (Mt. 24.43), and, second, to the sudden return of an absent master (κύριος) to his household (24.45-51). The first image represents the hearer as a householder who needs to be vigilant; the second, as a trusted servant exercising authority over other servants during the master's prolonged absence — and, perhaps, tempted to abuse that authority. Matthew's thief image is non-Markan, although it is used to illustrate the Markan theme of "watching," here detached from its original link with the image of servants awaiting their master's return (Mt. 24.42, 44; cf. Mk. 13.33-37). It is the householder who "watches," in order to defend his property against the thief; the question for Matthew's (single) servant is not whether he "watches" or sleeps but whether he administers the household faithfully in the master's absence. Matthew has developed the concluding Markan exhortation ("Watch therefore, for you do not know when the master of the house will come . . ." [Mk. 13.35; cf. Mt. 24.42]) into the sterner warning that "the master of that [wicked] servant will come on a day when he does not expect him and at an hour he does not know, and will dismember him and will place him with the hypocrites . . ." (Mt. 24.50-51).

Luke is more interested in the conventional image of the servant than in the surprising image of the thief. His version of *M46 thief/servant* is prefaced by *L8 blessed the servants,* in which the whole household is portrayed as looking eagerly for the master's return, and as certain to be praised by him when he does return (Lk. 12.35-38).[57] The thief passage is abbreviated slightly and treated as an appendage of the Lukan introduction, inculcating the same lesson: be ready (12.39-40).[58] Matthew's abrupt transition from the thief to the faithful servant is smoothed over by the insertion of a question from Peter:

---

57. Bovon considers it possible here to differentiate Lukan tradition (Lk. 12.36) from redactional additions (12.35, 37); v. 36 is the original Q image from which Mt. 25.1-13 was developed (*Lukas,* 2.323). It is more likely that the whole of *L8 blessed the servants* is the evangelist's composition, with vv. 35-36 reflecting the influence of Mt. 25.1-13 and v. 38 of Mk. 13.35. The passage provides an introduction to Luke's rendering of *M46 thief/servant,* just as vv. 47-48 provide a conclusion — again attributed to special Lukan tradition by Bovon (2.325), probably unnecessarily.

58. Luke's version lacks Matthew's emphasis on wakefulness (Mt. 24.42, 43; cf. 25.13). Catchpole argues that this is out of place in the Parable of the Thief, and that Matthew's version is thus secondary: "Protection against burglary is not watchfulness but prevention. . . . That being so, the theme of watching within the so-called parable of the watchful householder (24:43) is a damaging addition to a pre-Matthean parable, and it happens that Luke does not have it and is therefore more original" (*Quest for Q,* p. 57). Yet the linkage between the thief image and wakefulness is already established in 1 Thessalonians, where the fact that "the day of the Lord will come like a thief in the night" leads to the exhortation "So then let us not sleep, as others do, but let us keep awake and be sober" (1 Thes. 5.2, 6).

"Lord, does this parable apply to us or to everyone?" (12.41). The reference is probably to the supplementary Parable of the Watching Servants, to which the thief-in-the-night passage serves as a postscript. Peter's question marks a shift in subject matter, from the watchfulness required of all Christians to the specific responsibilities of leaders exercising authority over the household of the church during the Lord's absence. Jesus' counterquestion (v. 42) replies obliquely to Peter's question by providing a new parable intended "for us," in contrast to the parable of the servants which is addressed "to all."

Luke also provides a postscript to *M46 thief/servant*, in the form of a reflection on different degrees of culpability (Lk. 12.47-48a). Some servants know the master's will and others do not, and they will accordingly experience different levels of punishment. This passage serves to moderate the harsh Matthean reference to the unfaithful servant's dismemberment (Lk. 12.46).[59] The conclusion, that much will be required of those to whom much is given (v. 48b), confirms that Luke still has in mind the figure of the "faithful and wise steward, whom his master sets over his household . . ." (v. 42).

12.49-50	*L9 fire on earth*
12.51-53	*M18 division* (Mt. 10.34-35 →)
12.54-56	*M25 signs of the times* (Mt. 16.2-3 →)
12.57-59	*M4 accuser* (Mt. 5.25-26 →)
13.1-5	*L10 fate of Galileans*

L9 fire on earth and *M18 division* are both concerned with Jesus' mission. He came to cast fire on the earth (ἐπὶ τὴν γῆν), to endure his own unique baptism, and to bestow on the earth (ἐν τῇ γῇ) not peace but division (Lk. 12.49-50, 51-53). For Luke, fire is probably a reference to the Pentecost event (Acts 2.3), baptism to Jesus' death (cf. Mk. 10.38-39). Thus, *L9 fire on earth* sets *M18 division* in the context of a narrative situation in which Jesus has "set his face to go to Jerusalem" (Lk. 9.51, 53). It is in his journey to Jerusalem and its outcome that Jesus creates "division" within the intimate circle of the family.[60]

---

59. In Luke the dismembered servant is placed with "the faithless," in Matthew with "the hypocrites." Rather than attributing the former to Q and the latter to Matthean redaction (so Fitzmyer, *Luke*, 2.985), one might point to Lk. 11.39-48 as evidence that Luke can sometimes eliminate references to "hypocrites" found in his Matthean source (Mt. 23.25-31: "hypocrites" [4x]). Luke does use this term, however, in 6.42 (sing.); 12.56; 13.15.

60. According to Fleddermann, in vv. 49-50 Luke "borrows a metaphor from Mark and some vocabulary from Q to create an introduction to the Q pericope that integrates it into the theological framework of the Journey Narrative" (Q, p. 638). If the references to "Q" are replaced by "Mat-

M25 signs of the times continues to explore the theme of crisis — although it is marked off from the previous passage by the introductory formula, "And he said to the crowds . . ." (Lk. 12.54). Here, Luke completely rewrites the original Matthean version while retaining its underlying structure. The two meteorological observations are now based on the winds rather than the sun, and the hearers are therefore told that they know how to interpret "the face *of the earth and* of the sky" — but not the present time (12.56). The juxtaposition of *M25 signs of the times* and *M4 accuser* suggests a connection between the inability to understand "this time" and the sleepwalking into crisis or judgement against which the second passage warns. Addressing the crowds, Jesus speaks of the coming crisis by way of a parable in which the addressee is identified with a man who is imprisoned after failing to settle his debts, even when given the opportunity to do so.

The coming crisis is presented in more concrete form in *L10 fate of Galileans,* where Jesus teaches his contemporaries that their failure to repent will lead to a fate like that of the Galilean pilgrims Pilate recently slaughtered in the temple, or the eighteen people killed in the collapse of a tower in Siloam. Were the victims of these events "sinners" or "debtors" to a greater extent than anyone else (13.2, 4)? These events during Jesus' ministry anticipate the catastrophic events of forty years later, of which Luke's Jesus will later speak so clearly.[61] In Luke's historical perspective, the repentance of Jesus' contemporaries would have meant their turning to "the things that make for peace" (19.42), that is, to the practices of love for enemies and non-resistance as set forth in the Sermon on the Plain. The Matthean imagery of *M25 signs of the times* and *M4 accuser* is detached from contexts that have to do with the demand for a sign and the love of neighbour, and relocated within the Lukan perspective on the catastrophe of Israel.[62]

13.6-9	*L11 fig tree*
13.10-17	*L12 daughter of Abraham*
13.18-21	*M24 mustard seed/leaven* (Mt. 13.31-33 →)

---

thew," this is correct. At no point is it clear that Luke preserves the earlier wording: Mt. 10.34-35 is said to correspond more closely to Q than the Lukan parallel (pp. 641-44).

61. Cf. Lk. 19.41-44; 21.20-24; 23.27-31.

62. G. B. Caird entitles Lk. 12.54–13.9 "The Imminent Crisis: (3) for Israel," following from 12.35-48, "The Imminent Crisis: (1) for the Disciples," and 12.49-53, "The Imminent Crisis: (2) for Jesus" (*Saint Luke,* PNTC [Harmondsworth: Penguin, 1963], pp. 164, 167, 168). Caird argues that, for Luke, "To reject the way of Jesus was to choose the path leading directly to conflict with Rome and subsequent catastrophe" (p. 169).

L11 is a parable about an unproductive fig tree that may or may not bear fruit in the future. The context suggests that, like the later *L/Mk* Parable of the Vineyard (Lk. 20.9-18), *L11* is concerned with the fate of Jesus' contemporaries, "this generation" (cf. Lk. 11.50, 51). This is a parable of uncertain growth or productivity, in contrast to *M24 mustard seed/leaven*, where the topic is the assured hope of the triumph of God's kingdom, initiated in Jesus' ministry.[63] *M24* is presented as comment on *L12*, a Sabbath healing story in which Jesus' liberation of a "daughter of Abraham" is contrasted with the synagogue official's zeal for the sanctity of the Sabbath.[64] The fate of the fig tree may rest on whether "this generation" as a whole follows the official's lead in rejecting Jesus. The mustard seed is sown, and the yeast added to the dough, in "the glorious things done by him" (Lk. 13.17). If the fig tree eventually bears fruit, it will be assimilated to the great "tree" that grows out of the grain of mustard seed.

In locating the *M* material in this context, Luke shows his concern to provide it with a plausible setting in the life of Jesus. For Luke, Jesus' parables are not to be detached from his own life and ministry in its broader contemporary setting — as they are in the *Gospel of Thomas*.[65] Thus the parables remain *Jesus'* parables.

63. On the Q theory, the Parable of the Mustard Seed is a point at which Q overlaps with Mark; the Q version is preserved in Luke, without the Markan comparisons — "smaller than all seeds," "greater than all plants" — that recur in Matthew (*Critical Edition*, pp. 400-403). As usual, the appeal to a "Mark/Q overlap" serves to protect the Q hypothesis at points where so-called "minor agreements" of Matthew and Luke against Mark threaten to become major: here, Mt + Lk ὃν λαβὼν ἄνθρωπος vs. Mk ὃς ὅταν σπαρῇ, Mt ὅταν δὲ αὐξηθῇ + Lk καὶ ηὔξησεν vs. Mk ἀναβαίνει, Mt καὶ γίνεται δένδρον + Lk καὶ ἐγένετο εἰς δένδρον vs. Mk. καὶ ποιεῖ κλάδους μεγάλους, Mt τὰ πετεινὰ τοῦ οὐρανοῦ καὶ κατασκηνοῦν ἐν τοῖς κλάδοις αὐτοῦ + Lk τὰ πετεινὰ τοῦ οὐρανοῦ κατεσκήνωσεν ἐν τοῖς κλάδοις αὐτοῦ vs. Mk ὑπὸ τὴν σκιὰν αὐτοῦ τὰ πετεινὰ τοῦ οὐρανοῦ κατασκηνοῦν. Sanders and Davies note that in the synoptics this parable "exists in basically only one form" (*Studying the Synoptic Gospels* [London: SCM Press, 1989], p. 79). The second, Q version of the parable is demanded not by the textual evidence but by the refusal to contemplate Luke's knowledge of Matthew.

64. As I. Howard Marshall notes, "In the present Lucan context, the parables are a commentary on what has preceded" (*The Gospel of Luke: A Commentary on the Greek Text*, NIGTC [Exeter: Paternoster, 1978], p. 560).

65. The significance of this contrast is noted by Werner Kelber, for whom the narrative embodiment of parables and sayings is nothing less than a metaphysical fall from grace ("In the Beginning Were the Words: The Apotheosis and Narrative Displacement of the Logos," *JAAR* 58 [1990], pp. 69-87). "Aphoristic speech, parables and sayings arrangements were not allowed to stand on their own in the canon. . . . Employed as source materials or freely composed, sayings and discourses were now relegated to organized narrative space" (p. 85). Fortunately there is at

13.22-24   *M12 narrow gate* (Mt. 7.13-14 →)
13.25   *M47 exclusion* (Mt. 25.1-13 →)
13.26-27   *M13 depart* (Mt. 7.22-23 →)
13.28-29   *M14 east and west* (Mt. 8.11-12 →)
13.30   *M34 last first* (Mt. 20.16 →)

Luke reminds his readers that Jesus was at this time "passing through towns and villages, teaching and making his way to Jerusalem" (13.22). In response to the anonymous questioner who asks, "Lord, will only a few be saved?" (13.23), Jesus speaks of exclusion from the kingdom in words skilfully blended together from disparate Matthean origins.[66] The narrow gate of *M12* becomes the door closed against those the householder refuses to know, in spite of their desperate pleas.[67] In the original Matthean contexts, the excluded are identified as the unprepared bridesmaids *(M47 exclusion)* and as those who claim to have prophesied and performed mighty works in the name of Christ *(M13 depart)*. In Luke, the excluded represent Jesus' own contemporaries who experienced his ministry at first hand. Luke finds an affinity between the three Matthean passages, which he presents as an unbroken sequence.[68] *M14 east and west* and *M34 last first* continue the theme of exclusion, and indicate that Luke, like Paul, connects the exclusion of many within Israel with the inclusion of Gentiles.[69] Many will come from east and

---

least one gospel which avoided this error: "Unimpeded by narrative's spatio-temporal framework and in control of the discrete items of his proclamation, the 'living Jesus' of the *Gos. Thom.* seeks to elude entrapment in the past" (p. 79). The value judgements implicit in terms such as "not allowed," "relegated," "unimpeded," and "entrapment" originate in the modern Western "eclipse of biblical narrative," diagnosed so acutely by Hans Frei.

66. Contra Goulder, for whom "[t]hese texts do not always dovetail very neatly into each other" (*Luke*, 2.572).

67. The secondariness of the combination of *M12 narrow gate* and *M47 exclusion* is evident from the reference to the door as "narrow" in Lk. 13.24, a vestige of the Matthean passage which plays no role in the new context; *M47 exclusion* is thus a narrative fragment. It is unlikely that Lk. 13.24-30 preserves an original Q sequence which Matthew has broken up (Fleddermann, *Q*, pp. 676-92).

68. *M12 narrow gate* is abbreviated, and is connected to the fragment from *M47 exclusion* by the link-word θύρα (Lk. 13.24, 25 [2x]): a single door, which will in due course be shut by the householder, takes the place of the narrow and wide gates of Matthew. *M47 exclusion* is linked to *M13 depart* by the repetition of οὐκ οἶδα [ὑμᾶς] πόθεν ἐστέ (Lk. 13.25, 27a). Some Matthean wording is preserved in *M12* (εἰσελθ[ ] διὰ τῆς στένης [ ], ὅτι πολλοί, Lk. 13.24) and *M47* (κύριε ἄνοιξον ἡμῖν, ἀποκριθείς, οὐκ οἶδα ὑμᾶς, Lk. 13.25). In *M13* there is a clear parallel (Mt. 7.23 = Lk. 13.27), although the verbal overlap is confined to ἀπ' ἐμοῦ.

69. In Lk. 13.28 the typically Matthean reference to weeping and gnashing of teeth (cf. Mt.

west (Matthew), but also from north and south; and so the last will be first and the first last.[70]

The passage illustrates the variety of Luke's compositional procedures and his willingness to practise a radical rewriting of his source material — here, in the interests of creating a unified discourse out of thematically connected but formally disparate material. Luke does not simply reproduce this material, perhaps with a few stylistic modifications; he interprets it. Selecting, juxtaposing, and paraphrasing are all interpretative activities. Since this discourse is concerned with inclusion as well as exclusion, and with each as the corollary of the other, it is *M14 east and west* that stands at its heart.

13.31-33   *L13 Herod the fox*
13.34-35   *M39 Jerusalem* (Mt. 23.37-39 →)

M39 Jerusalem is extracted from Matthew's discourse against scribes and Pharisees, and provided with an introduction *(L13)* that links it to Jesus' journey to Jerusalem to suffer there (cf. Lk. 9.31, 51, 53). Luke has already incorporated much of the preceding part of the Matthean discourse in 11.37-52, in the context of a dinner hosted by a Pharisee. As the address to Jerusalem would not have been appropriate there, it is given a new role, which is to underline Luke's journey theme.[71] Jesus meets the news of Herod's hostility with a statement inspired by the Markan passion predictions.[72] He must proceed along his divinely appointed way, performing exorcisms and cures until the moment comes to complete his journey in his death in Jerusalem. This introduction to *M39 Jerusalem* concludes with the statement that "it

---

8.12; 13.42, 50; 22.13; 24.51; 25.30) makes best sense as derived from Matthew: so Sanders and Davies, *Synoptic Gospels*, pp. 93-94.

70. The sequence *last-first, first-last* is derived from Mt. 20.16 (the conclusion of the Parable of the Labourers in the Vineyard), and contrasts with Mk. 10.31 = Mt. 19.30, where the sequence is *first-last, last-first*. The variant makes excellent sense given *M/Mk* and *L/M*. Luke has expanded slightly and modified the word order. For debate about whether the saying is to be attributed to Q, see Fleddermann, *Q*, pp. 69-91.

71. *M39 Jerusalem* contains fifty-five words in Matthew, fifty-three in Luke. Luke's deviations from Matthew's wording are slighter here than in *M38 woe to Pharisees*, although in both passages most of Luke's rewordings are purely cosmetic. J. M. Robinson accepts that Luke here deviates from the Q sequence preserved in Matthew: the conclusion of the Lukan woes against Pharisees and lawyers (Lk. 11.52) involves a redactional transposition occasioned by the separation of the lament over Jerusalem with which the Q discourse and its Matthean equivalent conclude (*Sayings Gospel Q*, pp. 592-97). See also Catchpole, *Quest for Q*, pp. 257-58.

72. Note the δεῖ, Lk. 13.33; cf. 9.22 = Mk. 8.31; Lk. 24.7.

cannot be that a prophet should perish away from Jerusalem" (Lk. 13.33), which preserves the specific reference to Jesus while providing a link to the more general lament in *M39*, where Jerusalem is addressed as the murderer of the prophets. Luke's biographical concern is again clear: utterances collected from Matthew must be connected to Jesus' unique mission and destiny.

14.1-6   *L14 Sabbath healing <M21 Sabbath emergency (Mt. 12.11→)>*
14.7-14   *L15 guests and host <M37 exalt/humble (Mt. 23.12 →)>*
14.15-24 *M36 great feast (Mt. 22.1-10 →)*

Here it is again the role of *L* material to provide an introduction to a passage from *M*. Like the earlier woes against Pharisees (11.37-54) and the encounter with Simon the Pharisee and the sinful woman (7.36-50), this assemblage of *L* and *M* material has its setting at a dinner party. The Sabbath healing thus takes place in a Pharisee's home, not in the synagogue as in *L12 daughter of Abraham* and the Markan and Matthean prototype for the two additional Sabbath healing stories in Luke.[73] The expanded Matthean version of this story provided Luke with *M21 Sabbath emergency,* and the new story was probably created specifically to provide a setting for this. In Matthew, a sheep falls into a pit on the Sabbath (Mt. 12.11); in Luke, a son or an ox falls into a well (Lk. 14.5). In contrast, *L12 daughter of Abraham* justifies Sabbath healing with reference to normal Sabbath practice, leading an ox or ass to water (Lk. 13.15).[74]

L15 guests and host also has its origin in *M/Mk.* Jesus notes how his fellow guests choose the seats of honour (τὰς πρωτοκλισίας), and advises them not to do so when, in the future, they are invited to a wedding — not a dinner party, as at present (Lk. 14.7-8). This passage derives from *M38 woe to Pharisees,* which Luke has already incorporated into his text — but with one significant omission. Matthew claims that the scribes and Pharisees "love the seat of honour [τὴν πρωτοκλισίαν] at feasts and the best seats [τὰς πρωτοκαθεδρίας] in the synagogues . . ." (Mt. 23.6 = Mk. 12.39).[75] In Luke

73. Mk. 3.1-6 = Mt. 12.9-14 = Lk. 6.6-11.

74. On the Q theory, it may be argued either that Matthew and Luke have independently incorporated a self-contained saying about the Sabbath (Q 14.5) into Sabbath healing stories (Fleddermann, *Q,* p. 708), or that this saying does not belong to Q at all (*Critical Edition,* pp. 426-27). That this story is in reality L/M/Mk is evident from Jesus' question, ἔξεστιν τῷ σαββάτῳ θεραπεῦσαι . . . (Lk. 14.3 = Mt. 12.10 = Mk. 3.4).

75. Mk. 12.38-39 claims that scribes take pleasure in (1) walking in long robes, (2) greetings in the marketplaces, (3) the best seats in the synagogues, (4) places of honour at feasts. Mt. 23.6-7 in-

11.43, however, the Pharisees' conduct at feasts was passed over. Luke reserves this point for expanded use in *L15 guests and host,* a vignette which originates in the combination of this *M/Mk* passage with *M37 exalt/humble* (Lk. 14.11). "Everyone who exalts himself will be humbled" is applied to the guest who selects the seat of honour but is compelled by the host to surrender it to another. "Everyone who humbles himself will be exalted" is applied to the guest who selects the least conspicuous seat and is invited by the host to "go up higher." Luke's application of the general principle to the Pharisaic preference for the seat of honour is occasioned by the original context of the two Matthean passages on which he here draws (Mt. 23.6, 12). The Matthean principle will later be applied to another Pharisee, this one in the temple rather than at a feast (Lk. 18.14). In Luke, *M* is frequently generative of *L.* Unlike the fig tree in the parable, *M* bears fruit.

L15 guests and host concludes with an address to the host (Lk. 14.12-14), anticipating *M36 great feast,* which follows. It is the poor, the maimed, the blind, and the lame who should be the guests on such occasions — just as in the parable (14.13, 21). Together with an intervention from a guest (14.15), this passage connects the parable with the social event that is its Lukan context. In keeping with this context, the place of the Matthean "king" with his many servants is taken by a more modest "householder" with a single servant (Lk. 14.21), a person of comparable standing perhaps to Jesus' present host. Matthew's king has armies and servants to do his bidding, but it is not clear how Luke's protagonists have the authority to "compel them to come in" (Lk. 14.23). Matthew's version represents the destruction of Jerusalem in 70 CE as the occasion for broadening the scope of the invitation (Mt. 22.7-9). Luke omits the Matthean violence but distinguishes two stages in the broadening scope of the invitations that follow the initial refusal. The servant's two missions probably relate to the disadvantaged beneficiaries of Jesus' ministry ("the poor and maimed and blind and lame") and to the Gentiles, respectively (Lk. 14.21-23).

corporates items (2)-(4) in reverse order, but replaces (1) with being called "rabbi," introducing a passage that concludes with *M37 exalt/humble* (Mt. 23.8-12). Lk. 11.43 has just two items, in the Matthean sequence (3)-(2) and in wording influenced by Matthean redaction (ἀγαπᾶτε, cf. Matthew's φιλοῦσιν; the article with ἀσπασμούς; note Lk. 20.46, however, where the Markan material is reproduced in purely Markan form). (4) is reserved for expansion at Lk. 14.7-8. Matthew's dependence here on Mark is unambiguously clear, and so too would be Luke's on Matthew were this not disallowed on principle by the Q theory. It is the need to defend the theory, rather than the textual evidence itself, that underlies Fleddermann's claim that Matthew's singular reference to the best *seat* in the synagogues is derived from Q: "[I]f Matthew were borrowing it from Mark we would expect the plural instead of the singular" (Q, p. 537).

As in the parables of the pounds or talents (Lk. 19.11-27 = Mt. 25.14-30) and of the two sons (Lk. 15.11-32 = Mt. 21.28-32), the Lukan and Matthean wording diverges more widely than is usual in their shared material. In each case, Luke has chosen to rewrite these texts in his own way, drawing from the Matthean source no more than the plot-outline of the respective parables. The rewriting aims both to exploit narrative potential unrealized in Matthew (e.g. the excuses: Mt. 22.5; Lk. 14.18-20) and to suggest an alternative rationale for early Christian mission to the Matthean one, with its focus on the fall of Jerusalem.[76]

14.26-27 *M19 discipleship* (Mt. 10.37-38 →)
14.28-33 *L16 counting cost*
14.34-35 *M1 salt* (Mt. 5.13 →)

With the two linked discipleship sayings, on "hating" family members and on crossbearing, Luke's engagement with Matthew's Mission Discourse is almost complete. In both gospels, the sayings are linked by way of their conclusions: ". . . is not worthy of me" in Matthew (twice), altered to ". . . cannot be my disciple" in Luke.[77] The crossbearing saying is here *L/M/Mk*, occurring elsewhere in *Mk*, *M/Mk*, and *L/Mk* forms (Mk. 8.34 = Mt. 16.24 = Lk. 9.23).[78]

---

76. Equally radical rewriting is required on the Q theory, although mostly now on the part of Matthew. Here as elsewhere, the suggestion that the difference stems from independent oral tradition tends to overlook clear signs of Matthean and Lukan redaction in both versions. As for the version in *GTh* 64, Bovon argues that this "weist den einfachsten Aufbau auf und ist in diesem Punkt das ursprünglichste: Einladung der einen, ihre Absage, Einladung an andere" (*Lukas*, 2.506). But a simple structure is not necessarily the most original. The Thomas version appears to be post-Lukan in further elaborating the excuses, of which there are now four; the intention is to show that "businessmen and merchants will not enter the places of my Father."

77. Luke's version of the first saying adds, "If anyone comes to me . . . ," replaces Matthew's "loves . . . more than me" with "does not hate," includes three pairs of relationships (father/mother, wife/children, brothers/sisters) rather than Matthew's two (father/mother, son/daughter), and adds ". . . and even his own soul." In view of the other differences between the two versions, and Luke's earlier expansions of related Matthean discipleship material (Lk. 9.61-62; 12.52-53), there is no basis for the assumption that Luke's "does not hate" preserves the original wording of the saying. Citing 14.33, C. F. Evans suggests that this wording "may express Luke's rigorous outlook" (*Saint Luke* [London: SCM Press; Philadelphia: Trinity Press International, 1990], p. 577).

78. In Luke, Matthew's version is freely reworded although its structure is maintained; this contrasts with the more conservative treatment of the Markan version. Luke tends to treat the second occurrence of a doublet more freely than the first (cf. Lk. 9.26; 12.8-9 = Mk. 8.38; Mt. 10.32-33; Lk. 12.11-12; 21.14-15 = Mt. 10.19-20; Mk. 13.11).

Luke distributes the various components of Matthew's Mission Discourse as follows:

M^{seq} *harvest*	Mt. 9.37-38	→	Lk. 10.2
M^{seq} *instructions*	Mt. 10.7-16, 40	→	Lk. 10.3-12, *16
M16 testimony of Spirit	Mt. 10.19-20	→	*Lk. 12.11-12
M^{seq} *disciple, teacher*	Mt. 10.24-25	→	*Lk. 6.40
M17 nothing hidden	Mt. 10.26-33	→	Lk. 12.2-9
M18 division	Mt. 10.34-35	→	Lk. 12.51-53
M19 discipleship	Mt. 10.37-38	→	Lk. 14.26-27
M20 finding, losing	Mt. 10.39	→	Lk. 17.33

With minor exceptions (*), the Matthean sequence is maintained. The exceptions are easily explicable and correspond to Luke's compositional procedures elsewhere. The *disciple, teacher* saying has already been relocated within L/M^{seq}. At Luke 10.16 ("the one who *hears* you . . ."), a passage from the conclusion of the Matthean discourse provides a conclusion for the briefer Lukan equivalent. *M16 testimony of Spirit* and *M17 nothing hidden* are transposed. Otherwise the Matthean discourse remains largely intact in Luke. On the Q hypothesis, one or other evangelist would have to preserve the Q sequence. Either something very like Matthew's Mission Discourse already stood in Q, or Luke preserved a more extended Q sequence from which Matthew selected items for his Mission Discourse in their original order.[79] In either case, Q merely duplicates an extended section of Matthean or Lukan text. There is no need for either version of Q when the *L/M* theory can provide such a straightforward account of the compositional process.

M19 discipleship is amplified by *L16 counting cost*, a pair of parables or parable-like passages on the tower-builder and the king preparing for war.

---

79. The *Critical Edition* adopts the following Q sequence, normally following Luke: Q 10.2-16, 21-24; 11.2b-4, 9-15, 17-28, 16, 29-35, 39-52; 12.2-12, 33-34, 22b-31, 39-40, 42-46, 49, 51, 53-59; 13.18-21, 24-30, 34-35; 14.11, 16-23, 26-27; 17.33; 14.34-35 (the sequence is here simplified slightly). On that view, Matthew would have noted that passages on discipleship and conflict in Q 12.2-10, 51+53; 14.26-27 could appropriately be connected with the mission of the Twelve (Q 10.2-16) and with a passage from the Markan apocalypse (Mt. 10.17-22 = Mk. 13.9-13). The impression that Matthew has created order from the relative disorder of Q is occasioned by the abstraction of Q from its orderly Lukan contexts. Kloppenborg's attempt to find in this Q material a series of "sapiential speeches" (*The Formation of Q: Trajectories in Ancient Wisdom Traditions* [Philadelphia: Fortress, 1987], pp. 190-245) is undermined by his own acknowledgement of the "diverse" (pp. 199, 223) and "composite" (p. 206) character of the alleged speeches.

The link with the two *M19* discipleship sayings is underlined by the conclusion of *L16*: "So therefore, whoever of you does not renounce all his possessions *cannot be my disciple*" (Lk. 14.33, cf. vv. 26, 27). *M1 salt* is apparently out of place here, since Luke reproduces the Markan introduction, "Salt is good . . ." (Mk. 9.50), rather than the Matthean "You are the salt of the earth" (Mt. 5.13), which might have seemed more appropriate in a discipleship context. In spite of the Markan opening, Luke's familiarity with the Matthean version of the saying is clear. Underlinings represent verbal links between Mark and Luke, italics points at which Luke is influenced by Matthew:

> *You are the salt of the earth.* But if salt *is corrupted* [μωρανθῇ], how shall it be resalted? *It is good for nothing except to be thrown out for people to tread down.* (Mt. 5.13)

> <u>Salt is good</u>. But if salt becomes unsalted [ἄναλον γένηται], how shall you <u>restore</u> it [ἀρτύσετε]? Have salt among yourselves, and be at peace with one another. (Mk. 9.50)

> <u>Salt is good</u>. But if salt *is corrupted* [μωρανθῇ], how shall *it be* <u>restored</u> [ἀρτυθήσεται]? *Neither for the land nor for the dunghill is it useful.* The one who has ears to hear, let him hear.[80] (Lk. 14.34-35).

Luke's comment on the uselessness of adulterated salt tones down the violence of Matthew's. Elements from Mark have been recalled from a section which Luke otherwise omits (Mk. 9.41–10.12). Luke's understanding of the salt image clearly follows Matthew rather than Mark: Mark associates salt with peace; Matthew, with discipleship. By inserting the salt saying into a discipleship context, Luke betrays the influence of the Matthean equation: "You are the salt of the earth."[81]

15.1-7	*M30 lost sheep* (Mt. 18.12-14 →)
15.8-10	*L17 lost coin*
15.11-32	*M35 prodigal son* (Mt. 21.28-32 →)

80. This is the longer Markan form of the "ears to hear" saying, as in Lk. 8.8; cf. Mk. 4.9, 23. A shorter form, omitting "to hear," occurs at Mt. 11.15; 13.9, 43.

81. According to Fleddermann, the Markan version of the salt saying is secondary to the Q one: Mark inserts a second-person plural, omits the second half of the saying, and replaces the ambiguous μωρανθῇ with ἄναλον γένηται (Q, pp. 757-58). On the *L/M* theory too, the Matthean passage may be independent of Mark, although nothing definite can be said about its source.

M30 lost sheep is derived from the Matthean discourse on church order (Mt. 18.1-35), and Luke will later add an abbreviated version of some of the material that follows it:

M30 lost sheep	Mt. 18.12-14	→	Lk. 15.4-7
M31 brother who sins	Mt. 18.15	→	Lk. 17.3
M32 forgive repeatedly	Mt. 18.21-22	→	Lk. 17.4

In Matthew the Parable of the Lost Sheep introduces a passage addressed to church leaders who reenact the role of the shepherd as they seek to restore erring members of their congregation (Mt. 18.15-20). Luke breaks this connection by separating *M30 lost sheep* from *M31 brother who sins,* and by providing the parable with a new context which he derives from the earlier story of Levi's feast (*L/Mk;* italics = Lukan modifications):

> *And Levi made him a great feast in his house,* and there was a great crowd of tax collectors and others who were reclining with them *[ ].* And the Pharisees *and their* scribes *[ ] complained* to his disciples, saying, "Why do *you* eat and drink with tax collectors and sinners?" And Jesus answered and said to them, "Those who are *well* have no need of a doctor but those who are ill. I did not come to call the righteous but sinners *to repentance."* (Lk. 5.29-32)

> And all the tax collectors and sinners were drawing near to hear him. And the Pharisees and scribes complained saying, "This man receives sinners and eats with them." And he told them this parable, saying: "What man of you . . . ?" (Lk. 15.1-4)

Luke evidently sees an analogy between *M30 lost sheep* and the *L/Mk* saying in which Jesus' mission to sinners is compared with a doctor's responsibility to the sick. As a result, the Matthean parable is reassigned to a context within the ministry of Jesus similar to that of the Markan saying. The parable is no longer a directive for church leaders but a justification for a controversial aspect of Jesus' ministry.[82] Luke also carries over into his rendering of

82. It is Luke who is primarily responsible for the popular view that Jesus' acceptance of tax collectors and sinners is fundamental to his ministry (Lk. 7.36-50; 15.1-32; 18.9-14; 19.1-10). In Mark and Matthew, eating with tax collectors and sinners is something that Jesus does just *once* (Mk. 2.15-17 = Mt. 9.10-13; cf. Mt. 11.19; 21.31-32). Richard Burridge's question, "Jesus of Nazareth: Great Moral Teacher or Friend of Sinners?" represents a choice between the Jesus of Matthew and the Jesus of Luke (*Imitating Jesus: An Inclusive Approach to New Testament Ethics* [Grand Rapids: Eerdmans, 2007], pp. 33-79).

the parable the emphasis on repentance already introduced into the story of Levi. In the Matthean parable, the sheep is simply *found*. It plays no role in its own recovery. In Luke, the sheep is borne home on the shepherd's shoulders and there is rejoicing at its recovery, but the corresponding heavenly joy relates to "one repentant sinner" (Lk. 15.7), not to one who was lost but is now found.[83] This point recurs in the Parable of the Lost Coin, a Lukan composition modelled on *M30 lost sheep*[84] and indicating again Luke's predilection for paired male and female figures (here, the shepherd and the woman).[85] The disparity between the lost coin and the "one repentant sinner" (Lk. 15.10) is even more marked than in the case of the lost sheep. Yet the disparity is both deliberate and theologically significant. In the parable that follows, it is twice said of the prodigal son not that he is a repentant sinner but that he "was lost and is found" (Lk. 15.24, 32). This is a most unexpected description of the prodigal son, of whom it should rather be said that he "left home and has now returned." It is as if the prodigal son has changed places with the lost sheep and coin. The repentant sinner is twice described as "lost and found," the two lost objects are compared to a repentant sinner. The theological point is that repentance and being found are complementary descriptions of a single event. Jesus came to "find" sinners by calling them "to repentance" (cf. Lk. 5.32).

The Parable of the Prodigal Son opens by stating that "a certain man had two sons" (Lk. 15.11). Matthew includes a shorter parable that opens: "A man had two children" (Mt. 21.28). From that point on, the stories diverge. In Matthew, it is the father who takes the initiative, instructing each son in turn to labour in the vineyard (Mt. 21.28, 30). In Luke the initiative belongs to the younger son. Yet the two parables are still very similar. In both, one son creates a breach in the relationship with his father that he later puts right. In both, the other son is initially obedient to his father but later falls

---

83. In consequence, the application gives no explicit role to the shepherd (= Jesus?). In spite of these anomalies, Luke's verisimilitude has achieved its intended rhetorical effect on modern critical readers. According to Davies and Allison, "[I]t seems *overwhelmingly likely* that Jesus composed the similitude [of the lost sheep] in order to rebut criticism of his table fellowship with toll-collectors and sinners" (*Matthew*, 2.768-69; italics added).

84. So Goulder, *Luke*, 2.606-7; contrast Catchpole's claim that the Parable of the Lost Coin occurred in Q (*Quest for Q*, pp. 190-92).

85. So far in this gospel: Zechariah and Mary (Lk. 1.5-80); Simeon and Anna (2.25-38); the centurion of Capernaum and the widow of Nain (7.1-17); Simon and the sinful woman (7.36-50); the man sowing mustard seed and the women making bread (13.18-21). On this feature of Lukan composition, see Tannehill, *Narrative Unity*, vol. 1, pp. 132-35.

out with him. In both, the two cases are described in sequence.[86] Only in these two stories, taken together with their contexts, are tax collectors paired not just with sinners but with "prostitutes" (Mt. 21.31, 32; Lk. 15.30). The assumption that Luke's story must be independent of Matthew's overlooks the dynamic, generative nature of the Jesus tradition in its written embodiments.[87]

The dynamic of tradition would also be lost if we concluded that *Luke and not Jesus* is the author of the Parable of the Prodigal Son and the Parable of the Lost Coin.[88] That would be an utterly misleading claim. Luke composes these parables not as an independent author but as an interpreter, responsible for articulating the tradition that begins to form around Jesus during his ministry and that communicates him to ever-widening circles in the decades that follow, through preaching and writing. If oral and written tradition communicates Jesus, then it is also the case that Jesus communicates himself through the tradition. That is already so during his ministry, when certain traditions begin to take shape in response to the impulse proceeding from Jesus himself. From the start, he speaks through the medium of his own evolving reception. That is why the gospels are so concerned to represent not only what Jesus does and says but also the range of responses he evokes. Yet in and through the reception process Jesus truly speaks — when, for example, a later evangelist finds in parables handed down by a predecessor the possibility of articulating anew the universal significance of his engagement with "tax collectors and sinners." In the new text that results, it is still Jesus who is the speaker. The assertion that *"he said,* 'There was a man who had two sons . . .'" is not a fiction.

| 16.1-12 | *L18 unjust steward* |
| 16.13 | *M9 two masters* (Mt. 6.24 →) |

---

86. Mt. 21.28-29 = Lk. 15.12-24; Mt. 21.30 = Lk. 15.25-32.

87. In *Beyond the Q Impasse — Luke's Use of Matthew* (ed. A. J. McNicol et al.), it is assumed that this parable, like the Great Feast, is drawn from "Luke's non-Matthean tradition" (p. 219; cf. p. 211). While that is quite possible, direct literary relationships can take the form of free rewriting as well as cautious editing.

88. "As for the two sons and their father [Mt. 21.28-32], Luke has seen a way to make of them his masterpiece" (Goulder, *Luke*, 2.603). True though that may be, the only possibilities Goulder can envisage are his own view, which is that Luke is the author of this parable, and the view of Jeremias and others that it derives from the historical Jesus (pp. 609-16). The fact that Luke has attributed this "masterpiece" specifically to Jesus, and located it in the context of a narrative account of his identity, is ignored.

16.14-15	*L19 hostile Pharisees*
16.16	*M15 men of violence* (Mt. 11.12-13 →)
16.17	*M3 not an iota* (Mt. 5.18 →)
16.18	*M5 divorce* (Mt. 5.32 →)
16.19-31	*L20 rich man*

M9 two masters is added to a sequence of lessons drawn from *L18 unjust steward*. Luke has found a point of contact in the term "mammon." Positively, the unjust steward teaches us that we are to use the "mammon of unrighteousness" to make friends who will welcome us in our eternal dwelling place (Lk. 16.9). Negatively, we learn from him that if we are unfaithful in the matter of "unrighteous mammon," we will not be entrusted with treasure in heaven (16.10-12). We are not to serve two masters, but must make our choice between God and "mammon" (16.13 = *M9*). *M9* is only loosely related to the parable, however, and serves to introduce *L19 hostile Pharisees*, which underlines the shift in theme from the proper use of money (16.8-12) to the improper love of money said to characterize the Pharisees (16.13-15). The thematic shift suggests that *L19 hostile Pharisees* was composed as a sequel to *M9 two masters*, but that *L18 unjust steward* is pre-Lukan.[89] It is perhaps to be understood as an anecdote attributed to Jesus and based on some actual occurrence. Lessons are extracted from it, but it cannot have been composed for the sake of those lessons.

In the earlier Matthean context, *M15 men of violence* shares with *M3 not an iota* a common concern with the law. According to *M15*, the kingdom of heaven has been subjected to violence from the days of John the Baptist, who marks the terminus and goal of the prophets and the law (in that order). It is unclear how the two claims about the Baptist relate to one another. Perhaps they were not intended to do so. Luke, however, achieves a coherent sequence incorporating both *M15* and *M3*. He reverses the two halves of *M15 men of violence*, and restores the normal sequence of law and prophets. The negative reference to violence is replaced by a positive reference to the preaching of the kingdom.[90] By juxtaposing the new version of *M15* with *M3 not an iota*, Luke has constructed an important statement on the relation of law (and prophets) to gospel:

89. So Fitzmyer, who finds only minimal indications of Lukan redaction in vv. 1-12 (*Luke*, 2.1095-96).

90. Luke's εὐαγγελίζεται is widely regarded as secondary to Matthew's (and Q's) βιάζεται (so Catchpole, *Quest for Q*, pp. 233-34).

The law and the prophets were until John. From then on, the kingdom of God has been preached, and everyone is dragged into it. But it is easier for heaven and earth to pass away than for one dot of the law to fall. (Lk. 16.16-17)

John the Baptist marks the point at which law and prophets give way to the transformative preaching of the gospel; and yet the law retains its validity. Juxtaposed in this way, the two M^{res} passages point towards a dialectical view of the law with a long future in Christian theology and an equally long future of Marcionite criticism. *M5 divorce* is also related to the law in its Matthean form. Luke does not make the connection explicit, but in placing this saying after the two law-related sayings he appears to take it for granted.[91]

L19 hostile Pharisees touches on the theme of love of money, *M15 men of violence* and *M3 not an iota* are concerned with the law and the prophets, and the two themes are brought together in a third Lukan parable about a rich man (16.19; cf. 16.1; 12.16). The rich man's request for Lazarus to be sent to warn his brothers of the postmortem fate that awaits them is turned down on the grounds that "they have Moses and the prophets" (16.29; cf. v. 31). Luke 16 as a whole is a remarkable chiastic construct in which diverse *L* and *M* material is related to the themes either of wealth or law or both, without detriment to the integrity of the individual units.

17.1	*M29 temptations to sin* (Mt. 18.7 →)
17.2	*M28 millstone* (Mt. 18.6 →)
17.3	*M31 brother who sins* (Mt. 18.15 →)
17.4	*M32 forgive repeatedly* (Mt. 18.21-22 →)
17.5-6	*M27 little faith* (Mt. 17.19-20 →)
17.7-10	*L21 unworthy servants*
17.11-19	*L22 ten lepers*

The opening of Matthew's discourse on church order is drawn largely from Mark 9.33-47, where Matthew found the dispute about greatness and the example of the child together with the sayings about the millstone and self-mutilation (Mt. 18.1-9). Following this Markan opening, the Parable of the

---

91. For Fleddermann, Lk. 16.16 is identical to Q 16.16, apart from the substitution of the Lukan εὐαγγελίζεται for the Matthean βιάζεται (Q, pp. 781-83). Lk. 16.17 is similarly close to Q 16.17, and Lk. 16.18 to Q 16.18 (pp. 783-87). A thematic link is only possible, however, if Luke has carried over the Matthean association between the divorce saying and the law.

Lost Sheep (18.10-14) introduces a passage which tells how church leaders are to reenact the role of the shepherd in seeking to restore erring church members (18.15-20). A short dialogue about forgiveness (18.21-22) leads into the Parable of the Unforgiving Servant (18.23-35).

With the exception of the sayings on self-mutilation and the concluding parable, most of this material is represented in Luke:

M/Mk, L/Mk	Mt. 18.1-5 *greatness, child* [= Mk. 9.33-37, Lk. 9.46-48]		
L/M/Mk	Mt. 18.6 *M28 millstone* [= Mk. 9.42]	→	*Lk. 17.2
L/M	Mt. 18.7 *M29 temptations to sin*	→	Lk. 17.1
M/Mk	Mt. 18.8-9 *self-mutilation*		
M	Mt. 18.10 *little ones, angels*		
L/M	Mt. 18.12-14 *M30 lost sheep*	→	*Lk. 15.4-7
L/M	Mt. 18.15 *M31 brother who sins*	→	Lk. 17.3
L/M	Mt. 18.21-22 *M32 forgive repeatedly*	→	Lk. 17.4
M	Mt. 18.23-35 *unforgiving servant*		

When *M* and *M/Mk* material is removed, the only significant disruption to the Matthean sequence is the relocation of *M30 lost sheep* to a new context. The rationale for this has already been discussed. The Matthean connection is also evident in Luke's reference to "one of these little ones" (Lk. 17.2 = Mt. 18.6). In Matthew this refers back to the "child" mentioned in the previous verse; in Luke the phrase has no antecedent.

At first sight, the items collected in Luke 17.1-19 seem disparate. The brief rendering of parts of Matthew's church order discourse deals with the topics of offences (17.1-2) and forgiveness (17.3-4). This is followed by *M27 little faith*, extracted from the *M/Mk* version of the story of the epileptic boy, the conclusion of which Matthew has rewritten (Mk. 9.14-29 = Mt. 17.14-20). The disciples' attempt at exorcism has failed, and they ask: "Why could we not cast it out?" (Mk. 9.28 = Mt. 17.19). To this question Mark's Jesus replies, "This type can only be cast out by prayer" (Mk. 9.29), whereas Matthew's Jesus replies, "Because of your little faith" — to which is added the saying about faith moving mountains (Mt. 17.20 = *M27 little faith*; cf. Mt. 21.21 = Mk. 11.23). Luke passed over both conclusions in his own version of the exorcism story (Lk. 9.37-43), and he introduces the Matthean saying not with a question about failed exorcism but with the request, "Lord, increase our faith" (17.5). The request is probably suggested by the Matthean reference to "little faith" (ὀλιγοπιστία). For Luke, faith the size of a mustard seed has power to uproot a tree rather than a mountain.[92] Yet the saying leads directly into *L21 unworthy servants*, in order to present a more adequate account of the divine/human relationship than one based on a quantitative understanding of faith. This may also account for the placement of *L22 ten lepers*, a story that draws on the Markan account of the healing of a leper (Mk. 1.40-45 = Mt. 8.1-4 = Lk. 5.12-16), but makes its own distinctive contribution in highlighting the theme of gratitude.

17.20-22	*M41 kingdom in midst* (Mt. 24.23-25 →)
17.23-24	*M42 lightning* (Mt. 24.26-27 →)
17.25	*L23 suffering Son of man* (cf. Mk. 8.31 = Lk. 9.22)
17.26-27	*M44 days of Noah* (Mt. 24.37-39 →)
17.28-30, 32	*L24 days of Lot*
17.31	*M40 no return* (Mt. 24.17-18 →)
17.33	*M20 finding, losing* (Mt. 10.39 →)
17.34-35	*M45 one taken* (Mt. 24.40-41 →)
17.37	*M43 body, eagles* (Mt. 24.28 →)

In *M41 kingdom in midst*, Luke probably rewrites Matthew 24.23-25 (= Mk. 13.21-23), a warning against false Christs. Matthew follows this warning with a second, non-Markan warning reproduced by Luke as *M42 lightning*. Thus *M41* and *M42* correspond to the parallel Matthean warnings (italics indicate shared terminology):

> *M/Mk* Then if anyone says to you, "*Behold, here* is the Christ," do not believe. For false Christs and false prophets will arise and will perform great signs and wonders, so as to mislead, if possible, even the elect. *Behold*, I have told you beforehand. (Mt. 24.23-25)
>
> *L/M41* . . . The kingdom of God does not come with observation [μετὰ παρατηρήσεως], nor will they say, "*Behold, here* and there." For *behold*, the kingdom of God is in your midst. (Lk. 17.20-21)
>
> *M* Then if anyone *says to you*, "*Behold*, he is in the desert," *do not go* forth; "Behold, he is in the inner rooms," do not believe. *For as the*

---

92. On the Q theory, Luke preserves the Q reference to a tree, which Matthew has assimilated to the mountain in Mk. 11.23; the passage is therefore another Mark/Q overlap, and Mark is again secondary (Fleddermann, *Q*, pp. 804-7). On the *L/M* theory, the replacement of the mountain by the tree simply represents Luke's tendency to differentiate himself from Matthew when dependent on him — and also, perhaps, a recollection of the fig tree in Mk. 11.20 or Mt. 21.21 (Goulder, *Luke*, 2.642).

lightning comes from the east and shines as far as the west, *so will be*
the coming of *the Son of man.* (Mt. 24.26-27)
L/M42 . . . And they will *say to you,* "*Behold,* there, behold here." *Do not*
go, do not follow. *For as the lightning* flashes and lights up the sky
from one side to the other, *so will be [ ] the Son of man* in his day.
(Lk. 17.23-24)

That *M41 kingdom in midst* derives from the *M/Mk* passage is not certain, but the resulting correspondence to the Matthean sequence makes this
probable. Luke's rewriting of Matthew here would be no more drastic than
in the case of *M25 signs of the times* (Mt. 16.2-3 → Lk. 12.54-56). The addition
of Luke 17.21 creates a parallel between a false claim and the true one, along
the lines of *M42 lightning.* If Luke is independent of Matthew in *M41 king-*
dom in midst, we have yet another of the coincidences on which the Q theory
must rely so heavily. Matthew and Luke would both include two passages
warning in similar terms against false eschatological claims, deriving from
Mark and Q in the case of Matthew, L and Q in the case of Luke. It is more
likely that Luke here rewrites the Matthean passage.[93]

Luke has already relocated the conclusion of Matthew's extended eschatological discourse at 12.35-48 (*M46 thief/servant* = Mt. 24.43-51). Here, he incorporates the two preceding passages that Matthew has added to Mark: *M42 light-*
ning (Mt. 24.26-27) and *M44 days of Noah* (Mt. 24.37-39). As a result, he can
later engage with the eschatological discourse in its Markan form, without further reference to Matthew (Lk. 21.5-33 = Mk. 13.1-31). To *M44* Luke has added
L24 days of Lot as a parallel scriptural instance of sudden catastrophe. It was no
doubt the conjunction of *M44 days of Noah* and *M40 no return* in Matthew that
led Luke to think of Lot and his wife (cf. Gn. 19.12-26).[94] Also relevant here is the
original context of *M40,* where the urgent warning is occasioned by the imminent destruction of a city, as in the case of Lot (Mt. 24.15-16; cf. Lk. 21.20-21).[95]

---

93. Lk. 17.20b-21 is attributed to Lukan tradition by Fitzmyer, *Luke,* 2.1158-59; Kloppenborg,
Formation of Q, p. 155.

94. According to Kloppenborg, Lk. 17.28-30 derives from Q and 17.31 from Mark (*Formation*
of Q, pp. 156-58; cf. Catchpole, *Quest for Q,* pp. 248-50).

95. That *M40 no return* is derived from Mt. 24.17-18 rather than Mk. 13.15-16 is suggested by
Luke's retention of Matthew's single imperative (μὴ καταβάτω ἆραι) rather than Mark's double
one (μὴ καταβάτω μηδὲ εἰσελθάτω ἆραί τι); n.b. also ὁ ἐν τῷ ἀγρῷ (= Matthew) rather than ὁ εἰς
τὸν ἀγρόν (Mark). J. Lambrecht attributes these differences to Q ("Die Logia-Quellen von
Markus 13," *Bib* 47 [1966], pp. 321-60; pp. 342-46). It is methodologically questionable, however, to
postulate Q on the basis of minor agreements between Matthew and Luke against Mark.

Luke concludes his sequential rendering of the Mission Discourse of Matthew 10 by adding *M20 finding, losing*, before returning to the Matthean version of the eschatological discourse with *M45 one taken* and *M43 body, eagles*. His engagement with Matthew 24 as a whole takes the following form:

M40 no return	Mt. 24.17-18	→	*Lk. 17.31
M41 kingdom in midst	Mt. 24.23-25	→	Lk. 17.20-21
M42 lightning	Mt. 24.26-27	→	Lk. 17.23-24
M43 body, eagles	Mt. 24.28	→	*Lk. 17.37
M44 days of Noah	Mt. 24.37-39	→	Lk. 17.26-27
M45 one taken	Mt. 24.40-41	→	Lk. 17.34-35
M46 thief/servant	Mt. 24.43-51	→	*Lk. 12.35-48

Complicated though this material may be to analyze in detail, the compositional procedure is actually very simple. Luke is primarily interested in distinctively Matthean material in Matthew 24.43-51 (*M46 thief/servant*, already incorporated) and in 24.23-41 (*M41-45*). In Luke's rendering, the latter passage is supplemented by *L24 days of Lot*, linked to a further passage from Matthew 24 (*M40 no return*), and to *M20 finding, losing*. Allowing for the insertion of this material relating to Lot at Luke 17.28-33, this eschatological discourse only deviates from the Matthean sequence in its placement of *M43 body, eagles* at the conclusion.

Luke's presentation of this material goes far beyond rewording and rearranging. The primary interpretative goal is evidently to detach the supplementary Matthean material on the parousia from the Markan eschatological discourse, and thus from the fall of Jerusalem — which, for Luke, is the catastrophic event of which that discourse is speaking (cf. Lk. 21.20-24; cf. 19.41-44). According to Luke, the fall of Jerusalem ushers in not the parousia but "the times of the Gentiles" (21.24). As for Luke's understanding of the parousia itself, the radical rewriting suggests that *M41 kingdom in midst* may be the key to the entire presentation. Is the event in which "the kingdom of God is in the midst of you" identical to "the day of the Son of man," which dawns suddenly, like lightning (17.21, 24)?[96] In the rewriting of *M41*, are there anticipations of the Johannine reinterpretation of the parousia as insepara-

---

96. So George Caird, who writes: "The kingdom and the Son of man alike will come with the unpredictable ubiquity of a lightning flash, defying all calculations, so that no sentries can be posted to give warning of their approach" (*Saint Luke*, p. 197). A reference to the fall of Jerusalem seems implausible, however (*pace* Caird, pp. 199-200; followed by N. T. Wright, *Jesus and the Victory of God* [London: SPCK, 1996], p. 359).

ble from what takes place at Easter and in the coming of the Spirit? That is perhaps why the antecedent to the day of the Son of man is that "first he must suffer many things and be rejected by this generation" (17.25).

18.1-8   *L25 unjust judge*
18.9-14   *L26 two men in temple*

These parables are intended as a pair, as their similar introductions indicate. The Parable of the Unjust Judge inculcates the lesson that one "ought always to pray and not lose heart" (18.1). Yet the conclusion speaks not of answered prayer in general but of the eschatological vindication of the elect, who cry to God day and night (18.7). The evangelist may assume that what one ought always to pray is simply, "Thy kingdom come" (cf. 11.2). If the whole parable is intended to be taken eschatologically, then it is continuous with 17.20-37. Yet it is not clear whether either passage intends a purely future and cosmic eschatology. The event in which God vindicates his elect in the coming of the Son of man (18.7-8) cannot be unrelated to the event in which the tax collector "went down to his house justified rather than the other" — or, more generally, the event in which those who exalt themselves will be humbled while those who humble themselves will be exalted (18.13, 14; cf. 14.11). Whether these parables are pre-Lukan or not, their juxtaposition suggests that Luke here seeks to connect Jesus' characteristic advocacy of the sinner with the dawning of God's kingdom.

Luke continues to interpret the written tradition he inherits as he reverts to the Markan narrative framework at 18.15. In the extended final section of this chapter, the aim has been to show how he assembles the section of his gospel where he has no Markan or Matthean framework to guide him (11.33–18.14). This section is not at all the confused miscellany that it is sometimes supposed to be. At every point, Luke's juxtapositions of *M* and *L* material attest his own role as shaper and interpreter of the tradition he inherits from his predecessors.

In editing, rewriting, and interpreting the gospels of Mark and Matthew for Theophilus and other readers, Luke follows a simple compositional procedure that may be summarized as follows:

(1) Integration of the Markan and Matthean sequences is normally achieved by juxtaposing large-scale blocks of material. There is a concern to restore the original Markan sequence, subjected to significant

restructuring in the first half of Matthew. In consequence, Luke's editing of Mark is relatively independent of Matthew's (although he follows Matthean precedent in undertaking it at all). Luke's Matthean sequence is derived from the material that remains when Matthew's use of Mark has been eliminated. For that reason, its components normally occur in Luke at a later position relative to Mark than in Matthew.

(2) A substantial quantity of sayings material is extracted from the Matthean framework and gathered into a Sayings Collection. From this Luke constructs the latter part of his so-called "journey narrative," supplementing it with material unique to himself. Luke's interpretative activity is most evident here in the new juxtapositions he creates. Respect for Matthean sequence is still evident, however, in the presentation of material from the Matthean discourses on mission and church order.

In and through this editorial activity, simple to summarize yet complex in execution, Luke enters into the dynamic of the tradition itself: a tradition seeking to articulate anew the self-communication of the risen Jesus.

CHAPTER 5

Thomas versus Q

Luke is "dependent" on Matthew (as well as Mark) in the sense that he is Matthew's *interpreter.* Yet Matthew and Mark are themselves already interpreters. Matthew interprets the material he draws from Mark and elsewhere. And Mark is no less an interpreter than his successors — assuming that his gospel too contains preexisting material from oral or written sources, and is not a pure fiction composed out of nothing. The role of the evangelist is to present the traditions of Jesus' life, words, and destiny in coherent written form, and thereby to *interpret* the figure who speaks and is spoken of in those traditions. To retrace the literary relationships between the gospels is to uncover crucial moments in a reception process in which Jesus assumes his definitive canonical identity.

A canon-oriented view of the reception process is, however, a retrospective reconstruction that privileges certain moments and passes over others. In the definition of the fourfold canonical gospel, the reception process itself becomes the object of interpretation; and that interpretation takes the form of a *delimitation.* Authentic reception of the Jesus tradition is now confined to the gospels attributed to Matthew, Mark, Luke, and John, and other modes of reception as represented by other gospel literature are rejected as inauthentic — in principle if not always in practice. This delimitation has remained communally normative to this day. There is no good reason to reject it, belatedly taking up the cause of those it allegedly "marginalized." Yet it is important to recognize that the canonical recognition of Matthew, Mark, Luke, and John represents the construction of a new textual object, rather than a passive acknowledgement of what should have been obvious to all. Since individual gospels predate the decision that makes them "canonical" or "noncanonical," it should not be assumed that

217

gospels later assigned to the first category originated in isolation from gospels assigned to the second.

That assumption remains deeply embedded in modern scholarly discussion of gospel origins. Thus the so-called "synoptic problem" is constructed entirely within the space marked out by the canon. Even the hypothetical Q document contains nothing that is not already known from its canonical sources. Those who seek to exploit its difference from the canonical gospels must do so on the basis of what it lacks rather than what it contains.

The enduring influence of the canonical decision is also evident in connection with the *Gospel of Thomas* (henceforth *GTh*), which, some decades after its discovery, has still not been successfully integrated into any overarching account of gospel origins. Since much of the relevant sayings material is already found in the canonically derived Q document, it is difficult to find a role even for a nonhypothetical gospel within a "synoptic problem" whose conventional solution is supposed to be an assured result of modern scholarship. Even where Thomas is believed to contain early traditions, it is assumed that these existed in parallel with Q. Thus there are supposed to have been *two* literary embodiments of the sayings tradition, which — unlike the synoptic gospels — are formally quite distinct. *GTh* emphasizes the autonomy of each simple or composite saying by its use of the introductory formula, "Jesus said." In contrast, Q gathers individual sayings into more extended discourses supplemented by narrative fragments; formal or structural features are hard to identify. This coexistence of closely related material in the two different literary formats is an unrecognized problem in current scholarship. It stems from the attempt to graft the rediscovered text onto an older model of synoptic origins which is allowed to remain intact; this is the case even with scholars who consider themselves to be free of the bias towards the canonical.

According to Helmut Koester, "the sayings of the *Gospel of Thomas* consist for the most part of aphorisms, proverbs, wisdom sayings, parables, prophetic sayings about the 'Kingdom of the Father,' and community rules."[1] The author was "a collector and compiler who used a number of small units of collected sayings, some perhaps available in written form, and composed them randomly."[2] The Gnostic features evident in some of these sayings do

---

1. H. Koester, *Ancient Christian Gospels: Their History and Development* (Philadelphia: Trinity Press International; London: SCM Press, 1990), p. 80.

2. Koester, *Ancient Christian Gospels,* pp. 81-82.

not require a second-century date, since "the rise of Gnosticism must be dated earlier than the second century and . . . cannot be viewed as a relatively late Christian phenomenon."[3] Koester finds that, "[o]f the seventy-nine sayings of Thomas with Synoptic Gospel parallels, forty-six have parallels in Q, but the typical apocalyptic perspective of the later redaction of Q does not appear in any of these sayings."[4] While Thomas may derive in part from the earliest stratum of Q, it also seems to reflect a still earlier Sayings Collection on which Q[1] also drew, whose wording is at some points more faithfully preserved in the Thomas version.[5] It was, however, the developing Q tradition and not *GTh* that paved the way for the synoptic gospels.

It is possible, and perhaps probable, that Thomas does preserve some material in presynoptic form. Yet Koester's preoccupation with this possibility leads him to overlook the *formal* disparity between Q and Thomas. Q does not present sayings in random order or introduce them with a constantly repeated formula. Random individualized sayings are characteristic of parts of the wisdom tradition, but that tradition gives no precedent for the repeated introductory formula with its concern to emphasize the identity of the speaker. The editors responsible for the present *GTh* felt it important not only to preserve a saying but also to emphasize that it was Jesus himself who uttered it, and this concern may well go back to very early times. Whatever the date of the extant text(s) of Thomas, its *form* may still be archaic, deriving directly from primitive Christian Sayings Collections. If such Sayings Collections existed, however, there would be no need for Q. The Q document, which we have already seen to be implausible as an explanation of non-Markan parallels between Matthew and Luke, would also be redundant as a bridge between early Palestinian Christianity and the later gospels. If *GTh* can be shown to attest the existence of primitive Christian Sayings Collections, an important though indirect role in a historical reconstruction of gospel origins would now be played by a noncanonical text. Without Q, *GTh* would be still more significant than it is for Koester.

James Robinson finds the parallel between Q and Thomas in their shared *Gattung* or genre, that of the Λόγοι σοφῶν, extending beyond the early Christian Sayings Collections to texts as diverse as the book of Proverbs, *Pirke Aboth,* and the *Sentences of Sextus.*[6] Robinson is concerned to re-

---

3. Koester, *Ancient Christian Gospels,* p. 83.

4. Koester, *Ancient Christian Gospels,* p. 87.

5. Koester, *Ancient Christian Gospels,* pp. 87-99.

6. James M. Robinson, "ΛΟΓΟΙ ΣΟΦΩΝ: On the Gattung of Q" (1971), in his *The Sayings Gospel Q: Collected Essays* (Leuven: Leuven University Press, 2005), pp. 37-74; pp. 63n, 65-72.

trace the history of this genre, and he locates *GTh* at a late stage of "the trajectory from the hypostasized Sophia to the gnostic Redeemer" — at the very point where this *Gattung* was to be supplanted by "the *Gattung* of dialogues of the Resurrected with his disciples [which] provided a freer context for the imaginary gnostic speculations attributed to Jesus."[7] Q, then, is earlier than Thomas in its present form.[8] Yet we should envisage both texts as developing through time, from Q^1 to Q^{Mt} and Q^{Lk} and through whatever prior stages led to the Coptic version of Thomas.[9] Given that both texts "probably include authentic sayings of Jesus," they may be said to "overlap" chronologically; the late date of the final redaction of Thomas "cannot be validly used as an argument for leaving this text out of the study of the Synoptic tradition."[10] Above all, Q and Thomas both derive primarily from "the living oral tradition, even though smaller collections, perhaps even written collections, may have been incorporated in either or both."[11] Both texts "would seem to have received their first written impetus, initially determinative of their genre, from sapiential books."[12] It is almost as if these parallel texts are duplicates of one another. Working with an excessively broad concept of genre, Robinson offers no explanation for the formal characteristics that *differentiate* Thomas from Q, in spite of all they have in common. Although, like Koester, he supposes that Thomas may contain some very early material, the rediscovered gospel is accorded little *explanatory* value in the context of synoptic origins. Thomas represents an independent trajectory that ends with the dialogue gospels of Nag Hammadi, and Q remains unchallenged in its traditional role as the second source for Matthew and Luke.

The Q hypothesis is based on the dubious supposition that Luke is wholly independent of Matthew. But it also presupposes, equally dubiously, that canonical gospel origins can be adequately accounted for without recourse to noncanonical literature. The standard two-source model tacitly supposes that the retrospective distinction between canonical and noncanonical gospels corresponds to neutral historical reality, and that one can address the problem of gospel origins by attending to Matthew, Mark, Luke, and John alone. The enduring influence of the standard model is still

7. Robinson, "ΛΟΓΟΙ ΣΟΦΩΝ," p. 74.

8. Robinson, "On Bridging the Gulf between Q and the Gospel of Thomas" (1986), in *The Sayings Gospel Q*, pp. 203-58; pp. 219-45.

9. Robinson, "On Bridging the Gulf," pp. 243-44.

10. Robinson, "On Bridging the Gulf," pp. 244, 245.

11. Robinson, "On Bridging the Gulf," p. 249.

12. Robinson, "On Bridging the Gulf," p. 250.

perceptible even in the work of scholars such as Koester and Robinson, where *GTh* is presented as an unexplained double of Q whose "trajectory" simply bypasses all canonical literature.

In the absence of Q, the significance of Thomas must be reassessed. It will be argued here that Thomas preserves certain formal characteristics of the primitive Christian Sayings Collection (SC), a genre that predated the synoptic gospels and that remained important throughout the second century. In other words, what is attempted here is *a reading of Thomas in the light of its genre*. Generic features will be identified that are shared with other early sayings traditions; idiosyncratic features of this text are therefore of less interest. If evidence of an SC genre can be recovered from Thomas and elsewhere, this genre may provide the clue to the earliest, presynoptic inscription and transmission of Jesus' sayings. Although (contra Q) no primitive Christian SC can be recovered from later redaction, it is arguable that Thomas preserves isolated items — notably certain parables — in their oldest accessible form. Crucial evidence of presynoptic sayings transmission comes to light when the genre of Thomas is rightly identified and when that genre is seen to be compatible on occasion with a high degree of textual stability.

In this way the Q hypothesis may be replaced by an *SC hypothesis,* which finds an important key to synoptic origins not in a hypothetical document constructed within the canonical limit but in extant noncanonical material.

De-gnosticizing Thomas

The text that came to be known as "the Gospel according to Thomas" gives indications of a long and complex prehistory. This cannot be reconstructed in detail. Attempts to recover an early form of this gospel simply by stripping away late material rest on the questionable assumption that the text has evolved in a straightforwardly linear manner.[13] What can be more persuasively argued is that, whatever the process by which it came to be what it is, *GTh* is a later exemplar of an archaic genre, the primitive Christian Sayings Collection.

How "late" is Thomas, in approximately its present form? An answer to this question must begin from the Coptic codex (Nag Hammadi Codex II)

---

13. See April D. DeConick, *Recovering the Original Gospel of Thomas: A History of the Gospel and Its Growth* (London & New York: T. & T. Clark International, 2005).

in which the full form of this gospel is preserved, along with six other texts: *Apocryphon of John, Gospel according to Philip, Hypostasis of the Archons, On the Origin of the World, Expository Treatise on the Soul,* and *Book of Thomas the Contender.*[14] The *Gospel of Thomas* is the second item in this collection. These and other Nag Hammadi texts appear to have been translated from Greek.[15] According to the editors of the *Apocryphon of John,* these translations are to be set alongside

> the various translations into Coptic of biblical books made most likely during the latter part of the Third Century. These appear to have been un-coordinated efforts of individuals for their own benefit or that of other private persons. These biblical translations tend to be idiosyncratic and uncontrolled. . . . The various Coptic dialects are well represented among these fragments.[16]

The translations attest the spread of Christianity in Egypt from ethnic Greeks to Copts. As the manuscript tradition developed, texts that may originally have been translated into various Coptic dialects were increasingly copied in a standardized Sahidic form, that is, in "a new and artificial form of Coptic, a literary *Kunstsprache,* which was accessible to all Coptic speakers."[17] A mid- or late-fourth-century date for the Sahidic codices from Nag Hammadi "would correspond well with the beginning of the hegemony of standard Sahidic in Egyptian monasteries as evident from biblical manuscripts."[18] Codex II stands near the beginning of this development, however, and retains many morphological and orthographical features of the Subachmimic dialect in which the texts it contains may originally have been

14. For texts and introductions, see volumes XXXIII and XX-XXI in the series Nag Hammadi and Manichean Studies (ed. J. M. Robinson and H. J. Klimkeit) and Nag Hammadi Studies (ed. Martin Krause, James M. Robinson, and Frederik Wisse). These volumes are referred to henceforth as NHMS XXXIII and NHS XX or XXI. NHMS XXXIII contains *The Apocryphon of John: Synopsis of Nag Hammadi Codices II,1; III,1; and IV,1 with BG 8502,2,* ed. Michael Waldstein and Frederik Wisse (Leiden: Brill, 1995). NHS XX-XXI contain *Nag Hammadi Codex II,2-7,* ed. Bentley Layton, 2 vols. (Leiden: Brill, 1989).

15. For refutation of claims that *GTh* was originally composed in Syriac or Aramaic, see Simon J. Gathercole, *The Composition of the Gospel of Thomas: Original Language and Influences,* SNTSMS (Cambridge: Cambridge University Press, 2012), pp. 17-125.

16. Waldstein and Wisse, NHMS XXXIII, p. 7.

17. Waldstein and Wisse, NHMS XXXIII, p. 6. In contrast, Bentley Layton understands Sahidic as "the prestigious and orthodox dialect of the greater Nile valley and monasticism" (NHS XX, p. 7).

18. Waldstein and Wisse, NHMS XXXIII, p. 6.

translated, perhaps some decades earlier.[19] It may therefore be among the older Nag Hammadi codices, dating from the first half of the fourth century — together with the fragments of Codex XIII, written either by the same scribe or under his supervision.[20]

The standardization of Sahidic was evidently achieved through the monasteries. Waldstein and Wisse argue that

> without the rapid spread of cenobitic monasticism in Fourth Century Egypt the shift to and quick success of standard Sahidic becomes inexplicable. Only the scriptoria of the monasteries and their discipline could assure the remarkable degree of uniformity achieved in Sahidic orthography and scribal conventions during the second half of the Fourth Century.[21]

Evidence for a monastic origin has been found in the colophon to Codex II, where the scribe appeals to his "brothers," who are "the spiritual" (NIⲠⲚⲈⲨⲘⲀⲦⲒⲔⲞⲤ), to "remember me in your prayers."[22] *GTh* contains several references to "solitary ones" or "monks" (ⲘⲘⲞⲚⲀⲬⲞⲤ).[23] The Nag Hammadi codices were found near the Pachomian monastery at Chenoboskeia, and it has been widely supposed that they were produced and used there.[24] That would mean, as Robinson argues, that "the common presentation of the monastic movement of the fourth century C.E. as solidly orthodox is an anachronism, and more nearly reflects the situation of the later monasticism that recorded the legends about the earlier period."[25] Alternatively, the proximity to the Pachomian monastery may be coincidental, and the books may have been produced and used by a distinct group of Gnostic

19. See NHS XX, pp. 6-16. Layton here identifies the language of Codex II as "Crypto-Subachmimic," and draws attention to a fragmentary version of one of its tractates (*On the Origin of the World*) in pure Subachmimic (p. 7).

20. NHS XX, p. 4; *Nag Hammadi Codices XI, XII, XIII*, ed. Charles W. Hedrick (NHS XXVIII) (Leiden: Brill, 1990), p. 362.

21. Waldstein and Wisse, NHMS XXXIII, p. 6.

22. NHS XXI, p. 205.

23. *GTh* 16.4; 49.1; 75; cf. 23.1-2.

24. So James M. Robinson, "Introduction," in *The Nag Hammadi Library in English* (Leiden: Brill, 1984²) (henceforth *NHL*), pp. 16-21. "The headquarters monastery of the Pachomian order at Pabau, where the Basilica of Saint Pachomius was located, as well as the third Pachomian monastery at Chenoboskeia, where Pachomius himself began his Christian life as a hermit, are only 8.7 and 5.3 kilometers . . . respectively from the place where the library was buried" (p. 16).

25. Robinson, "Introduction," p. 18.

Christians.[26] A connection to the monastery seems plausible, however. Robinson also notes that the codices were found concealed in a jar at the foot of a cliff, in close proximity to caves probably used by monks or hermits associated with the monastery.

The texts of Codex II might seem to share a common orientation towards certain forms of "Gnostic" Christianity. If so, then the compiler of this volume has acted appropriately in placing *GTh* alongside such texts as the *Apocryphon of John*, the *Gospel of Philip*, and the *Hypostasis of the Archons*.[27] Thomas might then be regarded as a "Gnostic" text along with the others; that is, it would be the product of a relatively late development whose links to the formative period of Christian thought are unclear. It cannot be assumed that Thomas has been placed in the company of texts essentially alien to it, or that it finds its natural habitat in the vicinity of the canonical gospels. The location of Thomas between the canonical gospels and Gnostic Christianity needs to be clarified.

Most early publications on *GTh* saw the newly discovered text as closely related to Gnosticism. According to Grant and Freedman, writing in 1960,

> [t]he Gospel of Thomas shows how Gnostics understood, or rather, misunderstood, Jesus and his gospel. It shows how they constructed a bridge between their own faith and that of the Christian Church.[28]

Gnosticism is here understood to be a distinct religion with its own "faith," which can be contrasted with that of "the Christian Church," representing another distinct religion. Thomas embodies one religion's attempt to (mis)appropriate traditions belonging to another.[29] It is the expression of

26. So Alastair H. B. Logan, *The Gnostics: Identifying an Early Christian Cult* (London: T. & T. Clark, 2006), pp. 12-29. Logan appeals especially to evidence from Epiphanius.

27. Enno Popkes argues that the texts included in Codex II have undergone a common redaction: see his *Das Menschenbild des Thomasevangeliums: Studien zu seiner religionsgeschichtlichen und theologischen Einordnung*, WUNT (Tübingen: Mohr Siebeck, 2007). For discussion of this thesis, see also Jutta Leonhardt-Balzer, "On the Redactional and Theological Relationship between the *Gospel of Thomas* and the *Apocryphon of John*," in *Das Thomasevangelium: Entstehung — Rezeption — Theologie*, ed. J. Frey, E. E. Popkes, and J. Schröter, BZNW (Berlin & New York: De Gruyter, 2008), pp. 251-71. Criteria for distinguishing redactional assimilation from common motifs or terminology are, however, difficult to establish.

28. Robert M. Grant with David Noel Freedman, *The Secret Sayings of Jesus according to the Gospel of Thomas* (London: Collins, 1960), p. 16.

29. Cf. the remarkable claim of Michael Fieger, writing as recently as 1991: "Der Thomasjünger ist aufgrund seines Erkenntnisstrebens und seiner Glaubensabwehr Gnostiker und kein Christ" (*Das Thomasevangelium: Einleitung, Kommentar, und Systematik* [Münster: Aschendorff, 1991], p. 290).

a christianized Gnosticism, in which Christian elements are incorporated into an alien religious system. This interpretation of Thomas is untenable for at least three reasons.

First, it underestimates the dependence of most Gnostic texts on Jewish and Christian scripture. That dependence is no less evident when (as it seems to us) scriptural teaching is subverted. If the term "Gnosticism" is to be used at all, it should be used to refer primarily to Gnostic *Christianities* — just as "Paulinism" or "Arianism" refer to Pauline or Arian Christianities. If there are Gnostic texts with no significant Jewish or Christian affinities, these should be regarded as the exception rather than the rule. Ideological struggles between "catholics" and "gnostics" occurred *within* the Christian community.

Second, it is assumed that Thomas *can only* be regarded as a Gnostic text. Yet Thomas differs at least as much from representative Gnostic literature as it does from the synoptic gospels. On both sides, there are more or less profound differences as well as similarities. When Thomas is viewed as a "proto-gnostic" or "gnosticizing" text, its fundamental orientation is still supposedly *towards* Gnosticism (Gnostic Christianity or the Gnostic religion). In that case, there is a failure to read a highly distinctive text on its own terms.

Third, questions have been raised about the coherence of the term "Gnosticism" itself, quite apart from its relevance for Thomas.[30] No group defines itself as "Gnostic" in the Nag Hammadi literature. The author of the *Gospel of Philip* aspires simply to be worthy of the confession, "I am a Christian" (62.31-33). Irenaeus does refer to "the *hairesis* called 'Gnostic,'" but he is speaking of a specific sect or group of sects which may be differentiated from followers of Valentinus or Marcion.[31] The word is used in a positive sense by Clement of Alexandria, for whom "the Gnostic" is the ideal Christian.[32] While a concern with certain kinds of *gnosis* is widespread, the prom-

---

30. See Michael A. Williams, *Rethinking "Gnosticism": An Argument for Dismantling a Dubious Category* (Princeton: Princeton University Press, 1996); Karen King, *What Is Gnosticism?* (Cambridge, MA: Harvard University Press, 2003). For a defence of the traditional view, see the chapter "Gnosticism as a Religion," in Birger A. Pearson, *Gnosticism and Christianity in Roman and Coptic Egypt* (New York & London: T. & T. Clark International, 2004), pp. 201-23.

31. Irenaeus, *Adv. Haer.* i.11.1, 29.1; iii.4.23. On Irenaeus's usage see Alastair Logan, *Gnostic Truth and Christian Heresy: A Study in the History of Gnosticism* (Edinburgh: T. & T. Clark, 1996), pp. 1-13.

32. Thus the aim of Book 7 of the *Stromateis* is "to show the Greeks that only the Gnostic [τὸν γνωστικόν] is truly religious" (Clement of Alexandria, *Strom.* vii.1.1.1).

inence of this term owes much to Irenaeus's appropriation of the expression "*gnosis* falsely so-called" from 1 Timothy 6.20.[33]

The words "Gnostic," "Gnosticism," and *gnosis* need not be put under a ban, but they should be used with caution. The question whether and how far Thomas is a Gnostic text cannot simply be rejected as inadmissible; the challenge is to find the most appropriate way to address it. Rather than identifying a set of common Gnostic motifs against which Thomas may be checked, a more fruitful approach will be to compare it with a text usually regarded as stereotypically Gnostic: the *Apocryphon of John.* As we shall see, the *Apocryphon* differs fundamentally from Thomas in at least two crucial areas: in its appeal to secrecy and in its interpretation of Genesis.[34]

The Nag Hammadi codices (NHC) include three copies of the *Apocryphon of John,* and in each case it is placed first in otherwise diverse collections. For the producers and users of these texts, it appears to have acquired a foundational, quasi-canonical status as a surrogate "Old Testament" which discloses the cosmic background and context of what has taken place in Jesus. A fourth copy is found in the Berlin Gnostic Codex (*Codex Berolinensis 8502;* abbreviated BG), where it follows the *Gospel of Mary.* The four copies represent independent Coptic translations of a shorter version of the *Apocryphon* (NHC III; BG), and a single translation of a longer version (NHC II, IV). Differences between the shorter and longer versions are often significant, but a synoptic arrangement of the four texts poses no major difficulties.[35] The shorter version predates the longer one. Predating both is a

---

33. Irenaeus, *Adv. Haer.* i.23.4. Irenaeus's work was known to Eusebius under the title *Refutation and Overthrow of Knowledge Falsely So-called* [ἐλέγχου καὶ ἀνατροπῆς τῆς ψευδωνύμου γνώσεως], alluding to τὰς βεβήλους κενοφωνίας καὶ ἀντιθέσεις τῆς ψευδωνύμου γνώσεως (1 Tm. 6.20). This title may be original (Eusebius, *HE* v.7.1).

34. If the *Apocryphon* may be said to be characteristically "Gnostic," that does not mean that all themes normally associated with Gnosticism are necessarily to be found there. Thus Karen L. King argues convincingly that "[i]t would be wrong to suppose that the *Secret Revelation of John* envisages two types of humanity: those formed after the spiritual image of the first Human and those formed after the psychic likeness of the demiurge and his minions. Rather, all human beings participate in both genealogies" (*The Secret Revelation of John* [Cambridge, MA: Harvard University Press, 2006], p. 121).

35. The synoptic edition in NHMS XXXIII is indispensable, as the English translation in *NHL* is based only on the longer version. (See also the synoptic presentation of the BG and NHC II versions in King, *Secret Revelation,* pp. 26-81.) The longer version includes, and the shorter versions lack, an introduction (Synopsis 1.2-5 = II 1.1-4); a passage on the creator deity, Yaltabaoth (29.10–30.8 = II 11.7-22); additional detail on the primal revelation of the First Man (37.16–38.8 = II 14.20-30); a list of angels responsible for different parts of the body and attributed to the *Book of Zoroaster* (42.1–50.10 = II 15.29–19.10); and an extended passage of first-person address by

text summarized by Irenaeus, who may be dependent here on an earlier heresiological source (*Adv. Haer.* i.29-30).[36] In these texts, the early chapters of Genesis are so radically rewritten that a new myth of origins comes into being.[37]

In its longer form, the *Apocryphon of John* announces itself as "the teaching of the Saviour [and] the re[vela]tion of the mysteries [**NMMYCTHPION**] [and of the] things hidden in silence, [those things] which he taught John his disciple. . . ."[38] At the close of the book, when the revelation of hidden mysteries is complete, the Saviour instructs John to write them down and to pass them on in secret to his spiritual companions, members with him of "the immoveable generation."[39] This secrecy is essential: a curse is pronounced on anyone who divulges the hidden things to the unworthy, perhaps in exchange for a gift.[40] John duly passes on the teaching he has received to "his fellow disciples."[41] They are entrusted with the secret, but they are also subject to the

---

"Pronoia" (79.4–82.1 = II 30.12–31.25). Obscurities in the longer versions are frequently clarified by comparison with the shorter one.

36. NHMS XXXIII provides the Latin text only of Irenaeus, *Adv. Haer.* i.29 (pp. 188-93). In fact, the parallel with the *Apocryphon of John* resumes at i.30.4, where "her son" refers back to i.29.4. Thus i.30.1-3 is an interpolation, providing a simplified variant of the more complex account of heavenly origins in i.29.1-4. The variant interrupts the parallel with the *Apocryphon*, which continues up to i.30.10. Throughout, Irenaeus probably follows an earlier heresiological source, perhaps one based on the *Syntagma contra omnes Haereses* of Justin (*1 Apol.* 26.8; cf. Tertullian, *Adversus Valentinianos* 5; Irenaeus, *Adv. Haer.* iv.6.2; v.26.2; Eusebius, *HE* iv.11.8-10). On this see F. Wisse, "The Nag Hammadi Library and the Heresiologists," *VC* 25 (1971), pp. 205-23; pp. 213-18; for counterarguments, see P. Perkins, "Irenaeus and the Gnostics: Rhetoric and Composition in *Adversus Haereses* Book One," *VC* 30 (1976), pp. 193-200.

37. For a summary of the story told by the *Apocryphon*, see Gerard P. Luttikhuizen, "The Creation of Man and Woman in *The Secret Book of John*," in *The Creation of Man and Woman: Interpretations of the Biblical Narratives in Jewish and Christian Traditions*, ed. G. P. Luttikhuizen (Leiden: Brill, 2000), pp. 140-55.

38. *ApJn* II 1.1-4. The Christian frame story is present in both longer and shorter versions, but is not mentioned by Irenaeus. According to H.-M. Schenke, it represents a christianizing of a pre-Christian "Sethian" gnosticism ("The Phenomenon and Significance of Gnostic Sethianism," in *The Rediscovery of Gnosticism: Proceedings of the International Conference at Yale, New Haven, Connecticut, March 28-31, 1978*, vol. 2, *Sethian Gnosticism*, ed. B. Layton [Leiden: Brill, 1981], pp. 588-616; p. 612). The figure of Seth is important because he is the son of Adam, that is, "the Son of Man," who corresponds to a heavenly prototype identified with Christ (Irenaeus, *Adv. Haer.* i.30.1, 6, 9, 13; cf. NHC II 24.36–25.2 and parallels). The prominence and literalistic understanding of the "son of man" concept suggest a Gentile Christian origin.

39. *ApJn* II 31.27-31.

40. *ApJn* II 31.34-37.

41. *ApJn* II 32.4-5.

ban on communicating it to the unworthy. Given that John and the other disciples are already revered within the Christian community as the source of its common faith, the effect of the secrecy requirement is to create a sharp disjunction between the apostles' public and private communication, and thus between the addressees of the one and the privileged recipients of the other. Through the secrecy motif, it is claimed that what is elsewhere regarded as authoritative apostolic truth is insufficient.

As the revelatory discourse unfolds, it becomes clear that the disjunction between public and secret communication is inseparable from the content of what is revealed. Here the disjunction takes the concrete form of a subversive reinterpretation of the early chapters of Genesis, in which it turns out that the familiar narrative is systematically misleading. Moses wrote this narrative in the service of a deity whose claim to supremacy and uniqueness is false; the revelation to John exposes this falsehood by disclosing the truth concealed behind scriptural distortions. Christ the Revealer speaks of the true deity above the false god of scripture; of the train of events that engenders the latter and, through him, the nightmarish pseudoreality of our material world; and of the redemption or liberation of the elect that enables them to return from exile to their original divine home. The elect find themselves in a world ruled by a deity who has decreed his reality to be the only reality, and whose supremacist ideology is enforced by angelic and human minions, including Moses and the other scriptural authors.

Even the apostles must publicly conform to this ideology, accommodating their claims to Jewish scriptural teaching and providing warrant for them in the appeal to what is written. In the *Apocryphon*, however, there is no place for the claim "as it is written." When John asks the Saviour to interpret the language of Genesis, he is repeatedly warned: "Do not think it is as Moses said . . .";[42] "It is not as Moses wrote and you heard. . . ."[43] The secret teaching revealed by the Saviour is that the truth does *not* conform to Moses and that the Saviour himself is far greater than the deity of whom Moses speaks. Since this false deity is creator and ruler of the present world, however, even the gospel message must publicly be accommodated to him

---

42. *ApJn* II 13.19-20. John has requested an interpretation of the reference to the Spirit in Gn. 1.2 (LXX). The parallel in BG 45.7-11 reads as follows: "Do you think it is as Moses said, 'above the water'?"

43. *ApJn* II 22.22-23; BG 58.16-17, "It is not as Moses said . . ."; III.28.13, "Are you thinking it is as Moses said . . . ?" The reference is to the "trance" (ἔκστασις) of Gn. 2.21a LXX. Cf. also II 23.3-4 (= BG 59.17-19; III 29.21-24), with reference to Gn. 2.21b; II 29.6-7 (= BG 73.4-6; III 37.22-24), with reference to Gn. 7.7.

and the truth confined to the inner circle of the elect. The secrecy enjoined on the apostle John is of a piece with the content of the revelation he receives. A revelation as subversive as this *must* be secret, and the book that records it *must* be an "apocryphon." Ordinary Christians are not supposed to read it.

Thomas too writes "the secret sayings" (οἱ λόγοι οἱ ἀπόκρυφοι) of Jesus.[44] He acquires this privileged role by virtue of his special insight into the person of Jesus. One day Jesus asks his disciples to compare him to someone. The question is no longer, "Who do you say that I am?" as in the synoptic gospels, but, "Who am I like?" (*GTh* 13.1). In response, Simon Peter compares Jesus to a righteous angel; Matthew, to a wise philosopher. Yet the question is deceptive, for to seek an analogy of this kind is to suppose that Jesus is just another instance of an already familiar category, and so to deny his uniqueness. Thomas alone recognizes Jesus' incomparability and refuses to answer his question: "Master, my mouth is totally unable to say whom you are like" (13.4). In consequence, Thomas is acknowledged as Jesus' equal and is given secret instruction in the form of "three words" (13.6). His fellow disciples are curious to know what Jesus said to him (13.7). But the words or sayings are explosive, and cannot safely be divulged:

> Thomas said to them, "If I tell you one of the words he told me, you will pick up stones and throw them at me, and a fire will come out of the stones and burn you up." (13.8)

Here it is still clearer than in the *Apocryphon of John* that the disjunction between what is disclosed and what is to be concealed runs through the Christian community itself. In both texts, a disciple is singled out for a special revelation. In the *Apocryphon*, John communicates the newly revealed truths to his fellow disciples; in Thomas, these truths are withheld on the grounds that they would be rejected as blasphemous and heretical. The passage as a whole seems to reflect and to subvert Peter's confession in its Matthean form (Mt. 16.13-20). Together with Matthew, Peter now provides an inadequate answer to the question of Jesus' identity. The suggested analogies with a righteous angel or a wise philosopher are equivalent to "Some say John the Baptist, others Elijah, and others Jeremiah or one of the prophets" (Mt. 16.14). So Thomas's acknowledgement of Jesus' incomparability now takes over the role of Peter's confession. Like the Matthean Peter, Thomas is

---

44. *P. Oxy.* 654.1; *GTh*, introduction.

rewarded with the promise of a privileged relationship to Jesus. Thomas upstages Peter: that is why the inadequate answers are provided precisely by "Simon Peter" (cf. Mt. 16.16 for the dual form of the name) and Matthew. The text that *GTh* here intends to subvert is not Genesis — as in the case of the *Apocryphon* — but the Gospel of Matthew.[45] Yet Thomas resembles the John of the *Apocryphon* in that both are entrusted with teaching that must be withheld from ordinary Christian believers, who confess the one God as maker of heaven and earth or who think of Jesus as though he were an angel or a philosopher.

In the *Apocryphon*, the secrecy requirement is bound up with the entire content of this text. In Thomas, secrecy initially extends only to the "three words" of *Saying* 13.6. These words are apparently withheld even from the readers of Thomas, as they are from the other disciples. Nowhere else in this text are any such sayings referred to, and nowhere else is it supposed that Jesus confined his "real" teaching to a privileged disciple.[46] At first we might assume a connection between the three secret words of *Saying* 13 and "the secret words . . . which Didymus Judas Thomas wrote," which constitute the content of this gospel. Yet the gospel contains many more than three such sayings, and no further reference is made to secrecy. On a number of occasions Jesus responds to questions or comments attributed to "the disciples" as a whole, and it is everywhere supposed that they are his usual addressees.[47] The anomalous character of *Saying* 13 is highlighted by the previous saying, where a privileged role is assigned not to Thomas but to James:

> The disciples said to Jesus, "We know that you will depart from us. Who will exercise authority over us?" Jesus said to them, "Wherever you are, you shall go to James the Righteous, for whose sake heaven and earth came into being." (12.1-2)

---

45. The reference to Simon Peter in *GTh* 13 may also allude to his traditional link with the Gospel of Mark, as attested by Papias (on this see my "The Fourfold Gospel," in *The Cambridge Companion to the Gospels*, ed. Stephen C. Barton [Cambridge: Cambridge University Press, 2006], pp. 34-52; pp. 38-39; Richard Bauckham, *Jesus and the Eyewitnesses: The Gospels as Eyewitness Testimony* [Grand Rapids: Eerdmans, 2006], pp. 235-37). But the main point seems to be the parody of Peter's confession as attested by Matthew.

46. Individual disciples are referred to on only three further occasions (Mary in *Saying* 21.1, Salome in 61.2, Simon Peter in 114.1). In none of these cases is Jesus' teaching withheld from the others.

47. *Sayings* 6.1; 12.1; 18.1; 20.1; 24.1; 37.1; 51.1; 52.1; 53.1; 99.1; 113.1; cf. *Sayings* 14.1; 22.2-4; 60.1-6; 72.3; 91.1-2; 100.1-2; 104.1.

It is difficult to see how the Thomas to whom Jesus himself says, "I am not your master" (13.5), could later be subject to the authority of James the Righteous.[48]

Unlike the *Apocryphon of John,* Thomas is not an essentially or necessarily secret text. The introductory reference to "secret sayings" is probably dependent on *Saying* 13, which may itself be a relative latecomer to a gradually evolving text. Although the opening of Thomas is also attested in one of the Greek papyri (*P. Oxy.* 654), there are further indications that the references to Thomas and to secrecy may have been superimposed on an earlier sayings collection in which they were lacking.[49]

The Coptic and Greek versions of the opening of Thomas are similar but not identical. In its Coptic form, it runs as follows (differences are italicized):

These are the secret sayings which the living Jesus spoke and which *Didymus* Judas Thomas wrote. (1) And he said: "Whoever finds the interpretation of these sayings shall not taste death." (2) Jesus said: "Let not the one who seeks cease his seeking until he finds. And when he finds *he will be troubled. And when he is troubled* he will be amazed, and he will reign *over all.*"[50]

The Greek version begins:

These are the [secret] sayings [which] the living Jesus [sp]oke a[nd which Judas who is] also Thomas [wrote]. (1) And he said: "[Whoever finds the interpreta]tion of thes[e] sayings [shall not taste death.]" (2) [Jesus said:] "Let not the one who se[eks] cease [his seeking until] he finds. And when

---

48. J. D. Crossan finds in the tension between *GTh* 12 and 13 the basis for his theory of two strata, "one . . . composed by the fifties C.E., possibly in Jerusalem, under the aegis of James's authority," the other "possibly as early as the sixties or seventies, under the aegis of the Thomas authority" (*The Historical Jesus: The Life of a Mediterranean Jewish Peasant* [Edinburgh: T. & T. Clark, 1991], p. 427). According to Crossan, "the earlier James-layer is now discernible primarily in those units with independent attestation," whereas "the Thomas-layer is now discernible primarily in that which is unique to this collection" (pp. 427-48). While Crossan here makes the questionable assumption that Thomas is wholly independent of the synoptic gospels, he is right to note the significance of the James/Thomas polarity.

49. The attribution to Thomas would be a further instance of the "secondary authorial fiction" that assigns identities to "the originally unknown authors of the canonical gospels" (Ismo Dunderberg, *The Beloved Disciple in Conflict? Revisiting the Gospels of John and Thomas* [Oxford: Oxford University Press, 2006], p. 202).

50. ⲠⲦⲎⲢϤ = τὰ πάντα, as in Jn. 1.3.

he finds [he will be amazed, and being am]azed he will reign, an[d *reigning he will re*]*st*."[51]

In both Coptic and Greek versions, it is unclear whether Jesus or Thomas is the speaker in *Saying* 1, where the introductory formula, "And he said," lacks the normal reference to Jesus.[52] Is it the evangelist Thomas who here comments on the purpose and use of the sayings, or is Jesus already the speaker? The anomaly has been occasioned by the insertion of the reference to Thomas: ". . . and which Didymus Judas Thomas [Judas who is also Thomas] wrote." Without this insertion, the text runs smoothly: "These are the secret sayings which the living Jesus spoke. And he said . . ." Indeed, given Thomas's close association with secrecy in *Saying* 13, the earlier version of the introduction may have lacked any reference to secrecy: "These are the sayings which the living Jesus spoke. . . ." According to *Sayings* 1 and 2, it is the *interpretation* (ἑρμηνεία) of the sayings that is concealed and that must be zealously sought until one finds it. The sayings themselves are not secret.

As the Coptic text stands, there are three different models of secrecy or concealment in play: *(i)* "secret sayings" identified with the entire content of Thomas *(Introduction); (ii)* the concealed, unwritten interpretation of accessible written sayings *(Saying* 1); *(iii)* the three secret sayings not included in the text *(Saying* 13). These anomalies are best resolved by supposing a development from *(ii)* to *(iii)* to *(i)*. An anonymous sayings collection opens by promising eternal life to whoever finds the true, unwritten meaning of the sayings it contains. At some point, it is supplemented by *Saying* 13, where it appears that Jesus' most important and explosive revelations are *not* to be found in this gospel. Later still, this association of Thomas and secrecy leads to a rewritten introduction in which *all* the sayings are now secret and in which Thomas becomes their scribe. If *P. Oxy.* 654 is correctly dated to *c.* 200 CE, then these earlier developments push the text back at least into the middle of the second century. Unlike the *Apocryphon of John*, the text that came to be known as the *Gospel according to Thomas* was not originally intended for secret use.[53]

---

51. For the Greek text, see Harold W. Attridge (ed.), "The Greek Fragments," in NHS XX, pp. 95-128.

52. Elsewhere, "He said" at the start of a saying is attested only in *Sayings* 8.1; 65.1.

53. Other indications of textual fluidity in the existing texts of Thomas include (1) the different locations of the "split the wood saying" (*P. Oxy.* 1.29-30; *GTh* 77.2-3); (2) longer and shorter versions of the teaching about anxiety (*P. Oxy.* 655.1-17; *GTh* 36); (3) the displacement of Jesus' an-

Two pieces of external evidence support this reconstruction, one of them later than Thomas in its present forms, the other earlier.

(1) The final work in Codex II is entitled *The Book of Thomas the Contender*. Its opening is dependent on *GTh*, and seeks to resolve the tension in the earlier text between Thomas's roles as privileged recipient of secret unwritten revelation and as the scribe of the text as a whole:

> The secret sayings which the Saviour spoke to Judas Thomas, which I, Mathaias, wrote, as I was walking and listening to them speaking with one another.[54]

Thomas is relieved here of his scribal role in order to devote himself to the secret utterances that the Saviour intends for him alone. Another disciple takes upon himself the task of compiling a written record of the secret conversations. The dialogue or question-and-answer format sometimes employed in *GTh* here determines the presentation of the first half of the work. Jesus' utterances are introduced with the expression "The Saviour said" or, on one occasion, "Jesus said."[55] It is probably the three unwritten utterances of *Saying* 13 that have given rise to this text, which seeks to supplement the earlier work by elaborating the private conversation that was earlier felt too dangerous to communicate. Thus the anomalies generated by the inclusion of *Saying* 13 and the *Introduction* are resolved.[56]

(2) Evidence for this reconstruction is also found in Clement of Alexan-

---

swer to the disciples' questions about religious practices (*GTh* 6.1; 14.1-5). Nicholas Perrin overlooks this evidence of fluidity in arguing that *GTh* was "a carefully worked piece of literature, brought together at one place and at one time by an industrious Syriac-speaking editor," who structured the collection around "multiple catchword collections" (*Thomas, the Other Gospel* [London: SPCK, 2007], pp. 93, 94; see also his *Thomas and Tatian: The Relationship between the Gospel of Thomas and the Diatessaron* [Atlanta: SBL, 2002], pp. 49-170).

54. II 138.1-4.

55. II 139.21.

56. For the relationship between these texts, together with the *ActsTh*, see John D. Turner's introduction to *ThCont*, NHS XXI, pp. 173-78; p. 177. Turner proposes a "trajectory," from sayings collection to dialogue to romance, in which increasing significance is assigned to the figure of Thomas himself. Thomas is Jesus' twin brother in *ThCont* (II 138.5-12) and *ActsTh* (11, 31, 39), though not in *GTh*. The suggestion that *ThCont* contains two sources (one in question-and-answer format, the other a monologue), and that the incipit was originally attached to the second of these (pp. 174-76), seems questionable. The "discrepancy" between the opening reference to secret sayings and "the actual genre of the work" (p. 173) is explained by the intertextual connection with the incipit of *GTh*. Similarly, the emphasis on self-knowledge in *ThCont* (II 138.8-18, immediately following the incipit) is dependent on *GTh* 3 (II 33.1-5).

dria, who cites *Saying* 2 in a form close to *P. Oxy.* 654 but attributes it not to a secret *Gospel of Thomas* but to the *Gospel according to the Hebrews:*

> . . . So also in the Gospel according to the Hebrews [τῷ καθ' Ἑβραίους εὐαγγελίῳ], it is written: "The one who wonders will reign, and the one who reigns will rest."[57]

> The same sense is to be found in the words "The one who seeks will not cease until he finds, and when he finds he will be amazed, and being amazed he will reign, and reigning he will rest."[58]

In its full form, Clement's citation closely resembles the Greek version of *Saying* 2, further developed in the Coptic version.[59] At each of the minor points where the Greek version differs from Clement's, the Coptic version follows *P. Oxy.* 654 rather than Clement.[60] *P. Oxy.* 654 therefore represents an intermediate form in the evolution of this saying, Clement an earlier form. In view of the close relationship of the two Greek versions, it is probable that the text Clement knows as the *Gospel according to the Hebrews* is to some degree related to the *Gospel according to Thomas.*[61] A gospel "accord-

---

57. Clement of Alexandria, *Strom.* ii.9.45.5. Clement's wording, ὁ θαυμάσας βασιλεύσει, assimilates the original θαμβηθεὶς δὲ βασιλεύσῃ to the context. Greek texts of this and the following passage in *Synopsis Quattuor Evangeliorum*, ed. K. Aland (Stuttgart: Württembergische Bibelanstalt Stuttgart, 1967⁴), p. 94; O. Stählin, *Clemens von Alexandria*, II, GCS (Berlin: Akademie-Verlag, 1960³).

58. Clement of Alexandria, *Strom.* v.14.96.3. Clement has just cited a passage from the end of *Timaeus* (90D), in which the assimilation of perceiving subject to perceived object is seen as the divinely ordained goal of human life.

59. The Coptic version includes two pairings (*finds/troubled* and *troubled/amazed*) where the Greek and Clement have just one (*finds/amazed*). It omits the final pairings in the Greek and Clement (*amazed/reign* and *reign/rest*), replacing them with "and he will reign over all."

60. (1) In *P. Oxy.* 654, the saying opens with the imperative μὴ παυσάσθω, in Clement with οὐ παύσεται. (2) *P. Oxy.* 654 probably contained an infinitive absent from the Clement version: . . . ὁ ζη[τῶν τοῦ ζητεῖν ἕως ἄν] εὕρῃ, rather than . . . ὁ ζητῶν ἕως ἄν εὕρῃ. (3) There are minor differences in the construction of connections: καὶ ὅταν εὕρῃ and thereafter καί + participle in *P. Oxy.* 654, εὕρων δέ in Clement and thereafter participle + δέ. At all three points the Coptic version is closer to *P. Oxy.* 654 than to Clement: (1) ΜΝΤΡΕϤϨΟ, (2) ΝϬΙ ΠΕΤϢΙΝΕ ΕϤϢΙΝΕ, (3) ΑΥⲰ ϨΟΤΑΝ ΕϤϢΑΝϬΙΝΕ.

61. The suggestion that *GTh* incorporates material from *GHeb* was first made by G. Quispel ("Some Remarks on the Gospel of Thomas," *NTS* 5 [1958-59], pp. 276-90; "'The Gospel of Thomas' and the 'Gospel of the Hebrews,'" *NTS* 12 [1965-66], pp. 371-82; *Makarius, das Thomasevangelium und das Lied von der Perle*, NovTSupp [Leiden: Brill, 1967], pp. 75-111). For Quispel, *GTh* represents a conflation of the Jewish encratism of *GHeb* and the gnosticizing ten-

ing to the Hebrews" will have been an anonymous work named not after its author but after its presumed original readers, so no attribution to Thomas is likely here.[62] The fulsome endorsement of James the Righteous in *Saying* 12 is anomalous in its present context but would fit well into such a gospel for Hebrews; but it is naturally not possible to say what the text known to Clement contained.[63] What can be said is that, if the saying cited by Clem-

---

dencies of *GEgy*; readings from it are also preserved in the diatessaronic tradition. For a recent discussion, see P. Luomanen, "The Jewish-Christian Gospels and the *Gospel of Thomas*," in *Das Thomasevangelium: Entstehung-Rezeption-Theologie*, ed. J. Frey, E. Popkes, and J. Schröter, BZNW (Berlin & New York: De Gruyter, 2008), pp. 119-53.

62. The same is true of the *Gospel according to the Egyptians*, to which Clement also refers (*Strom.* iii.9.63.1, 9.93.1). This may also have been a Thomas-like Sayings Collection. The dialogue with Salome that Clement cites has affinities with *GTh* 22, 37, 61. For further discussion of these texts, see Chapter 8.

63. Origen knows both of a "Gospel according to Thomas" (*Homiliae in Lucam* 1; the reference may be to the infancy gospel) and a "Gospel according to the Hebrews" (*In Ioan.* ii.12). In the latter, according to Origen, "the Saviour himself says: 'My mother the Holy Spirit took me just now by one of my hairs and carried me away to the great Mount Tabor.'" This passage might have been found in a sayings collection rather than a narrative gospel; the tradition about the Holy Spirit as mother may be echoed in *GTh* 101.3; 105. Later, Eusebius, Didymus, and Jerome refer to a *Gospel according to the Hebrews* in the form of an Aramaic expansion of Matthew, identifying this with the original Hebrew Matthew of which Papias speaks. There is no trace of either identification in Clement or Origen. We may therefore differentiate a Greek *GHeb* attested by Clement and Origen from an Aramaic *GHeb* (the so-called "Gospel of the Nazareans") attested by the three later writers influenced by Papias. For the patristic texts, see Elliott (ed.), *The Apocryphal New Testament* (Oxford: Clarendon Press, 1999²), pp. 3-16, to which should be added (1) Eusebius, *HE* iii.25.4, where *GHeb* is excluded from the canon and connected especially with "those of the Hebrews who have accepted Christ"; (2) *HE* iv.22.7, where Hegesippus is said to have quoted from *GHeb* in Syriac and/or Greek; (3) Didymus the Blind, *ad* Ps. 33.1, where *GHeb* is said to correct the synoptic equation of Matthew and Levi (cf Mt. 9.9 = Lk. 5.27), showing that Levi is actually the Matthias of Acts 1. (On this last passage, see Dieter Lührmann, *Die apokryph gewordenen Evangelien*, NovTSupp [Leiden: Brill, 2004], pp. 182-91.) In spite of Jerome's explicit references to "the Gospel . . . which I lately translated into Greek and Latin" (*De Vir. Ill.* 2) and to "the Gospel written in Hebrew which the Nazarenes read" (*ad Is.* 11.2), Elliott and others assign non-Matthean narratives to the Greek *GHeb* attested by Clement and Origen: (1) "the story of a woman accused of many sins before the Lord" (Eusebius, *HE* iii.39.17); (2) an expanded, harmonizing passage about the descent of the Holy Spirit, who addresses Jesus as "my son" (Jerome, *ad* Is. 11.2); and (3) a post-Easter appearance to James (Jerome, *De Vir. Ill.* 2). If these stories belonged to the Greek *GHeb*, it must have been a narrative gospel rather than a sayings collection. But there is no reason why an expanded Aramaic Matthew should not contain additional non-Matthean narrative material. If the narrative passages are reassigned to a Matthew-like Aramaic *GHeb*, it is possible to view the Greek *GHeb* as a Thomas-like sayings collection, and perhaps even as an earlier form of *GTh*. If the Aramaic/Greek distinction is downplayed, however, the ref-

ent was associated with an invitation to seek out hidden interpretations, this should be differentiated from the later Thomasine motif of the secret text.

As *GTh* 13 illustrates, the secrecy motif is closely correlated with *opposition*. Secrecy seeks to contain the opposition that the revelation would otherwise engender on account of its content. In withholding the content of the revelation, secrecy reveals the sheer fact of opposition: in this case the opposition between Thomas and his fellow disciples, and the corresponding opposition between the intended readers of Thomas and ordinary Christians for whom the authority of Peter or Matthew is beyond challenge. Yet there are both internal and external indications that the secrecy motif has been superimposed on a previously anonymous sayings collection at a relatively late stage. If secrecy and the opposition it constructs are regarded as characteristically "Gnostic" features, then *GTh* is only superficially a Gnostic text. It has *become* a secret gospel, and it is thus drawn into the orbit of necessarily secret texts like the *Apocryphon of John* where opposition to conventional Christian beliefs is thematized in the content of what is revealed. Earlier, however, *GTh* or its precursor was simply a collection of Jesus' sayings, a useful supplement to narrative gospels and not a rival.

Even in its present form, *GTh* has little in common with the *Apocryphon* other than the secrecy motif. Above all, Thomas is concerned with the true interpretation of Jesus' sayings, whereas the *Apocryphon* is concerned with an interpretation of Genesis intended to counter the misinformation it contains. It is true that, in the context of Codex II, Thomas *can* be read against the background of the *Apocryphon,* which it directly follows. In Thomas, salvation is understood as a *return* to the original heavenly home, the Kingdom of the Father: "You are from it, and to it you will return."[64] The transition from the heavenly kingdom into the exile of embodiment *can* be interpreted by way of an elaborate cosmogony involving the fall of the heavenly Sophia, the production of the malevolent creator deity, and so on. But only a reader who comes to Thomas from an authentically "Gnostic" text such as the *Apocryphon of John* would find such a cosmogony in Thomas.

---

erences in Eusebius and Didymus may be assigned to the text known to Clement and Origen, resulting probably in a narrative gospel (so Lührmann, pp. 229-58; Andrew Gregory, "Jewish-Christian Gospels," in *The Non-Canonical Gospels*, ed. Paul Foster [London & New York: T. & T. Clark, 2008], pp. 54-67).

64. *GTh* 49.

The *Apocryphon* is concerned to unmask the Genesis narrative's claim to recount the truth about human origins. Only the exalted Christ who reveals himself to John can disclose the truth hidden behind the scriptural distortions.[65] If the *Apocryphon* is characteristically "Gnostic" here, the complete absence of any such Genesis subversion in *GTh* is a further indication of its un-gnostic character.

According to Genesis, the human being — man, *anthrōpos* — was made κατ᾽ εἰκόνα θεοῦ (Gn. 1.27). If *anthrōpos* is made "according to" or "in accordance with" the image of God, then the image of God represents an original heavenly *anthrōpos,* the preexistent pattern for humanity as we know it.[66] Yet this archetypal humanity also differs from our own. It is said that "male and female he made them," which might suggest that God made a number of humans all at once, some male and some female (v. 27c). Yet, for the author of the *Apocryphon,* that cannot be the case. It has just been said that "God made *the man,*" and that "according to the image of God he made *him*" (v. 27ab). The following chapter will speak of the creation of a single individual. We must therefore suppose that God made a single individual who was male-and-female. The division in which male and female are separated from one another has not yet taken place (cf. Gn. 2.18-25). Furthermore, this first individual is as yet neither embodied nor animate. Only later will we read that "God formed the *anthrōpos,* dust from the ground" and that he "breathed into his face the breath of life [πνοὴν ζωῆς]" (Gn. 2.7). It is therefore implied that the androgynous creature initially lacked materiality and remained inert.[67] Matter and animation were supplied only later. According to Genesis, then, an originally psychic creature is subsequently incarcerated in materiality and yet acquires the spirituality indicated by the reference to

65. In what follows, I attempt to reconstruct the interpretative logic underlying the *Apocryphon of John.* On this, see King, *Secret Revelation,* pp. 215-24; and, for the related material in Irenaeus, Thomas Holsinger-Friesen, *Irenaeus and Genesis: A Study of Competition in Early Christian Hermeneutics,* JTISupp (Winona Lake, IN: Eisenbrauns, 2009), pp. 56-103. The *Apocryphon* will be referred to either in its shorter Berlin Gnostic codex version or in the longer Codex II version. Occasional references to Codex III are to the alternative translation of the shorter version in Nag Hammadi Codex III.

66. The interpretation of the image of God as a divine hypostasis is already present in Philo, for whom it is the archetypal pattern for the whole created world, the νοητὸς κόσμος which is also ὁ θεοῦ λόγος (*De Opificio Mundi* 25). In the *Apocryphon,* the specific link with humanity is evident in the revelation of the heavenly world recounted in BG 47.14–48.14 (II 14.13–15.4).

67. BG 50.15–51.1, II 19.13-14; cf. Irenaeus, *Adv. Haer.* i.30.6. The difference between the incorporeal androgynous human of Gn. 1 and the embodied male figure of Gn. 2 is already noted by Philo (*De Opificio Mundi* 134).

"life." How are we to account for this three-stage origin of the androgynous *anthrōpos*, who is first psychic, then material, then spiritual? Why the humiliation of embodied fleshly existence, and why such a belated bestowal of spiritual life? What motivates the same deity to turn against his psychic creature in the one case but to elevate it to divinity in the other?

Pursuing such questions, we must look more closely at the creator deity himself. It is striking that God is said to have made the *anthrōpos* not "according to his own image" but "according to the image of God" (Gn. 1.27b). Who is this "God" whose image represents the pattern for the creative activity of another "God"? The one who makes is clearly inferior to the one who is imaged and whose image provides the maker with his pattern.[68] By what right, then, does the maker arrogate to himself the title "God," which (it now appears) belongs to another far above him? The groundlessness of his claim to exclusive deity is also evident in the remarkable plural, "Let *us* make man according to *our* image and likeness" (v. 26).[69] This maker evidently needs the cooperation of others who are like himself although subservient to him. Yet we are told by Moses that the maker of heaven and earth is unique. Everywhere else in this text the creator is unambiguously identified as "God," the ultimate beyond whom it is impossible to think. Only here, in the account of the making of *anthrōpos*, does the truth about the God above God slip out, as if by accident, revealing that the maker's claim to exclusive deity is false — and that the sacred text is likewise false insofar as it promotes that claim.

The sacred text does not leave us in complete ignorance of the true God. We have already learned that the initially psychic *anthrōpos* was modelled on an original heavenly *anthrōpos*, male-and-female, who is the image of God. Thus, the true God has an "image" as his counterpart, another in whom he acknowledges himself — like a reflection in a mirror. If the image of God is a hypostatized reflection, then God must dwell in the midst of light and in the presence of a reflective surface such as water. God would behold his image in the depths of his own deity, illumined by his own light. Moses refers to this,

---

68. This deity claims to be "God," but his claim is false (II 11.19-22, cf. II 12.8-9; *AH* i.29.4). In Gn. 1.27, however, "in the image of God" is taken to refer to the true God rather than the creator (cf. BG 47.20–48.10, II 14.18–15.4). The creator's subordinate status also reflects the Demiurge of Plato's *Timaeus* (cf. BG 44.7-9, II 12.33–13.5). Yet, "[r]ather than declare, as Plato did, that *mimesis* ensures that the mundane world is the best possible, the *Secret Revelation of John* exposes these likenesses as fundamental deception" (King, *Secret Revelation*, p. 94).

69. BG 38.10-14, II 15.1-4; cf. Philo, *De Opificio Mundi* 72-76; *Quaestiones et Solutiones in Genesin* i.4.

obscurely to be sure, when he speaks of "the Spirit of God" as "above the water" and of the coming into being of the light (Gn. 1.2, 3).[70] Scripture elsewhere identifies the reflected image of God with the feminine figure of Sophia or Wisdom, who is "the radiance of eternal light and a spotless mirror of the working of God and an image of his goodness" (Wis. 7.26).[71] If God is our Father, Sophia (here known as Pronoia) is our Mother, her androgyny notwithstanding.[72] If the psychic *anthrōpos*, Adam, is more masculine than feminine, the original *anthrōpos* is more feminine than masculine. Yet both the pattern and the copy must be male-and-female.

The Genesis narrative is becoming more densely populated than we had imagined. There is the true God and his image, the original *anthrōpos;* there is a false deity who arrogantly claims an exclusive divine right yet is accompanied by others like himself, over whom he rules; and there is an androgynous psychic man who is subsequently both entrapped in the material body and endowed with transcendent life, before the separation of male and female has taken place. If we enquire further about "God's" companions, we note that God is said to have created not only "the earth" but also "the heaven" (Gn. 1.1 LXX), or better, "the heavens." Plato taught that time is a moving image of eternity: and if so, the seven-day structure of the creator's time gives us the clue we need. In the creator's fake eternity, there must be seven heavens, and it is reasonable to suppose that each of these heavens must have its ruler or *archōn*. The creator is the chief ruler or *protarchōn* who generated the heavens and their rulers before he and they turned their attention to the creation of man, in imitation of the heavenly original. How they obtained a glimpse of that heavenly original is a question yet to be resolved. One more figure must first be added to the *dramatis personae,* that of "the Spirit of God" who, in the midst of profound darkness, "moved over the water" (Gn. 1.2).

God is Spirit, and the Spirit of God is therefore a being of divine origin. It is therefore disconcerting to find her moving as though agitated in the deep darkness of the primal chaos (cf. Gn. 1.2).[73] Why is she in darkness rather than in the light that is her true home? And why does she lack the eternal serenity proper to a divine being? Clearly, she has committed some

---

70. BG 27.1–28.4; II 4.22–5.11.

71. On this intertextual connection with the Wisdom of Solomon, see King, *Secret Revelation,* pp. 149-50. As King notes, however, the later text "split[s] the figure of Wisdom into two higher and lower characters: Pronoia and Sophia" (p. 226).

72. II 5.5-7.

73. BG 44.19–45.19; II 13.13-26.

error that has caused her to fall from the light above into the darkness below; and her error must be bound up with her proximity to the creator deity, for whom she is in some sense responsible. She is, in fact, his mother. Seeing her son claiming exclusive deity for himself, she becomes aware of her own entanglement in the darkness of error. Her agitation is her repentance for her own infringement of a divine prerogative which — she now sees — has generated a son in whom her error reaches its logical conclusion. In the arrogance of the creator who is also her son, the mother's primal error is writ large and reflected back to her. This second mother-figure is not to be confused with the original androgynous *anthrōpos*. One is the Image of God, the other the Spirit of God; one dwells in the heights, the other has fallen into the depths. Yet, oddly, it is the second, erring mother-figure who inherits the name Sophia or Wisdom.

Sophia's agitated repentance is a cry for help, and her cry is heard in the world above. A voice comes down to her: "The Man is, and the Son of man." The Man is the first man, the androgynous Image of God; the Son of man is Monogenes or Autogenes or Christ. The revelatory announcement is accompanied by a visionary appearance of the divine Image, which the announcement serves to interpret. The voice and the vision respond to Sophia's repentance and are intended for her, but they also reach her son, the chief archon, and his fellow archons. This revelatory moment is the necessary "prequel" to the proposal, "Let us create a man in the image of God and the likeness." Moses says nothing of this, of course, for he tells the story of the world's origins from the false standpoint of the chief archon who wishes to be the sole God. Yet, given that those who say, "Let us make . . . ," refer to "the image of God," it is clear that *something* must have occasioned their decision to make a man in imitation of the man above; and that something can only have been a revelation.[74]

Sophia's repentance does not lead directly to her restoration to the world above and her exit from the Genesis narrative. She is πνεῦμα, the Spirit of God, and she must somehow be involved in the bestowal of the πνοὴ ζωῆς on the androgynous psychic *anthrōpos*. We recall that, according to Moses, Adam is first punished by imprisonment in the flesh and then endowed with the breath of life. We also recall that the psychic *anthrōpos* is initially inanimate. The creator and his accomplices fail to bring him to life. When he eventually succeeds, it is at the instigation of his mother Sophia, who tricks her son into breathing out the divine spark he inherited from her

---

74. BG 47.15–48.14; II 14.14–15.4; Irenaeus, *Adv. Haer.* i.30.6.

into Adam's (psychic) nostrils.[75] The creator's loss is Adam's gain; Adam is superior to his creator, who now declares war on him in order to recover what has been lost. Adam's imprisonment in flesh is a first expression of the creator's hostility, and it will be followed by other acts of arbitrary violence recounted, or hinted at, by the Mosaic narrative. If Sophia and her children (the offspring of Seth) are to be restored to the perfection of the heavenly kingdom, they must outwit the powerful and malevolent creator.

This remarkable drama has its roots in biblical exegesis — an exegesis that can appeal to objective features of the text in its deconstruction of biblical ideology. For some at least of its early Christian readers, the Genesis text itself indicates that "God" is not God: in its reference to the image of God as pertaining to another, in the plural "let us . . . ," and in the contorted account of the creation of the *anthrōpos*. If the *Apocryphon of John* can be regarded as a characteristic product of Gnostic Christianity, then to be a Gnostic Christian is to be rooted in scripture — read, of course, against the grain.[76]

The essential simplicity of the exegesis underlying this reading of Genesis is illustrated by another text from Codex II, the *Hypostasis of the Archons* (or, *On the Reality of the Rulers*). Whatever its date in its present form, this text seems to preserve some of the original exegetical moves on which later exercises in deconstructive reading will depend. In its retelling of the story of Cain and Abel, the *Hypostasis* keeps close to the narrative of Genesis 4. Above all, the God-character in this narrative is still referred to as "God." In the retelling of Genesis 3, however, "God" has become "the Chief Ruler" or "the Ruler," whose high-handed treatment of the first human couple is bitterly resented. The scriptural narrative remains more or less intact, but it is retold from the perspective of "the serpent" who is also "the instructor." Elsewhere, the fact that Genesis is speaking of the archons rather than the true God is indicated by the simple device of extending the plural of Genesis 1.26 to other supposedly divine decisions:

> The Rulers took counsel and said, "Come, let us create a man that will be soil from the earth." They moulded their creature as one wholly of the earth.[77]

---

75. BG 51.1–52.1; II 19.15-33; Irenaeus, *Adv. Haer.* i.30.6.

76. Karen King suggests that this text "was plausible and persuasive to some people because it offered solutions to difficulties they had in reading *Genesis*" — difficulties with an anthropomorphic deity, for example (*Secret Revelation*, p. 221). That may underestimate the extent to which the *Apocryphon*'s reading of Genesis stems from genuine exegetical observations.

77. HypAr 87.23-27. This passage conflates Gn. 1.26 and 2.7. In consequence of the "let us cre-

The Rulers took counsel with one another and said, "Come, let us bring a sleep upon Adam." And he slept. (Now the "sleep" is Ignorance, which they "brought upon him and he slept.")[78]

The Rulers took counsel with one another and said, "Come, let us cause a deluge with our hands and obliterate all flesh, from man to beast." But when the Ruler of the Powers came to know of their decision, he said to Noah, "Make yourself an ark. . . ."[79]

Retelling the Genesis story on the assumption that "God" actually stands for the Chief Ruler or the Rulers is a comparatively straightforward procedure. Radical though its consequences may be, it is simply an extrapolation from the Pauline claim that the Christ event occurs within a world dominated by hostile "authorities," the "spirits of wickedness in the heavenly places" (Eph. 6.12).[80] If that is the nature of the world we live in, it is understandable that one should make further enquiries about "the reality of the rulers" and turn to scripture for answers.

Fundamental to these "Gnostic" texts are counterreadings of Genesis. They inhabit a different world from *GTh*, in which there are no clear signs of the exegetical concerns that preoccupy the "Gnostic" authors. Thomas's treatment of the figure of Adam is particularly significant in this regard, indicating that Gnostic counterreadings of Genesis are impossible here and that they are *not* silently presupposed.

Thomas refers to Adam on just two occasions.[81] The first of these is in *Saying* 46, which consists of five main elements distributed between the two parts of a single saying:

---

ate" of the former passage, the plural ⲀⲨⲢⲠⲖⲀⲤⲤⲈ replaces the singular ἔπλασεν of the latter. "Come, let us . . ." is also influenced by Gn. 11.7.

78. *HypAr* 89.3-7.

79. *HypAr* 92.4-10. "The Powers" (ⲚⲆⲨⲚⲀⲘⲓⲥ) are probably identical to "the Rulers."

80. The opening of the *Hypostasis of the Archons* explicitly refers to this teaching of "the great Apostle" (*HypAr* 86.1-27). The assumption that the Christian frame of this text is secondary (so Roger A. Bullard, NHS XX, p. 222) seems to reflect the old view of "Gnosticism" as an independent pre-Christian religion.

81. Most of the passages that April DeConick assembles under the heading "The Primordial Adam and the Encratic Ideal" do not require an Adam-related interpretation (*Recovering the Original Gospel of Thomas*, pp. 166-67; see also her *Seek to See Him: Ascent and Vision Mysticism in the Gospel of Thomas*, VCSupp [Leiden: Brill, 1996], pp. 16-21). Is there any clear evidence that "Thomasine Christians sought to recreate the youth of Adam within the present experience of their community" (*Recovering*, p. 189)?

Jesus said: "*(1a)* From Adam till John the Baptist, *(1b)* among those born of women there is no one greater than John the Baptist *(1c)* so that his eyes should not be lowered. *(2a)* But I have said, whichever of you becomes a child will know the kingdom *(2b)* and will be greater than John."

Elements *1a* and *1c* are unique to Thomas and serve to amplify *1b*. Elements *1b* and *2b* are closely related to versions of this saying found in Matthew and Luke:

(1b) Amen I say to you, there has not arisen among those born of women anyone greater than John the Baptist. *But whoever is least in the kingdom of heaven (2b)* is greater than he. (Mt. 11.11)

(1b) I say to you, among those born of women there is no one greater than John. *But whoever is least in the kingdom of God (2b)* is greater than he. (Lk. 7.28)

In *1b*, Thomas and Luke lack the Matthean verb ("there has not arisen"); Thomas and Matthew give the full name, "John the Baptist." At *2a*, superiority to John *(2b)* is grounded not in being "least in the kingdom of heaven/God" but on becoming a child and knowing the kingdom.[82] Here too Thomas amplifies Jesus's saying. "The least" is precisely the child,[83] and "becoming a child" is interpreted as "knowing the kingdom." The amplifications in *1a*, *1c*, and *2a* are obviously secondary. It is unlikely that the saying originally placed Adam in the category of "those born of women" or included a superfluous initial reference to John the Baptist. The link between the child and knowledge is characteristic of Thomas: thus it is the child seven days old who knows "the place of life" (4.1); and children at the breast are "like those who enter the kingdom" (22.2).[84]

The saying in its present form must be based on an earlier, less elaborate version, perhaps very similar to the Matthean and Lukan versions. This need not make it directly or indirectly dependent on Matthew or Luke. That Thomas is here independent of the synoptic evangelists is suggested by the lack of any reference to John the Baptist in the passage on the reed shaken by

82. A connection between the motifs of greatness, the kingdom, and childlikeness also occurs in Mt. 18.1-3.

83. Cf. Mt. 18.2-6; Mk. 9.37, 42.

84. In contrast, April DeConick regards the whole saying as part of the "kernel" of *GTh*, with the exception of "this person will know the kingdom" (*Recovering the Original Gospel of Thomas*, p. 70).

the wind which, in Matthew and Luke, immediately precedes the saying on greatness in the kingdom. This saying is given a quite different location in Thomas (*Saying 78*):

> Jesus said: "Why have you come out into the desert? To see a reed shaken by the wind, and to see a man clothed in fine garments like your kings and your great men? Upon them are the fine [garments], and they are unable to know the truth."

Thomas lacks the sequel in which Jesus suggests that the crowds have come into the desert to see a prophet — one greater than a prophet, indeed, whose coming was announced by a prophet.[85] And Thomas also lacks the preceding account of Jesus' answer to John's messengers, which establishes that the reed-shaken-by-the-wind passage has to do with the Baptist. In Thomas, it is evidently Jesus whom his addressees have come into the desert to see — and not the Baptist. While it is possible that Thomas has reshaped the passage after extracting it from an original context preserved by Matthew and Luke, it is more likely that Matthew (followed by Luke) has combined and coordinated passages whose original independence is still preserved in Thomas. In that case, *Sayings* 46 and 78 may derive neither from Matthew or Luke nor from purely oral tradition but from the early sayings collection(s) from which *GTh* is descended. These sayings in independent form would then predate the decision to incorporate them in a connected collection of sayings relating to John the Baptist — a decision for which Matthew was probably responsible.[86]

If the reference to Adam in *Saying 46* is secondary, it is all the more valuable as an indication of the theological stance of Thomas's later redactors. In Thomas, as in Matthew and Luke, the point of the saying is to draw a sharp distinction between an era that culminates in John the Baptist and the era of the kingdom. Even at its greatest, the old age is eclipsed by the new age disclosed in Jesus. The addition of "from Adam until John the Baptist" serves to connect the old era with the scriptural narrative in which — as is said else-

---

85. Mt. 11.9-10 = Lk. 7.26-27, citing Ex. 23.20 and/or Mal. 3.1. This passage might have been composed to connect Mt. 11.7-8 with 11.11, using a composite scriptural citation derived from Mk. 1.2.

86. The individual elements would then be *(i)* the reply to the Baptist's messengers (Mt. 11.1-6), followed by *(ii)* the saying on the reed shaken by the wind (11.7-8) and *(iii)* its application to the Baptist (11.9-10); together with the Baptist-related sayings on *(iv)* greatness (11.11), *(v)* violence (11.12), *(vi)* the law and the prophets (11.13), *(vii)* Elijah (11.14-15), and *(viii)* this generation (11.16-19).

where — "twenty-four prophets spoke in Israel" (*Saying* 52).[87] Adam marks the beginning of the old era, and is doubly inferior to the children of the new. Like all others, he is inferior to John the Baptist; and together with John he is also inferior to those who "know the kingdom." The point is not to disparage Adam. He remains a significant figure. Yet he lacks a knowledge of the one thing needful, the presence of the kingdom in Jesus.

In contrast, the Adam of the *Apocryphon of John* is endowed with spiritual knowledge as soon as his creator succeeds in animating him — inadvertently bequeathing to his creature the divine element received from his mother Sophia. The psychic Adam is cast down into the degradation of the material body because his creators immediately recognize him as one endowed with knowledge, superior to themselves. Knowing the kingdom himself, he is the father of the seed of Seth, with whom he will presumably reascend into the heavenly realms from where the divine element within him originates. This Adam has no need to lower his eyes in the presence of John the Baptist. He is a heroic figure with Promethean traits, and he is also the paradigm in whom the intended readers of the *Apocryphon* are to see their own origin, nature, and destiny. In contrast, there is nothing heroic or paradigmatic about the Adam of *GTh*. He simply marks the beginning of a past era now superseded by the presence of the kingdom. There is no place here for readings of Genesis that simultaneously deconstruct and remythologize the scriptural narrative.

In *Saying* 85, Adam is no longer an incidental figure. The saying speaks of both his origin and his fate:

> Jesus said: "Adam came to be from a great power and a great wealth, but he did not become worthy of you. For if he had been worthy, [he would] not [have tasted] death."

The saying is evidently related to *Saying* 46, according to which the one who knows the kingdom is superior to John the Baptist, who is himself superior to Adam and everyone else who belongs to the old era.[88] *Saying* 85 is

---

87. For discussion of the relationship of *Sayings* 46 and 52, see M. Moreland, "*Thomas* 52 as Critique of Early Christian Hermeneutics," in *Thomasine Traditions in Antiquity: The Social and Cultural World of the Gospel of Thomas*, ed. Jon M. A. Asgeirsson, April D. DeConick, and Risto Uro (Leiden & Boston: Brill, 2006), pp. 75-91; pp. 86-88.

88. *GTh* 85 has also been seen as the third of a trilogy of sayings interpreting key themes in Gn. 1–2 (so Stevan L. Davies, *The Gospel of Thomas and Christian Wisdom* [California: Bardic Press, 2005²], pp. 63-69). But in *GTh* 83-84 the difficult references to "the images," "your likeness,"

again concerned with the addressees' superiority to Adam, which is established indirectly and negatively by contrasting Adam's transcendent origin with his eventual fate. His death (recorded in Genesis 5.5) shows that he failed to attain the status that should have been his, and that the addressees *have* attained: "He did not become worthy of you." The emphasis on failure suggests that the author accepts the scriptural and Pauline correlation between sin and death. If so, there is no place here for a counterreading of Genesis 3 as narrating a justified act of rebellion against the tyranny of the archons. In *GTh*, Adam is not a heroic rebel against the cosmos. In spite of his origin, he is a prosaic figure.[89]

The claim that "Adam came to be from a great power and a great wealth" refers neither to a subordinate demiurge nor to the one God, as the Coptic indefinite articles misleadingly suggest in translation. For the contrast between origin and fate to be effective, the power and wealth in question must be intimately related to who and what Adam is; they must in some sense be *his* power and wealth. That there is no reference here to an archontic being is confirmed by similar or identical usage elsewhere in Thomas. Thus in *Saying* 21 the addressees are warned to arm themselves "with [a] great power," to prepare for the coming of thieves (21.7). The "great power" is their own strength. In *Saying* 29 Jesus expresses his amazement that "this great wealth has come to dwell in this poverty" (29.3). The "wealth" in question is that of the spirit, the "poverty" that of the body. Since this saying too is concerned with human origins, it is particularly relevant to the interpretation of the Adam saying:

> Jesus said: "If the flesh came into being on account of spirit, it is a wonder. But if the spirit came into being on account of the body, it is a wonder of wonders. Indeed, I am amazed at how this great wealth has come to dwell in this poverty."

---

and "your images" may be only indirectly related to Genesis. See however Enno Popkes, "The Image Character of Human Existence: *GThom* 83 and *GThom* 84 as Core Texts of the Anthropology of the *Gospel of Thomas*," in *Das Thomasevangelium*, pp. 416-34.

89. Nicholas Perrin finds here one of a number of parallels between *GTh* and Tatian, who is criticized by Irenaeus (*Adv. Haer.* i.28.1; iii.23.8) for denying the salvation of Adam (*Thomas, the Other Gospel*, pp. 121-22). Other parallels are found in Thomas's asceticism (vegetarianism, *GTh* 11; celibacy, 49, 75), and in verbal links with the *Diatessaron*, which are said to show that Thomas is dependent on Tatian throughout (pp. 81-106). In view of the fundamental differences between Thomas and the *Diatessaron*, it seems more likely that the parallels represent common traditions, textual or otherwise. In the case of the Adam saying, the common origin would be the Pauline claim that "in Adam all die" (1 Cor. 15.22; Irenaeus, *Adv. Haer.* iii.23.8).

In the two conditional clauses, alternative accounts are given of human origins, in one of which the flesh or body comes into being as the dwelling place of the preexistent spirit, in the other of which the spirit is a secondary element within fleshly or bodily existence. While both accounts seem counterintuitive, the second is still more incredible than the first. In the final part of the saying, it is the first account that is confirmed as true: amazing though it may seem, the great wealth of the spirit *has* made its dwelling place in the poverty of the flesh.

While *Saying* 29 does not allude directly to Genesis, it provides the key to the claim that "Adam came to be from great power and wealth." In the Greek text of Genesis, the name "Adam" is first used in connection with "the man [God] formed," that is, with the being formed from dust who was placed in the Garden and subjected to an initial prohibition (Gn. 2.15-16).[90] In contrast to the Masoretic Text, "the man" of Genesis 2 LXX is rapidly identified as the individual named "Adam," who was formed from the dust. The *anthrōpos* of Genesis 1, created male-and-female in the image of God, remains unnamed. Like Philo and "Gnostic" authors, Thomas assumes that Genesis speaks of the creation of humankind in (at least) two stages.[91]

This view was already familiar enough to Paul and his Corinthian readers to seem worth refuting. According to Paul, "it is not that the spiritual [Adam] comes first, then the animate one," alluding to εἰς ψυχὴν ζῶσαν in Genesis 2.7 in the use of ψυχικός in opposition to πνευματικός (1 Cor. 15.46a). "Rather, it is first the animate, then the spiritual" (1 Cor. 15.46b). Thus "the first man is ἐκ γῆς χοϊκός," alluding again to Genesis 2.7 (χοῦν ἀπὸ τῆς γῆς). He is not a discarnate, spiritual androgyne created in the divine image (1 Cor. 15.47a). Conversely, it is "the second man" who is "from heaven," not the first, and he is to be identified with the exalted Christ (15.47b).[92] The divine image theme of Genesis 1 plays virtually no role

---

90. τὸν ἄνθρωπον ὅν ἔπλασεν (Gn. 2.15) becomes Αδαμ thereafter, either with the article (2.16, 19, 20, 21, 22 [2x], 25) or without it (2.19, 20, 23); ἄνθρωπος is retained in 2.18. The MT reads הָאָדָם in each case; only at 4.25-5.3 is the article omitted (although there are ambiguous cases at 2.20; 3.17, 21).

91. See Philo, *De Opificio Mundi* 134; *Quaestiones et Solutiones in Genesin* i.4.

92. As Oscar Cullmann notes, v. 46 "is meaningful only if Paul thinks of a doctrine which asserts just what he denies here"; at this point, "Paul deliberately abandons — in fact, expressly attacks — the Philonic doctrine" (*The Christology of the New Testament*, Eng. trans. [London: SCM Press, 1959], p. 177). Arguments against this interpretation (e.g. C. Wolff, *Der erste Brief des Paulus an die Korinther*, ThHKNT 7/II [Berlin: Evangelische Verlagsanstalt, 1982], pp. 202-3) seem to me to be beside the point. Given the clear links between Philo, *GTh* 85, *ApJn*, and other Genesis-related texts, it is hardly possible to speak of a "Spärlichkeit ausserphilonischer Zeugnisse"

here.[93] Or rather, its role is confined entirely to the two-stage account of human origins that Paul seeks here to refute. That account is grounded in scripture, yet at this point scripture must give way to the eschatology of the gospel. It is no doubt unlikely that Paul is *specifically* refuting Thomas's claims that "Adam came to be from great power and great wealth," and that the great wealth of the spirit has made its home in the poverty of the flesh. Yet, while these sayings may not have existed in Paul's time, he is already familiar with the scripturally based anthropology that comes to expression in them.

There is no sign in Paul, Philo, or Thomas that anyone yet imagines that the Genesis creator deity is really an arrogant and misguided usurper. Although there is some common ground between the readings of Genesis presupposed in Thomas and the *Apocryphon of John,* they differ fundamentally from each other. Thomas has no intention of reading Genesis deconstructively, exploiting openings within the text so as to unmask and undermine its false ideology. Insofar as *GTh* is interested in Genesis at all, its interpretation is — in its own terms — straightforwardly literal. Initially, there is a spiritual *anthrōpos* possessing great power and wealth by virtue of its participation in the divine image. Then, strangely and wonderfully, this power and wealth are incarnated in the poverty of the flesh as the individual named "Adam" is formed from the dust of the ground. Adam fails to capitalize on the power and wealth that are his, and eventually falls victim to death.[94]

If the term "Gnostic" is appropriate to the deconstructive reading developed in the *Apocryphon,* it can hardly be stretched so far as to incorporate the literal one presupposed by Thomas.[95] While Thomas could be read in the context of texts such as the *Apocryphon* and the *Hypostasis,* these are not

---

(p. 202). The fact that Paul, unlike Philo, "geht . . . auf Gen. 1,27 gar nicht ein" (p. 202) is precisely the point: Paul here rejects the Genesis exegesis that produces a primal man in the image of God and focuses instead on an eschatological "last Adam" (1 Cor. 15.45). For Philo, it is human origin that provides the key to human nature; for Paul, human destiny.

93. The primary allusion in 1 Cor. 15.49 is to Gn. 5.3 rather than 1.26-27.

94. April DeConick rightly notes that this passage locates the original error not in the godhead but in the human (*Seek to See Him,* p. 16). Her suggestion that "a Great Power" is a reference to Christ seems unlikely, however, since the power and wealth must belong to Adam himself (pp. 16-17).

95. Compare the conclusion of A. Marjanen, that *GTh* is more closely related to the Gospel of John than to the *Apocryphon of John* or to the *Gospel of Philip* ("Is Thomas a Gnostic Gospel?" in *Thomas at the Crossroads: Essays on the Gospel of Thomas,* ed. R. Uro, SNTW [Edinburgh: T. & T. Clark, 1998], pp. 107-39; p. 138).

its native habitat. The intertextual context of Nag Hammadi Codex II enables the reader to view the *Apocryphon* as a kind of "Old Testament" that provides the essential background for the gospel containing "the secret sayings which the living Jesus spoke" and which point the way to eternal life.[96] Yet, extracted from its secondary literary context, Thomas would seem to have far more in common with the synoptic gospels than with the *Apocryphon*. The question is whether "the synoptic problem" can still be discussed as though Thomas did not exist.

Thomas and the Sayings Collection Genre

In terms of content, the *Gospel of Thomas* overlaps with the gospels of Matthew and Luke at point after point. The question is how these overlaps are to be explained. Is *GTh* dependent on the canonical gospels for this material? If so, does that dependence take the form of a purely literary relationship, or does it reflect the phenomenon of "secondary orality," that is, the "oralizing" of a written text as it becomes familiar through repeated public reading?[97] Or is *GTh* independent of the canonical gospels, either in its entirety or at least as regards its "core"? Is this text essentially early or late, original or secondary?[98]

A closely related issue has been less intensively discussed, and it concerns the *format* of *GTh*. This text consists of a series of sayings, whether shorter or longer, single or composite, normally introduced by the formula "Jesus said . . ." While Thomas is apparently dependent on Matthew and Luke for parts of its content, it is independent of them as regards its format. Nor does this format conform to the (now discredited) Q Gospel. Unlike Thomas, Q contains extensive narrative material (the ministry of John the Baptist, Jesus' baptism and temptations, the centurion's servant). Q presents Jesus' teaching

---

96. II 32.10-19.

97. On "secondary orality," see Risto Uro, "*Thomas* and Oral Gospel Tradition," in *Thomas at the Crossroads*, pp. 8-32; *Thomas: Seeking the Historical Context of the Gospel of Thomas* (London & New York: T. & T. Clark, 2003), pp. 106-33.

98. Uro rightly points to *GTh's* "mixture of early-looking traditions with features that very probably derive from the canonical gospels" (*Thomas: Seeking the Historical Context*, pp. 130-31). A theory of composition must therefore explain "both the influence of the canonical gospels and *Thomas'* access to traditions that are clearly independent of the canonical gospels" (p. 132). See too the balanced comments of Jörg Frey, "Die Lilien und das Gewand: *EvThom* 36 und 37 als Paradigma für das Verhältnis des *Thomasevangeliums* zur synoptischen Überlieferung," in *Das Thomasevangelium*, pp. 122-80; pp. 176-80.

in thematically organized blocks; Thomas does not. There is no basis for the common assumption that Thomas closely resembles Q, and that it thereby strengthens the case for Q. Q is far closer to Matthew and Luke than to Thomas — unsurprisingly, as Matthew and Luke are the sources out of which it has been constructed. In terms of format, Thomas is unique, the single surviving instance of a sayings collection to set alongside the narrative gospels.[99] The question is whether *GTh* was always unique or whether it attests the existence of a Sayings Collection genre, a class of writing whose existence ran parallel to that of the narrative gospels and that might conceivably have predated them. That is not to say that *GTh* itself may be earlier than the narrative gospels. If it contains early elements at all, predating the canonical evangelists, these can be identified only tentatively; they cannot be assembled into an "original core" to which a mid-first-century date might be assigned. Even within the more self-consciously literary genre of the narrative gospels, there is considerable fluidity as stories pass from unknown sources into Mark and from Mark into Matthew and Luke. Within an initially preliterary Sayings Collection genre, that fluidity is likely to have been greater still. It is therefore impossible to recover from *GTh* the text of a primitive sayings collection, along the lines of reconstructions of Q.[100] What may still be possible is to recover from *GTh* a primitive genre, one in which sayings of Jesus were simply listed one after the other with an introductory formula attached to each. This genre would be at least as old as the oldest written sayings in *GTh*. If Thomas preserves even a single saying or parable in a form that predates the synoptic versions, it most probably owes its preservation to an unbroken chain of written transmission. The links in the chain are beyond recovery — although, as we have seen, Clement of Alexandria's *Gospel according to the Hebrews* may have been one of them. Yet, if the Sayings Collection genre can be traced back behind *GTh* into the presynoptic era, it is plausible to suppose that texts of this kind may have been available to the synoptic evangelists. Before as well as

---

99. This distinction between independence of format and of content is rightly drawn by Jens Schröter, for whom the presentation of sayings without contexts indicates "daß dieses [das EvThom] ein ganz eigenes Konzept verfolgt (hier ist der Terminus 'unabhängig' sicher angebracht), daß dies jedoch andererseits kein ausreichendes Indiz ist, um auch eine sprachliche Beeinflussung auszuschliessen" (*Erinnerung an Jesu Worte: Studien zur Rezeption der Logienüberlieferung in Markus, Q und Thomas*, WMANT [Neukirchen-Vluyn: Neukirchener Verlag, 1997], p. 139). But it should not be too quickly concluded that the simple format of *GTh* is original to this work.

100. For an attempt along these lines, see DeConick, *Recovering the Original Gospel of Thomas*.

after the composition of their gospels, Jesus' sayings were transmitted by way of Sayings Collections (SCs). To the *L/M* hypothesis, which replaces Q, a Thomas-based SC hypothesis may be added. The two hypotheses are independent yet mutually reinforcing.[101]

If there is a Sayings Collection genre that predates the narrative gospels, then there is no need to envisage an extended period of purely oral transmission of Jesus' sayings. The writing of a saying would be an original rather than a secondary feature of the traditioning process. That does not mean that the precise wording of a saying or parable became "fixed" as soon as it was committed to writing (as Werner Kelber seems to suppose).[102] The "fixity" of a written saying is only provisional. The saying may be subjected to more or less radical revision whenever it is incorporated into a new manuscript or established within the sphere of orality through repeated public reading. Transmission entails interpretation: this is true of the sayings tradition as a whole, just as it is true of Matthew's use of Mark, or Luke's of Mark and Matthew, or Thomas's of earlier SCs. To contrast the fixity or deadness of writing with the fluidity of living speech is inappropriate in a context where writing and orality are interdependent and interact freely. The question is not whether this account of gospel origins is determined by the assumptions of "print culture" or other ideological commitments. The question is whether and how far extant evidence supports the SC hypothesis.

Early citations of Jesus' sayings are a good point at which to test this hypothesis. The more these citations *(i)* diverge from synoptic parallels and

---

101. For "Sayings Collections" as an early Christian genre, see Helmut Koester, *From Jesus to the Gospels: Interpreting the New Testament in Its Context* (Minneapolis: Fortress, 2007), pp. 26-28. Koester appeals to Q, Thomas, Justin, and *2 Clement*, but concedes that "[e]vidence for the continued existence of sayings collections is not easy to obtain" (p. 27). Paradoxically, such evidence as there is comes more sharply into focus in the absence of Q, since criteria for identifying SC material can then be derived from *GTh* alone.

102. A typical example of the overblown rhetoric accompanying this claim, complete with multiple mixed metaphors: "The objectifying, controlling power of the written medium, while taking the life out of spoken language, can freeze oral forms and preserve them in fossilized profiles" (*The Oral and the Written Gospel: The Hermeneutics of Speaking and Writing in the Synoptic Tradition, Mark, Paul, and Q* [Philadelphia: Fortress, 1983[1], 1997[2]], p. 44). In a more recent interview, Kelber partially retracts this claim, seeing a "conflictual relationship" between orality and literacy only as one possibility among their many potential modes of interaction (Werner H. Kelber and Tom Thatcher, "'It's Not Easy to Take a Fresh Approach': Reflections on *The Oral and the Written Gospel*," in *Jesus, the Voice, and the Text: Beyond the Oral and the Written Gospel*, ed. Tom Thatcher [Waco, TX: Baylor University Press, 2008], pp. 27-43; p. 30). For Kelber's account of *GTh* as an "interface" between orality and textuality, see his "In the Beginning Were the Words: The Apotheosis and Narrative Displacement of the Logos," *JAAR* 58 (1990), pp. 69-98, esp. pp. 78-82.

(ii) show formal similarities to *GTh,* the greater the likelihood that they have been derived neither from the synoptics nor from purely oral tradition but from Thomas-like SCs. The so-called *Second Letter of Clement* is particularly rich in such citations, which play a more significant part in this anonymous homily from the early or mid–second century than the scriptural citations that are also found here.[103]

Second Clement's eleven citations from the sayings tradition are introduced as follows:

And another scripture says [λέγει]: "I came not to call the righteous . . ." (2 *Clem.* 2.4)

And he himself also says: "Whoever confessed me before people . . ." (3.2)

For he says: "Not everyone who says to me, 'Lord, Lord . . .'" (4.2)

The Lord said [εἶπεν ὁ κύριος]: "If you are gathered together with me . . ." (4.5)

For the Lord said: "You shall be as lambs . . ." (5.2)

And the Lord says: "No servant can serve two masters . . ." (6.1)

For the Lord says in the gospel: "If you did not guard what is small . . ." (8.5)

For the Lord said: "My brothers are those who do the will of my Father." (9.11)

For when the Lord was asked . . . , he said: "When the two shall become one . . ." (12.2)

. . . that God says: "It is no credit to you if you love those who love you . . ." (13.4)

For the Lord said: "I come to gather all nations, tribes and tongues." (17.4)

---

103. On this see Helmut Koester, *Synoptische Überlieferung bei den Apostolischen Vätern* (Berlin: Akademie-Verlag, 1957), pp. 62-70; *Ancient Christian Gospels,* pp. 349-59; Andrew F. Gregory and Christopher Tuckett, "2 *Clement* and the Writings That Later Formed the New Testament," in *The Reception of the New Testament in the Apostolic Fathers* (Oxford: Oxford University Press, 2005), pp. 251-92.

The two most prominent characteristics of these introductory formulae are the references to speech ("says" [6x]; "said" [5x]) and the speaker ("the Lord" [7x]; "God" [1x]; "the scripture" [1x]). In the Greek fragments of *GTh*, *P. Oxy.* 654 preserves the introductory formula, λέγει Ἰη[σου]ς, on three occasions (*Sayings* 3, 5, 6), *P. Oxy.* 1, on six (*Sayings* 27-28, 30-33). The Greek present tense probably underlies the Coptic ΠΕΧΕ ΙC [ΧΕ]. The translator evidently took λέγει as a historic present meaning "said."[104] Both Greek and Coptic identify the speaker as "Jesus," given in the abbreviated form of a so-called *nomen sacrum*. The introductory formula, "Jesus says/said," is strikingly similar to the repeated "the Lord says/said" of *2 Clement*. In conjunction with other evidence, the parallel suggests a common origin within the SC genre. If so, it was not only *GTh* that used a citation formula to demarcate individual sayings and to emphasize the connection with a specific speaker. This would be a characteristic of the SC genre itself, a point at which it differentiates itself from collections of anonymous proverbs and from attempts to assemble Jesus' sayings into connected discourses.

An origin within a written text is suggested by two passages where "the Lord" is not the speaker in the *2 Clement* citations. In the first case, it is "another scripture" (in addition to Is. 54.1, previously quoted) that says, "I came not to call the righteous but sinners" (*2 Clem.* 2.4). The wording of this saying is identical to Matthew 9.13; the author may here be citing Matthew as scripture as he has just cited Isaiah.[105] Elsewhere, however, a non-Matthean passage is introduced with a formula that again implies a written text:

> For the Lord says in the gospel [ἐν τῷ εὐαγγελίῳ]: "If you do not guard what is small, who will give you what is great? For I say to you, the one who is faithful in little is also faithful in much."[106]

The final part of this saying is identical to Luke 16.10a, but the first part is only loosely related to Luke 16.12 ("*And if you are not faithful in another's, who will give you what is your own?*"). The difference is such that this can hardly be a free citation from Luke. Nor is it likely to stem from a purely oral tradition.[107] "In the gospel" identifies the location of the saying and must re-

---

104. With reference to the repeated λέγει of the Greek fragments, Lührmann speaks of "die damit signalisierte Zeitlosigkeit der einzelnen Worte Jesu" (Lührmann, *Die apokryph gewordenen Evangelien*, p. 178). The Coptic translation decision may make this less likely.

105. So Gregory and Tuckett, "2 Clement," p. 255.

106. *2 Clem.* 8.5.

107. As argued initially by H. Koester (*Synoptische Überlieferungen*, pp. 101-2). Later, Koester

fer to a written text. If a saying of Jesus can be described as "another scripture," the author clearly assumes that Jesus' sayings may be encountered in written form. "Gospel" here refers in general terms to written records of Jesus' teaching and life, rather than specifying a particular text. If the citation is drawn from an SC, this text would belong within the category "gospel" but would not itself be *a* or *the* gospel. At this point, the term "gospel" remains essentially anonymous and is not yet associated exclusively with the direct or indirect testimony of named apostles (Matthew; Mark/Peter; Luke/Paul; John). What matters about "the gospel" is that the Lord speaks in it, and there is no interest in its literary embodiments as such.

According to *GTh,* the purpose of an SC is to make the sayings of Jesus available for interpretation: "Whoever finds the interpretation [ⲈⲐⲈⲢⲘⲎ-ⲚⲈⲒⲀ] of these sayings shall not taste death" (*Saying* 1). Jesus' speech remains incomplete and ineffectual until it is accompanied by the speech of the interpreter who communicates its sense in his or her own words. Jesus' sayings are recorded not just for their own sake but in order to be *used,* taken up into the receiving community's ongoing discourse in order to shape its practice. That is also the case in 2 *Clement.* When Jesus says, "I came not to call the righteous but sinners," he *means* that it is those who are perishing who are to be saved (2 *Clem.* 2.7). When he speaks of guarding what is small in order to receive what is great, he *means* that we are to keep our flesh pure and our baptism undefiled, so as to attain eternal life (8.6). In a more complex saying, individual components can be interpreted separately. The author notes that,

> when the Lord himself was asked by someone when the kingdom would come, he said: "When the two shall be one [ὅταν ἔσται τὰ δύο ἕν], and the outside as the inside, and the male with the female neither male nor female."[108]

Although the Lord here responds to a question, his three-part answer is couched in obscure parabolic speech that evokes further questions. What is meant by "the two shall be one"? This might seem to allude to Genesis 2.24, ". . . *and* the two shall be one *flesh* [καὶ ἔσονται οἱ δύο εἰς σάρκα μίαν]," cited in the pericope on marriage and divorce in Matthew 19.5. But the author of 2 *Clement* prefers to take the statement in a broader sense:

---

rightly sees in this passage "possibly the earliest evidence for the designation of a sayings collection as 'gospel'" (*Ancient Christian Gospels,* p. 355).

108. 2 *Clem.* 12.2.

"The two are one" when we speak truth with one another, so that in two bodies there is one soul, without hypocrisy.[109]

Complete sincerity creates oneness of soul within two bodies, but the individual body and soul must also be in accord with each other. Jesus speaks of this in the second part of the saying:

"[T]he outside as the inside" is to be understood as follows: "the inside" means the soul, whereas "the outside" means the body. Just as your body is visible, then, so your soul is to be manifest in good works.[110]

Returning to the relationship of persons, the saying speaks finally about that relationship in its gendered form. Indeed, it seems to speak of the transcending of gender: ". . . the male with the female neither male nor female [οὔτε ἄρσεν οὔτε θῆλυ]." The male is with the female because "he who created them from the beginning made them male and female" (Mt. 19.4; cf. Gn. 1.27). For Christians, however, "there is neither male nor female [οὐκ ἔνι ἄρσεν καὶ θῆλυ], for you are all one in Christ Jesus" (Gal. 3.28). What is meant by this transcending of gender? For the author of 2 Clement, Jesus calls men and women to relate to one another as "brothers and sisters,"[111] in a familial love that is not determined by sexuality:

"[T]he male with the female neither male nor female" means that when a brother sees a sister he should not think of her as female, nor should she think of him as male. When you do these things (he says), the kingdom of my Father will come.[112]

The interpretation concludes with a reference back to the original question about the coming of the kingdom, to which Jesus' saying responded. In interpreting each of the three parts of the saying in turn, the author passes over the possibility that the second and third pairings (outside/inside, male/female) are exemplifications of the first (two/one).

The author's point-by-point interpretation is evidently based on a written version of Jesus' saying. Only in written form can a saying function as the object of a detailed, methodical interpretation such as this. Thus the author

109. *2 Clem.* 12.3.
110. *2 Clem.* 12.4.
111. The author addresses his hearers as ἀδελφοὶ καὶ ἀδελφαί in 19.1; 20.2.
112. *2 Clem.* 12.5.

elsewhere employs the same interpretative technique in expounding a scriptural passage (Is. 54.1), again in three stages (2 *Clem.* 2.1-3).

That the saying in question was available in written form is confirmed by a parallel passage in book 3 of Clement of Alexandria's *Stromateis.* Clement here contests the interpretation of the same saying with an opponent (Julius Cassianus), who uses it to deny the validity of marriage:

> Cassianus says: "When Salome enquired when she would know the answer to her questions, the Lord said, 'When you trample the garment of shame, and when the two become one and the male with the female neither male nor female.'"[113]

Clement quotes this passage from Cassianus's work, *On Self-Control* (Περὶ ἐγκρατείας) or *On Being a Eunuch* (Περὶ εὐνουχίας) — a reference to Jesus' saying about those who make themselves eunuchs for the sake of the kingdom of heaven (Mt. 19.12). Clement notes that the saying on the two becoming one occurs "not in the four gospels handed down to us, but in the one according to the Egyptians."[114] Cassianus himself cites this passage as authoritative, without further comment. The question-and-answer format is similar to 2 *Clement* 12.2, although the question is now concerned with the dawn of knowledge rather than the coming of the kingdom, and the questioner is identified as Salome and is no longer anonymous. The reference to the outside and the inside is lacking, with the result that the link between the pairings of two/one and male/female is clearer. The two become one not in marital intercourse, as a literal interpretation of Genesis 2.24 would suggest, but, on the contrary, in a transcending of gender that occurs (according to Cassianus) in the rejection of marriage and sexuality. The addition of ". . . when you trample the garment of shame" is thus taken to refer to the gendered body. For Cassianus, Adam and Eve's being clothed with "garments of skin" (Gn. 3.21) is a reference to their embodiment.[115] Although Clement acknowledges the subordinate status of the gospel in question, he is prepared to take the passage seriously — arguing, against Cassianus, that the "shame" that is to be overcome relates not to our created natures as male and female but to the sinful tendencies towards "anger" (θυμός) and "desire" (ἐπιθυμία), characteristic of male and female respectively.

It is clear from Clement's reference to the *Gospel according to the Egyp-*

---

113. Clement of Alexandria, *Strom.* iii.13.92.2.
114. Clement of Alexandria, *Strom.* iii.13.93.1.
115. Clement of Alexandria, *Strom.* iii.13.95.2.

tians that he and his opponent are debating the interpretation of a written tradition rather than an oral one. Evidently, writtenness is a necessary precondition for interpretations of this saying. The author of 2 *Clement* must have encountered it in written form just as Julius Cassianus and Clement of Alexandria did.[116] For the two earlier interpreters, the fact that this saying occurs in a text other than "the four gospels handed down to us" in no way diminishes its significance. They are presumably unaware of any such canonical limit.

The question is whether the author of 2 *Clement* draws his version of the two/one saying from the text Clement of Alexandria knows as the *Gospel according to the Egyptians*. On the one hand, the two versions are relatively close to each other; on the other hand, the version Cassianus uses seems to have been reworked to fit the saying for the ideological role he assigns to it. That this gospel shows a marked encratite bias is confirmed by another exchange between Salome and Jesus, which seems to have run more or less as follows:

> Salome asked the Lord: "How long shall people die?" He answered: "As long as you women bear children." Salome said: "I did well then in not bearing." The Lord answered and said: "Eat every herb, but that which is bitter do not eat."[117]

The final saying alludes to Genesis 2.16-17, the permission to eat of every tree in the Garden except the tree of the knowledge of good and evil. Cassianus understood this as a prohibition of sexual intercourse, arguing that the knowledge in question is identical to Adam's sexual knowledge of

---

116. In his early work Koester argued that the authors of 2 *Clement* and *GEgy* are both here "von einem frei umlaufenden Apophthegma abhängig" (*Synoptische Überlieferungen*, p. 104). Later, he states that this passage "must have been circulating in the free tradition of sayings from which the author of the sayings collection that 2 *Clement* knew and used obtained also other noncanonical materials" (*Ancient Christian Gospels*, pp. 359-60). Both statements presuppose the form-critical assumption of a homogeneous ongoing oral tradition whose individual components may, sooner or later, be independently reduced to writing. Koester does not see that his own sayings collection hypothesis — adopted no doubt under the influence of *GTh*, not yet available to him in the earlier work — actually represents an *alternative* mechanism for the transmission of Jesus' sayings, making the "free" oral tradition hypothesis redundant.

117. Clement of Alexandria, *Strom.* iii.9.64.1 (cf. iii.6.45.3); iii.9.66.1-2. Clement provides two versions of the first half of this dialogue. My rendering prefers the second version of Salome's question to the first (where she asks, "How long shall death prevail?") and the first version of Jesus' response to the second ("*you* women" rather than "women").

Eve in Genesis 4.1.[118] Thus, the Lord's prohibition of "that which is bitter" amounts to an endorsement of Salome's "I did well then in not bearing." While Clement argues that the Lord's cryptic utterance is compatible with the right to choose between continence and marriage,[119] the passage is at least open to the encratite reading. That this is indeed the *Tendenz* of this text is confirmed by a third passage cited by Clement, according to which the Lord said, "I came to destroy the works of the female."[120] Once again, the encratite interpretation is averted by way of an allegorical interpretation. It is clear from this saying and the two dialogues with Salome that *GEgy* is a vehicle for encratite ideology, and that Clement's opponent can therefore give a more compelling interpretation of it than Clement can.

In citing his own version of the two/one saying, the author of 2 *Clement* is unaware of these ideological issues. While his detailed, point-by-point interpretation presupposes a written SC, not an oral tradition, there is no sign here of the critique of marriage and sexuality evident in the later version of the two/one saying. It is possible that the author of 2 *Clement* draws on an earlier form of the SC that came to be known as the *Gospel of the Egyptians*, and that this text was later subjected to the encratite redaction that underlies the competing interpretations of Cassianus and Clement of Alexandria. Yet a direct, linear relationship between the two SCs is unlikely. The one fully extant SC is *GTh*, and its parallels with *GEgy* illustrate how one SC can overlap with another without any clear literary relationship between the collections as a whole. The fragments preserved by Clement seem to represent a text very different from Thomas.

In *GEgy*, the two/one saying is introduced with the assurance that the truth will be revealed "when you have trampled on the garment of shame. . . ."[121] In Thomas, this metaphor of the body has migrated to a new context:

> His disciples said to him, "When will you be manifested to us, and when will we see you?" Jesus said, "When you undress without being ashamed, and take your garments and place them under your feet like children, and trample on them, then you will see the Son of the Living One without being afraid."[122]

118. Clement of Alexandria, *Strom.* iii.17.104.1.
119. Clement of Alexandria, *Strom.* iii.9.66.3–67.1.
120. Clement of Alexandria, *Strom.* iii.9.63.2.
121. Clement of Alexandria, *Strom.* iii.13.92.2.
122. *GTh* 37.1-3; cf. *P. Oxy.* 655, i.17-23.

In *GEgy* the garment-of-shame motif is an addition to the two/one saying, whereas in both the Coptic and the Greek Thomas it is an independent saying in its own right. In Thomas, the two/one saying is presented in an expanded form that retains the structure of the *2 Clement* version (underlined, below):

Jesus saw infants receiving milk. He said to his disciples: "These children receiving milk are like those who enter the kingdom." They said to him: "Shall we then as children enter the kingdom?" Jesus said to them: "<u>When</u> you make <u>the two one, and</u> make <u>the inside as the outside</u> and the outside as the inside, and the above as the below, <u>and</u> when you make <u>the male with the female</u> one and the same, so that the male is <u>not male nor</u> the female <u>female</u>; when you form eyes for an eye and a hand for a hand and a foot for a foot, an image for an image; then you will enter the kingdom."[123]

While this elaboration of the two/one saying is a later expansion of the *2 Clement* version, that does not mean that the author of *2 Clement* had access to an early version of *GTh*. In its extant Greek and Coptic forms, this gospel may have been preceded by many other interrelated collections, only a few of which will have achieved the literary status conferred by a title. As we have seen, *GTh* is to some degree related to a text known to Clement of Alexandria as the *Gospel according to the Hebrews;* and Clement also knows of a *Gospel according to the Egyptians*. Otherwise titles for this SC literature are lacking. In the sayings, it is the Lord who speaks, not the scribe responsible for a particular collection. In this otherwise fluid literature, it is genre that represents the constant — the distinct genre of the collection of the Lord's sayings and dialogues, which, in spite of the growing popularity of narrative gospels, endured until at least the fourth century.

The author of *2 Clement* derived his sayings citations from a written source rather than oral tradition. He can refer to Jesus' sayings as "scripture," and he can subject them to a detailed interpretation that presupposes their objectification and stabilization in writing. As the source for his citations, he identifies only "the gospel" rather than any discrete literary embodiment. What is most striking, however, is how far his citations deviate from synoptic material:

1. Another scripture also says: "I came not to call the righteous, but sinners."[124]

---

123. *GTh* 22.1-7.
124. *2 Clem.* 2.4 (= Mt. 9.13).

2. And he himself also says: "The one who confessed me before people, I will confess him before my Father."[125]

3. For he says: "Not everyone who says to me, 'Lord, Lord,' will be saved, but the one who does righteousness."[126]

4. The Lord said: "If you are gathered with me in my bosom and do not do my commandments, I will cast you out and say to you, 'Depart from me, I do not know you [or] where you are from, workers of lawlessness!'"[127]

5. The Lord said: "You shall be as lambs in the midst of wolves." Peter answering said: "What if the wolves tear apart the lambs?" Jesus said to Peter: "Let not the lambs fear the wolves after their death, and you, do not fear those who kill you and can do nothing more to you, but fear the one who, after your death, has authority over soul and body to cast into the Gehenna of fire."[128]

6. The Lord says: "No servant can serve two masters. If we wish to serve God and Mammon, it is unprofitable to us. For what advantage is it if someone gains the whole world but loses his life?"[129]

7. For the Lord says in the gospel: "If you did not guard what is small, who

---

125. 2 *Clem.* 3.2. Cf. Mt. 10.32: "*Everyone who will* confess [*in*] me before people, I *too* will confess *in* him before my Father *who is in heaven.*"

126. 2 *Clem.* 4.2. Cf. Mt. 7.21: "Not everyone who says to me, 'Lord, Lord,' will *enter into the kingdom of heaven,* but the one who does *the will of my Father who is in heaven.*"

127. 2 *Clem.* 4.5. Cf. Mt. 7.23: "*And then* I will *confess to them,* '<I *never knew* you;> depart from me, workers of lawlessness.'" Lk. 13.27: "[ ] *And he* will say to you, '<I do not know you [or] where you are from;> depart from me, *all* workers of *unrighteousness.'*" According to Koester, "the source of 2 *Clem.* 4.2, 5 was probably the same collection of sayings that is used elsewhere in this writing, that is, a collection based on Matthew and Luke that also incorporated sayings from the free tradition" (*Ancient Christian Gospels*, p. 357).

128. 2 *Clem.* 5.2-4. Cf. Lk. 10.3: "*Behold I send you* as lambs [ἄρνας] in the midst of wolves" (Mt. 10.16a, πρόβατα). Lk. 12.4-5: "Do not fear those who kill *the body* and *after that have nothing further* to do. . . . Fear the one who after *killing* has authority . . . to cast into Gehenna." P. Oxy. LX.4009: "[*Be blame]less as the* [*doves a]nd wise* [*as the snakes*]. You will be as [lambs in the midst] of wolves." [*I* said to hi]m: "What then if *we* [*are* torn]?" [*He answering*] says to *me*: [ ] "*The* [*wolves tear]ing the* [*lamb can no*] longer do any[*thing*] to it. There[*fore*] *I say to y*]ou: Do [n]ot f[ear th]ose who k[ill yo]u and [*after killing*] are no *lon*[*ger a*]ble [to do anything]." On the relationship between the parallel passages from 2 *Clement* and P. Oxy. 4009, see Lührmann, *Die apokryph gewordenen Evangelien*, pp. 73-86.

129. 2 *Clem.* 6.1-2. Cf. Lk. 16.13: "No servant can serve two masters. *For either he will hate the one and love the other, or he will be devoted to the one and despise the other. You cannot* serve God and Mammon." Mt. 16.26: "For what *will it* advantage [ὠφεληθήσεται] *a person,* if *he* gain the whole world and lose his soul?"

will give you what is great? For I say to you, one who is faithful in little is also faithful in much."[130]

8. For the Lord said: "My brothers are those who do the will of my Father."[131]

9. For when the Lord himself was asked by someone when the kingdom would come, he said: "When the two shall be one, and the outside as the inside, and the male with the female neither male nor female."[132]

10. ... God says: "It is no credit to you if you love those who love you, but it is credit to you if you love your enemies and those who hate you."[133]

11. For the Lord said: "I come to gather all nations, tribes, and tongues."[134]

These citations may be drawn from a variety of sources, but it is at least equally likely that they all derive from a single, Thomas-like SC, itself partially dependent on the completed gospels of Matthew and Luke.[135] Where the sayings have synoptic parallels, striking divergences combine with close similarities to redactional elements in one or more of the synoptic gospels. The single reference to "scripture" (1) may imply direct acquaintance with Matthew, a text that can be cited as authoritative alongside Isaiah. Direct derivation from Matthew is also possible in the case of 2, 3, and 8, but the absence of a reference to "scripture" and the divergences in the wording make an origin in the SC at least as probable.[136] Elsewhere there are contacts with Lukan redaction (5, 7, 10), or with both Matthean and Lukan redaction (4, 6). Two sayings entirely lack a synoptic parallel (9, 11), and two find their

---

130. 2 *Clem.* 8.5. Cf. Lk. 16.12: "*And if you are not faithful in another's*, who will give you *what is your own?*" Lk. 16.10a: "The one who is faithful in little is also faithful in much."

131. 2 *Clem.* 9.11. Cf. Mt. 12.50: "<*For whoever does* the will of my Father *who is in heaven*> is my brother *and sister and mother.*"

132. 2 *Clem.* 12.2.

133. 2 *Clem.* 13.4. The reference here to "God" as speaker, rather than "the Lord," may reflect the conviction that "we must think about Jesus Christ as about God" (2 *Clem.* 1.1). Cf. Lk. 6.32: "*And if you love those who love you, what* credit is it to you?" Lk. 6.27 (cf. v. 35): "Love your enemies and *do good to* those who hate you."

134. 2 *Clem.* 17.4.

135. According to Gregory and Tuckett, 2 *Clement* may have used "a post-synoptic harmony for some of his traditions, but other, apocryphal gospels for other traditions" ("2 *Clement*," p. 278). Given that *GTh* contains both sayings dependent on Matthew and Luke and independent sayings, it is plausible to suppose a single SC in the case of 2 *Clement*.

136. Gregory and Tuckett conclude that 2 *Clement* presupposes Matthew's finished gospel in the case of 2 and 3, and Matthew and Luke in the case of 8 ("2 *Clement*," pp. 258-60, 270). Koester takes a similar view (*Ancient Christian Gospels*, pp. 349-53).

closest parallels in noncanonical gospels (5, 9).[137] Other passages contain additional nonsynoptic material (4, 5) or alternative wording (3, 7). Sayings that are combined in the synoptics are here separated (3, 4), and sayings separated in the synoptics are here combined (6). These differences are such as to make free citation from memory unlikely. The author is careful to reproduce his scriptural texts as accurately as possible, and the importance he assigns to Jesus' sayings suggests that he has taken similar care here too.[138]

The author's SC citations are formally similar to material in *GTh* and *GEgy*. The use of standardized introductory formulae has already been noted. In addition, SCs contain *(i)* short individual utterances, without context; *(ii)* juxtapositions in which one utterance serves to interpret another; *(iii)* responses to questions, requests, or remarks; *(iv)* passages of more extended dialogue; *(v)* extensions of a saying by addition of formally similar units.

(i) Individual utterances. Many of the sayings included in SCs are presented as brief, self-contained utterances:

GTh 34	Jesus said: "If a blind man leads a blind man, they will both fall into a pit."
GTh 42	Jesus said: "Become passers-by."
GTh 54	Jesus said: "Blessed are the poor, for yours is the Kingdom of heaven."
GEgy	. . . "I came to destroy the works of the female."
2 Clem. 9.11	The Lord said: "My brothers are those who do the will of my Father."

Such self-contained utterances may or may not represent the earliest extant form of the sayings in question. An utterance may originally have been transmitted either independently or as part of a larger unit. While there was clearly a tendency to create new units by juxtaposing one saying with another, there may also have been a contrary tendency to extract isolatable sayings

---

137. *P. Oxy.* LX.4009 (see above); *GEgy*.

138. *2 Clement* includes seven citations from the LXX. (1) *2 Clem.* 2.1 = Is. 54.1 LXX. (2) *2 Clem.* 3.5; Is. 29.13: minor differences with LXX are mostly accounted for by Mt. 15.8. (3) *2 Clem.* 6.8, summarizing Ez. 14.14, 18, 20. (4) *2 Clem.* 7.6 = Is. 66.24b. (5) *2 Clem.* 13.2 = Is. 52.5 (+ πᾶσιν); there is an additional unidentified citation here. (6) *2 Clem.* 14.1; Jer. 7.11: minor differences to accommodate the passage to its new context. (7) *2 Clem.* 14.2, summarizing Gn. 1.27. An unidentified prophetic word is cited in *2 Clem.* 11.2, also occurring in *1 Clem.* 23.3-4 where it is regarded as "scripture."

from larger units and to present them in self-contained form. This is the case in a series of sayings that Justin Martyr derives primarily from Matthew:

> On the subject of self-control, he speaks as follows: "Whoever sees a woman and desires her has already committed adultery in his heart before God." And, "If your right eye cause you to stumble, cut it out; for it is better for you to enter one-eyed into the kingdom of heaven than with two to be sent into the eternal fire." And, "He who marries a woman divorced from another man commits adultery." And, "There are some made eunuchs by men, others are born eunuchs, and others make themselves eunuchs for the sake of the kingdom of heaven. But not all receive this."[139]

The first two sayings are drawn from Matthew 5.28-29, although the wording of the second has been influenced by alternative versions elsewhere in this gospel.[140] In separating sayings that appear consecutively in Matthew, Justin may reflect an older tradition that individual utterances are the most fundamental components of Jesus' teaching.

(ii) Juxtaposition. The impact of one saying can be increased by juxtaposing it with another:

> GTh 39.1-3 Jesus said: "The Pharisees and the scribes took the keys of knowledge and hid them. They themselves did not enter, and those wishing to enter they prevented. But you, be wise [ϤⲢⲞⲚⲓⲙⲞⲤ] as serpents and blameless [ⲀⲔⲈⲢⲀⲓⲟⲤ] as doves."[141]

---

139. Justin, *1 Apol.* 15.1-4. On Justin's gospel citations, see Koester, *Ancient Christian Gospels,* pp. 360-402. Koester argues that, like *2 Clement,* Justin draws from "collections of sayings which were composed on the basis of harmonized gospel texts and which incorporated additional sayings from the non-canonical tradition" (p. 374). On this specific passage, see A. J. Bellinzoni, *The Sayings of Jesus in the Writings of Justin Martyr* (Leiden: Brill, 1967), pp. 57-61, 87-88, 96-97. According to Bellinzoni, "Justin did not quote the sayings of Jesus from memory but . . . used one or more written sources often quoted by other fathers in a form almost identical to Justin's version . . . , most often and most strikingly in Clement of Alexandria, Pseudoclementine *Homilies,* and Origen" (p. 95). Bellinzoni's claim is assessed positively by Annewies van den Hoek ("Divergent Gospel Traditions in Clement of Alexandria and Other Authors of the Second Century," *Apocrypha* 7 [1996], pp. 43-62), but more sceptically by G. Strecker ("Eine Evangelienharmonie bei Justin und Pseudoklemens?" *NTS* 24 [1977-78], pp. 297-316).

140. "If your right eye cause you to stumble, cut it out [ ]; for it is better for you *to enter one-eyed into* the kingdom of heaven *than with two* to be sent into *the eternal fire.*" Underlining = substitution from Mt. 5.30; italics, from Mt. 18.8-9.

141. Cf. Lk. 11.52: "*Woe to you lawyers, for you* took the key of knowledge. *You* did not enter

GEgy . . . The Lord said: "When you trample the garment of shame, and when the two become one and the male with the female neither male nor female."[142]

2 Clem. 6.1-2 And the Lord says: "No servant can serve two masters. If we wish to serve God and Mammon, it is unprofitable to us. For what is the advantage if someone gain the whole world and lose his soul?"[143]

Justin, *1 Apology* 15.11-12 "But you, do not store up for yourselves on earth, where moth and rust corrupt, and where thieves break through; store up for yourselves in heaven, where neither moth nor rust corrupts. For how does a person benefit if he gains the whole world but loses his soul? Or what shall he give in exchange for it? Store up therefore in heaven, where neither moth nor rust corrupts.[144]

In the first, third, and fourth cases, there is a secondary juxtaposition of originally separate sayings. In *GTh* 39, a redactor may have heard an allusion to Genesis 2–3 in each of the two distinct sayings, combining them for that reason. In the passage from *GEgy,* the garment-of-shame motif has been combined with the two/one saying but probably derives from an independent saying, a version of which occurs in *GTh* 37.2. This passage is best described as a conflation rather than a juxtaposition. Where sayings are conflated, their individuality is lost; where they are juxtaposed, it is retained. In the third passage, the SC underlying *2 Clement* has connected the sayings about the two masters and about gain and loss by way of a link passage related to both of them.[145]

Particularly striking juxtapositions occur when SC redactors draw on material associated with specific narrative contexts and assign it a more gen-

---

and those wishing to enter *you* prevented." Mt. 23.13: "*Woe to you,* <scribes and Pharisees>, *hypocrites! For you shut the kingdom of heaven.* . . ." Mt. 10.16: "*Behold, I send you as sheep in the midst of wolves. Be then* wise [φρόνιμοι] *as serpents and innocent* [ἀκέραιοι] *as doves.*"

142. Clement of Alexandria, *Strom.* iii.13.92.2; cf. *GTh* 22, 37.

143. Cf. Lk. 16.13: "*No servant can serve two masters. For either he will hate the one and love the other, or he will be devoted to the one and despise the other. You cannot serve God and Mammon.*" Mt. 16.26: "For what *will it* advantage *a person,* if *he* gain the whole world and lose his soul?"

144. Mt. 6.19-20 is here juxtaposed with Mt. 16.26 (6.20 being repeated). Divergences from Matthean wording are slight. See Bellinzoni, *Sayings,* pp. 61-62, 89-90 (although Bellinzoni does not focus on the phenomenon of juxtaposition).

145. "If we wish to serve God and Mammon . . ." derives from the conclusion of the two-masters saying (cf. Mt. 6.24c = Lk. 16.13c), while ". . . it is unprofitable to us" serves to introduces the commercial imagery of the following saying.

eral significance. In two similar examples, a blessing or a woe associated with the Lukan or Matthean passion narratives is connected to parenetic material occurring in the same gospel:

> *GTh* 79.1-3 A woman in the crowd said to him, "Blessed are the womb that bore you and the breasts that fed you." He said to her: "Blessed are those who have heard the word of the Father and have kept it in truth. For there will be days when you say, 'Blessed the womb that has not conceived and the breasts which have not given milk.'"[146]

> *1 Clem.* 46.7-8 Remember the words of Jesus our Lord; for he said [εἶπεν γάρ], "Woe to that man! It were good for him if he had not been born rather than to offend one of my elect. It were better for him that a millstone be put on him and he be drowned in the sea rather than to turn aside one of my elect."[147]

If the author of *1 Clement* expects his Corinthian readers to "remember" these words of Jesus, it will hardly be on the basis of their presumed knowledge of the Gospel of Matthew. The author draws here on an SC in which a woe elsewhere specific to Judas is given a more general application — thereby making it particularly applicable to the Corinthian situation as *1 Clement* understands it.

Juxtaposition is a literary phenomenon. When a saying is written down, it may be juxtaposed with another saying on a related theme and subsequently separated again for a new juxtaposition. In *P. Oxy.* 1, the saying "Raise the stone and there you will find me; split the wood and I am there" follows directly from another two-part saying: "Where there are three, they are without God; where there is one alone, I say, I am with him."[148] In the Coptic translation, a version of the three-and-one saying is found on its own in *Saying* 30, while "Raise the stone . . ." is juxtaposed with a saying about Je-

---

146. Cf. Lk. 11.27-28: "*And it came to pass as he said these things,* a certain woman from the crowd *raising her voice* said to him, 'Blessed are the womb that bore you and the breasts that fed you!' And he said [ ]: 'Blessed *rather* are those who hear the word of *God* and keep it [ ].'" Lk. 23.29: ". . . for *behold,* the days are coming when *they* will say: 'Blessed are *the barren and* the wombs that have not conceived and the breasts that have not fed.'"

147. Cf. Mt. 26.24: ". . . *but* woe to that man *by which the Son of man is betrayed.* It were good for *that man* if he had not been born." Mt. 18.6: "<*Whoever* offends one of *these little ones who believe in me,*> it would be well for him *that a* mill-*wheel be hung about his neck* and he be drowned in *the depth of* the sea."

148. *P. Oxy.* 1r, *ll.* 2-9. The reading is uncertain, however.

sus as the light, as τὰ πάντα, and as the origin of τὰ πάντα (*Saying 77*).[149] While it is unclear whether the direction of this redactional alteration is from *P. Oxy.* 1 to the Greek text underlying the Coptic or the reverse, this example indicates that a saying can migrate from one juxtaposition to another even within the same text. Normally, new juxtapositions occur as a saying is transferred from one text to another — a common occurrence within the synoptic tradition, as we have seen in the case of Luke's editing of Matthew. Juxtaposition is a characteristic feature of Jesus' sayings in their written form, but it is not unique to the SC genre.

(iii) Responses. In the SC, sayings of Jesus may be presented as responses to questions, requests, statements, or suggestions from others — whether an individually named disciple, the disciples as a group, or outsiders.[150]

> *2 Clem.* 12.2 When the Lord himself was asked by someone when the kingdom would come, he said: "When the two shall be one, and the outside as the inside, and the male with the female neither male nor female."

> *GTh* 113.1-4 His disciples said to him: "When will the kingdom come?" [Jesus said:] "It will not come by waiting; they will not say, 'Behold, here!' or, 'Behold, there!' But the kingdom of the Father is spread out on the earth and people do not see it."

> *GEgy* When Salome enquired when she would know the answer to her questions, the Lord said: "When you trample the garment of shame, and when the two become one and the male with the female neither male nor female."[151]

In such passages, sayings are provided with an occasion within Jesus' ministry, specifically within his relationships with others. Additional narrative detail is rare. In *GTh* 100.1, it is said that "[t]hey showed Jesus a gold coin

---

149. As in Logion 2, ⲠⲦⲎⲢϤ probably represents τὰ πάντα (as in Jn. 1.3).

150. Questions: *GTh* 12.1; 21.1; 37.1; 43.1; 51.1; 53.1; 113.1. Requests: *GTh* 18.1; 20.1; 24.1; 72.1; 91.1; 114.1. Statements: *GTh* 52.1; 79.1; 99.1; 100.1. Suggestions: *GTh* 104.1. Requests that Jesus should "tell" or "show" are interchangeable with questions. Requests for other types of action are found only in *GTh* 72.1 ("Tell my brothers to divide my father's possessions with me") and 114.1 ("Let Mary leave us, for women are not worthy of life"). In *GTh* 72.2-3, two alternative responses are provided, one addressed to the man who has made the request, the other to the disciples.

151. Clement of Alexandria, *Strom.* iii.13.92.2. Koester notes that the *2 Clem.* 12 version represents the "oldest and most original form" of this tradition (*Ancient Christian Gospels*, p. 359).

and said to him, 'Caesar's men demand taxes from us.'" The gold coin is redundant in this context and is probably a secondary feature derived from
narrative gospels (cf. Mt. 22.18-21 and parallels). Yet the references to others
already imply that Jesus' ministry is in principle narratable. If Jesus is addressed by Salome, Mary, Simon Peter, or the disciples as a group, a network
of ongoing relationships is presupposed. Jesus is not simply a disembodied
voice speaking from nowhere.

(iv) Dialogues. The single response to a question or request can be extended
into a longer dialogue.

> *GEgy* Salome asked the Lord: "How long shall people die?" He answered:
> "As long as women bear children." Salome said: "I did well then in not
> bearing." The Lord answered and said: "Eat every herb, but that which is
> bitter do not eat."[152]

> *GTh* 61.2-5 Salome said: "Who are you, O man? As though from One, you
> climbed onto my couch and ate from my table!" Jesus said to her: "I am he
> who came from the One who is equal. What belongs to my Father was
> given to me." [Salome said:] "I am your disciple!" [Jesus said to her:]
> "Therefore I say, when one is equal, he will be full of light, but when one is
> divided he will be full of darkness."

There are difficulties with the text, translation, and interpretation of the
GTh passage,[153] but its structure is clear. Both passages open with a question
from Salome; *GTh* adds a statement in which she seems to derive a possible
answer to her own question from Jesus' conduct.[154] In both passages, Jesus'
response leads Salome to an affirmation about herself, to which Jesus adds a
second response. The dialogue is constructed by a simple doubling of the
single response passages which, in Thomas, are far more common. Only here
and in *GTh* 13 and 60 is the response format extended into dialogue. Given
the popularity of gospels consisting almost entirely of dialogue, the relative
lack of extended dialogue in Thomas confirms the conservative nature of
this text, which preserves the basic forms of the early SCs. No such dialogue
occurs in the *2 Clement* citations, although there is a three-part passage in
which Jesus' saying evokes a question from Peter, to which Jesus responds

152. Clement of Alexandria, *Strom.* iii.9.64.1 (cf. iii.6.45.3); iii.9.66.1-2.
153. See Dunderberg, *The Beloved Disciple in Conflict?* pp. 89-101.
154. Compare the request + statement in *GTh* 24, and the statement + question in *GTh* 12.

(2 *Clem.* 5.2-4). Dialogue may have played a greater part in *GEgy* than in other SCs.

(v) Extensions. In these cases, a short saying is supplemented with analogous units that retain its formal structure, creating a coherent whole. In *GTh* 2 and the Greek parallels, the saying "Seek and you will find" is developed in precisely this way.

> *GTh* 2.1-4 Jesus said: "Let the one who seeks not cease his seeking until he finds; and when he finds he will be troubled; and when he is troubled he will wonder; and he will reign over all."

> *P. Oxy.* 654 [Jesus says]: "Let the one who seek[s not cease seeking until] he finds; and when he finds [he will wonder; and won]dering he will reign; an[d reigning he will rest]."

> *GHeb* "The one who seeks will not cease until he finds; and finding he will wonder; and wondering he will reign; and reigning he will rest."[155]

These carefully constructed extensions of the original saying are, once again, a literary phenomenon and not the product of purely oral tradition. They have not come into being spontaneously, but have been consciously crafted. The same is true of a citation in *1 Clement:*

> *1 Clement* 13.2 . . . especially remembering the words of the Lord Jesus, which he spoke teaching gentleness and patience. For he spoke thus [οὕτως γὰρ εἶπεν]: "Be merciful, that you may receive mercy.[156] Forgive, that it may be forgiven you.[157] As you do, so it shall be done to you.[158] As you give, so it shall be given to you.[159] As you judge, so shall you be judged.[160] As you are kind, so shall you receive kindness.[161] With what [ᾧ] measure you measure, with it [ἐν αὐτῷ] shall it be measured to you."[162]

---

155. Clement of Alexandria, *Strom.* v.14.93.3; cf. ii.9.45.5: "So also in the Gospel to the Hebrews it is written: 'The one who wonders shall reign, and the one who has reigned shall rest.'"

156. Cf. Mt. 5.7: "Blessed are the merciful, for they shall receive mercy."

157. Cf. Lk. 6.37c: "Forgive, and you will be forgiven."

158. No parallel.

159. Cf. Lk. 6.38a: "Give, and it shall be given to you."

160. Cf. Mt. 7.2a: "With what judgment you judge, you will be judged."

161. No parallel.

162. Cf. Mt. 7.2b; Lk. 6.38b: "With the measure you measure, [ ] it will be measured to you."

The author cites this complex passage to remind his Corinthian readers that Jesus taught "gentleness and patience." It is unlikely that he has assembled it himself, and it is also unlikely that such a carefully constructed passage came into being in a purely oral context.[163] The passage was probably drawn from a Sayings Collection.[164] It consists in seven parallel statements in which a specific or nonspecific ethical requirement is linked to a reciprocal divine action, eschatological or otherwise. The principle of reciprocity is stated in abstract form in the third statement ("As you do . . ."), and again in the final one ("With what measure . . ."). The first two statements present the principle of reciprocity as motivating the actions called for in the two imperatives (be merciful, forgive). The format is familiar from a number of synoptic parallels. In the following four statements, the principle of reciprocity is highlighted in the use of the less traditional *as/so* format. Imperatives and their corresponding motivations are only implicit here. The concluding statement is probably the inspiration for the preceding *as/so* statements, where the traditional imperatives give way to more precise formulations of reciprocity in connection with kindness, judging, giving, and action in general. With the measure with which we measure, it will be measured to us: as we judge, so we will be judged; as we give, so will it be given to us.[165]

The "reciprocal measure" saying seems to have developed in a closely analogous way in the synoptic tradition and its aftermath. In its earliest accessible form, it is relatively isolated:

Mk. 4.24 ". . . For in what measure you measure it will be measured to you."

In Matthew, the general principle of reciprocity is given a single specific application, combining an imperative with a motivational statement that is then repeated in the same format as the general principle:

Mt. 7.1-2 "Judge not, that you may not be judged. For in what judgment

---

163. Against Koester, who claims that *1 Clem.* 13.2 was "drawn from the oral tradition" (*Ancient Christian Gospels*, p. 20). Koester had earlier suggested that the passage may have been constructed by the author of *1 Clement* "aus irgendeiner schriftlichen Herrenwortsammlung, die wir nicht mehr kennen, die aber älter sein mag als unsere Evangelien" (*Synoptische Überlieferungen*, p. 16).

164. It is also cited in the same form by Clement of Alexandria (*Strom.* ii.18.91), who derives it from *1 Clement,* a text well known to him.

165. Cf. A. Gregory's discussion of this passage ("*1 Clement* and the Writings That Later Formed the New Testament," in *The Reception of the New Testament,* pp. 129-57; pp. 131-39). Gregory concludes "that Clement refers here to a collection of sayings that is independent of and earlier than the broadly similar sayings of Jesus that are preserved also in Matthew and/or Luke" (pp. 133-34).

you judge you will be judged, and in what measure you measure it will be measured to you."

Luke, dependent on Matthew, inserts three further applications:

Lk. 6.37-38 "Judge not, and you will not be judged. < Condemn not, and you will not be condemned. Forgive [ἀπολύετε], and you will be forgiven. Give, and it will be given to you; good measure — pressed down, shaken together, overflowing — they will place in your lap.> For in what measure you measure it will be measured back to you."

Luke's expansion of this teaching recalls the independent version cited by Clement of Rome. Yet another version is cited by Polycarp:

Polycarp, *To the Philippians* 2.3 . . . but remembering what the Lord said [ὧν εἶπεν ὁ κύριος], teaching: "Judge not, that you may not be judged. <Forgive [ἀφίετε] and it will be forgiven you. Be merciful, that you may receive mercy.> In what measure you measure, it will be measured back to you." And, "Blessed are the poor and those who are persecuted for righteousness' sake, for theirs is the kingdom of God."[166]

As in the equivalent passages in Clement of Rome, Matthew, and Luke, Polycarp concludes with the reciprocal measure saying. The expanded version of this saying is clearly marked off from the composite beatitude that follows, indicating that Polycarp intends to cite specific texts rather than summarizing the Lord's teaching in his own words.

The beatitude itself draws from both Luke and Matthew. Harmonized beatitudes are also found in *GTh* (Matthean elements underlined, Lukan italicized):[167]

GTh 54 Jesus said: "Blessed are *the poor, for yours is the kingdom* of heaven."

GTh 68 Jesus said: "Blessed are you when they *hate you* and persecute you. . . ."

---

166. According to Koester, Polycarp draws the first passage from *1 Clem.* 13.2, altering the order of the imperatives and bringing the wording into line with Matthew and Luke respectively at the beginning and end (*Synoptische Überlieferungen*, pp. 115-18). A derivation of both passages from a Sayings Collection influenced by Luke and Matthew seems at least as likely.

167. Cf. Mt. 5.3, 10, 11; Lk. 6.20, 22.

Polycarp, *To the Philippians* 2.3 "Blessed are *the poor* and <u>those who are persecuted for righteousness' sake, for theirs is the kingdom</u> *of God.*"

There is no need to suppose that Polycarp is quoting loosely from the synoptic gospels or that he draws on an oral tradition still unaffected by textuality. It is more probable that, like Clement of Rome and the author of *2 Clement,* he is quoting from a Thomas-like Sayings Collection. Even where the wording of a saying is influenced by Matthean or Lukan redaction, that influence is a secondary phenomenon within texts belonging to an essentially different genre.[168]

Before Mark

The Gospel of Mark is the earliest of the canonical gospels. But that does not make it the earliest venture into gospel-writing, a far-reaching experiment that single-handedly transformed the original traditions about Jesus by incorporating them into a connected narrative. Mark does not represent a fateful moment at which a fall occurred from the pristine oral paradise into the prosaic world of the text. There is no basis for speaking of "Mark's disruption of the oral lifeworld," or of his substitution of "devitalized, stable objects" for "living words" — belatedly taking up the cause of "those committed to speaking and to the oral gospel," for whom "the written gospel was neither desirable nor necessary."[169] On such a view, Mark becomes the focus for an ideological hostility to the text that can be traced back to Romanticism in the modern era and to Plato in the classical one.[170] In the early Christian context, this "great divide" between orality and textuality is most clearly articulated by Papias, who speaks of his preference for "a living and abiding voice" over "what comes from books."[171] This rhetorical appeal to

---

168. That a number of sayings in *GTh* betray the influence of Matthew and Luke has been well demonstrated by Simon Gathercole, who gives extensive attention to the relevant methodological issues (*The Composition of the Gospel of Thomas,* pp. 127-224). It should be noted that *GTh*'s "dependence on the synoptics" would not establish this work's secondary, postcanonical status, since both Matthew and Luke are also dependent on at least one of the synoptic gospels.

169. Kelber, *The Oral and the Written Gospel,* pp. 91, 95, 93.

170. This "anti-grammatological" tendency is a central concern in the earlier work of Jacques Derrida: see his *Of Grammatology,* Eng. trans. (Baltimore & London: Johns Hopkins University Press, 1976); "Plato's Pharmacy," in *Dissemination,* Eng. trans. (Chicago: University of Chicago Press, 1981), pp. 61-171; "The Linguistic Circle of Geneva," in *Margins of Philosophy,* Eng. trans. (Chicago: University of Chicago Press, 1982), pp. 137-53.

171. Eusebius, *HE* iii.39.3.

the living voice has to do with Papias's own project, specifically with his need to demonstrate his own links with apostolic figures of the first Christian generation; it should not be seen as indicative of early Christian attitudes in general.

It is much more likely that orality and textuality interacted with one another before Mark and that they continued to do so after Mark. The public reading of a text is already an oral event, and the creation of a new text on the basis of an old one may owe as much to oral performance as to the physical presence of a written text. The indirect dependence of one text on another by way of a so-called "secondary orality" is a possibility to be added to the more familiar model of direct dependence. Even here, however, the orality in question is textually determined. And there is no basis for the assumption that texts can *only* engage with one another through an oral medium, and that purely textual interactions can be ruled out a priori.

The Sayings Collection genre is independent of the narrative gospels. The question is whether it predates them. At the very least, the SC represents a simple and plausible mechanism for the transition between the oral and written transmission of a saying or parable of Jesus — whether the interval between utterance and inscription was longer or shorter. Jesus himself *spoke:* in that sense, the living voice does indeed precede the text. In the text the trace of the voice is preserved and protected against loss or distortion. Yet conservation is not an end in itself but merely a precondition for the text to fulfil its major function as a script for performance. Unlike the narrative gospels, the Sayings Collection is probably not formally read in the context of communal worship. Rather, it serves as an additional textual resource for preaching and other forms of Christian communication. Jesus' sayings are preserved with a view to practices of interpretation occurring within Christian discourse. In that sense, SCs are open rather than closed texts, pointing to the world of praxis within which they seek their own reinscription. Thus Thomas presents the sayings as objects not for passive contemplation but for active interpretation (ἑρμηνεία). The homily known as 2 *Clement* consists largely in interpretations of Jesus' sayings. Papias devotes his five-volume work to the "Exegesis of the Lord's Sayings" (Λογίων κυριακῶν ἐξηγήσεως),[172] to which the traditions that he received from the elders are supplementary.[173] Interpreting Jesus' sayings is so significant an

---

172. Eusebius, *HE* iii.39.1.

173. In his preface Papias writes, "I *also* will not hesitate to compile, *along with the interpretations* [συγκατατάξαι ταῖς ἑρμηνείαις], whatever I have learned well and remembered well from the

element within Christian discourse that interpretation already occurs within the SCs themselves. The boundary line between text and interpretation is fluid, and cannot be precisely drawn. Where one saying is juxtaposed with another, the aim is to enable the two sayings mutually to interpret one another. Where a saying is presented either as an independent artefact or as a response to a question, an interpretative decision has been made. Where a dialogue or an extended saying is constructed out of shorter traditional units, Jesus' utterances are again the objects of interpretation. *Ipsissima verba* are preserved only insofar as they seem the most effective vehicle for communication; if not, they may be adapted in order to realize more fully their semantic potential. Yet interpretation does not overwhelm the original textual datum, subsuming the person of Jesus into that of his interpreter. SCs and their users repeatedly insist that a given saying proceeds from the mouth of Jesus (or "the Lord," or "the Saviour"), and that it is therefore to be understood as *his own* utterance. An original act of communication from Jesus to ourselves is the foundation of all ongoing communicative action within the Christian community.

Narrative gospels are also engaged in practices of interpretation that are to some degree shared with SCs. Texts belonging to these different genres may include many of the same sayings, and it is plausible to suppose that this overlap comes about as a narrative gospel incorporates into itself material drawn from an SC. Although the only complete SC to have survived is relatively late in its present form, the genre itself may predate the synoptics. In order to give substance to this hypothesis, we will study a selected text — the parable material in Mark 4 — on the assumption that it has been constructed out of individual units derived from an SC. Since Mark 4 overlaps at a number of points with *GTh*, the hypothetical pre-Markan SC will also overlap with *GTh* at just those points. For example, both Mark and Thomas

---

elders" (Eusebius, *HE* ii.39.3). These traditions of the elders are thus supplementary to the exegesis or interpretation of the Lord's sayings, about which Papias must have spoken in the immediately preceding passage. On this see A. D. Baum, "Papias als Kommentator evangelischer Aussprüche Jesu: Erwägungen zur Art seines Werkes," *NovT* 38 (1996), pp. 257-76; pp. 270-73. According to Baum, referring to *HE* iii.39.3, Papias's work was in three parts: "Erstens dürfte Papias, wie in vergleichbaren Werken in der Regel üblich, die von ihm behandelten Herrensprüche (λόγια κυριακά) zitiert haben. Zweitens hat er diese Herrensprüche mit Erläuterungen (ἑρμηνεῖαι) versehen. Und drittens hat er in diese Auslegungen Mitteilungen der Presbyter (ὅσα ποτὲ παρὰ τῶν πρεσβυτέρων καλῶς ἔμαθον καὶ καλῶς ἐμνημόνευσα) eingefügt" (A. D. Baum, "Papias, der Vorzug der *Viva Vox* und die Evangelienschriften," *NTS* 44 [1998], pp. 144-51; p. 147). Since Papias states that "Matthew compiled the sayings [τὰ λόγια συνετάξατο]" (Eusebius, *HE* iii.39.16), it is likely that Matthew is a primary source of the Sayings Collection that Papias himself compiled and interpreted.

contain versions of the Parable of the Sower. If an early SC is in principle a plausible source for the Markan version of the parable, then the existence of this parable in a later SC may be cited as evidence for this source-critical hypothesis.[174]

Mark's introductory formulae provide initial evidence that a Thomas-like SC may have been used. The first of these serves as the introduction to the collection of parables and sayings that follows:

> And he taught them many things in parables, and in his teaching he said to them [ἔλεγεν αὐτοῖς]: "Listen! The sower went out to sow. . . ." (Mk. 4.2-3)

> Jesus said [ⲡⲉⲝⲉ ⲓⲥ]: "Behold, the sower went out. . . ." (*GTh* 9.1)

For Mark, the Parable of the Sower belongs to a collection of parables drawn from "many such parables" that Jesus uttered on the day in question (Mk. 4.33; cf. v. 13). For Thomas, the parable is a discrete unit in its own right. Mark's second introductory formula occurs at the close of the parable:

> ". . . yielding thirtyfold and sixtyfold and a hundredfold." And he said: "Whoever has ears to hear, let him hear!" (Mk. 4.9)

> . . . He said: ". . . he came quickly with his sickle and reaped it. Whoever has ears to hear, let him hear!" (*GTh* 21.2, 9-10)

The introductory formula ("And he said . . .") suggests that Mark's SC did not link the appeal to hear with the Parable of the Sower. Its redundancy is evident both from Matthew's omission (Mt. 13.9) and Luke's rewriting (Lk. 8.8: ταῦτα λέγων ἐφώνει). In Thomas, the appeal to hear belongs to the Parable of the Seed growing secretly, from which Mark may have transferred it.

---

174. For a thorough discussion of the "vormarkinische Sammlung" underlying Mk. 4.1-34, see Heinz-Wolfgang Kuhn, *Ältere Sammlungen im Markusevangelium* (Göttingen: Vandenhoeck & Ruprecht, 1971), pp. 127-46. Kuhn draws attention to (1) the catchword linkage between the three parables (σπείρειν, vv. 3, 31, 32, to which should be added γῆ, vv. 5, 8, 26, 28, 31 [2x]; καρπός, vv. 7, 8, 29; βασιλεία τοῦ θεοῦ, vv. 26, 30); (2) the non-Markan introductory formula καὶ ἔλεγεν (vv. 9, 26, 30); (3) the double conclusion (vv. 33, 34); (4) an inconsistency in relation to the addressees (vv. 10, 33); and (5) the shift from an original emphasis on comfort in adversity to the present concern with secrecy (pp. 129-136). Unfortunately Kuhn fails to engage with *GTh* and concludes from the catchwords that such a collection could have taken purely oral form (p. 144). On the general issue of pre-Markan sources and traditions, there is an extensive bibliography in W. R. Telford, *Writing on the Gospel of Mark* (Blandford Forum: Deo Publishing, 2009), pp. 338-41.

And he said to them: "To you has been given the mystery of the kingdom of God. . . ." (Mk. 4.11)

And he says to them: "Do you not understand this parable?" (Mk. 4.13)

The first passage responds to the disciples' nonspecific question "about the parables" (Mk. 4.10). Here a redactional insertion has taken place. In an earlier version of this material, the parable was more directly linked to its interpretation:

> And when he was alone, those who were about him [ ] asked him about the parable[ ]. And he said to them: "Do you not understand this parable? How then will you understand all the parables? The sower sows the word. . . ." (Mk. 4.10*, 13-14)[175]

If this reconstruction is correct, Mark 4.10-12 in its present form postdates the supplementation of the Parable of the Sower with a detailed interpretation (4.14-20).

> And he said to them: "Is a lamp brought in to be put under a bushel . . . ?" (Mk. 4.21)

> Jesus said: ". . . No one lights a lamp and puts it under a bushel. . . ." (*GTh* 33.1-2)

> And he said to them: "Take heed what you hear! The measure you give . . ." (Mk. 4.24)

In the repeated Markan introductory formula, "to them" lacks an antecedent (cf. Mk. 4.13). In Thomas, "he said to them" introduces a response to a request or question stemming from the disciples, and it corresponds to the formula, "His disciples said to him."[176] Mark 4.10*, 13 probably included

---

175. I here follow Bultmann, who sees Mk. 4.11-12 as "ganz sekundär" (*Die Geschichte der synoptischen Tradition* [Göttingen: Vandenhoeck & Ruprecht, 1967[7]], p. 215). In v. 10, σὺν τοῖς δώδεκα is Mark's addition to his source (p. 71), but more significant is his substitution of "parables" for "parable": "In V.10 wird nach dem Sinn der Parabelrede überhaupt gefragt, und darauf antwortet V.11f. Aber V.13 setzt voraus, daß nach dem Sinn der eben erzählten Parabel gefragt worden ist. Die Frage in V.10 muß also in der Quelle etwa gelautet haben wie Lk 8,9" (p. 351n). Such an approach is sharply criticized on narrative-critical grounds by J. Schröter (*Erinnerung*, pp. 301-9). While narrative-critical analysis may well lead one to question a given literary-critical hypothesis, the two approaches are not mutually exclusive in principle.

176. *GTh* 24, 51, 52, 53; cf. 20, 99 ("*The* disciples said to him"), 91 ("*They* said to him").

similar paired introductory formulae. In the lamp and measure sayings, the presence of the second member of the pair may suggest that the first too was present in the SC. If so, these sayings were once responses to questions.

The distinction between single and paired formulae is especially clear in the following passages:

And he said: "The kingdom of God is as if a man should scatter seed. . . ." (Mk. 4.26)

And he said: "With what can we compare the kingdom of God . . . ? It is like a grain of mustard seed. . . ." (Mk. 4.30-31)

The disciples said to Jesus: "Tell us what the kingdom of heaven is like." He said to them: "It is like a grain of mustard seed. . . ." (GTh 20.1-2)

Thomas too attests the formula "And he said" rather than the usual "Jesus said" (GTh 1, 8). Its presence in Mark suggests that it may be the older of the two. In retaining the traditional formula to introduce the Parable of the Seed growing secretly, Mark fails to note the shift from private instruction back to public address, as required by the narrative setting he himself has provided (cf. Mk. 4.33-34). In the Parable of the Mustard Seed, Mark's rhetorical question corresponds closely to the disciples' request in Thomas.

In Mark 4, the introductory formulae confirm that the evangelist's dependence on a Thomas-like SC is a real possibility.[177] Further support for this hypothesis may be found in individual parables and sayings.

In GTh 9, the Parable of the Sower is presented in the following form (differences from synoptic versions are italicized):

Jesus said: "Behold, the sower went out, *he filled his hand, he cast.* And some fell on the path; the birds came, they *gathered* them. Others fell on the rock, and *did not take root down into the earth and produced no ear up to heaven.* And others fell on the thorns; [ ] they choked *the seed and the worm ate them.* And others fell upon the good soil and gave *good*

---

177. The possible derivation of the Markan καὶ ἔλεγεν (4.21, 24, 26, 30, etc.) from a "Spruchsammlung" such as P. Oxy. 1 is already noted by Bultmann (*Geschichte*, p. 349). Bultmann assumes that the introductory formula λέγει ὁ Ἰησοῦς would have been original here: "Wurde eine derartig angelegte Sammlung in ein Evangelium aufgenommen, so war es natürlich, daß ὁ Ἰησοῦς fortfiel und etwa das Präsens in ein Tempus der Vergangenheit umgesetzt wurde" (p. 349). For Bultmann, a format such as this represents a primitive, presynoptic stage in the collecting of Jesus' sayings (p. 348).

fruit *up to heaven; it gave* sixty *per measure* and a hundred *and twenty per measure.*

As in the synoptic versions, the parable consists in a two-part introductory statement about the sower, the second part of which leads to a sequence of four further two-part statements which describe *(i)* where the seed fell, and *(ii)* what happened in consequence. It is striking that the divergences between *GTh* and the synoptic versions are concentrated in the second member of each of the five main statements, whereas the first member is in each case very similar.

Thomas provides no equivalent to the detailed, point-by-point interpretation that follows in all three synoptists, which requires not only a general distinction between the fruitful and unfruitful seeds but also clear differentiations among the unfruitful ones. In combination with the various types of soil, the birds, the sun, and the thorns all represent unfruitfulness, but, for the synoptic interpretation, they stand for different threats operating at different times and in different ways. This sober analysis of the fate of the word in a threatening environment has helped to shape the framing of the parable itself. On the other hand, the Thomas version seems to intend nothing more than the general contrast between fruitfulness and unfruitfulness. In each of the first three instances, the failure of the seed is total; there is no initial moment of fruitfulness that only later comes to nothing. In *GTh*, the parable not only *lacks* the synoptic interpretation, it also *excludes* it.[178]

We may suppose, then, that some precursor of the Markan evangelist had at his disposal an SC that included the Parable of the Sower without an accompanying interpretation. While it is not clear how far the Thomas version preserves actual pre-Markan wording, *GTh* does suggest the parable's original independence.[179] Yet the Markan provision of an interpretation is in keeping with the SC's basic intention, which is precisely that Jesus' sayings be interpreted. Thomas promises that "whoever finds the *hermeneia* of these sayings shall not taste death."[180] Similarly, the author of *2 Clement*

---

178. Compare the analysis of J. D. Crossan, *In Parables: The Challenge of the Historical Jesus* (New York: Harper & Row, 1973), pp. 39-44. Crossan too believes that the Markan interpretation has affected the parable itself, and draws attention especially to the intrusive reference to the sun (Mk. 4.6a), which aims to show what tribulation or persecution (4.16-17) is really like: "not slow withering but instant scorching" (p. 42).

179. This would be the case even if one accepted J. Schröter's claim that Thomas's version "läßt sich . . . am ungezwungensten als eine nachsynoptische Rezeption dieses Gleichnisses verstehen" (*Erinnerung*, p. 318). The text as a whole does not appear to require any such conclusion, however.

180. *GTh* 1.

cites sayings in order to interpret them. Since that text is actually a homily and not a letter, the primary context of sayings interpretation would seem to be preaching. If so, then the interpretation of the Parable of the Sower has a homiletic origin. It is "authentic" not because it represents *ipsissima verba* of Jesus but because it realizes the intention of the parable in its written form, which is to generate the supplementary discourse of interpretation.[181]

In Mark 4, the originally contextless parable is provided with a setting in Jesus' ministry (4.1-2), a conclusion (4.9), and an interpretation (4.10*, 13-20); and it is later supplemented again with a passage about the rationale for parables in general (4.10-12). In addition, two composite sayings are inserted between the interpretation of the Sower and the Parable of the Seed growing secretly, marked off from each other and the surrounding context by the use of introductory formulae. These sayings serve to outline a parable theory differing from that of 4.10-12. The first of these sayings comprises three main elements, a question, a supporting statement, and an appeal:

> And he said to them: "Does a light come so as to be put under the measure or under the bed, rather than on the lampstand? For there is nothing secret except in order to be revealed, nor is anything hidden except to come to light. Whoever has ears to hear, let him hear!" (Mk. 4.21-23)

The lampstand saying was transferred by Matthew to another context (Mt. 5.15). Luke, encountering the saying in both Mark and Matthew, retains it in the Markan context but relocates the Matthean version (Lk. 8.16; 11.33). With the exception of a minor transposition, the Thomas version is especially close to the second Lukan one (as underlining indicates):

> Jesus said: "[What you *[s.]* hear in your ears, proclaim from your rooftops.] For no one lights a lamp and puts it <under a measure>, nor does he

---

181. The familiar critical point about the secondariness of the interpretation must be differentiated from the negative evaluation that often accompanies it. Thus J. Wellhausen writes: "Er [d.h. der Kommentar] ist später als die Parabel und kann nicht von Jesus selbst herrühren. Das Wort im Sinne des Evangeliums, die Verfolgung wegen des Evangeliums und der Abfall davon liegen außerhalb des Gesichtskreises seiner Gegenwart; die apostolische Gemeinde wird vorausgesetzt und tritt an stelle des jüdischen Auditoriums" (*Das Evangelium Marci Übersetzt und Erklärt* [Berlin: Georg Reimer, 1909²], p. 32). In a nutshell, the problem is that the interpretation belongs within a "christlich-kirchliche" context, not that of a simple "Lehrer der Juden" (p. 32). There is no sense here that a logical development might be traceable between a parable, its inscription, and its ongoing interpretation within early Christian communities.

278

put it <in a secret place,> but he puts it on the lampstand so that everyone who enters and leaves will see its light." (*GTh* 33.1-3)[182]

It is likely that the lampstand saying developed in a linear manner, from Mark to Matthew to Luke to Thomas. It is variously linked with the "nothing secret" saying (Mk. 4.22; Lk. 8.17), the "city set on a hill" saying and the application to good works (Mt. 5.14-16), the saying about the eye as "lamp of the body" (Lk. 11.34-36), and the "rooftops" saying (*GTh* 33.1). Thus the linear development of the lamp saying is accompanied by a set of nonlinear juxtapositions, and it is this nonlinear development that is of the greater interpretative significance. Mark and Thomas confirm again that juxtaposition is a fundamental characteristic of the sayings tradition, both in SCs and in narrative gospels. It is a primarily literary phenomenon, in which free combinations and recombinations occur between relatively stable literary units.

The "nothing secret" saying recurs in Thomas in wording indistinguishable from Matthew 10.26, but, once again, in a different context. In Mark, the saying is a promise that the inner meaning of the parables will come to light; in Matthew, it is incorporated into a passage on fearless proclamation. For Thomas, its theme is truthful speech:

> . . . Jesus said: "Do not tell a lie, and do not do what you hate, for everything is disclosed in the sight of Heaven. For there is nothing hidden that will not become manifest, and there is nothing covered that will remain undisclosed." (*GTh* 6.2-6)

In Thomas, disclosure is the *fate* of hiddenness: thus, no secret falsehood will remain unexposed for ever. In Mark, disclosure is the *purpose* of hiddenness — an adaptation that accommodates the saying to the evangelist's parable theory. The wording preserved in Thomas could represent the original written form of this saying, on which other versions are dependent. The more important point is that both sayings incorporated in Mark 4.21-22 may have been made available to the evangelist by a Thomas-like SC. Even if the wording of a saying in Thomas shows synoptic influence, its SC context is independent of narrative gospels.

Mark's second composite saying comprises (*i*) an exhortation to hear, a mirror image of the exhortation that concludes the previous saying (4.23, 24a); (*ii*) a saying on reciprocity (4.24b); and (*iii*) a saying contrasting haves

---

182. The dependence of *GTh* 33 on Luke is rightly noted by Schröter, *Erinnerung*, pp. 374-75; Gathercole, *The Composition of the Gospel of Thomas*, pp. 194-96.

with have-nots (4.25). As we have seen, the second of these recurs in *1 Clement* in a form suggesting a nonsynoptic SC origin; the third has a parallel in *GTh*.

> And he said to them: "Take heed what you hear! In what measure you measure it shall be measured to you, and it shall be added to you. For whoever has, it will be given to him, and whoever does not have, what he has will be taken from him." (Mk. 4.24-25)

> "[. . . As you give, so it shall be given to you. As you judge, so shall you be judged. As you are kind, so shall you receive kindness.] In what measure you measure, *with it* shall it be measured to you." (*1 Clem.* 13.2)

> Jesus said: "Whoever has *in his hand,* it will be given to him, and whoever does not have, *the little* that he has will be taken from him." (*GTh* 41.1-2)

Apart from minor expansions (italicized), the wording of these sayings is relatively stable. Clement and Thomas suggest that, even prior to Mark, the sayings may have existed separately in a literary form distinct from the canonical gospels.

The connection between the first and the second of Mark's parables of growth is interrupted by the interpretation of the Parable of the Sower, and by the material comprising Mark's parable theory (4.10-12, 21-25). In the original SC, it is possible that the Sower was followed immediately by the Parable of the Seed sown secretly, just as the latter is followed immediately by the Parable of the Mustard Seed.[183] *GTh* 63-65 forms a collection of consecutive parables (the Rich Fool, the Great Feast, and the Wicked Tenants). Vestiges of a connection between the second and third parables may still be visible in *GTh* 20-21, though the order is reversed and the second parable survives only in fragmentary form in a composite context.

> And he said: "The kingdom of God is as if a man should cast seed upon the ground. . . . And when the fruit ripened, immediately he sends the sickle, because the harvest has come." (Mk. 4.26-29)

> [Mariam said to Jesus: "Whom are your disciples like?" He said: "They are like children. . . .] Let there be among you a man of understanding. When

---

183. This would then constitute the core of "eine schon dem Mk vorliegende kleine Sammlung" (Bultmann, *Geschichte*, p. 351). Bultmann believes, questionably, that this grouping of thematically linked parables could have occurred at the oral stage (p. 348).

the fruit ripened, he came immediately with his sickle in his hand, he harvested it. Whoever has ears to hear, let him hear!" (*GTh* 21.1-2, 8-10)

The conclusion of the Markan parable alludes to Joel 4.13 LXX;[184] the allusion is absent in Thomas. Thomas's concluding exhortation recurs in five other parables: the Fisherman (*GTh* 8), the Man of Light (24), the Rich Fool (63), the Wicked Tenants (65), and the Leaven (96). The original function of this exhortation was evidently to mark the conclusion of a parable. Mark uses it to conclude the Parable of the Sower, but extends it to the first of the composite sayings, and perhaps also to the later saying about defilement, where the text is uncertain (Mk. 4.9, 23; 7.16?). Matthew too can transfer the exhortation to hear out of a parabolic context (Mt. 11.15: the Baptist as Elijah), and also uses it to conclude his interpretation of the Wheat and the Tares (13.43). In Luke, it is attached to a short parable about salt (Lk. 14.35).

In the Parable of the Mustard Seed, Mark's version may represent an expansion of a form resembling Thomas's version. Here, if anywhere, Thomas has a strong claim to represent the oldest accessible form of a saying or parable of Jesus (see Figure 5.1).[185]

Luke places this parable in a non-Markan context, pairing it with the Parable of the Leaven. He is primarily dependent here on Matthew, who retains the Markan context but inserts the Parable of the Leaven (thus Mt. 13.31-33 = Lk. 13.18-21). In itself, the Matthean passage shows no knowledge of a second, Q version. At 1 Luke has material in common with Mark; in **2-6**, with Matthew; Luke's dependence on both Mark and Matthew is the most economical explanation. It is the Q hypothesis that generates a Q version of this parable, and not the texts as they stand.

Matthew and Luke present versions of the parable that are briefer than Mark's, but they retain his hyperbolic insistence that the smallest of all seeds produces the greatest of all plants — a great tree, indeed, in whose branches the birds of the sky can make their nests (Mt. 13.31-32 = Lk. 13.18-19). The conclusion of the synoptic parable again alludes to scripture, in this case to

---

184. Jl. 4.13: ἐξαποστείλατε δρέπανα ὅτι παρέστηκεν ὁ τρύγητος. Mk. 4.29: εὐθὺς ἀποστέλλει τὸ δρέπανον ὅτι παρέστηκεν ὁ θερισμός. Note that in the Markan context the ὅτι-clause is redundant.

185. See Richard Bauckham, "The Parable of the Vine: Rediscovering a Lost Parable of Jesus," *NTS* 33 (1987), pp. 84-101; pp. 93-94. "Like Jesus' parables in general, it [the *GTh* Parable of the Mustard Seed] does not break the bounds of naturalism and introduce mythological features such as are found in the Old Testament texts about the world-tree. . . . The other versions sacrifice naturalistic accuracy to closer correspondence with the Old Testament texts" (p. 94).

Figure 5.1

Lk. 13.18-19	Mt. 13.31-32	Mk. 4.30-32	GTh 20
1a So he said: **1b** "What is the kingdom of God like,	1 Another parable he set before them, saying:	**1a** And he said: **1b** "With what can we compare the kingdom of God,	1 The disciples said to Jesus: "Tell us what the kingdom of heaven is like." He said to them:
1c and to what shall I compare it?		**1c** or what parable shall we use for it?	
2 "It is like a grain of mustard, *which a man took and cast* into *his* garden,	**2** "The kingdom of heaven is like a grain of mustard, *which a man took and* sowed in *his* field.	**2** It is like a grain of mustard, which, <u>when sown upon the ground,</u>	**2** "It is like a grain of mustard, which
[3]	**3** It is the smallest of all the seeds,	**3** is the smallest of all the seeds <u>on the earth;</u>	**3** is the smallest of all seeds
4 and *it grew*	**4** but when *it is grown* it becomes greater than all plants	**4** but when it is sown it <u>springs up and becomes greater than all plants,</u>	**4** and when it falls upon tilled soil it grows great
5 and it *became a tree*	**5** and *becomes a tree*	**5** <u>and produces large branches</u>	[5]
6 and the birds of the sky dwelt *in its branches*."	**6** so that the birds of the sky come and dwell *in its branches*.	**6** so that the birds of the sky can dwell under its shadow."	**6** and gives shade to the birds of the sky."

Bold: common enumeration

Italics: Lk. = Mt.

<u>Underlining:</u> Markan elements absent from GTh.

Daniel 4.12.[186] Both the hyperbole and the allusion are absent in Thomas, where the image is of individual birds finding shade under a plant rather than flocks of them nesting in a great tree.[187] This conclusion results in a more coherent parable than the synoptic versions, and it may approximate more closely than they do to its earliest written form.[188]

Mark's compositional process in his parable chapter makes excellent sense if he has at his disposal an SC containing eight distinct items. This SC would overlap with *GTh* at all but one of these points. In Markan sequence and structure, these items are as follows:

1. The Parable of the Sower (= *GTh* 9; Mk. 4.3-8)
2. The Exhortation to hear (= *GTh* 21.10; Mk. 4.9, cf. v. 23)
3. The Lamp saying (= *GTh* 33.2-3; Mk. 4.21)
4. The Disclosure saying (= *GTh* 6.4-6; Mk. 4.22)
5. The Measure saying (= *1 Clem.* 13.2; Mk. 4.24)
6. Haves and have-nots (= *GTh* 41.1-2; Mk. 4.25)
7. The Parable of the Seed sown secretly (= *GTh* 21.9; Mk. 4.26-29)
8. The Parable of the Mustard Seed (= *GTh* 20.1-4; Mk. 4.30-32)

Items *1*, *7*, and *8* may already have been grouped together in the evangelist's SC. Item *1* is provided with a narrative introduction (Mk. 4.1-2), and item *8* is followed by a narrative conclusion (4.33-34). Item *2* has been transferred from the conclusion of another parable, perhaps the seed grown secretly, as the separate introductory formula indicates. Items *3-6* have been rearranged into two composite sayings, which the evangelist inserts into the parable collection in order to encourage receptive hearing. They complement the interpretation of the Parable of the Sower (4.13-20), which may be understood as a primitive Christian sermon outline. The interpretation was

186. Dn. 4.20-21 (Theodotion) reads as follows: "The great and strong tree [δένδρον = Mt., Lk.] that you saw . . . Under it the wild beasts made their home, and in its branches [ἐν τοῖς κλάδοις αὐτοῦ = Mt., Lk.] the birds of the sky dwelt [κατεσκήνουν τὰ ὄρνεα τοῦ οὐρανοῦ = Mk, Mt, Lk]."

187. As usual, the Q theory introduces unnecessary complications here. Thus John Dominic Crossan postulates a Q version of the parable, best preserved in Luke, which then provides supporting evidence for a reconstructed pre-Markan version (*In Parables*, pp. 44-49). Crossan is right, however, to point out that "the attempt to allude to the tree with the nesting birds of apocalyptic eschatological imagery" is secondary, and that *GTh* is here "much closer to the original," i.e. presumably the original *inscription* (p. 49).

188. Note, however, Simon Gathercole's critique of the assumption that an apparently simpler or more coherent version of a passage is necessarily earlier (*The Composition of the Gospel of Thomas*, pp. 132-38).

not present in the SC, and neither was the saying on the mystery of the kingdom, which disturbs the earlier link between the parable and its interpretation (4.11-12). The presentation of Jesus' parables and sayings is an ongoing interpretative process.

Interpretation proceeds, first, by locating the parabolic teaching in a credible and vivid situation within the historical ministry of Jesus. The effect is not to "historicize" Jesus' teaching, relegating it to the past, but rather to emphasize that the sayings are inseparable from the one who speaks in them. Second, the Parable of the Sower is marked out for special attention. The interpretative decision is made to regard this as a parable in four parts rather than two, and a key is provided that will also unlock the meaning of the other parables. The parable and its interpretation are carefully coordinated with one another, and the interpretation makes it impossible for hearers or readers to evade the existential question implicit within the parable. Third, originally unconnected sayings are juxtaposed with one another in order to clarify further the situation of parabolic address. In them, Jesus teaches that the aim of his parables is not to obscure the truth but to bring it to light; the basis for their reception lies in the hearer. Fourth, a passage is subsequently added which reflects on the distinction between the crowds, who hear the parables, and the disciples, who are taught what they mean (4.11-12; cf. vv. 33-34). This complex reception process takes its starting point from the initial inscription of discrete sayings and parables of Jesus in SC format.

This attempt to install the *Gospel of Thomas* at the heart of the so-called "synoptic problem" might be extended to the supposedly "Q" material of Matthew and Luke. In particular, the SC hypothesis would help to account for Matthew's expansion of Mark. Matthew's gospel would draw not only on Mark but also on one or more SC. Luke's use of Matthew as well as Mark would make this evangelist less dependent on SCs than his predecessors — although, as we have seen, he seems to have compiled his own SC in the process of editing his Matthean source material.

Thomas, then, is the point of departure for an "SC hypothesis" that should replace the implausible Q hypothesis. *GTh* itself is best understood as a *descendant* of the early SCs employed by Mark and Matthew, and as a *relation* of SCs known from second-century sources. The early SCs cannot be reconstructed as a whole; unlike Q, there can be no "critical edition." Yet items in *GTh* with synoptic parallels can plausibly be traced back to presynoptic collections. Even where a saying in its present form betrays the influence of synoptic redaction, that may be the result of secondary assimilation. In other cases, *GTh* may preserve sayings material in the closest available approximation to its earliest written form; in particular, it seems to incorporate a remarkably conservative transmission of some of Jesus' parables. And whatever the relation of a given saying to its synoptic equivalents, the SC genre itself remains essentially independent of the synoptics.

The SC hypothesis undermines the assumption that Jesus' sayings passed through an extended period of oral transmission during which there was no perceived need for inscription. It is true that, at least in the case of the oldest material, an interval between production and inscription is plausible, as there is no evidence that Jesus' sayings were committed to writing during his ministry. What is less plausible is the supposition that the Parable of the Sower was transmitted orally over three or four decades, acquiring a detailed interpretation along the way, before being finally committed to writing by the evangelist Mark. Such a view rests on a questionable analogy with processes of cultural transmission in non- or preliterate societies. It also fails to take into account the evidence of Thomas.

The SC hypothesis outlines a mechanism by means of which a saying of Jesus can pass into wider circulation. The inscription of such a saying is already an interpretative act even if Jesus' *ipsissima verba* are faithfully preserved, and it enables an unlimited series of further interpretative acts, including those that gave rise to the canonical gospels. From the outset reception entails an active shaping of the primary material, and the originary moment of the reception process is the event in which the word became text.

CHAPTER 6

Interpreting a Johannine Source (*Jn,* GEger)

In the three preceding chapters, a new approach to gospel origins has begun to take shape. It has been argued that Luke was "dependent" on Matthew, in the sense that Luke was Matthew's *interpreter*. The concept of "dependence" on a "source" draws attention only to the area of overlap between the secondary text and the primary one. Seeking to establish a genetic relationship between the two, one identifies those points where the secondary text has reproduced the wording and/or sequence of the primary text, and one ventures an explanation of the "changes" introduced by the second author. While these remain useful exegetical procedures which can still produce illuminating results, they imply too static an account of the intertextual relationship. They overlook the interpretative dynamic underlying early Christian gospel writing, reducing this dynamic to editorial processes of reproduction and emendation and failing to explain the phenomenon of *rewriting* itself.

Any new gospel rewrites its predecessors, whether that rewriting takes the form of revision, supplementation, or substitution. Matthew rewrites Mark both as he revises Markan material and as he supplements it with new narrative and sayings material. Luke rewrites Matthew both in his revised account of Jesus' temptations and in his substitution of a new birth narrative, inspired by and responsive to the Matthean one. The outcome of Matthean or Lukan rewriting is nothing less than a new interpretation of the figure of Jesus, qualitatively different from its precursor although the object of interpretation remains recognizably the same. Rewriting assumes that earlier gospel writing is not definitive, and that the traditions it embodies need to be articulated again in the light of new interpretative insights. Rewriting responds to an imperative perceived to stem from the tradition itself, and is not the autonomous act of the creative individual — as "redaction criticism" tends to suggest.[1] In the tradition, Jesus himself calls for the new interpretative activity that seeks to communicate his significance afresh. The interpretative dynamic underlying gospel writing and rewriting originates in the risen Lord who is also the earthly Jesus of the tradition. That is the context in which the "dependence" of one gospel on another is to be understood.

The limitations of the dependence model of gospel origins are also evident in its assumption that the genesis of canonical gospels can be explained purely internally, without recourse to noncanonical texts. As traditionally understood, dependence entails the preservation of much of the primary text within the secondary one. This model works well for the Markan substratum in Matthew and Luke; the Q hypothesis represents an attempt to extend it to the common non-Markan material. Matthew and Luke are supposed to be dependent on Q in the same way as they are dependent on Mark. The text of Q can therefore be recovered from Matthew and Luke, just as the text of Mark can be — although it is only possible to differentiate the two source texts because one of them is still extant. In this account, synoptic origins are explained by way of intracanonical evidence alone. Noncanonical texts are at best of marginal significance here. Canonical status coincides with historical reality; canonicity is historicized.

Prior to the discovery of the *Gospel of Thomas,* the Q hypothesis was perhaps the best available explanation for the early transmission of Jesus' sayings. Given the availability of *GTh,* however, the hypothesis is ripe for reconsideration. Unlike *GTh,* Q is not a pure sayings collection. Q includes a limited and apparently random assortment of narrative material; individual sayings remain undifferentiated within larger blocks of teaching material. In spite of overlapping content, the genre and format of *GTh* and of Q are quite different from one another. In principle, *GTh* might be seen as an anomaly, partially dependent on synoptic tradition for its content but unique as regards its genre. But the evidence points in another direction: *GTh* represents a relatively late instance of a much older Christian genre, that of the Sayings

---

1. Redaction criticism rightly views the evangelists as individual authors rather than mere collectors or editors, as implied by form and source criticism (on this see W. Marxsen, *Mark the Evangelist: Studies on the Redaction History of the Gospel,* Eng. trans. [Nashville: Abingdon Press, 1969], pp. 15-29). But it tends to see the authorial intervention as occasioned only by contingent situational factors and not as responsive to the dynamic of tradition itself. In consequence, the Jesus of the individual evangelist is considered in abstraction from Jesus himself; interpretation supplants its own object.

Collection. Since *GTh* demonstrably incorporates material from earlier Sayings Collections, it is possible that certain sayings or parables may be preserved here in presynoptic forms. Still more importantly, the Sayings Collection genre may itself precede the synoptics; *GTh* would then preserve the format in which Jesus' sayings were first committed to writing. If so, a noncanonical text would now play a crucial role in accounting for synoptic origins, shedding light not only on Matthew and Luke but also on the largely unknown situation prior to Mark. Canonical status and historical priority would no longer coincide.

Early Christian gospel production may be seen, then, as interpretative rewriting — a process that begins with presynoptic Sayings Collections and their incorporation into narrative gospels, and that extends to the creation of the fourfold canonical collection. This too is an act of gospel production, which sets each of four previously distinct texts within a normative intertextual context, thereby interpreting, limiting, and stabilizing the rewriting process itself. The creation of the canonical/noncanonical divide has a retroactive effect on the entire field, making it appear that canonical normativity is inherent to some texts while apocryphal marginality is equally inherent to others. This appearance cannot be dismissed as an illusion, for the fourfold canonical gospel remains a communally normative text which both includes and excludes. Yet this normative text can only be adequately understood if it is seen that the dividing line *might* have been drawn elsewhere, or in a different form, or not at all. Aided by texts and text fragments rediscovered in recent times, investigation of gospel origins must recognize that, at its point of origin, a particular gospel is not-yet-canonical or non-yet-apocryphal, and that *at this point* the canonical/noncanonical divide is irrelevant and potentially misleading. The rediscovered material is also a reminder that the dividing line was not universally acknowledged and that texts it seeks to exclude continued to be used and valued.

The question for the present chapter is whether a *precanonical* account can be given of the origins of the text traditionally known as "the Gospel according to John," and renamed "the fourth gospel" by critical scholars for whom the evangelist was no longer identifiable with the apostle John, son of Zebedee.[2] This critical rebranding is anachronistic, in spite of its appearance

---

2. Examples of this well-established terminology include W. Sanday, *The Criticism of the Fourth Gospel* (Oxford: Clarendon Press, 1905); W. F. Howard, *The Fourth Gospel in Recent Criticism and Interpretation* (London: Epworth Press, 1931); E. C. Hoskyns and F. N. Davey, *The Fourth Gospel*, 2 vols. (London: Faber, 1940); C. H. Dodd, *The Interpretation of the Fourth Gospel* (Cambridge: Cambridge University Press, 1953); J. L. Martyn, *History and Theology in the Fourth Gospel*

of historical integrity. There is no reason to suppose that, at its point of origin, the Gospel of John was *a* or *the* fourth gospel. Only in the context of the canonical collection did it come to be such, that is, a gospel that closes the collection it shares with its three synoptic precursors. In its original precanonical form, the Gospel of John may or may not predate the Gospel of Luke or the *Gospel of Thomas*. Since all three gospels seem to presuppose a complex development involving multiple earlier texts or text forms, we should in any case envisage a set of parallel and interconnected trajectories (synoptic, Johannine, and Thomasine) rather than a mere historical sequence fitted out with appropriate dates.[3] Even if the conventional datings are approximately correct, the canonical/noncanonical divide cannot be secured by imagining that the year 100 CE marks a kind of watershed, a secure *terminus ad quem* for the fourth gospel that separates it from noncanonical literature which can be dated no earlier than the first half of the second century. (It is easy to forget that the distinction between a first and a second century is itself a blatant anachronism for the period in question.) It is not clear why the twenty-to-thirty-year interval which may separate the gospels of Mark and John would be qualitatively different from the possibly similar interval between the Gospel of John and the *Gospel of Thomas*.[4] Even if it is true that "the four New Testament gospels were written earlier than any of the other 'gospels,'"[5] this conclusion does nothing to validate a four-gospel collection — as opposed to a collection of, say, the first three or the first ten gospels. If the later, noncanonical gospels are considered to be "dependent"

(New York: Harper & Row, 1968[1]); R. A. Culpepper, *Anatomy of the Fourth Gospel: A Study in Literary Design* (Philadelphia: Fortress, 1983); John Ashton, *Understanding the Fourth Gospel* (Oxford: Clarendon Press, 1991).

3. Traditional New Testament introductions tend to date the canonical gospels in the period 65-100 CE, with Mark dated earliest and John latest. For W. Marxsen, Mark can be precisely dated to 67-69 CE (*Introduction to the New Testament*, Eng. trans. [Philadelphia: Fortress, 1968], p. 143); Matthew may be dated to the 80s (p. 153), Luke to *c.* 90 (p. 161), John "towards the end of the first century" (p. 259). W. G. Kümmel dates Mark to *c.* 70 CE (*Introduction to the New Testament*, Eng. trans. [London: SCM Press, 1975], p. 98), Matthew to 80-100 CE (p. 120), Luke to 70-90 CE (p. 151), and John to "the last decade of the first century," a view which is "today almost universally accepted" (p. 246). Norman Perrin suggests 70-90 CE for the synoptic gospels, 80-100 for John (*The New Testament: An Introduction* [New York: Harcourt Brace Jovanovich, 1982[2]], p. 43).

4. Some such qualitative difference between the first and second centuries is presupposed when John P. Meier speaks of "the apocryphal gospels" as "a field of rubble, largely produced by the pious or wild imaginations of certain 2d-century Christians," in sharp contrast to "the earliest sources of 1st-century Christianity" (*A Marginal Jew: Rethinking the Historical Jesus*, vol. 1 [New York: Doubleday, 1991], pp. 115, 127).

5. Graham N. Stanton, *The Gospels and Jesus* (Oxford: Oxford University Press, 1989), p. 135.

or "secondary" in relation to earlier canonical ones, similar relationships of dependence and secondariness are evident within the canonical collection itself. If the *Gospel of Thomas* is found to be dependent on Matthew and Luke, then this dependence is not qualitatively different from Matthew's dependence on Mark, or Luke's on Mark and Matthew. A single dynamic process of gospel writing and rewriting runs through all these texts, and it is not the case that the beginning of the second century marks a turn from one kind of gospel writing (brought to completion by "the fourth gospel") to another (initiated perhaps by Thomas). This distinction is even less justifiable if the earlier datings for canonical gospels and the later datings for noncanonical ones turn out to be questionable: if, for example, the equally radical theologies of John and Thomas may have developed more-or-less simultaneously during the late first and early second centuries. The theological judgement represented by the fourfold canonical collection is, precisely, a *theological* judgement, needing no support from problematic arguments for historical priority.

The historicizing of the canonical decision affects other aspects of Johannine origins as well as the dating issue. As in the case of the synoptics, it is assumed that the origins of John are to be sought *either* in the other canonical gospels (by demonstrating that John is dependent on, say, Mark or Luke) *or* within the text of John itself (by reconstructing a so-called "Signs Gospel," or by identifying "later additions"). In themselves and in principle, these approaches are not without value. The question is whether a fuller and more adequate account could be given if the canonical boundary were to be removed and other texts brought into play. The present chapter is an attempt to answer that question. As in the case of Luke, we shall see that the origins of this gospel are to be found in the *interpretative process* embodied in it.

Moses, Jesus, and Two Evangelists

In 1935 H. I. Bell and T. C. Skeat published newly discovered fragments of an "Unknown Gospel" contained within a papyrus codex (*Egerton Papyrus* 2; henceforth *P. Eger.*) of which three leaves were partially extant. Introducing the new material, the editors wrote:

> Not since the discovery of the Sayings of Jesus at Oxyrhynchus has a Christian papyrus come to light which raises so many and such interesting problems as the present fragments. The Chester Beatty Papyri are of

far greater extent, but in some respects even they must yield in interest to these, since for the most part they merely provide new evidence for the text of existing books, whereas these, which reveal to us an entirely unknown work, open up new vistas altogether.[6]

The new material was to be dated still earlier than the other papyrus finds mentioned here.[7] Bell and Skeat found the closest similarities to the handwriting of *P. Eger.* 2 in three datable papyri, one stemming from the reign of Trajan (*d.* 117 CE), a second dating from *c.* 80 CE, and a third from 94 CE. The editors do not suggest a late-first- or early-second-century date for *P. Eger.* 2, however, stating only that it is "extremely improbable" that it "can be dated any later than the middle of the second century."[8] This slightly later dating was suggested by the (unsystematic) use of diaeresis over υ and ι, since this usage was "comparatively rare at the beginning of the second century" but "increas[ed] in frequency with each successive decade."[9] Also suggestive of a mid-second-century date was the lack of the iota adscript, used regularly until the late first century but falling into disuse in the course of the second.[10]

More recently, the original dating of *P. Eger.* 2 has been called in question by Michael Gronewald, editor of a further fragment (*P. Köln* 255) which belongs to the first of the extant leaves and provides several additional lines or part-lines on both sides.[11] At one point in the new fragment, an apostrophe is used between consonants (ανηνεγ'κον, line 4 recto) which, according to Gronewald, is more characteristic of the third century than the second.[12] Whether an isolated feature of this kind is a reliable indicator of date is un-

---

6. H. Idris Bell and T. C. Skeat, *Fragments of an Unknown Gospel* (London: British Museum, 1935), p. 1.

7. The references are to *P. Oxy.* 1, 654, 655, now known to stem from *GTh* but published by B. P. Grenfell and A. S. Hunt under the titles *Sayings of Our Lord from an Early Greek Papyrus* (London: Egypt Exploration Fund, 1897) and *New Sayings of Jesus and Fragment of a Lost Gospel* (London: Egypt Exploration Fund, 1904); and to the collection of biblical papyri from both Testaments published by Frederick G. Kenyon from 1933 (*The Chester Beatty Biblical Papyri* [London: Walker, 1933-58]).

8. Bell and Skeat, *Unknown Gospel,* p. 2.

9. Bell and Skeat, *Unknown Gospel,* p. 4.

10. Bell and Skeat, *Unknown Gospel,* p. 6.

11. M. Gronewald, "255. Unbekanntes Evangelium oder Evangelienharmonie (Fragment aus dem 'Evangelium Egerton')," *Kölner Papyri (P. Köln)* 6, Abhandlungen der Rheinisch-Westfälischen Akademie der Wissenschaften, PapyCol VII (Opladen: Westdeutscher Verlag, 1987), pp. 136-44.

12. Gronewald, "Fragment," pp. 136-37.

certain.[13] Yet even on the later dating, *P. Eger.* 2 remains among the oldest surviving Christian manuscripts. The later dating of the papyrus would not rule out an early date for the gospel itself.[14]

The "interesting problems" and "new vistas" to which Bell and Skeat refer have to do above all with the relationship of the Egerton gospel to the canonical gospels. The extant material

> is obviously part of a work designed on much the same lines as the canonical Gospels. It may perhaps seem rash to affirm this so positively on the basis of two leaves and a small fragment; but the whole scale of the narrative, the variety of incidents recorded, the mixture of sayings and miracles, irresistibly suggest this conclusion; and it is strengthened by ll. 28-9, which seem to point forward to the Passion.[15]

The Unknown Gospel includes two narratives with synoptic parallels — the healing of a leper and the question about taxes — yet these are so different from the synoptic versions that they seem to "represent a quite independent tradition."[16] If the author had ever read any or all of the synoptics, occasional synoptic words and phrases may have been reproduced from memory, but it is unlikely that he used Matthew, Mark, or Luke directly as a source.[17] *GEger* is, however, very closely related to John. It contains a dialogue about Moses' (or scripture's) testimony to Jesus and a subsequent attempt to arrest and stone him, and here close Johannine parallels abound (cf. Jn. 5.39; 9.29; 5.45 [+ 5.46, *P. Köln* 255]; 7.30; 10.31). According to Bell and Skeat,

> there can be no dispute that there is here a close connexion between 1 [= *GEger*] and John. The only question is what is the nature of this connexion. On the discovery of a new and non-canonical Gospel showing close verbal coincidences with John the assumption which naturally occurs first is that its author was using the existing Gospel of St. John as one of his

---

13. According to Larry Hurtado, Christian scribes were ahead of their contemporaries in their use of "reader's aids" such as punctuation, spacing, and so on (*The Earliest Christian Artifacts: Manuscripts and Christian Origins* [Grand Rapids: Eerdmans, 2006], pp. 177-85).

14. As suggested by H.-J. Klauck, *The Apocryphal Gospels: An Introduction*, Eng. trans. (London & New York: T. & T. Clark, 2003), p. 23, criticizing H. Koester.

15. Bell and Skeat, *Unknown Gospel*, p. 30. The concluding reference is to the phrase ὅτι οὔπω ἐ[ληλύθει] αὐτοῦ ἡ ὥρα τῆς παραδό[σεως].

16. Bell and Skeat, *Unknown Gospel*, p. 34.

17. Bell and Skeat, *Unknown Gospel*, p. 34.

sources; but a careful consideration of the evidence leads at least to some hesitation about this conclusion. The narrative in 1 makes no impression of being a mosaic of extracts from an earlier work. There is logical progression in the thought, so far as this can be determined from what remains.[18]

Bell and Skeat conclude that "it would be rash to reject off-hand the dependence of John on 1 in favour of the reverse theory," although they add, cautiously, that it would also be "rash and ill-advised in the present editors . . . to attempt a positive solution."[19] Yet their preference is clearly for regarding *GEger* as a source for John. That conclusion would indeed "open up new vistas altogether."[20]

The new vistas failed to materialize. There is little sign of them in the major works of subsequent Johannine scholarship, where *GEger* is largely ignored. In an article first published in 1936, C. H. Dodd argued against Bell and Skeat that *GEger* was dependent on John: in the parallel material, vocabulary and phraseology are characteristically Johannine, and are therefore unlikely to derive from a source.[21] Dodd also found the Johannine context of the parallel material more natural and less artificial than the Egerton one.[22] Echoing Bell and Skeat, he wrote:

> It would be rash to deny the possibility that the Fourth Evangelist found these sayings in a source represented by our papyrus, and made more effective use of them. But at least it seems clear that they are thoroughly "at home" in his work, and in view of the presumption created by our study of the language, it seems best to suppose that the author of the papyrus has excerpted the three sayings from the Fourth Gospel.[23]

The possibility which it would be "rash to deny" (or, as Bell and Skeat put it, "rash to reject off-hand") is nevertheless marginalized. For Dodd,

---

18. Bell and Skeat, *Unknown Gospel*, p. 35.

19. Bell and Skeat, *Unknown Gospel*, pp. 37, 38. Bell quickly retracted his pre-Johannine dating for *GEger* in the face of widespread criticism ("Recent Discoveries of Biblical Papyri: An Inaugural Lecture Delivered before the University of Oxford on 18 November 1936" [Oxford: Oxford University Press, 1936], p. 17). By 1949, however, he had reverted to his original position ("The Gospel Fragments P. Egerton 2," *HTR* 42 [1949], pp. 53-64, esp. pp. 56, 58-59, 61).

20. Bell and Skeat, *Unknown Gospel*, p. 1.

21. C. H. Dodd, "A New Gospel," in his *New Testament Studies* (Manchester: Manchester University Press, 1953), pp. 12-52; pp. 24-25.

22. Dodd, "A New Gospel," pp. 25-27.

23. Dodd, "A New Gospel," p. 27.

GEger is significant only because it supports a relatively early dating of John.[24]

Subsequent English-language Johannine scholarship has generally been content to repeat Dodd's conclusions.[25] Challenges have come mainly from those with a programmatic commitment to the early dating of noncanonical material.[26] German scholarship too has underlined the secondary, derivative character of *GEger*. According to J. Jeremias,

> There are points of contact with all four gospels. The juxtaposition of Johannine (*fr.* 1) and Synoptic material (*fr.* 2 and 3), and the fact that the Johannine material is permeated by synoptic expressions and the synoptic with Johannine usage, leads us to conclude that the author knew each and every one of the canonical gospels.[27]

This passage is quoted by Michael Gronewald, in the context of his 1987 publication of *P. Köln* 255, as indicative of the scholarly consensus ("[d]as bis heute gültige Fazit der gelehrten Diskussion").[28] At one crucial point, Gronewald's assumption that *GEger* is dependent on John has apparently affected his editorial judgement.

The new fragment belongs to the first leaf of *P. Eger.* 2, and includes a further Johannine-type saying on the verso and the conclusion of the healing story on the recto. As rendered by Gronewald and subsequent editors, the new saying is as follows:

εἰ γὰρ ἐπι[στεύσατε Μω(ϋσει)] ἐπιστεύσατε ἄ[ν ἐμοί πε]ρ[ὶ] ἐμοῦ γὰρ ἐκεῖνο[ς ἔγραψε]ν τοῖς πατ[ρά]σιν ὑμῶ[ν].

24. Dodd, "A New Gospel," p. 50.

25. See for example C. K. Barrett, *The Gospel according to St. John* (London: SPCK, 1978[2]), p. 110; R. E. Brown, *The Gospel according to John*, 2 vols., AB (New York: Doubleday, 1966), 1.229-30.

26. See H. Koester, *Ancient Christian Gospels: Their History and Development* (Philadelphia: Trinity Press International; London: SCM Press, 1990), pp. 205-16; Ron Cameron (ed.), *The Other Gospels: Non-Canonical Gospel Texts* (Guildford: Lutterworth Press, 1983), pp. 72-75; J. D. Crossan, *Four Other Gospels: Shadows on the Contours of Canon* (New York: Harper & Row, 1985), pp. 41-57.

27. W. Schneemelcher (ed.), *Neutestamentliche Apokryphen* (Tübingen: Mohr-Siebeck, 1990[6]), 1.83. German original: "Es finden sich Berührungen mit allen vier Evangelien. Das Nebeneinander von johanneischem (I) und synoptischem Stoff (II und III) und der Umstand, daß der johanneischen Stoff mit synoptischen Wendungen, der synoptische mit johanneischem Sprachgebrauch durchsetzt ist, läßt vermuten, daß der Verfasser die kanonischen Evangelien sämtlich kannte."

28. Gronewald, "Fragment," p. 137.

For if [you] be[lieved Moses] you would believe [me.] For [abou]t me he [wrot]e to your fathers.[29]

The additional phrase, "to your fathers," is the only significant difference from John 5.46. It recalls John 6.49, where Jesus states that "*your fathers* ate the manna in the wilderness and died," in contrast to those who come to Jesus himself as the bread of life. In both passages, Jesus appears to distance himself from the Jewish ancestry of his hearers. Such distancing is characteristic of the Johannine Jesus, who also speaks of "your law" (Jn. 8.17; 10.34; cf. 7.19) or "their law" (15.25). The Egerton evangelist's familiarity with John is apparently confirmed.

In reality, this confirmation is worthless, for it is based on a dubious editorial decision. The surviving letters of line 23 verso are as follows:

ΝΤΟΙϹΠΑΤ[. . .]ϹΙΝΗΜΩ

The third from last of the surviving letters is damaged, but it is evidently an *eta* rather than an *upsilon*. The left-hand vertical stroke has almost disappeared, but the right-hand vertical and the linking horizontal are clear. The reconstructed text should read:

[πε]ρ[ὶ] ἐμου γὰρ ἐκεῖνο[ς ἔγραψε]ν τοῖς πατ[ρά]σιν ἡμῶ[ν].

For [abou]t me he [wrot]e to *our* fathers.[30]

In *GEger*, then, Jesus speaks of the wilderness generation not as "your fathers" (as in Jn. 6.49) but as "*our* fathers" — a totally un-Johannine usage on the lips of Jesus, suggesting that the Egerton community sees itself as continuing to belong to the wider Jewish community. Since Gronewald's

---

29. Fragment 1 verso, ll. 20-23 (for the enumeration, see T. Nicklas, "The 'Unknown Gospel' on *P. Egerton 2*," in *Gospel Fragments*, ed. Thomas J. Kraus, Michael J. Kruger, and Tobias Nicklas, Oxford Early Christian Gospel Texts [Oxford: Oxford University Press, 2009], p. 76).

30. See Plate 5 in Nicklas's edition. In his initial transcription, Gronewald acknowledges that the letter in question is an *eta* but encloses it in double square brackets to indicate a scribal emendation ("Fragment," p. 138): "ημω[ist wahrscheinlich in 'ϋ'μω[korrigiert" (p. 139). Evidence for an emendation is presumably found in the faint and ambiguous markings above the intact right-hand vertical stroke of the H, interpreted as the upper part of Υ. The markings are poorly aligned with the vertical, however, and the horizontal cross-stroke of the H is left unerased. In the reconstructed text that follows (p. 140), Gronewald *replaces* ημω[with υμω[ν, with the υ now identified not as an emendation but simply as uncertain, along with three other letters in l. 23. Even if a scribal emendation had taken place, it would still be important to acknowledge the original reading.

publication, editors of *GEger* have failed to note that the text actually has Jesus speak of "our fathers," with the result that recent editions of *GEger* are seriously misleading at this point.[31]

In view of this unrecognized reference to "our fathers," the question of the relationship between *GEger* and John must be reopened. The reading "our fathers" does not in itself demonstrate that *GEger* is pre-Johannine. While the representation of Jesus as participating in a Jewish and scriptural heritage may imply a provenance closer to Judaism than John's, that does not provide direct evidence for its date. There was no singular "parting of the ways" between "Christianity" and "Judaism" that would make proximity to Judaism a criterion for relative datings.[32] Yet a singular parting of the ways may have taken place within the Johannine community. If *GEger* is most closely related to an earlier point on the trajectory that leads to the Johannine gospel, then its priority in relation to the canonical text begins to look plausible. The case for a pre-Johannine Egerton would have to show *(i)* that the reference to "our fathers" coheres with other elements in *GEger*'s representation of Jesus' relation to his Jewish milieu; *(ii)* that this representation itself coheres with an earlier stratum discernible within the present form of the Johannine text; and *(iii)* that the Johannine version of parallel material is secondary to the Egerton one. If the argument is successful, it will shed light on the development and logic of Johannine theology. We seek to recover what may lie *behind* the Johannine gospel in order to retrace the *forward* momentum that generates the canonical text.

Parallels between *GEger* Fragment 1 verso and John 5 are analysed in Figure 6.1. These parallels (**A B D**) are remarkably close, as is the further parallel with John 9 (**C**). A literary relationship between the two passages is indisputable, whether this took the form of scribal copying or reproduction from memory. Either one text draws from the other, or both draw on a com-

---

31. D. Lührmann, *Fragmente apokryph gewordener Evangelien in griechischer und lateinischer Sprache* (Marburg: Elwert, 2000), p. 148; A. Bernhard, *Other Early Christian Gospels: A Critical Edition of the Surviving Greek Manuscripts* (London & New York: T. & T. Clark, 2007), pp. 88-89; Nicklas, *Gospel Fragments*, pp. 24, 32; Bart D. Ehrman and Zlatko Pleše, *The Apocryphal Gospels: Texts and Translations* (New York & Oxford: Oxford University Press, 2011), pp. 248-49.

32. See Judith Lieu's critique of the "parting of the ways" model ("'The Parting of the Ways': Theological Construct or Historical Reality," *JSNT* 56 [1994], pp. 101-19; repr. in her *Neither Jew nor Greek? Constructing Early Christianity* [London & New York: T. & T. Clark, 2002], pp. 11-29). Lieu's point about social realities can be extended to texts: "[W]e can in different contexts speak of both separate identity and development, and of close interaction in combinations which defy any simple model" (p. 27).

Figure 6.1

P. Egerton 2 fr.3v + fr.1v +P. Köln 255v	John 5.37-47 (+9.29)
	5.37 ". . . The Father who sent me bears witness about me. You have never heard his voice or seen his form, 38 and you do not have his word abiding in you, because you have not believed him whom he sent.
1 [And] *knowing [their thought // Jesus said] to the lawyer[s: "Judge(?) ev]ery wrongdo[er and everyone who is law]less, and not me. *2* [. . .] what he does how [he] does . . ." [*3* And tur]ni[ng] to [the] rulers of the people he sa[id] this wor[d]:	
A *4* "[Se]arch the scriptures, in *which* you thi[nk] to have *life*. It i[s] they [that bear wit]ness about me.	**A** *39* *You* search the scriptures *because* you think in *them* to have *eternal* life. *And* it is they that bear witness about me.
	40 And you refuse to come to me that you may have life. *41* I do not receive glory from humans, *42* but I have known you, that you do not have the love of God within you. *43* I have come in the name of my Father, and you do not receive me; if another comes in his own name, him you will receive. *44* How can you believe, receiving glory from one another, and you do not seek the glory which is from the only God?
B *5* Do not th[ink] th[at] *I came* to accu[s]e [you] to *my* Father. Your [accu]ser is Moses, in whom you have hoped."	**B** *45* Do not *suppose* that I *shall* accuse you to *the* Father. Your accuser is Moses, in whom you have hoped."
C *6* When they s[aid], "We w[ell] know that God has spo[ken] to Moses, but as for *you*, we do not know [where *you are* from],"	**C** (*9.29* ". . . We know that God has spoken to Moses, but as for *this man*, we do not know where *he is* from.")
7 Jesus an[s]wering sa[id to the]m, "Now is accused [your un]belie[f in] // the things [attest]ed by him.	
D *8* For if [you] be[lieved Moses] you would believe [me.] For [abou]t me he [wrot]e to *our fathers. *[9* But if you do not believe h]i[s wri]t[ings, how will you believe my words?"]	**D** *5.46* "For if you believed Moses you would believe me. For about me he wrote. *47* But if you do not believe his writings, how will you believe my words?"

Verse enumeration in *GEger* is my own.

A B C D = parallels between *GEger* and John 5.

Italics = differences between *GEger* and John within parallel passages.

[   ] = approximate English equivalents to editorial restorations of Greek text.

// = approximate transition between fragments.

* = deviation from published texts of *P. Eger.* 2 or *P. Köln* 255.

mon source.[33] Since there seems no initial reason to suppose that the two texts are independent, the common source hypothesis may be left out of account unless and until it is needed. Does John derive **A B C D** from Egerton, or Egerton from John? Is Dodd right to claim that, while it would be "rash to deny" the former possibility, it is "best to suppose" the latter? This question should be approached indirectly, by way of a careful comparison between the two texts that remains open to both possibilities.

(i) Searching the Scriptures

Whatever the direction of the dependence, the two texts deploy the parallel material in very different ways. Here, as elsewhere in early Christian gospel writing, dependence is not subservience but rather the occasion for more or less radical reinterpretation. Thus, in spite of near verbal agreement over **A** (searching the scriptures), the contexts in which it is located are strikingly different. In *GEger*, **A** is an independent saying, linked without a break to **B** (Moses as accuser) and preceded by an elaborate introductory formula.

πρὸς [δὲ τοὺς] ἄ[ρ]χοντας τοῦ λαοῦ [στ]ρα[φεὶς εἶ]πεν τὸν λόγον τοῦτο[ν] . . . (1v 3)

A (together with **B**) is thus presented as a distinct saying with its own specific audience. The use of λόγος to refer to an individual saying is characteristic of John, although there is also an occurrence in Matthew:

"It is not what goes into the mouth that defiles a person but what comes out of the mouth that defiles the person." Then the disciples came and said to him, "You know that the Pharisees were offended on hearing *the saying*." (Mt. 15.11-12)

"Destroy this temple and in three days I will raise it." . . . So when he was raised from the dead, his disciples remembered that he had said this, and they believed the scripture and *the saying* which Jesus spoke. (Jn. 2.19, 22)

33. Cf. Jon Daniels's view that "Egerton's author and a Johannine hand have developed independently a common string of sayings" ("The Egerton Gospel: Its Place in Early Christianity" [unpublished diss., Claremont Graduate School, 1989; University Microfilms International, Ann Arbor, 1990], p. 263). Daniels apparently assumes that the "common string of sayings" derives from oral tradition.

Jesus said to him, "Go, your son will live." The man believed *the saying* that Jesus spoke to him, and went. (Jn. 4.50)

". . . The one who eats this bread will live for ever." . . . So many of his disciples on hearing this said, "This is a hard *saying,* who is able to hear it?" (Jn. 6.58, 60)[34]

In each case, the term λόγος is used to reflect back on what has just been said. There is no parallel to the *GEger* usage, where λόγος *introduces* a saying. If *GEger* is dependent on John, there might be a backward reference of a different kind, from *GEger* to John. *GEger* would then provide a new occasion for a familiar Johannine saying, cited almost as though it were itself scripture. But it is more likely that the introductory formula simply lends emphasis and solemnity to the saying, compelling the reader's attention and reminding him or her that matters of great moment are at stake.

In John, **A** is not separately introduced but occurs in the context of a lengthy discourse, addressed not to "the rulers of the people" but to "the Jews" (5.10-18 [4x]), on the themes of Jesus' oneness with the Father (5.19-30) and the testimony that substantiates his claim (5.31-47). Jesus cannot simply testify about himself, ἀπ' ἐμαυτοῦ (5.31), but has another (ἄλλος) to validate his words and to testify περὶ ἐμοῦ (5.32). Who is that other? Is it perhaps John the Baptist? John did indeed bear witness to Jesus when the Jewish leaders sent a commission of enquiry to investigate his activity (5.33, referring back to 1.19-28). In spite of John's importance at the opening of this gospel, his testimony is not what Jesus has in mind in the present discourse:

> You sent to John, and he bore witness to the truth. I do not receive testimony from a human source [παρὰ ἀνθρώπου], but I say these things so that you may be saved. He was a lamp, burning and shining, and you were willing to rejoice for a time in his light. But I have a testimony greater than John: for the works that the Father gave me to complete, these works that I do, testify about me that the Father sent me. And the Father who sent me, he it is who testifies about me. (Jn. 5.33-37a)

In contrast to John 1.8, John is himself a lamp or light which brought at least a temporary joy to those Jesus now addresses. He did indeed bear witness to Jesus, and yet his was a merely human witness and not the divine val-

---

34. Further examples in Jn. 7.36; 15.3.

idation that occurs in and through Jesus' works. His acts are also his Father's acts (cf. 5.19-30), and as such they are also the Father's testimony to him.

Having criticized his hearers for their lack of receptivity to this testimony (5.37b-38), Jesus now speaks of another kind of testimony:

> You search the scriptures because you think in them to have eternal life. And it is they that bear witness about me. And you refuse to come to me that you may have life. (5.39-40)

The statement about the scriptural testimony is strikingly similar to the earlier statements about the testimony of the Father:

ἄλλος ἐστὶν ὁ μαρτυρῶν περὶ ἐμοῦ, καὶ οἶδα ὅτι ἀληθής ἐστιν ἡ μαρτυρία ἣν μαρτυρεῖ περὶ ἐμοῦ. (5.32)

. . . αὐτὰ τὰ ἔργα ἃ ποιῶ μαρτυρεῖ περὶ ἐμοῦ ὅτι ὁ πατήρ με ἀπέσταλκεν. καὶ ὁ πέμψας με πατήρ, ἐκεῖνος μεμαρτύρηκεν περὶ ἐμοῦ. (5.36b-37a)

ἐραυνᾶτε τὰς γραφάς, ὅτι ὑμεῖς δοκεῖτε ἐν αὐταῖς ζωὴν αἰώνιον ἔχειν, καὶ ἐκεῖναί εἰσιν αἱ μαρτυροῦσαι περὶ ἐμοῦ. (5.39)

If *GEger* is dependent on John, then the noncanonical evangelist has drawn on characteristically Johannine phraseology in the parallel passage.[35] Yet phraseology characteristic of a particular author may still be drawn from elsewhere, in whole or in part. The motif of the testimony of Jesus' works is also known to the author of *GEger*, who at another point in the fragments appears to *coordinate* the testimony of Jesus' works with the testimony of scripture:

διδάσκαλε Ἰη(σοῦ) οἴδαμεν ὅτι [ἀπὸ θ(εο)ῦ] ἐλήλυθας ἃ γὰρ ποιεῖς μα[ρτυρεῖ] ὑπὲρ το[ὺ]ς προφ(ήτ)ας πάντας.

Teacher Jesus, we know that you have come [from God], for what you do bear[s witness] more than all the prophets. (*GEger* 2r, ll. 3-5)[36]

---

35. As argued by Dodd, "A New Gospel," p. 24. As G. Mayeda notes, however, the link between μαρτυρεῖν and scripture cannot be said to be Johannine: it is attested in Acts 10.43 and Rom. 3.21 but not elsewhere in John (*Das Leben-Jesu-Fragment Papyrus Egerton 2 und seine Stellung in der urchristlichen Literaturgeschichte* [Bern: P. Haupt, 1946], p. 22).

36. Lines 4-6 in Nicklas's edition, where the enumeration for Fragment 2 recto is unfortunately incorrect. Nicklas notes that the upper margin of Fragment 2r and v is extant (*Gospel Fragments*, p. 13) — as is clear from the photograph provided (Plate 3; compare the better quality im-

This statement stems from Jesus' opponents, who immediately afterwards test him with the question about taxes. Here, they evidently accept that "the scriptures . . . bear witness to me" (*GEger* 1v 4).[37] Yet the witness of Jesus' works (ἃ ποιεῖς) is seen as more significant — an indication, incidentally, that the complete gospel is likely to have contained a number of miracle stories in addition to the one or two partially extant. Whether or not the author shares this evaluation, the notion of a dual testimony is certainly his own, since he appeals both to the scriptural testimony (1v) and to the testimony of miraculous healing (1r).[38]

In contrast, the Johannine evangelist does not explain how the testimony of scripture relates to the testimony of the works, that is, the Father's testimony. John's testimony is carefully subordinated to the divine testimony on the grounds that it is merely human, and we might expect that the scriptural testimony will represent a second strand in the testimony of the Father, alongside the works. Yet the evangelist does not attempt to coordinate these forms of testimony. The appeal to scriptural testimony is introduced abruptly; the phraseology is similar to what has preceded, but the conceptual connection is loose. Furthermore, in John 5.45-47 it is Moses, the human author of scripture rather than the divine one, who comes to the fore. Is the scriptural testimony part of the Father's testimony to the Son, alongside the works, or is it a merely human testimony like John's (cf. 5.33-36)? It seems to hover between the two poles. If *GEger* is dependent on John, then the noncanonical evangelist has extracted **A** from a context in which it is not fully integrated. If John is dependent on *GEger*, then the lack of integration would reflect the incorporation of older material into a discourse which is primarily about something else.

The verbal differences between the two versions of **A** are less obvious than the contextual ones, but they too merit analysis:

1 ἐραυ[νᾶτε τ]ὰς γραφάς *2* ἐν <u>αἷς</u> ὑμεῖς δο[κεῖτε] ζωὴν ἔχειν *3* ἐκεῖναί εἰ[σ]ιν [αἱ μαρτ]υροῦσαι περὶ ἐμοῦ (*GEger* 1v 4)

---

age in the Bell and Skeat edition, Plate II). Despite this, Nicklas enumerates the first line of 2r as line 2 (p. 76). His line 1 consists simply in square brackets, probably owing to a misunderstanding of their use at the equivalent point in Bell and Skeat (*Unknown Gospel*, p. 10). 2v is enumerated correctly, however (*Gospel Fragments*, p. 66).

37. Following the verse enumeration introduced in Figure 6.1 above.

38. According to John W. Pryor, μαρτυρεῖ in the 2r passage "is far from certain as only the 'm' is clearly visible" ("Papyrus Egerton and the Fourth Gospel," *ABR* 37 [1989], pp. 1-13; p. 12). However, (1) the damaged fragment of the second letter is probably from an *alpha*; (2) the additional letters of μα[ρτυρεῖ] would fit the available space.

1 ἐραυνᾶτε τὰς γραφάς *2* <u>ὅτι</u> ὑμεῖς δοκεῖτε ἐν <u>αὐταῖς</u> ζωὴν <u>αἰώνιον</u> ἔχειν *3* <u>καὶ</u> ἐκεῖναί εἰσιν αἱ μαρτυροῦσαι περὶ ἐμοῦ (Jn. 5.39)

In both versions of **A** (**A**^Eg and **A**^Jn), the role of *2* is to support the reference to "searching the scriptures" in *1* by reminding the addressees of the high value that they already ascribe to scripture. If ἐραυνᾶτε is taken as an imperative ("*Search* the scriptures . . ."), then *2* is subordinated to *1* whereas *3* explains the rationale for *1*. The addressees are to search the scriptures (which they already regard as the way to life) *because* they bear witness to Jesus — and must therefore be *reread* with that in view. If ἐραυνᾶτε is taken as an indicative, *1* refers to an ongoing reading practice rather than a *re*reading, and *2* explains its rationale: "You search the scriptures *because* you think. . . ." In consequence of this coordination of *1* and *2*, the logical connection between *1* and *3* is lost and the passage simply juxtaposes an observation about a particular reading practice with a claim about the true sense of the texts.

In **A**^Eg, the ἐν αἷς at the beginning of *2* suggests that ἐραυνᾶτε τὰς γραφάς is to be taken as an imperative.[39] The addressees are to search the scriptures, in which they believe they have life, because their belief is misdirected so long as they do not recognize in Jesus the object of the scriptural testimony. In **A**^Jn, the ὅτι at the beginning of *2* suggests that ἐραυνᾶτε is to be taken as indicative. "Search the scriptures *because* you think . . ." makes little sense, especially since the assumption in question is misguided.[40] The addressees believe, wrongly, that the purpose of scripture is to give life; in fact, the purpose of scripture is to testify to Jesus. The logic of the saying seems to involve an *opposition* between *2* and *3* which emerges more sharply in **A**^Eg than in **A**^Jn. Thus the Johannine version requires a supplement which brings together its otherwise disparate references to "eternal life" and Jesus as the object of scriptural testimony: "And you refuse to come to *me* so that you may have life" (Jn. 5.40).

In **A**^Eg, the addressees think "to have life" through scripture; in **A**^Jn, "to have *eternal* life."[41] If John is dependent on *GEger*, then the Johannine evan-

---

39. So Mayeda, *Papyrus Egerton 2*, p. 19.

40. Cf. C. H. Dodd, *The Interpretation of the Fourth Gospel* (Cambridge: Cambridge University Press, 1953), pp. 329-30n. Dodd regards *GEger* as providing "the earliest witness for the text of this passage," i.e. Jn. 5.39 (p. 329n). The Johannine text is emended to account for the Egerton one, thereby safeguarding Johannine priority.

41. This distinction is preserved in the conflated version of Jn. 5.39 found in several Old Latin manuscripts. Ms a (fourth century) here reads: *scrutate scripturas in quibus vos existimatis in illis*

gelist is responsible for the additional term. If *GEger* is dependent on John, then the noncanonical evangelist has abbreviated the phrase, perhaps influenced by the fact that to "have life" is a Johannine idiom (14x in John; 1x in the synoptics). The crucial point here is the correlation between (eternal) life and scripture, which both evangelists will shortly identify very closely with the writings of Moses (Jn. 5.45-47; *GEger* iv 5-8). Nowhere in the Pentateuch or anywhere else in scripture is there a promise of ζωὴ αἰώνιος. If the Johannine Jews expect to find eternal life in and through scripture, they will seek in vain. What the Egerton text's "rulers of the people" will indeed find, however, is the promise of "life." For Paul too, there is a Jewish quest for salvation in and through the Law of Moses, and it can appeal to the promise of Leviticus 18.5 that "the one who does these things will live in them" — where "these things" refers to the commandments and prohibitions of the scriptural text (cf. Gal. 3.12; Rom. 10.5). Paul and his fellow Jews also reflect on the great appeal to choose life rather than death that Moses utters as the Torah and his own life draw to a close:

> Behold, I have set before your face today life and death, the good and the evil. If you hear the commandments of the Lord your God, which I command you this day . . . , you will live and you will be many. . . . I call heaven and earth to witness this day that I have set before your face life and death, the blessing and the curse. Choose life, so that you and your seed may live. . . . (Dt. 30.15-19)

The initial paired coordinates (life/death, good/evil) serve to structure Paul's argument in Romans 7.7-25.[42] The final pair (blessing/curse) is developed in Galatians 3.10-14. Other Jewish readers understood this passage more straightforwardly and less dialectically than Paul. According to Ben Sira:

---

vitam aeternam habere illae sunt quae testimonium dicunt de me in quibus putatis vos vitam habere hae sunt quae de me testificantur. Here, *in quibus* (2x) corresponds to A^{Eg} rather than A^{Jn} (cf. also the Curetonian Syriac at this point). The first *in quibus* has apparently been substituted for *quoniam* or *quia,* as the now redundant *in illis* indicates. Thus a translation that originally corresponded straightforwardly to the Greek text of Jn. 5.39 has had Egertonian readings superimposed and added. Ms ff2, and b (both fifth century) are similar to a, although ff2 replaces the imperative *scrutate* with the indicative or imperative *scrutamini* and lacks *in illis,* while b reads *scrutate scripturas quoniam . . .* [+ *in ipsis*] (= ἐραυνᾶτε τὰς γραφάς, ὅτι . . . [+ ἐν αὐταῖς]). In each case the distinction is maintained between *vitam aeternam habere* and *vitam habere.*

42. See my *Paul and the Hermeneutics of Faith* (London & New York: T. & T. Clark International, 2004), pp. 506-8.

If you will, you will keep the commandments, and to act faithfully is a matter of choice [εὐδοκίας]. He has placed before you fire and water: for whichever you wish, stretch forth your hand. Before humans are life and death, and whichever one wishes, it will be given to him. (Sir. 15.15-17)

Echoes of the Deuteronomy passage are clear. Those who hope to find life in and through the scriptures draw their hope from explicit scriptural utterances. The "rulers of the people" of *GEger* are in good company here. In contrast, when the Johannine Jews are told that they seek "eternal life" in the scriptures, the soteriological language is Johannine rather than scriptural.[43]

There are, then, several indications that A^{Eg} may represent an earlier form of the saying and that A^{Jn} is dependent on it. The Johannine version is not fully integrated into an otherwise coherent passage about Jesus' works as the Father's testimony; in *GEger,* the testimonies of scripture and of Jesus' works are coordinated. The Johannine understanding of ἐραυνᾶτε as indicative weakens the force of a saying that requires the imperative form of *GEger* for its full impact. A similar point can be made about *GEger*'s correlation between scripture and life, weakened by the substitution of the nonscriptural and Johannine expression "eternal life." Naturally these points are not decisive. But they do suggest that the first editors of *GEger* were right to appeal for an open mind on the direction of dependence. In spite of the long scholarly consensus, it is *not* "best to suppose" that the noncanonical is secondary to the canonical.

(ii) Moses the Accuser

B^{Eg} and B^{Jn} take the following forms:

1 μὴ ν[ομίσητε ὅ]τι ἐγὼ ἦλθον κατηγο[ρ]ῆσαι [ὑμῶν] πρὸς τὸν π(ατέ)ρα μου: *2* ἔστιν [ὁ κατη]γορῶν ὑμῶν Μω(ϋσῆς) εἰς ὃν [ὑμεῖς] ἠλπίκατε. (*GEger* 1v 5)

---

43. On the scriptural "life" motif in Paul and Second Temple Judaism, see Simon J. Gathercole, "Torah, Life, and Salvation: Leviticus 18:5 in Early Judaism and the New Testament," in *From Prophecy to Testament: The Function of the Old Testament in the New,* ed. C. A. Evans and J. A. Sanders (Peabody, MA: Hendrickson, 2004), pp. 131-50; Preston M. Sprinkle, *Law and Life: The Interpretation of Leviticus 18:5 in Early Judaism and in Paul,* WUNT (Tübingen: Mohr-Siebeck, 2008); and my *Paul and the Hermeneutics of Faith,* pp. 315-29, 481-510, and *Paul, Judaism, and the Gentiles: Beyond the New Perspective* (Grand Rapids: Eerdmans, 2007²), pp. 285-87.

1 μὴ <u>δοκεῖτε</u> ὅτι ἐγὼ <u>κατηγορήσω</u> ὑμῶν πρὸς τὸν πατέρα· *2* ἔστιν ὁ κατηγορῶν ὑμῶν Μωϋσῆς εἰς ὃν ὑμεῖς ἠλπίκατε. (Jn. 5.45)

If the opening phrase of **B**^{Eg} is correctly reconstructed as μὴ ν[ομίσητε ὅ]τι ἐγὼ ἦλθον,[44] then it is identical to the opening phrases of Matthew 5.17 ("Do not think that I came to destroy the law and the prophets") and 10.34 ("Do not think that I came to cast peace on the earth"). In the Matthean passages as in *GEger*, the opening phrase is followed by an infinitive. In *2*, however, *GEger* does not follow the format of the Matthean sequel ("I came not to . . . but . . ."), also attested in John 12.47: "For I came not to judge the world but to save the world" (cf. Jn. 3.17). In contrast, the Egerton saying provides an alternative candidate for the role that should not be attributed to Jesus. The addressees' accuser is not Jesus but Moses, in whom they have hoped — believing as they do that in and through the scriptures they have "life" (*GEger* 1v 4). Moses and the scriptures are virtually interchangeable in this passage: it can be said both that "it is they [the scriptures] that bear witness about me" and that "about me he [Moses] wrote to our fathers" (1v 4, 8). In **B**^{Eg}, *1* excludes a possible misinterpretation of Jesus' role here and now: that he has come to accuse his addressees to his Father. *2* names their real accuser. In **B**^{Jn}, what is excluded in *1* is apparently a future eschatological scenario: "Do not suppose that I *shall* accuse you to the Father." Since *2* is identical in the two versions, the shift in *1* from a hypothetical present role (**B**^{Eg}) to a hypothetical future one (**B**^{Jn}) creates an imbalance between Jesus and Moses: Jesus will not play the role of eschatological accuser since Moses already acts as accuser in the present.

In John, **B** is separated from **A** by the following passage:

And you refuse to come to me that you may have life. I do not receive glory from humans, but I have known you, that you do not have the love of God within you. I have come in the name of my Father, and you do not receive me; if another comes in his own name, him you will receive. How can you believe, receiving glory from one another, and you do not seek the glory which is from the only God? (Jn. 5.40-44)

Thus **B**^{Jn} follows a passage in which Jesus *accuses* his hearers of refusing to come to him, of lacking the love of God, of failing to receive him or to believe, and of seeking glory from one another rather than from God. "Do not

---

44. The initial letter of the word reconstructed here as ν[ομίσητε] is damaged, but is almost certainly a *nu* rather than a *delta*. Bell and Skeat's initial reading, μὴ δ[οκεῖτε], is thus incorrect.

think that I shall accuse you . . ." might be understood in connection with the Johannine insistence that Jesus came or was sent not to judge but to save (cf. Jn. 3.17; 12.47). That could explain the future tense: Jesus *does* accuse his hearers here and now, but that is incidental and subordinate to his real vocation, which is to save. On the other hand, it is not clear how a rejection of the role of eschatological accuser is compatible with the preceding claim that it is not the Son who refrains from judging but the Father, who "has given all judgment to the Son" (5.22; cf. v. 27). Can the Son call forth those who have done good to a resurrection of life and those who have done evil to a resurrection of judgment (5.29), while refraining from accusing people to the Father? In **B** as well as **A**, a superficial thematic link (accusation, testimony) masks significant problems of coherence.

In *GEger*, **A** and **B** form a single two-part saying, introduced as τὸν λόγον τοῦτο[ν] (1v 3). In both parts, positive and negative exhortations (ἐραυνᾶτε . . . , μὴ δοκεῖτε . . .) are followed by an explanatory statement (ἐκειναί εἰσιν . . . , ἔστιν ὁ κατηγορῶν . . .).[45] While there is a link between "the scriptures in which you think to have life" and "Moses in whom you have hoped," the emphasis falls on the contrast between the positive exhortation of **A** and the warning of **B**. The new element in **B** is the theme of accusation, and this may be related to the narrative situation indicated by the fragmentary opening of the extant material.

Following the single letter of line 1, lines 2-4 of Fragment 1v read:

[. . . . . . .] τοῖς νομικο[ῖς
[. . . πά]ντα τὸν παραπράσσ[οντα
[. . . . .]μον καὶ μὴ ἐμέ·

The initial lacuna may have been preceded by εἰδώς, the last extant word of fragment 3v. It is likely that, along with *P. Köln* 255, fragment 3 originally belonged to fragment 1.[46] εἰδώς is characteristic of controversy stories such

---

45. So Mayeda, *Papyrus Egerton 2*, p. 19. Mayeda also notes that "die beiden forensischen Wörter μαρτυρεῖν und κατηγορεῖν" serve to unite the two parts, divided by Jn. 5.40-44 (p. 23). In contrast, Norelli considers that the coherence of the Egerton equivalents of Jn. 5.39, 45 is secondary, reflecting a concern with "la controverse entre les chrétiens et juifs sur l'interprétation christologique de l'Écriture" ("Le Papyrus *Egerton* 2 et sa localisation dans la tradition sur Jésus," in *Jésus de Nazareth: Nouvelles approches d'une enigme*, ed. D. Marguerat [Geneva: Labor et Fides, 1998], pp. 397-435; p. 422).

46. Fragment 3v consists of six line-endings. As Bell and Skeat note, "It is just possible that this fragment [fr. 3] should be placed above fragment 1, giving the upper right portion of the first

as this, where it refers to Jesus' knowledge of what his opponents are thinking or saying (cf. Mk. 12.15; *GEger* fr. 2 ll. 9-10; Mt. 9.4?; Lk. 9.47).[47] A plausible reconstruction runs as follows: "[And] knowing [their thought Jesus said] to the lawyer[s: 'Judge(?) ev]ery wrongdo[er and everyone who is law]less, and not me.'" In line 3, -μον would then have read καὶ ἄνομον.[48] A less probable alternative would be παρὰ νόμον, in which case the reference is to "everyone who transgresses the law."[49] Either way, Jesus appeals to the experts in the law to judge, condemn, or reprove genuine transgressors rather than himself. He has evidently been accused of some breach of the Law of Moses, and he protests his innocence. Although the composite saying **A B** is addressed to the rulers of the people rather than the experts in the law, both groups evidently belong to a single hostile audience. The claim in **B** that Moses accuses Jesus' hearers turns the tables on the νομικοί, for whom Moses is Jesus' accuser.[50] Underlying the whole dialogue is the question *whose side Moses is on* in the controversy between Jesus and his critics.

Falsely accused of transgressing the Law of Moses, Jesus does not respond with a counteraccusation but warns his critics that Moses actually accuses them. In the Johannine context, where **B** is directly linked with **D**, Moses' accusation is identical to his testimony to Jesus:

> **B** Do not *think* that I *shall* accuse you to *the* Father. Your accuser is Moses, in whom you have hoped. **D** For if you believed Moses you would believe me. For about me he wrote. (Jn. 5.45-46)

---

page [= 1v], the upper left portion of the second [= 1r]. . . . In ll. 76-81 [= fr. 3v, ll. 1-6] we should then have the preliminaries to the conversation recorded on page 1: Jesus is apparently conversing with his interlocutors, and knowing (εἰδώς, l. 80 [= 3v, l. 5]) their intentions against him . . . , he addresses to them (the νομικοί) the remark recorded in ll. 2-5" (*Unknown Gospel*, p. 24). The case for what Bell and Skeat thought "just possible" is strengthened by the parallel with *P. Köln* 255.

47. The text linking fr. 3v to fr. 1v may be tentatively reconstructed as follows: εἰδὼς [δὲ ὁ Ἰη αὐτῶν τὴν διάνοιαν εἶπεν τοῖς] νομικο[ῖς . . .]. Cf. especially *GEger* 2r, ll. 9-10 (ὁ δὲ Ἰη εἰδὼς [τὴν δι]άνοιαν [αὐτ]ῶν); Mk. 12.15 (ὁ δὲ εἰδὼς αὐτῶν τὴν ὑπόκρισιν). With line breaks after εἰδώς and διάνοιαν, the proposed line (δὲ ὁ Ἰη αὐτῶν τὴν διάνοιαν) is an appropriate length (21 letters; the range for fr. 1v is *c*. 21-27 letters) and is compatible with the letter fragments at the beginning of fr. 1v (= the τ in τήν?) and the end of fr. 3v (= the -νοι- in διάνοιαν?).

48. So Bell and Skeat, Dodd, and others: for the various possibilities see Nicklas, *Gospel Fragments*, p. 24.

49. As Mayeda rightly notes, παραπράσσειν is characteristically used in an absolute sense (*Papyrus Egerton 2*, p. 16).

50. So K. Erlemann, "Papyrus Egerton 2: 'Missing Link' zwischen Synoptischer und Johanneischer Tradition," *NTS* 42 (1996), pp. 12-34; p. 18.

Moses wrote about Jesus, testifying to him in order to promote belief in him; but where unbelief prevails, his testimony becomes accusation. This is in line with the Johannine claim that "the one who does not believe in him is condemned already . . ." (Jn. 3.18). In *GEger*, however, there is intervening material between **B** and **D**, in the form of **C** (the critics' objection, closely related to John 9.29) and Jesus' response (unparalleled in John): "Now is accused [your un]belie[f in] the things [attest]ed by him," *i.e.* "Now it is your unbelief in the things attested by him that stands accused" (1v 7). While the theme of accusation is a continuation of **B**, its recurrence in 1v 7 represents a new phase of the argument. In **B**^{Eg} there is nothing to suggest that Moses' accusation relates *solely* to their failure to believe his testimony to Jesus. The scriptures bear witness to Jesus (**A**), but Moses (their primary author) *not only* bears witness to Jesus but *also* raises an accusation against his opponents. If, in contrast to John, the accusation is detached from the testimony, the reference will be to a broader range of pentateuchal material than those passages where the Egerton evangelist finds explicit messianic testimony. In neither case is it clear which passages he might have in mind, but Moses' role as accuser might plausibly be linked to the "Song of Moses" in Deuteronomy 32, which Moses was instructed to compose "as a testimony [εἰς μαρτύριον] to the sons of Israel" (Dt. 31.19) — that is, as an enduring testimony *against* them (cf. v. 21). Here the people of Israel is condemned as "a perverse and crooked generation" (v. 5), "a foolish and unwise people" (v. 6), "a nation devoid of counsel" (v. 28).[51] As with the reference to "life" (*GEger* 1v 4), the theme of Moses as accuser has its basis in Moses' text. In contrast, the two equivalent Johannine passages (Jn. 5.39, 45-46) have their basis within the evangelist's own theology.

It seems that in *GEger* Jesus *needs* Moses to testify on his behalf and to accuse his critics, just as they need and use Moses to accuse him (in the passage that must have preceded the extant material). Jesus *and* Moses, or Moses *against* Jesus? That is hardly a major issue in John. The Johannine Jesus brushes aside his critics' objection to his Sabbath healings (cf. Jn. 5.16-18; 7.19-23; 9.16). His controversy with them is focused on his christological claim, not on his positive or negative relationship to Moses. For the Johannine evangelist, "law was given through Moses, grace and truth came through Jesus Christ" (1.17). Moses and Jesus represent sheer difference; the

---

51. For Paul's use of the Song of Moses, see my *Paul and the Hermeneutics of Faith*, pp. 439-54. For the wider interpretative context, see David Lincicum, *Paul and the Early Jewish Encounter with Deuteronomy*, WUNT (Tübingen: Mohr-Siebeck, 2010).

question how they relate to one another is of little concern. Outside the Egerton parallels the theme of Moses as witness occurs only in John 1.45, and precisely here the awkwardness of the diction suggests the editing of a source:

> Philip found Nathanael and said to him, "We have found the one of whom Moses [and also the prophets] wrote in the law, Jesus son of Joseph from Nazareth!"[52]

Whoever added "and also the prophets" to Philip's testimony lacked the Egerton evangelist's sense that Jesus' relation to Moses is a crucial issue in its own right.

Like A^{Eg}, B^{Eg} is well integrated into its context — more so perhaps than the Johannine parallel. In its somewhat Matthean format, B^{Eg} offers a more coherent statement about Moses and Jesus than does B^{Jn}, where the eschatological orientation may reflect the strand in Johannine soteriology that emphasizes salvation at the expense of judgement. Also to be noted is the difference between "*my* Father" (B^{Eg}, 20x in John) and "*the* Father" (B^{Jn}, 98x in John). "The Father" occurs 11 times in John 5, whereas "my Father" occurs just twice (Jn. 5.17, 43). The main significance of B^{Eg} is to be found in the Mosaic concern that becomes fully explicit here, which, as we shall see, can be traced throughout the verso and recto material of Fragment 1. Outside the Egerton parallels, it is of marginal significance to the Johannine evangelist.

(iii) Moses against Jesus

In C^{Eg} (see Figure 6.1), Jesus' critics respond to his twofold λόγος, which combined the exhortation to search the scriptures, in order to find their true purpose in their testimony to him (A^{Eg}), with a warning that Moses (the primary scriptural author) not only testifies to Jesus but is also his critics' accuser (B^{Eg}). In both cases, Moses stands *alongside* Jesus and *against* his opponents, in spite of the fact that they place their "hope" in him and believe

---

52. ὃν ἔγραψεν Μωϋσῆς ἐν τῷ νόμῳ καὶ οἱ προφῆται εὑρήκαμεν . . . On the obtrusive reference to the prophets, see Robert T. Fortna, *The Fourth Gospel and Its Predecessor: From Narrative Source to Present Gospel*, SNTW (Edinburgh: T. & T. Clark, 1988), pp. 38, 41. Fortna assumes an original reference to Dt. 18.15. While Fortna's attempt to recover a complete "Signs Gospel" may be overoptimistic, his sensitivity to the stratified nature of the Johannine text is instructive.

that his writings point the way to "life." The question is which of the two sides in the controversy can legitimately claim Moses' support. Whose side is he on? Responding to Jesus' claim to Mosaic endorsement, we may expect his critics to deny this claim and to reclaim Moses for their own cause.

What they say at this point is: "We w[ell] know that God has spo[ken] to Moses, but you, we do not know [where you are from]" (1v 6).[53] This text corresponds closely to John 9.29, and may be reconstructed accordingly:

ἡμεῖς οἴδαμεν ὅτι Μωϋσεῖ λελάληκεν ὁ θεός, τοῦτον δὲ οὐκ οἴδαμεν πόθεν ἐστίν. (Jn. 9.29)

ε[ὖ] οἴδαμεν ὅτι Μω(ϋσεῖ) ἐλάλησεν ὁ θ(εό)ς, σὲ δὲ οὐκ οἴδαμεν [πόθεν εἶ]. (GEger 1v 6)[54]

Here Jesus' critics reaffirm their absolute confidence in Moses as the recipient of God's own words. Their confession is occasioned by Jesus' allegation that they themselves stand accused by Moses, and that Moses also validates his own claim. The two parts of their negative response balance each other and are intended to dissociate Moses from Jesus: ε[ὖ] οἴδαμεν ὅτι Μω(ϋσεῖ) . . . , σὲ δὲ οὐκ οἴδαμεν. . . . The contrast between God's speaking to Moses and the motif of Jesus' unknown origin arises from the fact that Jesus has confronted his opponents with his *words* (cf. τὸν λόγον τοῦτον, 1v 3). The question is whether Jesus' words are *his* words alone, or whether they are also *God's* words, as Moses' words are. While there is every reason to believe and confess that God spoke to Moses, there is no reason to think that Jesus and his words derive from God and possess any divine authorization.

In C[Jn], this hostile reaction takes third-person form and occurs in the context of a dialogue between the Pharisees and a man born blind, whose sight Jesus has controversially restored on the Sabbath.

So they called back the man who had been blind, and said to him: "Give glory to God! We know that this man is a sinner." And he answered, "Whether he is a sinner I do not know. One thing I know, that I was blind but now I see. . . . Why do you want to hear again? Perhaps you want to become his disciples?" . . . And they reviled him and said, "You are his dis-

53. For the apparently awkward idiom σὲ δὲ οὐκ οἴδαμεν πόθεν εἶ, cf. Lk. 13.25, 27.

54. Nicklas substitutes ὅ[τι] for Bell and Skeat's ε[ὖ] (*Gospel Fragments*, p. 24). The extant letter seems to be an *epsilon* rather than an *omicron*, however, although the slant of the (damaged) cross-stroke is uncharacteristic.

ciple, but we are disciples of Moses. <**C:** We know that God has spoken to Moses, but as for this man, we do not know where he is from."> The man answered and said to them, "This is amazing, that you do not know where he is from, and yet he opened my eyes! We know that God does not hear sinners, but if anyone is God-fearing and does his will, he hears him. . . . If he was not from God, he would be able to do nothing." (Jn. 9.24-25, 27b-31, 33)

Here, the antecedent of the Pharisees' confession (**C**) is their own claim to be "disciples of Moses" rather than of Jesus. Moses and discipleship play no further role in this passage, however, and it is their profession of ignorance about Jesus that is echoed and countered by the man born blind. Interwoven with the motif of Jesus' origin is the question whether he is a sinner. Initially, the Pharisees *know* that Jesus is a sinner whereas the man does *not know*. Subsequently, the Pharisees *know* that God spoke to Moses but do *not know* where Jesus is from. Tying together the conflicting themes of Jesus as "sinner" and as "from God," the man now *knows* that God does not hear sinners and is convinced that Jesus is from God. The contrast between *knowing* and *not knowing* is only formally articulated in **C**, but extends throughout the passage. If **C**^{Jn} is derived from **C**^{Eg}, a coherent account may be given of the Johannine evangelist's compositional procedure. In this dialogue, the *knowing/not knowing* contrast of **C**^{Eg} is extended in both directions, and an occasion is provided for the otherwise gratuitous reference to Moses. If **C**^{Eg} is derived from **C**^{Jn}, the later evangelist has moved it from a context in which its reference to Moses is largely superfluous to one in which it is crucial.

C. H. Dodd assesses the relationship between **C**^{Jn} and **C**^{Eg} as follows:

If the Fourth Evangelist took the saying in question from the "Unknown Gospel" he certainly showed great skill in fitting it into an entirely different context. If, on the other hand, we suppose that the borrowing was on the other side, we cannot perhaps admire so greatly the skill of our unknown author. Jesus has said, "Moses, on whom you have set your hope, is your accuser." The "rulers" reply, "We know that God spoke to Moses, but we do not know whence you come." In other words, "You appeal to the authority of Moses; we accept his authority, but we do not accept yours." It is, no doubt, an effective retort in its way, but it is no argument, and no real answer to what Jesus had said.[55]

---

55. Dodd, "A New Gospel," pp. 26-27. Nicklas similarly finds the rulers' reply "a bit abrupt" (*Gospel Fragments*, p. 40).

Dodd's conclusion is that C^{Jn} is fully at home in its context whereas C^{Eg} is not, and that it therefore "seems best to suppose" that the Johannine version is primary and the Egerton one secondary.[56] It is hard to understand the logic of this position. If C^{Eg} is "an effective retort in its way," how is it "no argument" and "no real answer . . ."? It is likely that Dodd's judgement is influenced by the familiarity of the Johannine context and the unfamiliarity of the Egerton one. In reality, C^{Eg} is a highly effective retort, argument, or answer, in a context in which Jesus has claimed that Moses stands with him and against his critics. In response, they seek to break this connection and reclaim Moses for themselves. How can Moses be the accuser of those who revere his words as God's words? What possible basis is there for a rival claim to divine authorization?

C consists in (C1) a statement about Moses, and (C2) a contrasting statement about Jesus: ". . . As for *you/this man,* we do not know where *you are/he is* from." As has already been noted, $C1^{Eg}$ is more fully integrated into its context than $C1^{Jn}$, where Moses is not directly relevant to the argument. A related point can be made about C2. In $C2^{Eg}$, the emphasis is not really on the rulers' ignorance, in spite of the wording, but rather on their complete rejection of Jesus' claim to divine authorization. In the Johannine context, however, C2 is taken literally as an acknowledgement of ignorance: "This is amazing, that you 'do not know where he is from,' and yet he opened my eyes!" (Jn. 9.30). Astonished as he is at the Pharisees' ignorance, the formerly blind man seeks to remedy it: if Jesus can open the eyes of the blind, he is clearly "from God" (Jn. 9.31-33). As these Pharisees have already stated that "this man is not from God, because he does not keep the Sabbath" (9.16), it would indeed be "amazing" if they subsequently pleaded ignorance on this point. While $C2^{Eg}$ serves to dismiss Jesus' claim to divine authorization, $C2^{Jn}$ is presented as a literal confession of ignorance which seems out of place in its context.

(iv) Moses' True Theme

In John 5.45-47, **B** leads directly into **D** (see Figure 6.1):

> **B** "Do not think that I shall accuse you to the Father. Your accuser is Moses, in whom you have hoped. **D** For if you believed Moses you would be-

lieve me. For about me he wrote. But if you do not believe his writings, how will you believe my words?"

Moses' accusation is concerned exclusively with the failure to believe in the one of whom he wrote. As we have seen, the link between the accusation and the testimony may be less direct in *GEger,* but it is more in line with the specifics of what Moses wrote. The Johannine connection between **B** and **D** may, of course, be original. In that case, *GEger* is responsible for separating them, inserting both **C** and a new introduction to **D**:

> 7 Jesus an[s]wering sa[id to the]m, "Now is accused [your un]belie[f in] the things [attest]ed by him. **D** 8 For if [you] be[lieved Moses] you would believe [me.] For [abou]t me he [wrot]e to our fathers. [9 But if you do not believe h]i[s wri]t[ings, how will you believe my words?"]

It may be significant that Moses is named both at the end of **B**^{Jn} and, immediately afterwards, at the beginning of **D**^{Jn} where a pronoun might have been expected: "Your accuser is *Moses,* in whom you have hoped. For if you believed *Moses...*" This contrasts with the evangelist's usage elsewhere in this chapter (cf. Jn. 5.33-36, on John), and may suggest that original intervening matter has been omitted.

The inclusion of an Egerton equivalent of John 5.47 is somewhat speculative. Yet the relationship between John 5.45-46 and *GEger* 1v 4-5, 8 is so close that one would expect the parallels to continue to the end of the Johannine discourse. In addition, traces of two letters can be seen beneath the last partially extant line of *P. Köln* 255 verso, one of which appears to be an *alpha,* the other a *tau* or a *pi.*[57] Their approximate positions in the missing line can be determined by correlating them with the line above (1v 23: [ἔγραψε]ν τοῖς πατ[ρά]σιν ἡμῶ[ν]). The (probable) α in line 24 is located below the final two letters of τοῖς, and the τ or π below the ν at the end of πατ[ρά]σιν and the following η. If, like line 23, the missing line contained around twenty-three letters, then the α will have been approximately the tenth or eleventh letter, and the τ or π fourth or fifth from the end of the line. If the missing line corresponded exactly to the first part of John 5.47, and if it consisted in twenty-four letters, it would read: εἰ δὲ τοῖς ἐκείνου γράμμασιν. . . . As the underlinings indicate, this does not correspond to the positioning of the two letter-fragments. A slight emendation gives a more promising result, how-

---

57. See Plate 5 in Nicklas's edition. Nicklas acknowledges that two letter-fragments may be seen, but does not attempt to identify them (*Gospel Fragments,* p. 24).

ever. A line of twenty-four letters might also have read: εἰ δὲ τοῖς γράμμασιν αὐτοῦ οὐ. . . . The α would then be the eleventh letter from the beginning of the line and the τ fifth from the end — corresponding exactly to the letter-fragments. A Johannine substitution of ἐκείνου for αὐτοῦ is plausible, given the evangelist's liking for this pronominal usage.[58]

In *GEger*, Jesus responds to **C** with the statement: νῦν κατηγορεῖται [ὑμῶν ἡ ἀ]πιστεί[α] τοῖς ὑπ᾽ αὐτοῦ [μεμαρτυρη]μένοις. Why does their unbelief in the things attested by Moses *now* stand accused? Moses was earlier identified as their accuser, but here the accuser is left unspecified; the emphasis falls on an accusation specifically against unbelief in what Moses attested, an accusation that sounds forth *now,* presumably in response to **C2** ("As for you, we do not know where you are from"). There is no Johannine parallel to the initial response to **C2**[Eg], which elegantly connects the accusation theme of **B** with **D**'s claim that Moses bears witness to Jesus. If the Egerton evangelist has added this passage to his Johannine extracts, it was not strictly necessary for him to do so. Having inserted **C** into **BD**[Jn], a simple excision of the initial γάρ would make **D**[Eg] an entirely adequate sequel to **C**[Eg]. If, on the other hand, the Johannine evangelist chooses *(i)* to reserve **C**[Eg] for later use, *(ii)* to omit the statement about unbelief, and *(iii)* to link **B** directly to **D** (without even substituting a pronoun for the resulting repetition of "Moses"), then this excision of dialogical material is in keeping with the monological context prevailing throughout John 5.19-47.[59]

Moses wrote of Jesus, and, according to **D**[Eg] in contrast to **D**[Jn], he wrote of Jesus "to our fathers." If **D**[Eg] is the source of **D**[Jn], then the omission makes good sense in view of the Johannine evangelist's tendency to distance Jesus from Jewish practices and traditions. In John 5.1, Jesus goes up to Jerusalem for a "feast of the Jews," and since "the Jews" will shortly emerge as his opponents (5.10, 15, 16, 18), it seems that Jesus is not included under that designation — although his Jewishness is not explicitly denied (cf. 4.9, 22). In John 6, Jesus' audience in the Capernaum synagogue speaks of "*our* fathers," who "ate the manna in the wilderness" (v. 31); but Jesus will later state that "*your* fathers ate the manna in the wilderness" (v. 49). The evangelist could perhaps have substituted "your" for "our" rather than omitting the phrase altogether: "For about me he wrote to *your* fathers." But that might still suggest

58. Cf. Jn. 1.8, 18, 33; 2.21; 3.28, 30; 4.25; 5.11, 19, 35, 37, 39, 43, 46; 6.29; 7.11, 45; etc. This pronominal usage is not unique to John, however: cf. Mt. 13.11; 17.27; 20.4; 24.43; Mk. 7.20; 16.20; Lk. 12.38; 18.14.

59. The contrast is noted by Erlemann, "Papyrus Egerton 2," p. 19.

too close a connection between Jesus and "your fathers." No such connection is envisaged when Jesus contrasts himself as "the bread of life" with the manna that "your fathers ate and died" (6.48, 49). Thus in John 5.46 the sentence concludes abruptly: "For about me he wrote."

If **D**^{Jn} is the source of **D**^{Eg}, then the Egerton evangelist is consciously seeking to counter the Johannine distancing of Jesus from Judaism, reincorporating him into the community that recollects the experience of "our fathers." In *GEger,* Jesus presents himself as continuing to belong within that community even as he engages in sharp controversy with its rulers.[60] This Jewish-Christian or Christian-Jewish feature of *GEger* is of a piece with its preoccupation with the Moses/Jesus relationship, which is a far more significant issue here than in John. It is not impossible that such an emphasis might be post-Johannine, in which case the aim is to reverse the trajectory of the source text. But it is more likely to be pre-Johannine. The evidence of *P. Köln* 255 is a crucial factor here, once the editorial misjudgement has been corrected.

(v) A Hostile Response

Fragment 1 recto is generally thought to follow directly from Fragment 1 verso, with a few lines missing at the bottom of the one and the top of the other.[61] The missing material will have comprised *(a)* the conclusion of Jesus' claim to Mosaic testimony and *(b)* the beginning of the account of the hostility it provoked. *(a)* probably took the form of an Egertonian equivalent of John 5.47, which would have occupied around three lines at the bottom of the verso; *(b)* would be accounted for by Fragment 3r. If Fragment 3 belongs to Fragment 1, as suggested above, then 3r will have been located at the top left-hand corner of the page containing 1r. Since the five (or six) line-fragments all contain only a few letters, no reconstruction is possible.[62] In

---

60. Compare Stephen's references to "our fathers" within a similar polemical situation (Acts 7.12, 38, 39, 44, 45; but contrast vv. 51, 52). Here too Moses testifies to Jesus (v. 37, citing Dt. 18.15, 18). The analogy between Jesus in *GEger* and Stephen in Acts is noted by Daniels, "Egerton Gospel," pp. 249-51.

61. Dieter Lührmann argues that the order ran from 1r to 1v, on the basis of the parallel between 1r, l. 23 ("Sin no more") and Jn. 5.14 (*Die apokryph gewordenen Evangelien*, pp. 136-37; followed by Norelli, "Le Papyrus *Egerton 2*," pp. 402-3). Nicklas rightly rejects literary dependence on Jn. 5.14, however (*Gospel Fragments*, p. 63).

62. Since only three letters are clearly legible in line 1, Dodd's attempt to find the conclusion of Jn. 10.30 there is overoptimistic ("A New Gospel," p. 44).

line 4, however, the letters KTEINΩ are legible and may represent something like: [ἵνα ἀπο]κτείνω[σιν αὐτόν] (cf. Jn. 11.53). That would fit the hostile context.

Figure 6.2

GEger 1r	John
1 [. . . so that . . .] stones togeth[er] they [might] s[tone h]im.	10.31 . . . The Jews again picked up stones so that they might stone him.
	[8.59 . . . So they took up stones to cast at him. But Jesus was hidden and went out of the temple.]
2 And the [ruler]s lai[d] their han[ds] on him [so tha]t they might arrest and ha[nd him over] to the crowd. 3 And they were not a[ble] to arrest him, because the hour of his hand[ing over] had not yet [come].	7.30 . . . So they were seeking to arrest him and no-one laid a hand on him, because his hour had not yet come.
	[8.20 . . . and no-one seized him, because his hour had not yet come.]
4 And the Lord going out [from their han]ds departed [from them].	10.39 . . . So they were seeking to arrest him, and he went out from their hands.

Ir *1* cannot be reconstructed as a whole.[63] "Stones together" is almost certainly correct, and "they might stone him" probably so. What is described here is evidently *preparation* for stoning Jesus, rather than an actual attempt to do so as in the Johannine parallels. In 1r *2*, the rulers seek to arrest Jesus and hand him over to the crowd, presumably for stoning, and it is therefore the crowd that is responsible for gathering the stones together, whether on its own initiative or at the behest of the authorities. Whereas the Johannine passages tell of a spontaneous action motivated by sheer fury at what Jesus has just said, *GEger* is more suggestive of a judicial process. A scriptural background is again perceptible. The "rulers" are "the rulers of the people" (1v *3*), and thus the "crowd," who are to carry out the stoning, are also "the people" (ὁ λαός). In the Torah, stoning is always a communal action. It is carried out by "all the congregation" (πᾶσα [ἡ] συναγωγή, Lv. 24.14; Nm. 15.35-36), by "the sons of Israel" (Lv. 24.23), or by "the hand of all the people"

63. Bell and Skeat here propose [?συνεβουλεύσαντο τῷ] ὄχλῳ [ἵνα βαστάσαντες] λίθους ὁμοῦ λι[θάσθωσι[ν αὐ]τόν (*Fragments*, pp. 9 + 26; see Nicklas, *Gospel Fragments*, p. 42, for other proposals). But (1) the λ in ὀ.χλῷ is probably a κ, and only the ω is clear; (2) this reconstruction would leave line 1 impossibly short. The final letter fragments visible in line 2 probably represent Λ, suggesting λ[ιθάσω]σι[ν], as in Jn. 10.31. If so, line 1 probably contained the ἵνα implied by the subjunctive.

(ἡ χεὶρ παντὸς τοῦ λαοῦ, Dt. 17.7).[64] Jesus is condemned in part for the action that occasioned the saying: "[Judge(?) ev]ery wrongdo[er and everyone who is law]less, and not me" (1v 1). That action may have been a Sabbath healing (cf. Jn. 5.9-16; 9.14-16). That breaches of the Sabbath may be punished by stoning is indicated by the fate of the man caught gathering firewood on the Sabbath (Nm. 15.32-36).[65] In addition, Jesus — like Stephen — is deemed to have spoken "blasphemous words against Moses and God" (cf. Acts 6.11). He has done so by claiming Mosaic authorization for himself, and he has used this authorization to denounce his critics — even though they "w[ell] know that God has spo[ken] to Moses" (1v 6), and find in those authoritative words the way to life (1v 4). That is why the authorities and the people seek to stone Jesus.

In John, spontaneous attempts to stone Jesus are occasioned by the sayings "Truly, truly I say to you, before Abraham was, I am" (Jn. 8.58-59) and "I and the Father are one" (Jn. 10.30-33). In the second passage, Jesus' opponents explain what they are doing: "It is not for a good work that we stone you but for blasphemy, because you being a man make yourself God" (10.33). The punishment of blasphemy by stoning is attested in Leviticus 24.10-23, where, in the course of a quarrel, an "Israelite woman's son" blasphemes by naming the name of God and cursing either his opponent or God.[66] Thus, according to the Mishnah, the blasphemer "is not culpable unless he pronounces the Name itself" (*mSanh.* 7.5). That is not the issue in the Johannine passages, however. These have no basis in any prior scriptural definition of "blasphemy," a term that does not even occur in the Torah.[67]

While stones are gathered for the expected stoning of Jesus, the rulers are concerned to arrest him. *GEger* 1r 2-3 shares three motifs with John 7.30: (1) laying hands on Jesus; (2) the failed attempt to arrest him; (3) the reference to Jesus' "hour" in explanation of that failure. In the Johannine parallel, (1) and (2) are reversed, (2) is abbreviated, and (1) is negated:

---

64. Or "all Israel," according to *mSanh.* 6.4, commenting on this verse. The first stones are to be thrown by the witnesses.

65. According to *mSanh.* 7.8, the person who profanes the Sabbath deliberately is to be stoned, but must offer a sin offering if this occurred in error. Acts punishable by stoning are collected in *mSanh.* 7.4.

66. ויקב בן־האשה הישראלית את־השם ויקלל (Lv. 24.11): "And the son of the Israelite woman pronounced the Name, and he cursed." LXX: καὶ ἐπονομάσας ὁ υἱὸς τῆς γυναικὸς τῆς Ἰσραηλίτιδος τὸ ὄνομα κατηράσατο. On this passage see J. Milgrom, *Leviticus 23–27*, AB (New York: Doubleday, 2000), pp. 2107-9.

67. On this see Barrett, *John*, p. 383.

317

So (2) they were seeking to arrest him and *no one* (1) laid a hand on him, (3) for his hour had not yet come." (Jn. 7.30)

Compare:

"the [ruler]s (1) lai[d] their han[ds] on him (2) [so tha]t they might arrest and ha[nd him over] to the crowd. And they were not a[ble] to arrest him, (3) because the hour of his hand[ing over] had not yet [come]. (*GEger* 1r 2-3a)

The Johannine account is more succinct, consisting in seventeen Greek words as opposed to a probable twenty-nine in *GEger*. In the transposition of (1) and (2) and the negation of (1), the Johannine evangelist also resolves a difficulty in the *GEger* account, where the rulers' laying hands on Jesus is somehow differentiated from an actual arrest. Alternatively, the Egerton evangelist may have created this difficulty in the course of rewriting the Johannine passage. Yet the Johannine negation, "*no one* laid a hand on him," suggests that the evangelist is here explicitly contradicting his source.

In *GEger* but not in John, we are told what the authorities intended to do with Jesus once they had arrested him: he was to be "handed over to the crowd," apparently for stoning. The un-Johannine reference to ἡ ὥρα τῆς παραδό[σεως] thus refers back to καὶ παρ[αδῶσιν] τῷ ὄχλῳ. The hour of Jesus' handing over is the moment when, after being arrested, he *is* handed over to his enemies for execution. This suggests that *GEger* originally included a passion narrative in which some such statement as John 19.16 was to be found: "So [Pilate] handed him over [παρέδωκεν] to them to be crucified." The same verb is repeatedly used of Judas's "betrayal" of Jesus (Jn. 6.64, 71; 12.4; 13.2, 11, 21; 18.2, 5) and of the authorities' handing over of Jesus to Pilate (Jn. 18.30, 35; 19.11). Had the Johannine evangelist used the phrase αὐτοῦ ἡ ὥρα τῆς παραδόσεως, it would have fitted perfectly into its wider context. In fact, the evangelist speaks here only of "his hour" (7.30; cf. 8.20; 2.4; 7.6), identified later as the hour not of Jesus' handing over but of his glorification (12.23; 17.1). The effect is to disconnect the hour motif from the concrete events of Jesus' passion and to connect it instead to the evangelist's overarching view of its theological significance.

For Dodd, the phrase οὔπω ἐ[ληλύθει] αὐτοῦ ἡ ὥρα τῆς παραδό[σεως] provides decisive evidence of dependence on John. "Are we to believe," he asks incredulously,

that it was that source [*GEger*] that provided him with the conception of the divinely-ordained 'Hour,' which controls the scheme of the Fourth

Gospel from its first introduction in ii.4 to the solemn proclamation in xvii.1, Πατέρ, ἐλήλυθεν ἡ ὥρα? It is no doubt conceivable that the evangelical tradition evolved the phrase ἡ ὥρα τῆς παραδόσεως αὐτοῦ, on the analogy of the Marcan phrase cited [Mk. 14.41], and that the Fourth Evangelist adapted it to his purpose. But to me it seems more likely that our unknown author took over the phrase from the Fourth Gospel without fully appreciating its import.[68]

Dodd's position remains possible, but it is not clear how he can be so convinced that dependence must run from the Johannine ἡ ὥρα αὐτοῦ to *GEger's* ἡ ὥρα τῆς παραδόσεως αὐτοῦ, and not the reverse.[69] The Egerton version is closely related to the vocabulary of the passion narratives, not least the Johannine one. In abstracting from this narrative context, the Johannine hour motif would seem to be secondary.[70] As in the case of *our/your fathers*, *GEger* may conceivably be reversing the trajectory of Johannine theology. But it seems more likely that it should be located at an earlier point on that trajectory.

In *GEger*, the narrative concludes with a brief reference to Jesus' escape from the hands of his enemies: "And the Lord going out [from their han]ds departed [from them]." A coherent account has been given of the hostile reaction to Jesus' Mosaic claims, consisting in (1) the preparation for stoning, (2) the attempted arrest, (3) the reason for its failure, and (4) Jesus' escape.[71] While a very similar range of motifs is to be found in the Johannine gospel, they are largely disconnected from one another. In addition, they are consciously repeated:

---

68. Dodd, "A New Gospel," p. 31.

69. Dodd's argument is restated by Charles E. Hill, *The Johannine Corpus in the Early Church* (Oxford: Oxford University Press, 2004), pp. 304-5. But Hill follows Jeremias rather than Dodd in viewing *GEger* as a gospel harmony reworking material from "the four Gospels" ([*sic*]; p. 305). Such a view can only be maintained if every minor coincidence of terminology is regarded as evidence that the noncanonical text is "dependent" on the canonical one, while overlooking the remarkable *independence* of Egerton's two synoptic-type stories from their synoptic counterparts.

70. Mayeda rightly notes the absence of distinctively Johannine theology here (*Papyrus Egerton 2*, p. 73).

71. That the Egerton account is coherent is denied by T. Nicklas: "The 'crowd' tried to stone Jesus (for reasons which cannot be known any longer), while the 'leaders of the people' try to capture him and hand him over to the crowd. How both actions logically relate to one another seems unimportant in the text" (*Gospel Fragments*, p. 54). This overlooks the possibility that the events described have a quasi-judicial character.

(1) *Stoning*

   A   "So they took up stones to throw at him. . . ." (Jn. 8.59a)

   B   "The Jews *again* lifted up stones so as to stone him." (Jn. 10.31)

(2) *Attempted arrest*

   A   "So they were seeking to arrest him, and no one laid a hand on him. . . ." (Jn. 7.30a, cf. v. 44)

   B   "So they were *again* seeking to arrest him. . . ." (Jn. 10.39a)

(3) *The hour*

   A   ". . . because his hour had not yet come." (Jn. 7.30b)

   B   "[These words he spoke in the treasury . . . but no one arrested him], because his hour had not yet come." (Jn. 8.20)

(4) *Escape*

   A   ". . . but Jesus hid himself and went out of the temple." (Jn. 8.59b)

   B   ". . . but he escaped from their hands." (Jn. 10.39b)

There are two possible explanations for these parallels between the two early gospels. Either the Johannine evangelist has found in the coherent Egerton account a set of motifs that can be individually deployed and repeated within the narrative framework of chapters 7, 8, and 10; or the Egerton evangelist has developed his account out of John 7.30 (attempted arrest, hour), 10.31 (stoning), and 10.39 (escape).[72] Have originally separate narrative fragments been conflated, or has an originally coherent narrative been broken up so that its parts can provide a framework for the dialogical material they enclose? An advantage of the latter hypothesis is that it can suggest a rationale for the compositional procedures of both evangelists. A brief account of a quasi-judicial process provides the later Johannine evangelist with a set of motifs that serve to highlight key moments in Jesus' controversies with his opponents.[73]

---

72. For the second view, see Norelli, "Le Papyrus *Egerton 2*," pp. 405-6.

73. According to Helmut Koester, "An explanation of this segment of *Papyrus Egerton* 2 as a secondary patchwork of Johannine passages does not seem very appealing" (*Ancient Christian Gospels*, p. 211). Such an explanation *is* appealing, however, to those who assume in advance that *any* noncanonical gospel will be some kind of "secondary patchwork."

(vi) "As Moses Commanded"

In the form published by Bell and Skeat in 1935, the story of the cleansing of a leper seems unconnected to the controversy from which Jesus has just made his exit. Since a parallel story appears in all three synoptic gospels, it was natural to regard this story as the key to the relationship between *GEger* and the synoptics, just as the preceding story is the key to its relationship to John.

Since the publication of *P. Köln* 255, however, it has become clear that this story too is concerned with the question of Jesus' relationship to Moses — in direct continuity with the controversy that has just concluded. The story is obviously related to the synoptics (see Figure 6.3). Equally important is its relation to the Johannine parallels within *GEger* itself.

Figure 6.3

GEger fr 1r + P. Köln 255r	*Mark 1.40-45*
5 And behold a leper comin[g to him]	40 And there comes to him a leper
says,	I <beseeching him and falling on his knees and> saying to him,
6 *"Teacher Jesus, while journeying [with] le[pers] and eatin[g with them] in the i[n]n, I too be[came a leper.] 7 If [th]en [you wish], I am cleansed."* 8 And	
	"If you wish, you can cleanse me."
	41 And II <having compassion, stretching
the Lord [says to him], "I wil[l], be cleansed." 9 [And immediately] the lep[rosy w]ent from him.	out his hand, he touched him and> he says to him, "I will, be cleansed." 42 And immediately the leprosy left him and he was cleansed.
	43 III <And being angry with him immediately he threw him out,>
10 And Jesus [says to him,]	44 and he says to him,
	IV <"See that you say nothing to anybody,
"G[o], // show yourse[lf] to th[e priests] and offer [for puri]fication as [Moses] com[manded.	but> go, show yourself to the priest and offer for your purification what Moses commanded, V <as a testimony to them.>"
And] s[i]n no more."	
	45 VI <But going out he began to proclaim much and to spread the word, so that he was no longer able to enter openly into a town, but was out in deserted places. And they were coming to him from everywhere.>

Italics = elements distinctive to *GEger*
I-VI < > = elements present in Mark (and other synoptics) but not in *GEger*
[ ] = reconstructed text.
// = approximate transition to *P. Köln* 255

Comparison of the Markan version with Matthew 8.1-4 and Luke 5.12-16 does not produce any significant findings in relation to *GEger*. Matthew and Luke include independent versions of **I**, of which Matthew's is abbreviated and Luke's extended. Both add "Lord" to the leper's address to Jesus, and omit the reference to compassion (or anger?) from **II** as well as the whole of **III**. Both include versions of **IV** and **V**, but Luke alone includes **VI**. *GEger* shares with Matthew 8.2 the opening of the story (καὶ ἰδοὺ λεπρὸς προσελθών), but there are no other significant convergences with Matthew or Luke.

The synoptic versions of this story are remarkably homogeneous when compared to the version in *GEger*. This noncanonical version lacks (**I**) supplementary detail about the leper's approach to Jesus, and (**II**) Jesus' response; in particular, it does not say that Jesus deliberately stretched out his hand and touched the leper. Like Matthew and Luke, *GEger* lacks the surprising Markan reference to Jesus' anger (**III**), which perhaps anticipates the healed leper's breach of the secrecy command. Unlike them, it also omits (**IV**) the secrecy command itself, and (**VI**) the reference to the reason for the act of law observance ("as a testimony to them"). Of these, **III** and **IV** at least are probably the product of Markan redaction. If so, the *GEger* story may derive from a version independent of Mark, although it too may contain secondary elements. Still more significant are the alternatives that *GEger* provides to **I** (the leper's approach to Jesus) and **V** ("as a testimony . . ."). In place of the synoptic references to the leper's prostration, *GEger* has him provide a straightforward account of how he contracted the disease: "Teacher Jesus, while journeying [with] le[pers] and eatin[g with them] in the i[n]n, I too be[came a leper]" (1r 6). As *P. Köln* 255 makes clear, Jesus' final words to the leper are "[And] s[i]n no more" (1r *10*), rather than ". . . as a testimony to them."

Before the ending of the story became available, the explanation about how the disease was contracted could be viewed positively. According to Dodd,

> The intention is apparently to enlist the sympathy of Jesus with a person who had had such bad luck as to contract a loathsome disease while travelling on his lawful occasions. The spirit of this *ad misericordiam* appeal reminds one of the version of the story of the man with the withered hand in the Gospel according to the Hebrews, where the man says, "I was a bricklayer, earning my living with my hands. I beg you, Jesus, restore to me my health, that I may not be disgraced by begging for food."[74]

---

74. Dodd, "A New Gospel," p. 35. For this passage, preserved by Jerome, see J. K. Elliott (ed.), *The Apocryphal New Testament* (Oxford: Clarendon Press, 1999²), p. 12.

In reality, the conclusion of the story in *GEger* indicates that the leper's autobiographical statement is more like a confession of sin than an appeal for sympathy. "Sin no more" is not a stray fragment from John 5.14, but refers back to the statement about association with lepers. Moses writes:

> As for the leper who has the disease, let his clothes be torn and his head uncovered and his mouth covered, and he shall call out, "Unclean!" All the days during which the disease is upon him, being unclean he shall be unclean. He shall dwell alone [κεχωρισμένος καθήσεται], outside the camp shall be his habitation. (Lv. 13.45-46)[75]

Anyone who voluntarily associates with lepers — travelling with them, eating with them, sharing their accommodation — is in flagrant breach of the Law of Moses.[76] Since uncleanness is contagious, it is inevitable that such a person will himself become a leper. From this standpoint, "eating with" unclean persons cannot be a matter of indifference, whether they are lepers (*GEger*), sinners (Lk. 15.2), or Gentiles (Acts 11.3; Gal. 2.12). The Jesus of the Egerton story is far removed from the figure who himself risks uncleanness by associating with the unclean. If in the previous narrative Moses wrote about Jesus, here Jesus strongly endorses Moses — both in the exhortation not to repeat the earlier transgression and in the demand that the Mosaic formalities be duly concluded:

> "G[o], show yourse[lf] to th[e priests] and offer [for puri]fication [περὶ τοῦ καθαρισμοῦ] as [Moses] com[manded. And] s[i]n no more." *(GEger 1r 10)*

When a leper is cleansed, he must first be brought to the priest (singular, as in the synoptics)[77] for an examination followed by a series of ritual actions (Lv. 14.1-9). On the eighth day, the cleansed leper brings offerings "for

---

75. Cf. also Nm. 5.1-4.

76. So Daniels, "Egerton Gospel," p. 142; Robert L. Webb, "Jesus Heals a Leper: Mark 1.40-45 and *Egerton Gospel* 35-47," *JSHJ* 4 (2006), pp. 177-202; pp. 195-96.

77. Mk. 1.44; Mt. 8.4; Lk. 5.14; but Lk. 17.14 and *GEger* 1r 10 have the plural τοῖς ἱερεῦσιν, in Luke's case no doubt because ten lepers were cleansed. The plural in *GEger* does not reflect dependence on Lk. 17.14, any more than συνοδεύειν and πανδοχεῖον are dependent on Lk. 10.34 and 15.2 (the view of F. Neirynck, "Papyrus Egerton 2 and the Healing of the Leper," in his *Evangelica 2: Collected Essays, 1982-1991*, BEThL 99 [Leuven: Peeters, 1991], pp. 773-83). In spite of the singular priest of Lv. 14, the protracted and complex rituals it envisages might well involve more than one priest (cf. *mNeg.* 14.8, where "two priests" receive the blood of the guilt offering).

his purification" (εἰς τὸ καθαρίσαι αὐτόν, Lv. 14.23). It is this two-stage process that Jesus enjoins, just as Moses commanded.

In the synoptics, the leper is told to fulfil the Mosaic prescriptions "as a testimony to them" (εἰς μαρτύριον αὐτοῖς, Mk. 1.44 = Mt. 8.4 = Lk. 5.14). Elsewhere, identical or very similar language is used to speak of the disciples' future testimony before governors and kings (Mt. 10.18; Mk. 13.9), and indeed before all nations (Mt. 24.14), and of their shaking the dust from their feet in protest against rejection (Mk. 6.11; Lk. 9.5). Whether the testimony is verbal or symbolic, positive or negative, the common factor is the gospel message. In the story of the cleansing of the leper, performing the Mosaic rituals is evidently viewed as a "testimony" that represents a challenge to the unbelief of the priestly authorities. None of the synoptists elaborates this point, since the Markan redaction represents a shift of emphasis onto the secrecy motif which Matthew and Luke maintain. While the nature of the "testimony" is not entirely clear, what is significant is that an explanation has had to be found for Jesus' insistence on the due performance of the Mosaic rituals. Since it cannot be taken for granted that the Law of Moses is to be observed, it is explained that Jesus on this occasion complied with the law so that the cleansing of the leper might be a "testimony" to his opponents. It is that special explanation that is lacking in *GEger,* where Jesus' fidelity to the Law is a central point of the story.[78] It may be for the same reason that Jesus here does not touch the leper, as he does in all three synoptists. The whole point of the Law's exclusion of lepers is to avoid defilement of this kind.

The Egerton version of this story is important here for two reasons. First, it shows few if any signs of dependence on the synoptic versions. This independence from the synoptics would be surprising if *GEger* were dependent on John. The compositional technique evident in passages derived from John — consisting in the almost verbatim reproduction of whole sentences — would be at odds with the independent narration of synoptic-type incidents. If John is dependent on *GEger,* the problem disappears. Second, the story of the leper confirms the significance for *GEger* of the relationship between Jesus and Moses. Although its primary affinities are with the parallel synoptic versions, its thematic continuity with the Johannine material indicates that this gospel has a distinctive character of its own, reflecting a largely Jewish milieu in which Jesus' relation to Moses is a sharply disputed

---

78. "What is striking in Egerton's account is that Jesus gives instructions to go to priests and to offer the proper sacrifices simply for their own sake. They are the proper Jewish things to do . . ." (Daniels, "Egerton Gospel," p. 148).

issue.[79] It is easier to view that milieu as predating the Gospel of John in its present form.

The Johannine Interpreter

The parallels between *GEger* and John are best explained on the hypothesis that the Johannine versions are dependent on those attested in *GEger*. In John 5.39 (= *GEger* 1v 4), "Search the scriptures in which . . ." becomes "You search the scripture because . . . ," and "life" becomes "eternal life." In John 5.45 (= *GEger* 1v 5), "Do not think that I came to accuse you . . ." becomes "Do not think that I shall accuse you . . . ," and "my Father" becomes "the Father." In John 5.46 (= *GEger* 1v 8), "About me he wrote" omits "to our fathers." This material is thematically linked to its Johannine context by way of the theme of "testimony," but its concern with scripture and Moses is not fully integrated. Similarly in John 9.29 (= *GEger* 1v 6), "We know that God spoke to Moses . . ." is removed to a context in which the relation of Jesus to Moses is of secondary importance. An original link between John 5.39 + 45 (= *GEger* 1v 4-5) is broken by the insertion of John 5.40-44, which represents a digression from the scriptural or Mosaic focus. Conversely, material has been omitted between John 5.45 + 46 (= *GEger* 1v 5, 8), resulting in a repetition of "Moses" where a pronoun might have been expected. Although John 5.47 (= *GEger* 1v 9) represents a direct challenge to Jesus' hearers, nothing is said about their response. Instead, we read that Jesus (who has been in Jerusalem) "crossed the sea of Galilee, that is, of Tiberias" (Jn. 6.1). The Johannine evangelist has reserved the Egerton account of the authorities' response for a later series of controversies, separating and repeating the motifs of the failed arrest (Jn. 7.30a; 10.39a = *GEger* 1r 2-3), the preparation for stoning (Jn. 8.59a; 10.31 = *GEger* 1r 1), the hour (Jn. 7.30b; 8.20 = *GEger* 1r 3), and the escape (Jn. 8.59b; 10.39b = *GEger* 1r 4), thereby dismantling a coherent account of a single quasi-judicial process.

Although the Johannine assimilation of the Egerton material gives every indication of secondariness, it is by no means arbitrary. As it is incorporated into the Johannine narrative, the Egerton material is also interpreted. In its new context, this material contributes to the Johannine presentation of a

---

79. "Egerton ist . . . nicht als antijüdische Schrift zu bezeichnen, sondern als Dokument eines in die Defensive gedrängten Judenchristentums, das trotz massiver Anfeindung um die Anerkennung ihres Herrn kämpft" (Erlemann, "Papyrus Egerton 2," p. 30).

controversy with "the Jews" in which Jesus' relation to Moses becomes one among several strands in the wider concern about his relation to God.

(i) Two Communities

In John 5, Jesus debates no longer with "the lawyers" or "the rulers of the people" (*GEger* 1v 1, 3; cf. 1r 2) but with "the Jews" (Jn. 5.10-18 [4x]). The reference is still to the Jewish *leaders,* who will later be described not only as "the Jews" (Jn. 7.1-15 [4x]) but also as "Pharisees" or "chief priests and Pharisees" (Jn. 7.32-47 [4x]), and as "rulers," as in *GEger* (Jn. 7.26, 48).[80] Whether as "the Pharisees" or as "the Jews," these leaders are clearly differentiated from "the crowd." "The Pharisees" refer dismissively to "this crowd which does not know the law" (7.47-49), and "the crowds" keep their views to themselves "for fear of the Jews" (7.12-13). "The Jews" are synonymous with Pharisees, chief priests, and rulers. In consequence, Jesus himself is not included among "the Jews" but is set over against them, and the same is true both of the "crowd" and of those he heals (cf. 5.10, 15; 9.18-23).

Why, then, does the Johannine evangelist speak generically of "the Jews" when he has in view quite particular groups (Pharisees, chief priests, rulers)? It seems that he does so because these groups articulate the dominant Jewish response to Jesus' claim, which is to reject it (even though many within the crowd — and, secretly, even among the rulers themselves — are more willing to give him a hearing). It is therefore "the Jews" who persecute Jesus for healing on the Sabbath and who seek to kill him because he makes himself equal to God (5.16, 18). For the Johannine evangelist, the term "Jew" is *defined* by a rejection of Jesus' claim stemming from loyalty to the Law of Moses. His use of the generic term must have contemporary relevance for himself and his readers, whereas Pharisees and chief priests must belong to what J. L. Martyn has called the *einmalig* dimension of the ministry of Jesus — its historical particularity.[81] Although the evangelist and his first readers may never have met a Pharisee or a chief priest, they do encounter Jews; and the

---

80. A clear and full analysis of the terminology is presented by Urban von Wahlde, who distinguishes between a "P" (Pharisees) and a "J" (Jews) stratum ("The Terms for Religious Authorities in the Fourth Gospel: A Key to Literary Strata?" *JBL* 98 [1979], pp. 231-53).

81. J. Louis Martyn, *History and Theology in the Fourth Gospel* (Louisville: WJK, 2003³). According to Martyn, Jn. 9 witnesses both to "an *einmalig* event during Jesus' earthly lifetime" (especially in the initial healing story of vv. 1-7) and to "Jesus' powerful presence in actual events experienced by the Johannine church" (p. 40).

two sides still have enough in common for that encounter to take sharply polemical form. The Johannine Jews belong to both levels of the "two-level drama" of the Johannine narrative. On one level, they are Pharisees or chief priests contemporary with Jesus; on the other, they are diaspora Jews contemporary with the evangelist and his first readers.[82] The common denominator that unites chief priests and Pharisees at the time of Jesus with diaspora Jews some decades later is rejection of Jesus' claim out of professed loyalty to Moses. The initial rejection articulated by Jesus' contemporaries has been perpetuated and, as it were, canonized. In *GEger*, the contemporary relevance of Jesus' dispute with the lawyers and rulers is only implicit; in the Johannine "Jews," that relevance becomes explicit. *GEger* reflects a schism within a community that still finds a common heritage in what God said through Moses to "our fathers." In John, one community speaks to another of "your law" (Jn. 8.17; 10.34; cf. 15.25; 18.31) and "your fathers" (Jn. 6.49).

This application of Martyn's "two-level" model to the Johannine Jews may be distinguished from interpretations of this motif that limit its significance, seeking a "way of clearing the Fourth Gospel from the ugly suspicion of anti-Semitism" (as John Ashton has put it).[83] In answering the exegetical question about Johannine usage, it is also important to address that suspicion and the hermeneutic that gives rise to it.

The Ἰουδαῖοι of John's Gospel are associated with Ἰουδαία. Thus in 7.1 Jesus avoids Ἰουδαία because the Ἰουδαῖοι seek to kill him. In 11.7-8, the disciples advise against returning to Ἰουδαία for the same reason. Jesus does return to Judea, however, where two bereaved sisters are being comforted by οἱ Ἰουδαῖοι, that is, by fellow Judeans (11.19, 31, 33, 45). The Johannine Ἰουδαῖοι may then reflect a distinctive Palestinian usage which differentiates inhabitants of Judea from inhabitants of, say, Samaria or Galilee. The term should perhaps be translated accordingly: the Johannine Ἰουδαῖοι are simply "Judeans."[84] In addition, and as already noted, the Ἰουδαῖοι are often

---

82. The distinction is illustrated within Jn. 9 by the terminological shift from "the Pharisees" (vv. 13-17 [3x]; Martyn's Scene 3 [*History and Theology*, p. 42]) to "the Jews" (vv. 18-23 [3x]; Martyn's Scene 4 [pp. 42-43]). Martyn, however, places the Johannine Pharisees on his second level, that is, as contemporaneous with the evangelist. While the chief priests were "the leading men of the Jerusalem Sanhedrin," Jesus' contemporaries, the Pharisees represent "the Pharisaic Bet Din in Jamnia" and the local "Gerousia" (p. 86). In my view, it is primarily in his use of the generic term "the Jews" that the evangelist indicates the existence of a second, contemporary level in his presentation.

83. John Ashton, *Studying John: Approaches to the Fourth Gospel* (Oxford: Clarendon Press, 1994), p. 52.

84. So Malcolm Lowe, "Who Were the ΙΟΥΔΑΙΟΙ?" *NovT* 18 (1976), pp. 101-30; p. 130.

specifically the Jewish *leaders,* not the Jewish people as a whole. If so, it may be argued that the evangelist's hostility is directed against a particular group, in the context of what is still an intra-Jewish debate; no generalized "anti-Semitism" is to be found in this gospel.[85] On this account, the Johannine Jews are not Jews in general, but specifically Judeans; and in most cases not even Judeans in general, but specifically the Judean authorities.[86]

These exegetical conclusions are not wrong, but they are too limited in scope. They reduce the two-level drama to a single level, as though the evangelist and his intended readers were interested only in the *einmalig* dimension of Jesus' story. The limitations of this exegesis are evident in two passages in John 6, where the Ἰουδαῖοι are neither Judeans nor leaders:

> So the Ἰουδαῖοι complained at him because he said, "I am the bread which descended from heaven." They said, "Is this not Jesus son of Joseph, whose father and mother we know? How can he now say, 'I have come down from heaven?'" Jesus answered and said to them, "Do not complain among yourselves. . . ." (Jn. 6.41-43)

> ". . . If anyone eats this bread he will live for ever, and the bread which I shall give is my flesh, for the life of the world." So the Ἰουδαῖοι argued among themselves saying, "How can this man give us his flesh to eat?" (Jn. 6.51-52)

These Ἰουδαῖοι have previously been identified as the "great crowd" present at the feeding miracle (6.5), which on the following day "came to Capernaum seeking Jesus" (6.22-24). They seek him because they are inclined to believe in him, and their questions and requests initially seem reasonable:

> "Rabbi, when did you come here?" (6.25)

> "What should we do so as to work the works of God?" (6.28)

> "So what sign do you do, that we may see and believe you? What do you do? Our fathers ate the manna in the desert, as it is written: 'He gave them bread from heaven to eat.'" (6.30-31)

> "Lord, give us this bread always." (6.34)

85. So Urban von Wahlde, "The Johannine 'Jews': A Critical Survey," *NTS* 28 (1981-82), pp. 33-60; p. 33.

86. See the nuanced discussion in Ashton, *Studying John,* pp. 36-70. But Ashton can only offer "glimmer[s] of light in this rather dark and impenetrable tunnel" (p. 68), because he does not give sufficient weight to the second, contemporary level of the evangelist's discourse.

Only when Jesus identifies the heavenly bread with himself, indeed with his own flesh, do his hearers turn against him. In so doing they constitute themselves as Ἰουδαῖοι. As with the Ἰουδαῖοι of Jerusalem in chapter 5, Moses represents the criterion by which Jesus' claim is judged and found wanting — here in his role as provider of manna from heaven rather than as lawgiver. The evangelist does not betray any particular hostility towards either group of Ἰουδαῖοι. Their own hostility towards Jesus is presented with a minimum of moralizing or polemic either from the evangelist or from Jesus himself, even where an intention to kill Jesus is in view (5.18; 7.1, 19-20, 25).[87] Jesus must indeed die, but his death is his enthronement in glory and its hour has been determined by his Father.

In Jesus' controversies with Ἰουδαῖοι in Jerusalem or Galilee, a boundary is established between two communities: Jesus' followers and "the Jews." Rejection of Jesus' claim will henceforth be part of the definition of the term "Jew." While the redefinition has been asserted from the Christian side of the boundary, where the evangelist stands, there is every reason to suppose that it is also asserted on the Jewish side. If the Johannine gospel dates from the late first or early second century, we may imagine that many on both sides are now agreed that being a Jew is incompatible with being a follower of Jesus the Messiah. Johannine references to expulsion from the synagogue are unlikely to be pure fabrication, whether or not such events were frequent and widespread (cf. Jn. 9.22; 12.42; 16.2).[88] Expulsion from the synagogue should not be seen as a unilateral and arbitrary act of violence, with non-Christian Jews as the aggressors and Christian Jews as the victims. All communities have boundaries and possess mechanisms for policing them which will normally include expulsion as a last resort. An early Christian community may expel a member for his irregular marital arrangements or for idola-

---

87. The situation is different in Jn.8.30-59, where, however, the Ἰουδαῖοι (vv. 48, 52, 57) are τοὺς πεπιστευκότας αὐτῷ Ἰουδαίους (v. 31). Even here, the polemical statement of v. 44 remains isolated.

88. According to Adele Reinhartz, the expulsion belongs to the *einmalig* level of the life of Jesus as imagined by the evangelist. His problematic portrayal of Jews is best seen as "a consequence of the community's ongoing struggle for self-definition rather than an external, Jewish act of expulsion"; this reading "removes responsibility for the anti-Jewish language from late first-century Jews or their authorities and restores it to the Johannine community, which embedded this portrayal in its formative text" ("The Johannine Community and Its Neighbors: A Reappraisal," in *What Is John? Volume II: Literary and Social Readings of the Fourth Gospel*, ed. Fernando F. Segovia, SBLSS [Atlanta: Scholars Press, 1998], pp. 111-38; p. 138). But if the Johannine community merely imagined its own persecution, was the same true of Paul (cf. 2 Cor. 11.24-25; 1 Thes. 2.14)?

trous practices;[89] a Jewish community may expel those who persist in a deluded and contentious messianic confession; and no neutral criteria are available to those who might wish to criticize such actions from outside their communal contexts. If opportunities for repentance have been given and declined, it cannot be said that such actions are unilateral. The persistent offender is no less the agent of his or her expulsion than the community officials who carry it out. Expulsion or separation takes place because *both* parties agree that it should. Paradoxically, the Johannine understanding of "Jews" in terms of the rejection of Christian claims about Jesus may represent common ground between the two sides. Separation can come about by consensus.[90]

(ii) A Mosaic Stratum

In contrast to this later consensus, *GEger* still tries to show that loyalty to Jesus is compatible with loyalty to Moses, and that messianic and non-messianic Jews share a common heritage in the form of the scriptures and of "our fathers." While Jesus' opponents seek to establish a new communal boundary in their hostile reaction to him, this text aims to show that no such boundary should exist: for Jesus observed the Law of Moses, and Moses bore witness to Jesus.

89. Cf. 1 Cor. 5.1-5; Mt. 18.15-17, read on the assumption that eating "food offered to idols" would have been a serious offence in the Matthean community (cf. Acts 15.20, 29; Rv. 2.14; *Did.* 6.3).

90. Contrast Robert Kysar's claim that "[t]he vitriolic attack on Judaism is nothing more nor less than the desperate attempt of the Johannine Christians to find a rationale for their existence in isolation from Judaism" ("Anti-Semitism and the Gospel of John," in *Anti-Semitism and Early Christianity: Issues of Polemic and Faith,* ed. Craig A. Evans and Donald A. Hagner [Minneapolis: Fortress, 1993], pp. 113-27; p. 122). Paradoxically, a "community that was founded on the sacrifice of an innocent person for their salvation now sacrificed [*sic*] their former brothers and sisters for the sake of their self-identity" (p. 124). Still more unfortunately, an "occasional piece designed for a particular situation and to meet certain needs has become part of the canon of the Christian church. . . . In its canonical status the Gospel of John has nurtured (if not conceived) repugnant attitudes and evoked abhorrent actions on the part of Christians toward their Jewish colleagues" (pp. 125, 126). This shallow polemic reflects an antipluralist strand in contemporary political discourse that typically issues in precisely the "vitriolic attack" on the other that it purports to denounce. A genuinely pluralist stance would require a recognition of communal boundaries and a willingness to differentiate between "normal" levels of the tensions that difference may entail and pathological deformations that issue in oppression, enslavement, or genocide. That there is nothing inherently virtuous about opposing boundaries in principle is illustrated by the ideologies that claim to do so, which include imperialism, communism, and global capitalism.

For many non-Christian Jews and non-Jewish Christians, however, the boundary is an established fact. The Johannine evangelist is concerned not to create a boundary that did not previously exist but to identify precisely *where it is to be located*. The boundary in the controversy between the Johannine Jesus and "the Jews" differs fundamentally from the one proposed by Jesus' opponents in *GEger*. In the Johannine appropriation, the concern with Jesus' relationship to the Law of Moses is displaced by a new concern: Jesus claims equality with God, "the Jews" reject that claim — and *at that point* the boundary becomes visible which enables each community to define itself by differentiation from the other. Jesus' relation to Moses is still an issue, but it has been displaced by the overriding question of his relation to God.

This displacement becomes visible in John 5.14-18:

> . . . After this Jesus found him in the temple and said to him, "See, you have become well; sin no longer [μηκέτι ἁμάρτανε], so that nothing worse should happen to you." The man went and told the Jews that it was Jesus who made him well. And for this reason [διὰ τοῦτο] the Jews were persecuting Jesus, because he was doing these things on the sabbath. And Jesus answered them, "My Father is working still, and I am working." So it was rather for this reason that the Jews were seeking to kill him, because he was not only annulling the Sabbath but was saying that God was his own Father, making himself equal to God [ἴσον ἑαυτὸν ποιῶν τῷ θεῷ].

In the healing story of John 5.1-9a, there is no apparent reason for controversy. A sick man, who has failed to recover despite so many years spent at a place of healing, is instantly healed by Jesus' word: "Rise, take up your pallet, and walk!" (v. 8). The command closely resembles Mark 2.11 ("Rise, take up your pallet, and *return to your house!*"), and is closer still to the preceding hypothetical version in Mark 2.9 (". . . or to say, Rise *and* take up your pallet, and walk?"). The Markan paralytic walks out carrying his mattress as a demonstration that his strength has been fully restored; the onlookers "glorified God, saying, 'We have never seen anything like this'" (Mk. 2.12). In the Markan story, the controversial element is Jesus' pronouncement of forgiveness. In the Johannine parallel the carrying of the mattress serves not to demonstrate the healing but to create a secondary, retrospective link with the Sabbath:[91]

> . . . And immediately the man became well and took up his pallet and walked. And it was the Sabbath that day. So the Jews were saying to the

91. As Martyn notes (*History and Theology,* p. 73).

healed man, "It is the Sabbath, and it is not lawful for you to carry your pallet." (Jn. 5.9b-10)

The compositional technique closely resembles John 9. There too, an initial healing story (the man born blind, 9.1-7) is retrospectively linked to the Sabbath (9.14), a conversation ensues between the healed man and the authorities (9.15-17; cf. 5.10-13), the healed man encounters Jesus again (9.35-38; cf. 5.14), and the outcome is hostility between Jesus and the authorities (9.39-41; cf. 5.16-18). While the basic structure of the two chapters is the same, it is elaborated differently.

In John 9, the encounter between the man and the authorities is expanded. It is preceded by a debate among the onlookers (vv. 8-12); the man's parents become involved (vv. 18-23); and he himself is brought back for further questioning (vv. 24-34). Jesus is absent from all but the beginning and end of this story, and the man born blind becomes its protagonist.[92] The elaboration of an originally self-contained miracle story is a literary strategy peculiar to John, and on this occasion it serves to exemplify Jesus' later warning that "they will put you out of the synagogues" (Jn. 16.2; cf. 9.22, 34-35). Although set within the life of Jesus, the story anticipates the experience of at least some Christians known to the evangelist — an experience that helps shape his conception of the boundary between two communities.

In John 5, the connection between the original miracle story and the Sabbath is developed in a different direction. The Sabbath issue leads not to an exemplary narrative illustrating the fate of the disciple but to a christological discourse in which Jesus announces his own participation in the work of his Father and speaks of the Father's witness to that participation (5.19-47). It is at the close of this monologue that the main Egerton parallels are embedded. The abrupt shift from the Sabbath issue to christology is striking. Initially it is said that "the Jews" were persecuting Jesus for his breach of the Sabbath. The reference is not to any specific hostile act such as the attempted arrests or stonings of later chapters (cf. 7.30, 32, 44-46; 8.59; 10.31, 39). Rather, this is a summary statement which presupposes that Jewish

---

92. "Three of the major characters in verses 8-41 (two are collective) play no part in verses 1-7: the blind man's neighbors, the Pharisees in council, the blind man's parents. The main accents are also new: that the healing occurred on a sabbath (an afterthought also in 5:10), Jesus' proper identity, synagogue discipline, discipleship to Moses versus discipleship to Jesus, faith in the Son of man. It scarcely needs further to be argued that verses 8-41 present material which someone composed as an addition to the simple healing narrative of verses 1-7" (Martyn, *History and Theology*, p. 37).

hostility to Jesus is a well-known fact and traces it back to his practice of Sabbath healing: "And for this reason the Jews were persecuting Jesus, because he used to do such things [ταῦτα ἐποίει] on the Sabbath" (5.16).[93] Here, ταῦτα ἐποίει refers to a habitual practice which the Bethesda or Bethzatha healing illustrates.[94] The narrator explains that the authorities' hostility to Jesus was occasioned by his actions on the Sabbath, which they considered to be in breach of the Law of Moses.

The authorities have said nothing to Jesus, yet he "answered" them by stating: "My Father is working still, and I am working" (v. 17). In restoring health and strength to a sick man, Jesus has "worked on the Sabbath" in spite of the Law's requirement that the seventh day be observed as a Sabbath and that "you shall do no work on it" (Ex. 20.10). He did so not because it is always lawful on the Sabbath to do good (cf. Mk. 3.4) but because his Father continues to work even on the Sabbath, and because he shares in that ongoing work rather than acting on his own initiative (cf. 5.19-20a). While in 5.20b Jesus begins to speak of "greater works" of resurrection and judgement, the theme up to that point is still his Sabbath healings.[95] In healing on the Sabbath, he shows himself to be above the Sabbath law by virtue of his cooperation as Son in the work of his Father. He "makes himself equal to God" both by speaking of God as his own Father (5.18) and by claiming to participate in an ongoing divine work which overrides the Sabbath (5.17, 19-20a).

The evangelist is aware that some of the Pharisees or their successors allege that "this man is not from God because he does not observe the Sabbath" (9.16). The conclusion is false, but the premise is true. Jesus does not observe the Sabbath. Why not? Because *God* does not observe the Sabbath, and because the Son's acts are also God's acts. What comes to light in the Sabbath healing incident is so important and so astonishing that *this* —

---

93. The Johannine idiom διὰ τοῦτο . . . ὅτι . . . is used to provide an explanation for some already-known fact or saying. In Jn. 5.16, the ὅτι clause explains the state of affairs referred to in the διὰ τοῦτο clause (i.e. persecution by "the Jews," cf. also v. 18): for analogies, see 1.31 (ἵνα; John's baptism); 8.47 (failure to hear); 10.17 (the Father's love); 12.39 (inability to believe). Elsewhere the same idiom is used differently, to indicate that an explanation has just been given of an earlier utterance, which is repeated: see Jn. 6.44 + 65; 9.21 + 23; 13.10 + 11; 16.14 + 15.

94. As Barrett notes, "John refers generally . . . to the healing ministry of Jesus (note the imperfect ἐποίει) and to his attitude to the sabbath law" (*John*, p. 255). For ταῦτα in Jn. 5.16, cf. 20.31; 21.24.

95. See Herold Weiss, "The Sabbath in the Fourth Gospel," *JBL* 110 (1991), pp. 311-21; pp. 315-18.

Jesus' "making himself equal with God" — must from now on be the theme of his controversy with "the Jews." The question about Jesus and Moses is subsumed into the question about Jesus and God.

The contrast with the Egerton gospel is striking. Fragment ɪᴠ of *GEger* opens with a (reconstructed) saying addressed to the νομικοί, the experts in the law: "[Judge(?) ev]ery wrongdo[er and everyone who is law]less, and not me." Jesus appeals to the law's guardians to recognize that he is no wrong-doer or lawless person; he must here respond to the accusation that he is in breach of the law, no doubt through some such action as a Sabbath healing. He will later demonstrate that he is no transgressor by ensuring that the cleansed leper conforms to the Mosaic regulations, and by identifying his former association with lepers as "sin." When Egerton's Jesus instructs a healed individual to "sin no more" (μηκέτι ἁμάρτανε, *GEger* ɪʳ 10), it is Mosaic criteria that identify what "sin" is. When the Johannine Jesus issues the same warning to another healed individual (Jn. 5.14), there is no trace of the Mosaic criteria. For the Egerton evangelist, it is crucially important to be able to show that Moses stands alongside Jesus as accuser of his critics, rather than alongside his critics as accuser of Jesus. For John, this issue has lost its urgency. The statements about Moses' testimony to Jesus are retained (Jn. 5.39, 45-47), but Jesus is now dependent on the Father's testimony, oc-curring in and through his own works, rather than the testimony of Moses. Far from rebutting the charge that Jesus is a transgressor, the later evangelist claims that Jesus' identity as Son places him above the law. This evangelist recognizes that Jesus' Sabbath healings were controversial, yet unlike his pre-decessor he insists that Jesus' relation to Moses is not the important issue. The authorities sought to kill Jesus because "he was not only annulling the Sabbath but was saying that God was his own Father, making himself equal to God" (Jn. 5.18). At this point, a major concern of *GEger* is displaced by Jo-hannine christology. Jesus' "making himself equal with God" marks the in-troduction of the christological theme as central to his Jerusalem ministry, forming an *inclusio* with John 10.33 where Jesus is threatened with stoning because "you, a man, make yourself God." The stoning theme is also sug-gested by *GEger*, as we have seen, but in this earlier context it is provoked by Jesus' offensive statements about Moses, his testimony and his accusation — statements that evoke no response at all in their Johannine context.

In *GEger*, Moses' authority remains unchallenged. The question is whose side he is on. This question arises within a community which is si-multaneously divided and singular, and the controversy around this ques-tion can only be resolved by persuasion or separation. From the later Johannine perspective, resolution has taken the form of separation. Figures who, in the earlier text, were simply leaders of the opposing faction have become οἱ Ἰουδαῖοι, without differentiation. Those who confess Jesus as the Messiah find that there is no longer a place for them in a synagogue where Moses retains his dominant role. And, in a certain sense, that separation is as it should be — so long as it is clear that the decisive reason for separation is that Jesus makes himself equal not with Moses but with God. This claim is either "blasphemy" (Jn. 10.33) or it is true. It is here that the line that divides and unites the two communities comes most sharply into focus.

The displacement of the Mosaic concern is visible above all in John 5.16-18, where the διὰ τοῦτο . . . ὅτι . . . of v. 16 is superseded by the διὰ τοῦτο οὖν μᾶλλον . . . ὅτι . . . of v. 18: "So it was rather for this reason that the Jews were seeking to kill him, because he was not only annulling the Sabbath but was saying that God was his own Father, making himself equal to God." At this point a differentiation of strata within the Johannine text becomes visible.[96] The Moses-related Egerton parallels (Jn. 5.39, 45-47; 9.29) are vestiges of an earlier stratum where the Sabbath is the chief concern (5.9b-16); and this in turn can be differentiated from a still earlier stratum in which the healing story is unconnected to the Sabbath (5.1-9a). While the intermediate stratum is characterized by its Mosaic focus, the focus shifts in the final stratum to the theme of Jesus' equality with God — a shift announced in 5.16-18 and further elaborated in the discourse that follows (5.19-38, 40-44).

In 5.16-19, the two explanatory διὰ τοῦτο statements (vv. 16, 18) are each followed by an "answer" from Jesus (vv. 17, 19), although no words are reported to occasion his answers. The Jews used to persecute Jesus because of his practice of healing on the Sabbath, and "Jesus *answered* them, 'My Father is working. . . .'" The Jews were seeking to kill Jesus because he made himself equal to God in calling God his Father, and "Jesus *answered* and said to them . . ." The second pairing of explanation and answer is modelled on the first, where the gap between explanation and answer might be filled by inserting a synoptic-type question:

> And for this reason the Jews were persecuting Jesus, because he was doing such things on the Sabbath. <And they said to him: "Why do you do what is not lawful on the Sabbath?"> And Jesus answered them . . . (Jn. 5.16, 17; cf. Mk. 2.24)

96. So Michael Labahn, *Jesus als Lebensspender: Untersuchungen zu einer Geschichte der johanneischen Tradition anhand ihrer Wundergeschichten*, BZNW (Berlin & New York: De Gruyter, 1999), pp. 247-49, 263-64.

In its present form, Jesus' answer belongs to the final, christological stratum. Yet something like the original version of his answer has been preserved elsewhere:

> Jesus answered and said to them, "I performed one work, and you all marvelled at it. Moses gave you circumcision (not that it is from Moses but from the fathers),[97] and you circumcise a man [ἄνθρωπον] on the Sabbath. If a man receives circumcision on the Sabbath so that the Law of Moses may not be nullified, are you angry with me because I made a whole man well on the Sabbath? Do not judge by appearances, but judge with right judgment." (7.21-24)[98]

In its present context, this *ad hominem* argument takes place at the Feast of Tabernacles many months after the incident to which it refers (7.2; cf. 6.4, 5.1).[99] The reference back to the Bethesda or Bethzatha healing becomes un-

---

97. The parenthesis represents an explanatory gloss probably inserted when the passage was moved to its present position; cf. the similar gloss in 4.2.

98. An earlier link between 5.16 and 7.19-23 was suggested by Harold Attridge ("Thematic Development and Source Elaboration in John 7:1-36," *CBQ* 42 [1980], pp. 160-70; p. 165-66), and accepted by Herold Weiss ("Sabbath," pp. 311-15). More commonly, 7.15-24 is connected to 5.47: so J. H. Bernard, *A Critical and Exegetical Commentary on the Gospel according to St. John*, 2 vols., ICC (Edinburgh: T. & T. Clark, 1928), 1.xix-xx; R. Bultmann, *The Gospel of John*, Eng. trans. (Oxford: Blackwell, 1971), p. 273, connecting γράμματα (7.15) to the references to Moses in 5.45-47; R. Schnackenburg, *The Gospel according to John*, 3 vols., Eng. trans. (London: Burns & Oates, 1968-82), 2.129-31, noting a number of other verbal links. While Bernard rightly states that "[i]t is very difficult to interpret 7.23 if we suppose it to refer to something which had happened months before" (p. xix), an original connection of 7.15-24 to the end of chapter 5 is not the only possible solution. In support of a link between 7.21-24 and 5.16, the following points should be noted. *(i)* Thematic and verbal connections between 7.15-18 and chapter 5 (e.g. 7.18 + 5.44) need not stem from an originally unified discourse (cf. 5.20 + 3.35; 5.30 + 8.16; 5.36 + 10.25). *(ii)* 7.19-20 was composed in order to integrate the older passage into a new context. Μωϋσῆς δέδωκεν ὑμῖν τὸν νόμον (7.19) is modelled on Μωϋσῆς δέδωκεν ὑμῖν τὴν περιτομήν (7.22). Comments from the "crowd" (v. 20) are typical of chapter 7 (cf. vv. 12, 31, 40, 43) but not of chapter 5. (The redactional character of 7.19-20 is noted by Labahn, *Jesus als Lebensspender*, pp. 250-51.) *(iii)* Unlike the proposed transposition, the "displacement" theory can explain *why* 7.21-24 has been removed from its original context within chapter 5. *(iv)* If *GEger* 1v precedes 1r, this gospel cannot have included parallels from Jn. 7 following *GEger* 1v 8-9 (= Jn. 5.46-47). *(v)* A connection between 7.21-24 and 5.16 resolves the problem noted by Labahn, criticizing the usual transposition hypothesis: "Entscheidend ist, dass das Sabbaththema in den Reden 5,19ff nicht mehr reflektiert wird und damit 7,19ff trotz des Mosethemas nach 5,47 zu spät käme" (p. 213).

99. Between the unspecified feast of Jn. 5.1 and the Feast of Tabernacles (7.2) comes the Passover (6.4), which precedes the Feast of Tabernacles by six months (cf. Lv. 23.5, 34).

ambiguously clear when Jesus indicates that the "one work" to which he refers consisted in "mak[ing] a whole person well on the Sabbath" (7.21, 23). The expressions "make whole" and "on the Sabbath" echo the earlier chapter and are hardly paralleled elsewhere. "Whole" or "well" (ὑγιής) derives from the original healing story (Jn. 5.6, 9; cf. v. 14), and occurs elsewhere in the canonical gospels only in Matthew 12.13 (in the context of another Sabbath healing) and 15.31 (a summary of Jesus' healing activity). "Make whole" is attested only in the two Johannine contexts: ὁ ποιήσας με ὑγιή (5.11); ὅτι Ἰησοῦς ἐστιν ὁ ποιήσας αὐτὸν ὑγιή (5.15); ὅτι ὅλον ἄνθρωπον ὑγιή ἐποίησα (7.23). "On the Sabbath" (ἐν σάββατῳ) occurs in John 5.16, three times in 7.22-23, and elsewhere only in Matthew 12.2 and Luke 6.1 (both textually uncertain).

Circumcision may be necessary on the Sabbath because it must be performed on the eighth day after birth (cf. Gn. 17.12; Lv. 12.3). If circumcision can override the Sabbath commandment, precisely to ensure that Moses' Law is faithfully observed, why should the healing of a whole human being be thought a transgression? This is essentially the same argument as the one Matthew inserts into a Markan story about another alleged Sabbath transgression. In this passage the Davidic analogy is Markan, the priestly one a Matthean addition:

> . . . And the Pharisees seeing it said to him, "Look, your disciples are doing what it is not lawful to do on the Sabbath." And he said to them, "Have you not read what David did when he was hungry, and those with him, how he entered the house of God and ate the consecrated bread, which it was not lawful for him to eat or for those with him, but was for the priests alone? Or have you not read in the Law how on the Sabbath the priests in the temple profane the Sabbath and are guiltless? I tell you, something greater than the temple is here." (Mt. 12.2-6)

In the original Markan passage, the point is that David's urgent need for food for himself and his followers occasioned a suspension of the law that the bread of the sanctuary "shall be for Aaron and his sons, and they shall eat it in a holy place . . ." (Lv. 24.9).[100] The double reference to "those with him" highlights the parallel with Jesus and his disciples, especially since, in the

---

100. Cf. Ex. 25.23-30; 40.22-23. According to 1 Sm. 21.6, the sacred bread eaten by David had just been replaced by fresh loaves; according to Lv. 24.8, loaves were to be replaced every Sabbath (cf. *mMenah.* 11.7-8). Underlying the Markan appeal to David is the deduction that he must have eaten the sacred bread on the Sabbath.

original story, David is alone and the "young men" are a fiction intended to convince the high priest Ahimelech that he has come on the king's legitimate business and is not an outlaw (1 Sm. 21.1-6).[101] The scriptural argument may presuppose a Davidic christology, in which case it is intended for use within the Christian community.

In contrast, Matthew's supplementary argument about the priests is better suited for an apologetic role, and the same is true of the Johannine argument about circumcision. The potential for tension between the Sabbath commandment and both the temple service and circumcision is acknowledged in the Mishnah. Rabbi Jose is reported to have exclaimed, "Great is circumcision, which overrides the rigour even of the Sabbath!"[102] It is agreed that "they may perform on the Sabbath all things that are needful for circumcision."[103] A detailed account is given of "acts pertaining to the Passover-offering" which "override the Sabbath."[104] According to the Johannine Jesus, the permission to circumcise on the Sabbath should be extended to cover his own healing activity. The repeated reference to "a man" being circumcised or receiving circumcision is intended to strengthen the analogy with the healing of a "whole man" (Jn. 7.22-23). It is a lesser thing for a man to "receive" the circumcision of just one of his members than for a "whole man" to be made well. If the Sabbath commandment may be suspended for the sake of a lesser good, it should all the more be suspended for the sake of a greater good.

John 7.21-24 belongs to an intermediate stratum within John 5. It originally followed on from 5.16, and has been displaced to its present context by the shift away from a Mosaic focus closely related to *GEger*. Like *GEger*, this Mosaic stratum reflects a Jewish Christian milieu.[105] The old miracle story (**1**: Jn. 5.1-9a) is initially linked to the issue of Jesus' attitude towards the Sabbath (**2a**: 5.9b-16). Jesus defends his conduct by appeal to the Mosaic precedent (**2b**: cf. Jn. 7.21-24), and lays claim to Moses' testimony (**2c**: 5.39, 45-47). The narrative probably concluded with an account of the authorities' hostile response (**2d**: cf. *GEger* 1r 1-4; Jn. 7.30; 8.59). In a subsequent revision (**3**: 5.17-38, 40-44), the earlier controversy about communal practice is displaced by a new controversy around Jesus' claim to equality with God — a claim mark-

---

101. On this see Joel Marcus, *Mark: A New Translation with Introduction and Commentary*, 2 vols., AYB (New Haven & London: Yale University Press, 2000-2009), 1.240-41.

102. *mNed.* 3.11.

103. *mShab.* 18.3; this is followed by detailed discussion in 19.1-5.

104. *mPes.* 6.1; 5.8–6.6.

105. See Labahn, *Jesus als Lebensspender*, pp. 254-55 (although without reference to *GEger*).

ing the boundary between two intimately related yet separate communities. In this rewriting, **1** and **2a** are retained; **2b** is transferred to a new location; **2c** is diluted by the insertion of additional material relating to the new theme; and **2d** provides resources for later accounts of a hostile response to Jesus' words.[106]

This Mosaic stratum (**2a-d**) has been reconstructed on the basis both of internal Johannine evidence and of *GEger*, and it provides a new context in which to view the relationship between the two early gospels. **2** is more closely related to *GEger* than **3**, with its radical christology of equality with God — and not only at **2c**, where the two texts coincide. As the first Egerton fragment opens, Jesus is defending himself, presumably against the charge that he has transgressed the law. The parallel with the conclusion of **2b** is striking:

". . . If a man receives circumcision on the Sabbath so that the Law of Moses may not be nullified, are you angry with me because I made a whole man well on the Sabbath? Do not judge by appearances, but judge with right judgment." (Jn. 7.23-24)

And Jesus said] to the lawyer[s: "Judge(?) ev]ery wrongdo[er and everyone who is law]less, and not me." *(GEger 1v 1)*

The Johannine appeal not to judge by appearances is only loosely connected to the Moses-related argument that precedes it, but is more closely related to the parallel Egerton appeal (whether or not the same verb was used). It is uncertain whether the Egerton Jesus would have made *ad hominem* appeals to the law to justify what would seem to be his breaches of it. In *GEger*, Jesus demonstrates that he conforms to the law and teaches others to do so when, in the sequel to the controversy with the lawyers and rulers, he cleanses a leper and sends him to the priests for the Mosaic rites to be carried out. In contrast, the Johannine Jesus transgresses the law himself (by healing

---

106. Compare H. Weiss's claim that "the story of the healing of the paralytic at the pool of Bethesda came to the Johannine community as a sabbath controversy story that ended with what is now 7:19-23," whereas "5.17-47 represents a secondary elaboration of the story within the Johannine community" ("Sabbath," p. 314). In the reference system I am using, this represents a differentiation between **1**, **2ab**, and **3**, although **2b** is identified with 7.17-23 rather than 7.21-24 (as in my own reconstruction). Weiss does not discuss the evidence of *GEger* which makes it possible to identify **2cd**. The three-stage reconstruction may be contrasted with the two-stage hypothesis of Robert Fortna, who ascribes Jn. 5.1-9a to his "Signs Source" and 5.9b-47 to Johannine redaction (*Fourth Gospel*, pp. 113-17).

on the Sabbath), and teaches the healed man to do the same (by carrying his pallet). **2** is a less conservative text than *GEger* appears to have been, although the issue of Jesus' relation to Moses is common to both. Much the most likely sequence is: *GEger* → **2** → **3**. In view of the differentiation of **2** from **3**, the sequence John → *GEger* is implausible, requiring a post-Johannine author to recover and reinterpret a pre-Johannine stratum from the full text in more or less its present form.

In the context of the fourfold canonical gospel and its reception, the Gospel of John is important not so much for its supplementary narratives as for its radical christology, which asserts Jesus' equality with God — not as a "second God" but by virtue of the mutually constitutive relationship of Father and Son. It has been asserted again and again that Johannine christology has little or nothing in common with the christology of Nicaea, that it is far from the evangelist's thoughts to see Jesus as "very God from very God," and that it is his subordinationist statements that express his real view. Yet the Nicene account arises in large part out of an ongoing dialogue with Johannine and other scriptural texts. Indeed, that dialogue — of which the object is Jesus — is already under way within the texts themselves. The Egerton fragments make it possible to recover a theological trajectory away from the Jesus/Moses issue that so preoccupied Christian Jews, towards ever more radical formulations of Jesus' relation to God.

CHAPTER 7

Reinterpreting in Parallel (Jn, GTh, GPet)

As preceding chapters have shown, a historical account of gospel origins must incorporate the evidence of gospels later deemed noncanonical. The *Gospel of Thomas* confirms the existence of the Sayings Collection genre within which Jesus' sayings were originally preserved and transmitted. In conjunction with the *L/M* hypothesis, the resulting SC hypothesis occupies the space left vacant by the demise of Q. Similarly, the extant fragments of the Egerton gospel contain pre-Johannine and presynoptic material that sheds light on the interpretative processes underlying the canonical gospels. It is simply wrong to suppose that canonical gospel origins can and should be explained without reference to extracanonical texts; there is no reason to assume any such correspondence between early gospel writing and a canonical/noncanonical divide first attested in the latter part of the second century. Precisely in order to grasp the historical, hermeneutical, and theological significance of this distinction, a precanonical stage must be envisaged in which gospel literature proliferates in the absence of any canonical limit.

In the present chapter, this argument will be further developed by investigating parallel interpretative processes in the gospels attributed to John, Thomas, and Peter. The fact that the Johannine gospel was later located on one side of the canonical boundary and *GTh* and *GPet* on the other is, of course, profoundly significant. But this canonical differentiation does not reflect differences inherent in the texts themselves. These gospels all claim apostolic authority, and they all present an image of Jesus rooted in early tradition and shaped by later interpretative developments. There is no reason to suppose that a canonical text must have been separated from its noncanonical counterparts by an interval of many decades, or that, even if such an interval could be demonstrated, it would possess any special significance. It is true that, within the ongoing tradition shaped by the fourfold gospel, a judgement in favour of the canonical text and against the noncanonical one is proper and necessary. One may indeed wish to affirm that the catholic church was right in its selection, and that these four gospels are individually and collectively adequate to the reality of divine self-disclosure in Jesus in ways that noncanonical gospels are not. Yet there is no standpoint from which such an affirmation could be made other than the one already shaped by the canonical decision.

In the gospels attributed to John, Thomas, and Peter, existing interpretations of early tradition are subjected to *reinterpretation*. Before engaging directly with these texts, the concept of reinterpretation must be developed in the context of a comprehensive outline of a reception process extending from the life of Jesus to the formation of the fourfold canonical gospel. The outline will draw on the findings of previous chapters, but will also anticipate points to be developed in the rest of this book.

Modelling Reception

"Dependence" is established as it becomes clear that one of two parallel versions of narrative or sayings material is the original of the other. On this basis it becomes possible to see how, in the later text, older material has been reformulated and recontextualized and thereby *interpreted*. Corresponding to the backward movement in which dependence is established is a forward movement, from earlier to later, in which an interpretative process is retraced. This double movement is evident as the Johannine evangelist refashions an older controversy story, itself dependent in part on the Egerton gospel; as Luke sets material extracted from Matthew's Sermon on the Mount in new juxtapositions; and as the *Gospel of Thomas* develops material from older sayings collections into its own distinctive account of Christian faith and practice. In each case, an evangelist interprets an older text.

The older text may already be an interpretation of one that is older still. As we have seen, the Johannine account of the Sabbath controversy interprets an earlier healing story not originally linked to the Sabbath. Whether or not this story once belonged to a "Signs Gospel," it appears to have existed in a written form stable enough to retain its distinctive identity even when a new narrative role was assigned to it. A three-stage compositional process is evident here: there is an original written text, an interpretation, and a reinterpretation. The same is true of *GTh*, which seems to have arisen not only from primitive Sayings Collections predating the synoptic gospels but also from intermediate texts such as the Greek *Gospel according to the Hebrews* attested by Clement and Origen. Since *GTh* betrays some awareness of Matthean and Lukan redaction, these gospels too belong to the intermediate phase between *GTh* and the earliest SCs. In the case of the Lukan sayings material, it is Matthew who represents the intermediate stage. While Luke may derive some "L" material directly from an SC, he is normally dependent on Matthew, who evidently transferred non-Markan sayings material from Sayings Collection format into a narrative context. At other points, it is Mark who plays the intermediary role for both Matthew and Luke: thus the parables in Mark 4 may be traced back through several stages of literary development to a Thomas-like Sayings Collection, and traced forward to the Matthean redaction.

The threefold pattern may be represented as follows:

SC	→	Mk. 4	→	Mt. 13
SC	→	Mt. 5–7	→	Lk. 6 + 11-17 *passim*
SC	→	Mt., Lk., *GHeb* →	*GTh*	
1/*GEger*	→	2	→	3 (= Jn. 5)

In each case, the analysis begins from an extant text (Matthew, Luke, Thomas, John) and postulates dependence on a prior text (Mark, Matthew, *GHeb,* proto-John) which may itself be dependent on a precursor (an SC, a collection of miracle stories, *GEger*). Later evangelists *re*interpret earlier interpretations whose object is an item in its original written form. At the primary and intermediate stages, an original account of a healing miracle is subsumed into a Sabbath controversy, along with material about Jesus' relationship to Moses. The simple saying, "Seek and you will find," is elaborated into a sequence in which finding leads to amazement, amazement to ruling, and ruling to rest. An interpretative key is provided for the Parable of the Sower. In each case, interpretative activity is evoked by an item whose original written form may still be perceptible — whether that interpretative activity takes the form of supplementary narrative, or the elaboration of a simple saying into a more complex one, or the provision of a point-by-point interpretative key. And in each case, this initial interpretation is subjected to more or less radical reinterpretation in later texts or text forms.

Intermediate and primary stages can often be identified only tentatively and approximately. There is no question of large-scale reconstructions of entire texts or text forms, as is sometimes attempted for Q or the Johannine

Signs Source. While the synoptic gospels do show evidence of comprehensive redaction (Matthean editing of Mark, Lukan of Matthew and Mark), redactional activity may also be highly localized. It would be hazardous to propose any kind of link between the later, christological stratum in John 5 and other apparently later passages such as John 15–17 or 21. Such passages may have been incorporated piecemeal into a text that developed incrementally, rather than reflecting a single and comprehensive editorial strategy. Moving back from the intermediate to the primary stage, the uncertainties increase. If the Mosaic controversy material in *GEger* is incorporated into successive editions of the Gospel of John, as argued in the previous chapter, it remains uncertain whether the saying "Search the scriptures . . ." is original to *GEger* or whether it already represents a redactional modification of a still earlier version of the saying. The same is true of the oldest material preserved in *GTh*. The oldest accessible form of a given item may or may not correspond to the original form in which that item was first put into writing. Although it is often wrongly assumed that writing the tradition is a Markan innovation, the Egerton account of the cleansing of the leper confirms that even a supposedly primitive Markan narrative may already incorporate significant redactional and interpretative activity. "Early" and "late" are purely relative concepts here. The Markan story is "early" vis-à-vis the Matthean and Lukan versions, but it may well be "late" in relation to the one attested in *GEger*.

Nevertheless, the oldest accessible form may be said to approximate to the original written form and to represent it. More precisely, what it represents and approximates is the moment of *inscription* — the moment when a prior tradition is articulated and stabilized as it is put into writing.[1] We must suppose that early oral tradition consisted in far more than a set of text-like verbal artefacts committed to memory. That model may be appropriate for (say) the Lord's Prayer or particularly concise and memorable sayings ("The Sabbath was made for man . . ." or "Render unto Caesar . . ."). But no precise formulation of the contexts of such sayings is plausible at the oral stage.[2]

---

1. "Inscription" represents the moment of transition between orality and writing for a given unit of material. It is a limitation of the form-critical project that this transition was never taken seriously. Thus Bultmann regards it as a matter of indifference "ob die Tradition mündlich oder schriftlich erfolgte, da bei dem unliterarischen Charakter des Überlieferungsstoffes ein prinzipieller Unterschied zwischen beiden nicht vorhanden ist" (*Die Geschichte der synoptischen Tradition* [Göttingen: Vandenhoeck & Ruprecht, 1967⁷], p. 7).

2. According to Bultmann, the Sabbath saying of Mk. 2.27 may have been added by the evangelist to an original unit consisting of 2.23-26; alternatively, vv. 25-26 (the scriptural proof) may

Stories of healings or exorcisms are still less likely to have circulated in fixed verbal form. At the oral stage, certain stories of Jesus' encounters with his opponents or with those in need would take the form of *anecdotes,* in which freedom of individual performance combines with a more stable underlying structure.[3] Transmission of such stories is no doubt aided by a repertoire of typical situations in which Jesus is expected to be found. In the earliest Christian communities, there is a collective knowledge or "social memory" that Jesus engaged in debate with Pharisees in Galilee and with Sadducees in Jerusalem, and that these debates were often concerned with the interpretation and practice of the law. It is also known that Jesus practised an itinerant ministry; that he was normally accompanied by a group of disciples; that he achieved fame as a healer, exorcist, and teacher; that he was put to death in Jerusalem; and so on. This generalized knowledge is a precondition for its written articulation in discrete items of gospel narrative. Thus, it is known that Jesus was "obedient unto death," in the sense that he consciously accepted his destiny rather than being the unwilling victim of an unexpected fate; and this generalized communal knowledge is presupposed in the three Markan "passion predictions," where the evangelist has no traditional sayings at his disposal but shares the conviction that Jesus *must have* known what lay in store for him as he took the road to Jerusalem.[4] In the act of inscription, a generalized conviction of this kind is identified and given a particular narrative shaping, and this is no less valid as an articulation of the tradition than one in which a

---

have been interpolated into an original unit consisting of 2.23-24, 27 (*Geschichte*, pp. 14-15). As for Mk. 12.13-17, the apophthegm represents the original context of the concluding saying, and no editorial interventions are perceptible after v. 13 (p. 25). Here and elsewhere, Bultmann's analysis appears to point only to earlier *written* versions of the material in question. It is unlikely that the introductory passages (Mk. 2.23-24; 12.14-15a) are exact transcripts of a prior oral tradition.

3. The supposition that such stories were "performed" orally before they were put into writing is admittedly hypothetical, given that inscription can occur at any point between the life of Jesus and the composition of the gospels. According to J. D. G. Dunn, individual synoptic narratives may be seen as *transcripts* of such performances: in many cases, "the more natural explanation for the evidence is *not* Matthew's or Luke's literary dependence on Mark, but rather their own knowledge of oral retellings of the same stories (or, alternatively, their own oral retelling of the Markan stories)" (*Jesus Remembered* [Grand Rapids: Eerdmans, 2003], p. 222; italics original). But the retelling of the same story in different words is no less possible within a literary relationship than within an oral one. A primarily literary explanation seems plausible where a story is retold within its Markan sequence — although an additional influence from oral tradition cannot be ruled out. In spite of these qualifications, however, it remains possible to extrapolate from free literary retelling to a prior oral stage, and to see a tradition of oral retelling as the basis for its literary equivalent.

4. But cf. J. Jeremias's attempt to recover a traditional saying from the Markan passion predictions (*New Testament Theology*, Eng. trans. [London: SCM, 1971], pp. 281-86).

specific saying is inscribed more or less verbatim. In its prewritten form, the tradition must be as concerned with the general as with the particular. Indeed, an overarching construal of the basic shape and orientation of Jesus' ministry is logically prior to the discrete items incorporated into it.[5] Even the oldest and most straightforwardly "authentic" of such items is dependent on the comprehensive construal for its meaning and significance. The Lord's Prayer is transmitted not just as a form of words (attested in Matthew and the *Didache* and in abbreviated form in Luke) but also and above all as a prayer *taught by Jesus,* who (it is recollected) habitually gave authoritative instruction about appropriate and inappropriate human responses to the divine — other instances of which lie to hand. In due course, such instances may find their way into an early written Sayings Collection. Other texts may gather together traditions about Jesus' actions and destiny. Through inscription, tradition becomes conscious of itself. It becomes its own object of reflection.

The oral tradition presupposed in the gospels is the social memory of the general and the particular in the life of Jesus. That memory is initially constructed within the earliest Christian communities in Jerusalem, Judea, and Galilee, and communities founded in Antioch, Asia Minor, Rome, and elsewhere will have come to participate in it later. We may assume that authoritative figures such as "the Twelve" played a major role in the shaping of social memory, but that they did so in a context in which general knowledge about Jesus' career was initially fairly widespread. We should also assume that the social memory has a pragmatic dimension and was constructed in the context of communal practices such as teaching, worship, controversy, initiation, scriptural interpretation, mutual aid, and ethical formation. Such practices represent the *Sitz im Leben* or "life-context" for the memory, although it is equally true that the life-context is itself already shaped by the memory. Baptism was presumably the context for the recollection that Jesus was baptized by John; but that remembered event was itself the basis for the ongoing practice of baptism. The life of the earliest communities is permeated by the remembered life of Jesus.

Jesus' sayings or actions are initially preserved as social memory and subsequently reduced to writing. Writing itself must have its *Sitz im Leben* within the early church. In general terms, writing bestows a degree of stabil-

---

5. In its own way, form criticism acknowledges the role of the general by placing the "Urelemente," "Einzelstücke," or "kleine Einheiten" of the synoptic tradition in generic categories which also correspond to certain types of content: controversies, miracles, parables, the passion, etc. (For the terminology cited, see Bultmann, *Geschichte,* p. 3; M. Dibelius, *Die Formgeschichte des Evangeliums* [Tübingen: Mohr-Siebeck, 1959³], p. 3.)

ity; it ensures preservation; it enhances communication. If the earliest Christian writings were informal, nonliterary Sayings Collections, their life-context was probably the increasing temporal and spatial distance between an expanding community and the time and place of Jesus' own activity. A written text that might have been superfluous in Jerusalem in the early 30s CE might be highly necessary a few years later in Antioch or Rome. Such collections were probably intended for teaching purposes and would not be formally read in the context of communal worship. That role was no doubt reserved for scripture, and these Christian writings were not yet "scripture." Since the Pauline letter *was* intended to be formally read (cf. 1 Thes. 5.27), the origin of a distinctively Christian "scripture" may be found there rather than in early collections of material relating to Jesus.

Inscription presupposes social memory or tradition, and memory presupposes the original datum that is the content of the memory. Jesus is baptized by John the Baptist, in the river Jordan, somewhere around the year 30 CE. It is later recollected that this event took place in the context of the ongoing practice of baptism. Those who recollect are above all the leaders of the earliest community, who have attained their leadership roles precisely because of their prior relationship with Jesus and their authoritative recollection of what he said and did.[6] They are the crucial link between the community and Jesus, uniquely positioned to determine the shaping of the present in the light of the remembered past and so to reshape the past in the light of the present. The "social memory" that is tradition begins with individual memories and is extended to the whole community as these memories are communicated. Subsequently, the memory is given a degree of verbal stability as it is articulated in writing, in the context of Mark or some proto-Mark or Sayings Collection. This original written account may be interpreted and reinterpreted by later evangelists, some of whose renderings are ultimately acknowledged as normative whereas others are not.

Thus the process of reception takes the following sevenfold form:

Datum → *recollection* → *tradition* → *inscription* → *interpretation* → *reinterpretation* → *normativization*

---

6. For Paul, in a particular polemical context, these leaders are "reputed to be pillars," although "what they once were [ὁποῖοί ποτε ἦσαν] is of no significance to me" (Gal. 2.9, 6). The majority opinion from which Paul here dissents is that James, Peter, and John are "pillars" by virtue of "their personal relation to Jesus while he was in the flesh, in the case of James as his brother, in the case of Peter and John as his personal followers" (E. de W. Burton, *A Critical and Exegetical Commentary on the Letter to the Galatians*, ICC [Edinburgh: T. & T. Clark, 1921], p. 87).

(1) *Datum.* The term refers to the necessary correlate and origin of reception. What is received must first be given. Reception is not pure construction; it is a response to the prior event in which the giving takes place. Reception participates in the event and cannot be sharply differentiated from it, but it does not initiate the event. At each point, from recollection through to normativization, reception responds to the initiative and impetus of the datum. What is given is not an unknown *x* that falls back into obscurity after occasioning a construction process with its own self-generated momentum. Nor is the datum given and received once for all; rather, giving and receiving occur in an ongoing process of initiative and response. The presence of the datum to recollection (in the earliest communities in Jerusalem, Judea, and Galilee) differs from its presence to reinterpretation (in the gospels of Thomas or John), but at each point the datum is nonetheless present. Rather than receding ever further into a lost past, its presence is the presence of its past. Jesus addressed his sayings and parables to his disciples, but as "the living Jesus" *(GTh)* he continues to speak what he once spoke.

This crucial correlation of datum and reception is noted by Paul Tillich, according to whom "the event on which Christianity is based has two sides: the fact which is called 'Jesus of Nazareth' and the reception of this fact by those who received him as the Christ."[7] As Tillich implies, the critical distinction between the two sides marks a significant advance in the *theological* interpretation of the gospels — in spite of the rhetoric of negation that sometimes accompanies it. If the early Christian interpretation of Jesus is viewed as reception, and if receiving corresponds to a prior act of giving, then there is no need to oppose "the historic biblical Christ" to the "so-called historical Jesus."[8] On the contrary, the demonstrable historicity of Jesus — *that* he existed and *how* he existed — is a necessary though not sufficient condition for the validity of the theological claim that Jesus is "given."[9] Concern with the historicity of Jesus only becomes problematic where the his-

---

7. Paul Tillich, *Systematic Theology 2: Existence and the Christ* (Chicago: University of Chicago Press, 1957), p. 97.

8. Stemming from Martin Kähler, this opposition has been reasserted by Luke Timothy Johnson: see his *The Real Jesus: The Misguided Quest for the Historical Jesus and the Truth of the Traditional Gospels* (San Francisco: HarperCollins, 1997).

9. For the role of historical Jesus scholarship in asserting the historicity of Jesus, see Schweitzer's survey of the controversy evoked by A. Drews's "Christ-myth" theory (*Geschichte der Leben-Jesu-Forschung* [Tübingen: Mohr-Siebeck, 1913^2], pp. 444-564; Eng. trans. *The Quest of the Historical Jesus: First Complete Edition* [London: SCM Press, 2000], pp. 355-436).

torical Jesus and the early church are seen as two separate and autonomous entities, divided rather than united by the Easter event.

(2) *Recollection.* Through reception the datum makes itself present, and it does not do so apart from recollection. In principle a living Jesus can be manifested directly and without recollection, as in the Johannine apocalypses.[10] Yet gospels are not apocalypses. The roots of the difference may be traced back to the earliest Christian communities, where Jesus is the object not only of eschatological anticipation and present experience but also and above all of recollection. Leadership roles in those communities are taken by those with close ties to Jesus, whether as disciples or as family members. Their authority rests on their ability to transmit and validate traditions of what Jesus said and did, thereby making him present again in spite of his bodily absence: "The one who receives you receives me, and the one who receives me receives the one who sent me" (Mt. 10.40). These leaders are variously known as "the Twelve" (1 Cor. 15.5), "the apostles" (1 Cor. 9.5; 15.7; Gal. 1.19), "the pillars" (Gal. 2.9), "the brothers of the Lord" (1 Cor. 9.5), "those who heard [the Lord]" (Heb. 2.3), or "those who from the beginning were eyewitnesses and ministers of the word" (Lk. 1.2). Communicating what they have seen and heard is integral to their leadership roles, and this requires them to *recollect* whatever will promote the upbuilding of the community. Thus an initial core of traditions comes into being, grounded in the corporate recollection of the earliest Christian leadership.

Purely individual recollections, in the form of traditions connected to specific named disciples, are conspicuously absent — *pace* Richard Bauckham, who finds evidence of individual transmission in Papias's ascription of traditions to named disciples, in the synoptic naming of individuals outside the circle of the Twelve, and in the prominence of Peter in Mark.[11] Yet Bauckham also rightly insists on the role of the Twelve in the transmission of the sayings and stories of Jesus.[12] This role may indeed have been in-

---

10. Rv. 1; *ApJn* 3.

11. Richard Bauckham, *Jesus and the Eyewitnesses: The Gospels as Eyewitness Testimony* (Grand Rapids: Eerdmans, 2006), pp. 12-38 (Papias), pp. 39-66 (synoptic naming), pp. 124-27, 155-82 (Peter in Mark).

12. "The status of the Twelve in relation to the renewed people of God explains their authoritative status in the early church. . . . It is not difficult to imagine that their role in the earliest Christian community would include that of authoritative transmitters of the sayings of Jesus and authoritative eyewitnesses of the events of Jesus' history. If any group in the earliest community was responsible for some kind of formulation and authorization of a body of Jesus traditions, the Twelve are much the most obviously likely to have been that group" (Bauckham, *Jesus and the Eyewitnesses,* pp. 96-97).

tended by Jesus himself, if what was later recollected corresponded to what had earlier been memorized; for, as a Jewish wisdom teacher, Jesus seems to have encapsulated his teaching in "carefully crafted aphorisms" with the intention that they should be remembered.[13] Jesus' relationship to the Twelve is that of the teacher to μαθηταί, students or learners, and we must assume that this teaching took place so that what was taught might be retained, acted upon, and communicated. It is indeed possible that "a formal transmission of Jesus' teaching by authorized tradents, his disciples, began already during Jesus' ministry."[14] The disciples communicate not only what they have heard but also what they have seen, and Bauckham envisages a formalizing of narrative traditions about Jesus after Easter, in place of the informal transmission that must have occurred during his ministry.[15] In any given case, it is impossible to know how far a saying or story rests on an underlying recollection, and what the nature of that recollection may have been. The way from a specific recollection to its formalization as tradition may have been highly indirect. Yet recollection broadly understood is the only historically credible explanation for the overwhelming emphasis on the past that characterizes the earliest gospel literature.[16]

(3) *Tradition*. Recollection becomes social memory or tradition when shared by the whole community. As tradition, an item such as the Lord's Prayer loses its original association with the individuals who were taught it by Jesus himself and becomes communal property. The original disciple plays a crucial role in ensuring continuity between Jesus and the community, but that role is no longer required once continuity has been established. The original eyewitnesses and ministers of the word communicated their recollections "to us" (cf. Lk. 1.2), and thereafter their recollections are indeed "ours," in the form of communal tradition. It is on that basis that written accounts of the life of Jesus come into being (cf. Lk. 1.1). Luke does not suggest that he and other writers have direct access to the eyewitnesses; these writers are indeed dependent on eyewitnesses, but only indirectly so. The eyewitness may retain a certain prestige in the communities to which he or she belongs, but the role is essentially a self-effacing one. In earlier gospel literature specific traditions are never traced to individual disciples, and this must reflect the anonymizing tendency of the earliest tradition itself and the corporate

13. Bauckham, *Jesus and the Eyewitnesses*, p. 282.
14. Bauckham, *Jesus and the Eyewitnesses*, p. 285.
15. Bauckham, *Jesus and the Eyewitnesses*, p. 285.
16. On this often overlooked point, see also Eugene E. Lemcio, *The Past of Jesus in the Gospels*, SNTSMS (Cambridge: Cambridge University Press, 1991).

recollection in which it originates. It is only at a later stage — in Papias, in the later redactions of John and Thomas, and in gospel titles — that specific traditions are connected with individual named disciples.

Luke's prologue already implies that tradition plays a mediating role between recollection and inscription, and it is the enduring achievement of "form criticism" to have brought this role into explicit consideration. It is true that, in Bultmann's version of this project, tradition does not mediate recollection but forms a virtual barrier against it. For Bultmann it is the needs of the early church that generate the tradition, and genuine recollection is preserved only incidentally and not because remembering Jesus was of any inherent importance. In consequence of this astonishingly one-sided yet influential account, eyewitness recollection and communal tradition are often seen as mutually exclusive alternatives: the gospels arise *either* from eyewitness recollection *or* from communal tradition, but not from *both*.[17] Yet there is no need for any such choice. An account that traces tradition back to recollection and recollection forward to tradition is proposed by Martin Dibelius:

> We must suppose that Jesus' words and stories of his life and death were kept alive in the circle of his disciples. If gospels written over a generation later are to be linked with these primary traditions [*Überlieferungs-Elementen*], we must ask how recollections preserved in the oldest congregations were disseminated, how they gained a certain stability of external and internal structure if not of precise wording, and above all what interests guided this process of dissemination and stabilization.[18]

It is the concept of "form" that best describes the transition from recollection to tradition.[19] According to Dibelius, the evangelists collected and connected independent units of tradition that already possessed a formal

---

17. See Bauckham, *Jesus and the Eyewitnesses*, pp. 290-318. Contrary to the form-critical attribution of the tradition to "the community as a collective," traditions were "originated and formulated by named eyewitnesses, . . . who remained the living and active guarantors of the traditions" (p. 290). It is typical of the English-language reception of *Formgeschichte* that for Bauckham form criticism and Bultmann are virtually synonymous.

18. Dibelius, *Formgeschichte*, p. 9 (my translation). The English translation of Dibelius's work (*From Tradition to Gospel* [London: Nicholson & Watson, 1934]) is unfortunately inadequate.

19. The difference at this point between Dibelius and Bultmann is rightly noted by Martin Hengel (*The Four Gospels and the One Gospel of Jesus Christ*, Eng. trans. [London: SCM Press, 2000], pp. 80, 144, 293-94).

structure. Whether by purely oral means or with the aid of writing, the tradition avails itself of a range of *Gattungen* or genres and thereby mediates between the original unformed recollections and the later gospel narratives. Tradition is simply *geformte Erinnerung* ("formed recollection"), and the reduction to form of an original *gestaltlose Erinnerungsschätze* ("repository of unstructured recollections") is occasioned by the needs of Christian mission and instruction.[20]

(4) *Inscription.* Use of this term is intended to highlight the moment at which an element in the tradition is given its first written expression. Inscription may occur at any point on the time line between the formation of the earliest Christian communities and the composition of narrative gospels. It may occur early on, as the compiler of a primitive Sayings Collections writes for the first time the text that came to be known as "the Parable of the Sower." But it may also occur much later, wherever an evangelist is himself the author of a particular story or saying. In either case, and whatever the degree of creativity exercised, inscription is the articulation of prior tradition. Even an entirely new story or saying will employ traditional motifs in giving fresh expression to what is already believed. The tradition that precedes inscription may already have been influenced by earlier textual articulations of related material. It is unlikely that an independent item of oral tradition will remain unaffected by the encounter with a written version of the same item; rather, it will tend to be assimilated to the written form. Thus, later evangelists inherit not only prior texts but also a tradition already permeated by textuality. A later gospel may be indirectly influenced by its predecessors even where there is no direct relationship of dependence.

Oral and textualized traditions are characterized by an ongoing dynamic interaction. Where a tradition is written, it is re-oralized whenever it is read and heard. In its new textual-oral form, it may be the occasion for new writing either indirectly or directly dependent on the old. There is no reason to suppose that oral traditions "that crossed the threshold to textuality were forced out of circulation and frozen into a static condition," as Werner Kelber has argued.[21] Writing is only frozen and static so long as it

---

20. Dibelius, *Formgeschichte*, pp. 12-13.

21. W. Kelber, *The Oral and the Written Gospel: The Hermeneutics of Speaking and Writing in the Synoptic Tradition, Mark, Paul, and Q* (Bloomington & Indianapolis: Indiana University Press, 1997²), p. 94. More recently, Kelber has conceded that orality and textuality interact with one another and that the very existence of a purely oral tradition uncontaminated by textuality is questionable ("The Oral-Scribal-Memorial Arts of Communication in Early Christianity," in *Jesus, the Voice, and the Text: Beyond the Oral and the Written Gospel*, ed. Tom Thatcher [Waco, TX: Baylor

remains unread. Nor is it appropriate to speak of "*Mark's* disruption of the oral lifeworld," as though writing the gospel tradition were a Markan innovation.[22] On the contrary, Mark's text in its present form is the product of an extended prehistory in which earlier text-forms were subjected to further editing and supplementation.[23] Although later in its present form, the *Gospel of Thomas* derives from pre-Markan Sayings Collections that may have contained written material as old as the Christian community itself. There is no "great divide" between gospel traditions in oral and written form. Even prior to inscription, the tradition will have displayed text-like characteristics of stability and iterability.[24]

(5) *Interpretation.* In one sense "interpretation" already occurs when an original datum is recollected and preserved as tradition, or when tradition is articulated through inscription. Even individual memory may be said to interpret, and that is still more the case when memory is corporate and social and when it is objectified in textual form. At this stage, however, "interpretation" can hardly be distinguished from its object. It is only where an earlier text is interpreted in a later one that the distinction is preserved and the nature of the interpretative act comes to light. When Mark assembles his parables of growth from a Thomas-like Sayings Collection, he *interprets* them as he sets them in a narrative context and employs a variety of means to draw out their fuller significance. When Luke extracts material from Matthew's Sermon on the Mount and reincorporates it in new contexts and juxtapositions, the outcome is an *interpretation* of the Matthean material. The object

University Press, 2008], pp. 235-62; p. 246). Yet Kelber's rhetoric is still shaped by a bias against textuality and by a propensity to argue on the basis of broad cultural generalizations.

22. Kelber, *Oral and Written Gospel*, p. 91; my italics. For a critique of Kelber's reading of Mark, see Joanna Dewey, "The Gospel of Mark as Oral Hermeneutics," in *Jesus, the Voice, and the Text*, pp. 71-87. But Dewey's account is still influenced by the assumption that speech and writing are fundamentally opposed to one another.

23. For literature on pre-Markan sources and traditions, see W. R. Telford, *Writing on the Gospel of Mark* (Blandford Forum: Deo Publishing, 2009), pp. 338-41.

24. According to Jan Assmann, "[t]exts are speech acts in the context of extended communication situations," requiring "acts of storage, transmission, and reproduction" that may or may not take written form ("Form as a Mnemonic Device: Cultural Texts and Cultural Memory," in *Performing the Gospel: Orality, Memory, and Mark*, ed. Richard A. Horsley, Jonathan A. Draper, and John Miles Foley [Minneapolis: Fortress, 2006], pp. 67-82; p. 75). Assmann distinguishes this pragmatic understanding of the text from the traditional correlation of *textus* and *commentarius*, in which "[t]extus is what a *commentarius* refers to, and *commentarius* is the kind of discourse that has a *textus* as its object" (p. 74). Assmann's account is a valuable corrective to antithetical accounts of the speech/writing relationship. I would myself prefer to view the text as a *written* artefact and to speak of "text-like" features of oral tradition.

of interpretation is in the first instance the text, but ultimately it is Jesus himself — Jesus as previously received in recollection, tradition, and inscription. Interpretation intends to move *towards* Jesus rather than away from him, and that remains the case even and precisely where the interpretative reshaping seems most radical. Each moment of the reception process marks a return to Jesus in a new mode.

No less than later evangelists, Mark is "a creative shaper of inherited tradition."[25] Joel Marcus's formulation of the characteristic redaction-critical programme intends to emphasize both the continuity and the discontinuity between the evangelist and his tradition. On the one hand, Mark is "constrained by the memories of Jesus' words and deeds that have been passed down to him in the church." On the other hand, "he has not reproduced these memories mechanically, but has elaborated them creatively to address the situation of his own time and place."[26] Mark, then, is neither the "totally unfettered author" imagined by some recent scholars, nor the "conservative redactor" envisaged by others.[27] True though this may be, however, it is less than adequate to locate the need for interpretation ("creative shaping") in a tension between the constraints of the past and the demands of a qualitatively different present. Interpretation arises out of the dynamic of the tradition itself, its own demand for fresh articulation in new situations.

(6) *Reinterpretation.* Interpretation is not just a single event but is also an ongoing process. The Markan parables of growth already incorporate at least two distinct interpretative stages: the addition of a detailed key to the first of these parables, and the subsequent insertion of the passage on the mystery of the kingdom of God. The Matthean redaction represents a further stage in the interpretation of this material. Similarly distinct stages came to light in the analysis of John 5: an original healing story is initially interpreted in the context of a Sabbath controversy, which is then subordinated to a christological controversy in a subsequent redactional layer. In this case, unlike the Matthean one, the later interpretation is characterized by its *discontinuity* with the earlier one. It is true that the Johannine redactional process preserves elements of continuity, and that discontinuities might also be identified in the Matthean redaction. The difference is one of degree only. Yet, where a secondary interpretation represents a more

---

25. Joel Marcus, *Mark: A New Translation with Introduction and Commentary,* 2 vols., AYB (New Haven & London: Yale University Press, 2000-2009), 1.59.

26. Marcus, *Mark,* 1.59.

27. Marcus, *Mark,* 1.60, 61.

or less radical reworking of an earlier one, it may be described as a *reinter-pretation*. Reinterpretation highlights again the disruptive element in the reception process, its resistance to closure and its ongoing quest for a more adequate articulation of Jesus' significance as understood by an evangelist and his interpretative community.

(7) *Normativization.* Interpretation and reinterpretation of earlier written tradition proliferate, and no single rendering of the tradition attains definitive status. In itself this need not be a problem. New gospel literature is produced in response to the demands of a growing Christian public, and there is no reason in principle why its proliferation should be an issue. From a precanonical perspective, early Christian gospel literature may be viewed as a single field within which an indefinite number of closely related texts circulate freely, eventually to be ascribed to Matthew or Peter, Mark or Mary, Luke or James, John or Thomas. Yet, at a certain point and for reasons that have yet to be clarified, a dividing line is retrospectively imposed on this single literary field, separating texts that previously coexisted in relative proximity to one another. Normativization is not just a pragmatic response to contingencies, but rather the production of a new textual object. The fourfold canonical gospel establishes a new field for the play of interpretation and reinterpretation, the object of which is not just the text as such but above all its protagonist, Jesus of Nazareth. He is the datum whose reception reaches its provisional, contested, yet (for many) definitive conclusion in the canonical decision.

Normativization will be the theme of Part Three of this work. In the present chapter we continue to focus on the precanonical phase of the reception process, when the datum handed down by tradition is subject to ongoing interpretation and reinterpretation within the single undivided field of early Christian gospel writing. As defined here, reinterpretation occurs in gospels later divided by the canonical boundary yet previously united in a concern to articulate the deeper meaning of the common tradition and its literary embodiments. Irrespective of the canonical boundary, reinterpretation can occur in parallel. As the three following studies will show, John, Thomas, and Peter engage with the same already-interpreted traditions, yet reinterpret them differently. That difference does not in itself establish the canonical boundary, which in its own way embraces and preserves difference rather than excluding it. Yet the boundary does at least invite reflection on theological differences that come to light as canonical and noncanonical texts are viewed in comparative perspective.

Seeking and Finding

In Matthew and Luke, the saying "Seek and you will find" occurs not in isolation but in the larger context of a repeated three-part instruction on prayer:

> a^1 Ask and it will be given you, a^2 seek and you will find, a^3 knock and it will be opened to you. b^1 For everyone who asks receives, b^2 and the one who seeks finds, b^3 and to the one who knocks it will be opened. (Mt. 7.7-8 = Lk. 11.9-10)

The three pairings *(ask/give[receive], seek/find, knock/open)* occur in two versions, with the imperatives of the first replaced by indicative statements in the second. There follows the assurance that the heavenly Father will give the "good gifts" requested, just as an earthly father will give bread, a fish, or an egg, rather than a malevolent substitute, when asked by his son (Mt. 7.9-11; Lk. 11.11-13). Here, asking and receiving take precedence over seeking and finding, knocking and being admitted. The second and third pairings serve to reinforce the first with the aid of synonyms. Asking is metaphorically identified with seeking and knocking, giving or receiving with finding and gaining entry.

The *seek/find* pairing can also exist on its own, without direct reference to prayer. This is clear from the Matthean parable in which a merchant *seeks* fine pearls and *finds* a single pearl of great price, which he acquires by selling all (Mt. 13.45-46). In Thomas's version of this parable, a wise merchant *finds* a pearl at the same time as he receives a "cargo" or "load" (ϤΟΡΤΙΟΝ) of goods belonging to himself — which he then sells in order to obtain the pearl (*GTh* 76.1-2). The point is that he chooses the pearl, which becomes available unexpectedly, at the expense of the goods in which he normally deals. This merchant is an exception to the normal rule that "businessmen and merchants will not enter my Father's realms" (*GTh* 64.12). Thomas's parable of the pearl is interpreted by way of a saying that occurs in different contexts in Matthew and Luke, to which the motif of "seeking" has been added: "You too *seek* his unfailing and enduring treasure . . ." (*GTh* 76.3; cf. Mt. 6.20; Lk. 12.33).[28]

---

28. In view of Thomas's interest in the "seeking" motif, its absence from the parable itself suggests that this version may be independent of Matthew's — contra W. Schrage, *Das Verhältnis des Thomas-Evangeliums zur synoptischen Tradition und zu den koptischen Evangelienübersetzungen* (Berlin: Töpelmann, 1964), p. 157. According to Schrage, the reference to "treasure" (76.3) may show

Elsewhere in the Coptic *GTh*, "Seek and you will find" occurs in no less than three affirmative versions and one negative one.[29] It will be convenient to consider these passages in reverse order:

(1) *GTh* 94 Jesus [sai]d: "The one who *seeks* will *find,* [the one who knock]s, they will open to him."
(2) *GTh* 92 Jesus said: "*Seek* and you will *find.* But the things you asked me about formerly and I did not tell you at that time, now I wish to tell them and you do not *seek* them."
(3) *GTh* 38 Jesus said: "Many times you have desired to hear these words which I speak to you, and you have no one else from whom to hear them. There will be days when you will *seek* me and will not *find* me."
(4) *GTh* 2 Jesus said: "Let the one who *seeks* not cease his *seeking* until he *finds;* and when he finds he will be troubled; and when he is troubled he will wonder; and he will reign over all."[30]

In each case, parallel interpretative processes are found in the Gospel of John. These parallels can be used to shed light on the phenomenon of *re-interpretation* — the more or less radical recasting of material that has already attained relatively stable literary form in earlier texts. Since *GTh* preserves material from various stages in the history of reception, it is particularly well suited to illustrate the often obscure distinctions between inscription, interpretation, and reinterpretation.[31]

---

an awareness of the Matthean link with the parable of the hidden treasure (*GTh* 109; cf. Mt. 13.44-46). If so, Thomas's separation of two thematically linked parables would have to be explained.

29. The view that these variants stem from oral tradition is rightly criticized by Simon Gathercole, on the grounds that textual transmission may be no less fluid than oral (*The Composition of the Gospel of Thomas: Original Language and Influences*, SNTSMS [Cambridge: Cambridge University Press, 2012], pp. 215-18).

30. Compare *P. Oxy.* 654: Jesus says: "Let the one who seek[s not cease seeking until] he finds; and when he finds [he will wonder; and won]dering he will reign; an[d reigning he will rest]." On this passage see also Chapter 5, above. In the Coptic version, ⲠⲦⲎⲢϤ probably represents τὰ πάντα (as in Jn. 1.3; etc.), and should be translated "all" or "all things" rather than "the All."

31. This comparison between John and Thomas is concerned to demonstrate parallel locations within the reception process, and is not dependent on any specific hypothesis about historical connections between these evangelists and their communities. Such hypotheses have been various; the following are representative examples. (1) In an article dating from 1962, Raymond Brown argued that Thomas is "ultimately (but still indirectly) dependent on John itself," a dependence mediated by the gnosticizing source(s) underlying the nonsynoptic material in this gospel ("The Gospel of Thomas and St. John's Gospel," *NTS* 9 [1962-63], pp. 155-77; p. 176). (2) An opposing view was maintained in 1992 by Stevan Davies, for whom *GTh* is "a text from the Christian

(1) *GTh* 94 might be seen as an abbreviation of the second of the matching three-part sayings of Matthew and Luke, in which the imperatives of the first are replaced by indicatives.[32] The *seek/find* and *knock/open* pairings are retained; the omission of the *ask/receive* pairing may reflect this evangelist's negative attitude towards prayer (cf. *GTh* 6.1-3, 14.2, 104.1-3). Yet *Saying* 94 may also be understood as adding the *knock/open* pairing to the otherwise independent *seek/find* pairing attested (in the imperative version) in *Saying* 92. The addition may reflect Matthean influence, along with the substitution of the indicative version for the imperative, but the continued emphasis on *seek/find* reflects the independent sayings traditions underlying Thomas itself.[33] The variants in *GTh* suggest that "Seek and you will find" was preserved as an independent saying in an early Sayings Collection, and that its incorporation into a doubled three-part saying may have been due to Matthew.

The original independence of the *seek/find* pairing is also suggested by its background in the wisdom tradition. Wisdom promises her devotees:

> I love those who love me, and those who *seek* me will *find* [me]. (Prov. 8.17)[34]

---

community that, in a later decade, produced the Gospel of John" ("The Christology and Protology of the Gospel of Thomas," *JBL* 111 [1992], pp. 663-82; p. 682). (3) In a monograph dating from 1995, Gregory Riley argued on the basis of the negative Johannine portrayal of Thomas (cf. Jn. 11.16; 14.5-7; 20.24-29) that the Johannine and Thomasine communities were engaged in controversy with one another about the physical reality of resurrection. As *Saying* 71 indicates, *GTh* is an "early witness to a Christianity which did not accept physical resurrection" (*Resurrection Reconsidered: Thomas and John in Controversy* [Minneapolis: Fortress, 1995], p. 154). (4) A similar "mirror-reading" of the doubting Thomas episode led April DeConick to argue that, "[f]or Johannine Christians, faith in Jesus was the basis of their salvation, whereas for the Thomasine Christians, the mystical visionary encounter was paramount" (*Voices of the Mystics: Early Christian Discourse in the Gospels of John and Thomas and Other Ancient Christian Literature*, JSNTSupp [Sheffield: Sheffield Academic Press, 2001], p. 84). (5) According to Elaine Pagels, John identifies Jesus exclusively with the divine light whereas for Thomas he participates in the light along with the whole of humanity (*Beyond Belief: The Secret Gospel of Thomas* [New York: Random House, 2003], p. 40); the theological controversy again comes to a head in the doubting Thomas episode (pp. 69-73).

32. Cf. Robert M. Grant with David Noel Freedman, *The Secret Sayings of Jesus according to the Gospel of Thomas* (London & Glasgow: Collins, 1960), pp. 174-75; Schrage, *Verhältnis*, p. 181; Michael Fieger, *Das Thomasevangelium: Einleitung, Kommentar, Systematik* (Münster: Aschendorff, 1991), p. 242.

33. Arguing against Schrage, April DeConick sees Matthean influence only at the level of the Coptic translations (*The Original Gospel of Thomas in Translation* [London & New York: T. & T. Clark, 2007], p. 266). This is puzzling, given that the Sahidic translation of Mt. 7.8bc actually *differs* from *GTh* 94 at three points (see Schrage, *Verhältnis*, p. 181, where the texts are set out in parallel).

34. MT: ‫ומשחרי ימצאנני‬ LXX: οἱ δὲ ἐμὲ ζητοῦντες εὑρήσουσιν.

A later writer elaborates this passage:

Radiant and unfading is Wisdom, and she is easily beheld by those who love her and *found* by those who *seek* her. (Wis. 6.12)[35]

Later still, Tertullian knows "Seek and you will find" as an independent saying. In the context of an attempt to explain the origins of "heresy," he writes:

I come now to the passage which our own people allege for entering into inquiry [*ad ineundam curiositatem*] and which heretics utilize for bringing in doubt [*ad importandam scrupulositatem*]. It is written, they say, "Seek and you will find."[36]

For Tertullian, this use of Jesus' saying is dangerous, suggesting that Christians do not already possess the truth but must still seek for it. He argues that the saying was uttered early in Jesus' ministry, when he was not yet acknowledged as the Christ, and that its meaning is clarified by the words addressed to a Jewish audience in John 5.39: "Search the scriptures, in which you hope for salvation, for it is they that speak of me."[37] To *seek* is to search the scriptures, to *find* is to discover that they bear witness to Christ. Since Jesus' sayings were initially addressed to Jewish hearers and have reached us "through Jewish ears," we should not assume that they apply directly to us.[38] For Christians, seeking lies in the past. Their calling is not to seek new truth but to hold fast the old truth summed up in the "Rule of Faith." The woman who lost one of her ten coins did not continue to seek once she had found it.[39] Tertullian's interpretation of Jesus' saying assumes a wider context within a narrative gospel and a more specific context between the two other injunctions of Matthew 7.7: "Ask and you will receive" and "Knock and it

---

35. . . . . καὶ εὑρίσκεται ὑπὸ τῶν ζητούντων αὐτήν. The relevance of these passages from Wisdom literature for the interpretation of *GTh* is rightly emphasized by Stevan Davies, *The Gospel of Thomas and Christian Wisdom* (California: Bardic Press, 2005²), pp. 36-40.

36. Tertullian, *De Praescr.* 8.1-2 (R. Refoulé, *Traité de la prescription contre les hérétiques*, SC [Paris: Éditions du Cerf, 1957]).

37. Tertullian, *De Praescr.* 8.3-6. Tertullian cites Jn. 5.39 in a form that recalls *GEger* and the Old Latin: "Scrutamini scripturas in quibus salutem speratis; illae enim de me loquuntur."

38. "Omnia quidem dicta Domini omnibus posita sunt, per aures Iudaeorum ad nos transierunt sed pleraque in personas directa, non proprietatem admonitionis nobis constituerunt, sed exemplum" (Tertullian, *De Praescr.* 8.16).

39. Tertullian, *De Praescr.* 11.4.

shall be opened to you."[40] Tertullian goes to such lengths to contextualize the *seek/find* saying precisely because it is in circulation (among both *nostri* and *haeretici*) as a freestanding saying addressed directly to later generations of Jesus' followers.

If this is correct, then *GTh* 92 and 94 derive ultimately from an old Sayings Collection in which Jesus was reported as saying simply: "Seek and you will find." In *Saying* 94, secondary Matthean influence has led to the substitution of the indicative for the imperative version and the addition of the *knock/open* pairing to *seek/find*.

The first of the three Matthean pairs occurs in two versions: *ask/give* (αἰτεῖτε καὶ δοθήσεται ὑμῖν) and *ask/receive* (πᾶς γὰρ ὁ αἰτῶν λαμβάνει).[41] Absent from Thomas, both versions occur in John 16.23b-24:

> Amen, amen, I say to you, whatever you ask [αἰτήσητε] the Father in my name, he will give you [δώσει ὑμῖν]. Until now you have not asked anything in my name. Ask and you will receive [αἰτεῖτε καὶ λήμψεσθε], so that your joy may be full.

To the Matthean pairings are added a Johannine introductory formula (possibly reflecting Luke's addition of "And I say to you . . ." [Lk. 11.9]), references to "the Father" as the one to whom asking is directed, Jesus' name as the basis for this asking, and joy as the consequence of receiving. While dependent like *GTh* 94 on the Matthew passage, the Johannine passage is concerned to develop its teaching on prayer. Along with "Seek and you will find," "Ask and it will be given you" may have been available to Matthew as an independent saying.[42]

(2) In *GTh* 92, "Seek and you will find" is followed by the complaint that "the things you asked me about formerly and I did not tell you at that time, now I wish to tell them and you do not seek them."[43] There is no trace here of the (probably earlier) Matthean and Lukan interpretation of the original saying, which incorporates it into a larger complex in which seeking is un-

---

40. Tertullian, *De Praescr.* 8.7-13.

41. Mt. 7.7a, 8a = Lk. 11.9aβ, 10a.

42. Cf. C. H. Dodd, *Historical Tradition in the Fourth Gospel* (Cambridge: Cambridge University Press, 1963), p. 350. But Dodd contrasts the Johannine λήμψεσθε with Matthew's δοθήσεται, failing to note that Matthew also attests λαμβάνει and John δώσει.

43. "Formerly" and "at that time" translate N̄NI2OOY and M̄ΦOOY ETM̄MAY (= ἐν ἐκείναις ταῖς ἡμέραις and ἐν ἐκείνῃ τῇ ἡμέρᾳ).

derstood as prayer and finding as the divine answer to prayer. While the say-ing is presumably addressed to Jesus' disciples, this is not made explicit. The logia of *GTh* are normally introduced with the phrase "Jesus said," rather than "Jesus said to his disciples."[44] The disciples sometimes pose questions to which Jesus' sayings provide answers[45] and occasionally take part in more extended dialogues,[46] but there is little interest in their role as addressees of the sayings. It is the readers or hearers of *GTh* who are addressed by the words of the living Jesus. Even in *Saying* 92, where the allusion to the disci-ples is clear, readers or hearers of *GTh* are closely identified with them.

In *Saying* 92, the complaint (". . . now I wish to tell them and you do not seek them") serves to interpret the original saying. The new interpretation understands seeking and finding in terms of addressing questions to Jesus and receiving answers from him, rather than addressing requests to God and receiving from him the objects of those requests. The relationship between seeking and finding is problematized here: "Seek and you will find" is ad-dressed to those who previously sought yet did not find. Seeking does not lead immediately and inevitably to finding, for finding is entirely dependent on Jesus and will only take place when persistence in seeking coincides with his will to reveal. The original saying is interpreted in the light of an under-standing of Jesus as the revealer who may temporarily withhold revelation. Those who seek revelation's answers to their questions must continue to seek even in the face of Jesus' silence. This is not the perpetual seeking that will never find, criticized by Tertullian. The promise "and you will find" still remains valid. Yet finding is closely tied to the will and person of the revealer, and it seems unlikely that, even when his answers are forthcoming, they will bring the dialectic of seeking and finding to a close. It will not be possible to locate seeking and finding in the past, contrasting that past with a present marked by secure possession of a Rule of Faith.

The original saying is interpreted here in the light of the view that Jesus withheld his clearest revelations from his disciples until the very end of his time with them. More developed versions of this schema are found in texts

---

44. Outside contexts of dialogue, an explicit reference to the disciples as addressees occurs only in *Saying* 14, probably under the influence of 13.

45. The disciples ask questions — or make comments implying questions — in *GTh* 12.1 (who will be our leader?), 18.1 (our end?), 20.1 (the kingdom of heaven?), 24.1 (the place where you are?), 37.1 (when will you be revealed?), 43.1 (who are you?), 51.1 (the repose of the dead?), 52.1 (twenty-four prophets?), 53.1 (circumcision?), 99.1 (Jesus' family), and 113.1 (coming of kingdom?). Cf. the nonspecific "they" (91.1; 100.1) and the use of named disciples (21.1; 61.2; 114.1).

46. *GTh* 13, 22, 60, 61.

such as the *Gospel of Mary* and the *Apocryphon of James*, where it has deter-mined the form of these texts as "revelatory dialogues." Yet a closer parallel to *GTh* 92 is found in John 16.4b-5:

> I did not tell you these things from the beginning, because I was with you. But now I depart to the One who sent me, and none of you asks me, "Where are you going?"

As in *GTh*, the possibility of definitive revelation is reserved for the end of Jesus' time with his disciples; yet, at the very moment where the revelation becomes possible, the disciples fail to inquire after it.[47] Precisely at this point of convergence, however, the two gospels diverge again. In John the disciples' failure to inquire is not a problem, for Jesus' promise to speak clearly and de-finitively is unconditional:

> These things I have spoken to you in parables [ἐν παροιμίαις]. The hour is coming when I will no longer speak to you in parables, but will tell you openly about the Father. (Jn. 16.25)

For Thomas, the promised revelation requires the disciples to resume their former seeking or questioning. The problem is that at present the basis for a revelatory dialogue does not exist: questions once asked are asked no longer. For John, no questioning is necessary: "In that day you will inquire [ἐρωτήσετε] nothing of me" (Jn. 16.23a). There will be finding without seek-ing. This point is given remarkable emphasis in John 16, and, equally re-markably, it is juxtaposed with the Johannine evangelist's elaboration of the first Matthean pairing, *ask/give[receive]*. In John 16.23-30, sayings on revela-tion *(R)* alternate with sayings on prayer *(P)*:

---

47. There is no reason to accept the proposal of Grant and Freedman that *GTh* 92 is "a gar-bled version of John 16:4-5" (*Secret Sayings*, p. 175). In Jn. 16 the disciples' failure to ask conflicts with 13.36–14.31, where both Peter and Thomas ask where Jesus is going (13.36; 14.5). In view of other parallels between these sections of the Farewell Discourses, chapter 16 is often rightly seen as a variant of chapter 14. R. Schnackenburg views Jn. 16 as "a 're-reading' of the original farewell dis-course" (i.e. chapter 14): "[S]ince the evangelist hardly ever repeats himself in this way elsewhere in the gospel, this discourse is probably the editorial work of a disciple or disciples" (*The Gospel according to St. John*, 3 vols., Eng. trans. [London & Tunbridge Wells: Burns & Oates, 1968-82], 3.90, 91). C. K. Barrett resolves the apparent contradiction between 16.5 and 13.36, 14.5 by empha-sizing the present tense of ἐρωτᾷ in 16.5 (*The Gospel according to St. John* [London: SPCK, 1978²], pp. 485-86). But one does not comment on the failure to ask a question if that same question has already been twice asked and answered.

R¹ "And in that day you will inquire [ἐρωτήσετε] nothing of me." (Jn. 16.23a)

P¹ "Amen, amen, I say to you, whatever you ask [αἰτήσητε] the Father in my name, he will give you. Until now you have not asked anything in my name. Ask and you will receive, so that your joy may be full." (Jn. 16.23b-24)

R² "These things I have spoken to you in parables. The hour is coming when I will no longer speak to you in parables, but will tell you openly about the Father." (Jn. 16.25)

P² "In that day you will ask [αἰτήσεσθε] in my name, and I do not say to you that I will inquire [ἐρωτήσω] of the Father on your behalf. . . ." (Jn. 16.26)

R³ His disciples said: "Behold, now you are speaking openly and uttering no parable. Now we know that you know all things and have no need for anyone to inquire [ἐρωτᾷ] of you. . . ." (Jn. 16.29-30)

As we have seen, *P¹* elaborates the Matthean *ask/give[receive]* pairing. *P²* repeats the motif of prayer in Jesus' name. In contrast, the *R* passages speak of the final, decisive revelation that will bring to a close the time of veiled, parabolic speech. *GTh* 92 shares the view that the revelation must occur towards the end of Jesus' way rather than at the beginning, but emphasizes that revelation or "finding" must have its correlate in a human "seeking." Jesus will reveal himself by answering questions; no revelation will be forthcoming if the questions have ceased. In the negations of *R¹* and *R³*, that view is explicitly rejected.[48] The definitive revelation is not contingent on the disciples asking the right questions. It is not subject to possibly indefinite postponement. It will take place "in that day" *(R¹)*; its "hour is coming" *(R²)*; according to the disciples, it is occurring "now" *(R³)*.

There is a theological basis for this Johannine confidence in the reality of a revelation that sums up the entire significance of Jesus' fleshly presence in the world. In *R¹*, "that day" refers back to the promise of reunion after a brief absence: "A little while and you will no longer see me, and again a little

---

48. That does not mean that Jn. 16 responds *directly* to *GTh*, only that the evangelist is familiar with the point of view underlying *Saying* 92. The view that John is in direct conflict with Thomas is rightly rejected by Ismo Dunderberg, *The Beloved Disciple in Conflict? Revisiting the Gospels of John and Thomas* (Oxford: Oxford University Press, 2006), pp. 14-46.

while and you will see me" (Jn. 16.16). Just as the pains of labour give way to joy at the birth of a child, so the grief of Good Friday will be overtaken by the joy of Easter (cf. 16.17-22). It is, then, the event of Easter that constitutes Jesus' definitive revelation of the Father and the corresponding possibility of prayer to the Father in Jesus' name. Since the Easter event is in no sense contingent on the disciples' seeking or inquiring, the revelation takes place as promised.

(3) In *GTh* 92, "Seek and you will find" is subjected to a pessimistic reinterpretation that highlights a failure to grasp the right moment for seeking. Seeking and finding are out of step with each other; the real possibility of finding is put into doubt by the failure to seek. Equally pessimistic is *GTh* 38, where seeking is fruitless since it does *not* lead to finding:

> Jesus said: "Many times you have desired to hear these words which I speak to you, and you have no one else from whom to hear them. There will be days when you will *seek* me and you will *not find* me."

This saying is almost a mirror-image of *Saying* 92. There, Jesus did *not* speak his revelatory words in former times, but wishes to do so *now*. In *Saying* 38, Jesus *still* speaks his revelatory words, as in the past, but will cease to do so *in days to come*. In one case, the time of Jesus' silence lies in the past; in the other, in the future. In one case, the original saying is problematized: the former seeking will only lead to finding if it is now resumed. In the other case, the original saying is negated: you will seek, but you will *not* find.[49] The parallel with John 7.34-36 is remarkable:

> So Jesus said to them: "Yet a little while I am with you and I depart to the One who sent me. You will *seek* me and you will *not find* [me], and where I am you cannot come." The Jews said to each other: "Where will this man go, so that we will *not find* him? Will he go to the diaspora of the Greeks and teach the Greeks? What is this word that he spoke, 'You will *seek* me and you will *not find* [me], and where I am you cannot come'?"

In *GTh* 38 the negation of the original saying is apparently addressed to disciples, in John 7 to "the Jews," who at this point are confused by Jesus' saying but not explicitly hostile to him. Later, the Johannine evangelist too has

---

49. Compare Prv. 1.28, ζητήσουσιν με κακοὶ καὶ οὐχ εὑρήσουσιν (cf. Davies, *Thomas*, p. 95, though the reference is incorrectly given).

Jesus readdress the negated saying to the disciples. At the transition between the foot-washing scene and the farewell discourses, a dialogue takes place between Jesus and Peter (Jn. 13.33, 36):

> "Children, yet a little while I am with you. You will *seek* me, and as I said to the Jews, 'Where I am going you cannot come,' so now I say to you." . . . Simon Peter said to him, "Lord, where are you going?" Jesus answered him, "Where I am going you cannot now follow me, but you will follow later."

Following his departure, Jesus is inaccessible. He can be sought, but he will not be found: the two evangelists agree on this point. It is the role of the Johannine farewell discourses to show how this *prima facie* absence creates space for new modes of presence — in the advent of the Paraclete, or through mutual indwelling, or through the Easter event. In *GTh* 38, absence appears to be unqualified. Yet this pessimism about revelation as an ongoing possibility is not typical of the work as a whole. Indeed, it is the text itself that mediates the words of the living Jesus. While both evangelists appear to reinterpret the saying "Seek and you will find" in the most drastic way possible, by negating it, the negation occurs in the context of an absence/presence dialectic which mirrors the structure of the saying itself.

(4) The Johannine evangelist is less concerned to develop the original saying than is Thomas. In John 16, it is the Matthean *ask/give[receive]* pairing that is reinterpreted, in a way that retains the focus on prayer; a position closely resembling Thomas's reinterpretation of seeking and finding is explicitly rejected. The most direct allusions to the original saying occur in John 7 and 13, where it is negated. While that is also the case in *GTh* 38, Johannine parallels to the positive counterparts in *GTh* 92 and 94 are so far lacking.

In contrast, Thomas's fascination with the original saying is evident at the start of his gospel, in the elaborate extended form it takes in *Saying* 2. In *Saying* 1, what is to be "found" is the true interpretation (ⲍⲉⲣⲙⲉⲛⲉⲓⲁ) of Jesus' sayings, and *Saying* 2 can therefore be seen as the hermeneutical key to the entire gospel:

> Jesus said: "Let the one who seeks not cease his seeking until he finds; and when he finds he will be troubled; and when he is troubled he will wonder; and he will reign over all."

We learn here that seeking requires persistence. It is lack of that persistence that occasions the disjunction between seeking and finding of which

Saying 92 speaks. Through incessant *seeking,* one may hope to *find* the meaning of Jesus' words, which will be both troubling and wonderful. Finding that revelatory and life-giving meaning enables one to participate in Jesus' own transcendence of τὰ πάντα, the created order which originally issued forth from him (cf. *GTh* 77) and within which he appeared in flesh (cf. *GTh* 28).[50]

The Johannine evangelist does not share this hermeneutical soteriology. Yet the *seek/find* pairing does occur in his account of the earliest encounter between Jesus and his future disciples (Jn. 1.37-41):

> . . . And the two disciples heard [John] speaking, and they followed Jesus. Jesus turning and seeing them following said to them, "What do you *seek?*" They said to him, "Rabbi" (that is, "Teacher"), "where are you staying?" He said to them, "Come and see." So they came and saw where he was staying, and remained with him that day. (It was about the tenth hour.) Andrew the brother of Simon Peter was one of the two who heard John and followed [Jesus]. He first found his brother Simon and said to him, "We have *found* the Messiah" (that is, "Christ").

This narrative reinterpretation of the *seek/find* saying corresponds closely to Tertullian's insistence that the most fundamental seeking and finding has already taken place, in the recognition of Jesus as the Christ.[51]

If this analysis is broadly correct, the saying "Seek and you will find" exemplifies each of stages 4-6 of the model of reception outlined earlier:

[Datum → recollection → tradition →] inscription → interpretation → reinterpretation [→ normativization]

Inscription represents the moment when an element in the tradition is first articulated in writing. The original written context of the *seek/find* saying was no doubt a Sayings Collection, an early precursor of *GTh.* Evidence of the

---

50. According to Richard Valantasis, in *Saying* 2 "a seeking that ends in finding inaugurates a process of spiritual transformation, and this thematization of spiritual desire . . . constitutes the primary characterization of the subjectivity promulgated in these sayings" (*The Gospel of Thomas* [London & New York: Routledge, 1997], p. 172).

51. For the use of ζητεῖν and εὑρίσκειν in John, see Mark Stibbe, "The Elusive Christ: A New Reading of the Fourth Gospel," *JSNT* 44 (1991), pp. 19-38; pp. 20-22. In John ζητεῖν occurs thirty-four times, εὑρίσκειν nineteen times. The "seeking" for Jesus is often hostile (7.1, 19, 20, 25, 30; 8.37, 40; 10.39; 11.8; 18.4, 7, 8), and on only three occasions is Jesus himself the object of "finding" (1.41, 45; 6.25).

saying's originally independent existence is still preserved in the only extant work in this genre. *Interpretation* marks the transition to a new and more coherent context: in this case, Matthean teaching about prayer subsequently taken over by Luke. *Reinterpretation* represents a more or less radical reworking of an earlier interpretation. While Luke is himself the interpreter of Matthew, as we have seen, his rendering of the *seek/find* saying represents a continuation of Matthew's interpretative strategy rather than a breach with it. It is Thomas who truly *re*interprets the saying. He does so not because he is committed to an alien Gnostic ideology but because he sees in it a potential to shed light both on Jesus' role as revealer (*GTh* 92) and on the spiritual discipline that Jesus' words require of their hearer or reader (*GTh* 2).

While the Johannine evangelist offers his own reinterpretation of the *ask/give[receive]* saying, his attitude towards the *seek/find* saying is more ambivalent. Twice he negates it (7.33-36; 13.33), and he does so implicitly a third time when he insists that Jesus' work as revealer is determined not by his disciples' seeking or questioning but by the event of Easter Day (16.16-30). The *seek/find* pairing is present in the story of the first disciples, but it is barely perceptible even there.

The issue between these two evangelists is whether and to what extent the *seek/find* saying represents a hermeneutical key to the revelation embodied in Jesus. They are agreed that fundamental interpretative questions of this kind can legitimately be put to the diverse written and oral traditions they inherit. Bringing Jesus' full significance to light is more important than passing on the traditions unchanged and uninterpreted. Yet their difference with regard to the *seek/find* motif goes deep into their respective theologies.

In *GTh*, the reader is immediately summoned to persistent, unwearied seeking (2.1). Seeking and especially finding — that is, *successful* seeking — are a constant theme of this text.[52] The disciples *seek* or inquire about the end without first discovering the beginning (18.1-3). They ask Jesus about "the place where you are," since "we are compelled [ΤΑΝΑΓΚΗ ΕΡΟΝ] to *seek* it" (24.1). Jesus confirms the urgency of their quest, instructing them to "*seek a place* for yourselves within Rest [ΑΝΑΠΑΥCIC], so that you do not become a corpse and be eaten" (60.6). The *place* (ΤΟΠΟC) of salvation (24.1, 60.6) is thus a place of rest — the *rest* that Jesus promises they will *find* if

---

52. Two different Coptic verbs are used for "find": ϬΙΝΕ, in conjunction with ϢΙΝΕ, "seek," no doubt because of the assonance (*GTh* 2.1; 92.1; 94.1), but otherwise 2Ε. (Only in *Saying* 110 does ϬΙΝΕ occur in the absence of ϢΙΝΕ.) Underlying the synonyms is the Greek εὑρίσκω: thus [ὃς ἂν] εὕρῃ in *GTh* 1 is translated as ΠΕΤΑ2Ε, whereas [ἕως ἂν] εὕρῃ in *GTh* 2.1 is translated as ϢΑΝΤΕϤϬΙΝΕ.

they come to him and take his yoke upon them (90.1-2). While persecutors will *find no place* (68.2), those who have suffered have *found life* (58). The solitary (**MONᴀXOC**) and elect will *find the kingdom* (49.1), whereas those who remain entangled in the world will fail to do so (27.1). To find the kingdom is also to *find* Jesus himself, mysteriously concealed within a piece of wood or under a stone, permeating the universe that comes from him and extends to him (77.2-3). If he is not found here and now, those who *seek to see him* after death will be unable to do so (59). Even the disciples are at risk of *seeking* Jesus yet failing to *find* him (38.2). Those who do find him also *find the world,* discovering it to be no more than a corpse and so showing that the world is unworthy of them (56, 80).[53] That superiority to the world is also evident in the one who *finds himself* (111.3). Finding oneself is indeed synonymous with finding the kingdom of the Father: for that kingdom is within as well as without, and "whoever knows himself will *find* it" (3.4 [Gk.]). Finding the kingdom (or Jesus, or oneself) occurs as one *finds the interpretation* of Jesus' secret sayings (1). There is, however, no finding without seeking. The promise that "you will *find*" is attached to the imperative to *seek* (92.1). Only the one who *seeks* will *find,* just as it is only the person who knocks to whom the door will be opened (94.2). Seeking and finding is a favourite theme of the parables in *GTh*. The fisherman's net is full of small fish, but he does *find* one large one (*GTh* 8.2). The merchant *finds* a pearl and sells his entire stock in order to obtain it; his example instructs us to *seek* the wealth that endures for ever (76.1, 3). The shepherd *seeks* for the lost sheep — it is the largest, and his favourite — until he *finds* it (107.2). The man who bought a field ploughs it and *finds* treasure (109.3).

The *seek/find* motif is central to this gospel's account of salvation and how it is to be attained. In contrast to John, this account requires a high degree of self-reliance on the part of the one who seeks. There is no promise of a Paraclete or Spirit of truth who will continue Jesus' teaching ministry after his departure. Readers of this gospel are not incorporated into Jesus as the true vine. The only vine mentioned here has been "planted outside the Father," and is destined to be destroyed (40). There is an occasional hint of assimilation to Jesus (108), but nothing corresponding to the Johannine "mutual indwelling" paradoxically occasioned by Jesus' departure, and finally comprehending Jesus, the Father, and those who are his in a network of relationships characterized by love. The short-lived sorrow of absence will be

---

53. "Finding the world" appears to have a negative sense in *Saying* 110, however — in spite of Stevan Davies' arguments to the contrary (*Thomas,* pp. 71-72).

transformed into the joy of reunion. In *GTh,* Jesus' departure is mentioned only in passing; we learn that his place was taken by James the Just (12.2), although that can hardly be of any concern to readers of the gospel in its present form. More significantly, Jesus is still present as the Living One (*Incipit,* 52.2, 59.1, 111.2) on account of his words as recorded and interpreted within this text. In these words of his, Jesus points out the way to life. Those who persist in their seeking have him as their companion and guide as they continue to engage with this text. Yet he is not concerned primarily to draw them to himself or to incorporate them into his own relationship with his Father. He is concerned that they should acquire *their own* knowledge of self, the world, and the kingdom, finding within themselves the necessary resources for their spiritual quest. The text in which Jesus' life-giving sayings are recorded serves as a mirror reflecting back what is already true about its readers but previously unrecognized. They *will* seek and find the kingdom, because they are from it and must return to it (49.2).

"Seek and you will find" places the emphasis on a movement towards the kingdom of the Father, initiated by the readers in response to Jesus' words. It is that movement in its many-sided complexity that is the fundamental theme of this gospel. In contrast, the theme of *divine* initiative is distinctly muted. At no point is "the Father" the subject of a verb — in sharp contrast to the Johannine usage of verbs such as "send," "give," "love," "show," "testify," "act," "work," "come," "dwell," "glorify," and "guard."[54] For Thomas, the Father is potentially the object of human worship (15), sight (27.2), and knowledge (69.1, 105), at least for those who are the "sons" or "elect" of "the living Father" (3, 50). Yet in other contexts he is hardly more than a synonym for "the kingdom." Finding the kingdom and seeing the Father are interchangeable (27.1, 2). The kingdom is within and without; it is spread out unseen upon the earth; and as such it is a space to be entered — though not a particular space about which one might say "here" or "there" (3.1-2, 113.3). How this space is also the kingdom "of the Father" (113.4) is left unclear. In comparison to John, this is a depersonalized soteriology in which divine initiative and agency play little part in the dominant movement from seeking to finding.

Conversely, the Johannine gospel is so dominated by the theme of divine agency embodied in Jesus himself that there is little scope for the human initiative represented by Thomas's *seek/find* motif. Johannine Chris-

---

54. In *GTh* 61.3 Jesus claims that "I was given the things of my Father" (2ⲚⲚⲀ ⲠⲀⲈⲒⲰⲦ = τὰ τοῦ πατρός μου?). According to *Saying* 28.1, Jesus is present in the world on his own initiative.

tians do not set out on a quest that will lead them to know or find themselves. They reinterpret the entire sayings tradition in line with their understanding of divine initiative, and their reinterpretation is so radical that even Jesus' proclamation of the kingdom of God is virtually replaced by a conceptuality of divine agency. From the standpoint of the more conservative Thomas, this is not reinterpretation at all but a substitution in which the real living and speaking Jesus is replaced by an alien figure, who happens to bear the same name.

In principle, might Thomas have been included within a canonical gospel collection and John excluded? From an a priori perspective, there is no reason to deny this possibility. It would be difficult to argue on neutral exegetical grounds that differences between the synoptics and Thomas are more fundamental than differences between the synoptics and John. Both later gospels have significant areas of overlap with their predecessors and equally significant points of divergence. Both lay claim to normative status, and compete with one another to have that claim acknowledged. The Johannine claim is significantly qualified by the presence of three other gospels within the canonical collection, which permits no single gospel to attain definitive status. Yet Thomas's claim was not qualified but simply rejected — which is why a previously popular text fell out of circulation into oblivion, at least until its modern rediscovery. From an a posteriori perspective, the fourfold canonical text that includes John but excludes Thomas may be seen as *stipulating* that differences within the canonical collection are to be viewed as unproblematic and indeed productive, whereas differences across the canonical boundary may raise issues of fundamental principle. One such issue has perhaps come to light here. Arguably, a nonnegotiable tension exists between the prioritizing of divine agency in John and of human agency in Thomas — not because divine and human agency are incommensurable in the abstract but because of the respective roles assigned to them within competing reinterpretations of the earliest tradition.

The Crucified King

All gospels embody a dynamic interpretative process. In principle, any passage in any gospel might represent the inscription of tradition, or its interpretation, or its reinterpretation. Interpretation and reinterpretation are not to be confused with free invention. They are not fictions but renewed attempts to articulate the significance of an already inscribed tradition. As

such they participate in the dynamic that the tradition derives from the recollected datum that generates it. Reinterpretation can be identified at any
point where the three moments in the writing of tradition can be differentiated from one another. Yet this threefold differentiation is most clearly visible in later, postsynoptic gospels, where a previous consensus about particular elements of the tradition is subjected to more or less radical revision.
This is no less the case with narrative texts than with sayings material.

In Mark's passion narrative, the events that accompany Jesus' crucifixion are organized by way of a chronological scheme. Jesus is crucified at the
third hour: his garments are divided, and a placard stating the charge against
him is attached to the cross; two other offenders are crucified to his right
and to his left; he is the object of derision from passersby, from chief priests
and scribes, and even from his fellow sufferers (Mk. 15.24-32). At the *sixth*
hour darkness descends, lasting until the *ninth* hour when Jesus laments his
God-forsakenness, is misunderstood as calling upon Elijah, and dies with a
wordless cry; the tearing of the temple veil and the centurion's confession
follow (15.33-39). In Matthew the reference to the third hour drops out. It is
noted that those who crucified Jesus and cast lots for his clothing were also
responsible for guarding him; that the placard was attached above his head;
and that the derision included reference to his claim to be Son of God (Mt.
27.36, 37, 40, 43). The most significant additions to Mark are reserved for the
moment of Jesus' death, when the tearing of the veil is accompanied by an
earthquake and the resurrection of the saints (27.51-53).

For present purposes, it is the motif of the placard that is of particular
interest. In the Markan account, the placard is duly noted but without interpretative comment:

> And they crucified him, and divided his garments, casting lots for them to
> decide who should take what. (And it was the third hour, and they cruci-
> fied him.) And the placard stating the charge against him [ἡ ἐπιγραφὴ τῆς
> αἰτίας αὐτοῦ] read: "The King of the Jews." And with him they crucified
> two criminals, one on his right and the other on his left. (Mk. 15.24-27)

The three main motifs — the parting of the garments, the placard, and
the two criminals — occur in all five early passion narratives, including the
Gospel of Peter.[55] Only the chronological note is absent in the post-Markan

---

55. GPet is included here among the early passion narratives on the assumption that the single manuscript (*P.Cair.* 10759), dating perhaps from the late sixth century, corresponds to the text
known to Serapion of Antioch in the late second century (Eusebius, *HE* vi.12.2-6), and to Origen,

texts, and in the first of Mark's chronological references the repeated reference to crucifixion — καὶ ἐσταύρωσαν αὐτόν (Mk. 15.25) following καὶ σταυροῦσιν αὐτόν (v. 24) — suggests a redactional addition.[56] If so, a written passion narrative predates a redaction in which all three chronological references, to the third, sixth, and ninth hours, were probably added.[57] Thus these references are absent from John, who seems at this point to reflect a pre-Markan version of the passion narrative in which Jesus died on the afternoon before Passover and in which the Last Supper was not yet a Passover meal (compare Jn. 13.1, 18.28 with Mk. 14.12-16).[58] For John, "the sixth hour"

Eusebius, and others. (For the relevant patristic texts see Thomas J. Kraus and Tobias Nicklas, *Das Petrusevangelium und die Petrusapokalypse: Die griechischen Fragmente mit deutscher und englischer Übersetzung* [Berlin & New York: De Gruyter, 2004], pp. 11-19.) The identification has been questioned by Paul Foster ("Are There Any Early Fragments of the So-Called *Gospel of Peter?*" *NTS* 52 [2006], pp. 1-28; mostly incorporated into his *The Gospel of Peter: Introduction, Critical Edition, and Commentary* [Leiden & Boston: Brill, 2010], pp. 57-91), and Peter van Minnen ("The Akhmîm *Gospel of Peter,*" in *Das Evangelium nach Petrus: Text, Kontexte, Intertexte,* ed. Thomas J. Kraus and Tobias Nicklas [Berlin & New York: De Gruyter, 2007], pp. 53-60; p. 60). Foster writes: "To make claims about the pre-history of this text in the second century (or even earlier) is to go beyond the available evidence, and in fact may be retrojecting this text into a period when it did not exist, even if some of its canonical and non-canonical sources are much earlier" ("Early Fragments," p. 28). The extent of the possible "retrojection" depends on the date assigned to the Akhmîm manuscript. Foster states that "a date of the late 6th to the early 9th century provides a highly probable period for the composition of the text," appealing — without bibliographical detail or assessment of the evidence — to Swete, Robinson, Lods, Omont, Vaganay, and Mara, while also keeping in play the twelfth-century *terminus ad quem* originally proposed by Bouriant (*Gospel of Peter,* pp. 56, 55n). Foster's conclusion may be contrasted with Kraus and Nicklas's, which is informed by recent scholarship rather than that of the early 1890s: "*Summa summarum* sind . . . Früh- wie Spätdatierungen (vom vierten bis zum 12. Jahrhundert) abzuweisen, das vielfach angesetzte achte oder neunte Jahrhundert auf das späte sechste . . . zu korrigieren" (*Das Petrusevangelium und die Petrusapokalypse,* p. 29). It is reasonable to assume that a manuscript dating from the late sixth century should be directly continuous with an εὐαγγέλιον κατὰ Πέτρον attested from the second century to the fifth (Serapion, Origen, Eusebius, Didymus, Theodoret). In addition, the Akhmîm scribe is probably working from a fragmentary exemplar that he transcribes in full even though its beginning and ending show it to be incomplete. This surviving remnant of a once-intact *Gospel of Peter* might itself date from a century or two earlier.

56. So Bultmann, *Geschichte,* p. 295.

57. As Joel Marcus argues, "The Markan scheme of third, sixth, and ninth hours . . . probably reflects the theological conception that the precise progression of events testifies to the purposefulness of divine providence in bringing about Jesus' death" (*Mark: A New Translation with Introduction and Commentary,* 2 vols., AYB [New Haven & London: Yale University Press, 2000-2009], 2.1043).

58. Mark's emendation of the pre-Markan chronology is acutely analyzed by Dibelius (*Formgeschichte,* p. 181): "Diese Einleitung [i.e. 14.1-2] weist auf das Ganze der Passion; sie kann

marks not the coming of darkness as Jesus hangs on the cross (which he does not mention), but rather the conclusion of the trial before Pilate (Jn. 19.14). In contrast, Mark has Jesus hanging on the cross between the third and the ninth hour of the day after Passover.[59]

Jesus is crucified as "the king of the Jews" (Mk. 15.26).[60] The placard plays an essential role in the narrative, explaining why Jesus was crucified. Yet for early Christian readers it raised a further question: how did Jesus come to be crucified on a political charge that was obviously unjustified?[61] Mark's answer is that Pilate was solely responsible for the title "king of the Jews," and that even he did not take it seriously. In the Markan passion narrative, the title fulfils a primarily apologetic role. It makes its first appearance in the Markan passion narrative as follows:

> And as soon as it was morning the chief priests with the elders and scribes and the whole Sanhedrin formed a plan, and binding Jesus they led him away and handed him over to Pilate. And Pilate asked him, "Are you *the king of the Jews?*" And he answered him and said: "You say so" [σὺ λέγεις]. And

---

nur am Anfang einer zusammenhängenden Darstellung ihren Platz haben. Aber diese Darstellung muss älter sein als Markus; denn sie widerspricht seiner Datierung. Sie gibt als entscheidendes Motiv für die heimliche Verhaftung Jesu die Nähe des Festes an; das hat nur Sinn, wenn Jesus noch vor dem Fest in die Gewalt seiner Gegner kam. Also war nach diesem Bericht jener Abend der Gefangennahme noch nicht der Passah-Abend; nach des Markus Meinung aber hielt Jesus und hielten die Juden an diesem Abend das Passah-Mahl. So kann Markus nicht der Autor dieser Einleitung und also auch nicht der Urheber des Zusammenhanges sein. Die Ausgestaltung der Leidensgeschichte ist älter als Markus."

59. For a brief account of the Markan and Lukan construction of a link between the Last Supper and the Passover, see my article "'I Received from the Lord . . .': Paul, Jesus and the Last Supper," in *Jesus and Paul Reconnected,* ed. Todd D. Still (Grand Rapids: Eerdmans, 2007), pp. 103-24; pp. 116-22. In Paul, the Passover is connected with the death of Jesus (cf. 1 Cor. 5.7) but not with the Lord's Supper (cf. 1 Cor. 11.23-34). Luke strengthens the link between Passover and Last Supper, already established by Mark, by providing Passover-related sayings as the context for the words of institution (cf. Lk. 22.15-20)

60. In this connection W. D. Davies and D. C. Allison, *A Critical and Exegetical Commentary on the Gospel according to St. Matthew,* 3 vols., ICC (Edinburgh: T. & T. Clark, 1988-97), cite Josephus, *Ant.* xvii.285, 295: after the death of Herod, leaders of rebel groups claimed to be "king," but were eventually captured and crucified, along with their supporters (3.615). Jesus' condemnation as "king of the Jews" represents the "Roman mockery of both Jesus and Judaism" (3.615).

61. On this A. E. Harvey writes: "It was precisely the suggestion that Jesus represented some kind of political threat to the Roman authorities that Christians of the early centuries had most strenuously to deny. It is hard to believe that they would have fabricated a piece of evidence which could so easily be turned against them" (*Jesus and the Constraints of History* [London: Duckworth, 1982], p. 13).

the chief priests accused him of many things. And Pilate again asked him, "Do you make no answer? See what things they accuse you of!" (Mk. 15.1-4)

Here, the "king of the Jews" title is entirely gratuitous. It precedes the barrage of unspecified accusations from Jesus' opponents and bears no relation to them.[62] As Jesus' response to Pilate's question indicates, "king of the Jews" is a designation specific to Pilate. Thus he continues to use it even though it bears no relation to reality, asking the assembled crowds:

"Do you want me to release to you *the king of the Jews?*" (Mk. 15.9)

"Then what shall I do with the one you call '*the king of the Jews*'?" (Mk. 15.12)

In both cases, Pilate uses the title because he wishes to release Jesus (cf. 15.10, 14) and mistakenly believes it will help secure a positive response.[63] In reality the crowds do *not* acknowledge Jesus as their king, and clamour instead for the release of Barabbas. While "king of the Jews" plays a significant role in Mark's Barabbas episode, however, it is not indispensable. In Matthew the title occurs in Pilate's initial question to Jesus (Mt. 27.11), but is replaced by more recognizably Christian terminology when he addresses the crowd:

"Whom do you want me to release to you, Jesus Barabbas or Jesus called Christ?" (Mt. 27.17)[64]

"What then shall I do with Jesus called Christ?" (Mt. 27.22)

62. The narrative awkwardness of Mk. 15.2 is noted by Bultmann, who sees in the "king of the Jews" motif (15.2, 12, 18, 26) the beginnings of a secondary dogmatic development which seeks to show "dass Jesus als der Messias gelitten hat und gestorben ist" (*Geschichte*, p. 307). Against this, Dahl rightly argues that the secondariness of Mk. 15.2 does not make the placard in v. 26 secondary: "More probably, the question of 15:2 was formulated in view of the inscription 'King of the Jews,' which is firmly fixed in the tradition" (N. A. Dahl, "The Crucified Messiah," in his *Jesus the Christ: The Historical Origins of Christological Doctrine*, ed. Donald H. Juel [Minneapolis: Fortress, 1991], pp. 27-47; p. 36).

63. On this reading, Pilate takes Jesus' σὺ λέγεις in v. 2 as a denial of the "king of the Jews" charge. There is no room for the "ambiguity" that Raymond Brown finds here (*The Death of the Messiah: A Commentary on the Passion Narrative in the Four Gospels*, 2 vols. [New York: Doubleday, 1999], 1.733). If Jesus' response to the crucial charge against him is ambiguous, it is incomprehensible that Pilate does not follow it up.

64. See Davies and Allison, *Matthew*, 3.584, on the text-critical issue. Matthew here highlights the choice between "political rebellion and passive waiting for the kingdom of God" (p. 586).

Matthew chooses here to break the chain of Markan references to the "king of the Jews" that lead directly from the trial to the placard on the cross. As a result, the soldiers' mockery ("Hail, king of the Jews") is less clearly motivated in Matthew (27.29) than in Mark (15.18), where the soldiers take up the title used by Pilate himself. The title is not strictly necessary within the Barabbas episode, but it *is* necessary if that episode is to provide the background for the placard, as Mark requires it to do. According to Mark, Jesus was crucified as king of the Jews because Pilate had three times referred to him as such — although this played no role at all in the decision to condemn him, which was occasioned by political expediency (Mk. 15.15). In Mark, Pilate's three questions about "the king of the Jews" anticipate and interpret the placard on the cross. That Jesus claimed to be king of the Jews was a misunderstanding by the soldiers who mocked and crucified Jesus, and who prepared the placard and attached it to the cross. The misunderstanding was occasioned by Pilate's use of the title precisely in the unsuccessful attempt to secure Jesus' release.

A pre-Markan version of the passion narrative might have seen something other than a mere misunderstanding in the "king of the Jews" title. A link between kingship and messianic claim is still perceptible when the chief priests mock the crucified Jesus as "the Christ, the king of Israel" (Mk. 15.32), although at his trial before the Sanhedrin he is condemned for blasphemous claims transcending messianic kingship (14.61-64). Earlier, at the triumphal entry, the crowds come close to acknowledging Jesus as Davidic king (11.9-10), and the unmistakable messianic and kingly allusions are confirmed by the announcement of "your king" in the underlying prophetic text, Zechariah 9.9 (cited in Mt. 21.4-5; Jn. 12.14-15). Yet, significantly, the Markan Jesus explicitly *contests* the link between Davidic kingship and the Messiah (Mk. 12.35-37).[65] In Markan context, the triumphal entry seems curiously disconnected from the account of Jesus' final days in Jerusalem that it ostensibly introduces. The "king of the Jews" title is traced back only to Pilate, and has no basis in reality. Are Mark's five linked references to Jesus as king of the Jews a substitute for an earlier chain of kingship references extending back to the tri-

65. The tension between Mk. 12.35-37 and Jesus' earlier acclamation as "Son of David" (10.47-48; 11.9-10) is rightly noted by Marcus (*Mark*, 2.847), whose preferred solution is that "[t]he Markan Jesus is not denying the Messiah's physical descent from David but the adequacy of the Davidic image to express his full identity" (p. 848). But if Jesus is not denying the Messiah's physical descent from David, why does he express himself so misleadingly? A better solution is to see 12.35-37 as the evangelist's retrospective rejection of a title understood positively in the tradition he inherits (cf. *Barnabas* 12.10-11).

umphal entry? If so, then Mark in its present form must be seen as a relatively "late" text in which the interpretation of earlier written tradition is already under way.[66] This interpretative intervention should not be understood merely as apologetically motivated fiction. For Mark's predominantly Gentile Christian readership, Jesus is *not* in any significant sense "king of Israel" or "king of the Jews." What he *is* is Son of God, rejected as such by the high priest but acknowledged by a Gentile centurion (Mk. 14.61-63; 15.39). From this confessional standpoint, the charge against Jesus — enshrined in the placard — can only seem perverse and in need of a purely ad hoc explanation.

In Matthew and Luke the placard and the charge are retained, but they are traced back not so much to Pilate as to the soldiers who mock Jesus prior to or during the crucifixion (Mt. 27.29; Lk. 23.36-38). Only the first of Pilate's three Markan references to the title is preserved (Mt. 27.11; Lk. 23.3).[67] The later synoptic evangelists make no significant attempt to reinterpret the motif of Jesus' kingship. Reinterpretation is undertaken, independently and in very different directions, by the gospels of John and of Peter. Whether these two evangelists were approximately contemporary or separated by half a century or more is unimportant. What is significant is that they reinterpret the older synoptic-type traditions in parallel with one another. This is illustrated by their attempts to rehabilitate the kingship motif.

In the *Gospel of Peter,* Jesus is mocked and crucified not as king of the Jews but as king of Israel (3.7; 4.11).[68] As king of the Jews, he is of special con-

---

66. As this account demonstrates, the tradition/redaction distinction is still a useful methodological tool for handling textual anomalies in Mark, although it should be employed with caution. The usefulness of this distinction has been widely rejected, however: see Werner H. Kelber (ed.), *The Passion in Mark: Studies on Mark 14–16* (Philadelphia: Fortress, 1976), especially the introduction (John R. Donahue, pp. 1-20) and conclusion (Werner H. Kelber, pp. 153-80). This groundbreaking work registered the methodological shift to a narrative-critical approach, which here takes the form of a radicalized redaction criticism in which virtually everything in Mark is the direct expression of the evangelist's theology. In my view, it is essential to retain diachronic alongside synchronic perspectives in order to ensure the connection between Jesus himself and his textual embodiments.

67. In Matthew, Pilate's initial question immediately follows the added episode of Judas's repentance and death, but is otherwise close to Mark (Mt. 27.1-2, 11-14 = Mk. 15.1-5). Luke reverses the Markan sequence, so that the accusations precede Pilate's question rather than following it, and he provides a specific antecedent for the question in the accusation that Jesus claims to be "Christ, a king" (Lk. 23.2). Luke has no independent tradition here but rewrites Mark for the sake of verisimilitude (cf. Gerhard Schneider, "The Political Charge against Jesus (Luke 23:2)," in *Jesus and the Politics of His Day,* ed. E. Bammel and C. F. D. Moule [Cambridge: Cambridge University Press, 1984], pp. 403-14; Brown, *Death of the Messiah,* pp. 736-37).

68. For the Greek text see Kraus and Nicklas, *Das Petrusevangelium und die Petrusapokalypse;*

cern to Pilate. It is presupposed in all the canonical passion narratives that an actual claim to kingship would represent a direct challenge to Roman authority. "King of the Jews" is a secular, politically oriented expression devised by Pilate himself, although (as the canonical evangelists hasten to add) he did not himself believe that Jesus laid claim to any such role. As king of Israel, however, Jesus' counterpart is no longer the Roman governor but "Herod the king," who is presiding over Jesus' trial as the extant text of *GPet* opens and who confirms the death sentence after Pilate has washed his hands in symbolic protest (1.1-2). In this gospel, King Herod presides over the crucifixion of the King of Israel, just as Pilate will later preside over the resurrection of the Son of God.[69] Herod's role here may be compared to the one assigned to him by Luke, who inserts a hearing before Herod within his broadly Markan account of the trial before Pilate. When Pilate learns that Jesus is a Galilean, "under the authority of Herod" (Lk. 23.7), he seeks to transfer the case to Herod's jurisdiction. His plan is thwarted by Herod's erratic behaviour, however. Although initially eager to witness a sign, Herod is provoked by Jesus' refusal to cooperate and subjects him to his soldiers' mockery before returning him to Pilate in royal garb (Lk. 23.8-12). In spite of this, the governor and the tetrarch are reconciled to each other and Pilate can claim Herod's support as he declares Jesus innocent for a second time (Lk. 23.12-16). Luke here shows how Herod and Pilate — in that order — fulfil the Davidic prophecy that "kings" and "rulers" will be "gathered together against the Lord and against his Christ," a prophecy that he will later cite in his second volume (Acts 4.25-28; Ps. 2.1-2).[70] There is a possible echo of the Lukan friendship theme in *GPet* 2.5, where Herod addresses the Roman governor as "brother Pilate," in spite of his earlier refusal to follow Pilate's lead

---

Andrew Bernhard, *Other Early Christian Gospels: A Critical Edition of the Surviving Greek Manuscripts* (London & New York: T. & T. Clark, 2007), pp. 49-83. Images of *P. Cairo* 10759 are available in the Nicklas-Kraus edition (with some errors in the pagination) and online at http://ipap.csad.ox.ac.uk/GP/GP.html (retrieved 17.2.12).

69. That "Herod" here is "Herod Antipas, the son of Herod the Great by his marriage to Malthace" (Foster, *Gospel of Peter*, p. 217) is barely relevant to the interpretation of this text.

70. In the application of the cited passage, Luke interprets the scriptural gathering of kings and rulers κατὰ τοῦ κυρίου καὶ κατὰ τοῦ Χριστοῦ αὐτοῦ as a reference to the "gathering" of Herod and Pilate ἐπὶ τὸν ἅγιον παῖδά σου Ἰησοῦν ὅν ἔχρισας (Acts 4.26, 27). Here, ἐπί means "over" (cf. Lk. 1.33; 12.14), emphasizing God-given authority rather than godless opposition. The significance of Ps. 2 for the Lukan account of Herod's role is rightly emphasized by M. Dibelius, "Herodes und Pilatus," in *Botschaft und Geschichte: Gesammelte Aufsätze I* (Tübingen: Mohr-Siebeck, 1953), pp. 278-92; pp. 286-91. For the later development of the Herod tradition, see J. D. Crossan, *The Cross That Spoke: The Origins of the Passion Narrative* (New York: Harper & Row, 1988), pp. 60-93.

in washing his hands (1.1). Yet it is not Herod but Joseph of Arimathea who is referred to as "the friend of Pilate" (2.3),[71] and there is otherwise little indication in the extant text that the Herod figure of *GPet* is influenced by Luke.[72] Underlying both Lukan and Petrine presentations is the early Christian interpretation of Psalm 2, which implies a priority of Herod over Pilate since Herod is more credibly identified as a "king" and Pilate as a "ruler." In Luke, Herod's priority is constrained by a Markan source in which Pilate is the sole arbiter of Jesus' fate and Herod is not mentioned. In *GPet,* Herod's authority is supreme. It is his instructions that Jesus' executioners are to follow (1.2). When Joseph asks for the body of Jesus, Pilate must forward his request to Herod (2.4). Herod's response to this request shows that as king he is responsible for ensuring that the law's requirements are duly carried out — in this case, the requirement that the sun should not set on the Murdered One (ἐπὶ πεφονευμένῳ), and that there should be no infringement of the Sabbath law (*GPet* 2.5).[73] This passion narrative is set within an intra-Jewish context in which the role of secular authority is marginal.

Jesus is mockingly referred to by his tormentors and executioners as

71. The phrase recurs in *P. Oxy.* 2949, probably a third-century fragment of *GPet* itself: so Lührmann, *Die apokryph gewordenen Evangelien,* pp. 60-73. Paul Foster's criticisms of Lührmann's reconstruction are too harsh ("Are There Any Early Fragments of the So-Called *Gospel of Peter?*" pp. 4-12). Kraus and Nicklas conclude more positively that "[d]ie Verbindungen zwischen beiden Texten fallen sofort auf, und es erstaunt dass auf relativ knappem Raum zahlreiche gleiche oder entsprechende Wörter anzutreffen sind, selbst wenn die Unterschiede in Wortwahl und grammatischer Form nicht unberücksichtigt bleiben dürfen" (*Das Petrusevangelium und die Petrusapokalypse,* p. 58). Similarly Peter Head states that, "[o]f sixteen recognisable words in POxy 2949, ten are identical with words in the Akhmîm fragment. Of the six which differ, four can be accounted for as synonymous variants" ("On the Christology of the Gospel of Peter," *VC* 46 [1992], pp. 209-24; p. 219n). Analogies might be found by comparing the Greek fragments of *GTh* with the Coptic translation.

72. In *GPet,* Herod presides over the Sanhedrin. This text is therefore unlikely to have followed the Lukan sequence of hearings before the Sanhedrin, Pilate, and Herod.

73. The alleged scriptural requirement, ἥλιον μὴ δῦναι ἐπὶ πεφονευμένῳ (*GPet* 2.5; 5.15), is loosely related to Dt. 21.22-23, where it is said that the body of a convicted criminal should be buried on the day of his execution. As Thomas Hieke notes, "[d]er wichtigste Unterschied zwischen Dtn 21,22-23 und EvPetr 5, 15 besteht wohl darin, dass aus dem, der aufgrund eines Kapitalverbrechens hingerichtet wird (Dtn 21,22: ἐὰν δὲ γένηται ἔν τινι ἁμαρτία κρίμα θανάτου), in EvPetr ein 'Ermordeter' (ἐπὶ πεφονευμένῳ) wird. Durch diese Abweichung vom alttestamentlichen Hintergrund wird der Leser gewahr, dass der EvPetr die Kreuzigung Jesu ziemlich unverblümt nicht als 'Hinrichtung', sondern als Ermordung versteht" ("Das Petrusevangelium vom Alten Testament her gelesen: Gewinnbringende Lektüre eines nicht-kanonischen Textes vom christlichen Kanon her," in *Das Evangelium nach Petrus,* pp. 91-115; p. 95).

"Son of God" and "King of Israel" (3.6, 7). Both titles have no doubt featured in his trial before Herod, in the lost material immediately preceding the extant fragment.[74] The mockery as well as the crucifixion stems from Herod's instruction, "What I ordered you to do to him, do" (1.2), apparently repeating more detailed instructions preceding the intervention by Pilate. Herod is also responsible for the mocking of Jesus in Luke 23.11, where Jesus is derisively clothed in a fine garment before being returned to Pilate. In *GPet*, the kingship theme is expressed more directly. When Herod delivered Jesus to the people, they

> pushed him as they ran, and said: "Let us drag away [σύρωμεν] the Son of God now we have him in our power!" And they clothed him in a purple robe and they sat him on a seat of judgement [ἐπὶ καθέδραν κρίσεως], saying, "Judge justly [δικαίως κρῖνε], King of Israel!" And one of them bringing a crown of thorns set it on the Lord's head. . . . (*GPet* 3.6-8)

Although *GPet* is generally nonspecific in its locations, it is clear that Jesus is dragged by a disorderly mob to Golgotha. There he is initially enthroned, receiving mock-supplicants who appeal for judgement in their favour. This motif derives in part from Isaiah 58.2, where it is said that "they ask of me righteous judgement [κρίσιν δικαίαν]." This passage is cited in Justin's first *Apology*, and the corresponding interpretation tells how, "mocking him [διασύροντες αὐτόν], they sat [him] on a judgement-seat [ἐπὶ βήματος] and said, 'Judge us!'"[75] The appeal for judgement derives from the Isaiah passage; the judgement-seat does not. Elsewhere in Justin's passion-related scriptural citations, his interpretative statements incorporate additional details drawn from the Matthean or Lukan passion narratives.[76] The

---

74. So L. Vaganay, *L'Évangile de Pierre* (Paris: Librairie Lecoffre, 1930), p. 238: "king of Israel" in *GPet* 3.7 and 4.11 "fait allusion aux débats du procès devant Hérode et rappelle que Jésus est déclaré le roi-Messie prédit par les prophètes," but also functions as unconscious prophecy "à la manière de Caïphe (Jn. xi, 50 sq.)."

75. *1 Apol.* 35.6. On this passage and the parallel in *GPet*, see M. Dibelius, "Die alttestamentlichen Motive in der Leidensgeschichte des Petrus- und des Johannes-Evangeliums," in *Botschaft und Geschichte I*, pp. 221-47; pp. 225-27. Dibelius argues that, here and elsewhere, *GPet* stands closer to the scriptural sources of the passion narrative than does John (p. 231).

76. In *1 Apol.* 35.3-4, the citation from Is. 58.2 ("Now they ask of me [righteous] judgement, and dare to approach God") follows directly from Is. 65.2 ("I *stretched out* my *hands* to a disobedient and *contradict*ory people . . ."). In the interpretations that follow (*1 Apol.* 35.6), Jesus is said to have "*stretched out* his *hands* when crucified by the Jews, *contradicting* him and claiming that he was not the Christ." The reference is probably to Lk. 23.35: "The rulers mocked him, saying, 'He saved others,

present passage seems to imply Justin's knowledge of *GPet*.[77] While the Petrine reference to Jesus as King of Israel is lacking here, Justin elsewhere appeals to Jews not to "mock the King of Israel, as your synagogue-leaders do after prayers."[78] The mockery continues: the passion narrative of *GPet* likewise reflects developing traditions of polemic that define the boundary between Christian and Jewish communities.

In Mark and Matthew, the inscription on the cross is anticipated in the mockery scene: "Hail, king of the Jews!" (Mk. 15.18; Mt. 27.29). In Luke, the link is still clearer as the kingship motif is oddly conflated with the offering of vinegar:

> The soldiers also mocked him, coming and offering him vinegar, and saying: "If you are the king of the Jews, save yourself!" And there was an inscription over him: "This is the King of the Jews." (Lk. 23.36-38)

In *GPet*, the link between the acclamation and the inscription is still more emphatic, as the kingship theme is given greater prominence. After the enthronement and acclamation, Jesus is crucified between two evildoers, remaining silent as though experiencing no pain.[79] Here the inscription reads:

---

let him save himself if he is the Christ of God, the Elect One!'" (cf. Mt. 27.41-43). Similarly, the citation from Is. 58.2 is related to an incident when, "mocking him, they sat [him] on a judgement-seat and said, 'Judge us!'" In both cases, the passion narrative provides Justin not only with correspondences but also with details that are not explicit in the scriptural citations. If one such detail derives from the Lukan passion narrative, the other seems to derive from the Petrine one.

77. Further support for this claim may be found in *1 Apol.* 40.6, where Justin interprets Ps. 2.2 as foretelling τὴν γεγενημένην Ἡρῴδου τοῦ βασιλέως Ἰουδαίων καὶ αὐτῶν Ἰουδαίων καὶ Πιλάτου τοῦ ὑμετέρου γενομένου ἐπιτρόπου σὺν τοῖς αὐτοῦ στρατιώταις κατὰ τοῦ Χριστοῦ συνέλευσιν. This corresponds closely to the situation in *GPet* 1, where Herod, the Jews, and Pilate are assembled together — although Pilate's soldiers are not mentioned till later. Both passages are much more directly shaped by the psalm text than is Lk. 23.6-15, where there is no συνέλευσις between Herod and Pilate; Justin summarizes the Lukan passage in quite different terms (*Dial.* 103.4). For arguments against this and other possible links between Justin and *GPet*, see Vaganay, *L'Évangile de Pierre*, pp. 150-61; for arguments in favour, P. Pilhofer, "Justin und das Petrusevangelium," *ZNW* 81 (1990), pp. 60-78.

78. Justin, *Dial.* 137.2; cf. Mt. 27.41-43; *GPet* 3.6-9.

79. Foster rightly emphasizes (1) that the "silence" motif is traditional, occurring in the trial scenes (Mk. 14.61; 15.4-5), and (2) that ὡς μηδέν[α] πόνον ἔχων is a comparison rather than a statement of fact (*Gospel of Peter*, pp. 292-93). The supposed link between *GPet* and docetism derives from Serapion of Antioch, according to whom this text was popularized by "those we call docetists" (οὓς Δοκητὰς καλοῦμεν) and contains a few later heretical additions (Eusebius, *HE* vi.12.6). Eusebius omits Serapion's listing of these supposed additions, but it is not necessary to suppose that ὡς μηδέν πόνον ἔχων was one of them. See also Jerry W. McCant, "The Gospel of Peter: Docetism Reconsidered," *NTS* 30 (1984), pp. 258-73; Head, "On the Christology of the Gospel of Peter."

"This is the King of Israel" (4.11). The shift from King of the Jews to King of Israel corresponds to the shift from Roman justice, maintained at least as a facade in the canonical gospels, to a Jewish justice exercised in the name of the Jewish law. But it also represents a shift from a misleading title to a revelatory one. In the synoptic gospels, Jesus is *not* "king of the Jews." The inscription on the placard is misleading, as even Pilate is well aware. In *GPet*, Jesus *is* "King of Israel" just as he is "Son of God" and "the Lord." Unlike "king of the Jews," King of Israel is a title for God himself:

> Thus says God the King of Israel, who delivers him, God Sabaoth: I am before and I am after these things, other than me there is no god. (Is. 44.6 LXX)

In the crucifixion of the King of Israel, is it *God* who is put to death, indeed "murdered" (πεφονευμένος, 3.5, 5.15)? In *GPet* Jesus is referred to not as "God" but as "Son of God" and "the Lord." Yet for at least one early reader of this text, the inscription on the cross speaks of God as it speaks of Jesus as King of Israel.

In the course of a long, passionate, and eloquent denunciation of those who put Jesus to death, Melito of Sardis — a contemporary of Justin — vividly evokes the crucifixion in the following terms:

> Now, in the middle of the street and in the middle of the city, in the middle of the day for all to see, has occurred the unjust murder of the just [δικαίου ἄδικος φόνος]. And so he is lifted up on a high tree, and a placard is attached indicating the Murdered One [τίτλος πρόσκειται τὸν πεφονευμένον σημαίνων].[80]

Who is this Murdered One? The *titulus* on the cross will give us the answer, but Melito is not yet ready to divulge what it says:

> Who is this? To say is hard, not to say more fearful still. Yet listen, trembling at the one for whom the earth quaked.[81]

---

80. Melito, *Pasch.* 94. For introduction and Greek text, see S. G. Hall, *Melito of Sardis, On Pascha, and Fragments* (Oxford: Clarendon Press, 1979). Translations here are my own. Paul Foster is dismissive of the evidence that *GPet* was known to second-century writers: "Contrary to certain suggestions, there is nothing in the writings of Justin or Melito of Sardis that makes their knowledge of this text even probable" (*Gospel of Peter*, p. 115). This judgement does not seem to rest on independent assessment of the primary texts (cf. pp. 97-101).

81. Melito, *Pasch.* 95. For the earthquake, cf. Mt. 27.51, 54; *GPet* 6.21. Other details that proba-

The answer takes the form of a list of six matching statements, all of which aim to bring to light the intolerable paradox of the crucifixion. The "unprecedented murder" is seen as a sacrilegious human act directed against the God who is its victim, and not as willed and intended by God himself:

ὁ κρεμάσας τὴν γῆν κρέμαται,

ὁ πήξας τοὺς οὐρανοὺς πέπηκται,

ὁ στηρίξας τὰ πάντα ἐπὶ ξύλου ἐστήρικται.

ὁ δεσπότης ὕβρισται,

ὁ θεὸς πεφόνευται,

ὁ βασιλεὺς τοῦ Ἰσραὴλ ἀνῄρηται ὑπὸ δεξιᾶς Ἰσραηλίτιδος.

The one who hung the earth is hanging,

The one who fixed the heavens is fixed,

The one who fastened all things is fastened to a tree!

The Lord is insulted,

The Deity is murdered,

The King of Israel is put to death — by an Israelite right hand![82]

The rhetorical impact of these six matching statements is achieved by contrasting the subject's all-embracing creative agency and status with his position as victim of an absolutely specific act of violence. These statements are intended as the deferred answer to the question, "Who is this?" The question itself arises from the "placard indicating the Murdered One," and the answer is that the Murdered One is God, the King of Israel, put to death by his own subjects. For Melito, then, the placard on the cross read: "This is the King of Israel," and referred to Jesus as God.[83] In *GPet*, the King of Israel who

---

bly derive from Matthew or *GPet* include Pilate's handwashing (*Pasch.* 92; cf. Mt. 27.24; *GPet* 1.1) and the vinegar and gall (*Pasch.* 79, 80, 93; cf. Mt. 27.34; *GPet* 5.16). References to the "unbroken lamb" may have a Johannine origin (*Pasch.* 4, 71; cf. Jn. 19.32-36), and there is an unambiguous reference to the raising of Lazarus (*Pasch.* 72; cf. Jn. 11.38-44). Other figures or events attested in at least two gospels include Judas (*Pasch.* 93), Caiaphas (*Pasch.* 93), the false witnesses (*Pasch.* 79, 93), the scourging (*Pasch.* 79), the crown of thorns (*Pasch.* 79, 93), and the darkness (*Pasch.* 97).

82. *Pasch.* 96.

83. As Hall notes, Melito "attribute[s] to Christ all the acts of God without exception" and "rarely uses expressions which clearly imply a personal distinction of the Son from the Father" (*Melito*, p. 43). Jesus is God, and as such he is both Father and Son: καθ' ὃ γεννᾷ πατήρ, καθ' ὃ γεννᾶται υἱός (*Pasch.* 9). Here and elsewhere, Jesus is simply "[a] Son" (*Pasch.* 5, 7, 8; cf. 44) rather than "the Son of God." Yet a distinction is drawn between God, addressed as Δέσποτα, and σοῦ τὸν υἱόν (*Pasch.* 76). At the close of the work, it is said of Jesus: οὗτος ὁ καθήμενος ἐν δεξιᾷ τοῦ

is also the Murdered One is identified not directly with God but with the Son of God who is also the Lord. Yet the coincidence is striking. In both cases, the true identity of the one crucified is clear for all to read in the placard attached to the cross. In both cases, the placard discloses the iniquity of those who put their own king to death. This act of regicide is also akin to deicide. Both reinterpretations of the passion story seek to expose the sacrilegious act of human malice in which God or the Son of God is, in the most direct and literal sense, the victim.[84] The possibility of exposure is already enshrined in the placard where the truth about the victim is inscribed.[85]

In the Petrine reinterpretation, the placard on the cross is of fundamental significance. The reinterpretation no doubt stems in part from contemporary polemics, but it has its textual basis in the displacement of Pilate by Herod in the light of Psalm 2. While the possibility of this displacement is already evident in Luke-Acts (cf. Lk. 23.6-16; Acts 4.24-28), its development is inhibited there by the earlier Markan account, to which Luke remains generally faithful. It is in *GPet* that a leading role is ascribed to Herod, so that the entire sequence of events is relocated within an intra-Jewish context in which Jesus is no longer "king of the Jews" (a victim of mistaken identity) but "King of Israel" (the Victim of deicide). The significance of Herod for

---

πατρός, φορεῖ τὸν πατέρα καὶ ὑπὸ τοῦ πατρὸς φορεῖται (*Pasch.* 105; cf. 103, 104). For analysis of the monarchian traits in Melito's christology, see R. M. Hübner, "Melito von Sardes und Noët von Smyrna," in *Oecumenica et Patristica*, ed. D. Papandreou, W. A. Bienert, and K. Schäferdiek (Stuttgart: Kohlhammer, 1989), pp. 219-40.

84. Jesus is murdered not only by crucifixion but also by poisoning: the drink of bile and vinegar is intended to hasten his death (*GPet* 5.15-17). On this see Vaganay, *Évangile de Pierre*, p. 254, following Zahn; Crossan, *The Cross That Spoke*, pp. 208-17.

85. Melito's dependence here on *GPet* 4.11 is noted by Hall, *Melito*, p. 53n, who also finds connections with *GPet* in *Pasch.* 72 (εἰς σφαγὴν συρείς; cf. *GPet* 3.6, σύρωμεν τὸν υἱὸν τοῦ θεοῦ), 93 (the role of Herod), and 94 (μέσης ἡμέρας; cf. *GPet* 5.15, ἦν δὲ μεσημβρία). The relationship of Melito and *GPet* is discussed by O. Perler, "L'Évangile de Pierre et Méliton de Sardes," *Revue biblique* 71 (1964), pp. 84-90. In contrast, Thomas Karmann finds here only parallels, without direct dependence ("Die Paschahomilie des Melito von Sardes und das Petrusevangelium," in *Das Evangelium nach Petrus*, pp. 215-35). Commenting on *Pasch.* 95, Karmann finds no definite link between the question-and-answer and the *titlos,* and sees βασιλεύς τοῦ Ἰσραηλ as an assimilation to the concern with Ἰσραηλ rather than Ἰουδαῖοι throughout this text: thus "king of Israel" here "hat mit dem Petrusevangelium . . . wohl nichts zu tun" (p. 226). Karmann does not discuss the possible relationship between τὸν πεφονευμένον in *Pasch.* 95 and ἐπὶ πεφονευμένῳ in *GPet* 2.5; 5.15. Cognate terms relating to murder occur eight times in *Pasch.* 94-96 (cf. also 72-73), in contrast to the more conventional language Melito uses elsewhere in this context (ἀπέκτεινας, *Pasch.* 92, 93; παθών, *Pasch.* 100; ὁ ἀμνός ὁ ὑπὲρ ὑμῶν σφαγείς, *Pasch.* 103). There is stronger evidence that Melito knew *GPet* than that he knew Matthew or John.

this reinterpretation is again confirmed by Melito, who follows Peter rather than Matthew in contrasting Pilate, who "washed his hands," with Herod, "whom you followed."[86]

Like *GPet* and unlike the synoptics, John finds the true significance of Jesus' death in the inscription on the cross. Both later evangelists reinterpret this motif, but do so differently. Unlike *GPet* and like the synoptics, John retains both a central role for Pilate and the "king of the Jews" charge. Indeed, the Johannine account of Jesus' trial before Pilate is based on the Markan references to Jesus as "king of the Jews," three in Pilate's questions and the fourth in his soldiers' mock-acclamation. As we have seen, Matthew and Luke play down the significance of this title in Jesus' trial. In contrast, John retains all four Markan references. The first is doubled; the fourth is located within the trial before Pilate rather than immediately after it. Yet this evangelist's use of a Markan template for his more elaborate trial scene is absolutely clear. Equally clear is the fact that he finds theological substance in the "king of the Jews" title. Mark's apologetically oriented use of this title is intended to show that, although Jesus was crucified as king of the Jews, Pilate himself believed him to be innocent of this charge. The Johannine evangelist, concerned with theology rather than apologetics, *reinterprets* "king of the Jews" in order that Jesus should be revealed as who he truly is precisely in the manner of his death.

The use of a Markan template is demonstrated by Figure 7.1 (p. 385).[87] John's use of Mark is highly selective, but here at least it is undeniable.[88] There are also indications that this evangelist can draw on Matthew and Luke to supplement Mark. In the discussion that follows, the enumeration is based on Figure 7.1, where it highlights the centrality of the "king of the Jews" issue for both Mark and John.

---

86. *Pasch.* 92, 95.

87. This "Markan template" creates potential difficulties for Robert Fortna's claim that the Signs Source (SG) underlying the Gospel of John included (or was attached to) a passion narrative, independent of Mark, that can be approximately reconstructed (*The Fourth Gospel and Its Predecessor: From Narrative Source to Present Gospel*, SNTW [Edinburgh: T. & T. Clark, 1989], pp. 163-76). Fortna argues that similarities between the SG and the synoptics derive from common tradition, and that the pre-Johannine author was also pre-Markan (p. 218). In the trial scene, however, the primary source would appear to be Mark, although individual motifs may have been drawn from elsewhere (e.g. "Gabbatha," 19.13; chronological data, 19.14).

88. On this see Maurits Sabbe, "The Trial of Jesus before Pilate in John and Its Relation to the Synoptic Gospels," in *John and the Synoptics*, ed. Adelbert Denaux, BEThL (Leiden: Leiden University Press, 1992), pp. 341-85. Sabbe, however, finds that the Johannine trial narratives have particular affinities with Luke, more than with Mark (p. 384).

Figure 7.1

Mark 15.2-18

1.1 And Pilate asked him,

> "Are you the king of the Jews?" And he answered him, "You say."

1.2 And the chief priests accused him of many things. And Pilate again asked him, "Have you no answer to make? See how many charges they bring against you." But Jesus made no further answer, so that Pilate wondered . . .

<*1.3* And Pilate asked him, *"Are you the king of the Jews?"* And he answered him, *"You say."*>

2. [Pilate asked them:]
> "*Do you* want *me to release for you the king of the Jews?*"
{Lk: And *they cried out* together *saying*, "Away with *this man*, release *Barabbas* for us!"}

<*3.1* And they robed him in *purple*, and {Mt: *weaving a crown of thorns they put it on his head*} they began to acclaim him: *"Hail, king of the Jews!"* And they beat him around the head with a reed, and they spat upon him and knelt in homage to him. And when they had mocked him, they stripped him of the purple robe and put his own clothes on him. And they led him out to crucify him.>

John 18.33-19.16

1.1 Pilate entered the praetorium again and called Jesus and said to him, *"Are you the king of the Jews?"* Jesus answered, "Do *you say* this of yourself, or did others tell you about me?"

1.2 Pilate answered, "Am I a Jew? Your own nation and the chief priests have handed you over to me. What have you done?" Jesus answered, "My kingship is not of this world. If my kingship were of this world, my servants would fight so that I might not be handed over to the Jews. But now my kingship is not from here."

1.3 Pilate said to him, *"Are you* not then a *king?"* Jesus answered, "*You say* that I am a king. For this I was born, and for this I have come into the world, to bear witness to the truth . . ."

2. [Pilate said:] "I find no crime in him. . . . *Do you* wish *me to release for you the king of the Jews?*"
So *they cried out* again *saying*,
> "Not *this man*, but *Barabbas!*"

3.1 And the soldiers *weaving a crown of thorns put it on his head,* and clothed him in a *purple* garment, and they came up to him and said, *"Hail, king of the Jews!",* and struck him with their hands. Pilate went out again and said to them, "See, I am bringing him out to you, that you may know that I find no crime in him." So Jesus went out wearing the crown of thorns and the purple robe. Pilate said to them, "Behold the man!" When the chief priests and the officers saw him, they cried out, "Crucify him, crucify him!"

[Pilate further questions Jesus, and again seeks to release him.]

3.2 . . . "If you release this man, you are not Caesar's friend; everyone who makes himself <u>a king</u> sets himself against Caesar." When Pilate heard these words, he brought Jesus out and sat on the judgment seat at a place called "The Pavement," in Hebrew "Gabbatha." Now it was the Day of Preparation for the Passover, at about the sixth hour.

4. . . . . "Then what shall I do with the man you call the king of the Jews?" And they cried out again, "Crucify him!" And Pilate said to them, "Why, what evil has he done?" But they shouted all the more, "Crucify him!" So Pilate, wishing to satisfy the crowd, released for them Barabbas, and after scourging *he handed* Jesus *over to be crucified.*

4. And he said to the Jews, "Behold your king!" They cried out, "Away with him, away with him, crucify him!" Pilate said to them, "Shall I crucify your king?" The chief priests answered, "We have no king but Caesar."

Then *he handed* him *over* to them *to be crucified.*

1.1 Pilate's initial question to Jesus is identical in all four canonical gospels: "Are you the king of the Jews?" (Jn. 18.33; Mk. 15.2; Mt. 27.11; Lk. 23.3). Like the other evangelists, John preserves Jesus' cryptic answer, "You say," but in the form of two different paraphrases, necessitating a repetition of Pilate's question *(1.3)*. The first paraphrase is a counterquestion about the source of Pilate's information: "Do *you say* this of yourself, or did others tell you about me?" These alternatives are represented by Mark and Luke respectively. In Mark, Pilate's question is "of himself" in the sense that he introduces the "king of the Jews" title on his own initiative. Jesus has been brought before him for trial, but no one has referred to a claim to be king of the Jews. In contrast, Luke has elders, chief priests, and scribes telling Pilate of Jesus' claim to be "Christ, a king." Here, Pilate asks whether Jesus is king of the Jews because "others t[old] you about me." In effect, the Johannine Jesus asks which of the earlier evangelists is correct, in providing an antecedent to Pilate's question (Luke) or in omitting to do so (Mark). Yet his question has already been answered by the narrator. The Johannine evangelist has noted that, in Mark, the initial question-and-answer *precedes* the chief priests' (unspecified) accusations *(1.2)*. Rather than following Luke in correcting Mark's awkward narration, this evangelist *exploits* the fact that Pilate's initial question seems to come from nowhere. Thus Jesus' opponents refuse to specify an accusation even when requested to do so. Insisting that it is Pilate's duty to put him to death, they merely assert that they have found him to be "an evildoer" (Jn. 18.29-32). Kept in the dark about the nature of his evildoing, Pilate hazards the guess that he may be a pretender to the vacant throne of Judea. Jesus' counterquestion highlights the fact that, without any external prompting, Pilate has testified to Jesus as king. It seems that the guess is an inspired one.

1.2 Pilate does not pursue the king-of-the-Jews issue and calls upon the prisoner to give an account of himself, in view of the "many charges" laid against him (Mark) or the sheer fact of his having been handed over (John). This makes it possible for Matthew and Luke to omit any further reference to "the king of the Jews" during the remainder of Jesus' trial. From the standpoint of the later synoptists, Mark's reversion to the title when Pilate offers the choice of Jesus or Barabbas, and then asks what is to be done with Jesus, is redundant. In John, Jesus confirms that Pilate has unwittingly spoken truth in referring to him as a king; that truth must now be elaborated. Jesus is indeed a king. Yet his kingship is defined in purely negative terms. It is not the normal worldly kingship that "king of the Jews" might suggest. Normal kings fight their way out of threatening situations. Jesus and his followers do nothing of the sort.[89]

1.3 This acknowledgement of a nonworldly kingship leads to the repetition of the original question and answer *(1.1)* in a new variant. The original question, *"Are you the king of the Jews?"* recurs here without reference to the Jews, in the form: *"Are you* not then a *king?"* The original answer, in which the Markan *"You say"* is paraphrased as "Do *you say* this of yourself . . . ?," now takes affirmative rather than interrogative form: "*You say* that I am a king" (Jn. 18.37). Remarkably, the affirmative version responds not only to the question immediately preceding it but also to the earlier interrogative version. "*You say* that I am a king" answers the question, "Do *you say* this of yourself . . . ?" In the cryptic Markan σὺ λέγεις, the later evangelist hears both a question about Pilate's insight into Jesus' kingly identity and its answer. This reinterpretation of the pre-Markan kingship motif is based on a close reading of the earlier interpretation. Jesus' claim to have come to bear witness to the truth is the positive counterpart to the preceding denial of worldly kingship. His kingship takes the form of testimony to the truth. But it is also Pilate who unwittingly testifies to the truth, by way of his questions about Jesus' kingship.

2 In the offer of release Mark's Pilate refers to Jesus as "king of the Jews," on the assumption that this is how he is regarded by the crowds (Mk. 15.9). This is the second in the sequence of occurrences of this title intended to explain the charge inscribed on the placard. John retains the Markan wording — unlike Matthew, where Pilate offers to release "Jesus who is called Christ" (Mt. 27.17), and Luke, where no such offer is made. In John, there is no differentiation between the Jerusalem authorities who have brought Jesus for trial and the crowds to whom the offer of release is made: the offer is addressed precisely to those who have already demanded that Jesus be put to

---

89. Cf. Jn. 18.10-11.

death (Jn. 18.31-32). The question is why the evangelist presents the offer motif in a form in which it has become meaningless. To compound the problem, he has associated the offer with an explicit declaration of Jesus' innocence (Jn. 18.38), in words that correspond closely to Luke 23.4 and in a context corresponding closely to Luke 23.15. Why would one who is declared innocent be the object of an act of clemency?[90] It seems that, here too, the evangelist hears in Pilate's offer an unwitting testimony to Jesus' kingship.

3.1 As in Mark, the Johannine Jesus is subjected to a mock coronation. In Mark, followed by Matthew, this event follows Jesus' condemnation and immediately precedes his crucifixion. The connection is still closer in *GPet*, where the mock coronation takes place at the site of Jesus' crucifixion. A throne is added to the purple garment and crown of thorns, and the acclamation takes the form of an appeal for just judgement, addressed to the "king of Israel" (*GPet*. 3.7-8). In contrast, the Johannine evangelist incorporates this event into Jesus' trial and in doing so further develops his theme of Pilate as witness. Pilate testifies to Jesus' kingship as he presents the mock kingly figure to his accusers with the words "Behold the man!" (Jn. 19.5). Here, however, the testimony is still indirect. It will later become more explicit in the words "Behold your king!" (19.15), and above all in the placard, written by Pilate himself (19.19-22).

3.2 Jesus' accusers here allege that he "makes himself a king" and so "sets himself against Caesar" (19.12), just as he "made himself Son of God" and set himself against the law (19.7). While the claim to be Son of God is the real reason for the authorities' hostility to Jesus (cf. 5.18), it is kingship rather than divine sonship that is the central concern of the Johannine passion narrative. Thus the authorities now echo Pilate's earlier reference to Jesus as "king of the Jews" (18.39), although their statement refers to kingship in general. The authorities (and the evangelist) seem less interested in the Jewish dimension of Jesus' alleged claim than in kingship as such.

90. Aware of this problem, Luke has the crowds demanding the release of Barabbas on their own initiative rather than in response to an offer from Pilate (Lk. 23.18-19). Luke attributes to Pilate three explicit statements of innocence (Lk. 23.4, 14-15, 22), which probably provided the model for the corresponding statements in John (Jn. 18.38; 19.4, 6). In Mark, there is no declaration of Jesus' innocence from Pilate, but only the question, "Why, what evil has he done?" in response to the demand that he be crucified (Mk. 15.14). In Matthew the declaration of innocence takes the form of a symbolic gesture (Mt. 27.24).

4 Earlier, the initial question, "Are you the king of the Jews?" (18.33), was re-peated but without the reference to "the Jews": "Are you not then a king?" (18.37). Similarly here, Mark's "the man you call the king of the Jews" twice becomes "your king" (19.14, 15). While the possessive ὑμῶν is formally equiv-alent to τῶν Ἰουδαίων, the effect of "your king" is to cast the addressees in the role of subjects, but not specifically *Jewish* subjects. In *GPet* Jesus is con-demned, mocked, and crucified as king *of Israel*. The theme of this passion narrative is the enormity of his regicidal murder by his own elect people. In John, Jesus is condemned, mocked, and crucified as *king* (king of the Jews). The outward event of his crucifixion, in which he is "lifted up," is in reality his exaltation and coronation. There is no particular interest in the human perpetrators of his death.

Mark's account of Jesus' Roman trial is dominated by the "king of the Jews" question. Pilate's use of this title creates the context in which Jesus' crucifixion as king of the Jews is intended to be understood. According to Mark, the initial question, "Are you the king of the Jews?" stems purely from Pilate and is unre-lated to the unspecified charges brought by the Jerusalem authorities. In the second question, "Do you want me to release for you the king of the Jews?" Pi-late continues to use the title but shows that for him it lacks all substance; Ro-man governors are not in the habit of releasing those they take seriously as a political threat. In the third question, "Then what shall I do with the man you call the king of the Jews?" it becomes clear that Pilate's use of the title is occa-sioned by a misreading of his audience's perception of Jesus. He expects a posi-tive response to his offer to release "the king of the Jews." Instead, the crowds demand his crucifixion. Thus it is *as king of the Jews* that Jesus is first subjected to a mock coronation and then crucified by Pilate's soldiers. The crucial point is that Pilate has put the king-of-the-Jews title into circulation precisely be-cause he wishes to secure Jesus' release, believing him to be innocent of all charges. Once in circulation, the title takes on a life of its own. That, for Mark, is the roundabout way in which Jesus came to be crucified beneath a placard which read: "The King of the Jews." The story as he tells it is an *interpretation* of an older version of the passion narrative, in which a more direct line may have been drawn between Jesus' crucifixion as king of the Jews and his accla-mation as such at his triumphal entry into Jerusalem. Whatever its relation to underlying historical facts, Mark's interpretation intends to show that Jesus' significance does not lie in any intention to replace existing political authority with an alternative messianic one centred upon himself. For Mark, Jesus' cru-cifixion as "king of the Jews" tells us nothing about who he truly is.

The placard on the cross presents itself as a satirical comment on a presumed claim to kingship. If Jesus never aspired to be king of the Jews and was never regarded as such, the satire loses its point. Mark's concern is precisely to show that the satire is pointless. For the later Petrine and Johannine evangelists, however, the placard is not misplaced satire but testimony to the truth. According to Peter, the placard read: "This is the King of Israel" (*GPet* 4.11). The King of Israel is the divine Son of God, God in person: Jewish regicide is also deicide. In contrast, John finds testimony to the truth in the original wording of the placard, which he cites in slightly extended form: "The King of the Jews" (Mk. 15.26) becomes "Jesus of Nazareth, the King of the Jews" (Jn. 19.19). This evangelist does not reproduce the οὗτος of Luke (Lk. 23.38) or the οὗτός ἐστιν of Matthew and Peter (Mt. 27.37; *GPet* 4.11). And it is specifically *Pilate* who testifies to the truth by inscribing the placard himself and refusing to emend it when asked to do so:

> And Pilate wrote the placard and set it upon the cross. And it was written: "Jesus of Nazareth, King of the Jews." Many of the Jews read this placard, for the place where Jesus was crucified was near the city, and it was written in Hebrew, Latin, and Greek. So the chief priests of the Jews said to Pilate, "Do not write, 'The King of the Jews,' but, 'This man said: I am King of the Jews.'" Pilate answered: "What I have written I have written." (Jn. 19.19-22)

As we have seen, the Johannine evangelist already casts Pilate in the role of a witness in his reinterpretation of the Markan trial narrative. Indeed, he is appointed to that role by Jesus himself. Pilate asks, "Are you the king of the Jews?" and Jesus replies by enquiring into the divine or human source of his insight (Jn. 18.33-34). Pilate then asks, "Are you not then a king?" and Jesus hears within his question a confession of the truth: "You say that I am a king . . ." (18.37). As his account of the controversy evoked by the placard indicates, the evangelist is concerned to emphasize the fundamental difference between identifying Jesus as king of the Jews or as one who claimed to be king of the Jews. Pilate does indeed speak of Jesus as king of the Jews, when he asks, "Do you wish me to release for you the king of the Jews?" (18.39), and when he invites his audience to "behold your king," a significant departure from the corresponding Markan reference to "the man you call the king of the Jews" (Jn. 19.14; Mk. 15.12). Not only does Pilate testify to Jesus as king, he also puts his testimony into writing, refusing the emendation that would convert it into a now falsified claim made by Jesus himself. Pilate takes his place alongside the other scriptural witnesses whose testimony is here cited (cf. Jn. 19.24, 28, 36-37).[91]

According to the written testimony of Pilate and the Johannine evangelist, Jesus is disclosed as king in his death on the cross. In crucifixion (unlike stoning), the victim is "lifted up," exposed to full public gaze (Jn. 3.14; 8.28; 12.32-34; cf. 18.32). In this case, it is a "king" who is lifted up. Although he is specifically king of the Jews, the three languages of the placard hint darkly at a wider significance: "I, when I am lifted up from the earth, will draw all people to myself" (12.32).[92] This "lifting up" is fundamentally not an execution at all, let alone a murder, but rather an epiphany of the king of all, exalted on the cross that is also his throne.[93]

In terms of the reception process, both the Johannine and the Petrine texts represent reinterpretations of earlier renderings of the passion narrative, themselves interpretations built on the foundation of the earliest written accounts of this sequence of events. In one sense, of course, the Markan interpretation is already subjected to reinterpretation by Matthew or Luke. Yet for heuristic purposes a distinction may be drawn between an ongoing process of interpretation and a *re*interpretation marking a radical departure from an earlier reading of events. In spite of emendations and expansions, Matthew and Luke basically follow Mark in presenting Jesus' death as king of the Jews as a case of mistaken identity. For Peter and John, Jesus' death is in reality the decisive disclosure of his true kingship. For one evangelist, that disclosure has a negative function. The placard speaks truth: on the cross the King of Israel who is also the divine Son of God is murdered by his own peo-

---

91. The point of Pilate's ὃ γέγραφα γέγραφα (Jn. 19.22) is to characterize him as a prophetic witness, not as "a true Roman in his respect for a legal document" (J. H. Bernard, *A Critical and Exegetical Commentary on the Gospel according to St. John*, 2 vols., ICC [Edinburgh: T. & T. Clark, 1928], 2.628).

92. As in Jn. 18.36-37, the emphasis in 19.19-22 is on kingship as such, not specifically kingship "of the Jews." It is therefore wrong to see here a reference to "the price paid by [Jesus'] accusers," that is, "the judgment of Judaism, which had surrendered the very hope that gave its existence its meaning" (R. Bultmann, *The Gospel of John: A Commentary*, Eng. trans. [Oxford: Blackwell, 1971], p. 669 [German original, 1941]). R. H. Lightfoot speaks in remarkably similar terms of "the price paid by the Jews for the rejection of their king, namely the condemnation and destruction of Judaism and of its age-long hopes" (*St. John's Gospel: A Commentary* [Oxford: Clarendon Press, 1956], p. 316). Both passages are cited approvingly by C. K. Barrett (*The Gospel according to St. John*, p. 549). All three commentators *also* see the cross as the locus of salvation — but at a cost.

93. As Joel Marcus has argued, the Johannine view presupposes an established, pre-Christian association of crucifixion with exaltation and kingship ("Crucifixion as Parodic Exaltation," *JBL* 125 [2006], pp. 73-87). I am less convinced by Marcus's claim (p. 74) that *Mark* intends his readers to see the truth about Jesus' kingship within the parody.

ple. The charge of deicide lies at the heart of this rendering of the passion story, serving to promote a supersessionist ideology. For the other evangelist, the disclosure intends universal salvation. Enthroned on the cross, lifted up in full public gaze, Jesus draws all people to himself. The human agent of the disclosure is, surprisingly, Pilate, whose role towards the end of the Johannine gospel corresponds to John the Baptist's at the beginning.[94] The disclosure of Jesus' identity is accessible to anyone who can read Pilate's unemended testimony in at least one of its three languages.

The two later evangelists do not "reinterpret" earlier renderings of the passion story in exactly the same sense of the term. As we have seen, the Johannine reinterpretation is closely bound to the precise wording of the Markan text: more so at the crucial points even than Matthew and Luke.[95] The Petrine reinterpretation deviates much further from any known exemplar. And yet, if Jesus was actually crucified as king of the Jews, and if the earliest recollection and tradition knew this and passed it on, then his crucifixion as the true king of Israel *must* represent an interpretative shift from an earlier rendering of the kingship motif to a later one.[96]

94. Thus the Johannine Pilate is not just a representative of "secular" political authority engaged in a power struggle with the Jewish leaders (the view of Ronald Piper, "The Characterisation of Pilate and the Death of Jesus in the Fourth Gospel," in *The Death of Jesus in the Fourth Gospel*, ed. G. van Belle, BEThL [Leuven: Leuven University Press, 2007], pp. 121-62). Piper seems to me to underplay Pilate's authorship of the trilingual *titulus*.

95. According to C. H. Dodd, the Johannine understanding of the crucifixion as an enthronement "presupposes a form of tradition in which the claim to kingship was prominent, as it is not in the Synoptics" (*Historical Tradition*, p. 122). Dodd fails to reckon with the possibility that a later evangelist may creatively reinterpret an earlier one.

96. Pace J. D. Crossan, who argues that the Petrine account of the passion predates the canonical ones (*The Cross That Spoke*, pp. 16-30). Crossan finds in the Petrine fragment (1) an early "Cross Gospel," later supplemented (2) by canonically oriented passages (Jesus' burial by Joseph of Arimathea [6.23-24], the empty tomb [12.50–13.57], apostles at the Sea of Galilee [14.60]), whose integration into the Cross Gospel is anticipated and facilitated (3) by redactional passages (Joseph's request [2.3-5a], the angelic descent [11.43-44], and the apostles' mourning [7.26-27, 14.58-59]). The primitive Cross Gospel thus extends from the trial before Herod and Pilate to the postresurrection dialogue between Pilate and the guards (1.1–11.49), with relatively minor additions (Joseph's request [2.3-5], the burial [6.23-24], the disciples' mourning [7.26-27], and the descent of the single angel [11.43-44]). The Cross Gospel predates Mark, and supplies Matthew with the story of the guard, Luke with the trial before Herod and the good thief, and John with the nonbreaking of the legs (p. 19). Along with its other difficulties, this elaborate hypothesis overlooks the Petrine evangelist's achievement of a *continuous* narrative, from Good Friday to Easter and beyond, that fills in perceived gaps especially in the Markan and Matthean versions (cf. *GPet* 9.34–11.45; 13.57–14.60).

Locating the Risen Lord

In the case of the king-of-the-Jews motif, the earliest accessible interpretative trajectory is to be found within Mark. That trajectory is decisively redirected by the Petrine and Johannine evangelists, acting in parallel although independently of each other at this point. A similar process may be traced within the Easter traditions — specifically, in the motif of Galilee as the site of the risen Lord's appearance. This motif is introduced by Mark in the context of Jesus' prediction of Peter's denials (Mk. 14.28). It is only loosely related to that context, however, and it is omitted from the parallel contained in the so-called "Fayum Fragment" (see Figure 7.2, to which the enumeration below corresponds).[97]

Figure 7.2

Mark 14.26-30 [Mt. 26.30-34]	*Fayum Fragment (P. Vindob. G 2325)*
1 And after singing a hymn they went out to the Mount of Olives.	*1* [After] leading [them/us] out,
2.1 And Jesus *said* to them, "*You will all fall away* {Mt: from me *this night*}, for it is written: '*I will strike the shepherd and the sheep* {Mt: of the flock} *will be scattered.*'	*2.1* as [*he sai*]*d*, "[*You will al*]*l fall away* [*this*] *night,* [according to] what is *written*: '*I will strike the* [*shepherd and the*] *sheep* [*will*] *be scattered,*'
2.2 But after I am raised I will go before you to Galilee."	
3 And *Peter said* to him, "*Even if they all* fall away, *I will not.*" {Mt: I will never be offended.}	*3* [and when] *Peter* / [I] *Peter* [said],* "*Even if they all* do so, [*I will no*]*t,*"
4 And *Jesus said* to him, "Amen I say to you that *you — today* {-Mt.}, this night, *before the cock* calls *twice* {-Mt.} *— will three times deny me.*"	*4* [*Jesus said, "Befor*]*e the cock* cro[ws] *twice* [*you will today d*]*e*[*n*]*y* [*me three times."*]

*Either [εἰπόντος το]ῦ Πέτ(ρου), or (Lührmann) [εἰπόντος ἐμο]ῦ Πέτ(ρου)

97. See Kraus and Nicklas, *Das Petrusevangelium und die Petrusapokalypse*, pp. 65-68. D. Lührmann argues that this text, first published in 1885, may be a fragment of *GPet*. Following Jesus' prophecy about the scattering of the sheep, the introduction to Peter's response can be reconstructed either as [εἰπόντος το]ῦ Πέτ(ρου) καὶ εἰ πάντες ο[ὐκ ἐγώ] (so Kraus and Nicklas) or as [εἰπόντος ἐμο]ῦ Πέτ(ρου) κτλ (Lührmann, *Die apokryph gewordenen Evangelien*, pp. 87-90). This would recall the ἐγὼ δὲ Σίμων Πέτρος in *GPet* 14.60 (cf. ἐγὼ δέ, 7.26) and the probable first-person singular reference to Peter in *P. Oxy.* 4009 (cf. *2 Clem.* 5.2). Lührmann connects the absence

In the Fayum Fragment, a series of subordinate clauses *(1-3)* serves to highlight Jesus' prediction of denial *(4)*, which was probably introduced by the formula λέγει Ἰη[σοῦς]. While there is one point where this text agrees with Matthew against Mark ("this night" at *2.1*), there are five points where it appears to agree with Mark against Matthew (omission of the Matthean "from me" and "of the flock" at *2.1*, retention of οὐκ ἐγώ at *3* and of "twice" and "today" [?] at *4)*. In view of these Markan links, the absence of *2.2* is striking, especially since the reference to a return journey to Galilee fits awkwardly into its Markan context. In *2.1*, Jesus announces the imminent dispersal of the group of disciples, citing scripture in doing so. While *2.2* might have spoken of the reconstituting of his "flock," it is not clear that this is what it does. The sheep/shepherd imagery is discontinued, and nothing is said about the purpose of the journey to Galilee. The ensuing dialogue with Peter *(3, 4)* makes no reference to Jesus' resurrection and its sequel, but is connected to *2.1*. It is likely that *2.2* is a secondary interpretative comment intended to mitigate the negative tenor of *2.1*, opening up the prospect of a miraculous new beginning. The Fayum text may be dependent on Mark in more or less its present form, in which case its author has rightly noted that the passage is more coherent if *2.2* is omitted. Alternatively it may stem directly from a pre-Markan version of this tradition.[98] Either way, the reference to the journey to Galilee in Mark 14.28 represents an interpretative intervention which allows post-Easter light to shine for a moment into the gathering gloom of the passion narrative.

This motif of the return to Galilee recurs in Mark's Empty Tomb story, and it is again apparently lacking in an otherwise closely related passage — this time from *GPet* (see Figure 7.3).[99]

1. In Mark, the women come to anoint Jesus' body with the spices they have bought. For the Petrine evangelist, an explanation along these lines seems

---

here of the Markan reference to Galilee (cf. Mk. 14.28) with the corresponding absence at *GPet* 13.56 (cf. Mk. 16.7).

98. According to Dibelius, this text "ist offenbar kein Evangelienfragment, sondern entstammt . . . einer Sammlung von Worten Jesu, die mit Zeitangaben versehen sind. Der Mk 14.27, 29-31 berichtete Dialog Jesu ist hier insoweit verkürzt, dass die Gegenrede des Petrus nur im Genitivus absolutus, also echt chrienmässig, eingeführt und aufs äusserste verknappt wird" (*Formgeschichte*, p. 161). Against Dibelius, (1) a genitive absolute is used in similar fashion in *GEger* 1v, ll. 14-17, in the context of a continuous narrative; (2) the Fayum Fragment is dependent on a larger narrative context, unlike the "chrienmässig" material in *GTh*.

99. See Foster's analysis of the relationship between *GPet* and Mark here (*Gospel of Peter*, pp. 465-68).

Figure 7.3

Mark 16.1-8	GPet 12.50–13.57
1. And when the sabbath was past *Mary the Magdalene* and Mary [the wife] of James and Salome bought spices so that they might come and anoint him. And very <u>early</u> on the first day of the week, they *come to the tomb,* when the sun had risen.	*1.* And <u>early</u> on the Lord's Day, *Mary the Magdalene,* a disciple of the Lord — being afraid of the Jews, for they were inflamed with anger, she had not done at the Lord's tomb what women are accustomed to do for those who die and are loved by them — *came to the tomb* where he was laid, taking her friends with her.
2. And they were saying to each other,	*2.* And they were afraid that the Jews would see them, *and they were saying,* "If we were not able to weep and mourn on the day he was crucified, let us do so now at his tomb. But *who will roll away for us the stone* laid against *the door of the tomb,* so that entering we may sit beside him and do what is right? *For* the stone *was great,* and we are afraid that someone may see us. And if we do not succeed, let us leave what we are bringing in memory of him, let us weep and mourn as we return to our house."
"Who will roll away for us the stone from *the door of the tomb?"*	
3. And they looked and saw that the stone had been rolled away; *for* it *was* very *great.* And entering the tomb they saw a young man seated on the right, *wearing a* white *robe,* and they were terrified.	*3.* And when they arrived they found the tomb open, and they came and bent down and *saw* there *a* certain *young man seated* in the middle of the tomb, beautiful and *wearing a* shining *robe,*
4.1 But he *said to them:* "Do not be terrified! *Do you seek* the *crucified* Nazarene? <u>He has been raised,</u> *he is not* here, *see the place* <u>where they put him!</u>	*4.1* who *said to them:* "Why did you come? Whom *do you seek?* Not the one who was *crucified?* <u>He is risen</u> and has departed. If you do not believe, bend down and *see the place* <u>where he lay,</u> *because he is not* [there].
4.2 But go, tell his disciples and Peter that he goes before you to Galilee. There you will see him, as he told you."	*4.2* For he is risen and has departed to the place from which he was sent."
5. And coming out they *fled* from the tomb, for trembling and terror had overcome them, and they said nothing to anyone, for they <u>were afraid.</u>	*5.* Then the women <u>were frightened</u> and *fled.*

Italics: exact parallels
<u>Underlining</u>: partial parallels

inadequate. What must be addressed is the difficulty that the visit to the tomb to perform customary burial rites is so belated. Normally a body is anointed prior to burial; but, we learn, Mary had been too paralyzed by fear to carry out the usual rites at the usual time. The explanation takes the form of a complete sentence inserted into the middle of another complete sentence. The awkward syntax suggests a later expansion of an opening that may once have corresponded closely to Mark's.

2. For Peter there is a further difficulty with the Empty Tomb story in the form in which he has received it. The stone that blocks access to the tomb is a problem not only for the women but also for the narrative itself. According to Mark, Mary Magdalene and her friends know that they are incapable of shifting the stone, and they are more than doubtful whether help will be on hand. Why, then, do they come to anoint Jesus' body when they are so unlikely to gain access to it? In the Petrine version of the conversation on the way to the tomb, the problem of the great stone is compounded by the possibility that there may be hostile onlookers. Since access to the tomb may be unrealistic, an alternative plan is proposed: the women will weep, mourn, and leave their spices *outside* the tomb, before returning home. This evangelist is concerned to enhance the verisimilitude of the story, which he knows in approximately its Markan form.

3. In Peter, unlike Mark, the reader already knows how the stone has been rolled away and how the young man comes to be seated inside the tomb. As they kept watch during the night, Pilate's soldiers

> saw the heavens opened and two men descending from there, having great radiance, and approaching the tomb. And the same stone that was placed against the entrance, rolling of its own accord, moved some way to the side, and the tomb was opened and both young men entered. (*GPet* 9.36-37)

This evangelist gives a different answer to Matthew's to the question who moved the stone. In Matthew, an angel of the Lord rolls back the stone and sits upon it (Mt. 28.2); in Peter, the stone moves without external agency as the angels approach. After their departure with the now risen Lord and the cross that followed (*GPet* 10.39), those gathered at the tomb again saw "the heavens opened, and a man descending and entering the tomb" (11.44). At this point the centurion, the other soldiers, and the Jewish elders hurry off to tell Pilate what has taken place, leaving the single angel to await the women within the tomb. Thus there is no trace of the guards when the women arrive, and the narrative can take its Markan course. Although Peter's story of the guards is probably inspired by Matthew's, this evangelist does not allow the guards to encroach on the women's visit to the tomb as Matthew does. In Matthew, the angel of the Lord arrives at the tomb just as the women do, and the terrified guards fall into a death-like trance so that the angelic message can be communicated without inconvenience (Mt. 28.4). The Petrine guards conduct themselves with greater professionalism than their Matthean counterparts; they are Romans rather than Jews. In Matthew the crucified Jesus is guarded by Roman soldiers (including a centurion) who confess him as Son of God, whereas his tomb is guarded by Jews (cf. Mt. 27.26, 36, 54, 65-66). In Peter Jesus is crucified by Jews, whereas his tomb is guarded by Romans (including a centurion) who confess him as Son of God (cf. *GPet* 8.31; 11.45). Here the Jewish authorities play a subordinate role at the tomb just as Pilate plays a subordinate role at Jesus' trial.

While Mark's young man in a white robe is surely an angel descended from heaven, the evangelist does not explicitly say so. Peter resolves the ambiguity by narrating his descent and by causing his white robe to shine. He also shifts the young man from "the right" to "the middle of the tomb," providing more headroom in a tomb so low that one has to stoop to look into it. The women remain outside a tomb too small to accommodate them.

4.1 In Mark, the first part of the angelic message consists in *(a)* an appeal not to be afraid; *(b)* a question about the presumed purpose of the visit; *(c)* the announcement of Jesus' resurrection and thus *(d)* of his absence; and *(e)* an invitation to confirm that absence by a visual inspection. In Peter the first part of the message consists in *(b)* a general question about the purpose of the visit followed by further questions suggesting the possible answer; *(c)* the announcement of Jesus' resurrection; *(e)* the invitation to carry out a visual inspection which will confirm the claim *(d)* that he is not here. At *(b)* Jesus is identified only as the crucified and no longer as the Nazarene. At *(c)* reference is made to Jesus' departure as well as his resurrection. The invitation to "see the place . . ." is presented as a remedy for unbelief; *(d)* and *(e)* are transposed.

4.2 In the second part of his message, the Markan angel speaks no longer of the emptiness of the tomb but of the risen Lord's journey to Galilee for the promised reunion with the disciples. The reference is clearly to Jesus' assurance in Mark 14.28 that "after I am raised I will go before you to Galilee," although a promise of reunion is only implicit there.[100] The risen Lord takes the road to Galilee as, in Luke, he takes the road to Emmaus, but walking ahead of his disciples so that they will catch up with him only when they arrive at their destination. Mark's present tense (προάγει, 16.7) suggests that Jesus has already begun his return to Galilee.[101] In the Petrine gospel, a journey on the horizontal plane is replaced by a vertical journey. "He is risen and has departed" *(4.1)* is repeated and elaborated: "He is risen and has departed to the place from which he was sent." This departure is symbolically depicted in the image of the Lord emerging from the tomb with his head surpassing the heavens (*GPet* 10.40). In this gospel there is no distinct ascension event; resurrection and ascension are fused. Also notable is the reference to preexistence. Here, the "Son of God" who is also "King of Israel" is a heavenly being.

The Petrine return to the heavenly homeland reinterprets the Markan return to the earthly homeland. In both gospels, the angel explains the emptiness of the tomb by referring not just to the resurrection but also to a departure and a destination, and the Petrine reinterpretation takes the simple form of substituting a vertical heavenward journey for a horizontal earthly one. A closely parallel reinterpretation is found in John, where Jesus himself takes over the angelic role:

> Jesus said to [Mary]: "Do not touch me, for I have not yet ascended to the Father. Go to my brethren and say to them, 'I ascend to my Father and your Father, to my God and your God.'" (Jn. 20.17)

As in Mark, Mary (but without her companions) is entrusted with a message for the male disciples. While there is little verbal overlap between the two references to Mary's commissioning, both sense and structure are similar. Also relevant here is the second Matthean version of the commissioning, in which, as in John, the risen Jesus is the speaker:

---

100. Aware of this problem, Matthew replaces Mark's καθὼς εἶπεν ὑμῖν with ἰδοὺ εἶπον ὑμῖν (Mk. 16.7; Mt. 28.7).

101. The reference to Jesus' journey makes it unlikely that "there you will see him" is a reference to the parousia (as argued by E. Lohmeyer, *Galiläa und Jerusalem* [Göttingen: Vandenhoeck & Ruprecht, 1936], p. 11).

1		2	3	
ὑπάγετε,		εἴπατε	τοῖς μαθηταῖς αὐτοῦ	(Mk. 16.7)
πορεύου δὲ	πρὸς τοὺς	καὶ εἰπὲ	αὐτοῖς	(Jn. 20.17)
	ἀδελφούς μου			
ὑπάγετε,		ἀπαγγείλατε	τοῖς ἀδελφοῖς μου	(Mt. 28.10)[102]

While the Johannine account of Mary's commissioning closely resembles Mark, the content of her message is reinterpreted. The message still has to do with Jesus' departure, but the journey to Galilee is replaced by an ascent to the Father in close analogy to *GPet*. Jesus ascends to the Father; he departs to the place from which he was sent. That might suggest that the two later gospels interpret "Galilee" allegorically, as a reference to heaven. Yet post-Easter stories set in Galilee occur both in *GPet* and in the final form of the Gospel of John. The Markan promise, "There you will see him," was no doubt fulfilled in the lost ending of *GPet* just as it is in John 21. In both cases, Jesus' appearances are probably to be understood as manifestations of the already ascended Lord, brief reenactments of the earthly life that concluded with his death and burial. Neither the Johannine "I am ascending . . ." nor the immediate Petrine return to heaven suggests the traditional forty days between resurrection and ascension (cf. Acts 1.3).

Jesus' announcement to Mary of his imminent departure recalls the "farewell discourses" of John 14 and 16, and here too language and concepts occur that may be traced back to the angelic message of Mark 16.7 and its antecedent in Mark 14.28. The statement "I go before you . . ." speaks of two journeys to the same destination, one preceding and enabling the other. The Johannine Jesus explains why his own journey must take precedence over his disciples': it is because "I go to prepare a place for you" (Jn. 14.2). Thus he can say to Peter, "Where I am going you cannot now follow, but you shall follow later" (13.36) — that is, when Jesus returns to escort his disciples to the heavenly home (14.3). Indeed, he himself is the familiar "way" that their journey must take (14.5-6). Yet the full reunion between the Lord and his disciples occurs only at their journey's end, for the purpose of the journey is that "where I am you may be also" (14.3). Here reunion is not represented in visual terms as it is in Mark 16.7 ("There you will see him, as he said"). Yet a

102. According to Dibelius, the Matthean and Johannine references to "my brothers" reflect the influence of Ps. 22.23a(22a), διηγήσομαι τὸ ὄνομά σου τοῖς ἀδελφοῖς μου ("Die alttestamentliche Motive," pp. 234-35). The promise, announced by Mary, is fulfilled in Mt. 28.16-20 and Jn. 20.19-23 respectively. The Johannine evangelist has "historisiert oder novellistisch verarbeitet" the scriptural motif, whose scriptural origin is "nicht mehr die Hauptsache" (p. 235).

Johannine paraphrase of this Markan promise occurs later in the discourses, when Jesus announces: "A little while and you will see me, and again a little while and you will not see me" (Jn. 16.16). As in 13.36, it is emphasized that the prospect of future reunion entails prior departure and absence. In chapter 16, the reunion occurs at Easter, as in Mark, whereas in chapter 14 it is apparently deferred to the parousia. The Johannine "little while" saying also fills a gap in the text of Mark, which does not itself contain the direct antecedent to "there you will see him" suggested by "as he said."

5. In Mark 16, Mary and her companions now *leave* the tomb they had previously *entered*: ἐξελθοῦσαι (v. 8) corresponds to εἰσελθοῦσαι (v. 5). In *GPet,* the space within the tomb is more limited: one has to stoop to look into it (*GPet* 13.55); it can accommodate a horizontal corpse or heavenly beings (cf. 9.37; 11.44) but not living humans.[103] More significantly, *GPet* lacks the Markan reference to the women's failure to pass on their message — since no message has been entrusted to them. The Petrine version of the story is entirely self-contained; the angel's words are addressed to the women alone, and there is no reference to the male disciples. Since "the twelve disciples of the Lord" were still grieving several days later, at the end of the feast, over what had happened (14.58-59; cf. 7.26), it seems that they still knew nothing of the resurrection.[104] While *GPet* lacks any equivalent to Mark's "they said nothing to anyone," it is evident here too that no communication has taken place. Indeed, in *GPet* the women are not only fearful but also unbelieving. The possibility of unbelief is explicitly thematized in the angelic message: "If you do not believe [εἰ δὲ μὴ πιστεύετε], bend down and see the place where he lay . . ." (13.56). Rather than responding to this invitation to see the empty tomb as a sign pointing to Jesus' resurrection, the women take fright and flee. In preserving and extending the negative tenor of the Markan narrative, the Petrine evangelist makes precisely the opposite editorial decision to Matthew's. In Matthew 28.8, the women do not "flee," they "leave quickly." Their "trembling and terror" is transmuted into "fear and great joy," and their failure to communicate what they have seen is replaced by an eagerness to inform the male disciples. In *GPet,* fear and grief predominate. Jesus' followers have absolutely no knowledge of his resurrection until they have returned to Galilee, through an encounter that must have been narrated shortly after the conclusion of the extant fragment. Both later evangelists seek to resolve the tension within Mark between the women's commis-

103. Vaganay rightly notes that "[l]es femmes n'entrent pas, elles ne font que se pencher" (*Évangile de Pierre,* p. 326).

104. So Vaganay, *Évangile de Pierre,* p. 331.

sion and their failure to discharge it — a failure that makes it seemingly impossible for the promised reunion in Galilee to take place. Matthew insists that the women *did* fulfil their commission, which was repeated when they encountered Jesus himself on their way back to the city. Here the angelic statement about Jesus' journey to Galilee ("he goes before you . . . ," Mt. 28.7) is replaced by an instruction to the disciples ("go and tell my brethren to go to Galilee," 28.10). A little later we learn that Jesus specified the precise place of the encounter, on a mountain (28.16). Peter adopts the opposite solution, eliminating not the women's failure but the commission itself.

As in the parallel passage in Mark 14.28, the angelic statement about Jesus' postresurrection journey to Galilee is not fully integrated into its Markan context. Both passages should probably be seen as editorial interventions by the evangelist, who intends to show that there are objective grounds for hope even where fear and despair are subjectively dominant: the fear and despair of both male and female disciples as they flee from the garden and then from the tomb (14.50; 16.8). Precisely in his inability to integrate these interpretive additions into the traditional narrative, Mark demonstrates that hope is grounded purely in Jesus' word and not in the empirical realities of the situation. Matthew and Peter reinterpret Mark's interpretation of the narrative, producing versions that differ radically from each other as well as from Mark.

In *GPet*, there is no reference to Jesus' journey to Galilee. His journey is transposed from the horizontal to the vertical plane. Nor is there any instruction to the disciples to meet him there. Yet this evangelist has not rejected the Markan claim that Galilee is the place where the risen Lord is to be encountered. The disciples make the journey to Galilee along with other pilgrims returning to their homes to resume their everyday lives after the interlude — in the disciples' case — not so much of the feast as of their entire discipleship of Jesus:

> It was the final day of Unleavened Bread and many were leaving to return to their homes with the ending of the feast. And we, the twelve disciples of the Lord, were weeping and mourning, and, grieving at what had happened, each departed for his own home. And I Simon Peter and Andrew my brother taking our nets went out into the sea, and there was with us Levi son of Alphaeus whom the Lord . . . (*GPet* 14.58-60)

At this point the fragment comes to an abrupt halt. The narrative may have proceeded to remind its readers that Levi son of Alphaeus was the tax collector whom Jesus called to follow him (cf. Mk. 2.13-14). The association of Simon Peter, Andrew, and fishing echoes another Markan story (cf. Mk. 1.16-20). In that case the original *GPet* may have followed Mark (as Matthew and Luke did) in including an account of Jesus' Galilean ministry as the prelude to the final journey to Jerusalem. The backward reference with which the Petrine fragment ends indicates a return to the situation preceding Jesus' original call. Presumably *GPet* proceeded to recount how, in the words of the Johannine parallel, "Jesus manifested himself . . . to his disciples by the Sea of Tiberias . . ." (Jn. 21.1). The Markan announcement that "he goes before you to Galilee," and that "there you will see him" (Mk. 16.7), is fulfilled — even though in *GPet* it is the already exalted Jesus who appears there, briefly reenacting his earthly life in a resurrection appearance just as the first disciples briefly reenact their former lives by going fishing in the lake.[105] This evangelist interprets the Galilean location of the resurrection appearance(s) as a return to the beginning. For a second time Simon Peter, Andrew, and Levi son of Alphaeus must be called away from their old life, now to become followers of the risen Lord.

In the Johannine parallel, Andrew and Levi are either absent or at least unnamed:

> Simon Peter, Thomas called Didymus, Nathanael from Cana of Galilee, the sons of Zebedee, and two others of his disciples were together. Simon Peter said to them, "I'm going fishing." They said to him, "We're coming with you." They went out and got into the boat. . . . (Jn. 21.2-3b)

In *GPet*, the smaller fishing party (three disciples rather than seven) is also more Markan in its composition. Thomas and Nathanael are characteristically Johannine figures (cf. Jn. 1.45-49; 11.16; 14.5; 20.24-29). Unlike John, *GPet* does not mention a boat. Simon Peter and Andrew wade into the sea in order either to set their nets near the edge of the lake or to cast them, as in Mark 1.16. Levi was "with us," but as a nonfisherman he is not said to have entered the water with the other two. In Mark 2.13-14 his tax office is located by the lake, so he too is where he was when first called by Jesus.[106]

---

105. The lake or "sea" is unspecified in *GPet* — "[n]ouvelle imprécision géographique," as Vaganay curtly notes (*Évangile de Pierre*, p. 339), contrasting the canonical references to the Sea of Galilee (Mk. 1.16; Mt. 4.18), the Sea of Tiberias (Jn. 21.1), and the Lake of Gennesaret (Lk. 5.1).

106. Origen knows of a copy of Mark in which Levi the tax collector is included among the Twelve (*Contra Celsum* i.62, cited by Foster, *Gospel of Peter*, p. 510). Presumably the reference is to Mk. 3.18, and a substitution of "Levi son of Alphaeus" (cf. Mk. 2.14) for "James son of Alphaeus."

There is no reason to suppose that *GPet* is dependent on John here,[107] and there are indications that the Johannine version is more developed than the Petrine one.[108] The extant opening of the Petrine version suggests that it took the form of a reenactment of the original call of the disciples, in which case the two essential elements are *(i)* the appearance of Jesus on the shore (cf. Jn. 21.4-7), and *(ii)* the renewed call to "follow me" (cf. Jn. 21.19b). In Mark, it is precisely Simon Peter, Andrew, and Levi to whom the original call to "follow me" is addressed (Mk. 1.17; 2.14). Johannine elements that may also have occurred in *GPet* include *(iii)* the miraculous catch of fish (Jn. 21.5-11; cf. Lk. 5.1-11); *(iv)* the initial nonrecognition of the risen Lord (Jn. 21.4, 7, 12); *(v)* the cooked breakfast on the shore (Jn. 21.9-13); and *(vi)* a conversation between Jesus and Simon Peter (Jn. 21.15-18; cf. 2 Pt. 1.14). Elements presumably absent from *GPet* include *(vi)* Simon Peter's subordination to the Beloved Disciple, an exclusively Johannine concern (Jn. 21.7, 20-24; cf. 13.23-26; 18.15-16; 20.2-10); and *(vii)* editorial comments seeking to integrate the story into the Johannine gospel (Jn. 21.1, 14, 24-25).[109]

107. On *GPet* 14.60 and its missing sequel Crossan states: "I presume this to be a redacted version of the incident in John 21:1-6" (*The Cross That Spoke*, p. 292; cf. Foster, *Gospel of Peter*, p. 511). Crossan's presumption is the product of his redactional theory — which cannot explain, however, why the Petrine redactor has made the opening of the Johannine story sound so Markan. Crossan also assumes that the redactor would have named all twelve disciples at this point, perhaps regarding Levi as a replacement for Judas Iscariot (pp. 292-93). This seems to be ruled out by the singular ἦν σὺν ἡμῖν Λευίς. Peter, Andrew, and Levi also feature in a post-Easter setting (along with Mary) in the *Gospel of Mary* 17.10–18.21.

108. According to Bultmann, John 21.1-14 was "originally an independent Easter story" which an editor has turned into an introduction to vv. 15-23, focused exclusively on the relation between Peter and the Beloved Disciple (*John*, p. 702). V. 7 is an editorial addition which serves to link the two parts, although it is inconsistent with v. 11: Peter leaps into the sea to meet the Lord in advance of the others but is also responsible for landing the catch of fish (pp. 702-3). Another inconsistency is the fact that Jesus has already procured and cooked fish (v. 9b; cf. v. 13), so that the miraculous catch is not needed (p. 703). Along with v. 7 and probably v. 4b, vv. 9b and 13 are no doubt redactional (p. 703). V. 14 indicates that "the redactor wished to combine the Matthean-Markan tradition of a Galilean appearance of the Risen Lord with the Johannine representation" (pp. 705-6). No clear link is provided between the narrative of vv. 1-14 and the conversations with Peter in vv. 15-23: "The other disciples are simply ignored in vv. 15-23; only the Beloved Disciple, whose appearance in v. 7 actually goes back to the redactor, appears again in vv. 18-23" (p. 706). The point here is that, "after Peter died as a martyr, the Beloved Disciple stepped into his place as an authoritative witness" (p. 706).

109. To the internal evidence for the secondary status of Jn. 21 should be added the evidence of *MS. Copt.e. 150(P)*. This has been edited by Gesa Schenke, who dates it to the fourth century ("Das Erscheinen Jesu vor den Jüngern und der ungläubige Thomas: Johannes 20,19-31," in *Coptica-Gnostica-Manichaica: Mélanges offerts à Wolf-Peter Funk*, ed. Louis Painchaud and Paul-

Absent in John but present in *GPet* is an explanation of how disciples last heard of in Jerusalem have returned to Galilee and their old way of life. The story told by the Petrine gospel is entirely coherent. The angelic message is disbelieved and there are no Jerusalem appearances of the risen Lord. As yet the disciples know nothing of the resurrection, and they return grieving to their Galilean homeland so as to pick up the threads of their former lives. In Galilee, by the lake, Jesus appears to three of them, reenacting their original call. In John 21, however, the disciples have already encountered the risen Lord; they have been commissioned by him and have received the Holy Spirit and the power to forgive or retain sins (Jn. 20.19-23). In this context their sudden appearance in Galilee, after the conclusion of 20.30-31, is hard to understand — as is their reversion to a former way of life which has not been mentioned before in this gospel (cf. Jn. 1.35-42). The story recounted in John 21 must have had its original context elsewhere, and the evidence of *GPet* indicates that it develops out of the Markan promise that the risen Jesus will appear to his disciples in Galilee. The same is true of Matthew 28.16-20, where the promised encounter occurs on a Galilean mountain rather than at the lakeside. As we have seen, the Markan passage is reinterpreted in Jesus' address to Mary in John 20.17, and the Galilee connection is only reestablished when the lakeside call story is developed into a supplement to an already complete gospel.

The Johannine and Petrine gospels reinterpret Mark's interpretation of the Empty Tomb story in its pre-Markan form. The Markan interpretation

---

Hubert Poirier [Louvain: Peeters; Quebec: Les Presses de L'Université Laval, 2006], pp. 893-904). This single incomplete sheet of papyrus contains Jn. 20.19-25 in Coptic translation on the recto, and 20.26-31 on the verso (with three lines missing in between). At Jn. 20.30-31, the Coptic reads (as reconstructed by Schenke, pp. 900-902): ⲀⲞ̅P ⲌINKEMⲀⲈIN ⲆⲈ ON ⲈNⲀⳣⳣOY N̅Ō̅I I̅C̅ [ⲈNⲤⲈⲤⲎ]Ⲍ ⲀN ⲈⲠⲈIⳤⲰⲘⲈ. ⲈNⲦⲀYⲤⳬⲀI NⲀI N̅ⲆⲈ ⳤⲈⲔⲀ[Ⲥ ⲈⲦⲈⲦN̅]ⲀⲠIⲤⲦⲈY(?) ⳤⲈ ⲠⳤOIC ⲠⲈ ⲠⲈⳤⲢIⲤ[Ⲧ]OⲤ Ⲡ̅ⳟ[ⲎⲢⲈ M̅]ⲠNOYⲦⲈ ⲠⲈ ⟨ⳤⲈⲔⲀⲤ [ⲈⲦⲈⲦNⲀⳤ]I⟩^del ⟨ⲀYⲰ N̅ⲦⲈⲦNⳤ(I)⟩^corr N̅OYⲰN̅Ⲍ N̅ⳣⲀ ⲈNⲈⲌ 2M̅ ⲠⲈⳤⲢⲀN ("Jesus performed many other signs which are not written in this book. But these are written so that you may believe that the Lord is the Christ, the Son of God, ⟨so that you may receive⟩^del ⟨and may receive⟩^corr eternal life in his name"). There are three main deviations from standard Coptic and Greek readings here. In v. 30, "in the presence of his disciples" is lacking. In v. 31, "the Lord" is substituted for "Jesus" and the participle "believing" is omitted (although there are complications here owing to scribal error: Schenke, pp. 900-901). Following the close of Jn. 20.31 and a scribal correction, there is an empty space equivalent to about three lines. The scribe considers that he has completed his task: either he chooses not to continue into Jn. 21, or he is using an exemplar in which this chapter is lacking. There is no subscribed title, although it might have been present at the missing foot of the page. (My thanks to Joel Marcus for alerting me to Schenke's article, and to the Bodleian Library, Oxford, for images of the papyrus.)

sets the terror of Easter morning in the context of a journey to Galilee, where the Lord and his disciples are to be reunited. The later evangelists reinterpret Jesus' journey as heavenward rather than earthly. They nevertheless preserve the Galilean reference, somewhat fortuitously in John but more cogently in *GPet*. In reinterpreting the earlier interpretation, the later evangelists attempt to rearticulate the significance of Jesus' resurrection, understood now as an exaltation to heaven which removes him from the earthly sphere into the immediate presence of God. Yet his continuing concern for his followers and their mission is expressed in the one appearance story that the two gospels have in common, in which Jesus' original calling of his disciples is re-enacted and renewed.[110]

There is one fundamental difference between the Petrine account of the Easter events and its canonical counterparts. The Petrine version is concerned to fill gaps in the narrative and to eliminate anomalies. Events preceding the women's arrival at the tomb are narrated in full. The women acknowledge that they are unlikely to gain access to Jesus' body, and plan accordingly. The young man in the tomb is unambiguously identified as an angel whose descent from heaven was actually observed. The women's failure to deliver their message is eliminated, and a plausible naturalistic explanation for the disciples' return to Galilee is substituted. In contrast, gaps and anomalies abound in the other four accounts of the Easter event — to the despair of harmonizers and the delight of rationalists. In theological perspective, the canonical decision can be seen as the rejection of the Petrine assumption that only a continuous and coherent Easter narrative can expect to be cogent and persuasive. Gaps and anomalies are integral to the canonical testimony to an event transcending narration, just as the *via negativa* is integral to discourse about God.

---

110. Points of contact between *GPet* and John are otherwise slight. The nonbreaking of Jesus' bones (Jn. 19.32-33) is only loosely connected to the nonbreaking of the criminal's bones (*GPet* 4.14). In *GPet* 3.7, ἐκάθισαν αὐτὸν ἐπὶ καθέδραν κρίσεως may be compared with ἐκάθισεν ἐπὶ βήματος in Jn. 19.13, which could be understood transitively; cf. Justin, *1 Apol.* xxxv.6, αὐτὸν ἐκάθισαν ἐπὶ βήματος (on this see Vaganay, *Évangile de Pierre*, p. 158; Foster, *Gospel of Peter*, pp. 264-66). According to Charles Hill, such points are sufficient to demonstrate Johannine influence on *GPet*, and make it possible to characterize this text as an attempt at gospel harmonization along with *GEger* and Tatian's *Diatessaron* (*The Johannine Corpus in the Early Church*, pp. 306, 309). In reality, *GPet* has little in common with either text. Brown's comment is nearer the mark: "It is virtually inconceivable that the author of *GPet* had John before him and copied so little distinctively Johannine" (*Death of the Messiah*, p. 1331). It is, however, entirely conceivable that the author of Jn. 21 had before him something closely related to the lakeside appearance story of *GPet*.

In their different ways, the gospels that go under the names of Thomas, John, and Peter all exemplify the tendency for later evangelists not simply to continue the interpretative work of their predecessors but rather to subject it to more or less radical *re*interpretation. Naturally, the line between interpretation and reinterpretation cannot be sharply drawn; the purpose of the distinction is simply to draw attention to significant discontinuities and disruptions within the interpretative tradition. While there is always discontinuity and disruption within the transmission of oral or written tradition, this can be more clearly seen at some points than at others. It may be seen in the programmatic development of the traditional seeking-and-finding saying in *GTh* and in its more ambivalent treatment in John; in the contrasting Petrine and Johannine transpositions of the "king of the Jews" charge from an apologetic context into the sphere of revelation; and in the various attempts to negotiate the negative testimony of the empty tomb.

This investigation of the phenomenon of reinterpretation within a more comprehensive model of reception has demonstrated again that canonical and noncanonical gospels are intimately related and that they can and should be read in the light of each other. In other words, they can and should initially be read as though the distinction between canonical and noncanonical did not exist. Early Christian gospel literature does not display one or another of two distinct sets of attributes, foreshadowing either canonical recognition or apocryphal marginalization. While a comparison between a canonical and a noncanonical gospel may bring striking divergences to light, these are not necessarily any greater than divergences among the canonical gospels themselves. At the same time, the proliferation of interpretations and reinterpretations raises in acute form the question of *normativity*. Interpretations are not all equally good and reliable. There is such a thing as *mis*interpretation — or so it is generally believed. Where interpretations and reinterpretations proliferate, so too does the possibility of misinterpretation, with potentially disastrous consequences. It seems that, beyond interpretation and reinterpretation, the reception process will require a moment of *normativization* in order to establish limits within which it will henceforth operate. Normativization may take various forms, of which the fourfold canonical gospel has been the most enduring and successful. This fourfold textual object stipulates that each of the texts it comprises must be read in the light of the other three, without detriment to its individual integrity, and that it must not be read in the light of apparently similar texts outside the canonical boundary. Previously intermingled, early Christian gospels are divided from one another like wheat and tares, sheep and goats. This is fundamentally a creative move as well as a restrictive one. It brings into being a new composite textual object which enshrines the principles of plurality and relativity and excludes any monopolistic claim to embody "the gospel of Jesus Christ" rather than a self-limiting "gospel according to . . ." (εὐαγγέλιον κατά). At the same time, the new construct represents a fundamental disruption within the community of gospel readers. Precisely by stipulating the canonical boundary, it acknowledges that this is not a natural barrier like a river or mountain range but an artificial construct, more like a wall that imposes a new political order on communities affected by it. The fourfold gospel represents a decision about community order and organization rather than a historical, literary, or theological judgement about the nature of early gospel literature. At the same time it establishes a new field for the exercise of historical, literary, or theological judgement, a field full of potential for the upbuilding of the community.

It seems that any individual gospel can be viewed under two distinct perspectives. It can be viewed as a further contribution to the single ongoing project of writing the gospel. Or it can be viewed in its relation to a canonical boundary that defines it as something which, in itself, it is not. The second perspective is much the more familiar. In consequence, the distinction between Matthew and John on the one hand, and Thomas and Peter on the other, *looks as though* it were natural and self-evident rather than the construction of something new. In the absence of the precanonical perspective, the canonical perspective will inevitably be misunderstood. It is only as the texts deemed noncanonical are taken into account that the true significance of the canonical boundary becomes clear.

PART THREE

THE CANONICAL CONSTRUCT

CHAPTER 8

The East: Limiting Plurality

According to one account of gospel origins, Mark and Q are rapidly succeeded by Matthew and Luke; Q disappears, but by the end of the first century John has been added. The canonical collection is now essentially complete, and is increasingly recognized as such during the mid- to late second century. Meanwhile, other gospels were composed. But these were never acknowledged as equal in standing to the proto-canonical four, on which they are in any case dependent. The canonical inclusion of one group and the exclusion of the other correspond to the historical circumstances of their origin and earliest reception. The canon formalizes a prior historical reality: the four New Testament gospels significantly predate all extant noncanonical texts and are fundamentally different from them in literary and theological character.[1]

On a second account of gospel origins, the relationship of canonical to noncanonical gospels is simply reversed. As far as possible, one seeks to show that texts later deemed noncanonical actually predate those later deemed canonical. So it is argued that the *Gospel of Thomas* is wholly independent of the synoptics and that it preserves many of Jesus' sayings in an earlier and more original form.[2] Other texts from the Nag Hammadi collection are in-

---

1. So Graham N. Stanton, *The Gospels and Jesus* (Oxford: Oxford University Press, 1989), p. 135. Elsewhere Stanton argues that four-gospel codices were already in use in the 140s, and indeed that the codex format was adopted precisely so as to accommodate it ("The Fourfold Gospel," *NTS* 43 [1997], pp. 317-46; pp. 337-40). If so, then the canonical/noncanonical divide is already embodied in the codex format itself. This seems unlikely, however. The unequal distribution in the papyrus attestation of canonical gospels suggests that, in the earliest period, gospels normally circulated singly.

2. S. Davies, *The Gospel of Thomas and Christian Wisdom* (California: Bardic Press, 2005²), pp. x-xxxi.

serted into the prehistory of the Gospel of John.[3] Far from being dependent on the canonical gospels, the *Gospel of Peter* is said to preserve the early source from which all the canonical passion and Easter narratives are drawn.[4] The so-called "Secret Gospel of Mark" is also pressed into service at this point.[5] Although it is presented as a second edition of canonical Mark in the "letter of Clement to Theodore" in which its fragments are contained, attempts are made to establish its priority to the canonical text — while passing over the overwhelming evidence that both the letter and the secret gospel are a modern forgery.[6] No clearer indication could be given of a programmatic commitment to the priority of the noncanonical over the canonical.

In both accounts, the canonical/noncanonical distinction plays a decisive role. In the first, the canonical texts straightforwardly precede the noncanonical ones. In the second, the (correct) hypothesis that the noncanonical *may* predate the canonical hardens into a systematic prioritizing of the noncanonical. On both sides of the argument, early or late datings serve as proxies for positive or negative value-judgements about the texts in question — as the debate around the *Gospel of Thomas* illustrates all too clearly.[7] As Dieter Lührmann notes, the terms "canonical" and "apocryphal" are, like "heresy" and "orthodoxy," almost unavoidably value-laden.[8] The two accounts continue to operate within these dichotomies, reproducing them rather than subjecting them to critical reflection. In consequence, a simple point is overlooked. As Lührmann notes,

3. H. Koester, *Ancient Christian Gospels: Their History and Development* (Philadelphia: Trinity Press International; London: SCM Press, 1990), pp. 173-200.

4. J. D. Crossan, *The Cross That Spoke: The Origins of the Passion Narrative* (New York: Harper & Row, 1988), pp. 16-30.

5. Koester, *Ancient Christian Gospels*, pp. 293-303; J. D. Crossan, *Four Other Gospels: Shadows on the Contours of Canon* (Sonoma, CA: Polebridge, 1992[2]), pp. 59-83; Ron Cameron, *The Other Gospels: Non-Canonical Gospel Texts* (Guildford: Lutterworth, 1983), pp. 67-71.

6. See my article "Beyond Suspicion: On the Authorship of the Mar Saba Letter and the Secret Gospel of Mark," *JTS*, n.s., 61 (2010), pp. 128-70. For a summary of the hypotheses of Koester and Crossan, see pp. 141-42 n. 41.

7. According to Stevan Davies, "[T]he significance of the Gospel of Thomas for contemporary religious life depends in great part on whether it can be shown to be dependent and gnostic and second-century or not" (*The Gospel of Thomas and Christian Wisdom*, p. xxxi). For an equally questionable conflation of dependence, gnosticism, the second century, and theological/historical value, but from an opposing ideological standpoint, see John P. Meier, *A Marginal Jew: Rethinking the Historical Jesus*, vol. 1 (New York: Doubleday, 1991), pp. 124-39.

8. D. Lührmann, *Die apokryph gewordenen Evangelien: Studien zum neuen Texten und zu neuen Fragen* (Leiden & Boston: Brill, 2003), p. 1.

The term "canonical" does not represent an attribute inherent to the gospels in question. Rather, it presupposes that this status has in some way been ascribed to them: canonical gospels have *become* such. Until this occurs, however, there can equally be no gospels which deviate from this standard from the outset. "Noncanonical" gospels have *become* "apocryphal" through the canonization of the others.[9]

In consequence, all early Christian gospels must be viewed from within two distinct perspectives, the precanonical and the canonical. In the precanonical phase, gospels proliferate unchecked. Each adds its own distinctive material while selecting, interpreting, and reinterpreting material derived directly or indirectly from its predecessors. There is no difference in this respect between the Gospel of Luke and the *Gospel of Peter*. Of course, some gospels are more successful than others, circulating more widely and establishing themselves in liturgy, catechesis, or private use. In Rome, Justin is already familiar with Luke in the middle of the second century; towards its close, Serapion (bishop of Antioch) encounters the *Gospel of Peter* for the first time.[10] Yet Serapion initially approves the latter text's liturgical use in the church of Rhossus, although this is an innovation there.[11] Only when the shadow of heresy falls on the Petrine gospel does the bishop change his mind about it; and even then he simply requires that heretical passages be deleted, not that it should no longer be read. If "gospels" are memoirs of the apostles and their first followers, as Justin held,[12] then the memoirs of Peter or Thomas would be a highly significant addition to the memoirs of Matthew or John. Far from implying closure, the attribution of gospels to named figures invites imitation. Equally open to proliferation is an older anonymous and singular usage,

---

9. Lührmann, *Die apokryph gewordenen Evangelien*, p. 2. German original: "'Kanonisch' ist freilich keine Eigenschaft, die den so bezeichneten Evangelien von sich aus zukommt; vorausgesetzt wird damit vielmehr, dass ihnen ein solcher Rang in irgendeiner Weise beigemessen worden ist — kanonische Evangelien sind also zu solchen erst *geworden*. Solange das aber nicht geschehen ist, kann es ebensowenig Evangelien geben, denen diese Qualität von vornherein abgeht, und 'nicht kanonische' sind ebenso durch die Kanonisierung der anderen erst 'apokryph' *geworden*." Italics original.

10. Among the items Justin draws from Luke are the annunciation (*Dial.* 100.5; Lk. 1.35, 38), the worldwide census (*Dial.* 78.4; Lk. 2.1-5), Jesus' age at the time of his baptism (*Dial.* 88.2; Lk. 3.23), the blood-like sweat of Gethsemane (*Dial.* 103.6; Lk. 22.44), and "Father, forgive them . . ." (*Dial.* 105.5; Lk. 23.34). For Serapion, see Eusebius, *HE* vi.12.1-6 (and further below).

11. Eusebius, *HE* vi.12.4.

12. Justin, *1 Apol.* 66.3; *Dial.* 106.3.

which survives in Justin and later writers.[13] Here the focus is on the Lord's sayings, preserved "in the gospel," that is, in some unspecified textual form. In a given context, the primary reference might be to the text that came to be known as the "Gospel according to Matthew."[14] Yet "in the gospel" might also refer to the text eventually attributed to Luke,[15] or to an unknown sayings collection.[16] In this usage, "the gospel" is not a fixed literary entity, for any true saying of Jesus is precious wherever it may happen to be preserved in writing.[17] While Matthew and Luke are the main sources for these sayings, they remain unnamed and there is no concern to differentiate them.

The fourfold canonical gospel represents a delimitation within the larger field of early gospel literature as a whole. A new, composite textual object is constructed, and authors and circumstances of origin are assigned to its component parts. While textual boundaries are preserved, free movement across them is unhindered. On the other hand, the boundary separating the included from the excluded is absolutized. Here there is no freedom of movement. One might proceed — in a homily, for example — from a Matthean text to a related Johannine one; but to add a quotation from the *Gospel of Peter* would be an egregious error, no matter how apposite it might seem. The fourfold canonical gospel is constituted not only by the four distinct texts it contains but also by their radical differentiation from all other related texts. It is not simply a "collection," capable in principle of coexisting alongside other similar but less important texts. Exclusion is as fundamental to its being as inclusion: the fourfold canonical gospel is what it is only in

13. Justin's Trypho states that he has read "your commandments in the so-called gospel [ἐν τῷ λεγομένῳ εὐαγγελίῳ]" (*Dial.* 10.2).

14. According to the *Didache*, we are to pray the Lord's Prayer in its Matthean form, "as the Lord commanded in his gospel" (*Did.* 8.2).

15. Clement of Alexandria, *Strom.* iii.6.56.3: ". . . the Lord says in the gospel that this man's land produced plentifully" (cf. Lk. 12.16). The originally anonymous circulation of "Luke" is evident from Tertullian, who states that Marcion "ascribes no author to his gospel — as if attaching a title were prohibited to one who thought it acceptable to undermine the text itself" [*Marcion evangelio, scilicet suo, nullum adscribit auctorem, quasi non licuerit illi titulum quoque affingere, cui nefas non fuit ipsum corpus evertere*] (*Adversus Marcionem* iv.2.3). Tertullian anachronistically assumes that Marcion *deleted* a title that had probably not yet been added.

16. 2 *Clem.* 8.5.

17. Compare Jens Schröter's view that "gospel" refers not to a specific literary genre but to any text containing Jesus tradition ("Die apokryphen Evangelien und die Entstehung des neutestamentlichen Kanons," in *Jesus in apokryphen Evangelienüberlieferungen*, ed. J. Frey and J. Schröter, WUNT [Tübingen: Mohr Siebeck, 2010], pp. 31-60; pp. 42-45).

this double gesture. It is *kanōn,* both norm and truth, and what it excludes is thereby constituted as aberration and falsehood. The canonical gospel severs the historical and literary ties that bind Matthew and Thomas, John and Peter, realigning Matthew with John on one side of the great divide, Thomas with Peter on the other. It is an attempt to create order out of the chaos of interpretations and reinterpretations.

The fourfold canonical gospel is a construct rather than a quasi-natural object, and as such it is vulnerable to alternative proposals. Internal boundaries might be removed and the individual texts subjected to *conflation* into a single narrative. The rigidity of the external boundary might be relaxed, allowing for *supplementation* by gospel-like texts purporting to fill perceived gaps in the canonical narrative. New gospel-writing might occur within the sphere of the excluded texts, with a view to the *subversion* of the canonical norm; beyond subversion lies the possibility of *displacement,* the substitution of a new image of Jesus for the old. The possibilities of conflation, supplementation, subversion, and displacement are inherent to the fourfold canonical gospel, as illustrated by texts such as the *Diatessaron,* the *Protevangelium of James,* the *Gospel of Judas,* and the material relating to Jesus in the Qur'an. Yet these proposed modifications may also be resisted. Since first theorized by Irenaeus, the fourfold canonical gospel has endured. It should not be seen merely as an unstable compromise, "striking a precarious balance between an unmanageable multiplicity of gospels on the one hand and a single, self-consistent gospel on the other."[18] It was not established only by "tortured" arguments, "special pleading," and "implausible legend[s]."[19] Nor do the circumstances of its origin undermine theological perspectives on canonical status. Indeed, in social contexts shaped by the fourfold gospel the church's decision *can only* be seen as "its avowal of a norm beneath which it already stands and beneath which it [must] stand if it is to perceive the truth."[20] The canonical decision marks the proximate goal of a reception process that may be traced back through the written texts to Jesus' initial impact on his contemporaries.

In this chapter and the next, we shall try to catch sight of the familiar canonical object at the historical moment when it begins to take shape. In view of the originally close relationships between gospels subsequently divided by

---

18. Harry Y. Gamble, *The New Testament Canon: Its Making and Meaning* (Philadelphia: Fortress, 1985), p. 35.

19. Gamble, *New Testament Canon,* pp. 32, 33, 34.

20. John Webster, *Holy Scripture: A Dogmatic Sketch* (Cambridge: Cambridge University Press, 2003), p. 64.

the canon, we should not expect to find an early consensus embracing all who have not wilfully located themselves on the margins. In second-century literature, the fourfold gospel is only demonstrably present in the two late texts where there is explicit reference to it: in Irenaeus emphatically, in Clement of Alexandria incidentally.[21] Clement's writings are particularly significant in shedding light on the transition from early proliferation to the construction of the canonical limit. While the four-gospel collection no doubt had earlier roots, perhaps in local liturgical usage, Clement reflects the emerging consensus about its normative status which Irenaeus strives to promote.[22]

Attempts to trace the fourfold gospel back to earlier times run into insuperable difficulties. Thus Papias refers only to accounts of the Lord's words (and deeds) drawn up by Mark, on the basis of Peter's preaching, and by Matthew, writing in "Hebrew" or Aramaic. As has been argued in chapter 3, Papias understands Matthew as a response to the perceived inadequacies of Mark; but neither work is viewed as "canonical" in any clear sense. Eusebius was evidently unable to find any reference to, or citation from, Luke or John in Papias's five-volume work.[23] There was, however, "another story about a woman wrongfully accused of many sins before the Lord, which," Eusebius notes though Papias presumably did not, "occurs in the Gospel according to the Hebrews."[24] In sum, Papias "records other things purportedly reaching

21. On the dating and provenance of the incomplete "Muratorian Canon," see below.

22. A conceptual distinction between the "four-gospel collection" and the "four-gospel canon" is proposed by Theo K. Heckel, who argues that the four gospels were viewed "als enger zusammengehörige Gruppe, bevor deren explizite Hervorhebung gegenüber anderen Schriften belegbar ist. Statt vom Vierevangelien*kanon* ist zunächst von der Vierevangelien*sammlung* zu reden" (*Vom Evangelium des Markus zum viergestaltigen Evangelium,* WUNT [Tübingen: Mohr-Siebeck, 1999], p. 4; italics original). Heckel's attempts to show that a "four-gospel collection" is already implicit in Jn. 21, Papias, and Justin are in my view unsuccessful.

23. According to Richard Bauckham, "it was by comparison with John that Papias could not but see Mark and Matthew as lacking order. . . . Presupposed is his very high evaluation of John" (*Jesus and the Eyewitnesses: The Gospels as Eyewitness Testimony* [Grand Rapids: Eerdmans, 2006], pp. 423-24). Thus, "Papias must have said something about the origin of John's Gospel, comparable with his statements about the Gospels of Mark and Matthew" (p. 424). Bauckham has no adequate answer to the question why Eusebius should have omitted what Papias "must have said" about John (and Luke?). Shortly before his discussion of Papias, Eusebius has provided a lengthy defence of John's place within the canonical collection (*HE* iii.24.1-16). Later he will cite testimonies to the fourfold collection from Irenaeus (*HE* v.8.2-4), Clement (*HE* vi.14.5-7), and Origen (*HE* vi.25.4-6). Given his general interest in the fourfold gospel and his specific concern with John, it is inconceivable that Eusebius would fail to exploit an early testimony to Johannine origins and genuineness. If so, Papias does not associate his "elder John" with any "fourth gospel."

24. Eusebius, *HE* iii.39.17.

him from the unwritten tradition [ἄλλα . . . ὡς ἐκ παραδόσεως ἀγράφου εἰς αὐτὸν ἥκοντα], such as some strange parables of the Saviour, his teachings, and other more legendary matters."[25] Through Papias's endeavours, previously unwritten parables, teachings, and legends now take their place within the sphere of gospel and gospel-related literature, *alongside* the earlier productions ascribed to Mark and Matthew. Even if Papias had some knowledge of Luke and John, there is no place for a normative fourfold gospel within his perspective on the oral and written tradition.

Evidence for an early origin of the fourfold collection cannot be found in the common format of the traditional gospel titles, εὐαγγέλιον κατά . . . These titles presuppose the concept of a singular gospel embodied in a number of parallel texts, and their function is to differentiate these texts while acknowledging their common substance. It is not clear that these titles were originally assigned only to the four canonical texts, and that the use of the same format in the case of gospels ascribed to Peter, Thomas, the Hebrews, and so on must be seen as later imitations.[26] What is clear is that the titles recognize the fact and legitimacy of plurality, whether in open or closed form. As such, they represent a later attempt to formalize the prior reality of proliferation; they cannot belong to the period of the gospels' composition and initial reception. Although Martin Hengel has argued that an original anonymous circulation could not have given rise to the common format,[27] the reality appears to be just the opposite: the common format indicates a later interest in the individuality of the previously undifferentiated and anonymous texts that constitute "the gospel."[28] The titles presuppose traditions of the kind that Papias attests in the case of Mark and Matthew, and they are unlikely to predate Papias. Texts already named and differentiated could not have given rise to the generalized references to "the gospel" in

25. Eusebius, *HE* iii.39.11.

26. According to Brevard Childs, the titles indicate that "there is only one Gospel, but it has been rendered by four different evangelists" (*The New Testament as Canon: An Introduction* [London: SCM Press, 1984], p. 152). In itself, however, the κατά-formulation implies only a plurality, and not specifically the number four.

27. M. Hengel, *Studies in the Gospel of Mark,* Eng. trans. (London: SCM Press, 1985), p. 82: "Circulation of anonymous works without a title would of necessity have led to a multiplicity of titles."

28. The earlier transition from oral proclamation to written text may derive from Mk. 1.1 and is already attested in the *Didache* and *2 Clement* (so James A. Kelhofer, "'Gospel' as a Literary Title in Early Christianity and the Question of What Is (and Is Not) a 'Gospel' in Canons of Scholarly Literature," in *Jesus in apokryphen Evangelienüberlieferungen,* ed. J. Frey and J. Schröter, WUNT [Tübingen: Mohr-Siebeck, 2010], pp. 399-422; pp. 414-17).

early citations of Jesus' sayings. It is "the gospel" that explains "the gospel according to . . . ," and not the reverse.

The starting point for an account of the emerging fourfold gospel must be in late-second-century Alexandria. Clement of Alexandria is particularly significant because, in spite of his awareness of the church's fourfold gospel, he continues to cite ostensibly noncanonical material as authoritative. Showing relatively little interest in the distinctive character of individual gospels, he continues to represent an older inclusive account of the gospel in which the content is more important than its precise textual location.

Clement: The Inclusive Gospel

In Book 3 of his *Stromateis,* Clement addresses the issue of "marriage" — by which he means the role of sexual intercourse in the life of the Christian.[29] Positioning himself and the church midway between the opposite extremes represented by the "heresies" or "sects," Clement directs suitable outrage against those followers of Carpocrates and his son Epiphanes who claim that private property of any kind is incompatible with the divine creator's bestowal of his gifts equally on all, humans and animals alike. In his sensational and precocious book *On Righteousness,* Epiphanes argued that Moses and other human legislators oppose the divine law of equality when they introduce the concept of private property. Male desire has been decreed by God, as we learn from the command to "be fruitful and multiply" (Gn. 1.28). Yet Moses blatantly contradicts the divine law when he attributes to God the command that "thou shalt not desire thy neighbour's wife" (Ex. 20.17 LXX). In writing of the neighbour's wife, Moses makes a private possession (ἰδιότης) out of what should be held in common (κοινωνία). According to Clement, these Carpocratians put their communistic doctrines into practice at their love-feasts. It was against such people that Jude wrote in his epistle.[30]

If followers of Carpocrates appeal to the natural order to justify their li-

---

29. Greek text in *Clemens Alexandrinus,* ed. O. Stählin, L. Früchtel, and U. Treu, 4 vols., GCS (Berlin: Akademie-Verlag, 1960-80³), vol. 2. The ANF translation of Clement gives the whole of Book 3 in Latin; English translations are available in *Selected Translations of Clement and Origen with Introductions and Notes,* ed. J. E. L. Oulton and H. Chadwick, Library of Christian Classics (Philadelphia: Westminster Press, 1954); *Stromateis I-III,* trans. John Ferguson, FC (Washington, D.C.: Catholic University of America Press, 1991).

30. Clement summarizes Epiphanes' work in *Strom.* iii.2.5.1–10.2. Epiphanes is said to have lived only seventeen years (iii.2.5.2).

centiousness, followers of Prodicus look instead to the spiritual unions in the realm of the Pleroma, of which they have learned from an anonymous Valentinian tract.[31] Imitating these sacred couplings, they "sacralize carnal and sexual intercourse and suppose that it leads them into the kingdom of God."[32] They regard themselves as "sons by nature of the first God," "lords of the Sabbath," "royal children," superior to the rest of the human race and free from petty restrictions imposed by angelic or human powers.[33] These people like to cite the Lord's words, "To everyone who asks, give" (Lk. 6.30), especially in the company of young and attractive female church members.[34] They ignore the Lord's stern condemnation of the lustful look and the adultery of the heart (Mt. 5.28).[35]

Annoying though these groups are to Clement, they pose a less serious threat than those at the opposite extreme who in the name of self-control (ἐγκράτεια) renounce marriage and intercourse entirely. This is a view associated especially with Marcion and his followers, who refuse to replenish the tragic world of the creator deity after learning of the God who is goodness rather than mere justice.[36] Abstinence from marriage and intercourse is also counselled by Tatian, in his book *On the Saviour's View of Perfection* (Περὶ τοῦ κατὰ σωτῆρα καταρτισμοῦ). From this work Clement quotes a forceful exegesis of 1 Corinthians 7.5, where Paul countenances a temporary abstinence, by mutual agreement and for the sake of prayer: "Agreement promotes prayer, corrupt intercourse destroys intercession. . . ." If one avails oneself of the apostle's reluctant permission, one will be serving two masters: God insofar as one abstains for the sake of prayer, and the devil insofar as one succumbs again to desire.[37] Similar doctrines to Tatian's are being taught, closer to home, by one Julius Cassianus, formerly a follower of Valentinus and author of the multivolume *Exegetica* from which Clement has previously drawn arguments about the antiquity of the Hebrew philosophy.[38] This formidable figure is Clement's chief opponent in Book 3 of the

---

31. Clement of Alexandria, *Strom.* iii.4.29.1-3. Clement considers the authentic Valentinian view of marriage to be essentially sound (*Strom.* iii.1.1.1; 4.29.3).

32. Clement of Alexandria, *Strom.* iii.4.27.5, 30.1.

33. Clement of Alexandria, *Strom.* iii.4.30.1.

34. Clement of Alexandria, *Strom.* iii.4.27.3.

35. Clement of Alexandria, *Strom.* iii.4.31.1.

36. Clement of Alexandria, *Strom.* iii.3.12.1-3.

37. Clement of Alexandria, *Strom.* iii.12.81.1.

38. Clement of Alexandria, *Strom.* iii.12.92.1; i.21.101.2 (where Cassianus is again linked with Tatian, this time approvingly).

Stromateis. It is, Cassianus argues, a gross mistake to attribute the formation of our bodies and specifically our generative organs to the true God or to the Saviour, rather than to angelic powers. How could the Saviour have created that from which he came to deliver us? Cassianus's book on this matter is entitled either *On Self-Control* or *On Being a Eunuch* (Περὶ εὐνουχίας), a reference to the Lord's commendation of those who make themselves eunuchs for the sake of the kingdom of heaven (Mt. 19.12).[39] But Cassianus also has other supportive texts at his disposal, and the most important of these are drawn not from Matthew but from the *Gospel according to the Egyptians.*

In his debate with Cassianus, Clement turns to this otherwise unknown gospel on three occasions, on each of which he provides his own counter-interpretation of the material in question. In passing, Clement mentions that these passages "do not occur in the four gospels handed down to us [ἐν τοῖς παραδεδομένοις ἡμῖν τέτταρσιν εὐαγγελίοις], but in the one according to the Egyptians [ἐν τῷ κατ' Αἰγυπτίοις]."[40] This is the one and only occasion on which Clement speaks of a fourfold gospel, and he develops his point no further. Far from disqualifying the text in question, he assumes that it contains authentic sayings of Jesus whose correct interpretation is critically important for Christian practice. The interpretative contest between Clement and Cassianus sheds considerable light on attitudes towards gospel writing in late-second-century Alexandria.

The exclusion of *GEgy* from the four gospels of the church is mentioned only on the third and final occasion on which Clement discusses this text. On the second occasion, its title is provided; on the first, it is introduced anonymously, as follows:

> To those who in the fair name of self-control [ἐγκράτεια] dishonour the creation and the holy creator [τὸν ἅγιον δημιουργόν] who is the almighty and the only God, teaching that marriage and the begetting of children are to be rejected and that no further unfortunates are to be brought into the world as fodder for death, this is what must be said. First, in the words of the apostle John: "And now many antichrists have come, so that we know it to be the last hour. They went out from us but they were not of us, for if so they would have remained with us." Next, they must be convicted of misinterpreting the passages they cite [τὰ ὑπ' αὐτῶν φερόμενα]. For example, when Salome asked the Lord, "How long shall death prevail?"

39. Clement of Alexandria, *Strom.* iii.13.91.1–92.2.
40. Clement of Alexandria, *Strom.* iii.13.93.1.

(not implying that life and the creation are evil), he replied, "So long as you women bear children" (but with reference to the normal course of nature, in which birth is always followed by death).[41]

This passage marks the point in Clement's argument at which he turns from the antinomians to the ascetics. A brief preview is therefore given of the position he will seek to refute and of the means by which he will do so: first, he will cite scriptural testimonies that attack his opponents or undermine their views, and, second, he will correct their misreadings of testimonies they themselves cite. The ascetic position grounds the call to ἐγκράτεια in a disjunction between the creator or "demiurge" and the supreme God. The creator deity has imprisoned elect souls within material bodies. To marry and practise sexual intercourse is to affirm one's imprisonment and to collude with the hostile power responsible for it; and it is also to drag further souls down into the miseries of bodily confinement. The Christian who indulges in marital intercourse sins both against him- or herself and against others. But if the creator and the supreme God are one and the same, as Clement believes, this extreme platonizing view loses its appearance of rectitude. Rather, it is the perversion of the truth foreseen by the apostle John, when he spoke against former Christian brothers and sisters now unmasked as "antichrists" (cf. 1 Jn. 2.18b-19). Yet antichrists too can quote scriptural testimonies, citing the words not of an apostle but of the Lord himself when, in answer to Salome's question, he traces death's power back to women's reproductive capability. Death, they claim, is engendered by women. Clement agrees with the exegesis but not with its ontological assumptions: the Lord speaks simply of the ordinary course of nature, and does not suggest that birth and creatureliness are evil. Together with the citation from the apostle John, the citation and counterinterpretation of the Lord's answer to Salome illustrate the way Clement's argument will proceed.

Nothing in the Salome passage implies that Clement regarded it as nonauthoritative or nonscriptural. It is assumed that Salome did indeed ask the Lord about death and that the Lord answered her in the specified way. What is at issue is how the question and the answer are to be interpreted. In themselves they have the same status as another question and answer that Clement proceeds to cite, which recounts "what the Lord said to those who asked about the 'bill of divorce,' whether it was lawful to divorce a wife, as Moses commanded." In answer to this question, the Lord said:

---

41. Clement of Alexandria, *Strom.* iii.6.45.1-3.

Because of your hardness of heart Moses wrote this. But have you not read that [God] said to the first-formed man [τῷ πρωτοπλάστῳ], "The two of you shall be one flesh"? So he who divorces his wife (except on grounds of immorality) makes her an adulteress.[42]

While this passage has been extensively redacted, its origin in the Matthean divorce pericope is clear. Yet Clement makes no reference to the fact that he is here dependent on Matthew whereas his earlier citation was drawn from the *Gospel according to the Egyptians*. His concern is purely with what the Lord said, and the Lord's words are no less significant on one occasion than on the other. The Salome passage might seem to favour those who reject marriage, whereas the passage prohibiting divorce might seem to affirm it. Yet Clement does not assert the superiority of the "canonical" passage over the "apocryphal" one. No such distinction is mentioned here. In any case, his opponent too is deeply interested in the Matthean passage, especially in its conclusion. There, he can claim that Jesus affirms his disciples' suggestion that one should not marry when he commends those who "make themselves eunuchs for the sake of the kingdom of heaven."[43] According to Clement, the disciples were referring only to remarriage after a divorce occasioned by adultery: the words "if this is the case of a man with his wife . . ." (Mt. 19.10a) refer not to the prohibition of divorce but to the Matthean exception to that prohibition. In this passage, as in the dialogue with Salome, Clement finds himself on ground selected by his opponent. Yet it is the words of Jesus and their correct interpretation that are at stake, not their literary context.

Precisely because the Lord's sayings are so important, their wording and sequence may be varied in order to do fullest justice to the desired sense. In Clement's redacted citation from the divorce pericope, "Moses wrote this" abbreviates the Matthean "Moses permitted you to divorce your wives" (Mt. 19.8). Citations from Genesis 1.27 and 2.24a are omitted (cf. Mt. 19.4), and Genesis 2.24b is cited as direct divine speech to "the first-formed man": *the two of you*, rather than *they*, shall be one flesh. The prohibition of divorce is derived not from Matthew 19.9, as one would expect here, but from the parallel in Matthew 5.32.[44] The accurate rendering of this latter passage and of

---

42. Clement of Alexandria, *Strom.* iii.6.47.2.

43. Clement of Alexandria, *Strom.* iii.6.50.1-3, citing Mt. 19.11-12 with two minor omissions.

44. Clement here is clearly dependent on Matthew rather than Mark. In the Markan version of the divorce pericope, "have you not read . . . ?" is absent, and the prohibition of divorce is differently worded and constructed (cf. Mk. 10.6, 11-12).

the saying about eunuchs suggests careful construction rather than imprecise citation from memory.

This is confirmed by an important passage in Book 4 of the *Stromateis*, where Clement explicitly acknowledges that Jesus' sayings may be shaped by their interpreters. The relevant passage occurs within an extended exegesis of the beatitudes in their Matthean form (cf. Mt. 5.3-12), itself located within a discussion of martyrdom. While the Matthean wording is followed closely in the earlier beatitudes, "Blessed are the peacemakers" lacks its sequel (". . . for they shall be called sons of God"). Surprisingly this sequel is reattached to the beatitude that follows, to which Clement ascribes special significance:

> It is, I consider, the sum of all virtue [κεφάλαιον πάσης ἀρετῆς] when the Lord teaches us to despise death, in fullness of knowledge [γνωστικώτερον] and for love of God. "Blessed," he says, "are those who are persecuted for righteousness' sake, for they shall be called sons of God." Or, according to some who transpose the gospels [ὡς τινες τῶν μεταθέντων τὰ εὐαγγέλια]: "Blessed," he says, "are those who are persecuted for righteousness' sake, for they shall be perfect." And, "blessed are those who are persecuted for my sake, for they shall have a place where they shall not be persecuted." And, "blessed are you when people hate you, when they exclude you, when they cast out your name as evil for the Son of man's sake."[45]

There are people, we learn here, who "transpose the gospels."[46] Clement cites and approves the results of their transpositions. Indeed, he engages in this practice himself when he attaches the sequel of the blessing of the peacemakers to the blessing of the persecuted. The transposition entails the reversal of Matthew 5.9b and 5.10a and the suppression of 5.10b (". . . for theirs is the kingdom of heaven"). Clement proceeds to give three further examples of this practice. In the first, 5.10b is again replaced by a new sequel, adapted from 5.48 ("You then shall be perfect . . ."). In the second, "for my sake" is drawn from 5.11; the sequel ("for they shall have a place . . .") is unattested elsewhere and is probably a new formulation. The final example is a near-verbatim citation of Luke 6.22, selected in preference to its parallel in Mat-

---

45. Clement of Alexandria, *Strom.* iv.6.41.1-3. Since beatitudes always start with "Blessed . . . ," it is Clement who has linked originally discrete items with "and."

46. The context does not suggest a reference to followers of Marcion (the view of E. Molland, *The Conception of the Gospel in the Alexandrian Theology* [Oslo: Jacob Dybwad, 1938], p. 14, and Hengel, *The Four Gospels and the One Gospel of Jesus Christ*, p. 17).

thew 5.11. In this case, the transposition involves a juxtaposition of related material from two gospels — as Clement may hint in his use of the plural εὐαγγέλια. New versions of old sayings are constructed by way of substitutions drawn from another gospel or from elsewhere in the same gospel, or by new formulations. An example may be seen in *GTh* 68-69:

> Jesus said: "Blessed are you whenever they hate you and persecute you. And wherever they persecuted you, they will find no place." Jesus said: "Blessed are those who are persecuted in their heart. It is they who know the Father in truth."

While Clement's four versions of the blessing of the persecuted are more closely related to the canonical material than Thomas's two, both authors show a tendency to preserve the blessing itself but to provide it with a new explanatory sequel. The Clement passage is especially valuable for its explicit acknowledgement that constructing new variants of Jesus' sayings is an accepted and legitimate practice.[47]

This practice is further exemplified in Clement's rendering not only of the divorce pericope but also of the Salome dialogue. Returning to this dialogue later in Book 3, Clement gives both question and answer in a modified form. In the first version, Salome asks, "How long shall *death prevail?*" and the Lord replies, "So long as *you women* bear children."[48] In the second version, Salome asks, "How long shall *humans die?*" and the Lord replies, "So long as *women* bear children."[49] Clement's exegesis focuses especially on the word "humans" (ἄνθρωποι) in Salome's question:

> The Word no doubt reveals the end of the age when Salome says: "How long shall humans die?" The scripture here understands "human" in a double sense, the visible person [τὸν φαινόμενον] and the soul, and again the one who is being saved and the one who is not. And sin is said to be the death of the soul. Thus the Lord answers guardedly, "So long as women bear children," that is, so long as the desires are active.[50]

---

47. In some cases at least, this possibility of deliberate construction may be preferable to the conventional appeal to citation from memory — on which see Carl P. Cosaert, *The Text of the Gospels in Clement of Alexandria* (Atlanta: SBL, 2008), pp. 25-32.

48. Clement of Alexandria, *Strom.* iii.6.45.3: μέχρι πότε θάνατος ἰσχύσει/μέχρις ἂν ὑμεῖς αἱ γυναῖκες τίκτητε.

49. Clement of Alexandria, *Strom.* iii.7.64.1: μέχρι τίνος οἱ ἄνθρωποι ἀποθανοῦνται/μέχρις ἂν τίκτωσιν αἱ γυναῖκες.

50. Clement of Alexandria, *Strom.* iii.7.64.1.

The passage in question is regarded as *scripture,* the utterance of the Logos, and as scripture it requires interpretation. Salome's reference to humans dying is to be understood in connection both with the natural separation of body and soul and with the dire consequences of sin among those who are not saved. Since Clement's interpretation is dependent on the term ἄνθρωποι, present in this version of the question but absent from the first, it is likely that the new version accurately represents the scriptural text from which it is drawn. In the case of the Lord's reply, the reverse is the case: the saying has been emended so as to connect it more closely to the desired interpretation. In the earlier version, "So long as *you* women bear children" links the reply with the female questioner and provides a straightforward literal sense. Death will prevail for as long as "you women" give birth. Omission of the possessive pronoun loosens the link with the questioner and makes possible the allegorical equation of women with desires and of children with the fruits of those desires. The earlier literal interpretation is based on the scriptural wording, whereas the allegorical interpretation requires a minor adjustment to the text.

Clement's allegorical interpretation is occasioned by his opponents' similarly allegorical interpretation of another saying derived from the same source:

> Those who oppose God's creation in the fair name of self-control also appeal to what was said to Salome, as we mentioned earlier. (This is found, I believe [οἶμαι], in the *Gospel according to the Egyptians.*) For, he says, "the Saviour himself said, 'I came to destroy the works of the female [ἦλθον καταλῦσαι τὰ ἔργα τῆς θηλείας], where 'female' refers to desire and 'works' to birth and death [γένεσιν καὶ φθοράν]."[51]

The new saying is a quotation within a quotation drawn from Julius Cassianus.[52] It is, however, Clement, not Cassianus, who identifies *GEgy* as the source both of the Salome passage cited earlier and of the independent but thematically related saying cited here.[53] Clement has no objection to the

51. Clement of Alexandria, *Strom.* iii.7.63.1-2.
52. Clement of Alexandria, *Strom.* iii.13.91.1.
53. J. Ruwet, S.J., assumes that Clement only identifies the source of this material in the course of writing Book 3 of the *Stromateis,* and that *GEgy* was previously barely known to him ("Clement d'Alexandrie: Canon des écritures et apocryphes," *Bib* 29 [1948], pp. 77-99, 240-68, 391-408; p. 397). Given the scarcity of attributions to any named gospel in Clement, this is an unnecessary conclusion. Ruwet is concerned to find Clement engaging seriously with "un écrit rejeté par

equation of the female with desire, but proposes that "the works of the female" refers to sins and vices rather than to natural functions. It is this allegorical reinterpretation of the "works of the female" saying that leads to the second interpretation of the Salome passage.

In spite of his modest disclaimer, "I believe," Clement has independent access to *GEgy* and can therefore cite the remainder of the Salome dialogue on his own initiative and not in response to Cassianus:

> Why do they not cite the sequel to what was said to Salome, these people who would do anything rather than follow the truth of the gospel norm [τῷ κατὰ ἀλήθειαν εὐαγγελικῷ κανόνι]? For when she said, "I did well not to bear," implying an inappropriate view of childbirth, the Lord responded: "Eat every plant, but that which is bitter do not eat." For in this way he indicates that it is up to us [ἐφ' ἡμῖν εἶναι] whether to choose celibacy or marriage, and that there is no obligatory commandment to restrain us.[54]

Salome here exempts herself from the Lord's collective reference to "you women" and from the cycle of birth and mortality they are said to engender.[55] (In this gospel she is celibate, although in Matthew she may be identified as "the mother of the sons of Zebedee," while in Thomas she scandalously claims to have shared bed and board with Jesus himself.)[56] Clement implausibly argues that Jesus regards Salome's celibacy as a purely personal choice: if marriage seems "bitter" to her, celibacy might seem equally "bitter" to someone else. The saying is better understood as a cryptic endorsement of

l'Église" (p. 397), and suggests that he is motivated merely by "le désir de confondre la mauvaise foi des hérétiques" (p. 398).

54. Clement of Alexandria, *Strom.* iii.9.66.1-3.

55. Her words are καλῶς οὖν ἐποίησα μὴ τεκοῦσα. English translations sometimes give a conditional sense: "I would have done better had I never given birth to a child" (Oulton), or "I would have done better if I never had a child" (Ferguson). The conditional is occasioned by the difficult phrase that follows, ὡς οὐ δεόντως τῆς γενέσεως παραλαμβανομένης, understood to mean "suggesting that she might not have done right in giving birth to a child" (Oulton). But the phrase need not imply that Salome herself has experienced childbirth: compare J. K. Elliott (ed.), *The Apocryphal New Testament* (Oxford: Clarendon Press, 1999²), p. 18 ("When she said, 'I have done well in not giving birth,' imagining that it is not permitted to bear children . . ."), and Cameron, *The Other Gospels*, p. 51 ("When she said, 'I have done well in not bearing children,' as if it were improper to engage in procreation . . ."). My translation assumes that what is improper or inappropriate is not procreation but Salome's "received" view of it — as the adverbial οὐ δεόντως seems to imply.

56. Mt. 27.56 (cf. Mk. 15.40; Mt. 20.20); *GTh* 61.

her choice, in keeping with the encratistic tendency evident throughout the cited *GEgy* material in spite of Clement's arguments to the contrary. One might expect him simply to reject this gospel, exploiting the fact that it is not one of the canonical four (as he will later note). Yet for Clement it is counterintuitive to reject any literary record of the Lord's words, even if it is relatively unfamiliar. It is none other than the divine Logos who instructs us in and through the record of what the incarnate Lord said to Salome. Here too we encounter "scripture" and "the gospel norm."

In this passage and in the final reference to the Salome dialogue, Clement names the source from which he and Cassianus draw this material: the *Gospel according to the Egyptians*. Like other gospels, *GEgy* derives its authority from the fact that it preserves the Lord's sayings. In itself, however, it does not possess the same kind of authority as the four handed down within the church. The point is noted in passing before Clement again proceeds to reinterpret the passage in question, so as to bring it into line with his own positive view of marriage:

> Cassianus says: "When Salome enquired when she would know the answer to her questions, the Lord said, 'When you trample the garment of shame, and when the two become one and the male with the female neither male nor female.'" First, we do not find this saying in the four gospels handed down to us but in the one according to the Egyptians [ἐν τοῖς παραδεδομένοις ἡμῖν τέτταρσιν εὐαγγελίοις οὐκ ἔχομεν τὸ ῥητόν, ἀλλ' ἐν τῷ κατ' Αἰγυπτίους]. Next, he seems to me unaware that it speaks symbolically [αἰνίττεται] of anger as the male impulse and of desire as the female one.[57]

Cassianus is "unaware" of Clement's allegorical interpretation because he understands the saying along more literal lines, as implying a rejection of the gendered body with its desires. Cassianus may also be unaware of the very existence of a fourfold gospel that excludes the gospel on which he is here dependent. Clement's comment seems to represent a transitional moment in which a differentiation within the field of gospel literature is beginning to take shape, while excluded texts may still be valued insofar as they preserve authoritative utterances of the Lord himself.[58] The reference to four

---

57. Clement of Alexandria, *Strom.* iii.13.92.2–93.1.

58. According to Hengel, "We could almost say that precisely because the unique authority of the four Gospels was indispensable for [Clement], he could sometimes bring himself also to use 'apocryphal' texts which helped him in his argument . . ." (*Four Gospels*, p. 19). But the distinction

gospels may reflect the influence of Irenaeus, whose work Clement is elsewhere said to have known.[59]

GEgy is twice referred to by name,[60] and the title serves to identify material distinctive to this gospel as opposed to others. Similarly formed titles occur on just seven further occasions in Clement's extant writings, once each in the case of the gospels according to Matthew, Luke, and the Hebrews, and twice each in the case of Mark and John.[61] In each case the point is to highlight the uniqueness of the cited material to the gospel in question:

> And in the Gospel according to Matthew [ἐν δὲ τῷ κατὰ Ματθαῖον εὐαγγελίῳ] the genealogy extends from Abraham to Mary the mother of our Lord.[62]

> Our Lord was born in the twenty-eighth year, when a census was first ordered by Augustus. To show that this is true, it is written thus in the Gospel according to Luke [ἐν τῷ εὐαγγελίῳ τῷ κατὰ Λουκᾶν γέγραπται οὕτως], "In the fifteenth year of Tiberius Caesar the word of the Lord came to John son of Zechariah."[63]

> These things are written in the Gospel according to Mark [ἐν τῷ κατὰ Μᾶρκον εὐαγγελίῳ]. And while in all the other corresponding passages he [the Holy Spirit] slightly alters the wording of each of them alike, everything shows the same harmony of sense.[64]

> In the Gospel according to Mark [*in euangelio secundum Marcum*] the Lord was asked by the High Priest if he was "Christ the Son of the blessed God," and said in response: "I am. . . ." In other gospels, however, the Lord does not reply directly to the High Priest when asked if he was the

---

between the canonical and the noncanonical is itself relativized by the presence of genuine words of the Lord in texts belonging to both categories.

59. Eusebius, *HE* vi.13.9.

60. Clement of Alexandria, *Strom.* iii.7.63.1; 7.93.1.

61. Hengel's listing omits the passages preserved in Cassiodorus and includes a passage where "John" is a reference not to the evangelist but to the Baptist (*Four Gospels*, pp. 16n, 220).

62. Clement of Alexandria, *Strom.* i.1.147.5. On another occasion, the first and fourth beatitudes are attributed to "Matthew," perhaps because in this context Clement is engaging primarily with Mark (Clement of Alexandria, *Quis Dives Salvetur* 17.4).

63. Clement of Alexandria, *Strom.* i.21.145.2.

64. Clement of Alexandria, *Quis Dives Salvetur* 5.1. The reference is to Mk. 10.17-31, which Clement has just cited.

Son of God. But what does he say? "You say so" — a quite sufficient response.[65]

The Lord referred to such food in symbolic language in the Gospel according to John [ἐν τῷ κατὰ Ἰωάννην εὐαγγελίῳ], saying, "Eat my flesh, and drink my blood."[66]

"That which was from the beginning, which we have heard, which we have seen with our eyes." In full agreement with the Gospel according to John [*consequenter evangelio secundum Iohannem et convenienter*], this letter maintains the spiritual beginning [*principium spirituale*].[67]

The beginning [of wisdom] is to wonder at things, as Plato says in the *Theaetetus*, and Matthias enjoins in the *Traditions*, saying, "Wonder at what is before you," establishing this first of all as the foundation of further knowledge. It is also written in the Gospel according to the Hebrews [ἐν τῷ καθ᾽ Ἑβραίους εὐαγγελίῳ], "The one who wonders will rule, and the one who rules will rest."[68]

The second of the passages that mention *GEgy* by name is unique in its reference to a fourfold canonical collection. Nevertheless, as in all the above passages, this gospel is named in order to *differentiate* it from other gospels or related literature. *GEgy* is differentiated from the traditional four just as Mark is differentiated from other unspecified gospels containing parallel accounts of Jesus' conversation with the rich young ruler or his trial before the Sanhedrin. Clement's more usual practice is to introduce a gospel citation with nonspecific formulae such as "the Lord says" or "the Lord says in the gospel."[69] The cited material may be drawn from Matthew, Luke, John, or (occasionally) from other sources, although Clement's tendency to rephrase the sayings he cites often makes exact attribution difficult. But the crucial point is that Clement himself is generally uninterested in specific attribution:

65. Clement of Alexandria, *In Epistola Iudae Catholica*, preserved in Cassiodorus's Latin translation of parts of Clement's *Hypotyposes* (at v.24; text in *Clemens Alexandrinus*, III, pp. 203-15). Cassiodorus translated Clement's outlines of 1 Peter, Jude, and 1 and 2 John. Eusebius assigns a passage from the 1 Peter outline (on Peter and Mark) to Book 8 of the *Hypotyposes* (*HE* ii.15.2).

66. Clement of Alexandria, *Paed.* i.6.38.2.

67. Clement/Cassiodorus, *In Epistola Iohannis Prima* (at 1.1).

68. Clement of Alexandria, *Strom.* ii.9.45.4-5.

69. On Clement's introductory formulae, see Cosaert, *Gospels in Clement*, pp. 26-29.

I do not now mention what the parable says *in the gospel* [ἐν τῷ εὐαγγελίῳ], "The kingdom of heaven is like a man who cast a net into the sea. . . ."[70]

The Lord *in the gospel* bluntly calls the rich man who had stocked up his barns . . . a fool.[71]

It says *in the gospel* that the Lord, standing on the shore, called out to the disciples (who happened to be fishing), "Children, do you have anything to eat?"[72]

These passages are drawn from Matthew, Luke, and John respectively, and there are no parallels in other canonical gospels. Yet for Clement "the gospel" is in the first instance a singular, anonymous literary entity.[73] An individual gospel need be named only on the rare occasions when the distinctiveness of the cited passage needs to be highlighted.[74] The nonspecific formula "The Lord says in the gospel . . ."[75] contrasts sharply with the precise attributions Clement provides elsewhere: "As the apostle also says in the Letter to the Romans . . .";[76] "Clement says in the Letter to the Corinthians . . .";[77] "As John says in the Apocalypse . . ."[78]

Further consideration of the six named gospels will help to ascertain how far the concept of the fourfold canonical gospel has developed in Clement's work.

---

70. Clement of Alexandria, *Strom.* vi.11.95.3, citing Mt. 13.47; cf. *GTh* 8. That Clement here cites Matthew rather than Thomas or his source is argued by Tj. Baarda, *Essays on the Diatessaron* (Kampen: Kok Pharos, 1994), pp. 291-98.

71. Clement of Alexandria, *Paed.* ii.12.125.2, referring to Lk. 12.16-20.

72. Clement of Alexandria, *Paed.* i.5.12.2, citing Jn. 21.4-5.

73. A literary understanding of the term "gospel" is also implied where reference is made to "law, prophets and gospel" (Clement of Alexandria, *Strom.* iii.10.70.3). Since for Clement Christ or the Logos is the author of all three, "gospel" cannot in itself be a designation of "true Christianity," as E. Molland claims (*The Conception of the Gospel in the Alexandrian Theology*, p. 15).

74. It is misleading to claim that, in Clement, "Matthew, Mark, Luke, and John are quoted by name and in such a way as to indicate that they possessed the highest authority for him" (James A. Brooks, "Clement of Alexandria as a Witness to the Development of the New Testament Canon," *SecC* 9 [1992], pp. 41-55; p. 42). Evangelists are named only exceptionally; the "highest authority" belongs to the Lord himself.

75. Clement of Alexandria, *Strom.* iv.4.15.4.

76. Clement of Alexandria, *Strom.* ii.6.29.3.

77. Clement of Alexandria, *Strom.* vi.8.65.3.

78. Clement of Alexandria, *Strom.* vi.13.106.2.

(i) *Matthew and Luke.* These two gospels are normally quoted anonymously and without differentiation. In the passages cited above, they are named in the course of an elaborate attempt to coordinate Jewish and Christian history with the history of Greece and Rome — a context in which accurate citation is especially important. Clement refers to the numerical structure of Matthew's genealogy and to the chronological notice in Luke 3.1. Both passages are unique to the respective evangelists, and are their own composition rather than recording a dominical saying. Although Clement is aware of the evangelists' names, he gives no further details about the composition of their gospels.

(ii) *Mark.* Two later writers preserve a passage or passages from Clement's lost *Hypotyposes* in which he gives an account of the origins of Mark, presumably dependent in part on Papias. In Cassiodorus's sixth-century Latin translation of short commentaries on four of the Catholic Epistles (1 Peter, Jude, 1 and 2 John), Clement is said to have commented as follows on 1 Peter 5.13, where Peter refers to "my son Mark":

> Mark, a follower of Peter, while Peter publicly preached in Rome before members of Caesar's cavalry [*coram quibusdam Caesareanis equitibus*] and presented many testimonies to Christ, at their request, so that they might remember what was said, composed from what Peter had said the gospel called "according to Mark" [*evangelium quod secundum Marcum vocitatur*].[79]

Eusebius gives a somewhat different version of Clement's account:

> When Peter publicly preached the word in Rome and in the Spirit proclaimed the gospel, those present, who were many, requested Mark, as he had long followed him and remembered what he had said, to put it into writing [ἀναγράψαι τὰ εἰρημένα]. This he did, and gave the gospel to those who had requested it of him. When Peter became aware of this, he neither explicitly prohibited it nor endorsed it [μήτε κωλῦσαι μήτε προτρέψασθαι].[80]

These passages clearly go back to the same original.[81] The most striking

---

79. Clement/Cassiodorus, *In Epistola Petri Prima Catholica*, at 1 Pt. 5.13. In view of the parallel in Eusebius, it is not clear whether the naming of the gospel stems from Clement or from Cassiodorus.

80. Eusebius, *HE* vi.14.6-7.

81. A comparison between Cassiodorus's translation of Clement (C) and Rufinus's of

difference is the absence in Cassiodorus of the surprising statement about Peter's indifference to his follower's literary endeavours. Cassiodorus explains exactly why such passages are missing from his translations. In Clement's commentaries, he states, "many things are acutely said, but others incautiously, which we have translated into Latin in such a way that, with certain offensive elements [*quibusdam offendiculis*] removed, his purified doctrine may be more securely extracted."[82] Clement's claim that Peter refused to endorse a gospel written precisely to preserve his own teaching might well seem an incautious or offensive element. Peter's indifference to the Gospel of Mark probably mirrors and expresses Clement's own attitude. For Cassiodorus, a disparaging remark about a canonical text is unacceptable and must be suppressed. For Clement, Mark adds little or nothing of substance to Matthew and Luke and is therefore unworthy of endorsement by the chief of the apostles. Mark is one of the "four gospels handed down to us," but in Clement's eyes it might just as well not have been. Genuine Petrine tradition is to be found elsewhere: Clement claims access to it in both oral and written forms (through the "elders," and in 1 Peter and the *Preaching of Peter*).[83] In contrast, Mark's unauthorized work excites little enthusiasm.

(*iii*) *John*. Clement also speaks in his *Hypotyposes* of the origins of the Gospel of John. Eusebius again preserves the passage but conflates it with the anecdote about the origins of the Gospel of Mark discussed above, thereby obscuring Clement's view of the relationship between John and his predecessors.[84]

Eusebius (R) confirms this identification: *praedicante Petro evangelium palam Romae* (C) = *cum Petrus Romae publice praedicasset verbum dei* (R); *Marcus, Petri sectator . . . petitus ab eis* (C) = *auditores rogasse Marcum, qui olim iam sectator ipsius fuisset* (R); *scripsit ex his, quae a Petro dicta sunt* (C) = *conscribere ea, quae sciebat ab apostolo praedicata* (R).

82. Cassiodorus, *De Institutione Divinarum Litterarum* i.8.4.

83. Clement claims to have been initiated by three unnamed instructors into "the true tradition of the blessed teaching derived directly from Peter, James, John, and Paul, the holy apostles" (*Strom.* i.1.11.3). He cites at length what "Peter in his epistle says" (*Strom.* iv.20.129.2-4). From the *Kergyma Petrou* he quotes passages in which the risen Lord commissions his apostles (*Strom.* vi.5.43.3; vi.6.48.1-2), and in which Peter differentiates Christianity from pagan idolatry and Judaism (*Strom.* vi.5.39.1–41.7) and appeals to the fulfilment of prophecy (*Strom.* vi.15.128.1-3).

84. The interpolation is generally overlooked, and in consequence seems to provide early support for the "Griesbach hypothesis" (so David L. Dungan, "The Two-Gospel Hypothesis," in *The Interrelations between the Gospels*, ed. D. Dungan, BEThL [Leuven: Leuven University Press & Peeters, 1990], pp. 125-56). The interpolation is, however, noted by H. Merkel, who argues that (1) the basic contrast is between the two gospels with genealogies and John; (2) only the Mark passage is anecdotal in character; (3) connections with the statement about the gospels with genealo-

Omitting the interpolated Mark passage, Eusebius cites or summarizes Clement's account in the following terms:

> In the same books Clement records the tradition of the earliest elders about the order of the gospels [περὶ τῆς τάξεως τῶν εὐαγγελίων], as follows. He says that the first gospels to be written were the ones containing genealogies. . . . Last of all John, noting that the bodily facts [τὰ σωματικά] had been set forth in the [earlier] gospels, at the encouragement of his acquaintances and by inspiration of the Spirit, produced a spiritual gospel [πνευματικὸν ποιῆσαι εὐαγγέλιον].[85]

Eusebius's concern with the order of the four canonical gospels results in an unusual sequence in which Mark and Luke change places. Matthew and Luke were written first, then Mark, then John.[86] When the Markan passage is removed, however, it is clear that the relationship between Matthew and Luke on the one hand and John on the other has to do with the way the respective gospels *begin*. This explains the otherwise curious identification of Matthew and Luke by way of their genealogies rather than the evangelists' names. The genealogies present the σωματικά, the "bodily facts" about the Lord's earthly origins, and this starting point can be contrasted with the Johannine gospel which traces the origins of his earthly life back into the

gies are lacking ("Clemens Alexandrinus über die Reihenfolge der Evangelien," *ETL* 60 [1984], pp. 382-85). Merkel traces the interpolation to Clement's own conflation of earlier source material (pp. 384-85), overlooking the probable source of the passage on Mark in the comment on 1 Pt. 5.13 preserved by Cassiodorus.

85. Eusebius, *HE* vi.14.5, 7.

86. According to Stephen Carlson, the passage is not about the sequence of the gospels at all, either in the original context in Clement or in Eusebius's rendering of it: "Clement merely discussed the public nature, not the chronology, of the gospels" ("Clement of Alexandria on the 'Order' of the Gospels," *NTS* 47 [2001], pp. 118-25; p. 124). Carlson does not give a satisfactory explanation of the use of ἔσχατον in relation to John, which appears to confirm the chronological interpretation of προγεγράφθαι in relation to Matthew and Luke, and of περὶ τῆς τάξεως τῶν εὐαγγελίων in relation to the whole passage (Eusebius, *HE* vi.14.5-7). As Denis Farkasfalvy rightly states, "There is hardly any doubt that Eusebius wants his reader to think that the text he quotes from Clement is, indeed, about the chronological order of the four canonical gospels" ("The Presbyter's Witness on the Order of the Gospels as Reported by Clement of Alexandria," *CBQ* 54 [1992], pp. 260-70; p. 262). According to Farkasfalvy, "[t]he quotations lined up by Eusebius do not seem to constitute a continuous text by Clement" (p. 262). The insertion of the Mark passage is suggested by its use of εὐαγγέλιον (singular) in connection with Peter's preaching rather than εὐαγγέλια (plural) as in the references to the other gospels (pp. 262-63). But Farkasfalvy also breaks the link between the "genealogies" reference and the John passage, arguing unconvincingly that the former has to do with longer and shorter versions of Matthew and Luke (pp. 265-67).

"spiritual" sphere of the preexistent Logos. The point is repeated when Clement elsewhere turns his attention to 1 John, noting the parallel between the "spiritual beginning" *(principium spirituale)* of the letter and that of the gospel.[87] Elsewhere Eusebius himself notes that "the genealogy of our Saviour's fleshly origins [τὴν μὲν τῆς σαρκὸς τοῦ σωτῆρος ἡμῶν γενεαλογίαν], which had previously been written by Matthew and Luke, John passed over so as to begin with the doctrine of his divinity [τῆς δὲ θεολογίας ἀπάρξασθαι]".[88] Eusebius's dependence on the Clement passage (minus the Markan interpolation) is clear. The Johannine evangelist and his gospel are named insofar as they have their own distinctive contribution to add to earlier renderings of the gospel that are allowed to remain anonymous.

Clement's enthusiasm for John contrasts with his indifference towards Mark. We might conclude, then, that Clement sees the fourfold gospel as a descending hierarchy, in which John as the "spiritual gospel" is followed by Matthew and Luke as providing adequate renderings of the "bodily facts," leaving Mark a virtually redundant supplement to an essentially threefold gospel. Yet such an account would give too much weight to the rare occasions when Clement identifies an individual gospel at all. Gradations between them are relativized by the fact that their primary rationale is to preserve the words of the Lord. It is in his words that true authority lies, not in the texts as such.

(iv) Hebrews and Egyptians. Clement's references to specific gospels amplify the original phrase, ἐν τῷ εὐαγγελίῳ, and follow an almost identical format:[89]

ἐν τῷ κατὰ Ματθαῖον εὐαγγελίῳ
ἐν τῷ εὐαγγελίῳ τῷ κατὰ Λουκᾶν
ἐν τῷ κατὰ Μᾶρκον εὐαγγελίῳ
ἐν τῷ κατὰ Ἰωάννην εὐαγγελίῳ
ἐν τῷ καθ᾽ Ἑβραίους εὐαγγελίῳ
ἐν τῷ κατ᾽ Αἰγυπτίους [εὐαγγελίῳ]

The titles of *GHeb* and *GEgy* follow the pattern of the others, although they presumably refer not to authors but to the original readers. While these titles imitate and adapt the original κατά formula, they need not imply that

87. Clement/Cassiodorus, *In Epistola Iohannis Prima* (at 1.1).
88. Eusebius, *HE* iii.24.13.
89. See above for contexts and references.

precisely four instantiations of that formula were already established. As argued in Chapter 5 above, the Greek *GHeb* known to Clement and Origen is to be distinguished from later references to a gospel in the Hebrew or Aramaic language, used by Jewish Christians. This text was probably a sayings collection related — perhaps closely — to *GTh*. The excerpts from *GEgy* are largely or exclusively dialogical, and Salome's questions seem to have played a major structural role in this work.[90] In view of the analogy between the titles, it is likely that *GEgy* was compiled in response to *GHeb*. If *GEgy* indeed implied opposition to the created order, as its promoter Julius Cassianus believed, then its opposition to the creator deity of Jewish scripture would also reflect the antagonism between "Egyptians" and "Hebrews." An age-old Egyptian antipathy towards Jews is already noted by Josephus, who states that "the slanders against us originated with the Egyptians."[91] Tensions will have been heightened by Jewish uprisings in Alexandria, Egypt, and Cyrene during the reign of Trajan,[92] and such tensions may well find their echoes in the two opposed gospel titles, as also in the anti-Jewish sayings in *GTh*.[93]

Clement himself is unaware of any such tension. Both *GHeb* and *GEgy* are cited positively, although he knows that they do not belong to the fourfold collection he regards as traditional. They are no doubt named because they are relatively unfamiliar. The same may also be true of Mark — although the content of Mark is known indirectly in the Matthean and Lukan parallels, and Clement's citations sometimes show the influence of specifically Markan wording. Mark, unendorsed by Peter, is a marginal case. In contrast, the naming of John expresses Clement's view of its distinctive character as an important complement to earlier gospels.

Clement's citational practice represents a moment of transition between the earlier nonspecific appeal to "the gospel" and the emergence of four "gospels" differentiated by the names of their purported authors. Yet there is no consciousness of innovation in his single Irenaeus-like reference to "the four gospels handed down to us," nor is it explained how this "handing down" has taken place or how it differentiates one set of gospel texts from others. One factor may simply be relative familiarity. Clement assumes that Matthean, Lukan, or (to some degree) Johannine sayings will be well known

90. Clement of Alexandria, *Strom.* iii.13.92.2. For a possible analogy, see the *Dialogue of the Saviour* (NHL, III.5), which consists almost entirely of question-and-answer dialogues between Jesus and Matthew, Judas, and Mariam.
91. Josephus, *Contra Apionem* i.223.
92. Dio Cassius, *Hist. Rom.* lxviii.32.1-3; Eusebius, *HE* iv.2.1-5.
93. Cf. *GTh* 52-53 (scripture, circumcision).

to his readers, whether from liturgical usage, catechetical instruction, or private reading.[94] Sayings from *GHeb* and *GEgy* may be equally valuable, but Clement anticipates that these texts may not be known to many of his readers and identifies them accordingly. If so, then a precondition for the fourfold gospel is the operation of the developing market in Christian literature, where, in response to public appetite for such works, gospels or gospel-like texts proliferate alongside novelistic accounts of apostolic exploits, apocalypses, letter collections, and so on. As ever, some books achieve a wide circulation whereas others are known only within limited circles or areas. If, hypothetically, two gospel texts are popular in Alexandria whereas only one of them is known in Rome, then the consensus about the one will seem to give it an ecclesial sanction that the other lacks. The fourfold gospel is an attempt to articulate, formalize, and enforce a convergence around a common usage.

Clement himself articulates this perceived convergence, but shows no interest in formalizing or enforcing it. Indeed, he refers to it only in passing and in a single passage that does not reflect his eclectic citational practice as a whole. Nevertheless, an emerging trend may retrospectively be identified in this single passage, especially if we look back at Clement and his contemporaries from the perspective of Eusebius, the first great historian of the Christian canon.

Eusebius: Constructing the Boundary

Clement's unusually generous use of "disputed scriptures [ἀντιλεγομένων γραφῶν]" is noted by Eusebius without a hint of criticism.[95] In his *Stromateis,* Clement had used citations from the Wisdom of Solomon, the

---

94. For the liturgical use of "gospels," see Justin, *1 Apol.* 66.3 + 67.3, where, however, the number four is not specified. References to personal reading occur in the *Dialogue with Trypho*, where Trypho refers to τὰ ἐν τῷ λεγομένῳ εὐαγγελίῳ παραγγέλματα, and claims to have studied them: ἐμοῖ γὰρ ἐμέλησεν ἐντυχεῖν αὐτοῖς (*Dial.* 10.2); and in the Valentinian *Treatise on the Resurrection*, where the addressee, Rheginus, is invited to "remember reading in the gospel [ⲉⲕⲱϣ 2Ⲙ̄ ⲡⲉⲩⲁⲅⲅⲉⲗⲓⲟⲛ] that Elijah appeared and Moses with him" (NHC I,4, 48.8-9; cf. Mk. 9.4).

95. Eusebius, *HE* vi.13.6. For analysis of Eusebius's categorization of canonical, disputed, noncanonical, and heretical writings, see Bruce M. Metzger, *The Canon of the New Testament: Its Origin, Development, and Significance* (Oxford: Clarendon Press, 1987), pp. 201-7; David L. Dungan, *Constantine's Bible: Politics and the Making of the New Testament* (London: SCM Press, 2006), pp. 69-87.

Wisdom of Jesus son of Sirach, and several disputed letters: Hebrews, *Barnabas, Clement of Rome,* and Jude.[96] In his *Hypotyposes,* Clement's brief summaries of "every canonical text [πάσης τῆς ἐνδιαθήκου γραφῆς]" also covered disputed works such as "Jude and the rest of the catholic epistles and Barnabas and the so-called *Apocalypse of Peter.*"[97] Concerned as he is to establish the canonicity of Hebrews, Eusebius cites passages where Clement asserts its Pauline authorship, explains its anonymity, and identifies Luke as its translator from Hebrew into Greek.[98] It is in this context that (as we have seen) passages on Mark and John are combined. Mark wrote his gospel at the request of Peter's audience; John wrote his to complement the two whose genealogies retraced Jesus' human origins.[99]

So Clement becomes one of Eusebius's star witnesses to the fourfold canonical gospel. By focusing on the accounts of Markan and Johannine origins, Eusebius deftly sidesteps Clement's citations from gospels which from a later standpoint are wholly unacceptable. Clement's writings refer to named gospels linked with the Hebrews and the Egyptians. There is a gospel whose name Clement does not know, containing the dominical saying "My mystery is for myself and for the sons of my house."[100] In this or another gospel there occurs the saying "Ask and I will act, think and I will give," attributed on one occasion to the Lord and on another to "the scripture."[101] These and other texts, valued by Clement as preserving authentic information about the Lord although not formally gospels, are also passed over by Eusebius as unworthy

96. Eusebius, *HE* vi.13.6.

97. Eusebius, *HE* vi.14.1. Eusebius's information here is not entirely reliable. He himself regarded 1 John and 1 Peter as canonical and the other Catholic Epistles as disputed (*HE* iii.25.2-3). Cassiodorus seems to have found in Clement discussion of only four catholic epistles (1 Peter, 1 and 2 John, and Jude), in spite of a probably erroneous reference to "James" where "Jude" is apparently meant (*Institutiones Divinarum Litterarum* i.8). According to Photius, the *Hypotyposes* contained notes on Genesis, Exodus, the Psalms, the letters of Paul, the Catholic Epistles, and Ben Sira (*Bibliotheca*, codex 109; PG ciii). For a history of the Catholic Epistles collection, see David R. Nienhuis, *Not by Paul Alone: The Formation of the Catholic Epistle Collection and the Christian Canon* (Waco, TX: Baylor University Press, 2007), pp. 29-90.

98. Eusebius, *HE* vi.14.2-4. Three passages relating to Hebrews are here combined, of which the first (on Luke as translator) is also preserved in Cassiodorus's translation of Clement's commentary on 1 Peter (at 5.13). Having mentioned the relationship between Peter and Mark, Clement sees a parallel in the relationship between Paul and Luke.

99. Eusebius, *HE* vi.14.5-7.

100. Clement of Alexandria, *Strom.* v.10.63.7, a saying recorded ἐν τινι εὐαγγελίῳ. Hengel mistakenly substitutes "heart" for "house" (*Four Gospels*, p. 17).

101. Clement of Alexandria, *Strom.* vi.9.78.1; vi.12.101.4: αἴτησαι καὶ ποιήσω, ἐννοήθητι καὶ δώσω.

of note.[102] Having worked carefully through the *Stromateis* and noted texts used and named there, Eusebius must have grasped the full extent of Clement's scriptural eclecticism. Yet he is highly selective in his use of the information he has acquired. From his perspective, it is one thing to cite material from Barnabas or Clement of Rome, quite another to relax the barrier separating true from false gospels. If Clement did just that, the fact must be suppressed.[103] The fourfold gospel must be established not in name only but unambiguously and without leaving room for doubt. The reason for this selective use of Clement is simply that, for Eusebius, some questions are still open whereas others have been definitively closed. One can still engage in free debate about the status of, say, 2 Peter or *Barnabas;* but the normative status of the fourfold gospel is now beyond doubt. If that issue was considerably more open in the past, it is time to move on.[104]

Eusebius's vindication of the canonical gospel is carefully assembled, piece by piece, in Books 1-6 of his history of the church. Particularly striking is the extent of his dependence on Clement.

(i) Christological origins. Eusebius's story begins where for a Christian historian it has to begin: not with the circumstances of Jesus' human origins but with his divinity.[105] Strictly speaking, only the Father is in a position to comprehend the Light who predates the world, the Word who was in the beginning with God and who was God.[106] Yet, as this language already suggests, scripture comes to aid us in our semantic perplexity. The scriptures contain passages that speak plainly of Christ's transcendent divine being, and the first such passage to be cited here is the opening of the Gospel of John.[107] With its special focus on Christ's divine origin, this gospel goes

103. Eusebius notes that Clement refers to Cassianus as "the author of a chronological work" (*HE* vi.13.7; cf. Clement of Alexandria, *Strom.* i.21.101.2), but not that he also engages him in exegetical dispute about the interpretation of *GEgy.*

104. Eusebius's selective account of Clement's citations is echoed in H. von Campenhausen's claim that, "as in Irenaeus, it is the four great Gospels and the apostle Paul . . . which for [Clement] constitute the hard permanent core of a New Testament which at its edges is fluid" (*The Formation of the Christian Bible,* Eng. trans. [Philadelphia: Augsburg Fortress, 1972], p. 298). For Clement, the core of early Christian literature is to be found in "the gospel," and the gospel is to be found wherever Jesus' sayings are preserved in literary form.

105. Eusebius, *HE* i.1.8-9.

106. Eusebius, *HE* i.2.2-3.

107. Eusebius, *HE* i.2.3, citing Jn. 1.1, 3.

some way towards dispelling the blank incomprehension expressed in the scriptural question, "Who shall declare his generation?"[108] The theme is further developed with the help of passages drawn exclusively from the Old Testament;[109] also relevant to this prehistory is the prophetic anticipation of the incarnate life.[110] Thus the stage is set for Christ's appearance in the flesh, which can be dated with the help of material drawn from Luke, Josephus, and Daniel.[111]

While the Word's heavenly generation is a sacred mystery, his earthly origin should in principle be more easily grasped. Yet it seems doubtful whether we have reliable information on this, since Matthew and Luke provide us with quite different genealogies which many suppose to be in conflict with one another.[112] For a demonstration that this is not the case, we are indebted to Julius Africanus, in his letter to Aristides, cited here at length.[113] Africanus's simple and elegant solution purports to show how the apparently discordant genealogies converge in the two generations preceding Joseph. One genealogy traces the Davidic line through Solomon (Mt. 1.6-7), the other through a lesser-known son of David, Nathan (Lk. 3.31). According to Matthew, Joseph was the son of Jacob, who was the son of Matthan (Mt. 1.15-16). According to Luke, Joseph's immediate forebears were Heli and Melchi (Lk. 3.23-24).[114] To reconcile the genealogies, all that is necessary is to explain the relationships between Matthan and Melchi in the second generation before Joseph, and between Jacob and Heli in the first. Let us suppose that on Matthan's death Melchi married his widow. In that case, Matthan's son Jacob would be the brother of Melchi's son Heli. Let us further suppose that Heli died childless. In that case, it would be Jacob's responsibility to marry his widow in order to "raise up seed for his brother," in accordance with the institution of "levirate marriage" to which the Sadducees referred when they questioned Jesus about resurrection (Mt. 22.23-28; cf. Dt. 25.1-10). So Jacob becomes the father of Joseph, thereby bestowing posthumous fa-

---

108. Eusebius, *HE* i.2.2, citing Is. 53.8 LXX.

109. Eusebius, *HE* i.2.4–16, citing Gn. 1.26; 18.1–19.29; 32.28-30; Jos. 5.13-15; Ex. 3.4-6; Ps. 106.20; Prv. 8.12-16, 22-31. Appeal to these texts goes back at least as far as Justin's *Dialogue with Trypho.*

110. Eusebius, *HE* i.2.23–3.20.

111. Eusebius, *HE* i.5.1–6.11.

112. Eusebius, *HE* i.7.1.

113. Eusebius, *HE* i.7.1-17.

114. Eusebius, *HE* i.7.5. Africanus apparently follows a text that omits the names Matthat and Levi between Heli and Melchi. The structure of his solution is unaffected by this omission.

therhood on the deceased Heli. Joseph, then, has two (equally Davidic) genealogies because he has two fathers, one natural and the other legal.[115]

Eusebius's unreserved endorsement of Africanus's brilliant hypothesis is understandable. From a modern critical standpoint, of course, the hypothesis is no longer persuasive. There is (so one might argue) no evidence that either Matthew or Luke was aware of Africanus's ingenious family drama; their genealogies may be independent, or the Lukan one may have been composed to rival the Matthean one; the information they provide is in any case of dubious historical worth.[116] Such points are valid within a *precanonical* perspective on the gospels, inaccessible to Africanus or Eusebius. Within a canonical perspective, however, the patristic solution may still have its place, not least in view of its appeal to other intracanonical material (primarily from Deuteronomy). It demonstrates that Matthew and Luke *can* be read together, as components within a larger canonical whole, even if this does not correspond to the intentions or expectations of the evangelists themselves. None of the canonical evangelists intended their own incorporation into a fourfold collection or the corresponding semantic shifts, but that is nevertheless the objective *form* in which their work has survived.

We recall how, for Clement, the Gospel of John was written to complement the gospels that include genealogies. The earlier gospels tell of the Lord's fleshly descent, the later one traces his origin not to David, Abraham, or Adam, but to eternity. That is the sense in which John is the "spiritual gospel," complementing the earlier gospels' emphasis on "the bodily facts" (τὰ σωματικά).[117] It is, however, Eusebius who preserves and endorses this account, and it is now clear how the distinction derived from Clement has shaped his entire presentation of the Lord's entry onto the earthly scene. In the first book of his history, interpretation of the relevant passages from John, Matthew, and Luke is supplemented with material drawn from the prophets, Josephus, and the Abgar legend.[118] The supplementary texts pro-

---

115. Eusebius, *HE* i.7.5-9, 17. Africanus finds supporting textual evidence for his theory in the Lukan statement that Jesus "was the son (as was supposed) of Joseph, [son] of Heli, [son] of Melchi" (Lk. 3.23-24), extending "as was supposed" to cover Joseph's relation to Heli and noting the omission of the Matthean ἐγέννησεν (*HE* i.7.10). He also provides an account of the survival of Jesus' genealogy, supposed to stem from Jesus' family (*HE* i.7.11-14).

116. On this issue see Chapter 3, above.

117. Eusebius, *HE* vi.14.7.

118. Josephus supplies information about the date of Jesus' birth, the life and death of Herod, the Roman governors of Judea and the Jewish high priests, and indeed about John the Baptist and

vide a context, the gospels the content. Following in the steps of Clement, Eusebius derives from the canonical collection a contrast between the temporal and fleshly on the one hand and the eternal and divine on the other. When Mark is inserted into the picture at a later point in Eusebius's history, Clement's double-sided construal of the canonical collection is obscured.[119] Yet it is clear from Eusebius's first book that this construal has shaped his own thinking. Indeed, the function of his endorsement of Africanus is to resolve the problem inherent in Clement's claim that "the gospels containing the genealogies were written first."[120] By referring to the two gospels by way of their genealogies rather than the respective evangelists, Clement unwittingly focuses attention on a well-known point of discord — to which Africanus provides a compelling canonical solution.

(ii) Gospel origins. In the original form of Clement's schema, there is no place for Mark. This gospel opens not with a genealogy or a birth but with the ministry of John the Baptist and the baptism of Jesus. While the evangelist believes that these events represent "the beginning of the gospel of Jesus Christ" (Mk. 1.1), they represent not the beginning but the middle of the story from the standpoint of the canonical collection. Indeed, the implication that the descent of the Spirit at the baptism marks the beginning of Jesus' significant history is now theologically suspect, since it may seem to suggest an adoptionist christology.[121] Clement's ambivalence towards Mark is clearly expressed in the reaction he attributes to Peter, who "neither prohibited nor endorsed it," even though it is supposed to be a written record of his own teaching.[122] Unlike Clement, however, Eusebius is concerned to show that the fourfold canonical gospel is firmly established and that the line dividing the canonical from the noncanonical is absolutely clear. The inclusion of Mark is therefore a problem that must be addressed.

Eusebius has little to say about the origins of Matthew and Luke, merely repeating the traditional view that Matthew was written for the Hebrews and that Luke is the work of a disciple of Paul.[123] With the problem of the genealogies satisfactorily resolved, it can be taken for granted that Matthew

---

Jesus himself (Eusebius, *HE* i.5-6, 8-11). The Abgar legend tells of the founding of the church in Edessa, following correspondence between King Abgar and Jesus (*HE* i.13).

119. Eusebius, *HE* vi.14.6-7.
120. Eusebius, *HE* vi.14.5.
121. Cf. Irenaeus, *Adv. Haer.* i.26.1-2; iii.11.7.
122. Eusebius, *HE* vi.14.7.
123. Eusebius, *HE* iii.18.6; iii.4.7-8.

and Luke belong together. Eusebius might have explained that Matthew and Luke were originally intended for different readerships, the one Jewish, the other Gentile, but he evidently feels no need to do so.[124] In contrast, Eusebius provides an elaborate account of Markan origins in Book 2 of his history, well before his citation of the important early testimonies of Papias, Irenaeus, and Clement.[125] While dependence on Clement and Papias is explicitly acknowledged, or rather asserted,[126] the account is of Eusebius's own construction. The context for Mark's composition is now Peter's victory over Simon Magus in Rome, a tradition which in Eusebius's version combines Justin's claim that the Romans erected a statue to Simon[127] with a summary account of his final defeat drawn from the *Acts of Peter*,[128] a text elsewhere rejected as noncanonical.[129]

Within this new context Eusebius gives his own rendering of the Clement tradition:

> . . . When the divine word had thus been established among them [*sc.* the Romans], Simon's power was extinguished and immediately destroyed, along with the man himself. So greatly did the lamp of piety enlighten the minds of Peter's hearers that they were not satisfied with a single hearing or with unwritten instruction in the divine message, and with all kinds of appeals begged Mark, whose gospel is extant, as he was a follower of Peter, to provide them with a written record of the teaching they had received in oral form. Persisting in their request until they had persuaded him, they were thus responsible for the writing known as the Gospel according to Mark. It is said that, when what had happened was revealed to him by the Spirit, the apostle was delighted by their enthusiasm [ἡσθῆναι τῇ τῶν ἀνδρῶν προθυμίᾳ], and authorized the work [κυρῶσαί τε τὴν γραφήν] for reading in the churches. Clement gives this account in the sixth book

124. See Margaret Mitchell, "Patristic Counter-Evidence to the Claim That 'The Gospels Were Written for All Christians,'" *NTS* 51 (2005), pp. 36-79. Mitchell finds an ethnic and/or geographical explanation for the composition of Matthew and Luke in the so-called "Anti-Marcionite Prologues" (pp. 56-57), Origen (pp. 65-67), Gregory of Nazianzus (pp. 67-69), and Chrysostom (pp. 72-73).

125. Eusebius, *HE* ii.14.1–16.1 (Eusebius's account); iii.39.15 (Papias); v.8.3 (Irenaeus); vi.14.6-7 (Clement).

126. Eusebius, *HE* ii.15.2.

127. Eusebius, *HE* ii.14.1-3, citing Justin, *1 Apol.* 26.

128. Eusebius, *HE* ii.14.1-6; compare the Vercelli fragment of the *Acts of Peter*, Eng. tr. in Elliott, *ANT*, pp. 399-421.

129. Eusebius, *HE* iii.3.2; cf. iii.25.6.

of his *Hypotyposes,* and it is also attested by Papias, bishop of Hierapolis.[130]

When Eusebius later cites the sources here referred to, we learn that Papias is barely relevant and that Clement's authentic account has been significantly modified.[131] As noted earlier, what Clement actually wrote was:

> When Peter publicly preached the word in Rome and in the Spirit proclaimed the gospel, those present, who were many, requested Mark, as he had long followed him and remembered what he had said, to put it into writing. This he did, and gave the gospel to those who had requested it of him. When Peter became aware of this, he neither explicitly prohibited it nor endorsed it.[132]

Eusebius's preemptive rewriting of Clement's original statement makes three closely related changes.[133] First, he stresses the urgency of the request for a written record, together with its pious motivation. If Peter's hearers have to overcome an initial reluctance on Mark's part, this underlines how much they wanted the written record and how precious it was to them when it eventually became available. Second, Peter learns what has happened through divine inspiration. Whereas the original account is tacitly critical of an unauthorized initiative, the new version implies that this initiative is already approved by the Holy Spirit, who is Peter's informant. Third, Peter's refusal to acknowledge the work written in his name is directly contradicted. Far from turning his back on this transcript of his own preaching, the apostle commended the new gospel for public use and approved the conduct of those who had brought it into being. The reader of Mark's gospel should not imagine for a moment that this work has gone out into the world as an orphan, unblessed by its apostolic progenitor. If that had been the case, it would be impossible to justify its place within the canonical collection. Although Eusebius will later cite statements by Papias as well as Clement which imply that Mark is a work of limited value, that is emphatically not his own view. The church acknowledges four gospels, neither more nor less, and

130. Eusebius, *HE* ii.15.1-2.

131. Eusebius, *HE* iii.39.15 (Papias); vi.14.6-7 (Clement).

132. Eusebius, *HE* vi.14.6-7.

133. Margaret Mitchell misunderstands the Eusebian paraphrase, viewing it as "another version of [the] tradition about Mark's gospel, also attributed to Clement's *Hypotyposes,*" and thus as an authentic "fragment from Clement" ("Patristic Counter-Evidence," pp. 50, 51).

there must be absolute clarity about this point. Mark's canonical status must be vindicated, and the early sources must be rewritten accordingly — even if, from a scholarly perspective, it is also desirable to preserve them in their original uncensored form.

Having prefaced the new story with the defeat of Simon Magus, Eusebius also provides a sequel which tells of Mark's mission to Egypt, where he "proclaimed the gospel he had written and established churches first of all in Alexandria itself."[134] Mark, then, is an evangelist in the full sense and in his own right, and establishes the church of Alexandria in the apostolic succession. He is said to have been succeeded as bishop of Alexandria by Annianus in "the eighth year of Nero," i.e. in 62 CE, implying a considerably earlier date for the composition of the gospel.[135] By the time of Eusebius, we may presume, the church of Alexandria has forgotten earlier reservations about Mark and his gospel, and has taken both to its heart.[136] While these older and newer traditions contain little if any reliable historical information about Markan origins, they do register shifting evaluations of Mark with some precision. In its developed Eusebian form, the legend of Peter and Mark is an expression of newfound confidence in the value of this work as integral to the canonical collection.

Alongside Mark, the Gospel of John is also singled out for special consideration. Having introduced the apostle John by way of a legend drawn (once again) from Clement, Eusebius turns to the subject of his writings. In the first place, the gospel that bears his name is to be acknowledged as genuine.[137] The point is emphasized because the authority of other works attributed to John is more doubtful; there is no dispute about the gospel or the first epistle, but the status of the two shorter epistles and the book of Revelation is unclear.[138] But the genuineness of the gospel must also be emphasized because there *are* grounds on which it might hypothetically be challenged. After all, it is very different from the others. If we focus again on gospel beginnings, John asserts the divinity of Christ in order to complement and balance the Matthean and Lukan stress on his human origins: here

---

134. Eusebius, *HE* ii.16.1.

135. Eusebius, *HE* ii.24. There are further references to the succession of Alexandrian bishops, up to the time of Clement, in *HE* iii.14; iii.21.1-2; iv.1.2; iv.4; iv.5.5; iv.11.6; iv.19; v.9.1; v.22.

136. Shortly after Eusebius, the link between Mark and Egypt is also asserted by Epiphanius: "Mark, who came directly after Matthew, was ordered to issue the Gospel by Peter in Rome, and after writing it was sent by Peter to Egypt" (*Pan.* 51.6.10).

137. Eusebius, *HE* iii.24.1-2.

138. Eusebius, *HE* iii.24.17-18; iii.25.1-4; vi.25.9-10; vii.25.1-27.

too, Eusebius anticipates material he will later cite from Clement.[139] But an additional explanation for the composition of John is also provided. Like his fellow apostles, John saw the oral proclamation of the gospel as his primary vocation. He was moved to write for the following reason:

> When the three previously composed gospels were already circulating widely and had reached him too, they say that he accepted them and confirmed their truthfulness, except that they lacked an account of what Christ did first of all, at the beginning of his ministry. This claim is indeed true. For it is clear that the three evangelists recorded what the Saviour did only in the year after John the Baptist was confined to prison. . . . They say then that John, when requested to do so for this reason, gave an account in his own gospel of the period about which the earlier evangelists had remained silent, and of the things the Saviour did at that time (that is, before the Baptist's imprisonment). . . .[140]

In its full form, the argument is carefully constructed and unusually detailed. It is noted that all three synoptic evangelists begin their accounts of Jesus' public ministry after John's arrest (cf. Mt. 4.12; Mk. 1.14; Lk. 3.20), and that the fourth evangelist makes clear his concern with an earlier period when he states that "John had *not yet* been thrown into prison" (Jn. 3.24).[141] This argument is largely drawn from a source, as Eusebius indicates by inserting his citation formula, "they say" (φασίν), on four occasions, along with parenthetic remarks of his own. While the source is unnamed, Eusebius uses it just as he has earlier used Julius Africanus's harmonization of the Matthean and Lukan genealogies, to demonstrate that apparent contradictions can be resolved by careful exegesis and to secure the canonical status of the texts in question.[142]

---

139. Eusebius, *HE* iii.24.13.

140. Eusebius, *HE* iii.24.7-8, 11.

141. Eusebius, *HE* iii.24.8-11. For a recent restatement of this argument, see Richard Bauckham, "John for Readers of Mark," in *The Gospels for All Christians: Rethinking the Gospel Audiences*, ed. R. Bauckham (Grand Rapids: Eerdmans, 1998), pp. 147-71; pp. 150-56.

142. Charles E. Hill implausibly argues that Eusebius's source here is none other than Papias ("What Papias Said about John (and Luke)," *JTS*, n.s., 49 [1998], pp. 582-629; *The Johannine Corpus in the Early Church* [Oxford: Oxford University Press, 2004], pp. 385-96). According to Hill, Eusebius bases his main argument on a single written source, to which he refers in the phrases κατέχει ὁ λόγος and ἀληθής γε ὁ λόγος (*HE* iii.24.5, 8) as well as in the citation formula φασίν ("What Papias Said," pp. 589-90; *Johannine Corpus*, pp. 387-88). This source contained not only the passage about John but also an account of Matthew's composition so closely linked to the familiar

Eusebius is in no doubt whatsoever about "the holy tetrad of the gospels."[143] Although dependent on Clement at a number of points, little of the diversity of the earlier usage is allowed into his own text; only the single startling statement about Peter's indifference to the gospel written in his honour, which, by the time it is cited, has already been emphatically contradicted. Yet echoes of earlier debates may still be detected in the special care taken to secure the canonical status of Mark and John.

In his engagement with Clement's contemporary, Serapion, bishop of Antioch, the other side of Eusebius's contribution to canon construction comes into view. The canonical status of the holy tetrad requires not only that the right texts be safely incorporated but also that the wrong texts be decisively repudiated.

(iii) Peter without Mark? Clement may have been personally acquainted with Serapion. Having left Alexandria at a time of persecution in *c.* 202,[144] he is next heard of around a decade later as bearer of a letter from Alexander, bishop of Jerusalem, congratulating the church of Antioch on the appointment of a new bishop after Serapion's death.[145] Divine providence has led Clement to Jerusalem (Alexander writes), and there he has greatly strengthened the church; he is a man "whom you too know and will recognize."[146] If this means that Clement was known to the Antiochene church from an earlier visit, then an acquaintance with Serapion is plausible.

Of Serapion's writings, Eusebius quotes from a violently anti-Montanist letter addressed to Caricus and Pontius (or Ponticus), written "that you may

---

Papias statement cited elsewhere (iii.39.16) that the two should be identified (*Johannine Corpus*, pp. 388-90). If the John passage is from the same source as the Matthew one, and if the Matthew passage is drawn from Papias, then the John passage too must stem from Papias. The problem with this hypothesis is that, while the Matthew passage is directly or indirectly *influenced* by Papias, it is actually very different. According to Papias, "Matthew compiled the sayings in the Hebrew language, and each person interpreted them as he was able" (*HE* iii.39.16). In the other passage, it is said that "Matthew, having first preached to the Hebrews, as he was about to go to others, wrote his gospel [τὸ κατ' αὐτὸν εὐαγγέλιον] in the ancestral language so that, for those whom he was about to leave, his absence should be filled up by a written text" (iii.24.6). The two passages have little in common beyond a reference to the gospel's original language, expressed in different terminology (Ἑβραΐδι διαλέκτῳ or πατρίῳ γλώττῃ).

143. Eusebius, *HE* iii.25.1.

144. Eusebius, *HE* vi.6; vi.1; vi.3.1.

145. Eusebius, *HE* vi.11.4-6. Eusebius's *Chronicle* dates Serapion's episcopacy from the eleventh year of Commodus (190 CE) to the first year of Caracalla (211).

146. Eusebius, *HE* vi.11.6. Cosaert's claim that Alexander is writing from Cappadocia, and that it was there that Clement came to know him, appears to be incorrect (*Gospels in Clement*, p. 10).

know that the working of the fraudulent movement of the so-called 'New Prophecy' is abhorred by the Christian community throughout the world."[147] The point is reinforced by further episcopal signatures and by the enclosure of the polemical work of Claudius Apolinarius, bishop of Hierapolis.[148] Then there is a letter to Domninus, who converted to Judaism fearing persecution as a Christian.[149] And there is also a letter which, in the collection used by Eusebius, has been entitled "On the So-called Gospel of Peter" (Περὶ τοῦ λεγομένου κατὰ Πέτρον εὐαγγελίου).[150] This was addressed to the church at Rhossus, a port on the Gulf of Issus around twenty miles northwest of Antioch. According to Eusebius, it was written to refute the falsehoods this gospel contains, which had led some members of the church to adopt heterodox views.[151] We would expect Serapion's critique of a heterodox gospel to be at least as robust as his attack on Montanism. Yet in the excerpt preserved by Eusebius he is remarkably circumspect, partly out of embarrassment at what he now regards as his own earlier lapse of judgement. Careful, sentence-by-sentence reading of this excerpt will again expose the gulf between the canonical orthodoxy of Eusebius's day and the attitudes of leading figures such as Serapion and Clement, a century or so earlier.

The excerpt opens as follows:

> For we, brothers, accept both Peter and the other apostles as if they were Christ, but as people of experience [ἔμπειροι] we reject the writings falsely ascribed to them [τὰ ὀνόματι αὐτῶν ψευδεπίγραφα], knowing that such things we did not receive [οὐ παρελάβομεν].[152]

Gospels genuinely written by Peter or other apostles such as Matthew or John would come to us with the full authority of Christ. Yet we should not naively assume that a gospel bearing an apostolic name and written, perhaps, in the first-person singular is actually the work of that apostle. When we read in a gospel the words "I, Simon Peter . . ." (*GPet* 14.60), we must judge whether to take these words at face value or ascribe them to a more recent author, who has

---

147. Eusebius, *HE* v.19.1-2.

148. Eusebius, *HE* v.19.3-4; cf. iv.27. On Serapion's letter, see Christine Trevett, *Montanism: Gender, Authority, and the New Prophecy* (Cambridge: Cambridge University Press, 1996), pp. 51-54.

149. Eusebius, *HE* vi.12.1.

150. Eusebius, *HE* vi.12.1.

151. Eusebius, *HE* vi.12.2.

152. Eusebius, *HE* vi.12.3.

usurped the apostolic persona and who possesses no authority whatever. In raising the issue of pseudepigraphy, Serapion at the same time flatters his readers by associating them with himself as persons capable of making critical decisions of this nature. A preliminary test for pseudepigraphy is indicated. Writings that the church has "received" *cannot* be pseudepigraphal; those that the church did not receive *may* be. The question of pseudepigraphy does not arise in the case of a familiar and widely used gospel bearing an apostle's name. A previously unknown gospel bearing an apostle's name should be treated with greater caution, however, even where the apostle in question is a more prestigious figure than any of the traditional evangelists. Pseudepigraphy is a real possibility. Yet Serapion does not here endorse Eusebius's own view, which is that heretically motivated pseudepigraphy should be *assumed* in the case of gospels attributed to the likes of Peter, Thomas, or Matthias.[153] For Serapion, there might in principle be a legitimate gospel authored by one or another of these apostolic figures, which we would be bound to receive as embodying the authority of Christ. Indeed, such a gospel may actually exist, in the form of the text attributed to Peter that is currently in use at Rhossus. The question of authenticity seems genuinely open.

Clement himself does not betray any knowledge of a Petrine gospel. But if Peter is dissatisfied with Mark's well-intentioned attempt to compose a gospel in his name, he might in principle respond by composing a gospel of his own that would rectify Mark's deficiencies and thereby supersede it. For Clement as for Serapion, an authentically Petrine gospel is in principle entirely plausible. If there is an *Epistle of Peter*, a *Kerygma of Peter*, and an *Apocalypse of Peter*, why not also a gospel?[154]

Such may perhaps have been Serapion's initial thoughts when he first encountered a *Gospel according to Peter* during a visit to Rhossus:

When I visited you, I assumed that everyone held the true faith [ὀρθῇ πίστει], and, not having read the Gospel produced by them in the name of

153. Eusebius, *HE* iii.25.6.

154. The *Epistle of Peter* is, of course, 1 Peter, so named to differentiate it from 2 Peter, which Clement does not know; see the lengthy citation of what "Peter says in his epistle" in *Strom.* iv.20.129.2-4. For the *Kergyma Petrou*, see *Strom.* vi.5.39.1–41.7, 43.3; vi.6.48.1-2; vi.15.128.1-3. For the *Apocalypse of Peter*, see Eusebius, *HE* vi.14.1; Clement of Alexandria, *Eclogae Propheticae* 41.1-3; 48.1–49.2 (*Clemens Alexandrinus*, III [GCS], pp. 135-55). There is an analysis of these passages in Thomas J. Kraus and Tobias Nicklas, *Das Petrusevangelium und die Petrusapokalypse: Die griechischen Fragmente mit deutscher und englischer Übersetzung* (Berlin & New York: De Gruyter, 2004), pp. 89-92.

Peter [τὸ ὑπ᾽ αὐτῶν προφερόμενον ὀνόματι Πέτρου εὐαγγέλιον], I said, "If it is only this that seems to you to produce a mean-spirited attitude, let it be read!"[155]

What had happened at Rhossus? Serapion arrived there, perhaps on a regular visitation, and was confronted by a group agitating to be permitted to read a gospel they attributed to Peter. There is no indication that this gospel has occasioned controversy within the congregation itself. If there had been a Rhossian faction opposed to this gospel, Serapion could hardly have approved it without even reading it through. Yet the Rhossians recognize that they need his permission before they include this gospel in their liturgical readings, since this would be a departure from normal practice.[156] The clear distinction between tradition and innovation suggests that, like Clement, the Rhossians know of "the four gospels handed down to us" yet continue to value gospel literature beyond the canonical boundary. Unlike Clement, they wish to expand the liturgically authorized collection itself, arguing that it would be "mean-spirited" to insist on limiting it to four. Stung by a charge that applies potentially to himself, and assuming that the gospel's impressive credentials are authentic, Serapion gives the Rhossians the permission they want. In the Antiochene sphere of influence it seems that the fourfold gospel is established, but not securely. One can appeal against it with some prospect of success; apostolic authorship trumps the fact that this gospel is not yet widely known. Only later does Serapion raise questions about authenticity.

But now, having learnt from what has been told me that their mind lurks in some den of heresy [αἱρέσει τινί . . . ἐφώλευσεν], I am anxious to come to you again. So, brothers and sisters, expect me shortly.[157]

---

155. Eusebius, *HE* vi.12.4. This translation of τὸ δοκοῦν ὑμῖν παρέχειν μικροψυχίαν is to be preferred to the NPNF rendering ("which occasions dispute among you"); cf. Paul Foster, *The Gospel of Peter: Introduction, Critical Edition, and Commentary* (Leiden & Boston: Brill, 2010), p. 106 ("that seemingly causes captious feelings among you"). The NPNF mistranslation seems to derive from Rufinus's Latin rendering of Serapion's pronouncement: *Si hoc est solum, quod inter vos simultatem videtur inferre, legatur codex.* Kraus and Nicklas translate μικροψυχία as *Kleinmut,* "faintheartedness," "timidity" (*Das Petrusevangelium und die Petrusapokalypse,* p. 13), which is hardly more appropriate to the Greek word than "dispute."

156. It is likely to be public rather than private reading that is at issue here (*pace* C. Hill, *Who Chose the Gospels? Probing the Great Gospel Conspiracy* [Oxford: Oxford University Press, 2010], p. 82). A group of Christians does not normally consult its bishop about what may be read in the privacy of the home.

157. Eusebius, *HE* vi.12.4.

The addressees are now told that the situation has changed, and that the permission earlier granted is in jeopardy. Serapion has been listening to informers. It seems that the Rhossians who agitated for that permission were secretly cherishing heretical notions in their hearts. The bishop does not divulge his sources, but he believes them and is preparing to act on them; the letter warns the congregation of an imminent second visit during which the accused will be interrogated about their beliefs and, if guilty and unrepentant, expelled from the church.

> And we, brothers and sisters, comprehended the heresy of Marcianus, who contradicts himself because he does not understand what he says, as you will learn from what has been written to you.[158]

It is presumably the leader of the newly exposed Rhossian heretics who is here named. Serapion understands him better than he understands himself; the rest of the congregation is invited to take the same view as Serapion does, enabled by his letter to recognize the fallacies on which the heretics' position rests.

> For, having obtained this same gospel from others of its exponents, that is, from the successors of those who introduced it, whom we call "Docetae" (for most of their views are from that school of thought [διδασκαλίας]) . . .[159]

The relationship between heresy and the Petrine gospel is very close. Comprehending Marcianus's heresy has required Serapion to track down the gospel that he had previously not bothered to read. He knows that it is used and valued not only in Rhossus but also by a group characterized by opinions that Serapion identifies with the "Docetae."[160] Unlike Marcianus, these people are not directly accused of heresy. Yet their association with a particular school of thought prepares the addressees for the possibility that the gospel they use in all innocence may have been corrupted in transmission. The Rhossians are already aware that this gospel has not yet circulated widely, and they put this down to the "mean spirit" of those who recognize

158. Eusebius, *HE* vi.12.5.
159. Eusebius, *HE* vi.12.6.
160. The name occurs in a heresiological list in Clement (*Strom.* vii.17.108.2). It is doubtful whether the Docetae of Clement or Serapion are to be identified with the group responsible for the elaborate mythological system outlined by Hippolytus (*Refutatio Omnium Haeresium* viii.1-4; x.12).

only the familiar four. They now learn that this limited circulation may have more to do with the special concerns of the sect-like group that is so closely associated with this text. Petrine though it may be in origin, its provenance gives cause for concern.

> ... we were able to read through it and to find that most of it conforms to the true doctrine of the Saviour [τοῦ ὀρθοῦ λόγου τοῦ σωτῆρος], but that some things have been added, which we list for you below [ἃ καὶ ὑπετάξαμεν ὑμῖν].[161]

The self-contradictions of the Rhossian heretics are rooted in the corruption of the text to which they appeal. Most of that text is entirely orthodox and no doubt authentically Petrine. But there are other passages of which this cannot be said, and — since heresy is always subsequent to truth — these must be regarded as secondary additions stemming presumably from the "docetae."[162] Serapion lists the corrupt and corrupting passages. The implication is clear: the Rhossians must eliminate these passages and thus restore the Petrine gospel to its original form. Having done so, however, they may continue to use it.[163]

At this point, Serapion and Eusebius part company. Serapion's list is not preserved. For Eusebius, the Petrine gospel is not an authentic text that has suffered corruption but a wholly corrupt text that must be rejected.[164] There are indeed gospels attributed to Peter, Thomas, or Matthias in circulation, but these are cited as authentic only by heretics.[165] The boundary between the canonical and the noncanonical is now absolutely clear. It is the bound-

---

161. Eusebius, *HE* vi.12.6.

162. Paul Foster suggests that Serapion was actually acquainted with two different texts of *GPet*, and that the version found in the Akhmîm codex is "a witness to the first edition of the *Gospel of Peter*, since there are no blatantly docetic features . . ." (*Gospel of Peter*, p. 108). It is much more likely that Serapion's identification of supposedly added passages rests on the dogmatic assumption that heresy is always later than orthodoxy.

163. According to Harnack, "Serapion hat um 200 die öffentliche Vorlesung des Petrusevangeliums im Gottesdienst gestattet, und er hat bald darauf diese Erlaubniss zurückgezogen, nicht weil er nun erklärte, dass neben den vier Evv. kein fünftes gelesen werden dürfe — im Gegentheil: was wirklich als von Aposteln stammend erkannt wird, steht so hoch wie das Wort Christi selbst und soll gelesen werden — , sondern weil jenes Evangelium häretisch und gefälscht sei" (*Das Neue Testament um das Jahr 200* [Freiburg i.B.: J. C. B. Mohr, 1889], p. 49). But the list of falsified passages appended to Serapion's letter indicates an intention to restore the authentic Petrine text rather than regarding it as heretical through and through.

164. Eusebius, *HE* iii.3.2.

165. Eusebius, *HE* iii.25.6.

ary between truth and error, light and darkness. There can be no movement from either side of the boundary in the direction of the other. There is no more interest in differing degrees of falsehood on one side of the boundary than in differing degrees of truth on the other. Congregations under the sway of powerful individuals will no longer be able to negotiate with bishops about which gospels are to be read in church. Theologians will no longer be permitted to assume that authentic words of the Lord are to be found in any text that calls itself a gospel.

Whether the Eusebian boundary is regarded as "repressive" is a matter of perspective.[166] Bishop Serapion might not have been displeased at this draconian solution to his embarrassing Petrine problem. Clement might have been distressed to learn that cherished Petrine texts were to fall into such disfavour. Yet awarding praise or blame is beside the point. What comes to light in Eusebius is nothing less than a new, composite, and definitive gospel text, its boundary sharply defined following the severance of intertextual links with other gospel literature. The new text is an instrument of repression for advocates of the Petrine gospel, just as the Petrine gospel can only be an occasion of error for advocates of the fourfold gospel. There are no neutral criteria by which such a dispute might be adjudicated. What is undeniable is that the fourfold canonical gospel rapidly acquires an enduring social embodiment whereas gospels on the wrong side of the canonical boundary do not. What is also undeniable is that this need not have been so. The boundary is a construct, not a natural barrier that has always been the case.

166. Eusebius's imperial connections are often thought to give substance to this charge. Eusebius was commissioned by the emperor Constantine to produce fifty complete Bibles of the highest quality (Eusebius, *Vita Constantini* iv.34-37). It has been argued that these works contribute to the "closure" of the New Testament canon, with the addition of the five Eusebian *antilegomena* ("catholic epistles" other than 1 Peter and 1 John) to his twenty-two *homologoumena* (so Dungan, *Constantine's Bible,* pp. 121-22). Plausible though this may be, Constantine could have had no influence on Eusebius's view of the fourfold gospel, since the first edition of the *Historia Ecclesiastica* belongs to an earlier period (313/14, according to Andrew Louth, "The Date of Eusebius' *Historia Ecclesiastica*," *JTS* 41 [1990], pp. 111-23).

CHAPTER 9

The West: Towards Consensus

In one sense the fourfold gospel is simply a collection of texts, like the Pauline letters. Yet Paul's letters differ from each other fundamentally, in spite of overlaps. Each letter covers different ground, and parallels are incidental. In the case of the gospels, parallels are everything. Here the same story is told in four different ways, so that a gospel is far more closely bound to other gospels than a letter is to other letters. The singularity of the letter collection is to be found in the figure of its author; its plurality derives from different addressees and occasions. In the case of the gospel collection, singularity is located in a common content, plurality in the divergent authorial perspectives on that content. Each gospel is to be read not only as itself but also in its relation to the others. From a canonical standpoint, the interrelatedness precedes the individuality.

In view of this fundamental interrelatedness, the fourfold canonical gospel may be seen not only as a collection but also *as a new text* — like Matthew in relation to Mark. As Mark is to Matthew so is Matthew to the fourfold gospel: in both cases, an earlier text is preserved yet also subsumed into a larger text. The analogy is not exact; the fourfold gospel adds no new textual material but reorders material that already exists. Yet the reordering has hermeneutical consequences so profound that here too one must speak of a new text, more than and other than the sum of its parts. The fourfold gospel is intended as a final and definitive act of gospel production, incorporating just four of the many available works in the gospel genre and representing itself as the intended goal of the individual writings. While the teleology is fictive, this is a fiction that immediately converts itself into fact and social reality in the form of the normative fourfold text.

In the previous chapter it became clear that the fourfold gospel remained a work in progress until well into the fourth century. While Eusebius is able to cite passages from Irenaeus and Origen which testify to the four-fold gospel as clearly as he could wish, he is aware that this testimony is not universal. Papias does not mention the gospels ascribed to Luke and John, in spite of his supposed access to the traditions of apostles and elders. Serapion initially sanctions the public use of a gospel according to Peter, later requiring that it be reedited but not abandoned. Clement quotes from a wide range of gospel literature, and hands down a tradition disparaging to Mark; only by suppressing or manipulating his statements can Eusebius make him a witness to the gospel's true canonical form. At points such as these, the fictive or constructed nature of the fourfold gospel is patent. Yet what matters is not that the construction is problematic or ill-founded but that it is precisely *construction* that Eusebius undertakes as he tells how the four gospels came to be written and acknowledged. He and other early theorizers of the fourfold gospel do not merely assert or defend this composite textual object — rather, they *produce* it.

If Eusebius stands at the end of the process of articulating the fourfold gospel, Irenaeus stands at its beginning. At this beginning an initial rationale for the gospel's canonical form comes clearly to light.

Irenaeus: The Politics of Gospel Origins

Eusebius preserves the Greek text of an important passage in which Irenaeus lists four canonical gospels and indicates their circumstances of origin:

> Matthew, among the Hebrews and in their own language, produced a written account of the gospel [γραφὴν ἐξήνεγκεν εὐαγγελίου], while Peter and Paul were in Rome evangelizing and founding the church. After their departure [ἔξοδον] Mark also, the disciple and interpreter of Peter, handed down to us in written form [ἐγγράφως] what was preached by Peter. And Luke, the follower of Paul, set down in a book the gospel preached by him. Then John the disciple of the Lord, who reclined upon his breast, gave out a gospel while living in Ephesus in Asia.[1]

Eusebius carefully notes that this passage occurs in the third book of Irenaeus's work against heresies, and adds further citations from the same work indicative of its author's view of the scriptural canon. Irenaeus is an im-

---

1. Eusebius, *HE* v.8.2-4, citing Irenaeus, *Adv. Haer.* iii.1.1.

portant early witness to the alleged Johannine authorship of Revelation.[2] He quotes from the first epistle of John and the first epistle of Peter, but also from the *Shepherd of Hermas* and the Wisdom of Solomon.[3] He affirms the divine inspiration of the Septuagint, defending it against more recent translations and rehearsing the traditional story of its origin.[4] Thus the passage on the four canonical gospels is set alongside other passages relating to the history of the canon, an area in which Eusebius takes a special interest.[5] In consequence it is uprooted from its original context, and its possible significance within Irenaeus's own work is overlooked. Eusebius is concerned with the question *which books* should be deemed to belong to the New Testament scriptures. The answer to his question would take the form of a list, and he himself has already provided just such a list — although a rather tentative one — at an earlier point in his work.[6] What is at issue for Eusebius is simply inclusion or exclusion. It cannot be assumed that this is true also of Irenaeus.

Eusebius refers to Irenaeus's major work under two titles, one shorter ("On the Heresies")[7] and one longer ("Exposure and Refutation of Knowledge Falsely So-Called").[8] The second of these corresponds exactly to the last of Irenaeus's own attempts to provide his work with a title, all of which represent "exposure" and "refutation" as its primary concerns.[9] "Exposure" covers the contents of Book 1, where Irenaeus displays firsthand knowledge of certain post-Valentinian soteriologies filled out with material on earlier heresies probably derived from Justin.[10] "Refutation" covers the contents of Book 2, where Irenaeus attempts to demonstrate the incoherence and im-

---

2. Eusebius, *HE* v.8.5-7.

3. Eusebius, *HE* v.8.7-9.

4. Eusebius, *HE* v.8.10-15.

5. Eusebius introduces the passage on the fourfold gospel by referring to his earlier stated intention to note church writers' statements relating to the canonical books (*HE* v.8.1; cf. iii.3.3, i.1.1).

6. Eusebius, *HE* iii.25.1-4. In spite of remaining doubts about six writings (five catholic epistles and Revelation), Eusebius's list is essentially the same as the one provided by Athanasius in his "Easter Letter" of 367.

7. πρὸς τὰς αἱρέσεις (Eusebius, *HE* iii.18.2). In Rufinus's Latin translation this is rendered as *adversus haereses*, the origin of the familiar Latin title and its English equivalent.

8. ἔλεγχος καὶ ἀνατροπὴ τῆς ψευδονύμου γνώσεως (Eusebius, *HE* v.7.1).

9. In the preface to Book 5, Irenaeus entitles his work *De traductione et eversione falso cognominatae agnitionis*, a slight modification by himself or his Latin translator of the earlier *De detectione et eversione falsae cognitionis*, in the preface to Book 4; cf. *detectio et eversio sententiae ipsorum*, preface to Book 2.

10. See F. Wisse, "The Nag Hammadi Library and the Heresiologists," *VC* 25 (1971), pp. 205-23; pp. 213-18.

plausibility of the Valentinian scheme. The exposure is even more important than the refutation. We are told that earlier defenders of the faith failed in their attempts to refute the heretics because they lacked an understanding of their secret teachings — like doctors trying to treat a disease without an adequate diagnosis.[11] Irenaeus, however, has read the Valentinians' texts and debated their tenets.[12] The refutation in Book 2 can be expected to succeed, since it is grounded in the exposure elaborated in Book 1.

Irenaeus's two main tasks have apparently been completed by the end of his second book.[13] In the preface to the third, he tells us that he has fulfilled the request of his anonymous addressee. This third book is therefore an unexpected bonus, like the rich and unstinting love of God which gives more generously than anything we can ask or imagine; it will contain additional "proofs from the scriptures" *(ex scripturis . . . ostensiones)*.[14] The passage on gospel origins (cited above) occurs at the beginning of the scriptural proofs and serves to establish the reality of an apostolic scripture arising from the apostolic preaching. While Irenaeus continues to speak of "refutation," his scriptural *ostensiones* refute only by elaborating the truth in relation to which falsehood can be identified as such. They negate only as they also construct. Irenaeus shows himself here to be a creative theological thinker and not just a "proto-orthodox heresiologist."[15] The question, then, is whether the concept of a fourfold gospel is developed primarily as a polemical weapon, to be directed against such targets as the Marcionite minimalism that acknowledges only a truncated Gospel of Luke.[16] It is one thing to note that the fourfold gospel is *put to use* in the refutation of heresies, another to demonstrate that its *origins* lie in the antiheretical struggle.

---

11. Irenaeus, *Adv. Haer.* iv, *praef.* 2.

12. Irenaeus, *Adv. Haer.* i, *praef.* 2.

13. As Richard A. Norris notes, Book 2 "seems intended not as a first step, but as a complete refutation in its own right" ("Irenaeus of Lyons," in *The Cambridge History of Early Christian Literature*, ed. Frances Young, Lewis Ayres, and Andrew Louth [Cambridge: Cambridge University Press, 2004], pp. 45-52; p. 48).

14. Irenaeus, *Adv. Haer.* iii, *praef.* The unspecific reference to "the scriptures" indicates that Irenaeus does not yet have in view the plan he announces in retrospect, where Book 3 focuses on "the teaching of the apostles," Book 4 on "the words of the Lord," and Book 5 on "the rest of the Lord's teaching and the apostolic letters" (*Adv. Haer.* v, *praef.*; cf. iv, *praef.*, 1; iii.25.7).

15. The phraseology is Bart Ehrman's; see his *Lost Christianities: The Battles for Scripture and the Faiths We Never Knew* (New York & Oxford: Oxford University Press, 2003), p. 192.

16. For recent examples of this familiar claim, see M. Hengel, *The Four Gospels and the One Gospel of Jesus Christ*, Eng. trans. (London: SCM Press, 2000), p. 34; Ehrman, *Lost Christianities*, pp. 238-40.

Cited out of context as it usually is, the passage on gospel origins gives the impression that Matthew, Mark, Luke, and John wrote on their own initiative and without any mandate to do so. For Irenaeus, however, the writing of gospels originates in the authorization the Lord gave his apostles: "Whoever hears you hears me, and whoever despises you despises me and the one who sent me."[17] It is from the apostles that the knowledge of salvation has come to us as we encounter their proclamation in its written form: "for what they once proclaimed they afterwards by the will of God handed down to us in writings [*in scripturis*], to be the foundation and pillar of our faith [*fundamentum et columnam fidei nostrae*]."[18] The apostles first speak and later write, and their mandate to preach the gospel to the ends of the earth is fulfilled in their writing just as it is in their speaking. In no sense is writing here subordinated to speaking, as though an essentially oral and living discourse would be diminished when reduced to lifeless letters on a page. That trope is familiar to Papias who, in authorizing his own project, contrasts "what is drawn from books" unfavourably with "the living and abiding voice," that is, with the words of the Lord's disciples communicated to Papias by those who had heard them.[19] The books subordinated to the oral traditions presumably include the gospels of Mark and Matthew, to which Papias refers elsewhere. No such antithesis between speech and writing is found in Irenaeus.[20] What the apostles spoke they also wrote. Even if, as we will learn shortly, only two them actually wrote while two others had their speaking transferred into writing by disciples, the writing of the gospel is as much a collective apostolic endeavour as its oral proclamation. The gospels are apostolic not just because they derive directly or indirectly from apostles, but also because those individual apostles — Matthew, John, Peter, Paul — represent the apostles as a whole, fulfilling their mandate to preach the gospel to every creature as their gos-

---

17. Irenaeus, *Adv. Haer.* iii, *praef.*, citing Lk. 10.16.

18. Irenaeus, *Adv. Haer.* iii.1.1; cf. 1 Tm. 3.15, where the *columna et firmamentum veritatis* is the church.

19. Eusebius, *HE* iii.39.4. The Papias passage is often said to attest "the abiding vitality of the living testimony/memory that existed within the early communities" (Richard C. Beaton, "How Matthew Writes," in *The Written Gospel*, ed. Markus Bockmuehl and Donald A. Hagner [Cambridge: Cambridge University Press, 2005], pp. 116-34; p. 118). This claim should be treated with caution, however. Papias's speech/writing contrast is intended to promote the value of his own (written) work as based on firsthand testimony rather than written records.

20. The well-known passage about illiterate barbarian Christians (Irenaeus, *Adv. Haer.* iii.3.2) is no exception here. While it is possible to be Christian solely on the basis of the rule of faith, without written gospels, Irenaeus does not regard this as desirable.

pel proclamation is extended through writing to hearers yet to come. The universal scope of the apostolic mandate can only be realized through the technology of writing.

While Irenaeus's account of gospel origins is directly or indirectly dependent on Papias,[21] the differences between them are still more striking than the similarities. Irenaeus constructs a fourfold gospel out of passages in Papias which intend no such thing. Papias has this to say about the origin of the Gospel of Matthew:

> Matthew therefore compiled the sayings in the Hebrew language [Ἑβραΐδι διαλέκτῳ], and each person translated them as he was able.[22]

Irenaeus rewrites this passage as follows:

> Matthew, among the Hebrews in their own language [ἐν τοῖς Ἑβραίοις τῇ ἰδίᾳ αὐτῶν διαλέκτῳ], produced a written account of the gospel, while Peter and Paul were in Rome evangelizing and founding the church.[23]

In Eusebius's excerpts from Papias, the passage on Matthew follows on directly from the passage about Mark. It is likely that Papias assumes Markan priority and sees Matthew as responding to the deficiencies he identifies in Mark. If so, Irenaeus has (1) reversed the sequence, giving the priority to Matthew that it has retained ever since. He has also (2) added a reference to the intended readers to Papias's remark about language; (3) substituted "gospel" for "sayings"; and (4) replaced the supplementary comment about translation with the reference to Peter and Paul in Rome.

(1) According to Irenaeus, Matthew is enabled and authorized to transfer the gospel from speech to writing because he is an apostle, entrusted like all other apostles with the commission to proclaim the gospel of God to the ends of the earth. If the writing of the gospel is no less an *apostolic* task than its preaching, then a fully apostolic gospel must come first. Papias's Mark-Matthew sequence must give way to a Matthew-Mark sequence; Matthew

---

21. Against Hengel, who claims that Irenaeus is independent of Papias here and draws his information from the Roman church archive (*Four Gospels*, p. 36). Hengel optimistically argues that "Irenaeus, or probably the Roman archive, is amazingly well informed about the circumstances and chronological order of the composition of the Gospels" (p. 39). For analysis of Irenaeus's relation to Papias, see F. Loofs, *Theophilus von Antiochien adversus Marcionem und die anderen theologischen Quellen bei Irenaeus*, TU (Leipzig: J. C. Hinrichs, 1930), pp. 325-37.

22. Papias, in Eusebius, *HE* iii.39.16.

23. Irenaeus, *Adv. Haer.* iii.1.1.

must write as an apostle and not just as the compiler who rectifies the deficiencies of Mark. This prioritizing of the apostle over the apostle's disciple is taken further by Tertullian, who proposes the order John-Matthew, Luke-Mark on the following grounds:

> We assert in the first place that the gospel documentation [*evangelicum instrumentum*] has apostles as its authors, to whom this office of proclaiming the gospel was given by the Lord. If apostolic followers [*apostolici*] are also involved, they are not alone but with apostles and after apostles; for the preaching of disciples might be suspected of self-seeking if unaccompanied by the authority of their masters — or rather, of Christ who made them their masters. Of the apostles, then, John and Matthew instil faith into us; of the apostolic followers, Luke and Mark renew it. . . .[24]

Tertullian here places John ahead even of Matthew because of the fundamental importance of the Johannine prologue in establishing the creed-like "Rule of Faith," the hermeneutical key to the gospels and to scripture as a whole.[25] His downgrading of Luke (and consequently Mark) is largely motivated by his anti-Marcionite agenda. Nevertheless, the distinction between apostles and *apostolici* is already evident in Irenaeus's reversal of the original Mark-Matthew sequence. Unlike Tertullian, Irenaeus is still close enough to Papias to list the two gospels the earlier writer explicitly mentions before the two that he does not.

(2) Matthew's composition in the Hebrew language and for Hebrew addressees is intended to connote authenticity, for it is within just this milieu that Jesus lived and taught.[26] Behind the Greek Matthew familiar to Irenaeus and his readers there is said to be a Hebrew original in which Jesus' *ipsissima verba* are preserved. Papias implies a contrast between the variant forms in which Jesus' sayings currently circulate in Greek and the stability of the Hebrew original; the variants are said to derive from different attempts at trans-

---

24. Tertullian, *Adversus Marcionem* iv.2.1-2; cf. v.5.3.

25. On this see Richard Cornell, "'I and the Father Are One': Scriptural Interpretation and Trinitarian Construction in the Monarchian Debate" (Ph.D. diss., University of Aberdeen, 2010), pp. 154-222.

26. "Hebrew" here refers not to the language of Jewish scripture but to Aramaic (cf. the use of ῾εβραϊστί in Jn. 5.2; 19.13, 17, 20; 20.16; Rv. 9.11; 16.16; and τῇ ῾Εβραΐδι διαλέκτῳ in Acts 21.40; 22.2; 26.14). Within scripture, the scriptural language is referred to not as "Hebrew" but as "the language of Canaan" (Is. 19.18) and as יהודית (2 Kgs. 18.26, 28; Neh. 13.24). It is first referred to as "Hebrew" in the Greek prologue to Ben Sira.

lation, some displaying more ability than others.[27] In contrast, Irenaeus is uninterested in variants and substitutes an original Hebrew readership for the Greek one implied by Papias's reference to translation.[28] As a result, it is left unclear how Irenaeus envisages the transmission of this Hebrew text into the Greek-speaking world. He must assume that the Greek text is an absolutely faithful rendering of the Hebrew and that nothing of significance would be gained if one had direct access to the original.[29] For Irenaeus, Jerome's later identification of an expanded Aramaic Matthew with the original "Hebrew" Matthew would have been highly problematic.[30]

(3) Irenaeus's reference to "a written account of the gospel" (γραφὴν εὐαγγελίου) is intended to emphasize the close relationship between Matthew's text and the gospel proclaimed throughout the world by the apostles, "who all possessed the gospel of God both equally and individually."[31] In this context Irenaeus does not and cannot speak of "four gospels," as Origen will later do in an otherwise similar passage.[32] "Gospels" in the plural is rare

27. According to Papias, ἡρμήνευσεν . . . αὐτὰ ὡς ἦν δυνατὸς ἕκαστος (Eusebius, *HE* iii.39.16). This statement need not imply multiple translations of the whole text.

28. J. Kürzinger attempts unconvincingly to show that Irenaeus and Papias refer not to the "Hebrew" language but to Matthew's Hebraic style ("Irenäus und sein Zeugnis zur Sprache des Matthäusevangeliums," *NTS* 10 [1963-64], pp. 108-15).

29. As Clement's teacher Pantaenus did, according to a tradition preserved by Eusebius (*HE* v.10.3). When Pantaenus arrived in India, he is said to have encountered a Christian community founded by the apostle Bartholomew which still preserved the Hebrew Matthew he had left with them.

30. Jerome says that he obtained this expanded Aramaic/Hebrew Matthew "from the Nazarenes of Beroea in Syria," also identifying it (wrongly) with the "Gospel according to the Hebrews" known to Clement, Origen, and Eusebius; see J. K. Elliott (ed.), *The Apocryphal New Testament* (Oxford: Clarendon Press, 1999²), pp. 6-14. Surprisingly, Jerome's quest for an original Hebrew Matthew differing from the Greek has recently been revived by Hans-Martin Schenke, who finds in a deviant Coptic Matthew text evidence of an independent Greek translation of the Hebrew original alongside the canonical one (*Das Matthäus-Evangelium im mittelägyptischen Dialekt des Koptischen (Codex Schøyen)*, Coptic Papyri in the Schøyen Collection I [Oslo: Hermes Publishing, 2001], pp. 31-33). Schenke notes the problems his hypothesis would raise for standard accounts of synoptic origins, but seems untroubled by them.

31. Irenaeus, *Adv. Haer.* iii.1.1. This phrase (*qui quidem et omnes pariter et singuli eorum habentes evangelium Dei*) immediately precedes the statement about Matthew. The term *evangelium* has been used on two earlier occasions in this context. The Lord *dedit apostolis suis potestatem evangelii, per quos et veritatem, hoc est, Dei Filii doctrinam, cognovimus* (*Adv. Haer.* iii, *praef.*). It was, then, the apostles *per quos evangelium pervenit ad nos* (iii.1.1).

32. The relevant excerpt from Origen's commentary on Matthew is preserved in Eusebius, *HE* vi.25.3-6. Origen has "learned by tradition *about the four gospels*, which alone are undisputed in the church of God under heaven, that the first to be written was the one according to the former

in Irenaeus. When, later in Book 3, he explains why there must be precisely four gospel texts, the plural usage is still outnumbered by the singular one. The four living creatures of Revelation 4.7 correspond to "the gospels," but also to the "quadriform gospel" (τετράμορφον εὐαγγέλιον), the "character of the gospel" (χαρακτὴρ τοῦ εὐαγγελίου), the "form of the gospel" (τὴν ἰδέαν τοῦ εὐαγγελίου), and the "aspects of the gospel" *(personas evangelii)*.[33] What Marcion rejects is not three gospels but "the whole gospel" *(totum evangelium)*.[34] An individual text may be referred to as "this gospel" (Matthew) or "that gospel" (John), but also as the gospel *according to* Matthew or John (κατά, *secundum*), that is, as an individual instance of a singular gospel.[35] Just as Matthew produces not "a gospel" but "a written account of the gospel," so Mark composes a "gospel writing" *(evangelica conscriptio)*.[36] Irenaeus does not object to plural formulations,[37] but singular ones are of particular value to him in establishing a seamless continuity between apostolic preaching and apostolic writing.

(4) Matthew produced his written account "while Peter and Paul were in Rome evangelizing and founding the church." Peter and Paul will shortly be associated with Mark and Luke; Irenaeus's statement serves to coordinate the first three gospels but also, more significantly, to emphasize again the relationship between oral and written renderings of the gospel. Matthew writes, Peter and Paul preach, and all three discharge the same apostolic commission as they do so. Mark and Luke write their gospels on the basis of prior apostolic preaching just as Matthew does; Peter must be named before

tax-collector, later an apostle of Jesus Christ, Matthew, who published it for those who had believed from Judaism, composed in the Hebrew language [τοῖς ἀπὸ Ἰουδαϊσμοῦ πιστεύσασιν, γράμμασιν Ἑβραϊκοῖς συντεταγμένον]."

33. Irenaeus, *Adv. Haer.* iii.11.8-9. A surviving Greek excerpt gives a plural here, probably incorrectly.

34. Irenaeus, *Adv. Haer.* iii.11.9.

35. Irenaeus, *Adv. Haer.* iii.11.7: *evangelium quod est secundum Matthaeum; id quod est secundum Lucam/Marcum/Ioannem.* iii.11.8: τὸ μὲν κατὰ Ἰωάννην . . . τὸ δὲ κατὰ Λουκᾶν. iii.11.9: *secundum Ioannis evangelium.* Irenaeus's usage here may actually have influenced the gospel titles; there is no indication here or anywhere else in Irenaeus that the title "gospel according to . . ." is already firmly established. In my view, early datings of the titles do not take the lack of attestation seriously enough: see Hengel, *Four Gospels,* pp. 48-56; Theo K. Heckel, *Vom Evangelium des Markus zum viergestaltigen Evangelium,* WUNT (Tübingen: Mohr-Siebeck, 1999), pp. 207-17; David Trobisch, *The First Edition of the New Testament* (Oxford: Oxford University Press, 2000), pp. 38-43; Silke Peterson, "Die Evangelienüberschriften und die Entstehung des neutestamentlichen Kanons," *ZNW* 97 (2006), pp. 250-74, p. 273.

36. Irenaeus, *Adv. Haer.* iii.1.1, 10.5.

37. Further examples occur in Irenaeus, *Adv. Haer.* i.20.2; ii.22.3, 27.2.

Mark, and Paul before Luke, emphasizing the priority of the apostle in the communication of the gospel in both spoken and written forms. There is no interest here in the priority of speech over writing, which in the case of Matthew, Peter, and Paul occur simultaneously. Rome is tacitly juxtaposed with Judea or its vicinity, where Matthew wrote his gospel "among the Hebrews." Judea represents the church's origin, Rome its destiny; the two leading apostles must therefore make their way there.

Irenaeus's statement about Mark is again modelled on Papias's, and the corresponding statement about Luke follows a similar pattern. The two *apostolici* now write after their teachers' deaths, so that their writings substitute for the apostolic presence and embody it in a new medium:

> After their departure Mark also, the disciple and interpreter of Peter, handed down to us in written form what was preached by Peter. And Luke, the follower of Paul, set down in a book the gospel preached by him.[38]

Mark, who is now the "disciple" as well as the "interpreter" of Peter, has his counterpart in Luke, the "follower" (ἀκόλουθος) of Paul and indeed of the apostles as a whole.[39] As the Mark/Peter link is derived from 1 Peter 5.13, where Peter refers to "my son Mark,"[40] so the Luke/Paul link is derived from 2 Timothy 4.11, where Paul states that "Luke alone is with me" (cf. Col. 4.14, where Luke is "the beloved physician"). In both cases the apostles are assumed to be in Rome — code-named "Babylon" by Peter (1 Pt. 5.13), whereas Paul anticipates imminent martyrdom there (2 Tm. 4.6-8). Rome's status within the Christian world is established not only by the joint apostolic foundation and martyrdom but also by gospels written there under the direct impact of the apostolic teaching.

One gospel was written among the Hebrews, two are closely connected with Rome, and a fourth was written in Ephesus:

> Then John the disciple of the Lord [ὁ μαθητὴς τοῦ κυρίου], who reclined upon his breast, gave out a gospel while living in Ephesus in Asia.[41]

38. Eusebius, *HE* v.8.2-4, citing Irenaeus, *Adv. Haer.* iii.1.1.

39. Irenaeus, *Adv. Haer.* iii.10.1, where Irenaeus probably has Lk. 1.1-4 in mind.

40. If Papias was familiar with 1 Peter, as Eusebius claims (*HE* iii.39.16), then Peter's reference to "my son Mark" may have been the origin of the attribution of the gospel to Mark/Peter — in spite of the strictures of M. Hengel (*Studies in the Gospel of Mark*, Eng. trans. [London: SCM Press, 1985], p.150n). Cf. Clement/Cassiodorus, *In Epistola Petri Prima Catholica*, at 1 Pt.5.13; Origen, *In Mattheum* 1 (cited in *HE* vi.25.5); Eusebius, *HE* ii.15.2.

41. Eusebius, *HE* v.8.2-4, citing Irenaeus, *Adv. Haer.* iii.1.1.

The figure known as "John the disciple of the Lord" is drawn from Papias, who refers to "Aristion and the Elder John" as τοῦ κυρίου μαθηταί.[42] Seven named members of the Twelve have previously been referred to both as "elders" and as "disciples of the Lord": Papias used to enquire about "the words of the elders," that is, about "what Andrew or Peter said, or Philip or Thomas or James or John or Matthew or any other of the Lord's disciples." He also enquired about "what Aristion and the Elder John, the Lord's disciples, say." Papias's list of disciples has been said to demonstrate his knowledge of the fourth gospel.[43] While the first three names *(Andrew-Peter-Philip)* are common to John 1.40-44 and Papias, the rest of Papias's list *(Thomas-James-John-Matthew)* is only loosely related to John 21.2 *(Simon Peter–Thomas–Nathanael–sons of Zebedee)*. Papias's list is better explained as deriving from Matthew, a text he certainly knows, where the sequence is: *Simon Peter–Andrew–James–John–Philip–Thomas–[Bartholomew]–Matthew . . .* (Mt. 10.2-3). Papias promotes Andrew over Peter, and Philip and Thomas over James and John, suggesting that he rejects the tradition that gives Peter, James, and John a special status (cf. Mt. 17.1; 26.37). The claim that Papias drew on the Gospel of John here is without substance.

It is not clear whether or not the Elder John is to be distinguished from John the son of Zebedee, previously listed between his brother James and Matthew. The contrast between εἶπεν and λέγουσιν may suggest that one belongs to a past apostolic generation whereas the other is a contemporary. If the two are different, however, Papias has failed to make this unambiguously clear. Indeed the ambiguity may even be deliberate, giving greater weight to the traditions Papias ascribed to the Elder John along with Aristion, his two most important witnesses.[44] The oral nature of these traditions is underlined by Papias's contrast between "things drawn from books" and "the living and abiding voice" whose utterances are preserved in his own books.[45] It is in these books alone that authentic Johannine tradition is to be found, for Papias has drawn it not from other books but from those who heard the Elder's teaching at first hand. Papias's relation to John is only one step removed from Mark's to Peter.[46]

42. Eusebius, *HE* iii.39.4.

43. So M. Hengel, *The Johannine Question*, Eng. trans. (London: SCM Press, 1989), pp. 16-23; R. Bauckham, *Jesus and the Eyewitnesses: The Gospels as Eyewitness Testimony* (Grand Rapids: Eerdmans, 2006), pp. 20-21.

44. Eusebius, *HE* iii.39.7, 14.

45. Eusebius, *HE* iii.39.4.

46. T. Heckel wrongly assumes that the link Papias alleges between himself and the Elder

In Irenaeus, Aristion has dropped out of sight and the expression "the disciple of the Lord" has replaced "the Elder" as a unique designation of a single "John," who now authors his own writing rather than communicating oral traditions that are reduced to writing by someone unknown to him. The process by which Papias's Elder is transformed into the Fourth Evangelist can be reconstructed with some certainty — once we abandon the assumption that the authorship tradition must have grown seamlessly out of the gospel's actual circumstances of origin.[47] The transformation begins (1) with the identification of Papias's Elder with the apostle John, who must therefore have lived to a great age. (2) Meanwhile the "John" who authored the book of Revelation was similarly identified with the apostle, thereby securing the work's authoritative status. Just as the Elder John is assimilated to the apostle and the author of Revelation by virtue of the common name, so (3) he becomes an evangelist by virtue of the common title, "Elder" (cf. 2 Jn. 1); it is assumed that the author of the letters and the gospel is one and the same. Subsequently, (4) John sheds the title "Elder" and comes to be known as "John the disciple of the Lord" — another expression derived from Papias, which (5) also makes it possible to connect the authorship tradition with the internal evidence of John 21. Finally, (6) the link between John and Ephesus is established by way of a deduction from the letters to the seven churches in Revelation 2–3.

(1) The ambiguous relationship between the Elder John and John son of Zebedee is resolved: Irenaeus assumes that the two are identical, and that Papias's older contemporary was therefore an apostle who lived to a great age, surviving into the reign of Trajan (98-117 CE).[48] Thus Polycarp, the

---

John entails a knowledge of the fourth gospel (*Vom Evangelium des Markus zum viergestaltigen Evangelium*, p. 262). Papias is said to have cited material from 1 John (Eusebius, *HE* iii.39.16), but it is not clear whether he identifies its author with his Elder.

47. There is no "unsolved riddle" in the shift from the multiauthored text postulated by Bultmann and others to a later consensus about the sole authorship of John of Ephesus, as Hengel claims (*Johannine Question*, p. 24). "Why," Hengel asks sceptically, "do we possess no independent reference to th[e] 'Johannine' school with its plurality of authors and teachers . . . , but only to *one* John . . . ?" (p. 24). Yet a gap in the external historical attestation is as unsurprising as the tradition's eagerness to fill it.

48. Irenaeus, *Adv. Haer.* ii.22.5; iii.3.4. According to Bauckham, however, Irenaeus maintains a distinction between John the son of Zebedee and John the evangelist (*Jesus and the Eyewitnesses*, pp. 452-63). Since both the son of Zebedee and the evangelist are identified as "apostles" (Irenaeus, *Adv. Haer.* i.9.2, 3; iii.1.1, 12.5, 21.3), Bauckham must argue that Irenaeus dissociates the word "apostle" from the Twelve (pp. 461-62). Yet Irenaeus barely deviates from the predominant scriptural usage, in which there are twelve apostles (*Adv. Haer.* ii.21.1; cf. iii.12.13, 14) plus the apostle Paul (iii.13.1).

bishop of Smyrna whom Irenaeus himself had known in his youth, is said to have received John's teaching at first hand,[49] and Papias can be described as "the hearer of John and a companion of Polycarp."[50] If, following Eusebius, we assume that Papias is referring to two different individuals named "John," the second might be a source of authoritative tradition, along with Aristion, but he would not be an aged apostolic eyewitness. If the two are identified, however, extreme longevity is required in order to bridge the gap between the ministry of Jesus and the time of Papias and Polycarp. John's longevity is confirmed by Irenaeus's late dating of Revelation, which was written "not long ago but almost in our own times, towards the end of Domitian's reign."[51]

(2) Perhaps independently of Papias, the identification of an individual named John with the apostle of that name was suggested by the book of Revelation, whose author presents himself as "[Christ's] servant John," and as "John, your brother" (Rv. 1.1, 9; cf. 1.4; 22.8). According to Justin,

> There was among us a man whose name was John, *one of the apostles of Christ,* who prophesied in an apocalypse granted to him that there would be a thousand years in Jerusalem for those who believe in our Christ, and after that (to abbreviate somewhat) the general and eternal resurrection and judgement of all.[52]

The claim to apostolic authorship follows simply from the author's self-identification as "John," combined with a desire to establish the authority and authenticity of the revelation. Thus those who later question that authority and authenticity do so by denying its apostolic origin. It was, perhaps, written by the heretic Cerinthus, falsely laying claim to an apostolic name.[53] Or, more plausibly, it was written by an individual with the same name as the apostle's,[54] a view which can find support in Papias (*pace* Irenaeus) and in the two Johannine tombs in Ephesus.[55] Debates about the Apocalypse were evoked by its suspiciously "carnal" concept of the millen-

---

49. Eusebius, *HE* v.20.5-6, 24.16.

50. Irenaeus, *Adv. Haer.* v.33.4 (cf. v.33.3, 30.1). As Eusebius points out, this claim that Papias heard John at first hand is incompatible with Papias's own statements (*HE* iii.39.1-2).

51. Irenaeus, *Adv. Haer.* v.30.1.

52. Justin, *Dial.* lxxxi.4, also cited in Eusebius, *HE* iv.18.8; cf. Rv. 20.4-6, 11-13.

53. Eusebius, *HE* iii.28.2 (Gaius, also cited by Dionysius of Alexandria, *HE* iii.28.3-5 = vii.25.1-3).

54. Eusebius, *HE* vii.25.6-27 (Dionysius).

55. Eusebius, *HE* iii.39.5-6 (Eusebius).

nium — a concept initially popularized by Papias's appeal to traditions supposed to emanate from "the Elder John," depicting the miraculous fertility and universal harmony of the coming millennial age.[56] Yet for those who accept the authenticity of Revelation, John the Seer is identical to John the Apostle, already identified with Papias's Elder of that name — who thus becomes an author.

(3) The question is how the Elder's literary activity is extended to cover not only Revelation but also the Gospel of John. The missing link is found in a citation from 2 John 10-11, where Irenaeus attributes the injunction not to greet the heretical teachers to "John the disciple of the Lord."[57] This short letter is addressed to "the elect lady and her children" by "the Elder" (2 Jn. 1). Is this "the Elder" whom Papias can cite anonymously but whom he also identifies as "the Elder John"?[58] So it must have seemed to whoever first sought to name the author of the anonymous Johannine literature.[59] From 2 John it was a short step to 1 John and the Gospel of John, given the close verbal and thematic links between these texts and the apparent claim to eyewitness status in 1 John 1.1-3.[60] In this way, thanks to Papias, an anonymous gospel acquired an author, who would now be known not as "the Elder John" but as "John the disciple of the Lord," or simply as "John." Only later did the difficulty present itself of attributing Revelation and the gospel and epistles to the same author.[61]

(4) While the title "John the disciple of the Lord" is evidently not yet known to Justin, it predates Irenaeus, occurring already in a lengthy excerpt from a Valentinian exegesis of the Johannine prologue attributed to Ptolemaeus.[62] Irenaeus introduces this excerpt as follows:

56. Irenaeus, *Adv. Haer.* v.33.3-4.

57. Irenaeus, *Adv. Haer.* i.16.3.

58. Eusebius, *HE* iii.4, 7, 14, 15.

59. The identification is repeated by Martin Hengel (*Johannine Question*, p. 30), although Hengel follows Eusebius in differentiating this John from the son of Zebedee (p. 31).

60. Cf. Irenaeus, *Adv. Haer.* iii.16.5, 8, where texts from the first and second Johannine epistles and from the gospel are juxtaposed. Irenaeus does not quote from 1 Jn. 1.1-3, but see the *Muratorian Canon*, ll. 26-34.

61. Eusebius, *HE* vii.25.6-27. In an admirable piece of critical analysis, Dionysius of Alexandria points out (1) that the opening of the letters to the seven churches ("John to the seven churches that are in Asia . . . ," Rv. 1.4) is at variance with the anonymity of all three Johannine epistles; (2) that "John" does not identify himself as the apostle, and that this may have been a common name within the early church; and (3) that closely similar vocabulary and style in the gospel and epistles are unparalleled in Revelation.

62. Irenaeus, *Adv. Haer.* i.8.5; the attribution occurs at the end of the excerpt, in the Latin but

They teach that John the disciple of the Lord referred to the first Ogdoad [i.e. the first set of conjunctions within the *Plērōma*], substantiating their claim as follows: "John the disciple of the Lord, wishing to express the genesis of all things and how the Father brought forth the All. . . ."[63]

Irenaeus and his Valentinian precursor are both directly or indirectly dependent on Papias for these references to "John the disciple of the Lord," for that is what Papias's Elder John becomes when Aristion drops out of the picture and there is no further need of the title "the Elder" to differentiate one of "the disciples of the Lord" from the other. In his singularity, the "disciple of the Lord" evokes the figure of "the disciple whom Jesus loved," the author of the fourth gospel according to John 21.20-24. He is also the author of the Johannine apocalypse. According to Irenaeus, it was "John the disciple of the Lord" who "saw in the Apocalypse this new [Jerusalem] descending upon the new earth," and whose oral teaching about the age of peace and plenty is said to be preserved in the fourth of Papias's five books.[64]

(5) In Irenaeus's statement about the origins of the Gospel of John, the evangelist is identified not only as "the disciple of the Lord" but also as "the one who reclined on the Lord's breast." In the first instance the reference is to John 13.23-25, where "one of his disciples, whom Jesus loved" is placed in intimate proximity to him at the Last Supper and so is in a position to pass on Peter's urgent and confidential question about the identity of the betrayer. Yet there is a still more direct antecedent to Irenaeus's language in John 21.20, where Peter sees following Jesus "the disciple whom Jesus loved, who reclined at the supper on his breast, and who had said, 'Lord, who is it who will betray you?'" Irenaeus has selected the second of the three relative clauses, abbreviating it slightly ("who reclined on the Lord's breast" rather than "who reclined at the supper on his breast") but using it in an exactly comparable way to identify the disciple in question. In John 21.24, it is said that this disciple is also the author of the gospel. In Irenaeus's reference to "John the disciple of the Lord, who reclined on his breast," the pre-Irenaean, Papias-derived deduction about authorial identity is linked to the internal evidence of the gospel itself.

(6) John is said to have written his gospel "while living in Ephesus in Asia." The Ephesian origin of the fourth gospel corresponds to the Roman

---

not in the Greek. Irenaeus has already signalled the importance of Ptolemaeus in the preface to *Adv. Haer.* i.

63. Irenaeus, *Adv. Haer.* i.8.5.

64. Irenaeus, *Adv. Haer.* v.35.2, 33.3-4.

origin of the second and third. The John/Ephesus connection is also presupposed in a legend recounted by Clement of Alexandria, loosely based on the Parable of the Prodigal Son, which opens with John's return to Ephesus following the death of the unnamed tyrant (presumably Domitian) supposed to have exiled him to Patmos.[65] If John was in Patmos "because of the word of God and the testimony of Jesus" (Rv. 1.9), and if the first of his seven letters is addressed to the church of Ephesus, it may seem reasonable to suppose that he was exiled to Patmos from Ephesus and would return there after the death of the persecutor. Irenaeus, then, extends an existing link between John and Ephesus to the composition of the gospel. The four canonical gospels are attributed not only to named authors — apostles or *apostolici* — but also to specific places: Judea (the land of the Hebrews), Rome, and Ephesus in Asia. If Rome takes pride in Peter, Paul, and the gospels composed by their followers, Ephesus can appeal to John and to a gospel reflecting his own unique intimacy with Jesus.

This Rome/Ephesus axis in Irenaeus's account of gospel origins recurs in its sequel, where he lists the series of twelve bishops who inherited their primacy over the church of Rome from Peter and Paul, up to and including Eleutherius, the present incumbent (*c.* 177-89 CE),[66] and matches it with an account of the apostolic foundation of the church in Asia, where for many years Polycarp of Smyrna proved himself a staunch defender of apostolic truth.[67] Through the Roman succession, "the tradition imparted to the church by the apostles and the proclamation of the truth has reached also to us."[68] Yet Rome is not self-sufficient. In the time of Anicetus (*c.* 154-165), it was Polycarp who came to Rome from Asia, confronted Marcion, and turned many back from heresy to the church.[69] The church of Ephesus, "founded by Paul and having John resident there until the time of Trajan, is a true witness [μάρτυς ἀληθής] of the apostles' tradition."[70] Within the fourfold canonical gospel, it is the role of John to maintain the distinctive Asian contribution to the tradition in its written expression — without detriment to the special place of Peter and Mark, Paul and Luke, within the church of Rome. From this perspective, then, the fourfold canonical gospel may be seen as a plea for East-West consensus, one that acknowledges the contributions of both.

---

65. Clement of Alexandria, *Quis Dives Salvetur* 42.2.
66. Irenaeus, *Adv. Haer.* iii.3.2-3.
67. Irenaeus, *Adv. Haer.* iii.3.4.
68. Irenaeus, *Adv. Haer.* iii.3.3.
69. Irenaeus, *Adv. Haer.* iii.3.4.
70. Irenaeus, *Adv. Haer.* iii.3.4.

East-West consensus in other matters was a central concern of Irenaeus's public career. One such matter was the celebration of the *pascha*, the Christian passover. Is this *pascha* exactly parallel to the Jewish one, celebrated on the fourteenth day of the month Nisan?[71] If so, the *pascha* will be focused on the Lord's suffering (πάσχειν), and the preparatory fast will be ended at evening with a eucharistic meal corresponding to the passover meal of the local Jewish community. Or does the Christian *pascha* celebrate the Lord's resurrection, in which case the fast will end on a Sunday, without any relation to the Jewish calendar? The churches of Asia took the first view; churches elsewhere took the second.[72] At the request of Victor of Rome, the issue was debated in Gaul, Italy, Greece, Asia, and Palestine, in an unsuccessful attempt to impose the majority practice on the Asian churches and to eliminate their traditional christianized passover. Responding no doubt to Victor's claim to Petrine and Pauline authority, Polycrates of Ephesus vigorously defends the Asian churches' right to maintain the "quartodeciman" practice hallowed by their own saints and martyrs:

> For in Asia too great luminaries [στοιχεῖα/*luminaria*] have fallen asleep, who will rise in the day of the Lord's coming when he comes with glory from heaven to seek out all the saints: Philip, one of the twelve apostles, who fell asleep in Hierapolis, and his two aged virgin daughters and another daughter who lived in the Holy Spirit and rests in Ephesus; and John, who reclined on the Lord's breast, who as a priest bore the [sacerdotal] plate [πέταλον] and was a witness and teacher, falling asleep in Ephesus; and Polycarp in Smyrna, both bishop and martyr, and Thraseas from Eumenia, also bishop and martyr, who sleeps in Smyrna. Must I tell of Sagaris, bishop and martyr, who sleeps in Laodicea, or of Papirius the blessed or Melito the eunuch who lived entirely in the Holy Spirit, who lies in Sardis awaiting the visitation [ἐπισκοπή] from heaven? These all observed the *pascha* on the fourteenth day as the gospel teaches [κατὰ τὸ

---

71. The passover lamb is to be slaughtered, and eaten with unleavened bread, on the evening of the fourteenth day of the first month of the year (Ex. 12.2, 6, 18). This month is earlier known as *Abib* (Ex. 13.4; 23.15; 34.18; Dt. 16.1) — the name referring to ears of barley (cf. Ex. 9.31; Lv. 2.14) — but later as *Nisan*, a Babylonian loanword (Neh. 2.1; Est. 3.7). The English term "passover" derives from YHWH's promise, "I will pass over you," Heb. ‏ופסחתי עלכם‏ (Ex. 12.13), hence "the Lord's passover" (KJV), Heb. ‏פסח הוא ליהוה‏ (Ex. 12.11). The Greek πάσχα (Ex. 12.11 LXX) derives from the Aramaic ‏פסחא‏. The coincidental resemblance of πάσχα to πάσχειν is exploited by Melito of Sardis, who identifies τὸ πάσχα (the slaughtered passover lamb) as a type of Christ, ὁ πάσχων (*Pasch.* 46, cf. 66-67).

72. Eusebius, *HE* v.23.1-3.

εὐαγγέλιον], in no way deviating from it but following the rule of faith [τὸν κάνονα τῆς πίστεως].[73]

As in Irenaeus, John is identified as the one who "reclined on the Lord's breast," and in both cases there may be an implied contrast with Peter's more distant relationship to the Lord (cf. Jn. 13.23-25; 21.20-23). If Rome is represented by Peter and Ephesus by John, then Ephesus can lay claim to a unique intimacy with the Lord. Polycrates does not refer to John's gospel, but his language implies familiarity with it and an identification of John with the anonymous "beloved disciple." It is likely that the otherwise inexplicable claim that John was a priestly figure derives from the gospel's claim that the "other disciple" who accompanied Simon Peter to Caiaphas's house was "known to the high priest" (Jn. 18.15).[74] It is, then, probable that κατὰ τὸ εὐαγγέλιον refers primarily to the Gospel of John, seen as justifying the practice of commemorating the Lord's death at the time of the passover sacrifice (cf. Jn. 18.28, 39; 19.14, 31-37). Johannine chronology makes possible Melito's claim, addressed to "Israel," that "you killed your Lord at the great feast."[75] A contemporary of Melito's, Claudius Apollinarius of Hierapolis, makes a more direct allusion to the Gospel of John as he refutes those who appeal to Matthew in support of their claim that "on the fourteenth day the Lord ate the sheep with the disciples, and himself suffered on the great day of unleavened bread" (that is, on 15 Nisan).[76] In reality, it is the fourteenth day that is

> the true passover of the Lord, the great sacrifice, the servant of God in place of the lamb; bound, though he bound the strong one; judged,

73. Eusebius, *HE* v.24.2-5 (also cited more briefly in iii.31.3).

74. John's πέταλον derives from the golden plate attached to the high priestly turban, inscribed with the words "Holy to the Lord" (Ex. 28.36; cf. 29.6; 36.37 LXX); Polycrates may here see it as a mark of priesthood in general, however. The influence of Jn. 18.15 is more likely than R. Bauckham's suggestion that Polycrates identifies John the evangelist with the "John" named in Acts 4.6 as a member of the high-priestly family, indicating that the Asian tradition differentiates the evangelist from the son of Zebedee (*Jesus and the Eyewitnesses*, pp. 445-52).

75. Melito, *Pasch.* 79. Eusebius refers to two books by Melito on the *pascha*, one of them occasioned by controversy in the church of Laodicea at the time of Sagaris's martyrdom (*HE* iv.26.3), the other perhaps to be identified with the work cited here (but see the discussion in S. G. Hall [ed.], *Melito of Sardis, On Pascha, and Fragments* [Oxford: Clarendon Press, 1979], pp. xix-xxi). Polycrates' letter of *c.* 190 confirms that Melito and Sagaris belong to an earlier period.

76. Cited in the introduction to the seventh-century *Chronicon Paschale* (ed. L. Dindorf [Bonn: E. Weber, 1832], pp. 13-14; henceforth *Chron. Pasch.*). It is likely that the controversy about the date of the Lord's death, to which Apollinarius refers, also occasioned one of Melito's two works on the *pascha* (Eusebius, *HE* iv.26.2-3).

though judge of living and dead; delivered into the hands of sinners to be crucified, *exalted* on the horns of the unicorn; whose sacred *side* was *pierced*, who poured out from his side the two purifications, *water and blood*, word and spirit, and who was buried on the day of the passover, being laid in a stone tomb.[77]

(Johannine allusions are italicized.)[78] Even clearer reference to John is made by Clement of Alexandria. On the night of his arrest, the Lord broke with his previous custom and celebrated the passover early, on the thirteenth day:

Appropriately, then, to the fourteenth day when he suffered, the chief priests and scribes brought him early to Pilate but *did not enter into the praetorium, so as not to be defiled* and be unable to *eat the passover* in the evening.[79]

The Gospel of John, then, informs debate about the Christian passover, in Asia and beyond, from as early as the 160s.[80] When in the 190s Polycrates appeals to the apostle John in defence of the Asian churches' *pascha*, his appeal has deep roots in local use of the gospel attributed to the apostle — to which he alluded, in the reference to John as reclining on the Lord's breast, but which he does not mention. John here is "witness and teacher," but, in deference perhaps to Roman prejudices, he is not explicitly identified as a gospel-writer.

Victor, Peter's successor, responded to Polycrates' letter by breaking fellowship with the Asian churches, branding them as heretical — and earning himself a sharp rebuke from none other than Irenaeus, who reminded him of his predecessor Anicetus's more conciliatory attitude towards Polycarp, in

77. *Chron. Pasch.*, p. 14. In the previous fragment, Apollinarius opposes those who, appealing to Matthew against John, argue that the Lord ate the passover with his disciples on 14 Nisan and suffered on the following day: καὶ διηγοῦνται Ματθαῖον οὕτω λέγειν ὡς νενοήκασιν, ὅθεν ἀσύμφωνός τε νόμῳ ἡ νόησις αὐτῶν καὶ στασιάζειν δοκεῖ κατ' αὐτοὺς τὰ εὐαγγέλια (p. 14).

78. ὁ ὑψωθείς . . . , cf. Jn. 12.34, δεῖ ὑψωθῆναι τὸν υἱὸν τοῦ ανθρώπου (the identification of the cross with "the horns of the unicorn" is drawn from Ps. 21.22 [22.21] LXX). ὁ τὴν . . . πλευρὰν ἐκκεντηθείς, cf. Jn. 19.34, 37, τὴν πλευρὰν ἔννυξεν/εἰς ὃν ἐξεκέντησαν (cf. Zec. 12.10). ὁ ἐκχέας ἐκ τῆς πλευρᾶς αὐτοῦ . . . ὕδωρ καὶ αἷμα, cf. Jn. 19.34, καὶ ἐξῆλθεν εὐθὺς αἷμα καὶ ὕδωρ.

79. *Chron. Pasch.*, p. 15: οὐκ εἰσῆλθον εἰς τὸ πραιτώριον ἵνα μὴ μιανθῶσιν ἀλλ' . . . τὸ πάσχα φάγωσι, cf. Jn. 18.28, οὐκ εἰσῆλθον εἰς τὸ πραιτώριον ἵνα μὴ μιανθῶσιν ἀλλὰ φάγωσιν τὸ πάσχα. This is undoubtedly an excerpt from Clement's lost work on the *pascha*, written in response to Melito (Eusebius, *HE* iv.26.4).

80. For the dating, see Hall, *Melito of Sardis*, pp. xxi-xxii, on Melito's reference to "Servillius/Sergius Paulus proconsul of Asia" (Eusebius, *HE* iv.26.3).

spite of the real disagreements between them.[81] Here too Irenaeus appeals to the apostle John: Anicetus remained in communion with Polycarp even though he failed to persuade him "to abandon traditions he had always observed with John the disciple of our Lord and the other apostles with whom he had associated."[82] Irenaeus himself is in favour of celebrating the mystery of the Lord's resurrection on the Lord's Day, but sees no reason why the alternative tradition should be regarded as heretical.[83] The Roman and Asian churches must agree to differ, now as in the time of Anicetus and Polycarp some thirty years earlier.

This appeal to John (and other unspecified apostles) again underlines the antiquity and apostolicity of the Asian traditions. It also casts fresh light on Irenaeus's reference to "John the disciple of the Lord, who reclined on his breast" as the author of the fourth gospel. Here too Irenaeus upholds the usage of the churches of Asia, where this gospel is highly regarded, in the face of Roman devaluing of the John/Ephesus tradition. Irenaeus actually enhances the Roman claim by associating the gospels of Mark and Luke with Peter and Paul, founders and proto-martyrs of the church of Rome. Yet Ephesus too has its claim, in the form of a fourth gospel associated with the apostle who enjoyed the closest intimacy with Jesus. For Irenaeus, then, the fourfold gospel has to do with achieving consensus between Rome and Ephesus, West and East — a consensus achieved, here too, by embracing difference within a greater unity. As presented by Irenaeus, the fourfold gospel is an ecumenical construct.[84] It is not directed primarily against heretics who use the wrong gospels, or just one of the right ones. Irenaeus does more than refute heresies. As Eusebius notes, Irenaeus the peacemaker (Εἰρηναῖος εἰρηνοποιός) was most appropriately named.[85]

81. Eusebius, *HE* iv.24.10-18.

82. Eusebius, *HE* iv.24.16.

83. Eusebius, *HE* iv.24.11.

84. Thus E. Käsemann's claim that the unity of the church is compromised by "the fact that the canon presents us with four Gospels instead of one" is the opposite of the truth — precisely from the standpoint of "the historian" ("The Canon of the New Testament and the Unity of the Church," Eng. trans., in *Essays on New Testament Themes*, SBT [London: SCM Press, 1964], pp. 95-107; p. 95).

85. Eusebius, *HE* iv.24.18.

Rome and the Gospel from Asia

Irenaeus is not the first to speak of "gospels" in the plural,[86] but he is the first to insist that there must be precisely four of them: "The gospels cannot be more in number than they are, nor again can they be fewer."[87] Earlier, the number of gospels is indeterminate. Some are more widely used and known than others, but there is no agreed answer to the question how many there are because the question itself has not yet been raised. Local usage no doubt varied. Gospels popular in parts of the East — *GPet, GTh, GEgy* — may have been virtually unknown in the West. The question, *how many?* arises from the decision to draw a line through the extant gospel literature, separating gospels that are henceforth to be acknowledged by the universal church from those that are not. For some communities, the number *four* will represent a restriction; for others, an expansion. More precisely, the fourfold gospel will represent a restriction in parts of the East and an expansion in parts of the West, notably in Rome itself. In Rome, the gospel associated with John, Ephesus, and Asian factionalism had yet to establish itself. Although the claim that John met with "orthodox" resistance has recently been strenuously denied, there are a number of clear indications that this was indeed the case.[88]

(1) Evidence of the early Roman reception of gospel literature may be seen in Justin's two major works, dating from the middle of the second century. Material from Matthew is cited frequently, often supplemented by or conflated with material from Luke, with a focus on the birth narratives,[89] John the Baptist,[90] Jesus' baptism and temptations,[91] his relation to his disci-

---

86. For early occurrences of the plural see Justin, *1 Apol.* 66.3; Apollinarius of Hierapolis, cited in *Chron. Pasch.*, p. 14D; slightly later, Clement of Alexandria, cited in *Chron. Pasch.*, p. 15C; *Strom.* iv.6.41.2; *Hypotyposes*, cited in Eusebius, *HE* vi.14.5.7; Clement/Cassiodorus, *In Epistola Iudae Catholica* (at v.24).

87. Irenaeus, *Adv. Haer.* iii.11.8.

88. In his important but problematic monograph, *The Johannine Corpus in the Early Church* (Oxford: Oxford University Press, 2004), Charles Hill seeks to demolish what he describes as "the orthodox Johannophobia theory": that is, the view that "so deep was the affinity for this Gospel among Valentinians and gnostics, and so close was its identification with these groups in the popular Christian mind, that many Church leaders suspected it or opposed it" (p. 3).

89. Justin, *1 Apol.* 33.5-6 (Lk. 1.32; Mt. 1.21); *Dial.* 77.4–78.8 (Mt. 1.18–2.18; Lk. 2.1-4); *Dial.* 100.5 (Lk. 1.35, 38); *Dial.* 102.2; 103.3 (Mt. 2.13-22); *Dial.* 106.4 (Mt. 2.2, 9-11).

90. Justin, *Dial.* 49.3-5 (Mt. 3.11-12; 14.1-12; 17.12-13); *Dial.* 88.7-8 (Mt. 3.4, 11; Lk. 3.15; cf. Jn. 1.20, 23).

91. Justin, *Dial.* 88.2-3, 8 (Lk. 3.22-23; Mt. 3.13-16); *Dial.* 103.6 (Lk. 3.22; Mt. 4.3-10); *Dial.* 125.5 (Mt. 4.10).

ples,[92] the sayings tradition,[93] the last days in Jerusalem,[94] his suffering and death,[95] and his resurrection.[96] In many cases the primacy of Matthew is clear. The whole of the Matthean infancy narrative is recounted, at least in outline, and Luke provides only supplementary details relating to the annunciation and the journey to Bethlehem. Justin's discussion of the Baptist's ministry and of Jesus' baptism and temptations is almost entirely Matthean. The sayings material is more evenly distributed between Matthew and Luke, however, and the tendency to conflate parallel texts is here particularly marked. Justin uses both gospels for the incidents of Jesus' passion: from Matthew comes his silence at his trial and the taunting at the cross; from Luke, the hearing before Herod, the blood-like sweat in Gethsemane, and the last words.

Justin's gospel citations differ from Irenaeus's in three main ways. First, they are almost entirely confined to Matthew and Luke. It is quite misleading to view Justin as a witness to a fourfold gospel in which John is of the same standing as the other three.[97] Second, they are often presented in conflated or harmonized form. This suggests that Justin has at his disposal a considerable quantity of harmonized material drawn from Matthew and Luke, although not a complete harmony of these gospels.[98] Third, the attributions to

92. Justin, *Dial.* 100.3 (Lk. 9.22); *Dial.* 100.4 (Mt. 16.16-17); *Dial.* 106.3 (Mk. 3.16-17).

93. Justin, *1 Apol.* 15.1–17.4 (material selected from Mt. 5–7; Lk. 6; etc.), 63.3-5 (Mt. 11.27; 10.40); *Dial.* 35.3 (Mt. 24.5, 24; 7.15); *Dial.* 76.3-7 (Mt. 7.22-23; 8.11-12; 25.41; Lk. 9.22; 10.19); *Dial.* 81.4 (Lk. 20.35-36); *Dial.* 96.3 (Lk. 6.35-36; Mt. 5.45); *Dial.* 100.1 (Mt. 11.27); *Dial.* 101.2 (Lk. 18.18-19); *Dial.* 105.6 (Mt. 5.20); *Dial.* 107.1 (Mt. 12.38-39); *Dial.* 120.6; 140.4 (Mt. 8.11-12); *Dial.* 125.1-2 (Mt. 13.3-8).

94. Justin, *1 Apol.* 66.3 (Lk. 22.19; Mt. 26.28); *Dial.* 17.3-4 (Mt. 21.12-13; 23.16, 23, 27 [Lk. 11.42, 52]); 53.2 (Mt. 21.1-2, 7, 10); *Dial.* 93.2 (Mt. 22.32-35); *Dial.* 112.4 (Mt. 23.7, 23, 24, 27); *Dial.* 122.1 (Mt. 23.15).

95. Justin, *1 Apol.* 38.7-8 (Mt. 27.39); *Dial.* 99.2 (Mt. 26.39); *Dial.* 101.3 (Mt. 27.40, 43); *Dial.* 103.4 (Lk. 23.7); *Dial.* 102.5 (Mt. 27.12-14); *Dial.* 103.8 (Lk. 22.42, 44); *Dial.* 105.5 (Lk. 23.46).

96. Justin, *Dial.* 106.1 (Lk. 24.6-7, 36, 44-46); 108.2 (Mt. 28.13, 15). As Koester rightly notes, "Justin Martyr is the first Christian writer who makes extensive use of narrative materials from written gospels," in the context of "the proof of the truth of the Christian proclamation from scripture" (*Ancient Christian Gospels: Their History and Development* [Philadelphia: Trinity Press International; London: SCM Press, 1990], p. 376).

97. Cf. Hill, *Johannine Corpus*, pp. 337-42.

98. On the harmonized sayings material, see A. J. Bellinzoni, *The Sayings of Jesus in the Writings of Justin Martyr* (Leiden: Brill, 1967); on Justin's gospel citations as a whole, Koester, *Ancient Christian Gospels*, pp. 360-402. The case for Justin as a harmonizer is strengthened by William L. Petersen's demonstration of links between his gospel citations and the *Diatessaron* ("Textual Evidence of Tatian's Dependence on Justin's ΑΠΟΜΝΗΜΟΝΕΥΜΑΤΑ," *NTS* 36 [1990], pp. 512-34).

"the memoirs of the apostles" imply some form of collective rather than individual authorship. In consequence, there is virtually no acknowledgement of gospel differences.

In his harmonizations of Matthew and Luke, Justin also inserted individual motifs drawn from other gospel literature. There is a single clear reference to a Markan passage, suggesting that Justin is aware of the traditional link with Peter.[99] Elsewhere it is said that Jesus' mother was descended from David, and that Jesus was born in a cave; both motifs occur in the *Protevangelium of James*.[100] We also learn from Justin that

> when Jesus went down into the water a fire was kindled in the Jordan, and when he came up out of the water the Holy Spirit lighted on him like a dove — [as] his apostles wrote of this our Christ.[101]

A similar baptism of Spirit and fire (or light) occurs in the *Diatessaron*, in a text identified by Epiphanius as the *Gospel according to the Hebrews*, and elsewhere.[102] In another passage Jesus himself speaks of baptism: "If you are not born again [ἀναγεννηθῆτε], you will not enter into the kingdom of heaven."[103] It is not clear how this saying relates to the two further variants in John 3.3, 5. As argued in an earlier chapter, Justin's claim that Jesus was set on the judgement-seat and told to "judge us" is related to *GPet*.[104]

For Justin, all such information about Jesus must derive from "the

---

Justin's harmonizations seem to be confined to individual items rather than to whole gospels: for example, one would not expect conflation of the Lukan annunciation to Mary with the Matthean annunciation to Joseph within a whole-gospel harmony (cf. *1 Apol*. 33.5-6 [Lk. 1.32; Mt. 1.21]).

99. Justin, *Dial*. 106.3 (Mk. 3.16-17). On Justin and Mark, see C.-J. Thornton, "Justin und das Markusevangelium," *ZNW* 84 (1993), pp. 93-110. In its context Justin's phraseology (ἐν τοῖς ἀπομνημονεύμασιν αὐτοῦ) suggests a reference to Peter. M. Marcovich suggests that the text originally read ἐν τοῖς ἀπομνημονεύμασιν <τῶν ἀποστόλων> αὐτοῦ (as in *Dial*. 100.4; 101.3; 102.5; 104.1; 106.4), and that τῶν ἀποστόλων has been omitted by a copyist (*Iustini Martyris Apologiae pro Christianis, Dialogus cum Tryphone*, ed. M. Marcovich [Berlin & New York: De Gruyter, 2005], p. 252). Though possible, the emendation seems unnecessary given the other variants among Justin's formulations.

100. Justin, *Dial*. 100.3; *PJas* 10.1 (Mary and David); *Dial*. 78.5-6; *PJas* 18.1 (the cave).

101. Justin, *Dial*. 88.

102. See W. L. Petersen, *Tatian's Diatessaron: Its Creation, Dissemination, Significance, and History in Scholarship*, VCSupp (Leiden: Brill, 1994), pp. 14-20; Elliott, *Apocryphal New Testament*, p. 15.

103. Justin, *Dial*. 61.4.

104. Justin, *1 Apol*. 35.6; *GPet* 3.6-8. See P. Pilhofer, "Justin und das Petrusevangelium," *ZNW* 81 (1990), pp. 60-78.

memoirs of his apostles,"[105] or rather, from "the memoirs which I claim were composed by his apostles and their followers."[106] While this longer formulation accompanies a reference to Luke's Gethsemane narrative, there is otherwise no distinction between Luke and Matthew in these references to apostolic memoirs — seven of which apply to Matthean material,[107] four to Lukan,[108] one to Markan,[109] and one of which is indeterminate.[110] Whether directly or indirectly, all three gospels are to be regarded as apostolic. Justin does not say how many other apostolic memoirs he thinks there are, but they appear to include the source for his distinctive account of Jesus' baptism. With the exception of the Petrine memoirs recorded by Mark, there is no differentiation between these texts. Each item that Justin cites is traced back not to an individual memoir but to the apostolic memoirs as a whole — that is, to the entire body of extant gospel literature insofar as it can be regarded as authentic. Justin does not tell us that any given item may be derived from one specific text to the exclusion of others. He is uninterested in whether something is peculiar to Matthew or to Luke, since what is found in one gospel is regarded as common to all. His language implies that writing is a normal part of the apostles' vocation: however many memoirs may have been written, they represent the twelve as a whole.[111] Undifferentiated and anonymous though these texts are, Justin does acknowledge that they constitute a plurality. Only rarely does he revert to the old singular formulation, "in the gospel."[112]

If "the gospel" consists in apostolic memoirs, and if there is an indeterminate number of these works, there is room in principle for a Gospel according to John. In practice, however, John is at best marginal for Justin.

---

105. Justin, *Dial.* 100.4; 101.3; 102.5; 104.1.

106. Justin, *Dial.* 103.8: ἐν τοῖς ἀπομνημονεύμασιν ἅ φημί ὑπὸ τῶν ἀποστόλων αὐτοῦ καὶ τῶν ἐκείνοις παρακολουθησάντων συντετάχθαι. This hardly makes Justin "the first witness to the collection of four Gospels," as Hengel claims on the grounds that it must refer to at least two apostolic gospels and at least two authored by their followers (*Four Gospels*, pp. 19-20). If he had intended to contrast two types of gospel, one directly apostolic, the other only indirectly so, we would expect ἤ rather than καί. Gospels associated with two apostolic followers (Mark and Luke) are also memoirs of apostles (Peter and Paul), along with the Gospel of Matthew and, perhaps, the *Protevangelium of James* and the *Gospel of Peter*. There is no suggestion of a fourfold gospel here.

107. Justin, *Dial.* 100.4; 101.3; 102.5; 103.6; 105.6; 106.4; 107.1.

108. Justin, *Dial.* 103.8; 105.1; 105.5; 106.1.

109. Justin, *Dial.* 106.3.

110. Justin, *Dial.* 104.1 (the division of Jesus' garments).

111. Justin refers to twelve apostles in *1 Apol.* 39.3; *Dial.* 42.1.

112. Justin, *Dial.* 10.2 (where it is Trypho who is speaking); 100.1.

While his Logos christology may echo the Johannine prologue, this is never explicitly cited.[113] Matthew and Luke are much the most important of the apostolic memoirs, with Matthew enjoying a certain primacy over Luke. Other such works are peripheral. This estimation appears to have been typical of Roman Christian communities in the mid–second century, differing markedly from the Eastern churches' Johannine enthusiasm. Whether in the East or the West, however, no one as yet has tried to fix the number of the gospels or proposed this as a point of consensus.

(2) Searching through the library at Aelia (Jerusalem) for the theological works of previous generations, Eusebius comes across a "dialogue of Gaius, a man of great learning, with Proclus, an advocate of the Phrygian heresy, held in Rome in the time of Zephyrinus," that is, at the beginning of the third century.[114] In this dialogue (probably a literary record of an actual event), Proclus initially seeks to justify the new prophecy by appealing to the "four prophetesses, daughters of Philip, at Hierapolis in Asia";[115] Gaius refers his opponent to the tombs of Peter and Paul in the Vatican and on the Ostian Way, countering Proclus's appeal to the great figures of Christian Asia

---

113. The Λόγος is the Son of God (Justin, *1 Apol.* 32.9; 63.4), God's πρωτότοκος (*1 Apol.* 33.6; 46.2), and rules in second place μετὰ τὸν γεννήσαντα θεόν (*1 Apol.* 12.7). It was διὰ Λόγου that God made the κόσμος (*1 Apol.* 64.5); indeed, δι' αὐτοῦ πάντα ἔκτισε καὶ ἐκόσμησε (*2 Apol.* 6.3). He became man (ἀνθρώπου γενομένου, *1 Apol.* 5.4), being made flesh (σαρκοποιηθείς, *1 Apol.* 32.9; 66.2). Hill appeals to this material to argue that "John's Prologue is a primary source for Justin's Christology" (*Johannine Corpus*, p. 324). Even if this is so, Hill fails to reflect on the distinction between the unacknowledged use of a source and explicit citations from "the memoirs of the apostles." No satisfactory explanation is offered for the absence of Johannine material in Justin's citations.

114. Eusebius, *HE* vi.20.3. See the Yale Ph.D. thesis of Joseph D. Smith, "Gaius and the Controversy over the Johannine Literature" (1979); also August Bludau, *Die ersten Gegner der Johannesschriften* (Freiburg: Herder, 1925). Smith and Bludau both provide synthetic interpretations of material drawn from Eusebius, Irenaeus, Epiphanius, and two late Syriac writers, Dionysius Bar Salibi and 'Abdisho' Bar Brika. Two more recent works have sought to dismantle synthetic accounts of this kind. Allen Brent's hypothesis about the alleged statue of Hippolytus leads him to a systematically sceptical account of all the primary source material on which the synthesis relies (*Hippolytus and the Roman Church in the Third Century: Communities in Tension before the Emergence of a Monarch-Bishop* [Leiden: Brill, 1995], pp. 144-84). Heavily dependent on Brent, Charles Hill's presentation is determined by his rejection of the "orthodox Johannophobia thesis" (*Johannine Corpus*, pp. 172-204). Hill does his utmost to show that Gaius was not an "orthodox Johannophobe," or that, if he was, he was unrepresentative and uninfluential.

115. Eusebius, *HE* iii.31.4. Here, μετὰ τοῦτον indicates that Proclus had previously referred to another prophetic figure. For Montanist appeal to Philip and his daughters, see also *HE* v.17.3, where the other early prophets referred to are Agabus, Judas, and Silas (cf. Acts 11.27-28; 15.32; 21.10-11).

with the still more prestigious saints and martyrs of Rome.[116] According to Eusebius, local Roman traditions are also in play in Gaius's refusal to debate on the scriptural terrain selected by his opponent. Gaius,

> curbing his opponents' haste and presumption in composing new scriptures [περὶ τὸ συντάττειν καινὰς γραφάς], mentions only thirteen letters of the holy apostle, not enumerating [μὴ συναριθμήσας] the one to the Hebrews with the others. To this day, some of the Romans do not regard this as the work of the apostle.[117]

In the course of a debate about the legitimacy or otherwise of the "new prophecy," Gaius *(i)* criticizes his opponents for ascribing scriptural status to texts allegedly composed among themselves, and *(ii)* refers to a Pauline collection containing just thirteen letters, excluding Hebrews. Yet Eusebius does not say that Gaius explicitly rejected Hebrews or accused his opponents of fabricating it, only that he "enumerated" thirteen rather than fourteen Pauline letters and that Hebrews was not included. Something similar could be said of the *Muratorian Canon,* where Paul's letters are not simply listed but also enumerated:

> The blessed apostle Paul, following his predecessor John's example, writes in his own name to seven churches, in this order: to the Corinthians a first, to the Ephesians a second, to the Philippians a third, to the Colossians a fourth, to the Galatians a fifth, to the Thessalonians a sixth, to the Romans a seventh. Although another is added to the Corinthians and the Thessalonians for the sake of correction [*pro correctione*], one church is signified as extended through the whole world. For John too in the Apocalypse writes to seven churches yet speaks to all. Furthermore, one to Philemon, one to Titus, and two to Timothy, out of affection and love; yet they are to be held in honour in the catholic church for the ordering of churchly discipline.[118]

116. Eusebius, *HE* ii.25.6.

117. Eusebius, *HE* vi.20.3.

118. *Muratorian Canon*, ll. 47-63; corrected Latin text in A. Souter, *The Text and Canon of the New Testament* (New York: Scribner, 1913), pp. 208-11. In l. 48, *non nisi nominatim* appears to mean that Paul does not write anonymously, in which case Pauline authorship of Hebrews is here rejected. The uncorrected text is found in Geoffrey M. Hahneman, *The Muratorian Fragment and the Development of the Canon* (Oxford: Clarendon Press, 1992), pp. 6-7. Hahneman notes that "[e]xcerpts from the Muratorian Fragment discovered in a Prologue to Paul's Epistles confirm that the poor Latin of the Fragment is not that of the original" (p. 9).

This enumeration of the Pauline letters is not Gaius's. Its division into two parts is occasioned by the analogy with the seven Johannine letters of Revelation 2–3, with the result that the enumeration is broken off at that point. As we shall see, Gaius rejected Revelation. Yet the parallels are striking. As in the case of Gaius, Paul's letters are not only listed but also enumerated; there are thirteen of them, and Hebrews is not included.

Gaius, then, enumerated thirteen Pauline letters in the course of a critique of the "new scriptures" to which his opponents appealed. The context was presumably a listing of the texts that ought to be acknowledged as scriptural.[119] Like the *Muratorian Canon*, Gaius sought to identify the authentic and authoritative Christian scriptures; certain texts to which Proclus wished to appeal were thus eliminated. Hebrews itself does not seem to be at issue. It is Eusebius himself who has chosen to highlight its absence, which he sees as symptomatic of a broader Roman ambivalence towards this text. Yet it is one thing to omit Hebrews from an enumeration of the Pauline letters, quite another to accuse one's opponents of presumptuously "composing new scriptures." The "new scriptures" to which Proclus the Montanist wishes to appeal, and which Gaius disallows, must be texts other than Hebrews.

One of these texts is the Revelation of John, crucial to the prophetic movement within the churches of Asia but forthrightly rejected by Gaius, who attributes it to the heretic Cerinthus, arch-opponent of the apostle John:[120]

> But Cerinthus too, by means of revelations purportedly written by a great apostle [δι᾽ ἀποκαλύψεων ὡς ὑπὸ ἀποστόλου μεγάλου γεγραμμένων], falsely presents us with amazing things supposedly disclosed by angels, saying that after the resurrection the kingdom of Christ will be earthly and that the flesh will dwell in Jerusalem, subject again to desires and pleasures. And being an enemy of the scriptures of God, he says that there will be a thousand-year marriage festival — intending only to deceive.[121]

119. If Gaius listed what he regarded as canonical texts, then it is not the case that "there are no catalogues of the Christian canon until the fourth century," as Hahneman argues (*Muratorian Fragment*, p. 132). For a critique of Hahneman's late dating of the fragment, see J. Verheyden, "The Canon Muratori: A Matter of Dispute," in *The Biblical Canons*, ed. J.-M. Auwers and H. J. de Jonge, BEThL 163 (Leiden: Peeters, 2003), pp. 487-556.

120. Cf. Irenaeus, *Adv. Haer.* iii.3.4 (= Eusebius, *HE* iii.30.6), where John refuses to enter the public baths with Cerinthus inside.

121. Eusebius, *HE* iii.28.2. Cf. Rv. 1.1 (where an angel is sent to communicate a "revelation of Jesus Christ" to "his servant John"); 1.11 (John is commanded to write what he sees); 20.4-9 (the first resurrection, followed by the saints' thousand-year reign on earth, dwelling in "the camp of

Gaius here rejects outright a text accepted not only by his opponent but also, some decades earlier, by Justin.[122] This, then, is one point at which he seeks to "curb his opponents' haste and presumption in composing new scriptures."[123] The crucial question is whether the other major Johannine text — the gospel — was among the "new scriptures" accepted by Proclus but rejected by Gaius. Proclus himself seems to have appealed to the Gospel of John to establish fundamental Montanist tenets. A later writer attributes to his followers the claim

that the Holy Spirit was in the apostles but not the Paraclete [*in apostolis . . . spiritum sanctum fuisse, paracletum non fuisse*], and that the Paraclete spoke more things in Montanus than Christ revealed in the gospel — and not only more but also better and greater things [*meliora atque maiora*].[124]

The Johannine basis of this argument is clear. We learn from John 20.22 that the apostles received the Holy Spirit, and yet that event did not fulfil the promise of the Paraclete who would reveal "all things" and guide into "all the truth" (Jn. 14.26; 16.13). If such was Proclus's argument, his opponent might very well respond by rejecting the Johannine gospel as well as the Johannine apocalypse. And he would have to give reasons for doing so, as he did in the case of Revelation.

The key to this issue lies in lost works of Hippolytus, known through later Syriac writers and, with the help of evidence they provide, in Epiphanius. In a catalogue of scriptural and ecclesiastical writings dated 1298, Ebed-Jesu ('Abdisho' bar Brika) attributes to Hippolytus works enti-

the saints and the beloved city"); 19.7, 9 (the marriage of the Lamb). Allen Brent attempts to distinguish between the "revelations" contained in the Apocalypse attributed to John and the "amazing things" found in a second apocalyptic text, based on or appealing to the Apocalypse and authored by Cerinthus (*Hippolytus and the Roman Church*, pp. 133-37). Brent's claim that the contents of the work described here *differ* markedly from Revelation (p. 134) is hard to understand, as is his further assertion that Cerinthus claimed to have written *both* texts (p. 135). The view that Gaius refers to two texts rather than one is traced back to articles published in the *Theologisches Jahrbuch* for 1853, by "V. Baur" ([*sic*], p. 135n; cf. pp. 129n, 542).

122. Justin, *Dial.* 81.4. The disagreement in the Roman church about the status of Revelation is acknowledged in the *Muratorian Canon*, ll. 71-73.

123. This disagreement about Revelation indicates that Gaius's polemical attribution of "new scriptures" to Montanist authors does not refer to explicitly Montanist writings such as the "catholic epistle" of Themiso (Eusebius, *HE* v.18.5).

124. Ps.-Tertullian, *Adversus Omnes Haereses* 7. Citing this passage, A. Bludau draws attention to its Johannine logic: "Die Verheissung Jo 14, 16 wäre nach ihm [i.e. Proclus] nicht für die Aposteln sondern für das nächste Zeitalter bestimmt gewesen" (*Die ersten Gegner*, p. 66).

tled *Heads against Gaius (Rêšē d-luqbal Gaios)* and *Apologia for the Revelation and Gospel of John Apostle and Evangelist (Mappaq b-ruḥā d-ʿal gelyānā w-kārōzutā d-yōḥanan šliḥā w-ewangelisṭā).*[125] The first title indicates simply that Hippolytus wrote a work in opposition to Gaius: "heads" corresponds to κεφάλαια, probably "main points," in which case this work may be an epitome of a more extensive work. The second title corresponds closely to the title of a work listed on the plinth of a marble statue, evidently of Hippolytus himself, discovered in 1551:[126] ὑπὲρ τοῦ κατὰ Ἰωαννὴν εὐαγγελίου καὶ ἀποκαλύψεως.[127] The later and longer Syriac title may contain secondary features — notably the placing of the apocalypse first, reflecting ongoing concern about its canonical authority, and the addition of "apostle and evangelist" to differentiate this John from the others known to ecclesiastical tradition. Yet the Syriac implies an original Greek ἀπολογία ὑπέρ . . . , which could have been abbreviated to ὑπέρ in the inscription. Hippolytus, then, wrote a work against Gaius and an apologia for the Johannine gospel and apocalypse; the first was perhaps an epitome of the second. While it is possible that the apologia has nothing to do with Gaius, the fact that Gaius is known to have been a critic of Revelation makes it natural to assume that he

---

125. Cited in J. B. Lightfoot, *The Apostolic Fathers, Part I: S. Clement of Rome*, 2 vols. (London: Macmillan, 1885), p. 350. Lightfoot drew these titles from G. S. Assemani's *Bibliotheca Orientalis Clementino-Vaticana* (1719-28), volume III of which is devoted to the works of Syriac Nestorian writers. An English translation of Ebed-Jesu's catalogue had earlier been published by G. P. Badger (*The Nestorians and Their Rituals* [London: John Masters, 1852], vol. 2, pp. 361-79), although this is based on a different and inferior text to the ones used by Assemani.

126. On the discovery and authentication of the statue, see Brent, *Hippolytus and the Roman Church*, pp. 3-114. The mutilated statue of a seated figure was apparently discovered in the vicinity of the cemetery of St. Hippolytus on the Via Tiburtina. The cemetery itself was first excavated in the nineteenth century and supports the original identification with Hippolytus, which was based on the listed literary works. On one side of the chair is a table calculating the Passover from 222-333 CE in sixteen-year cycles; on the other, a table with corresponding dates for Easter on the following Sunday (Brent, pp. 3-4). In the original restoration, the statue was supplied with a male head. Brent speculates that it was originally a female figure representing Wisdom and alluding to the Hippolytan group's proto-trinitarian beliefs (pp. 69-76). In that case, the works listed would not necessarily stem from a single author (p. 115). Yet a list of works on the plinth of a statue strongly implies an association with the individual represented — as in the exactly parallel case of a statuette of Euripides with a list of his plays (Louvre MA 343; Brent, plate 14). Could a seated human figure, male or female, plausibly depict the procession of the divine Logos from the Father?

127. Brent argues that the ὑπέρ in this title was preceded by τά (*Hippolytus and the Roman Church*, p. 172). In his reproduction of the list (plate 5), the Υ of ΥΠΕΡ is itself almost illegible, and there is no visible trace of any letter preceding it. While there would be space for τά at the beginning of the line, there are other lines that are offset from the uneven left-hand margin.

may have been the occasion for Hippolytus's defence of both major Johannine writings. If the two works are related, then the title of the longer one identifies the issue whereas the title of the abbreviated version identifies the opponent.[128]

It is probably a passage from the *Heads against Gaius* that Dionysius (or Jacob) Bar Salibi quotes or summarizes in the preface to his commentary on Revelation. Having completed his "exposition of the gospel," this twelfth-century writer turns his attention to Revelation and immediately acknowledges that its status is disputed, with Eusebius and Dionysius of Alexandria ranged on one side of the argument and Irenaeus and a certain Hippolytus of Bosra on the other.[129] Most relevant here is the controversy between another Hippolytus and Gaius:

> Hippolytus the Roman said: There appeared a man named Gaius, who claimed that the Gospel was not John's, nor was the Apocalypse, but that they were written by the heretic Cerinthus. And against this Gaius Hippolytus arose and demonstrated that John's teaching in the Gospel and in the Apocalypse was different from that of Cerinthus.[130]

Bar Salibi proceeds to express his agreement with Hippolytus: the gospel and the Apocalypse are in harmony with the rest of scripture, and those who say that John did not write the Apocalypse are wrong.[131] Associating the rejection of the Apocalypse with the (manifestly heretical) rejection of the gos-

---

128. According to Brent, Ebed-Jesu has invented the two titles on the basis of an earlier and equally fictitious reference to Hippolytus, Gaius, and the Johannine literature, in the preface to Dionysius Bar Salibi's commentary on Revelation — to be discussed below (*Hippolytus and the Roman Church*, pp. 170-74). The pretext for this arbitrary conclusion is that "Ebed-Jesu's title does not correspond precisely with that on the Statue" (p. 172). Even though "the ancient convention was not to fix titles accurately," the differences are such as to "give grounds for doubting their equivalence" (p. 172). In reality, as we have seen, the differences are slight and readily explicable. Brent cites no evidence that the scholarly Ebed-Jesu was in the habit of inventing new literary works to add to his catalogue, or that he was intimately familiar with the work of Bar Salibi (who is not included in the catalogue). Brent's case is summarized by Hill, who considers it to be "potentially devastating" to the consensus on "the Gaian controversy" (*Johannine Corpus*, pp. 183-86; p. 183).

129. This figure may be the product of a misreading of Eusebius, *HE* vi.20.10.

130. Text from J. Sedlaèek, *Dionysius Bar Salibi, In Apocalypsim, Actus et Epistulas Catholicas*, CSCO 60 (I, 20 [Latin] = II, 101 [Syriac], Leuven: Peeters, 1909-10); I 1.30–2.3/II 4.4-9 (page and line references to the Latin and Syriac texts respectively). An English translation of the preface had previously been published in T. H. Robinson, "The Authorship of the *Muratorian Canon*," *The Expositor* 7 (1906), pp. 481-95.

131. I 2.10-12/II 4.16-19.

pel is an effective rhetorical strategy, although it is only the status of the Apocalypse that is of direct concern in this context. The introduction of Hippolytus and Gaius as sparring partners also prepares the way for their return on five occasions later in this commentary, where criticisms of Revelation attributed to "Gaius the heretic" are refuted by Hippolytus. The significance of these five passages was first noted by John Gwynn, in an article dating from 1888.[132] Four of them are from the section on the seven angels with their trumpets (Rv. 8.6–9.21). Gaius objects to the lurid apocalyptic accounts of disasters preceding the end, since authentic scriptural texts indicate that the end will come suddenly and without warning. At the blast of the second angelic trumpet, a great mountain falls into the sea, a third of which is turned to blood (Rv. 8.8-9); Gaius holds this to be incompatible with the promise that the Lord will come suddenly, like a thief in the night (1 Thes. 5.2).[133] At the fourth trumpet a third part of the sun, moon, and stars is destroyed (Rv. 8.12). Yet, according to Paul, the final destruction will occur while people are still saying, "There is peace and security" (1 Thes. 5.3).[134] At the fifth trumpet locusts emerge out of the bottomless pit to torture the human race (Rv. 9.1-11). On the contrary, Gaius argues, the apostle teaches that the righteous will be persecuted while the unrighteous will prosper until the very end (2 Tm. 3.12-13).[135] At the sixth trumpet four angels are released from the river Euphrates in order to kill a third of humankind (Rv. 9.13-19): "On this Gaius says that it is not written that angels are to make war, nor that a third part of humanity is to perish but that 'nation will rise up against nation'" (Mt. 24.7).[136] At one point the Syriac material corresponds especially closely to Eusebius's summary of the *Dialogue with Proclus*, where Gaius criticizes the idea of a materialistic millennium. In the fifth of Bar Salibi's confrontations between Gaius and Hippolytus, Gaius objects to the claim that Satan's binding lies in the millennial future (Rv. 20.1-3), since Satan, the "strong man," has already been bound by Christ (Mt. 12.29).[137] There is, therefore, no future millennium in prospect. At each of these five points Bar Salibi cites and approves the counterarguments of Hippolytus, which demonstrate the worthlessness of Gaius's attack on the Johannine apocalypse.

---

132. J. Gwynn, "Hippolytus and His 'Heads against Gaius,'" *Hermathena* 6 (1888), pp. 397-418. Gwynn did not have access to Bar Salibi's preface, which was missing from his text.

133. I 8.13-15/II 11.16-18.

134. I 9.14-17/II 12.24-29.

135. I 10.1-5/II 13.17-21.

136. I 10.25-27/II 14.11-13.

137. I 19.18-20/II 25.3-6.

What did Bar Salibi's Gaius have to say about the Johannine gospel? The Syriac author's commentary on John remains unpublished, but an excerpt from a seventeenth-century Latin translation was published by J. Rendel Harris in 1896.[138] The structure of the encounter between the heretic and Hippolytus is similar to those in the Revelation commentary: the heretic claims that a Johannine writing contradicts the synoptic gospels (or Paul), and Hippolytus replies by showing how the alleged contradiction can be resolved. The repetitions in this passage (indicated below by the enumeration) suggest that a still more extensive response to Gaius's argument is here being summarized, either by Bar Salibi or in the *Heads against Gaius,* his most probable source:

> <Gaius> a heretic criticized John because he did not agree with his co-authors, saying that after the baptism Jesus went into Galilee and performed the miracle of the wine in Katna [*sic*]. Saint Hippolytus opposed him: [1] Christ after he had been baptized went into the desert, and when a search was made for him by John's disciples and by the people, they sought him and did not find him, because he was in the desert. When the temptation was completed and he returned, he came into inhabited regions not to be baptized (for he had already been baptized), but so that he might be revealed by John, who said looking at him, "Behold the Lamb of God!" [2] So he was baptized and departed into the desert while they were seeking for him, and when they saw him they were fully persuaded who he was. Although they did not know this when he departed, he persuaded them when he returned through what was revealed by John: "On the next day John saw him and said, Behold the Lamb of God!" [3] For those forty days they sought him and did not see him. When the days of the temptation were over and he had returned and had been seen, he went into Galilee. [4] So the evangelists agree with each other that — after our Lord had returned from the desert and when John had revealed him, [on account of] those who had seen him being baptized, heard the Father's voice, then saw him no more because he had gone into the desert — John needed to bear witness to him again, to the effect that "this is the one whom you seek"; and from there he departed into Galilee in the power of the Spirit.[139]

138. J. Rendel Harris, "Presbyter Gaius and the Fourth Gospel," in his *Hermas in Arcadia and Other Essays* (Cambridge: Cambridge University Press, 1896), pp. 43-57; pp. 47-48 (citing the Latin translation of Dudley Loftus [1619-95]).

139. Rendel Harris notes that two manuscripts of the John commentary in the British Mu-

Gaius's point is that John's account of the sequel to Jesus' baptism is inconsistent with the other gospels. In John, Jesus departs for Galilee (Jn. 1.43), whereas in the others he goes into the desert to be tempted (Mt. 4.1; Mk. 1.12; Lk. 4.1-2). In [1], Hippolytus offers his basic solution to this difficulty, which is to locate the forty days of the temptations prior to the Baptist's testimony to Jesus (Jn. 1.29-34). The synoptists narrate the baptism, the divine voice, and the temptations; John narrates the *later* revelation through the Baptist. In [2], the argument is repeated from the perspective of Jesus' potential disciples, who did not fully grasp who he was on the occasion of his baptism and sought for him in order to know more. In [3], mention is made of the return to Galilee, while in [4], the conclusion is drawn that the whole scenario is agreed by all the evangelists. Here the reference to a further testimony of the Baptist may allude to John 1.36, where the lamb-of-God saying of 1.29 is repeated in abbreviated form. The synoptists report the forty days of temptation, John adds that Jesus returned to the Baptist in order to be revealed through him, and the outcome is a coherent narrative. The Baptist's repeated testimony is necessary because those who had seen Jesus being baptized and heard the divine voice were slow to grasp who he was. The motif of the fruitless quest for Jesus during the forty days is suggested by Jesus' question, "What do you seek?" (Jn. 1.38), as is the Baptist's implied reference to "the one whom you seek." The concluding reference to the power of the Spirit is a Lukan touch (Lk. 4.14). Bar Salibi's Hippolytus does not follow up Gaius's reference to the miracle at Cana.

Very similar arguments and counterarguments occur in the work of Epiphanius of Salamis. In the fifty-first of his eighty treatises against heresies, Epiphanius proposes a new name for adherents of the anti-Johannine tendency:

> Since they do not accept the *Logos* proclaimed by John, they shall be called *Alogi*. Being alienated in every way from the proclamation of the truth, they deny the purity of the proclamation, and accept neither the Gospel of John nor his Apocalypse. If indeed they accepted the Gospel but re-

---

seum lack the name "Gaius" at the start of the passage, and read "A certain heretic . . ."; in one case the name Gaius has been added above the line ("Presbyter Gaius," p. 48). Harris argues that this identification is correct on the basis of formal similarities to the Revelation passages (pp. 49-50). This identification was to be confirmed by the reference to Gaius's opposition to the Johannine gospel in the (as yet unknown) preface to the Revelation commentary. It is possible that Gaius *was* named in the original copy of the John commentary, and later anonymized by a scribe to whom the name was unfamiliar. The name is present in the Dublin manuscript used by Loftus.

jected the Apocalypse, we might suppose that they did so out of fastidiousness [ἀκριβολογία], not accepting an apocryphon because what is said in the Apocalypse is uttered in deep and dark riddles. But since they absolutely reject all the books proclaimed by Saint John, it is clear to all that these people resemble those of whom Saint John speaks in the catholic letters: "It is the last hour, and you have heard that the Antichrist is coming; and now there are many antichrists," and so on.[140]

Epiphanius or his source is responsible for naming the "heretics," and the term *Alogi* is his rather than theirs.[141] Although their beliefs are otherwise orthodox,[142] these people attributed both the gospel and Revelation to Cerinthus, like Bar Salibi's "Gaius the heretic."[143] In contrast, Eusebius's Gaius attributes only Revelation to Cerinthus, and his reputation as a learned and orthodox churchman is not impugned. Here Eusebius again conceals a problematic view on the fourfold gospel, as in his suppression of Clement's use of the *Gospel according to the Egyptians*. In reality, Bar Salibi's Gaius is to be identified with Epiphanius's *Alogi*.[144]

---

140. Epiphanius, *Pan.* li.3.2-5, citing 1 Jn. 2.18. Greek text of *Pan.* li in *Epiphanius, Ancoratus und Panarion*, ed. K. Holl and H. Lietzmann, 3 vols., GCS (Leipzig: Hinrichs, 1915-33), 2.248-311; Eng. trans., Frank Williams, *The Panarion of Epiphanius of Salamis, Books I-III*, 2 vols. (Leiden: Brill, 1987-94), 2.26-67. Translations here are my own.

141. The term is used on five occasions in *Pan.* li, in 3.1-2 (3x), 17.10, and 28.4, and on one further occasion in liv.1.1, where "a certain Theodotus" is described unreliably as "an offshoot of the aforementioned heresy of the Alogi" (see Smith, "Gaius," pp. 215-19). According to Brent, Epiphanius's *Alogi* consist of "disparate groups of people not necessarily doctrinally united," including non-Christian critics of the gospels such as Porphyry, Celsus, and Philosabbatius (*Hippolytus and the Roman Church*, p. 140). Yet Epiphanius mentions these individuals not as *Alogi* (which has a precise reference to the rejection of John from within the Christian community) but in connection with discrepancies they allege between the Matthean and Lukan birth narratives (*Pan.* li.8.1-4). Epiphanius's point is that the *Alogi*'s rejection of John on the basis of contradictions with other gospels resembles the approach of non-Christian critics to contradictions between Matthew and Luke. The *Alogi* claim that John is ἀδιάθετος, "noncanonical" (li.18.6), a term that only makes sense within a Christian context.

142. Epiphanius, *Pan.* li.4.3. For a thorough analysis of *Pan.* li, see Smith, "Gaius," pp. 211-55.

143. Epiphanius, *Pan.* li.3.6.

144. The older assumption that the *Alogi* were a distinct group within the churches of Asia, held by both Zahn and Harnack, was in principle superseded by publication of Bar Salibi's prefaces, linking Gaius the Roman presbyter with rejection not only of Revelation but also of the Johannine gospel. See A. Harnack, *Das Neue Testament um das Jahr 200: Theodor Zahn's Geschichte des Neutestamentlichen Kanons (Erster Band, Erste Hälfte)* (Freiburg i.B.: J. C. B. Mohr [Paul Siebeck], 1889), pp. 59-70. According to Zahn's modernizing interpretation, the *Alogi* "leugneten die Thatsache der von jeher bestandenen Autorität der vier Evv. und der johanneischen Schriften

Like "Gaius the heretic," these *Alogi* criticize the Johannine gospel on the grounds that its account of the beginnings of Jesus' ministry (Jn. 1.19–2.11) is incompatible with the synoptic temptation narrative. The so-called *Alogi* are simply those persons who accept the anti-Johannine views of an individual teacher and author. Epiphanius has converted this teacher and his real or presumed influence into a heretical sect, summarizing as follows his major anti-Johannine argument:

> And what, *he says* [φησίν], did he [the pseudo-Johannine evangelist] say? That "in the beginning was the Word, and the Word was with God, and the Word was God" [Jn. 1.1]; and that "the Word became flesh and dwelt among us, and we saw his glory, glory as of the only Son from the Father, full of grace and truth" [1.14]; and immediately afterwards, that "John bears witness and cried saying, This is he of whom I said to you . . ." [1.15]; and that "this is the lamb of God who takes away the sin of the world" [1.29]. And next he says, "Those who heard him said, Rabbi, where are you staying?" [1.38], together with this, "The next day Jesus wished to go to Galilee, and he finds Philip, and says to him, Follow me" [1.43]. And shortly afterwards he goes on to say, "And after three days there was a wedding in Cana of Galilee, and Jesus was invited with his disciples to the wedding, and his mother was there" [2.1-2]. But the other evangelists say that he spent forty days in the wilderness being tempted by the devil, and then returned and chose his disciples.[145]

From this discrepancy we can only conclude that "the Gospel that goes under the name of John is lying [τὸ δὲ εὐαγγέλιον τὸ εἰς ὄνομα Ἰωάννου ψεύδεται]."[146] In opposing this conclusion, Epiphanius (like Bar Salibi's Hippolytus) must show that there is a place for the temptation narrative within this apparently unbroken sequence, and he too does so by arguing that John the Baptist testified to Jesus as the lamb of God not on the occa-

---

nicht," but took up their position "im Namen des unverjährbaren Rechts der innern Kritik" (cited by Harnack, p. 60). Opposing this, Harnack argues that, "als diese Aloger auftraten, gab es in Kleinasien weder eine bestimmte kirchliche Christologie noch ein fertiges N. T. . . . Der Widerspruch der Aloger gegen die johanneischen Schriften ist . . . für den Einblick in die Entstehungsgeschichte nicht nur des N. T.s, sondern auch des Evangelienkanons, von höchster Bedeutung" (p. 70). While Harnack mislocates the Alogi in Asia Minor, sidelines Gaius of Rome, and substitutes a christological concern for the actual Montanist one, his basic criticism of Zahn's early dating of the four-gospel collection remains valid.

145. Epiphanius, *Pan.* li.4.7-10; cf. li.17.11–18.1.
146. Epiphanius, *Pan.* li.18.1.

sion of his baptism but on his return from the temptations in the wilderness (cf. Jn. 1.29-34).[147] The synoptic gospels narrate the baptism, the temptations, and the return to Galilee; John has no need to repeat the first two items, but inserts a return to the Jordan for the testimony of John. Unlike Bar Salibi's Hippolytus, Epiphanius does not reflect on the rationale for the return; there is no reference here to potential disciples who heard the divine voice at the baptism, who sought in vain for Jesus during the forty days, and who were finally persuaded by the Baptist's testimony. If Bar Salibi's Hippolytus is derived from a genuine Hippolytan source, as he appears to be, then Epiphanius is not simply reproducing that source without modification. Hippolytus is interested in the development of the early disciples' faith from its first beginnings, and finds an opportunity to explore this theme as he harmonizes the Johannine and synoptic narratives. Epiphanius is concerned here solely with the harmonization itself, though he later reflects at length on the disciples' developing relationship to Jesus as reflected in the various distinct accounts of their call.[148] Like Hippolytus, however, Epiphanius sees the Baptist's revelatory role in his testimony to Jesus as "the Lamb of God" (Jn. 1.29, 36), rather than, say, as "the Son of God" (Jn. 1.34).[149] Internal exegetical evidence that this testimony occurs during a second visit of Jesus to the Jordan, subsequent to his baptism and temptations, is found in retrospective elements in the Baptist's testimony: "This is he of whom I said . . ." and "I saw the Spirit descend as a dove . . ." (Jn. 1.30, 32).[150] Overall, Bar Salibi's debate between Hippolytus and Gaius is so similar to Epiphanius's engagement with his *Alogi* that it is plausible to suppose that Epiphanius is heavily dependent on material derived from Hippolytus.[151] In that case the *Alogi* are to be identified not with some obscure Asian sect but with Gaius, the proto-orthodox Roman churchman, together with his presumed followers.[152]

A further problem addressed by Epiphanius is that "John said that the Saviour kept two passovers over a two-year period, but the other evangelists

147. Epiphanius, *Pan.* li.12.6–13.10.

148. Epiphanius, *Pan.* li.14.1–15.13.

149. Epiphanius, *Pan.* li.13.8, 16.4.

150. Epiphanius, *Pan.* li.13.9, 21.12-13.

151. There is no suggestion in Epiphanius that the *Alogi* are opposed to the Logos christology: so rightly Bludau, *Die ersten Gegner*, pp. 77-87, against Harnack and others.

152. As J. D. Smith writes: "All evidence of criticisms against the Gospel of John and Revelation . . . can be traced back to Gaius of Rome and to no other person or group" ("Gaius," p. 427, italics removed).

describe one Passover."[153] As for the other major Johannine writing, the *Alogi* ask: "What good does the Revelation do me by telling me about seven angels and seven trumpets?"[154] In particular, they seek to discredit the account of the loosing of the four angels bound at the river Euphrates, whose task is to kill a third of the human race.[155] This coincides precisely with the fourth of Bar Salibi's Gaius passages; the previous three are also drawn from the vision of angels with trumpets (Rv. 8.2–9.21).[156] Since Bar Salibi provides considerably more detail than Epiphanius, there can be no question of dependence here; the only reasonable explanation is that both draw from a common Hippolytan source. The *Alogi* also deny the authenticity of the letter to the church in Thyatira (Rv. 2.18), on the grounds that no church has existed there since it was taken over by the "Phrygians" or Montanists.[157] As in Gaius's *Dialogue with Proclus,* the rejection of Revelation and its attribution to the heretic Cerinthus are linked with anti-Montanist polemic. In Hippolytus's responses as in Epiphanius's, the Montanist issue is in the background and the primary concern is with the Johannine literature itself.[158] In Epiphanius's controversy with the *Alogi* we overhear Hippolytus's controversy with Gaius.

It is therefore highly probable that both the gospel and the Apocalypse of John were among the "new scriptures" rejected by Gaius and affirmed by Proclus, his Montanist opponent. Echoes of this controversy can be heard in the *Muratorian Canon,* which is much preoccupied with the issue of Johannine difference:

The fourth of the gospels: John, one of the disciples, exhorted by his fellow-disciples and bishops, said, "Fast with me today and for three days, and whatever is revealed to anyone we will tell one another." That same night it was revealed to Andrew, one of the apostles, that, with the acknowledgement of them all [*recognoscentibus cunctis*], John should write everything in his own name [*suo nomine*]. And so, although different be-

---

153. Epiphanius, *Pan.* li.22.1. There are actually three Johannine passovers, as Epiphanius points out (*Pan.* li.23.6; Jn. 2.13; 6.4; 11.55).

154. Epiphanius, *Pan.* li.32.3; cf. Rev. 8.2–9.21; 11.15-19.

155. Epiphanius, *Pan.* li.34.2.

156. Brent is therefore wrong to claim that there is no parallel in Bar Salibi to the ridiculing of the angels with their trumpets (*Hippolytus and the Roman Church,* p. 164). Four of the five Gaius passages are from precisely this section of Revelation.

157. Epiphanius, *Pan.* li.33.1-3.

158. This distinction is rightly emphasized by Smith, "Gaius," p. 341.

ginnings [*varia principia*] are taught by the individual gospel books, this does not affect the faith of those who believe, since by one and the same Spirit all things are declared in all of them about his birth, his passion, his resurrection, his association with his disciples, and his double advent — the first in humility and contempt, which has occurred already, the second according to the kingly power of the Father, which is clearly future. What wonder is it, then, that John repeatedly asserts each of these things in his letters, saying of himself, "What we have seen with our eyes and heard with our ears and touched with our hands, these things we have written to you"? Thus he shows himself not only an eyewitness and hearer but also a writer of all the wonderful works of the Lord, in sequence.[159]

The order of the gospels, with John in fourth place and Luke in third, follows Irenaeus.[160] Presumably on the basis of John 21.24 (". . . *we know* that his testimony is true"), the author claims that John wrote his gospel at the instigation and with the subsequent authorization of the other apostles. That is the first of three reasons why believers' faith need not be shaken by the disconcertingly different gospel beginnings, the *varia principia*. The second reason is that, in spite of their narrative diversity, the gospels all inculcate the catholic church's rule of faith. The third is that John explicitly refers to himself as the author of the gospel attributed to him (1 Jn. 1.4): the reference to the gospel is secured by substituting a past tense *(scripsimus)* for a present (γράφομεν). This elaborate apologia for the fourth gospel takes up almost a third of the extant document, and demonstrates that this gospel and its opening chapters were perceived as problematic. The implied reader of the *Muratorian Canon* is one who has felt the impact of the case against John.[161]

---

159. *Muratorian Canon*, ll. 9-34. My translation assumes that *uno ac principali spiritu* in l. 19 is a free or erroneous rendering of the Pauline τὸ ἓν καὶ τὸ αὐτὸ πνεῦμα (1 Cor. 12.11). In ll. 32-33, I assume that *sed auditorem et scriptorem* should read *et auditorem sed scriptorem*.

160. The (presumed) order Matthew-Mark-Luke-John is seen by Hahneman as an indication of a late Eastern provenance, in contrast to the characteristic Western sequence of Matthew-John-Luke-Mark (*Muratorian Fragment*, pp. 183-87). Hahneman fails to note that different sequences are occasioned by different needs: for example, the need to correlate the gospels with the four living creatures of Rv. 4 (Irenaeus, *Adv. Haer.* iii.11.8), or the need to prioritize gospels with apostolic authors in reaction against the Marcionite privileging of Luke (Tertullian, *Adversus Marcionem* iv.2.2). Like Irenaeus (*Adv. Haer.* iii.1.1) and Origen (Eusebius, *HE* vi.25.4-6), the *Muratorian Canon* is concerned with the presumed order of composition.

161. The Roman provenance of this text is suggested by the reference in ll. 38-39 to the *profectio Pauli ab urbe ad Spaniam*, in spite of Albert C. Sundberg's claim to the contrary ("Canon

(3) Gaius is said to have been active during the episcopacy of Zephyrinus (198-217). The question is whether Roman resistance to the gospel attributed to John may be traced any further back, thus making it plausible that Irenaeus's concept of the fourfold gospel seeks to overcome this resistance and to achieve consensus between the West and the East.

Irenaeus is well aware of those who reject the Gospel of John, and who do so in part for anti-Montanist reasons. There are, he tells us, people who,

> in order to evade the gift of the Spirit poured out on the human race in these last times by the will of the Father, do not accept the perspective represented by John's Gospel [*illam speciem . . . , quae est secundum Ioannis Evangelium*], where the Lord promises to send the Paraclete. And so they reject this gospel and the prophetic Spirit together — these wretches who aspire to be false prophets and thrust aside the prophetic gift from the church, endorsing the conduct of those who refuse to communicate with the brethren because a few may be hypocritical. It must be assumed that such people do not accept the apostle Paul either, who, in his Epistle to the Corinthians, speaks at length about the prophetic *charismata* and knows of both men and women as prophesying in the church. In all these ways, then, they sin against the Spirit of God and fall into the unforgivable sin.[162]

Irenaeus here seems to refer to Roman support for anti-Montanists in Asia who refuse communion with supporters of the "new prophecy," alleg-

---

Muratori: A Fourth Century List," *HTR* 66 [1973], pp. 1-41; pp. 5-7). Sundberg argues that this text's uncertainty about the canonicity of Revelation suggests an original eastern milieu (pp. 20-26), but does not adequately address the case of Gaius of Rome. As Sundberg notes (pp. 9-11), a second-century dating of this text is dependent on a questionable interpretation of the reference to the composition of the *Shepherd of Hermas* "most recently in our own times" *(nuperrime in temporibus nostris)* during the episcopacy of Pius (ll. 74-75). The point here is to contrast the *Shepherd* with the canonical books previously listed, written by apostles and thus to be dated within an apostolic age distinct from "our own times." Sundberg's proposed fourth-century dating (p. 38) is too late, however, overlooking the apologetic character of the discussion of the Gospel of John and the plausibility of a *Sitz im Leben* in the aftermath of Gaius's critique and Hippolytus's apologia — i.e. in the mid–third century.

162. Irenaeus, *Adv. Haer.* iii.11.9. In my translation, "endorsing the conduct of those . . ." paraphrases *similia patientes his*. For detailed discussion of this passage, see Smith, "Gaius," pp. 140-68; Smith also draws attention to a parallel passage in Irenaeus's *Demonstratio,* 39 (pp. 162-63). Irenaeus's opponents "aspire to be false prophets" in the sense that they assume the mantle of the false prophet by opposing true prophecy. The older assumption that the opponents were themselves Montanists is untenable (so Smith, pp. 153-58).

ing that the occasional excesses of a few are characteristic of the movement as a whole.[163] In Rome though not in Asia, rejection of the new prophecy is associated with rejection of the Johannine gospel.[164] Yet, Irenaeus argues, the gospel that promises the coming of the Paraclete can only consistently be rejected if one is also prepared to reject Paul's first letter to the Corinthians, where the lengthy commendation of prophecy (1 Cor. 14) follows an earlier acknowledgement that women as well as men exercise a prophetic ministry within the church (1 Cor. 11.4-5).[165] The denunciation of those who reject both gospel and prophecy is born of personal experience. While still a presbyter, Irenaeus had visited Rome as a representative of the Gallic churches, who at this time were seeking to exploit their own recent martyrdoms to bring about peace among the competing factions in "Phrygia and Asia" — a strategy for which the support of Rome would be needed.[166] This attempt to secure "the peace of the churches"[167] was evidently a failure.[168] In the passage from *Against Heresies* 3, Irenaeus appears to blame this on the Roman anti-Montanist faction, which rejected not only the new prophecy but also the Johannine gospel.[169] There is no indication here of an exegetical debate

163. For Asian anti-Montanist exploitation of the actions of those whom Irenaeus regards as unrepresentative "hypocrites" (*eos qui in hypocrisi veniunt*), see the excerpts from Apollonius preserved in Eusebius, *HE* v.18.1-13, esp. 18.6-10. An anonymous anti-Montanist writer commends the refusal of fellowship to Montanists even when members of the competing factions are suffering martyrdom together (*HE* v.16.22). It is unlikely that the Montanism opposed in Rome was itself Roman (so R. Heine, "The Role of the Gospel of John in the Montanist Controversy," *SecC* 6 [1987], pp. 1-19; p. 11).

164. Unlike Gaius of Rome, Asian anti-Montanists make positive use of Johannine texts and traditions (cf. Eusebius, *HE* v.18.13). There is no evidence of anti-Johannine polemic in Asia (against H. von Campenhausen, *The Formation of the Christian Bible*, Eng. trans. [Philadelphia: Augsburg Fortress, 1972], p. 238).

165. Irenaeus seems unaware of 1 Cor. 14.33b-35, which is probably an anti-Montanist gloss. On Montanism and women, see Christine Trevett, *Montanism: Gender, Authority, and the New Prophecy* (Cambridge: Cambridge University Press, 1996), pp. 151-97.

166. Eusebius, *HE* v.3.4–4.2; cf. v.1.3.

167. Eusebius, *HE* v.3.4.

168. At a later date, Tertullian claims that his opponent Praxeas persuaded the bishop of Rome (Zephyrinus, Victor, Eleutherus?) to revoke his previous endorsement of Montanism, partly on the grounds that this was inconsistent with the attitude of his predecessors. Irenaeus's visit to Rome took place early in the pontificate of Eleutherus, *c.* 175 CE.

169. This Irenaeus passage is an embarrassment for Charles Hill, since it might seem to refer to "orthodox Johannophobes," to whose nonexistence his entire lengthy monograph is devoted. Hill first draws attention to the sharpness of Irenaeus's criticism (*Johannine Corpus*, pp. 113-15), which in reality demonstrates nothing more than Irenaeus's own Montanist sympathies. Second, Hill suggests that these anti-Montanists may possibly have been related to the group responsible

about possible contradictions with the other gospels, as in the case of Gaius some years later. At this point, it seems that a novel and unfamiliar gospel is rejected purely because it seems to lend support to the Phrygian heresy.[170]

This defence of John in the face of Roman reservations confirms that Irenaeus's fourfold gospel seeks to promote ecumenical consensus and understanding between the churches of the East and the West — a concern also expressed in his interventions in the controversies around the new prophecy and the passover. Here too, Irenaeus has the attitude of the Roman church in view. He stands near the beginning of the process in which Rome came to accept the legitimacy of the gospel from Asia. In the East, additional gospels will have to be proscribed if the fourfold collection is to be firmly established. It will no longer be possible for an impeccably orthodox bishop to permit a congregation to use the *Gospel according to Peter,* or for theologians to debate authentic teaching of Jesus preserved in the *Gospel according to the Egyptians.* Serapion and Clement are still influenced by the old assumption that the singular gospel of the Lord's words and deeds may have an indefinite number of literary attestations. But that assumption begins to fade as attention is focused on specific texts now directly or indirectly associated with leading apostles: Matthew and John, Peter and Paul. In contrast, four gospels represent one more than the West is accustomed to, rather than several fewer. The Ephesian gospel must therefore be defended against those who believe this unfamiliar text to be tainted with Montanism.

Contested Beginnings

From the later second century onwards, a gradual consensus formed around the fourfold gospel both in the West and in the East. The motivation was not

---

for the *Apocalypse of James,* a "heretical" text in which he implausibly claims to detect anti-Montanist and anti-Johannine tendencies (pp. 115-18). Arguments of this quality do nothing to establish that these "Johannine antagonists" are "well outside the bounds of right belief," or to confirm that the Roman church too had "prized the Fourth Gospel as inspired scripture" from time immemorial (p. 118). Perhaps aware of the weakness of his position, Hill resorts to intemperate language about unnamed interpreters who "charge Irenaeus with fabrication and deception on a grand scale," who accuse him of "playing psychological games with his unsuspecting readers," and who elevate him "to the soaring heights of an evil genius" (p. 118). Hill fails to explain why an Irenaeus who advocates a disputed gospel should lay himself open to such charges.

170. On Montanist appeal to the Johannine Paraclete, see Trevett, *Montanism,* pp. 62-66, 92-95.

the need to defend the true faith against heretics such as the Marcionites, countering one version of a canon of Christian scripture with another. Irenaeus does report that Marcion provided his followers with a version of the Gospel of Luke that lacked the birth narratives and those sayings in which Jesus appeared to assume that his Father was also the creator. This is "not the gospel but rather a fragment of the gospel" *(non evangelium sed particulam evangelii).*[171] In rejecting the gospel in its entirety *(totum evangelium),* Marcion separates himself from the gospel of which he boasts.[172] Yet Irenaeus does not view the fourfold gospel primarily as a weapon against Marcion, whom he seems to know only at second hand.[173] Nor does he show much awareness of heretical appeal to additional gospel texts.[174] Heresy is dangerous not because it uses the wrong gospels but because it misuses the right ones.[175]

While Irenaeus is apparently the first to *advocate* a four-gospel collection, he is not the first to *use* such a collection or to regard it as inspired scripture. This is clear from his engagement with the primary objects of his critique, the "disciples of Valentinus," or, more specifically, "those around Ptolemaeus, an offshoot of the school of Valentinus."[176] As presented by

171. Irenaeus, *Adv. Haer.* i.27.2.

172. Irenaeus, *Adv. Haer.* iii.11.9.

173. Following Harnack, the Marcionite background to Irenaeus is strongly emphasized by Hans von Campenhausen (*Formation of the Christian Bible,* pp. 148, 171-72, 203-4). The argument seems to rest on considerations of general probability rather than a close reading of Irenaeus's text. Irenaeus's relative lack of interest in Marcion is rightly noted by Elaine Pagels ("Irenaeus, the 'Canon of Truth,' and the *Gospel of John*: 'Making a Difference' through Hermeneutics and Ritual," *VC* 56 [2002], pp. 339-71; p. 346).

174. Irenaeus mentions a *Gospel of Judas* (*Adv. Haer.* i.31.1), and a Valentinian *Gospel of Truth* (iii.11.9). In *Adv. Haer.* i.20.1, he does claim that the heretics use "an unspeakable number of apocryphal and spurious writings" (ἀμύθητον πλῆθος ἀποκρύφων καὶ νόθων γραφῶν), but can offer only a single instance in support of this claim, a story about Jesus' childhood attested in the *Infancy Gospel of Thomas.*

175. Cf. Irenaeus, *Adv. Haer.* iii.11.7.

176. Irenaeus, *Adv. Haer.* i, *praef.,* 2; i.11.1; ii, *praef.,* 1; ii.31.1; iii, *praef.;* iv, *praef.* See Ismo Dunderberg, "The School of Valentinus," in *A Companion to Second-Century Christian "Heretics,"* ed. Antti Marjanen and Petri Luomanen (Leiden: Brill, 2005), pp. 64-99. Dunderberg sees the closest analogy to Irenaeus's account not in the extant fragments of Valentinus himself but in the *Tripartite Tractate* from Codex I of the Nag Hammadi collection (pp. 70-71). As Christoph Markschies has emphasized, it is uncertain whether and how far Valentinus himself was regarded by his contemporaries as a "heretic" (*Valentinus Gnosticus? Untersuchungen zur valentinianischen Gnosis mit einem Kommentar zu den Fragmenten Valentins,* WUNT [Tübingen: Mohr-Siebeck, 1992], pp. 388-407).

Irenaeus, this post-Valentinian theology supports its major claims by appealing to the evidence of all four of the gospels that Irenaeus too acknowledges. Yet it coordinates their testimony in such a way that the decisive event in the gospel narrative is the descent of the Spirit at Jesus' baptism — a fundamentally Markan orientation on which are superimposed the perspectives first of Matthew and Luke and later of John. At least as significant as Irenaeus's well-known argument for a four-gospel collection is his substitution of a new point of coherence, which he finds not at the baptism but at the annunciation and birth. He is less concerned with the fourfold gospel in itself than with the fundamental interpretative decision that determines whether or not this gospel is rightly understood. Here as elsewhere, canon formation is inseparable from theological hermeneutics.

Irenaeus's work opens with an account of the post-Valentinian system attributed to Ptolemaeus, including samples of the scriptural exegesis with which it is supported.[177] Most of the cited exegesis relates to the canonical gospels, which are here said to reveal in parabolic form the strange story of the world's origin and destiny. The function of this story is to bridge the ontological gulf between the creator deity of Genesis, who mistakenly believes himself the only true God, and the transcendent realm of the *Plērōma* as revealed by Jesus. The *Plērōma* consists of thirty paired aeons, starting from a primary Tetrad which expands into an Ogdoad from which a Decad and a Duodecad are subsequently generated.[178] Sophia, the twelfth and youngest aeon of the Duodecad, conceives a presumptuous and dangerous passion to comprehend the greatness of the Father, Bythus. She is quickly restored to her proper position within the hierarchy, and three new aeons come into being: Christ and his bride, the Holy Spirit, who teach the aeons about the unknowable Father, and Jesus (or the Saviour), who is the combined product of the entire *Plērōma*. (As Paul says, "In him the whole *Plērōma* was pleased to dwell.")[179] But Sophia's rash action has lasting consequences. Her passion has been conceived apart from her husband Theletos, so that she gives birth to it as a "formless substance" (οὐσίαν ἄμορφον) which must be excluded from the *Plērōma*.[180] This excluded being is named Sophia or Achamoth. She receives form from Christ, but his departure causes her to conceive a

177. The exegesis is presented separately from the main exposition in Irenaeus, *Adv. Haer.* i.3.1-6; i.8.1-5; cf. i.18.1–21.2.

178. Irenaeus, *Adv. Haer.* i.1.2.

179. Col. 1.19. This text is not cited but obviously underlies the account of the Saviour's origin in Irenaeus, *Adv. Haer.* i.2.6.

180. Irenaeus, *Adv. Haer.* i.2.2-4.

longing for the inaccessible light that reenacts the passion of her mother before her.[181] She is liberated from her passion by a visitation from the Saviour, by whom she conceives the spiritual offspring with whom the Valentinian Christians are identified. Her passion then becomes the substance of the Demiurge and the material world he creates, into which the spiritual offspring are secretly inserted — to be awakened in due time by the advent of the Saviour from on high, who descends onto the man Jesus in the form of a dove and reveals the unknown Father and the mysteries of the *Plērōma*.[182] The role of Jesus and the gospels that bear witness to him is to disclose and substantiate this tale of the realms above, in parabolic form. All four canonical gospels are enlisted in the service of this radical theology.

(1) *Matthew*. The fundamental premise of this theology is that the God revealed in Jesus was previously unknown, in sharp contrast to the well-known deity of Jewish scripture. For the Valentinian Christian, it is just this difference that the Matthean Jesus announces when he says:

> I thank you, Father, Lord of heaven and earth, because you have hidden [these things] from the wise and understanding and revealed them to children. Yes, my Father, for such was your will for me [ὅτι ἔμπροσθέν σοι εὐδοκία μοι ἐγένετο]. All things have been given to me by my Father, and no one knew the Father except the Son and no one knows the Son except the Father and the one to whom the Son reveals him.[183]

This passage is "the crown of their system" (κορωνίδα τῆς ὑποθέσεως αὐτῶν), because it establishes the distinction between the Father of Jesus and the creator deity that the myth seeks to elaborate.[184] The creator himself is ignorant of the God above him, believing himself to be the one true God — a limitation attested throughout Jewish scripture.[185] Yet this ignorance is not culpable. This Valentinian deity is the Platonic Demiurge, a being whose power, wisdom, and justice are limited but real. He is not the malevolent

---

181. Irenaeus, *Adv. Haer.* i.4.1-2.

182. Irenaeus, *Adv. Haer.* i.4.5–5.6; 7.2.

183. Irenaeus, *Adv. Haer.* i.20.3. The Valentinian citation is drawn from Mt. 11.25-27 rather than from the close parallel in Lk. 10.21-22. Matthew's τὸν υἱὸν εἰ μὴ ὁ πατήρ . . . is expanded slightly in Luke's τίς ἐστιν ὁ υἱὸς εἰ μὴ ὁ πατήρ . . . In Irenaeus, this passage follows immediately after the citation of its sequel, Mt. 11.28-30 (*Adv. Haer.* i.20.2). In v. 27b, the order Father/Son–Son/Father (rather than the reverse) is attested in Justin (*1 Apol.* 63.3) and later by Irenaeus himself (*Adv. Haer.* ii.6.1; but cf. iv.6.7).

184. Irenaeus, *Adv. Haer.* i.20.3.

185. Irenaeus, *Adv. Haer.* i.5.4.

Ialdabaoth of alternative versions of the myth, also known as *Sakla*, the "fool" who "says in his heart, There is no God" (Ps. 13.1 LXX). When the Saviour reveals the truth through Jesus, the Demiurge responds positively to this new knowledge, even though it shows his previous claim to supreme deity to be illusory. Thus the Demiurge is represented by the Matthean figure of the centurion, placing himself and his substance at the Saviour's disposal in the words, "I am one having soldiers and servants under my authority, and whatever I command they do."[186]

(2) *Mark.* Valentinian appeal to passages from Matthew is only to be expected, in view of the widespread popularity of this gospel. What is more striking is the nonassimilation of Mark to Matthew. It is Mark who preserves crucial details in the double story in which Jesus heals the woman who has been haemorrhaging for twelve years and restores Jairus's twelve-year-old daughter to life (Mk. 5.22-43). For truly spiritual readers, the flow of blood signifies the passion of Sophia, the twelfth aeon whose identity was endangered by the flow of her being into the sea of divinity,[187] whereas the restoration of the twelve-year-old girl discloses the bestowal of form and light on Sophia-Achamoth.[188] In the Markan conjunction of stories concerning female figures associated with the number twelve, both parallels and differences between the upper and lower Sophia-figures come to light. The passion of Sophia-Achamoth is also attested by the Markan cry of dereliction (Mk. 15.34), which signifies Sophia's lament at the prohibition that prevents her return to the realm of light.[189] Her abandonment by the Christ who bestowed form and recollection of the light corresponds to the Saviour's abandonment of the human Jesus at or prior to his crucifixion. This exegesis may be a vestige of an earlier version of the myth in which the aeon Sophia was herself expelled from the *Plērōma*, rather than her offspring and

186. Irenaeus, *Adv. Haer.* i.7.4, citing Mt. 8.9 in a compressed and emended form, with ἄνθρωπος omitted and no reference to the authority under which the centurion himself is set. The absence of the Lukan τασσόμενος (Lk. 7.8) confirms the Matthean origin of this exegesis.

187. Irenaeus, *Adv. Haer.* i.3.3. The question τίς μου ἥψατο, cited here, occurs only in Mk. 5.30.

188. Irenaeus, *Adv. Haer.* i.8.2. The age of Jairus's daughter is given only in Mark (Mk. 5.42; cf. Mt. 9.25; Lk. 8.55). Jairus is an ἀρχισυνάγωγος in the Irenaeus passage and in Mk. 5.22 (Mt. 9.18: ἄρχων; Lk. 8.41: ἄρχων τῆς συναγωγῆς, but cf. Lk. 8.49). Although Mark Edwards argues that the doubling of the Sophia figure may be original (*Catholicity and Heresy in the Early Church* [Farnham: Ashgate, 2009], p. 27n), it is more likely to be a secondary product of reflection on the double narrative of Mk. 5.25-43.

189. Irenaeus, *Adv. Haer.* i.8.2 (cf. i.4.1): ὁ θεός μου . . . , εἰς τί ἐγκατέλιπές με (Mk. 15.34), rather than θέε μου . . . , ἱνατί με ἐγκατέλιπες (Mt. 27.46)

double.[190] The cry of dereliction reenacts and discloses the lament of Sophia-Achamoth, but it also represents Jesus' grief at the departure of the divine Christ who had descended upon him at his baptism.[191] To Valentinian exegetes, this tragic earthly occurrence suggested the heavenly tragedy of Sophia's abandonment by the divine Christ, who left her in the dark and with no immediate possibility of return to the *Plērōma*. Just as Mark testifies to the end of the liaison between the human Jesus and the divine Christ, so he testifies to the beginning: for his gospel alone opens with the baptism of Jesus and the descent of the Spirit, and is highly valued by those who seek to build their christology on this foundation.[192]

(3) *Luke.* Whether or not Irenaeus's selection is representative, his Valentinian exegetical material shows a pronounced Lukan bias. When Simeon acclaims the Christ child in the temple, he represents the Demiurge, who praised God when he learned from the Saviour of his coming elevation into the sphere left vacant when Sophia-Achamoth is finally admitted to the *Plērōma*.[193] The widowed Anna signifies Achamoth's patient waiting for her eventual union with the Saviour.[194] The Lord was twelve years of age when he disputed with the teachers of the law; he was thirty when he began his ministry; and thus he revealed both the Duodecad and the number of aeons in the original *Plērōma*.[195] In a three-part passage on discipleship, the Lukan Jesus identifies the three classes of humans as *pneumatikoi, psychikoi,* and *hylikoi.*[196] Those under the dominance of the material ask, "Shall I follow you?," to which Jesus responds with a statement about the homelessness of the Son of man. Those who have attained the level of the *psychē* (that is, ordinary church members) allow this-worldly responsibilities to take precedence over discipleship, putting their hand to the plough but looking back. Those who have attained the highest plane of all, the spiritual, obey Jesus' command to "let the dead bury their dead." The threefold anthropological

---

190. Cf. Irenaeus, *Adv. Haer.* i.2.3 with i.4.1-2; i.11.1.

191. Cf. Irenaeus, *Adv. Haer.* i.25.1; i.26.1; i.30.12-13. The *Gospel of Philip* applies the cry of dereliction solely to the earthly event, not to any heavenly analogy: "He uttered these words on the cross, for he [the divine Saviour] had departed from that place" (68.27-28).

192. As Irenaeus notes, *Adv. Haer.* iii.11.7. Mark was used in support of a christology in which "Jesus was not the Christ but only the temporary instrument of the Christ" (Douglas Farrow, "St. Irenaeus of Lyons: The Church and the World," *Pro Ecclesia* 4 [1995], pp. 333-55; p. 337).

193. Irenaeus, *Adv. Haer.* i.8.4 (cf. i.7.1); Lk. 2.25-35.

194. Irenaeus, *Adv. Haer.* i.8.4 (cf. i.7.1); Lk. 2.36-38.

195. Irenaeus, *Adv. Haer.* i.3.1-2; Lk. 2.42, 3.23.

196. Irenaeus, *Adv. Haer.* i.8.3; Lk. 9.57-62. Here, ἀκολουθήσω σοι is understood as an incredulous question.

terminology is based on Paul,[197] but the corresponding typology of responses to Jesus is Lukan. In the Parable of the Leaven, the woman is Achamoth, the three measures of meal again represent the three classes of humans, and the leaven itself is the Saviour.[198] Achamoth is the lost sheep wandering in the desolate realms outside the *Plērōma;* she is also the lost coin, and the woman who searches for her is her mother, the Sophia of the *Plērōma.*[199]

(4) *John.* Johannine material is almost absent from Irenaeus's sampling of Valentinian gospel exegesis, with the highly significant exception of a lengthy excerpt in which an attempt is made to harmonize the Johannine prologue with the Valentinian Ogdoad.[200] "In the Beginning was the Word": according to Irenaeus's Valentinian exegete, we learn here that the aeon known as *Logos* derives its being from *Archē,* the aeon otherwise known as *Nous* (or *Monogenēs*).[201] *Nous* belongs to the first Tetrad along with his spouse *Alētheia* and their progenitors *Buthos* (or *Proarchē*) and *Sigē* (or *Charis*). It is already notable that either the original or the supplementary names echo Johannine terminology. They have been incorporated into this account of the genesis of the aeons precisely so as to establish a secondary connection with the fourth gospel.

"All things were made by him": that is, the *Plērōma* derives from *Logos.* But *"in* him is Life, *Zōē."* This pairing of *Logos* and *Zōē* provides Johannine support for the masculine-feminine conjunctions that characterize the entire *Plērōma* and that are so important for Valentinian Christianity as a whole. Other versions of the *Plērōma* are less concerned about gender balance or assimilation to John.

"The Life was the light of humans": here the Valentinian author finds a reference to the fourth and final conjunction within the Ogdoad, between *Anthrōpos* and *Ekklēsia;* the feminine partner is said to be implied in the Johannine plural. Thus the secondary Tetrad that completes the Ogdoad consists in *Logos* and *Zōē, Anthrōpos* and *Ekklēsia.* So far, this secondary Tetrad has been more fully attested in the Johannine text than the primary one, of which only *Archē (Monogenēs)* has been mentioned. But then we read that the glory of the enfleshed *Logos* was "glory as of *Monogenēs* from the Father,

---

197. Irenaeus, *Adv. Haer.* i.8.3; 1 Cor. 15.48 (ὁ χοϊκός); 2.14, 15 (ψυκικὸς ἄνθρωπος, ὁ πνευματικός).

198. Irenaeus, *Adv. Haer.* i.8.3; Lk. 13.20-21.

199. Irenaeus, *Adv. Haer.* i.8.4; Lk. 15.3-10.

200. Irenaeus, *Adv. Haer.* i.8.5; Jn. 1.1-5, 14.

201. Irenaeus, *Adv. Haer.* i.1.1.

full of *Charis* and *Alētheia.*" Since the Saviour is the fruit of the entire *Plērōma,* whose fullness dwells bodily within him, it is fitting that in his human manifestation he is here associated with the primary Tetrad. In sum, a careful reading of the opening of John's gospel confirms the structure and nomenclature of the Ogdoad:

> Accurately, then, he refers to the first Tetrad, the Father and *Charis, Monogenēs* and *Alētheia.* And so John has identified the primary Ogdoad, the Mother of the whole system of Aeons: for he has identified the Father and *Charis,* and *Monogenēs* and *Alētheia,* and *Logos* and *Zōē,* and *Anthrōpos* and *Ekklēsia.* (Or so Ptolemaeus claims.)[202]

Here as elsewhere in these Valentinian exegeses, there are clear indications of secondary assimilations to the gospel texts, a willingness to modify an earlier account of the *Plērōma,* the passion of Sophia, or the character of the Demiurge in order to be able to demonstrate a scriptural basis. This procedure reflects a growing recognition of the status of the gospels as scripture, a recognition in which the Valentinian "pneumatics" participate along with those they disparage or patronize as the "psychics." Also evident here is a logical sequence within the four-gospel collection. As we have seen, a certain interpretation of Mark is foundational to the Valentinian theology: the divine Saviour or Christ descends upon the human Jesus at his baptism and returns to heaven at his crucifixion. In contrast, the Johannine material represents a late development within the superstructure of this theology. Evidence for this may be seen in the Valentinian claim that Jesus suffered in the twelfth month of his ministry, thereby signifying the passion of the twelfth aeon. To Irenaeus's puzzlement, his opponents appeal to the scriptural reference to "the acceptable year of the Lord" (Lk. 4.19, citing Is. 61.2), while overlooking the clear Johannine evidence that, during his ministry, Jesus visited Jerusalem for *three* celebrations of the passover.[203] The explanation is obvi-

---

202. Irenaeus, *Adv. Haer.* i.8.5. The concluding reference to Ptolemaeus is found in the Latin only, and may be a gloss (so Dunderberg, "School of Valentinus," p. 77n).

203. Irenaeus, *Adv. Haer.* ii.22.1-6. On the basis of Jn. 8.57, Irenaeus here argues that Jesus died in his forties, presumably after a ministry of around fifteen years. A one-year ministry is presupposed in information provided by Clement about the followers of Basilides, who dated Jesus' baptism and passion a year apart (*Strom.* i.21.145.1.1–146.4). Unlike Irenaeus, Clement does not criticize this claim. As W. A. Löhr notes, this implies a Lukan orientation with no awareness of the Johannine chronology (*Basilides und seine Schule,* WUNT [Tübingen: Mohr-Siebeck, 1996], pp. 45-46). Mark Edwards's claim that Eusebius attributes to Basilides a commentary on John in twenty-four books is incorrect (*Catholicity and Heresy,* p. 20). What Eusebius actually says is that

ously that an established Lukan model of a one-year ministry remains in place because the fourth gospel as a whole has yet to make its full impact — in spite of growing interest especially in its prologue. As we have seen, the chronological divergence is still regarded as a major problem by Gaius of Rome.[204]

In this Valentinian christology, the foundational role of the baptism is clear. This is the moment at which the earthly Jesus is united with the heavenly Christ (Mark) and the Word becomes flesh (John).[205] When the Matthean and Lukan birth stories are incorporated into this account, they are understood to refer to the beginning of the human life of the creator's son:

> There are some who claim that [the Demiurge] produced Christ as his own son, but with a psychic nature [ἀλλὰ καὶ ψυχικόν]. He it was who was spoken of through the prophets, and who passed through Mary like water through a pipe. At the baptism there descended upon him that Saviour who was from the *Plērōma* and from all its members, in the form of a dove, bearing within him the pneumatic seed of Achamoth. They claim then that our Lord combined these four elements, preserving the type of the original and primary Tetrad: the pneumatic from Achamoth, the psychic from the Demiurge, the economic constructed with indescribable skill [ἐκ τῆς οἰκονομίας ὃ ἦν κατασκευασμένον ἀρρήτῳ τέχνῃ], and the Saviour who descended onto him as a dove and who remained without suffering [ἀπαθῆ] — for it was not possible for him to suffer, being ungraspable [ἀκράτητον] and invisible. And so the Spirit of Christ who had come upon him was removed when he was led before Pilate.[206]

In this Valentinian christology much is conceded to the psychic majority and to their reading of the gospels. Jesus is indeed the Messiah predicted by the prophets. The "indescribable skill" with which the creator "constructed" a body for his Messiah is acknowledged, a further sign that this creator deity is a being of real power and wisdom in spite of his defective

---

Basilides wrote twenty-four books εἰς τὸ εὐαγγέλιον (*HE* iv.7.7). Johannine traits in the Basilidean system criticized by Hippolytus (summarized in *Catholicity and Heresy*, pp. 21-23) probably stem from the later Basilidean tradition.

204. Epiphanius, *Pan.* li.22.1.

205. Thus Heracleon draws from Jn. 1.29 a distinction between the earthly Jesus and the heavenly Christ: the "lamb of God" refers to the body, whereas "who takes away the sin of the world" refers to the one who was in that body (Origen, *In Ioan.* vi.38.306).

206. Irenaeus, *Adv. Haer.* i.7.2.

self-understanding. The psychics are also right to accept the testimony of Matthew and Luke that the creator's Christ was born of the Virgin Mary. What they fail to understand is the descent and reascent of the dove-like Spirit, the Saviour who communicates the innermost secrets of the *Plērōma* through the words of Jesus. They learn from the gospels the outward course of Jesus' life, but they lack all perception of the higher mysteries revealed in and through that life.

The Valentinian theology appeals to the same four gospels as Irenaeus but coordinates them differently. Here, the descent of the dove-like Spirit heralds the revelation of the unknown Father who transcends the well-known deity of Jewish scripture. This event is the common starting point of all four gospels; the birth stories of Matthew and Luke should be seen as a prelude to the real story, for the unique creative act of which they speak generates not the Saviour himself but only his human bearer or vehicle. Through the descent of the Spirit, the teaching and career of Jesus are shaped into a complex parable of the *Plērōma,* the unknown world of the Father which is the home of the true Christian.

Irenaeus does not oppose this theology by arguing that the gospel is fourfold, as this is common ground between the two sides. His argument for a fourfold gospel is illustrated with examples of heretical appeal to a single gospel or to additional gospels, but his main concern is to achieve ecumenical consensus by securing Western recognition of the gospel from Asia. There is no direct link between the fourfold gospel and opposition to heresy. The debate with heresy is focused not on the contents of the church's gospel but on its interpretation — more specifically, on the coordination of gospel beginnings. In its emphasis on the descent of the Spirit, the Valentinian theology subordinates Matthew and Luke to Mark and John. Irenaeus achieves a quite different outcome by the simple expedient of aligning John with Matthew and Luke rather than with Mark. The Word becomes flesh not in the descent of the Spirit but in the miraculous conception. As a result, the human and the divine in Jesus no longer have fundamentally different origins, the one proceeding from the creator through Mary, the other from the *Plērōma.* Jesus is no longer the *bearer* of the Christ, or the Son, or the Word. Rather, he *is* the Christ, the Son, and the Word-made-flesh. The protagonist of the gospel narrative is singular, not doubled; there is no shadowy deity assuming temporary possession of the humanity. Just as there is no *Plērōma* above and beyond the creator of heaven and earth, so there is no Saviour above and beyond the human Jesus, the Messiah of Israel. Irenaeus underlines this point in connection with each gospel in turn.

(1) *Matthew.* In various ways, the opening chapters of Matthew are said to confirm that the God revealed in the gospel is one and the same as the God attested by the law and the prophets. This oneness and self-identity of God entail a corresponding oneness and self-identity of Jesus, as the Matthean baptism account makes clear:

> Matthew has this to say about the baptism: "The heavens were opened to him, and he saw the Spirit of God, like a dove, coming upon him. And behold, a voice from heaven, saying: 'This is my beloved Son, in whom I am well-pleased.'" For Christ did not then descend onto Jesus, nor was there one who was Christ, another who was Jesus; but the Word of God — who is the Saviour of all and ruler of heaven and earth, who is Jesus (as we demonstrated earlier), who both took flesh and was anointed by the Spirit from the Father — became Jesus Christ.[207]

According to Irenaeus, the divine voice acclaims Jesus, rather than the dove-like Spirit or a Christ who is other than Jesus. In focusing on the dove, the Valentinians have missed the point of this trinitarian story, which is precisely that a human (*this* human) is acknowledged by God as the beloved Son. This is so because of an event prior to the anointing with the Spirit, the Word's assumption of flesh at the moment of Jesus' conception. The Matthean story evokes Johannine echoes, and as a result the distinctive being of the Spirit as well as the Son is maintained.

Matthew maintains that the beloved son is identical to the man Jesus of Nazareth, with whose human genealogy his gospel opens. Here it is not difficult for Irenaeus to find the corresponding evangelist's symbol from among the "four-faced cherubim" of Revelation 4.6-8, whose faces are images or reflections of Christ's saving activity. Matthew's is the "anthropomorphic" gospel, the gospel with a human face.[208]

(2) *Mark.* This gospel actually opens not with Jesus' baptism but with the prophetic announcement of the coming of John the Baptist to "prepare the way of the Lord" (Mk. 1.1-3). There is no indication that the Lord's being

---

207. Irenaeus, *Adv. Haer.* iii.9.3. The cited passage is Mt. 3.16-17, lacking the expected *descendentem* before *quasi columbam.* The reference to an earlier demonstration that the Word is Jesus is to *Adv. Haer.* i.9.2-3.

208. Irenaeus, *Adv. Haer.* iii.11.8. While Irenaeus describes the "cherubim" collectively as τετραπρόσωπα, he follows Revelation rather than Ezekiel in assigning one face to each creature: compare Ez. 1.6, τέσσαρα πρόσωπα τῷ ἑνί. The reference to cherubim is derived from Ps. 79.2(1): ὁ καθήμενος ἐπὶ τῶν χερουβίμ, ἐμφάνηθι (cited *Adv. Haer.* iii.11.8).

is subject to an ontological gulf between an earthly Jesus and a heavenly Christ:

> As for those who separate Jesus from Christ, and claim that Christ remained impassible whereas Jesus suffered, preferring the Gospel according to Mark, their error can be corrected if they read it with a love of truth.[209]

If this gospel is read *without* this love of truth, that is, in the light of the Valentinian theology, it will seem to contain a cacophony of voices: for, between the advent and the departure of the Saviour from above, Jesus is variously the mouthpiece either of the Saviour, or of the mother (Achamoth), or of the creator.[210] Thus the identity of the protagonist will be constantly shifting, and he will be Jesus only in name. In contrast, the lover of truth will understand that the protagonist of this text is singular and self-identical, and that the quest for mysterious presences behind and above his self-manifestation is perverse.

Mark's opening Isaiah citation suggests to Irenaeus the image of the prophetic Spirit descending from on high — like the fourth living creature, which resembled a flying eagle.[211] Formally, these correspondences between earthly and heavenly entities bear some resemblance to the Valentinian hermeneutics that Irenaeus opposes. Yet the relation of symbol to reality is reversed here. For the Valentinian, the fourfold gospel might be seen as an image of the primary Tetrad, in which the supreme heights of the divine world are occupied by the aeons Depth and Silence, Only-begotten and Truth. In Irenaeus, it is the heavenly creatures who symbolize both the earthly mission of the Son of God, seen from various perspectives, and the humanly authored gospels that bear witness to it.

(3) *Luke.* The opening chapters of the Gospel of Luke again provide abundant material for Irenaeus's demonstration of the divine unity. According to Luke,

> the angel of the Lord appeared to shepherds, announcing joy to them "because there is born in the house of David a Saviour who is Christ the Lord." Then there appeared a multitude of the heavenly host, praising God and saying, "Glory to God in the highest, and on earth peace to peo-

---

209. Irenaeus, *Adv. Haer.* iii.11.7.
210. Irenaeus, *Adv. Haer.* i.7.3.
211. Irenaeus, *Adv. Haer.* iii.11.8.

ple of good will." The gnostic falsifiers claim that these angels came from the Ogdoad and disclosed the descent of the Christ from above. But they fall into further error when they say that he who was from above, Christ or the Saviour, was not born at all, but that after the baptism of the Jesus of the economy [*de dispositione*] he descended upon him as a dove. And so, on these people's view, the angels of the Ogdoad are lying when they say, "To you is born this day a Saviour who is Christ the Lord, in the city of David." For neither Christ nor the Saviour was born then, on their view, but rather the Jesus of the economy who is of the creator of the world, on whom they say that the Saviour from above descended after the baptism — that is, thirty years later.[212]

Again, Irenaeus contends against the same misreading of the gospel story — a misreading that is nevertheless compelling enough to make its own kind of sense of the entire fourfold gospel. On Valentinian premises, one might expect that the angels of the nativity would represent a lower Ogdoad, acclaiming the birth of the creator's Christ. Yet it seems that angelic representatives of the supreme Ogdoad are somehow present in the skies over Bethlehem, acclaiming the Saviour's birth — or rather the birth of the creator's Christ, upon whom the true Christ or Saviour was destined to descend thirty years later. This passage illustrates the difficulties that Valentinian hermeneutics faced in accommodating a soteriology focused on the baptism to the birth narratives of post-Markan gospels. It also illustrates again Irenaeus's acute sensitivity to the danger of distinguishing Jesus from Christ, reading a divided subject into the gospel narrative. From his perspective, the birth narratives confirm that the descent of the Spirit is not in itself the fundamental saving event. Jesus' being as Christ and Saviour embraces his entire life from beginning to end. He himself is Christ and Saviour, and he is never anything other than that.

Luke's identification with the calf-like figure of Revelation is the only one of Irenaeus's correspondences to survive in both the influential later versions of this scheme developed by Jerome and Augustine. In itself, the correspondence seems unimpressive: the calf is a sacrificial animal, the Lukan narrative opens with a priest offering incense, and this is therefore a priestly gospel.[213] Yet, for those familiar with the scheme in any of its versions, the four heavenly symbols effectively communicate the legitimacy of the four

---

212. Irenaeus, *Adv. Haer.* iii.10.3, citing Lk. 2.10-14.
213. Irenaeus, *Adv. Haer.* iii.11.8.

canonical gospels irrespective of the grounds on which particular symbols are assigned. They achieve their impact by rhetorical rather than rational means, and their rhetoric is that of the image.[214]

(4) *John*. Valentinian theology is characterized by its distinctions — between the Father and the creator, between the Christ from above and the human Jesus. According to Irenaeus, John wrote his gospel precisely to counter these doctrines, already popularized by Cerinthus.[215] That is why he states that "all things were made through him" (Jn. 1.3):

> In "all things" is included this creation of ours [*haec, quae secundum nos est, conditio*]. For it cannot be granted to them that "all things" refers to the contents of their Pleroma.[216]

If there is any remaining doubt about this, John finally dispels it when he states that "he was in the world, and the world was made through him, and the world knew him not," and that "he came to his own, and his own received him not" (Jn. 1.10, 11). For Marcion and the Gnostics, these statements are simply untrue; for Valentinians, they require yet another distinction, between the Demiurge who actually made the world, and the Saviour, who converted Achamoth's passion into unorganized material for the Demiurge's use.[217] Valentinian exegesis requires a maximalist reading of the Johannine prologue, exploiting every possibility of a distinction so as to populate this text with the aeons and their offspring. Irenaeus offers a minimalist reading in which the creative and incarnate Logos, the Only-begotten, the Son, and the Christ are identical to Jesus.[218] He strives to convince his opponents and his readers

---

214. In dismissing them as "theosophische Spielereien," Harnack merely discloses his own rationalistic prejudices (*Das Neue Testament um das Jahr 200*, p. 45).

215. Irenaeus, *Adv. Haer.* iii.11.1; on Cerinthus, see *Adv. Haer.* i.26.1; on Cerinthus and John, *Adv. Haer.* iii.3.4.

216. Irenaeus, *Adv. Haer.* iii.11.1. In Heracleon's more straightforward interpretation of Jn. 1.3, however, the *Plērōma* is excluded from "all things"; the text speaks of the *Logos* as causing the Demiurge to make the world (Origen, *In Ioan.* ii.8). For this Valentinian exegete, the Johannine prologue does *not* disclose the structure of the *Plērōma*. It is possible that, as Hill suggests, Heracleon's commentary shows an awareness of Irenaeus's refutation of the earlier Valentinian interpretation of the Johannine prologue (*Johannine Corpus*, p. 209).

217. Irenaeus, *Adv. Haer.* iii.11.2; i.4.5.

218. For Irenaeus "Jesus is the Logos and the Logos is Jesus," so that there can be "no other Word before him or behind him or above him" (Farrow, "St. Irenaeus," p. 340). In twentieth-century theology this christological point has been restated especially by Karl Barth and Hans Frei.

that Jesus, who suffered for us and who dwelt among us, is himself the Word of God. For if any other of the aeons had become flesh for our salvation, the Apostle would surely have said so. But if the Word of the Father who descended is the same as the one who ascended, that is, the only-begotten Son of the only God who by the will of the Father became flesh for humans, then he [John] did not refer to any other nor to an Ogdoad, but to the Lord Jesus Christ. On their view, however, the Word did not actually "become flesh." They claim that the Saviour was clothed with a psychic body [σῶμα ψυχικόν], prepared with indescribable care for the purpose of the economy so as to be visible and palpable. But "flesh" is what was originally formed from dust by God for Adam, which, as John asserts, the Word of God truly became. And so their first and primal Ogdoad disappears. For since "Word," "Only-begotten," "Life," "Light," "Saviour," "Christ," "Son of God," and "he who became flesh for us" have been shown to refer to one and the same person, the structure of the Ogdoad is destroyed.[219]

In its double emphasis on the creative and incarnate Word, the Johannine prologue is Irenaeus's most effective anti-Valentinian weapon.[220] No other gospel opening seems to him to confront the main heretical errors as directly as this one. In its explicit and implicit backward references to Genesis 1–2, this passage can be viewed as the hermeneutical key to the fourfold gospel as a whole.[221] If the Word made flesh is the one through whom heaven and earth were created in the beginning, and through whom flesh itself was moulded out of dust (cf. Gn. 2.4-7, 23-24), then there is no ontological space available for any *Plērōma*. It is in their differing construals of the relation between John and Genesis that the opposed readings of the fourfold gospel part company.

While Irenaeus may seem to approximate to a "literal" reading of the Johannine prologue, and thus to have the advantage over his opponents, there is one crucial point that he fails to discuss. Within the prologue itself and the subsequent narrative, attention is focused on the testimony of John (Jn. 1.6-8, 15-36), which in its most concrete form consists in a testimony to the descent of the dove-like Spirit (1.32-33). If Mark's baptism story can be read as

---

219. Irenaeus, *Adv. Haer.* i.9.3.

220. The close connection between Irenaeus's "rule of truth" and the Johannine prologue is noted by Elaine Pagels ("Irenaeus, 'the Canon of Truth,' and the *Gospel of John*," pp. 361-67).

221. See Thomas Holsinger-Friesen, *Irenaeus and Genesis: A Study of Competition in Early Christian Hermeneutics*, JTISupp (Winona Lake, IN: Eisenbrauns, 2009).

narrating the descent of the divine Christ upon the human Jesus, the same is true of the more elaborate Johannine account. If we ask *when* and *where* the Word became flesh, it is not self-evident that the Fourth Evangelist directs us to unnarrated events in Nazareth or Bethlehem rather than to the descent of the Spirit at the river Jordan.[222] The Johannine prologue will only yield the desired theological outcome if it is detached from Mark and reread in the light of the Matthean and Lukan birth stories, in such a way that the Word's becoming-flesh is seen to encompass the whole of Jesus' human life rather than merely being the defining event within that life.

The crucial link with Matthew and Luke is found in John 1.13, where Irenaeus discovers a reference to the virginal conception tradition. While Greek manuscripts take this to refer to "the children of God" (cf. v. 12), there is Latin evidence for the singular reading, ". . . who believe in the name of him who was born [*in nomine eius, qui . . . natus est*] not of bloods nor of the will of the flesh nor of the will of a man but of God."[223] Irenaeus alludes to this passage in christological contexts where the birth of Jesus is at issue. In Matthew's citation of Isaiah 7.14, it is said both that a virgin shall bear a child and that his name will be Emmanuel, God with us (Mt. 1.23). Scripture speaks in this way,

> lest perhaps we should regard him as merely human (for not by the will of the flesh nor by the will of a man but by the will of God was the Word made flesh), and that we should not imagine that Jesus was one and Christ another but know them to be one and the same.[224]

The singular reading of John 1.13 ties the Johannine prologue firmly to Matthew and Luke, while detaching it from Mark and from the christo-

---

222. Thus A. Loisy could plausibly argue that the Johannine incarnation takes place at Jesus' baptism, when "l'union permanente de l'esprit divin à l'humanité de Jésus fait le Christ et constitue sa filiation divine" (*Le Quatrième Évangile* [Paris: Picard, 1903], p. 230). At the baptism there occurred "l'adoption de cette humanité par la personne divine du Verbe" (p. 232). See also R. H. Fuller, "Christmas, Epiphany, and the Johannine Prologue," in *Spirit and Light: Essays in Historlcal Theology,* ed. M. L. Engle and W. B. Green (New York: Seabury Press, 1976), pp. 63-73; F. Watson, "Is John's Christology Adoptionist?" in *The Glory of Christ in the New Testament: Studies in Christology in Memory of George Bradford Caird,* ed. L. D. Hurst and N. T. Wright (Oxford: Clarendon Press, 1987), pp. 113-24.

223. See Tertullian, *De Carne Christi* xix, where this reading is defended and expounded in detail.

224. Irenaeus, *Adv. Haer.* iii.16.2; cf. the further allusions to Jn. 1.13 in *Adv. Haer.* iii.19.2; v.1.3. The verb "was born" (*natus est*) is found only in the second of the three passages.

logical dualism that appeals to Mark. This is another of the fundamental hermeneutical moves that ensure that Irenaeus's readers will construe the fourfold gospel quite differently from the Valentinians.

In Irenaeus's allocation of evangelists' symbols, John is identified with the lion-like creature rather than the eagle in flight, as in the later versions.[225] As with Mark's eagle and Luke's calf, the allocation is fairly arbitrary. Yet the four heavenly creatures as a group provide Irenaeus with exactly what he needs, a vivid and memorable image of fourfoldness. This is an image which highlights the differences between the gospels while retaining their common orientation to the Lord who sits enthroned among the cherubim, manifesting himself in and through their divergent forms. The prestige of the heavenly symbolism furthers the ongoing process in which four gospels are singled out from the mass of early Christian gospel literature. Yet Irenaeus does not use this symbolism primarily to exclude, but rather to propose a consensus that will accommodate the traditions of both West and East, especially Rome and Asia. While the fourfold gospel in itself provides no defence against Valentinian and related heresies, a consensus encompassing not just the texts but also the principles of their interpretation might prove more effective. Everything stands or falls with the way in which gospel beginnings are coordinated. Is the saving event attested in the fourfold gospel to be identified with Jesus' human existence in its entirety? Or should we envisage a purely divine Saviour who simply *uses* that humanity as a vehicle of occasional revelations, as and when required?

---

225. Irenaeus, *Adv. Haer.* iii.11.8.

CHAPTER 10

Origen: Canonical Hermeneutics

Traditions about Jesus — his sayings, his deeds, his controversies, his sufferings — were shaped and formed within the communities founded by his first followers. As we saw in the model of the reception process developed in Chapter 7, Jesus himself is the original datum or given, the object of the recollection that gives rise to tradition, further articulated in inscription and in the interpretation and reinterpretation that ensue. In its written forms, tradition is subject both to rewriting and to reoralization. The relation of the spoken to the written word is a circular and interactive one, and any antagonism between the deadness or fixity of the letter and the freedom of purely oral transmission is alien to it. Where such an antagonism is read into the world of the first Christians, this is the projection of neuroses from a later era. The dynamic of tradition lies precisely in this interaction of speech and writing, as speech becomes writing and writing reverts to speech when publicly read and opened up in preaching and teaching. As reception, the dynamic of tradition is not self-generated but arises from its object who is also a subject constantly present to it. As the prologue to the *Gospel of Thomas* puts it, this subject is "the living Jesus" (᾽Ιη[σου]ς ὁ ζῶν, ĪC ЄΤΟΝϨ). There is no place here for anxiety about an ever-increasing temporal distance from the datum, or nostalgia for an unrepeatable moment of pure gift. The gift once given and received continues to be given and received; the Jesus who once spoke to his disciples speaks still in what was once spoken. This possibility is enshrined in the writing in which the original speech-act is preserved and elucidated, and in the new speech-acts this writing continues to generate.

In Irenaeus and his successors there occurs the new development in the reception process which we have called *normativization*. At this point a division is created across the textual field of gospel writing. The anonymous, undifferentiated texts that constitute "the gospel" acquire names and distinct identities. While the Lord can still be said to speak "in the gospel," there is a dawning awareness that this "gospel" must have a *form* and that this form must be fourfold. It is determined that the living Jesus is to be received in and through four specified texts and no others. The circle drawn around the selected four is also a dividing line severing the intertextual links that previously bound all early gospels together. The rejected are consigned — in principle if not always in practice — to outer darkness and oblivion. In the case of the four, however, intertextual links are not only recognized but also actively shaped. The four must be appropriately coordinated with one another; it is this concern that explains the preoccupation with gospel beginnings. Simply marking them off from the others does not in itself achieve the intended stabilization of the gospel tradition. If the Logos who was in the beginning is associated primarily with the Spirit who descended at Jesus' baptism, the outcome will be a quite different construal of the gospel narrative from one in which the Logos is Mary's child. The difference is an expression of incompatible worldviews and theologies, and cannot be allowed to stand. And so (as we have seen) the Matthean and Lukan beginning is given priority over the Markan one as the key to the Johannine prologue, where the beginning of all beginnings is recounted. It is this fundamental interpretative move that establishes the canonical norm, in and alongside the selection of the four. The fourfold gospel is immediately the object of interpretation, and is made to articulate a theology not present in any one gospel apart from the others — a theology concerned with the correct identification of the protagonist of the gospel narrative. The exclusion of the alternative coordination of gospel beginnings is just as fundamental as the exclusion of the newly noncanonical texts.

Normativization creates its canonical image of the protagonist by way of a double act of severance, from texts deemed unreliable and from interpretations deemed untrue. These gestures of rejection are not ethically neutral; they entail a claim to power of some over others. Yet that is the case at every point in the reception process. In the beginning certain elite individuals play a privileged role in the shaping of recollection into tradition. While many others may also have cherished memories of Jesus, theirs are not selected for communal use. Next, inscription divides the sphere of tradition by creating a distinction between the written and the unwritten: Jesus was remembered to have done many things that might have been written but were not (cf. Jn. 20.30), and it is the writers' choices that determine which traditions — and *whose* — will come to embody the tradition as a whole as the unwritten gradually decays. Where texts are subjected to interpretation, other potential interpretations are excluded; *re*interpretation likewise is always also *counter*interpretation. There is, then, nothing unique or uniquely problematic about the selection of four gospels to the exclusion of all others. Acts of selection and rejection have occurred all down the line, and are themselves in turn the objects of selection and rejection. An item of tradition may be inscribed, interpreted, and reinterpreted, but the texts in which these processes occur may in due course be passed over in favour of other texts where other traditions are preserved and interpreted. In the abstract these acts of selection and exclusion are all claims to power, but at no point is power exercised in such a way as to reduce reception to passive submission. In itself, the claim that there are no more and no fewer than four legitimate gospels is simply a proposal which may or may not be accepted, not an infallible decree binding on all the faithful by virtue of some supremely authoritative source. Peter himself knows nothing of a fourfold gospel, and is associated with rival gospels that eventually fall on either side of the canonical boundary. Whatever binding and loosing takes place here is the collective work of the extended community.

In the West a focus on the literary form of the gospel is first attested by Irenaeus, who is concerned that the Johannine gospel be fully recognized and rightly coordinated with the others. In the East, a decade or so later, Clement of Alexandria knows that just four gospels are endorsed by tradition but still betrays the influence of the older view that the Lord's words are preserved in a wider and undefined range of texts which together constitute "the gospel." In one context, the point is that there are no fewer than four gospels; in the other, that there are no more than four. But *why* no more than four, when sayings or narratives preserved in other texts are valued by the likes of Clement and cautiously endorsed even by the impeccably orthodox bishop Serapion of Antioch? The answer, implied in Eusebius, is that an ecumenical consensus gradually forms around these four texts as they become familiar through extended usage. As ever, some texts but not others circulate widely and establish themselves in communal usage, in consequence of the collective judgements of their readers together with chance factors such as availability and patronage. That is the social reality underlying normativization.

The question, *why four?* receives a different kind of answer from a key figure who has so far featured little in the discussion: Origen. In the first of a series of homilies on the Gospel of Luke, preached probably in Caesarea in the late 230s or early 240s, Origen comments as follows on Luke 1.1, where the evangelist refers to the "many" who have "attempted" to compose an account of what has taken place:

> Just as, among the people of old, "many" claimed to prophesy, yet some of them were false prophets while others were true, and the people possessed the gift of discernment of spirits [χάρισμα . . . διάκρισις πνευμάτων] by which the true prophet was distinguished from the false; so now, in the new covenant, "many" wished to write gospels, but the "experienced money changers" did not approve them all but selected some of them [τινα αὐτῶν ἐξελέξαντο]. The word "attempted" seems to imply an accusation against those who undertook the writing of gospels without a gift [χωρὶς χαρίσματος]. For Matthew did not merely "attempt" but wrote by the Holy Spirit, and so too Mark and John and likewise Luke. But as for the ones entitled *Gospel according to the Egyptians* or *Gospel of the Twelve*, their authors indeed "attempted." Basilides too presumed to write a *Gospel according to Basilides*. Indeed, there were "many" who "attempted." For there is a *Gospel according to Thomas* in circulation, and another *according to Matthias,* and many others. These are the work of those who "attempted." But the church of God selected [προκρίνει] only the four.[1]

In this parallel between the false and true prophets of the old covenant and the false and true evangelists of the new, it is said that the Pauline *charisma* of discernment or differentiation of spirits made it possible for the people of Israel to distinguish true prophecy from false (cf. 1 Cor. 12.10). Jerome's Latin translation cites Hananiah, Jeremiah's opponent, as an example of a false prophet (cf. Jer. 35.1 LXX [28.1]).[2] Nine of the ten Septuagintal occurrences of the term ψευδοπροφήτης are found in Jeremiah, where it renders

---

1. Origen, *In Lucam, Homilia i,* Greek and Latin texts in GCS, Origenes Werke IX, *Die Homilien zu Lukas in der Übersetzung des Hieronymus und die griechischen Reste der Homilien und des Lukas-Kommentars,* ed. Max Rauer (Berlin: Akademie-Verlag, 1959²), pp. 3-4; Eng. trans. (of Latin text and commentary fragments only), FC 94 (Washington, D.C.: Catholic University of America Press, 1996). In the passage cited, as elsewhere, the Greek text is shorter than the Latin. Since the Greek fragments are preserved only in later commentaries or catenas (see Rauer, pp. xxxiv-lx), some of these may have been abbreviated. In other cases it is more likely that Jerome's translation has elaborated the original. As Ronald E. Heine notes, "Origen's thought could be altered by rewriting in Greek, even while using some of his own words, as well as by translating his Greek into Latin" ("Can the Catena Fragments of Origen's Commentary on John be Trusted?" *VC* 40 [1986], pp. 118-34; p. 131).

2. . . . *et quidam erant pseudoprophetae — e quibus unus fuit Ananias filius Azor —, alii vero veri prophetae . . .* (Rauer, *Die Homilien zu Lukas,* p. 3).

the Hebrew נביא in contexts where prophets are aligned with priests among Jeremiah's opponents; Hananiah is the only individual so designated.[3] Whether or not the reference to Hananiah goes back to Origen, the point is that the difference between true and false prophecy does eventually come to light. A divine gift of discernment was at work in the historical process that led to the inclusion of some texts and the exclusion of others: the scriptures of the old covenant contain a book of the prophet Jeremiah, but no such book is attributed to Hananiah. It is the same within the new covenant, where the gift of discernment is exercised by "experienced money changers" (οἱ δόκιμοι τραπεζῖται) who know the difference between genuine and counterfeit coins. The allusion is to an unattributed "scripture," also cited by Clement in the form: "Be experienced money changers, rejecting some things but retaining the good."[4] Clement applies the saying to the art of dialectic; Origen, to the formation of the fourfold gospel, here presented as a selection from a much larger body of writings that look very similar to the inexperienced eye. While the divine gift of discernment of spirits is surely operative here as it was under the old covenant, the emphasis now falls on the communal wisdom that differentiates the true image of Jesus from the false. The "experienced money changers" are those early readers of gospel literature who weighed and tested the gospels attributed to Matthew and Matthias, Mark and Thomas, Luke and the Twelve, John and the Egyptians, and found that some were genuine while others were not. They therefore *selected* the four gospels they regarded as genuine, rejecting the others. The four gospels did not simply impose themselves on the Christian community, marginalizing all other gospel literature by their sheer presence. Early gospels looked broadly similar, sharing many of the same generic conventions. There was no prior reason to suppose that some would be counterfeits, that precisely four would prove genuine, and that a gospel attributed to Matthew would be included in that number whereas one attributed to Thomas would not. Informed critical reading of all early Christian gospels was required, and it was informed readers who *chose* the texts that would henceforth be normative, just as their predecessors in ancient Israel chose Jeremiah at the expense of Hananiah.

3. Plural: Jer. 6.13; 33(26).7, 8, 11, 16; 34(27).9; 36(29).1, 8; Zec. 13.2. Singular (Hananiah): Jer. 35(28).1.

4. Clement of Alexandria, *Strom.* i.28.177: Γίνεσθε δὲ δόκιμοι τραπεζῖται, τὰ μὲν ἀποδοκιμάζοντες, τὸ δὲ καλὸν κατέχοντες. In the *Clementine Homilies*, this saying without the interpretative gloss is attributed to Jesus and applied to a distinction between true and false within scripture itself (ii.51; xviii.20). Origen alludes to the saying in his homilies on Leviticus (iii.6) and Ezekiel (ii.4), and presents it as a command of Jesus in his commentary on John (xix.2.44).

By what criteria was this differentiation between genuine and counterfeit gospels established? For Jerome, Origen's Latin translator, the answer is clear. Counterfeit gospels are heretical, genuine ones are orthodox. In Jerome's translation, the listing of noncanonical gospels known to Origen is introduced with the claim that "the church has four gospels, heresy many."[5] Origen himself does not seem to have raised the issue of heresy here. Noncanonical gospels are not necessarily heretical. Rather, as the Lukan prologue suggests, they are the work of evangelists who "attempted" to write gospels but did not succeed, not because they were tainted with heresy but because they wrote without the leading of the Holy Spirit, χωρὶς χαρίσματος. Canonical gospels are those that are divinely gifted to an evangelist and his readers, being written ἀπὸ πνεύματος ἁγίου. Like the people of Israel, those who created the canonical norm were entrusted with a corresponding χάρισμα of discernment of spirits, enabling them to distinguish ungifted attempts at gospel writing from those given from above. It is through the Holy Spirit that the work of the Holy Spirit is discerned as such. Unlike "heresy," this criterion has no possibility of demonstration. It is more like a *stipulation:* that only the gospels according to Matthew, Mark, Luke, and John are to be regarded as gifted, the authentic and normative mediation of the original gift or datum that is Jesus himself. The search for an explanation and a rationale comes to an end in the sheer empirical fact that "the church of God selected only the four." To be a member of the church of God is to belong to a community to which just four gospels have been given. In selecting four gospels, the church of God also engages in communal self-definition.

There is, then, a limit to what can be said about the rationale of the fourfold gospel. On this point Origen is uncharacteristically terse. He does not know, or is not interested in, the Irenaean appeal to the four cherubim of Ezekiel and Revelation. What matters to him is not the speculative question, *why?* but the pragmatic question, *so what?* Given that there are four acknowledged gospels, how are we to proceed with them? More specifically: how are we to interpret one gospel in a way that takes due account of the other three? How is a gospel to be read in its primary canonical context?

These questions arise for Origen as the author of the first substantially extant gospel commentary, the commentary on John that occupied him for around three decades yet remained incomplete at his death.[6] Nine of its

---

5. *Ecclesia quatuor habet evangelia, haeresis plurima* (Rauer, *Die Homilien zu Lukas,* p. 4).

6. Greek text in A. E. Brooke, *The Commentary of Origen on S. John's Gospel,* 2 vols. (Cambridge: Cambridge University Press, 1896); *Der Johanneskommentar,* Origenes Werke IV, ed.

thirty-two completed books have survived, together with fragments of some of the others.[7] In Books 1, 6, and 10 in particular, Origen demonstrates in a variety of ways that the gospel's fourfold form is of fundamental hermeneutical significance.

Commentary as Pilgrimage

In the preface to Book 32 of his commentary on the Gospel of John, Origen compares the gradual progress of this monumental work with the journeying of the Israelites through the wilderness. Scripture recounts how the Israelites encamped at forty-two different locations during their forty-year pilgrimage (Nm. 33.1-49). In the present book Origen journeys on to his own thirty-second encampment, working through the Johannine account of the foot washing and the conversation that follows (Jn. 13.2-33). He may perhaps have hoped to complete his own pilgrimage through the Gospel of John in forty-two books, accompanied still by his patron Ambrosius who had commissioned this work many years earlier — and who from time to time expressed anxiety about the rate of progress.

> Guided by God through Jesus Christ, let us walk in the great and life-giving way of the gospel, in hope that we may know and traverse it until we reach its end. For the moment, however, let us strive to attain the thirty-second encampment, as it were, in the things that are to be said; and may the pillar of shining cloud that is Jesus be with us, holy brother Ambrosius, leading us on when necessary and halting us when needful, until we have finished dictating our exposition of this gospel — not discouraged by the length of the journey or wearied by our own weakness, but impelled to follow in the tracks of the pillar of truth. But whether it is God's will that we should complete this intellectual journey-by-

---

E. Preuschen, GCS (Leipzig: J. C. Hinrichs, 1903); Eng. trans. Allan Menzies, ANF 10 (repr. Grand Rapids: Eerdmans, 1974), pp. 297-408 (Books 1-10); Ronald E. Heine, FC, 2 vols. (Washington, D.C.: CUA Press, 1989-93). My understanding of Origen's Greek is often at odds with one or both of the available English translations. The referencing system used here is intended to facilitate checking any of these Greek or English editions. The final number refers to the sentence enumeration in Preuschen's edition (followed by Heine), the penultimate number to the second (bracketed) system of section enumeration used by Brooke, Preuschen, and the ANF translation.

7. For a general account of the commentary, see J. A. McGuckin, "Structural Design and Apologetic Intent in Origen's *Commentary on John*," in *Origeniana Sexta: Origène et la Bible/Origen and the Bible*, ed. G. Dorival and A. Le Boulluec, BEThL 118 (Leuven: Peeters, 1995), pp. 441-57.

dictation through the whole text of the Gospel according to John, God alone knows.[8]

The image of the forty-year journey punctuated by numerous encampments suggests that the composition process has been intermittent, with longer or shorter intervals between the various books of the commentary. Allusion is made here to Numbers 9.22: "Whether it was for two days or a month or for a longer time that the cloud remained upon the tabernacle . . . , the children of Israel encamped and did not set forth; but when it was removed they did set forth." On some occasions Origen seems to have proceeded directly from one book to the next.[9] Elsewhere a lengthy preamble marks the resumption of a work that had been set aside for some time.[10] This journey too may yet take forty years if it is completed at all.

In a homily on the forty-two stages of Numbers 33, dating from the same period as later books of the John commentary, Origen applied this passage to the life of the Christian.[11] There is, he tells his hearers, nothing superfluous in Holy Scripture. Even a passage like this one — a bare itinerary consisting of little more than a list of obscure place-names — is there for our spiritual nourishment. When we hear it read in church, we should not long to return to familiar, safe passages in the gospels, epistles, or psalms. Rather, we should be open to receive its unique testimony to our ultimate concern.[12] The forty-two stages in the Israelites' journey from Egypt to the Promised Land correspond to moments in the Christian's ascent from worldly defilement to the divine life.[13] In passing it is noted that, according to the Matthean genealogy, there are also three-times-fourteen or forty-two stages in Christ's descending movement in the opposite direction. His descent enables our ascent — to which, however, he and the Holy Spirit are also present

8. Origen, *In Ioan.* xxxii.1.1-3.

9. This is implied by anticipations of the following book that occur in some of the conclusions. Book 2 closes with the words "Next, the meaning of *so that all might believe in him* must be considered" (Origen, *In Ioan.* ii.30.229, referring to Jn. 1.7b). Similar anticipatory conclusions occur in xiii.64.455, xx.33.422, and xxviii.21.249. A direct continuation from the previous book is implied in xiii.1.1-2.

10. Origen, *In Ioan.* v.1; vi.1.1-12.

11. Latin text in *Homilien zum Hexateuch in Rufins Übersetzung (Die Homilien zu Numeri, Josua, und Judices)*, Origenes Werke VII, ed. W. A. Baehrens, GCS (Leipzig: J. C. Hinrichs, 1921); Eng. trans. in ACT, *Homilies on Numbers*, ed. Thomas P. Scheck (Downers Grove, IL: IVP Academic, 2009).

12. Origen, *Hom. in Num.* xxvii.1.1–2.1.

13. Origen, *Hom. in Num.* xxvii.2.3; 4.1.

in the form of the pillars of fire and cloud.[14] Yet the main interest lies in recovering hints of hidden meaning in each of the place-names. Two of these are already translated by the Septuagint, *Marah* as *Bitterness* and *Kibroth-hattaavah* as *Tombs-of-Desire* (Nm. 33.8, 16). Origen offers translations and brief comments on the remaining forty place-names, using the text to construct an image of the Christian life as an extended pilgrimage through a varied terrain in which every point has its own distinct character, in the form perhaps of a challenge, a failure, or a promise.[15]

Applying the Numbers passage to himself and his John commentary, Origen is no doubt conscious of the link between each of the thirty-two books and a specific moment in his own eventful life, over a period of perhaps thirty years. According to Eusebius, Origen died at the age of sixty-nine at around the same time as the emperor Decius (249-51), under whom he had endured imprisonment and torture.[16] It is unlikely that the John commentary had progressed any further. In the preface to his Latin translation of Origen's homilies on Luke, Jerome refers to this commentary as a work of thirty-two books, translation of which is (he says) quite beyond his powers.[17] (Did he even have access to all thirty-two? Eusebius earlier stated that just twenty-two volumes had survived into his own day.)[18] In Book 32 Origen himself refers to these homilies on Luke,[19] which cannot have been delivered earlier than the 240s if Eusebius is right to claim that Origen only allowed his sermons to be taken down by stenographers after he had reached the age of sixty.[20] Eusebius also notes that Book 22 of the John commentary referred to an earlier period of persecution under Maximinus (235-38), during which his patron Ambrosius had suffered, receiving from Origen an *Exhortation to Martyrdom* that is still extant.[21] Reference to this period of persecution presumably occurred in the preface to Book 22 of the commentary,

14. Origen, *Hom. in Num.* xxvii.3.1-2; 5.1.
15. Origen, *Hom. in Num.* xxvii.9.1–12.13.
16. Eusebius, *HE* vii.1; vi.39.5.
17. Rauer, *Die Homilien zu Lukas,* p. 1.
18. Eusebius, *HE* vi.24.1.
19. Origen, *In Ioan.* xxxii.2.5.
20. Eusebius, *HE* vi.36.1. Origen is said to have been a little under seventeen years old when his father Leonidas died in the persecution that occurred in the tenth year of Septimius Severus (202). For discussion of the literary conventions deployed in Eusebius's biographical material on Origen, see C. Markschies, "Eusebius als Schriftsteller. Beobachtungen zum sechsten Buch der Kirchengeschichte," in his *Origenes und sein Erbe: Gesammelte Studien,* TU (Berlin & New York: De Gruyter, 2007), pp. 223-38.
21. Eusebius, *HE* vi.28.

where Origen may have congratulated his patron on his faithful endurance; Ambrosius is addressed by name in all the prefaces that survive in full.[22] The lost Book 22 would then date from *c.* 238-40, and the final book of the commentary must have been composed during the late 240s.

Further information about the progress of the commentary is provided in the preface to Book 6, written after Origen's final move from Alexandria to Caesarea in the year 231.[23] If the individual books retrace the Israelites' pilgrimage towards the Promised Land, Book 6 marks the moment of exodus from Egypt, with pharaonic oppression assimilated to Jesus' stilling of the storm:

> Up to the fifth book [τόμου] we dictated what was imparted to us [τὰ διδόμενα], although the Alexandrian storm seemed to hinder us [εἰ καὶ ὁ κατὰ τὴν Ἀλεξανδρείαν χειμὼν ἀντιπράττειν ἐδόκει]; for Jesus rebuked the winds and the waves of the sea. And after we had proceeded for a while with the sixth book, we were brought out of the land of Egypt, the God who led his people out from there delivering us too. Then, when the enemy bitterly attacked us with new writings truly hostile to the gospel and all the ill winds of Egypt were roused up against us, the Word was calling us instead to stand firm in the fight and to guard my own mind [τὸ ἡγεμονικόν], lest evil thoughts should prevail over the storm and direct it into my own soul. So it would have been untimely to turn to the next section of scripture, until my mind had recovered its calm. (In addition, the absence of my usual stenographers made dictation impossible.) But now the many flaming missiles directed against us have ceased to threaten, extinguished by God, and our soul has adjusted to what has happened on account of the heavenly word and has learned to live with the treacherous proceedings that have occurred [τὰς γεγενημένας ἐπιβουλάς]. Since calm has been restored, we intend to delay the continuation of this work no longer, praying that God may be present as teacher to speak in the sanctuary of our soul, so that the building of this exposition of the Gospel according to John may be completed [ἵνα τέλος λάβῃ ἡ τῆς διηγήσεως τοῦ κατὰ Ἰωάννου εὐαγγελίου οἰκοδομή].[24]

---

22. Origen, *In Ioan.* i.3.9; ii.1.1; vi.22.6; xiii.1.1; xx.1.1; xxviii.1.6; xxxii.1.2. For Origen's relationship to Ambrosius, see A. Monaci Castagno, "Origene e Ambrogio: L'indipendenza dell' intellettuale e le pretese del patronato," in *Origeniana Octava,* ed. L. Perrone, BEThL (Leuven: Peeters, 2004), pp. 165-93.

23. Eusebius, *HE* vi.26, referring to the tenth year of the emperor Alexander Severus (222-35).

24. Origen, *In Ioan.* vi.2.8-10.

The composition of the first six books or "tomes" of the commentary covers four distinct phases of Origen's recent biography, recounted here so as to explain the delay to Book 6. First, Books 1-5 are composed in spite of adverse conditions in Alexandria. That Origen maintains the peace of mind needed to continue with his work is the gift of the Jesus who rebukes winds and waves and bestows inward calm. Second, having embarked on the composition of Book 6, Origen is delivered from the land of Egypt. Evidently the winds and waves continued to threaten, even if there was calm within. The preceding reference to Alexandria shows that the departure is to be understood literally. Third, Origen comes under renewed attack even after leaving Egypt. The "new writings" directed against him stem from the old pharaonic enemy, as do the "treacherous proceedings" that follow.[25] A difficult situation prior to departure has now become a crisis, and for a while Origen is unable to proceed with literary work. Fourth, the winds again subside and the fiery darts are quenched; building work may therefore be resumed. The building image runs throughout this preface. The commentary is a "house," which must be built in fine weather if it is to stand firm against storm and flood.[26] It is a construction of the mind (λογικὴ οἰκοδομή), sheltering truths and insights expressed in its letters.[27] It is the temple of Solomon, built in peacetime and rebuilt in the time of Ezra after truth had gained its victory over a hostile king — another displaced refer-

---

25. The Pharaoh figure is Demetrius, bishop of Alexandria since 189. Only distant echoes of the conflict are audible in Eusebius, who states that Origen was "sent to Greece because of an urgent necessity of ecclesiastical affairs," and, passing through Palestine, "received ordination [πρεσβείου χειροθεσίαν] from the bishops of that place." This occasioned certain unspecified "agitations" (τὰ κεκινημένα) and "decrees" (τὰ δεδογμένα) from church leaders (HE vi.23.4). Eusebius has previously claimed that Demetrius objected to Origen's ordination on the supposed grounds that his self-castration made him ineligible, although his real reason was jealousy of Origen's spreading fame (HE vi.1-5). The story of the overzealous ascetic action is unlikely and is disbelieved even by the usually credulous Epiphanius (Pan. lxiv.3.11-13); Origen's harsh criticism of self-castration betrays no sign of self-consciousness (In Mattheum xv.1-5, on Mt. 19.12). As a letter from Origen appears to suggest, Demetrius may have refused to ordain Origen because of his unhealthy interest in philosophy and heresy (cf. HE vi.19.11-14). Other parts of what may be the same letter are preserved by Rufinus (De Adulteratione Librorum Origenis 7) and Jerome (Apologia adversus Libros Rufini ii.18-19), and they indicate that Demetrius's concern about an uncanonical ordination by foreign bishops was accompanied by an accusation of heresy arising from Origen's doctrine of apokatastasis: Origen here defends himself against the charge that he believes that the devil will be saved. According to Jerome, the Roman church supported Demetrius's condemnation of Origen, although the bishops of Palestine, Arabia, Phoenicia, and Achaia dissented (Epistulae xxxiv.4).

26. Origen, In Ioan. vi.1.1.

27. Origen, In Ioan. vi.1.2.

ence to the pharaoh of the exodus.[28] It is the tower referred to in the gospel (τὸν εὐαγγέλικον πύργον), whose builder must count the cost of completion, including the parapet that will preserve one who has climbed so high from a fall.[29] Autobiographical references in this preface explain why building work was interrupted but can now be resumed. The explanation is addressed to Ambrosius, the wealthy patron who has provided Origen with his stenographers (ταχυγράφοι) and who therefore has a financial stake in the progress of the commentary project.

This preface represents a renewed determination to work through the Gospel of John in its entirety, after the relatively slow progress of previous years. The first five books of the commentary cover only John 1.1-18, and were written between Origen's return to Alexandria from Caesarea in *c.* 217 and his final departure from Alexandria in 231. The earlier date is suggested by Origen's reference to his commentary as the "firstfruits" of the period of his return to Alexandria after a period of separation from Ambrosius.[30] The implication is that the commentary represents a new start, and the most likely occasion for this is Origen's return from an earlier period of exile in Caesarea during *c.* 215-17.[31] If these dates are approximately correct, progess on the John commentary was initially slow in comparison to the productivity of later years. In the preface to Book 5 Origen responds to a letter in which Ambrosius, concerned about the rate of progress, suggested that he take the opportunity of his current short absence from Alexandria (in an unidentified location) to resume work on the commentary. Ambrosius is here playfully compared to the Egyptian taskmasters, urgently demanding that the people fulfil their quota of work.[32] The building project that Origen

28. Origen, *In Ioan.* vi.1.3-5: "About the time of Ezra, when truth conquers wine, the enemy king, and women, the temple to God is rebuilt" (5). The allusion is to the debate in 1 Esdras 3–4, in which Zerubbabel shows that truth is greater than wine, the king, and women, and receives permission from King Darius to rebuild the temple (4.33-63). Origen has turned the king into an "enemy" to adapt the story to his own situation.

29. Origen, *In Ioan.* vi.2.6-7.

30. Origen, *In Ioan.* i.1.4.

31. Eusebius, *HE* vi.14.16-19. These dates are suggested by Eusebius's reference to "war" in Alexandria (vi.14.16), which seems to refer to massacres carried out by Caracalla during his visit to the city in 215 (Dio Cassius, *Hist. Rom.* lxxvii.22-24; Herodian, *Hist. Rom.* iv.8-9), and also by Origen's claim to have discovered a psalms scroll in a jar in Jericho during the reign of Caracalla (Eusebius, *HE* vi.16.3).

32. Origen, *In Ioan.* v.1 (Preface). In relation to Origen, Ambrosius takes on the ἔργον τῶν τοῦ θεοῦ ἐργοδιωκτῶν, demanding that he devote himself τῷ πρὸς σε καθήκοντι (cf. Ex. 5.13: οἱ δὲ ἐργοδιῶκται κατέσπευδον αὐτοὺς λέγοντες, Συντελεῖτε τὰ ἔργα τὰ καθήκοντα καθ᾽ ἡμέραν . . .).

will make his own in the later preface is here imposed on him by another. Good-humoured though the comparison may be, it indicates that particular importance is ascribed to this project and that Origen is under semiformal obligation to see it through to completion.

If progress on the commentary was slower than intended, the explanation must lie in Origen's other literary activity. During his Alexandrian period, from the beginnings of his literary career (*c.* 210) until the move to Caesarea (231), Origen wrote not only the first five books of the John commentary but also eight of the twelve books of commentary on Genesis 1–3,[33] commentaries on Psalms 1–25 and Lamentations (the latter in five books), two books on the resurrection, the four books of the *De Principiis,* and ten books of *Stromata.*[34] Parts of this literary corpus predate the beginnings of the John commentary in *c.* 218. This is the case with the books on the earlier psalms and the resurrection, probably also with *De Principiis* and the earlier books on Genesis.[35] Eusebius notes that the *Stromata* — consisting no doubt of philosophical and literary excerpts and comments, following the precedent of Clement — date from the later years of Origen's Alexandrian period, during the reign of Alexander Severus (222-35).[36] The same may be true of the books on Lamentations. Yet the John commentary seems to have been especially significant to both Origen and Ambrosius, and the preface to Book 5 proceeds to explain why this is so.

33. According to Socrates the church historian, the typological relationship between Adam and Eve and Christ and his church was elaborated in Book 9 (*Historia Ecclesiastica* iii.7). This would have been in connection with Gn. 2.18-25. Critics such as Epiphanius are probably referring to the Genesis commentary when they object to Origen's suggestion that the χιτῶνας δερματίνους of Gn. 3.21 are a reference to embodiment (*Pan.* lxiv.4.9; cf. also 4.11). If Origen required nine of his twelve books to reach the end of Gn. 2, it is unlikely that the remaining books extended beyond Gn. 3.

34. Eusebius, *HE* vi.24.1-3.

35. In his preface to Ps. 1 (cf. Epiphanius, *Pan.* lxiv.6.1–7.4), addressed to Ambrose, Origen states that this represents the beginning of his literary activity. Since the comment on Ps. 1.5 provides an important statement of Origen's doctrine of resurrection (Epiphanius, *Pan.* lxiv.9.5–16.7), it may be linked with the books on the resurrection; these are said to have predated the Lamentations commentaries, which referred back to them (Eusebius, *HE* vi.24.2). If *De Principiis* and the earlier books on Genesis belong to the same period, the result would be a systematic focus on beginnings and corresponding endings. *De Principiis* seems to have lacked the usual dedication to Ambrosius, which may suggest that the relationship was not yet as firmly established as it would later be (but cf. Jerome, *Epistulae* lxxxiv.9). As in the case of his *Hexapla* (Eusebius, *HE* vi.16.1-3), Origen's early work would then be intended as the foundation for what was to follow in years to come.

36. Eusebius, *HE* vi.24.3.

Having referred to his patron's urgent requests that he give the commentary his full attention, reiterated by letter even when he is away, Origen ruefully contrasts the prolixity of his expositions with the succinctness of the scriptural text itself. In devoting four whole books to the brief opening sentences of John and in embarking on a fifth, he seems to have disregarded the warning of Solomon the Preacher: "My son, beware of making many books [βιβλία πολλά], for there is no limit [περασμός], and much study is weariness of the flesh."[37] Is prolixity a sin? It seems that it may be. Solomon elsewhere wrote: "In many words [ἐκ πολυλογίας] you will not escape sin, but in sparing the lips you will be wise" (Prv. 10.19). As he obeys Ambrosius, does Origen disobey God?[38] Origen claims to have found a solution to his dilemma, which he hopes is not just wishful thinking born of reluctance to disappoint his friend. Surely the mere fact of λέγειν πολλά, saying a lot, is not to be condemned as sinful πολυλογία, if what is said has to do with holiness and salvation? If much speech is sinful then Solomon himself is condemned, as the author of three thousand proverbs and five thousand songs.[39] So too is Paul, whose interminable discourse led the unfortunate Eutychus to fall into a deep sleep and to suffer a serious accident.[40] It seems that the πολυλογία and the βιβλία πολλά criticized by Solomon cannot consist in the proliferation of speech or writing per se. The argument that demonstrates the point is set on Johannine terrain. The Word that was in the beginning with God (Jn. 1.2) is here identified with the scriptural Word of God. This Λόγος is singular: it is not πολυλογία or λόγοι, for its many aspects or themes are all contained within it. The unfolding of the divine Word does not consist in a supplementation by many more words, for the many words of scripture are uttered within the sphere of the one Word. The words of God are the Word of God. Throughout scripture multiplicity tends towards singularity; a single gospel is articulated in four texts bearing that name, though written by different hands. The crucial question is whether

---

37. Eccl. 12.12, the text on which the preface to Book 5 of the commentary is based (Preuschen, *Johanneskommentar,* p. 100). While Book 5 is otherwise lost, it must have concluded at Jn. 1.18, for Book 6 commences at 1.19.

38. Origen, *In Ioan.* v.4 (Preface). In the following sentences I continue to paraphrase this preface, virtually all that survives of Book 5.

39. Cf. 1 Kgs. 5.12 (4.32). In MT the second figure is reduced to 1005, חמשה ואלף rather than המשת אלף.

40. Cf. Acts 20.7-12. According to Luke, Paul spoke until midnight; according to Origen, from morning to midnight. Origen emphasizes Paul's hearers' dismay at Eutychus's apparent death; Luke, their comfort at his miraculous restoration.

multiple books of commentary can also participate in the singularity of the one Word of God, Jesus Christ as attested in holy scripture. At this point there are grounds for caution. Commentary may provide a pathway through the text, it may occupy itself with the scriptural words of truth, and yet stand outside the sphere of the one Word and fall under the Solomonic condemnation. In its many conflicting and contradictory words and books, the one Word is lost. As the analogy of holy scripture shows, however, a multitude of words and books may not only harmonize with the one Word but also be necessary to articulate its many aspects. The one Word — Christ or scripture, Christ embodied in scripture — is internally complex, as scripture's many books and Christ's many names bear witness. Insofar as it serves to elucidate that complexity, commentary belongs within the sphere of the one Word and the one Book. In that case, even a multivolume commentary will not transgress the divine prohibition of the making of many books.

This theological rationale for commentary is also pragmatically motivated. Multivolume commentaries already exist in which the one Word is indeed lost amidst confusion and contradiction. Before Origen lies not a blank page or a clean sheet but deviant commentary which he seeks to counter by *overwriting* it, rendering it almost illegible:

> If we are persuaded by this differentiation of the one book from the many, I must now be concerned not about the quantity of my writings but about the tendency of my thinking [οὐ διὰ τὸ πλῆθος τῶν γραφομένων ἀλλὰ διὰ τὴν δύναμιν τῶν νοουμένων], in case I should fall into transgressing the commandment. If I present as truth something opposed to the truth, even in just one of my writings, then I shall be writing "many books." Now, however, the heterodox are rising up against Christ's holy church with their pretended knowledge [προφάσει γνώσεως], producing works in many books that provide an exposition of the gospels and the apostolic texts [διήγησιν τῶν εὐαγγελικῶν καὶ ἀποστολικῶν λέξεων]. If we remain silent and do not oppose them with true and sound teaching, they will get a hold on inquiring minds who, for lack of wholesome fare, would hasten after forbidden and truly unclean and hateful foods.[41]

Ambrosius, himself a convert from the Valentinian heresy, has asked Origen to devote special attention to refuting an earlier, heretical John commentary in many books.[42] Its author is Heracleon, described favourably by

---

41. Origen, *In Ioan.* v.8 (Preface).
42. Ambrosius's earlier Valentinianism is mentioned by Eusebius, *HE* vi.18.1. Jerome's claim

Clement as "the most distinguished of the school of Valentinus" as he introduces a lengthy citation in which the theme of "confession" is discussed in connection with Matthew 10.32.[43] While Heracleon disappears from view in the later books of Origen's commentary, his interpretations are repeatedly cited and refuted at least until Book 20. These interpretations and refutations are concerned with matters great and small. Heracleon assumes that Jesus' encounter with John the Baptist takes place in "Bethany beyond the Jordan" (Jn. 1.28). Origen, who claims to have visited the relevant sites, insists that the text should be emended to "Bethabara"; for Bethany is located near Jerusalem, not beyond the Jordan.[44] It is not that Heracleon is heretical at this point, it is simply that Origen is more knowledgeable. When Jesus is said to "go down" to Capernaum (Jn. 2.12), Heracleon finds a hidden reference to the lower, material world into which Christ descends at his incarnation. Its inappropriateness as a place of residence for Christ is indicated by the lack of any reference to what he did there — an interpretation which overlooks everything recorded about Capernaum in the other gospels, a survey of which Origen provides.[45] Heracleon thinks that the words "Zeal for your house will devour me" (Jn. 2.17) are uttered by one of the angelic powers cast out by the Saviour, overlooking the fact that this is a scriptural citation (from Ps. 69.9), and failing to appreciate that the Saviour genuinely subjects himself to ill treatment and suffering.[46] When the Samaritan woman is said to have left her water jar behind as she hurried back to the city (Jn. 4.28), Heracleon argues that the water jar represents the capacity to receive life, left behind with the Saviour as the woman returns to the world to tell the elect of his coming. But why would she have left her capacity to receive life with the Saviour? In any case, the water jar was not left "with the Saviour"; it was simply left.[47] The evangelist proceeds to recount that Jesus stayed with the Samaritans for two days (Jn. 4.40), and Heracleon contrasts the superficial relationship implied by "with them" with the more authentic relationship that "in them" would have implied. Origen refutes this distinc-

---

that he was actually a Marcionite (*De Vir. Ill.* 56.1) seems to stem from the unreliable Epiphanius (*Pan.* lxv.3.1).

43. Clement of Alexandria, *Strom.* iv.9.71.1. For discussion of Heracleon's possible links with Alexandria, see C. Markschies, "Valentinianische Gnosis in Alexandrien und Ägypten," in his *Origenes und sein Erbe*, pp. 155-71; pp. 160-62.

44. Origen, *In Ioan.* vi.24.204-7.

45. Origen, *In Ioan.* x.9.48-60.

46. Origen, *In Ioan.* x.19.222-24.

47. Origen, *In Ioan.* xiii.30.187-92, paraphrased in what follows.

tion by referring to Matthew 28.20, "I am *with* you always. . . ."[48] The refutations always occur after Origen has presented his own interpretation of a passage, ensuring that Heracleon's interpretations are redundant from the outset and that any possible dependence on them remains concealed.

Nevertheless, in the preface to Book 5 Origen does acknowledge that it was the heterodox who invented the gospel commentary genre, which arises out of the hermeneutical conviction — shared by Origen — that there is a hidden or nonobvious sense behind the plain sense of scripture which it is the interpreter's task to bring to light. Subsequent commentary, whether ancient or modern, presupposes the same hermeneutical conviction. If there is only a plain sense requiring no enrichment from beyond itself, commentary is unnecessary.

It is true that even the plain sense leaves some of its readers' questions unanswered. According to the plain sense of John 4.28, the Samaritan woman left her water jar behind at the well when she returned to the city. Was this deliberate, or did she forget it in her haste to communicate what had happened? A commentary might content itself with responding to questions such as this which arise out of the gaps in the narrative.[49] Yet even a modern commentary may find this insufficient. Raymond Brown writes as follows on the abandoned water jar:

> We are not to seek a practical reason for this (e.g., that she left it for Jesus to drink; that she was in a hurry to get back to the town). This detail seems to be John's way of emphasizing that such a jar would be useless for the type of living water that Jesus has interested her in.[50]

48. Origen, *In Ioan.* xiii.51.349-51.

49. By leaving her water pot, the woman "shewed that her absence was to be but for a brief space" (B. F. Westcott, *The Gospel according to St. John* [London: John Murray, 1887], p. 74). "The woman left the waterpot presumably in order that Jesus might drink — thereby incurring uncleanness. . . . Others take the point to be simply that the woman forgot her pot in her haste to report what had happened; or that she is making a complete break with the past. The last suggestion seems very improbable" (C. K. Barrett, *The Gospel according to St. John* [London: SPCK, 1978²], p. 240). "Dem Zug, dass die Frau ihren Krug . . . stehen lässt, ist ein tieferer Sinn nicht abzugewinnen; er illustriert, falls er nicht einfach aus einer Vorlage . . . übernommen ist, nur den Eifer der Frau" (Walter Bauer, *Das Johannesevangelium*, HNT [Mohr-Siebeck, 1925²], pp. 68-69). Even those commentators who insist that a water jar is just that and nothing more may still find hidden meanings elsewhere in this vicinity — as with Bauer's *Vorlage*, the text concealed behind the text.

50. Raymond E. Brown, *The Gospel according to John*, 2 vols., AB (New York: Doubleday, 1966), 1.173.

Brown's comment still displays the bias from plain to hidden sense that is integral to the commentary genre. Potential amplifications of the plain sense are mentioned, but only in order to be marginalized. The narrative detail means more than it actually says. By means of it the evangelist practises an indirect communication that leads beyond what is manifest, presenting the abandoned water jar as a symbol of the difference between the material and the spiritual, and the woman whose action establishes that difference as a model for the reader to emulate. Or rather, "this detail *seems* to be John's way" of making some such point. John does not *seem* to say that the woman left her water jar behind, he simply *says* it. Seeming-to-say is pertinent only to the hidden sense, where the commentator lacks full and unrestricted access to realities communicable only indirectly. And yet it is in this seeming-to-say that the commentator discerns the evangelist's most fundamental communicative intent.

Origen's interpretation of the abandoned water jar is richer and more complex.[51] This narrative detail is, he insists, by no means redundant. Like everything in scripture, it has a purpose, and it is the commentator's task to discern what the evangelist had in view when he wrote the words ἀφῆκεν οὖν τὴν ὑδρίαν αὐτῆς ἡ γυνή καὶ ἀπῆλθεν εἰς τὴν πόλιν . . . (Jn. 4.28). At a literal level (κατὰ τὴν λέξιν), these words tell us of the woman's eagerness to communicate Jesus' significance, giving priority to others' well-being over her own physical needs. These others need to hear her account of the man whose knowledge of the human heart marks him out as the Christ, and this supremely urgent task takes precedence over the daily drudgery of water-carrying. According to Origen, we are to follow her example in making communication of what we have received our own priority: that is the lesson the evangelist intended to teach in tacitly commending the Samaritan's action. Yet there is a further level of meaning beyond this literal-ethical one; Origen calls it ἀναγωγή, the anagogical, up-leading or uplifting sense.[52] We must look more closely at that water jar: the interpreter draws the reader into a shared search for meaning, and, because we now enter upon uncharted territory, the results will be necessarily tentative. Perhaps, Origen suggests, the Samaritan may be said to have left behind

> the container of a water — that is, a teaching — revered for its depth [τὸ δοχεῖον τοῦ σεμνοποιουμένου ἐπὶ βαθύτητι ὕδατος, τῆς διδασκαλίας],

---

51. Origen, *In Ioan.* xiii.29.173-75.

52. See W. A. Bienert, "Ἀναγωγή im *Johannes-Kommentar* des Origenes," in *Origeniana Sexta*, pp. 419-28.

despising her former opinions, receiving in a better container than the water-jar the beginnings of that water that springs up into eternal life.[53]

Valentinian gnosis discloses "the depths of God" (1 Cor. 2.10), and its supreme deity may be known simply as Depth.[54] According to the Samaritan woman, the well too is deep (Jn. 4.11). The depths from which the water jar is to be filled signify a profound teaching that is profoundly wrong, misstating or contradicting basic Christian beliefs about God and world. That is why the water jar must be left behind at the well. Origen can therefore exploit the fact that the narrative has no further use for the water jar. Unlike more recent commentators who project modern conventions of narrative realism onto the ancient text, he does not need to explain that the water jar is the pledge of the woman's eventual return or that it is left for the use of Jesus or his disciples — issues of no interest to the text. Even the anachronistic allusion to Valentinianism has its own logic. In assimilating the Samaritan woman to Ambrosius, in his shift of allegiance from the Christ of Valentinus and Heracleon to the Christ of the church, it further elaborates the exemplary character of the woman's action. In the Johannine narrative Samaritans hold beliefs about God and world that are erroneous yet closely related to the truth (cf. Jn. 4.20-22; 8.48). The ideological conflict of orthodox Jews and heterodox Samaritans is all the more intense because it occurs between neighbours (cf. Jn. 4.9). A deep Samaritan well can therefore signify a deeply heretical teaching, just as an abandoned Samaritan water jar can signify both the individual's assimilation of that teaching and its renunciation.[55]

Commentary presupposes normativization. Only the normative text contains a hidden sense, withholding yet preserving the intent of the evangelist who wrote it or the Spirit who inspired it. Yet commentary also demonstrates that normativization does not bring the reception process to a halt, as though what was previously dynamic and creative here became rigid and impervious to change. On the contrary, normativization establishes a channel in which characteristic features of the reception process are reenacted. There is again a moment of inscription, in the form of the writing of the gospel; and this gives rise to interpretation and reinterpretation, as illustrated here by Heracleon's commentary and Origen's countercommentary. Previously it was gospel literature itself that proliferated, on the assumption

---

53. Origen, *In Ioan.* xiii.29.175, alluding to Jn. 4.14.
54. Irenaeus, *Adv. Haer.* i.1.1.
55. Cf. Origen, *In Ioan.* xiii.13.81, 17.101.

that the world itself could not contain all that might be written of Jesus' words and deeds. Now it is commentary that proliferates. A limit has been set for the canonical gospel, but there is no limit to the work of interpretation it calls forth. The one book inscribed by the evangelist John gives rise to the thirty-two books of Origen's uncompleted commentary, written (it is to be hoped) within the margins of the one book and so evading the Preacher's strictures.

Scripture's Firstfruits

At the beginning of Origen's commentary, the dominant scriptural image is not the stages on the pilgrimage towards the Land of Promise but that of the "firstfruits." The source of this image is again the book of Numbers. In Numbers 18.8-12 LXX, the Aaronic high priest is allocated the firstfruits (ἀπαρχή) of the children of Israel. Occurring eight times in this chapter, ἀπαρχή represents three different Hebrew words, and as a result a distinction in the Hebrew text between what is due to Aaron and what is due to the Levites is blurred.[56] Firstfruits of wheat, wine, and oil are to be presented both to Aaron (vv. 8-12) and to the Levites (vv. 29-32). It is not said that firstfruits are to be shared between Aaron and the Levites; rather, two different recipients are specified for what appears to be the same produce. Noting this apparent contradiction, Origen resolves it by assuming that the Levites' firstfruits are to be identified with their "tithe" (ἐπιδέκατον, vv. 21, 26; 24, 28 [pl.]). Receiving a tithe from the children of Israel, the Levites are required to offer a tithe of the tithe to Aaron (vv. 26-28). If tithe and firstfruits are identical, this offering to Aaron is also a tithe of the Israelites' firstfruits, which Aaron receives not directly but through the mediation of the Levites — or rather, according to Origen, Levites and priests. Assuming a distinction between the high priestly family and other priests, Origen sets the latter alongside the Levites, no doubt recalling the apparent equation of priests and Levites in Deuteronomy 18.1, and the reference in Hebrews 7.5 to "those of the sons of Levi who assume the priestly office," and who "have a commandment in the law to take tithes from the people."[57] By means of these

---

56. תרומה (vv. 8, 11), ראשית (v. 12), חלב (vv. 12 [2x], 29, 30, 32).

57. H. Attridge rightly notes that οἱ μὲν ἐκ τῶν υἱῶν Λευί κτλ here "may reflect the distinction between priests and non-priestly Levites, although neither here nor elsewhere does the author make that distinction explicit" (*Hebrews*, Hermeneia [Philadelphia: Fortress, 1989], p. 195n).

two equations of tithes and firstfruits, Levites and priests, Origen can claim that Levites and priests together present firstfruits to Aaron, consisting in a tithe of the tithe or firstfruits they themselves received from the children of Israel.

In the preface to Book 1 of Origen's John commentary, this complex exegesis underlies the passage in which he introduces himself as commentator and Ambrosius as dedicatee and reader. Origen is interested in the Levites because, unlike other tribes, they are wholly consecrated to God and possess nothing they can call their own (cf. Nm. 18.24).

> Members of the tribes offer tithes and firstfruits to God through the Levites and priests, and not everything they possess is firstfruits or tithes. But the Levites and priests, using only tithes and firstfruits, offer tithes to God through the high priest, and I believe also firstfruits. As for those of us who approach the teachings of Christ, the majority devote themselves mainly to this life and dedicate only a few of their actions to God. They resemble those of the tribes who have few dealings with priests and do little to support the service of God. But those who are dedicated to the divine word and genuinely live for the service of God, aware of the excellence of what is provided for this purpose [κατὰ διαφορὰν τῶν εἰς τοῦτο κοινωνημάτων], will not improperly be called Levites and priests. Indeed, the most distinguished, who have assumed the first rank in their generation, will be high priests — after the order of Aaron, not of Melchizedek. . . . Now, since our entire activity and life is dedicated to God, as we aspire to the highest things, and since we desire to offer that firstfruits derived from the many firstfruits . . . , what else can our firstfruits be, after our physical separation from one another, than the study of the gospel [τὴν περὶ εὐαγγελίου ἐξέτασιν]? For we may venture to claim that the firstfruits of all the scriptures is the gospel. What other firstfruits of our labours could there be, since we came home [ἐπιδεδημήκαμεν] to Alexandria, than that which concerns the firstfruits of the scriptures?[58]

In this elaborate typology, Origen casts himself as a Levite or priest and Ambrosius as high priest. Author and reader are members of the tribe wholly dedicated to God, whose inheritance is not the land but the deity itself. The Levitical tribe combines with the other eleven to make up the Christian community (consisting, according to Revelation 7.4-8, of 144,000

58. Origen, *In Ioan.* i.3.9-13.

believers in Christ), but it is also distinguished from them by its absolute consecration to God's service.[59] Origen is interested not in the Levites' mediating role between people and high priest but only in the contrast between partially and wholly consecrated lives, reflected in the different resources from which the respective offerings are taken: ordinary wheat, wine, or oil in the one case, already-consecrated produce in the other. The firstfruits the Levite presents to God through the high priest are an expression of the consecrated life. As such, it must be the choicest produce of the land. As the Levites offer Aaron the firstfruits of the firstfruits, a tithe of a tithe, so Origen offers Ambrosius the firstfruits of his exegetical labours (ἀπαρχὴ πράξεων) on the firstfruits of the scriptures (ἀπαρχὴ τῶν γραφῶν).

At this point the root of the complex imagery is laid bare. It serves to link a significant moment in Origen's biography — a new start in Alexandria after prolonged absence — with the choice of this particular scriptural text. Before retracing Origen's elaboration and defence of the thesis that the fourfold gospel is the firstfruits of all the scriptures, we will see how the biographical background sheds further light on the theme of the interpreter as Levitical priest.

As we have seen, the preface to Origen's Book 6 speaks of his recent exodus from pharaonic persecution in Egypt. In conjunction with information from Eusebius, it is clear that Origen has now settled in Palestine.[60] Some years earlier, the preface to Book 1 seems to speak of a journey in the opposite direction, following a period in which Origen has been resident elsewhere, separated from Ambrosius and his other Alexandrian students and supporters. According to Eusebius, the earlier departure was occasioned by the outbreak of "war" in Alexandria, which probably means that it occurred at the time of Caracalla's massacres there in the year 215.[61] But

---

59. Origen, *In Ioan.* i.1.1–2.8. In Rv. 14.4, cited here, the 144,000 are ἀπαρχὴ τῷ θεῷ καὶ τῷ ἀρνίῳ.

60. Eusebius, *HE* vi.23.4.

61. Eusebius, *HE* vi.19.16; Dio Cassius, *Hist. Rom.* lxxviii.22-24; Herodian, *Hist. Rom.* iv.8.6–9.8. According to Herodian's version of events, Caligula was secretly enraged at reports of Alexandrian disrespect yet initially joined in the celebrations to mark his arrival. "When he observed that the city was overflowing with people who had come in from the surrounding area, he issued a public proclamation directing all the young men to assemble in a broad plain. . . . He ordered the youths to form in rows so that he might approach each one and determine whether his age, size of body, and state of health qualified him for military service. Believing him to be sincere, all the youths, quite reasonably hopeful because of the honour he had previously paid the city, assembled with their parents and brothers, who had come to celebrate the youths' expectations. . . . At a given signal the soldiers fell upon the encircled youths, attacking them and any others present. They cut

the real reason had to do with Origen's relationship to Demetrius, his bishop.

Prior to this, Eusebius tells how Origen resumed his role as catechist on his return from a visit to Rome, Demetrius "urging him and virtually pleading with him to work unstintingly for the welfare of the brethren."[62] The language ostensibly emphasizes the bishop's confidence in his young catechist's extraordinary abilities, yet it also hints at real tensions. Bishops urge and plead only when they have cause for concern. The grounds for Demetrius's anxiety become clear in Eusebius's very next sentence, where we learn that Origen did not entirely share the bishop's overriding concern for the Christian community as a whole. People were coming to him for instruction from morning to evening, one after another in a steady stream, barely leaving him time to breathe; so Eusebius reports, sympathetically. Time was lacking for "deeper theological discourse or study and interpretation of the holy scriptures" (τῇ τῶν θείων βαθυτέρᾳ σχολῇ τῇ τε ἐξετάσει καὶ ἑρμηνείᾳ τῶν ἱερῶν γραμμάτων). So Origen handed over to his colleague Heraclas the task of elementary instruction for the Christian masses, reserving to himself the continuing training of the intellectual elite.[63] Demetrius's urging and pleading were evidently directed against this division of labour.

It was presumably this episcopal hostility to his literary and philosophical ambitions that led Origen to leave Alexandria, around the time of Caracalla's murderous visit to the city in 215, and to take up residence in Caesarea. His preaching activity in Caesarea and Jerusalem led to a formal complaint from Demetrius, on the grounds that a layman should not be permitted to preach in the presence of bishops. Following a robust response from Alexander and Theoctistus, bishops of Jerusalem and Caesarea, Demetrius changed tack and sent a delegation to Origen with a letter requesting his return to Alexandria.[64] It is this new start in Alexandria to which Origen refers in the preface to Book 1 of the John commentary.[65]

---

them down, these armed soldiers fighting against unarmed, surrounded boys, butchering them in every conceivable fashion" (iv.9.4-6, trans. Edward C. Echols, *Herodian of Antioch's History of the Roman Empire from the Death of Marcus Aurelius to the Accession of Gordian III* [Berkeley and Los Angeles: University of California Press, 1961]). Dio's less circumstantial account suggests that further atrocities may have occurred.

62. Eusebius, *HE* vi.14.11: Δημητρίου . . . παρορμῶντος αὐτὸν καὶ μόνον οὐχὶ ἀντιβολοῦντος ἀόκνως τὴν εἰς τοὺς ἀδελφοὺς ὠφέλειαν ποιεῖσθαι.

63. Eusebius, *HE* vi.15.

64. Eusebius, *HE* vi.19.19.

65. For the link between the John commentary and the return from exile in Caesarea, see

Ambrosius may have been a member of Demetrius's delegation. At any rate, he immediately becomes a key figure in Origen's second Alexandrian career, providing him with nothing less than a ready-made publishing house for the production of his future commentaries: a team of seven "speed-writers" (ταχυγράφοι) to take down Origen's dictations, the same number of "book-writers" (βιβλιογράφοι) to produce fair copies, and specialist female calligraphers.[66] Book 1 of the John commentary is the firstfruits of Origen's second Alexandrian phase, but it is also the firstfruits of Ambrosius's publishing house.

In this biographical context, the significance of the priestly and high priestly roles Origen assigns to himself and to Ambrosius becomes clear. These roles bypass the episcopal hierarchy. Ambrosius rather than Demetrius is the Aaronic figure to whom firstfruits are due. Origen is not ordained, and yet he is a Levitical priest who offers the firstfruits of his interpretative labours to God and his patron. From an episcopal perspective, the story of Korah, Dathan, and Abiram in Numbers 16–17 is a cautionary tale warning against disobedience to the legitimate ecclesial authority represented by Moses and Aaron.[67] For Origen, appealing instead to Numbers 18, Aaron and the Levitical priest are figures of *spiritual* authority and do not correspond to any visible worldly authority structure, even an ecclesial one.[68] In the circumstances of Origen's second Alexandrian career a certain distance between the biblical scholar and the bishop is acknowledged and formalized, although both view themselves as wholly committed to the service of the church.

The firstfruits that Origen has to offer relate to the firstfruits of scripture, and *the firstfruits of scripture is the fourfold gospel*. This is the proposition that must be elaborated and defended.[69] Still more than the English "firstfruits,"

Preuschen, *Johanneskommentar*, pp. lxxviii-lxxix (followed by Ronald E. Heine, *Origen: Scholarship in the Service of the Church* [Oxford: Oxford University Press, 2010], pp. 86-89). Overlooking Eusebius's evidence of early tensions between Origen and Demetrius (*HE* vi.14.11–15.1), Preuschen assumes that Origen left Alexandria when Caracalla sent the city's scholars into exile — an event for which the only ancient evidence seems to be Origen's own departure (*Johanneskommentar*, p. lxxix). P. Nautin's dating of the beginning of the John commentary to 230-31 does not adequately explain why Origen presents the commentary as the beginning of a new phase in his life (*Origène: sa vie et son oeuvre* [Paris: Beauchesne, 1977], pp. 425-27).

    66. Eusebius, *HE* vi.23.1-2.

    67. Cf. Jude 11; *1 Clem.* 40–43; Cyprian, *Epistulae* lxiv.1; lxvii.1-3; lxxiv.16; lxxv.8-9.

    68. Cf. Origen's sharp attack on the appeal to Mt. 16.18-19 in support of episcopal authority (*In Mattheum* xii.14). For the interpretation Origen rejects, see Cyprian, *Epistulae* xxvi.1; lxxiv.16.

    69. In what follows I paraphrase Origen, *In Ioan.* i.4.13-14.

the Greek ἀπαρχή suggests chronological priority. Yet the gospel is not chronologically prior to other parts of scripture; it is more nearly last than first. For a solution to this difficulty, Origen again turns to Numbers 18, where Aaron is promised both the ἀπαρχή of the land and the πρωτογενήματα, the first produce (vv. 12, 13). Chronological priority belongs to the Law of Moses, theological priority to the gospel; thus the law is πρωτογενήματα, the gospel ἀπαρχή. In insisting that these terms are not just synonyms, Origen is influenced both by his habitual *semantic maximalism* (the assumption that everything in scripture has more meaning rather than less), and by the requirements of his own argument. Here and elsewhere in this prefatory material, he is not interpreting the Numbers passage for its own sake, he is *using* it to develop a sophisticated argument about the nature of his own interpretative activity. For Origen, the idea of interpreting a passage "for its own sake" would be barely comprehensible: what would it mean for a passage to benefit from being interpreted? Interpreted or not, an *unused* scripture would be simply useless. All scripture is inspired and as such *use-full*. Here, then, Origen's distinction between the scriptural ἀπαρχή and πρωτογενήματα is pragmatically motivated. It serves him as a conceptual tool for the task in hand, which is to determine the relative significance of the different parts of scripture. The law came first, but the heart of the matter is to be found in the gospel. Only when the harvest of the prophetic writings had been gathered in did the perfect word (ὁ τέλειος λόγος) come to fruition.

The gospel comes after the prophets, but the apostolic Acts and epistles come after the gospel. If scriptures' firstfruits come last rather than first, why should we not find them in writings about or by apostles rather than in gospels?[70] A singular yet differentiated "new testament" is already in view, and the question is how its component parts are to be coordinated with one another and with the "old" scriptures. The basic distinction between the old and the new gives rise to further distinctions between the law and the prophets, the gospels (τὰ εὐαγγέλια) and the apostolic writings (τὰ ἀποστολικά). Moses represents the law, but from a Christian perspective he is also and preeminently a prophet; "prophets" can therefore assimilate "law." As we shall see, "gospel" likewise can assimilate "apostles," and indeed "prophets" too, so that even the basic old/new divide is ultimately relativized. Gospel is the heart of Christian scripture and may be encountered in many and various ways throughout scripture. Yet the distinctions must be put in place before they can be relativized. There are prophets, gospels, and apostolic texts. The

70. Origen, *In Ioan.* i.5.15-16.

534

letters of the apostles are works of high authority, full of wise and beneficial instruction, yet they lack the supreme authority of direct divine discourse. When Paul tells Timothy that "all scripture is inspired and useful" (2 Tm. 3.16), he differentiates the prophetic discourse from his own. The apostolic ". . . as I command in all churches" (1 Cor. 7.17) is not on the same level as "Thus says the Lord." Paul explicitly acknowledges this difference when he identifies two sources for his instructions to the Corinthians: "I command, or rather not I but the Lord . . ." (1 Cor. 7.10), "I say, not the Lord . . ." (1 Cor. 7.12). In the first case, the Lord's commandment stems not from the law or prophets but from the gospel which, containing the words of Jesus, is the supreme scriptural instance of direct divine discourse. In both cases, Paul subordinates his own word to the Lord's, while nevertheless expecting that it will carry weight with his addressees. Also relevant here is the fact that the apostolic discourse must frequently appeal to the higher authority of the law and the prophets in order to ensure its own credibility. In asserting a congruity between the apostolic and the scriptural word, the introductory formula "as it is written" seems to acknowledge a deficiency in apostolic discourse that must be filled from the substance of the past. If the apostolic letters (and Acts) are not gospel, however, neither are the old scriptures. The old is not gospel because it does not *show,* but only *foretells,* the one who is to come. Gospel is articulated in the testimony of John: "*See* [ἰδού] the Lamb of God . . ." (Jn. 1.29). The Baptist is more than a prophet, for no mere prophet points to a present Christ.

God has set within the church prophets, apostles, and evangelists (Eph. 4.11), and we must grasp both the distinctive features of their respective testimonies and their common orientation towards the one gospel.[71] Once we recognize that the role of the evangelist is not simply to give a narrative account of Jesus' deeds and words, it becomes clear that gospel is also present within the apostolic and prophetic texts. Here, gospel takes the form of exhortation to place full confidence in Jesus — an extension, we might say, of the Baptist's imperative, "See . . ." If gospel is articulated in and through apostolic discourse, the same is true of the prophets.[72] Or rather, this *comes to be* the case, in retrospect:

> When Christ had not yet come to interpret the mysteries they contain, the law and the prophets lacked the promise integral to the definition of "gos-

71. Origen, *In Ioan.* i.5.18-20.
72. Origen, *In Ioan.* i.8.32-36.

pel." But when the Saviour came and caused the gospel to be embodied [καὶ τὸ εὐαγγέλιον σωματοποιηθῆναι ποιήσας], by the gospel he also made everything gospel. . . . So before the gospel came with the coming of Christ none of the old texts was gospel [οὐδὲν τῶν πάλαι εὐαγγέλιον ἦν]. But the gospel, which is the new covenant, released us from the oldness of the letter and illumined with the light of knowledge the never-ageing newness of the Spirit, proper to the new covenant yet present in all the scriptures.[73]

Christ embodies the gospel, the gospels are gospel insofar as they point to him, and, once we have seen what they invite us to see, we may also see Christ as embodied gospel elsewhere: behind the veil of the Old Testament, and in apostolic letters to the churches. In these initial prefatory remarks to Origen's commentary, a hermeneutic is sketched out for Christian scripture as a whole. It is of a piece with the hermeneutic everywhere operative in Origen's scriptural interpretation, and indeed in the classical tradition of Christian exegesis that he did much to shape. Scripture is viewed here as a differentiated unity, its coherence grounded in a christological centre and its rich diversity in the divine plenitude. Interpretative practice arises from that prior construal of its object.[74] In the modern era the hermeneutic and the practice have been subject to repeated criticism as "premodern" or "supersessionist," ethically as well as intellectually indefensible under current conditions. They would be better described simply as canonical, that is, as arising out of a communal decision to treat selected books — previously undifferentiated perhaps from many other comparable books — in certain distinctive ways. There is no neutral vantage point from which such a decision could be either approved or condemned. These books can be read noncanonically, when some other interpretative context is substituted for an ecclesial one, or they can be read in the context of different canonical collections shaped by other interpretative communities. No book is inherently canonical: texts become canonical because their readers stipulate that they shall henceforth be so, and they stay that way only insofar as later readers uphold the earlier decision. Equally, no book is inherently noncanonical: only an uncritical essentialism will claim that a text is *really* just an occasional letter, or that it *is* only what its putative author is supposed to have meant it to be, or that its true being is invariably distorted in the reception

73. Origen, *In Ioan.* i.8.33, 36.
74. The concept of the "construal" of scripture is drawn from David Kelsey, *The Uses of Scripture in Modern Theology* (Philadelphia: Fortress, 1975).

process, or that it is meaningful to uphold the "rights" of a text over against the very community that has selected and preserved it for use.[75] Since canonicity is a secondary phenomenon that presupposes a text's non- or precanonical origin, there can be no question of a corresponding essentialism here too. The hermeneutic outlined by Origen and his successors is best understood as a reasoned prescription for communal usage.

Yet it is only at a high level of abstraction that one can attribute a singular hermeneutic to Origen and the later interpretative tradition. In the John commentary and elsewhere, hermeneutical reflection typically occurs in connection with specific interpretative tasks; the hermeneutical principles appropriate to the reading of Leviticus or the psalms or a gospel will overlap but will also diverge. The distinction between literal-historical and anagogical-spiritual senses may mean different things in different contexts.[76] In the case of the Gospel of John, the hermeneutical guidelines Origen seeks at the beginning of his interpretative project are to be found within the term "gospel" itself.

Four of the canonical books are entitled εὐαγγέλιον, "good news," and Origen proposes a general definition of this term which he then applies to the gospels.[77] The term εὐαγγέλιον may be defined as "speech conveying an announcement of events that, rightly and because of the benefits they bring, give joy to the hearer on receiving the announcement."[78] Thus, as Origen points out, this particular discourse is defined in terms of its impact on the hearer. If other types of discourse can be defined in abstraction from the hearer's response, that cannot be the case here. An announcement (ἀπαγγελία) is always addressed *to* someone; one cannot announce in solitude. Nor does one announce trivia or irrelevances, however interesting or

---

75. On this point compare R. W. L. Moberly, "Theological Interpretation, Presuppositions, and the Role of the Church: Bultmann and Augustine Revisited," *JTI* 5 (2011-12), pp. 1-22.

76. This possibility is overlooked when it is assumed that Origen's hermeneutic is everywhere essentially the same, unaffected by differences of genre among the scriptural texts or by specific issues arising in interpretative practice. Thus, according to E. A. Dively Lauro, "Origen defines three senses of scriptural meaning within his exegetical theory [*De Principiis* iv] and applies them within his homilies and commentaries" (*The Soul and Spirit of Scripture within Origen's Exegesis* [Atlanta: JBL, 2005], p. 238). While there is clearly a close relationship between hermeneutical theory and interpretative practice, it seems unlikely that exactly the same theory could determine the interpretation of texts as diverse as (e.g.) Genesis, Leviticus, Ezekiel, John, and Romans.

77. For this paragraph, see Origen, *In Ioan.* i.7.27-31.

78. ἔστι τὸ εὐαγγέλιον λόγος περιέχων ἀπαγγελίαν πραγμάτων κατὰ τὸ εὔλογον διὰ τὸ ὠφελεῖν εὐφραινόντων τὸν ἀκούοντα ἐπὰν παραδέξηται τὸ ἀπαγγελόμενον (Origen, *In Ioan.* i.7.27).

engaging. An announcement lays claim to its hearers' attention by communicating events or decisions of which they are so far unaware yet which have potentially significant impact on their own future. That impact might be positive, negative, or indeterminate; but where the announcement is εὐαγγέλιον, "*good* news," the prospect of future benefits or well-being occasions joy. Good news and joy are inseparable: the angel who announces the birth of the Saviour brings good news of a great joy, but the same might be said of the messenger who announces a victory in battle. Elaborating the initial definition slightly, it can be said that εὐαγγέλιον is "speech communicating to the one who believes it the arrival of good, or speech announcing the presence of an expected good."[79] The military victory and the birth of the Saviour may be expected, good news may be awaited, and in that case good news transforms hope into reality, anticipation into fulfilment. These general definitions also apply specifically to the gospel, which at every point announces the coming of Jesus Christ for our well-being and the copresence in him of the Father who is God of all, thereby evoking joy as the only reasonable response. Testimonies from Matthew, Luke, and John make it clear that, for Jesus' first followers, the good realized in him had been expected. When Andrew tells his brother Simon Peter that "we have found the Messiah" (Jn. 1.41), he announces the coming of a long-awaited good. His announcement is already gospel, good news, even though the narrative of Jesus' life is at this point barely under way. The sheer fact of his "coming" (παρουσία), his "residence" (ἐπιδημία) in our midst, is already gospel insofar as it is announced by one person to another as a guarantee of coming good. In the fourfold gospel Andrew's announcement to Simon Peter is writ large.

There is an important difference, however, between Andrew's announcement and the written gospel. Each gospel is most fundamentally a structure composed of announcements beneficial to whoever believes them (σύστημα τῶν ἀπαγγελομένων ὠφελίμων τῷ πιστεύοντι).[80] Yet Andrew needed no interpreter — except in the trivial sense that the term "Messias" must be translated for the benefit of Greek-speaking readers (Jn. 1.41). Andrew's confession seems to contain no hidden meaning requiring advanced exegetical skills to extract it. What he meant was what he said, and what he said successfully communicated his meaning. In contrast, the written gospel *does* need an interpreter — which is why Ambrosius has asked Origen to un-

---

79. λόγος περιέχων ἀγαθοῦ τῷ πιστεύοντι παρουσίαν ἢ λόγος ἐπαγγελόμενος παρεῖναι τὸ ἀγαθὸν τὸ προσδοκώμενον (Origen, *In Ioan.* i.7.27).

80. Origen, *In Ioan.* i.7.28.

dertake his commentary, and why Origen has agreed to do so. But why is interpretation necessary at all?

Interpretation is necessary because the text exists on two levels. In terms of its literary form the gospel is fourfold, but in terms of its meaning its structure is dual.[81] Meaning has a beginning and an end, a starting point in the plain sense of the text and a goal in the spiritual substance to which the text points. Interpretation is a journey that sets out from the gospel in its "bodily" (σωματικόν) or "perceptible" (αἰσθητόν) form, in quest of the gospel that is "spiritual" (πνευματικόν) or "eternal" (αἰώνιον [cf. Rv. 14.6]). The law provides the nearest analogy. Just as the law contains "a shadow of the good things to come" (Heb. 10.1), so the gospel teaches a shadow of the mysteries of Christ. The plain sense of both texts is where we are meant to start; they are a primer for children learning the rudiments of Christian literacy; but we are not intended to remain there. While there are spiritual preconditions for progress on this road, these are effectual in and through a second bodily or perceptible text, the commentary. Having acquired a basic familiarity with the text of the evangelist, we must now allow ourselves to be led by the commentator into that text's *beyond:*

> The task that now lies before us is to transform the perceptible gospel into the spiritual. For what is the narrative of the perceptible if it is not transformed into the spiritual? Nothing at all, or very little, merely enabling ordinary readers to assure themselves of the facts indicated. But for us the challenge lies in striving to attain the depths of the gospel's meaning [εἰς τὰ βάθη τοῦ εὐαγγελικοῦ νοῦ] and to search out the pure truth underlying the types.[82]

This is a further expression of Origen's programme of *anagogical* interpretation, leading us upward into the heights; it seems that the way up and the way down are one and the same.[83] Whichever the direction of travel, there is need of a guide. The need for interpretation or commentary arises from the assumption that the apparently straightforward surface of a text conceals hidden depths.

81. Origen, *In Ioan.* i.9.37–10.46. As H. de Lubac rightly points out, for Origen "the spiritual understanding of the New Testament" is "as extensive as that of the Old Testament" (*History and Spirit: The Understanding of Scripture according to Origen* [San Francisco: Ignatius Press, 2007], p. 240).

82. Origen, *In Ioan.* i.10.45-46.

83. ὁδὸς ἄνω κάτω μία καὶ ὡυτή (Heraclitus, fr. 60, cited by Hippolytus, *Refutatio Omnium Haeresium* ix.10; H. Diels and W. Kranz, *Die Fragmente der Vorsokratiker*, vol. 1 [Berlin: Weidmann, 1960⁹], p. 164).

It is not that the "pure truth" is only loosely connected to the "facts" or "types." The truth in question is simply Jesus himself. As we have seen, εὐαγγέλιον means an announcement of good things, and the pure truth can be nothing other than the good things embodied in Jesus, "good" in the sense that they are supremely beneficial to us. Thus Jesus is identified in the gospel with a plurality of goods.[84] He is the way, the truth, and the life. He is the light of the world. He is the resurrection. He is the door.[85] As such he delivers us from lostness, falsehood, death, darkness, and exclusion. What he is corresponds to what we need him to be. His being is not the abstract existence of a deity living to and for itself alone but an infinitely rich being-for-us. The limitless plurality of goods Jesus embodies has its correlate in the many writings required to attest them; we learn that "Jesus is a multitude of goods" from "writings about him hardly to be numbered [τὰ γεγραμμένα περὶ αὐτοῦ δυσεξαρίθμητα]."[86] Yet even this proliferation of writings — gospels and commentary — cannot exhaust the plurality, for, as John tells us, even a deluge of books would still leave much that Jesus did unwritten.[87] From this standpoint, the fourfold form of the gospel is *as such* already a testimony to Jesus' manifold being-for-us. If there were no spiritual gospel beyond the perceptible surface, and if acquaintance with the facts were all that the gospel had to offer, its plural form would be a hindrance rather than a help. Acquaintance with the facts would be best acquired through a single clear, comprehensive, and coherent narrative, not through four divergent and often contradictory ones. Yet these texts *together* constitute "gospel," good news about who Jesus is for us. Good news is good because it announces good things that benefit us, and the interpreter's task is to indicate how this good news is articulated in and through the gospel narratives at every point — even and especially where the surface historical sense may seem implausible. The gospel's spiritual sense is that which makes it gospel. It is nothing other than the text's subject matter, its *res* or substance. Without gospel the fourfold narrative would be worth "nothing at all, or very little."

Since the good news of the event that benefits us is communicated primarily through the gospels and only secondarily and derivatively through the other scriptures, these four texts are the firstfruits of scripture. Origen here synthesizes all three early Christian uses of the term εὐαγγέλιον. In the first

84. Origen, *In Ioan.* i.11.52-54.
85. Jn. 14.6; 8.12; 11.25; 10.9.
86. Origen, *In Ioan.* i.11.60.
87. Origen, *In Ioan.* i.11.61, citing Jn. 21.25.

instance the gospel is the proclaimed word, the core Christian message. This originally Pauline usage may have been influenced by the language of Isaiah 52.7: ὡς ὡραῖοι οἱ πόδες τῶν εὐαγγελιζομένων ἀγαθά (as cited in Rom. 10.15). Origen quotes the same text in the same form,[88] and it underlies his general definition of εὐαγγέλιον as an announcement of an event whose occurrence benefits the hearers. Second, the gospel is the literary record of the sayings and deeds of Jesus. Early writers appeal to what "the Lord said in the gospel," and there is initially no interest in differentiating one part of the fluid and open-ended literary record from another. The core Christian message is already contained in Jesus' sayings, and if these are gospel then so too is any text that records and preserves them. Third, names are attached and boundaries are drawn; the earlier focus on the gospel's content now expands to include its form. Association with named figures individualizes the texts and makes it possible to refer to them in the plural as "gospels." In Origen's synthesis, the good news of the infinite good bestowed in Jesus is articulated both in the singularity of the written gospel and in its plural form. The gospel is the hermeneutical key to the gospels, the spiritual sense that flows out through the texts like the four rivers of Paradise. In announcing Jesus' incarnate life, the text mediates between the past event of bestowal and the reader/hearer's present and future in which the bestowal is continually realized.

The firstfruits of scripture are the gospels, and the firstfruit of the gospels is the Gospel of John.[89] This text is ἀπαρχή because its ἀρχή lies not in a human genealogy stemming from Abraham (Matthew) or in the ministry of the Baptist (Mark) but in the beginning of all beginnings when the eternal Word already "was."[90] The word existing ἐν ἀρχῇ (Jn. 1.1) is also the word that was ἀπ' ἀρχῆς (1 Jn. 1.1), and the Johannine author's insistence on an absolute rather than a relative starting point makes the term ἀπαρχή peculiarly appropriate to his gospel. The absolute beginning belongs within the sphere of the divine, yet Origen shows no interest here in a divinity abstracted from Jesus' humanity. In John the primary revelation of Jesus' divinity occurs in his "I am" sayings, which indicate that no distinction can be drawn between his being-in-itself and his being-for-us. To draw such a distinction, seeking to rise above the being-for-us to a simple being-in-itself, would be to abandon the gospel narrative in its fourfold testimony to the incarnation. It

88. Origen, *In Ioan.* i.10.51. Some Pauline manuscripts read τὰ before ἀγαθά.
89. Origen, *In Ioan.* i.6.21-22.
90. For this contrast Origen is evidently indebted to Clement (Eusebius, *HE* vi.24.5-7, on which see Chapter 8 above).

would be to assume that the "spiritual" gospel can be detached from the "perceptible" one, rather than representing a substance and content that articulates itself through the external literary form. If "gospel" is good news of an event from which we stand to gain, there can be no transcending of Jesus' fleshly human history.[91]

Gospel Difference

Origen develops these reflections about gospel and the gospels in the context of an extended preface to Book 1 of his commentary. What is constructed here is therefore an *a priori* theological hermeneutic, in the sense that hermeneutical principles are laid down in advance of the work of interpretation. Analysis of the term "gospel" leads to the conclusion that the interpreter's goal is to hear good news for here and now in the narrated event there and then. The interpreter is to expect this past event to open up to the here and now and to transform it, through the mediation of the text and its interpretation, for this event does not lie inert and silent in the past but continues to declare itself. That at least is the interpreter's *hope*. Aware that he is embarking on a lengthy interpretative journey, Origen cannot as yet anticipate what he will learn along the way. Hermeneutical resources mustered at the outset may or may not prove adequate to the practical task of interpreting the text, word by word and sentence by sentence. At certain points the initial *a priori* hermeneutic may need to be supplemented by *a posteriori* principles of interpretation arising from exegetical practice. This is indeed what happens as the commentary develops, and it happens at just the point where Origen begins to negotiate parallels between John and the synoptic gospels. His object of interpretation is the Gospel of John not in isolation but within its fourfold context, and this wider context becomes highly relevant at points where the narratives converge. As we shall see, Origen is compelled by the complex realities of the fourfold text to set aside one set of interpretative tools and to develop new ones.

Towards the end of Book 2 Origen comments on John 1.7, where it is said that John the Baptist "came for witness so as to bear witness to the light,

91. That Origen sets the christology of the Johannine prologue in a trinitarian rather than binitarian context has been ably demonstrated by Christoph Markschies, "Der Heilige Geist im Johanneskommentar des Origenes. Einige vorläufige Bemerkungen," in his *Origenes und sein Erbe*, pp. 107-26. Markschies's discussion focuses especially on the important discussion of the Holy Spirit in *In Ioan.* ii.6.73-78, in connection with Jn. 1.3.

that all might believe through him," and he takes the opportunity to outline the fuller account of the witness of John given later in the chapter (Jn. 1.15-37).[92] His outline maps out the ground that will be covered in more detail in Book 6 and the lost Book 7, and it is attractively clear and simple. There are, Origen argues, six testimonies of the Baptist. The first occurs in John 1.15-18: "John testified about him and cried out saying, 'This is he of whom I said, "He who comes after me ranks before me, for he was before me"' . . ." (1.15). An earlier testimony is here recalled, but Origen is more concerned to establish that it is John the Baptist rather than John the evangelist who continues to speak in the verses that follow (1.16-18), where there is no indication of a change of speaker.[93] This is significant because the Baptist here represents the prophets and the evangelist the apostles, and because some falsely assert that the prophets lack the knowledge of the true God that Jesus revealed to the apostles. If it is the Baptist rather than the evangelist who states that "the only-begotten God [or Son] who is in the bosom of the Father has declared him" (Jn. 1.18), then the past tense suggests that the Son's disclosure of the Father occurred in and through the prophets.

> He who was in the bosom of the Father did not now "declare" for the first time, as if it was previously inappropriate for anyone to receive what he explained to his apostles. Does he who was before Abraham not teach us that Abraham rejoiced and was glad to see his day? The words, "From his fullness we all received," and "grace for grace," show that the prophets drew their gift from the fullness of Christ, and received a second grace in place of the first. For, after being initiated into the types, they were led by the Spirit to attain to the vision of the truth [τὴν τῆς ἀληθείας θέαν].[94]

Since John the Baptist's first testimony opens by referring to the preexistence of the Coming One, it is entirely possible to take the past tense verbs that follow in 1.16-18 as continuing to develop that theme. Modern commentators hold that John 1.15 is parenthetical and that 1.16 is to be connected back to 1.14 as the community's testimony to the incarnation. As a conjecture about what was intended by an author or early editor, that may be correct.[95] Origen, however, argues that it is "forced and inconsistent with

---

92. Origen, *In Ioan.* ii.29.212-23.

93. Origen, *In Ioan.* ii.29.212-14; vi.2.13–3.42 (a more detailed discussion, on which my paraphrase is based).

94. Origen, *In Ioan.* vi.2.15, alluding to Jn. 8.58, 56.

95. The disadvantage is that this leaves Jn. 1.15 entirely isolated. As W. Bauer writes, "So

the context [βεβιασμένην καὶ ἀνακόλουθον τὴν ἐκδοχήν]" to suppose that "the speech of the Baptist is so suddenly and inappropriately interrupted by the speech of the disciple."[96] Right or wrong, he has a point, and his point is motivated by factors both theological and exegetical. He has not merely imposed an irrelevant theological concern for continuity on a text that can only mean something else. The passage is clearly open to Origen's reading. It contains no equivalent of the quotation marks that modern translations insert at the close of v. 15; its past tenses cohere with the theme of preexistence; and its openness to more than one construal is in keeping with its role as canonical scripture intended for use.

The words "This is the testimony of John . . ." (1.19) introduce the second testimony. Questioned by priests and Levites from Jerusalem, John identifies himself as the Isaianic voice crying in the wilderness rather than as the Christ or Elijah or the Moses-like prophet (1.20-23).[97] Origen finds the introduction to a third testimony in the reference to those sent from the Pharisees (1.24-28).[98] Here John explains why he baptizes; it has to do with the unknown one in the midst whose sandal he is unworthy to untie. The break between the third testimony and the fourth is emphasized by statements about place ("This took place in Bethabara beyond the Jordan . . .")[99] and time ("The next day . . ."). The fourth testimony takes place in the presence of Jesus, who is identified as the Lamb of God (1.29-31).[100] The following account of the descent of the Spirit forms the fifth testimony, introduced with the words "And John testified, saying . . ." (1.32-34).[101] Finally, "the next day" John repeats his testimony to Jesus as Lamb of God, with the result that two of his disciples follow Jesus (1.35-37).[102]

Origen's structuring of this material is based on the six introductory formulae in the text (Jn. 1.15, 19, 24, 29, 32, 35). Here, his concern with the text's theological depths does not lead him to disparage or neglect its surface.

---

plötzlich, wie der Täufer aufgetaucht war, verschwindet er wieder, was neuerdings als Symptom der Ueberarbeitung gewertet wird und entweder zur Streichung von 15 oder zu seiner Verpflanzung hinter 18 führt" (*Johannesevangelium,* p. 26, parentheses omitted).

96. Origen, *In Ioan.* vi.3.34.

97. Origen, *In Ioan.* ii.29.214; vi.2.43–4.118.

98. Origen, *In Ioan.* ii.29.215; vi.5.119–29.251.

99. Origen explains his conjectural substitution of "Bethabara" for "Bethany" in *In Ioan.* vi.24.204-16, where the Gadara/Gergesa issue is also discussed.

100. Origen, *In Ioan.* ii.29.216; vi.252-307. The loss of the end of Book 6 and of Books 7-9 means that detailed treatment of the Baptist's testimony extends only as far as Jn. 1.29.

101. Origen, *In Ioan.* ii.29.217.

102. Origen, *In Ioan.* ii.29.218.

Indeed, it is precisely this carefully ordered textual surface that poses the question of the theological significance of testimony, already touched on in connection with the first testimony. According to Origen, there are some

> who claim that the Son of God has no need of witnesses, since he brings all that is necessary for belief in the saving and powerful words he proclaimed and in wonderful works that would immediately convince anyone at all. They say: If Moses was believed because of his words and miracles, not needing any witnesses to announce him in advance, and if each of the prophets was received by the people as from God, how should one greater than Moses and the prophets not accomplish what he wills and benefit the human race without prophets to testify to him?[103]

In the testimony of John the scriptural testimony to Jesus reaches its definitive articulation. John is himself foreshadowed in scripture, but as representing the preparatory voice characteristic of the prophet — at least until the moment when he points to Jesus as the Lamb of God, anticipating the ministry of the apostles. Or so Origen interprets John's significance. But it is also possible to claim that the divine self-disclosure in Christ has its own immediate power of conviction, operating in sharp discontinuity with any prior norms; the possibility that these may have been shaped in advance by the preexistent Christ is not recognized. It is those who seem to think most highly of Christ who are inclined to take up such a position.[104] For Origen, the testimony of John demonstrates that Christ's coming is not without a context which both shapes it and is shaped by it.

In John's second and third testimonies Origen confronts for the first time the issue of gospel parallels. Differences in wording between the four versions of the citation from Isaiah 40 are carefully noted, showing "how the evangelists abbreviate the prophetic words."[105] The Johannine description of

---

103. Origen, *In Ioan.* ii.28.199-200.

104. Compare a current model of "apocalyptic interpretation," associated with Paul rather than John: on this account, "the starting-point for Christian reflection as attested by Paul, and hence its ongoing governing criteria, must be derived from the revelation of Christ . . . , not overlooking of course the role of the Spirit within that revelation" (Douglas A. Campbell, *The Quest for Paul's Gospel: A Suggested Strategy* [London & New York: T. & T. Clark International, 2005], p. 65). Thus, "preceding states and situations like Israel and creation" must be understood "retrospectively" (p. 65), that is, as objects on which the gospel may unilaterally shed its light but not as testifying subjects. For a response to Campbell on this point, see my "Paul the Reader: An Authorial Apologia," *JSNT* 28 (2006), pp. 363-73; pp. 369-72.

105. Origen, *In Ioan.* vi.14.138.

the Pharisees' hostile questioning about John's baptism (Jn. 1.24-25) may be connected with the Matthean account of John's denunciation of Pharisees and Sadducees as a "generation of vipers" (Mt. 3.7).[106] The Matthean passage itself has a parallel in Luke, where it is the crowds who are denounced in those terms; the Matthean addressees are to bring forth "*fruit* worthy of repentance," the Lukan ones "*fruits*" (Mt. 3.8; Lk. 3.8), perhaps because the Pharisees and Sadducees are required to bring forth the specific fruit of faith in Jesus whereas the crowds must produce a wider range of fruits.[107] These investigations of synoptic parallels are intended to be programmatic. Origen writes:

> Since it appears important to us to compare [παρατιθέναι] the passage under consideration with similar passages in other gospels, and to do so in each case until the conclusion of this work, showing that those that seem to clash [τὰ μὲν συγκρούεν δοκοῦντα] are in agreement [σύμφωνα], and explaining what is distinctive to each one, that is what we shall do with the present passage.[108]

Perhaps because of the intricate and protracted nature of these comparisons, Origen twice apologizes for them:

> Do not suppose that we have acted inappropriately in comparing passages from the other gospels with the one we are investigating, concerning those sent from the Pharisees to inquire of John.[109]

> If it seems that we have digressed in comparing passages from the other gospels, it does not appear out of place to me nor alien to the present subject.[110]

Comparisons are necessary and appropriate because the Gospel of John does not stand alone but belongs within the fourfold canonical gospel. That is its primary literary context, and its words should therefore evoke echoes from the other three as they are heard. The comparisons have the potential to illuminate the text from a new angle; any text will look different when viewed from the perspective of another. For the most part, parallel texts are

106. Origen, *In Ioan.* vi.14.132-34.
107. Origen, *In Ioan.* vi.14.139-41.
108. Origen, *In Ioan.* vi.14.127.
109. Origen, *In Ioan.* vi.14.135.
110. Origen, *In Ioan.* vi.14.146.

here simply juxtaposed. There is no attempt to organize the parallel passages into a single sequential narrative, as in a gospel harmony such as Tatian's. Nevertheless the harmonizer's perpetual anxiety about *apparent contradictions,* passages that "seem to clash" and that must be shown to be "in agreement," is also evident here. In John 1.26-27 the Baptist speaks of his baptism as preparatory for "the one who comes after me, the thong of whose sandal I am unworthy to untie." Apart from the preceding Isaiah quotation, this is the first Johannine passage with direct synoptic parallels, and Origen fulfils his promise to consider these in detail. One difference between the various versions of the saying causes him particular concern. According to Matthew, John the Baptist pronounced himself unworthy to *carry* his successor's shoes; according to Mark, he felt unworthy to *stoop and untie* them (Mt. 3.11; Mk. 1.7). Luke and John broadly agree here with Mark against Matthew, but Origen does not discuss them at this point. Why does Mark diverge from Matthew here? The difference is not a trivial one:

> It is one thing to carry the sandals, obviously already loosed from the wearer's feet, and quite another to stoop and untie the sandal-thong. Since none of the evangelists errs or lies, as believers must claim, it follows that the Baptist said both things at different times, being moved to express different meanings. For the writers were not led to record the same things differently, as some suppose, as if they did not accurately recollect [μὴ ἀκριβοῦντες τῇ μνήμῃ] the individual things said or done.[111]

Origen claims here that a more relaxed view of this gospel difference would conflict with the believer's commitment to the evangelists' absolute truthfulness, and this leads him to engage in the dubious practice of manufacturing separate sayings or incidents out of gospel variants. This practice will later be systematically developed by Augustine, who is just as concerned as Origen about exactly what the Baptist was unworthy to do with the messianic footwear.[112] Origen is able to make the difference theologically fruitful, suggesting that the passage about the sandals is μυστικός, containing a hidden meaning.[113] The shoes of the Son of God represent his twofold descent into our world and into Hades, one downward step followed by another. To "stoop" and "unloose" is to bend down with Jesus in order to grasp the meaning of this double mystery. To "carry" his sandals is to retain that

111. Origen, *In Ioan.* vi.18.171-72.
112. Augustine, *De Cons. Evang.* ii.12.29.
113. Origen, *In Ioan.* vi.18.172-78.

meaning in one's memory. Further scriptural citations help make the proposed mystical sense vivid and appealing.[114] What is problematic is not the imaginative theological application of this gospel difference but rather the incongruous historical claim that the Baptist *must* have spoken on different occasions both of untying and of carrying — one recorded by Mark, the other by Matthew — because otherwise the evangelists' veracity and trustworthiness would be compromised. The mystical or theological interpretation presupposes an inspired *text* and has no need of speculations about the historical John's *ipsissima verba*. A canonical hermeneutic requires that gospel parallels be noted and differences exploited, but not that each such difference must have its own discrete link to a piece of empirical reality.

Origen's anxiety attack when faced with his first significant gospels parallel is uncharacteristic.[115] When he returns to this issue in Book 10 of his commentary, he subjects his own earlier assumptions to radical criticism. Having dealt with the miracle at Cana in the lost Book 9, Origen arrives at the innocuous-sounding statement of John 2.12, that "after this he and his mother and brothers and disciples went down to Capernaum and stayed there a few days."[116] If we ask the Johannine narrator to specify more broadly *when* it was that this visit to Capernaum took place, he tells us that it *followed* the six-day period that covers Jesus' identification as the Lamb of God, his first encounters with his disciples, his return to Galilee, and his first sign (Jn. 1.29–2.11), and that it *preceded* the imprisonment of John the Baptist (3.24). If we put the same question to the synoptic evangelists, the answer is very different. When did Jesus first visit Capernaum? All three synoptists locate this event after the forty days of temptation in the wilderness. Matthew tells how Jesus returned to Galilee after the arrest of John, leaving Nazareth and taking up residence in Capernaum so as to fulfil the prophetic announcement of the dawning of the light by the sea (Mt. 4.12-16). Mark's

---

114. Ps. 15[16].10; 1 Pt. 3.18-20; Rom. 14.9.

115. That is, uncharacteristic of this work in its extant form. For a broad survey of Origen's practice in relation to gospel parallels, see H. Merkel, *Die Widersprüche zwischen den Evangelien: Ihre polemische und apologetische Behandlung in der Alten Kirche bis zu Augustin*, WUNT (Tübingen: Mohr-Siebeck, 1971), pp. 94-121. Summarizing his discussion of relevant material in the John and Matthew commentaries and the Luke homilies, Merkel writes: "Während er sich oft zu sehr von dem Bemühen, die völlige Irrtumlosigkeit der Evangelisten nachzuweisen, bestimmen lässt, hat er in anderen Fällen den richtigen Ansatz, die Evangelien als kerygmatische Schriften mit verschiedenen theologischen Anliegen zu sehen und Differenzen in der Darstellung von daher zu begründen" (p. 121).

116. Origen, *In Ioan.* x.1.3-9.

sequence is broadly similar, although he does not mention Nazareth and places the visit to Capernaum after the call of the first disciples (Mk. 1.12-21). Luke does not explain exactly when John was arrested (cf. Lk. 3.18-20), but he like Matthew has Jesus proceed from his baptism to the wilderness and from the wilderness to Nazareth and then Capernaum (Lk. 4.1-31). In the synoptics, then, Jesus first visits Capernaum after his temptations and John's arrest. In John he visits Capernaum before John's arrest and without any reference to the temptations.

On reaching John 2.12 Origen again fulfils his self-imposed obligation to cite and discuss the synoptic parallels. This time there is no trace of the anxiety that led him to insist that the Baptist must have spoken on different occasions both of untying and of carrying. He might have followed the line taken by Hippolytus in his dispute with Gaius over the authority of the Gospel of John, locating the baptism and temptations *before* Jesus' first appearance in the Johannine narrative (see Chapter 9 above). Or he might have anticipated Augustine's claim that apparently continuous narratives can conceal substantial breaks in historical continuity, thus creating space for a lengthy Johannine sequence to be inserted between the synoptic temptation accounts and the start of the public ministry in Galilee (see Chapter 1). Gospel harmonizers face multiple difficulties, yet these present themselves one by one, and, with the help of a few guiding principles, solutions of a sort can always be found. It is striking, then, that Origen here confronts and opposes the assumption shared by Hippolytus, Gaius, and Augustine, which is that the authority of a gospel narrative stands or falls with the possibility of successful harmonization at the empirical-historical level.[117] The ultimate harmony that resolves the surface dissonance is not to be found in a composite account of the life of Jesus. On the contrary,

the truth of these matters must lie in the spiritual sphere [ἐν τοῖς νοητοῖς]. Otherwise, if the discord [διαφωνία] be not resolved, our trust in the gospels must be abandoned and we may no longer regard them as true or divinely inspired [θειοτέρῳ πνεύματι γεγραμμένων] or as the reliable record they are supposed to be. As for those who accept the four gospels but do not consider that the apparent discord is to be resolved anagogically [λύεσθαι διὰ τῆς ἀναγωγῆς], let them tell us, in connection with the difficulties raised above about the forty days of temptation for which

117. Origen analyzes the differences between John and the synoptics here "with a precision worthy of Bultmann" (B. Childs, *The New Testament as Canon: An Introduction* [London: SCM Press, 1984], p. 146).

there is absolutely no room in John, when it was that the Lord came to Capernaum.[118]

The apparently trivial issue of chronology arises precisely because there are four gospels rather than one. It is significant as a harbinger of many similar difficulties that Origen's comparative approach may bring to light as he makes his way through the Johannine text and the relevant parallels. Faced with this dissonant plurality, there are just two possibilities: either to select one of the gospels as a historically reliable guide and to disregard the others, or to accept that the truth of the four is not to be found at the literal-historical level, ἐν τοῖς σωματικοῖς χαρακτῆρσιν.[119] Thus the fourfold gospel marks the end of all attempts to reconstruct the life of the historical Jesus. Each individual gospel has its own sequence of events, and taken on its own there is no reason to suppose it to be unreliable. The Marcionite Christian will naturally assume that Marcion's edition of Luke provides a trustworthy account of the life of Jesus, since the conflicting accounts provided by other gospels are rejected on principle. Modern concern with the historical Jesus has gone hand in hand with the selection of one gospel as a reliable guide in preference to the others, whether the favoured gospel is John (Schleiermacher), Mark (Holtzmann), or Matthew (Schweitzer). If the individual gospel appears to provide a reliable record of Jesus' life, the fourfold gospel exposes that appearance as an illusion. The object or protagonist of the fourfold gospel is not a historical figure artificially isolated from his own reception; rather, he is a historical figure received as the Christ and Son of God, so infinitely rich in his many aspects that he must necessarily break free of the confines of purely historical narration. What is undermined by gospel plurality or difference is direct access to a Jesus who is not yet or no longer what he is for Christian faith. From the standpoint Origen here attains, the assumption that difference threatens the gospel itself — a view shared by harmonizers (Tatian, Augustine) and their critics (Reimarus, Lessing) — can only be regarded as perverse. The gospel is *constituted* by difference. The difference that problematizes empirical correspondence does so in order to open up the spiritual sense that makes the gospel gospel: good news bringing joy to the hearer on account of the ultimate well-being it promises. That well-being would in no way be enhanced if all four gospels provided the same account of the sequence of events from Jesus' baptism to his first visit

118. Origen, *In Ioan.* x.2.10.
119. Origen, *In Ioan.* x.2.14.

to Capernaum. Their failure to do so indicates their concern to articulate the gospel in the history rather than a neutral history without gospel.

In concrete terms, that concern led the four evangelists to

> avail themselves of many things done and said by the wonderful and ex-
> traordinary power of Jesus, at times interweaving within their writing
> that which was disclosed to them in a purely spiritual manner [τὸ
> καθαρῶς νοητῶς αὐτοῖς τετρανωμένον] in language apparently con-
> cerned with perceptible realities [ὡς περὶ αἰσθητῶν]. I do not condemn
> them for incorporating material that is other than historical [τὸ ὡς κατὰ
> τὴν ἱστορίαν ἑτέρως γενόμενον] in the service of their innermost aim:
> transferring an event from one location to another, or from one time to
> another, and subjecting what was said in a particular way to certain modi-
> fications. Their intention was, where possible, to speak spiritual and em-
> pirical truth together [ἀληθεύειν πνευματικῶς ἅμα καὶ σωματικῶς], and,
> where that was not possible, to prefer the spiritual to the empirical, fre-
> quently preserving (as one might put it) the spiritual truth in the empiri-
> cal falsehood [σωζομένου πολλάκις τοῦ ἀληθοῦς πνευματικοῦ ἐν τῷ
> σωματικῷ . . . ψεύδει].[120]

It is the fourfold gospel that brings the working methods of the evangelists to light. Only when John is set alongside Matthew, Mark, and Luke does
it become clear that the cleansing of the temple is here transferred from the
end of Jesus' ministry to the beginning (Jn. 2.13-22),[121] that the main site of
that ministry is relocated from Galilee to Jerusalem, and that Jesus' characteristic modes of speech have been transformed. The fourfold gospel represents
a hermeneutical framework for each of its four components that is both critical and evangelical: critical in that it bars access to much that we might like to
know about the historical Jesus, evangelical in that it prioritizes a spiritual
truth which is that of the gospel, good news bringing joy to the hearer.

---

120. Origen, *In Ioan.* x.4.18-20. De Lubac plays down the significance of Origen's radicalism
here, arguing that "too strict an idea of agreement between the evangelists" leads him into an "au-
dacity that is at times worrisome" (*History and Spirit*, pp. 232, 234). De Lubac's anxiety is
prompted by his emphasis on historical reality as the bedrock of Origen's spiritual interpretation,
an emphasis that passages such as this one may seem to threaten. Yet there is no risk of "timeless
allegorizing" in a context where the spiritual sense is identical to the gospel, defined as "speech
conveying an announcement of *events* that, rightly and because of the benefits they bring, give joy
to the hearer . . ." (*In Ioan.* i.7.27).

121. Origen will later discuss this point at length, going so far as to question the historicity of
the incident itself (*In Ioan.* x.15.118–18.209).

Origen's hermeneutical reflections represent a profound early *reinter-pretation* of the complex textual object still known as "the gospel" though consisting of four "gospels." This is *re*interpretation because Origen is well aware of an existing interpretative practice that is concerned to demonstrate the harmony of the gospels on the empirical rather than the spiritual plane. Indeed, he exemplifies just this practice in his first substantial discussion of gospel parallels — before subjecting his own former viewpoint to devastating critique in the second extant discussion.

No interpretation of the fourfold gospel is mandatory because integral to its object from the outset. The form of the gospel is theologically underdetermined and could be put to a variety of uses; Irenaeus competes with his Valentinian opponents on the same textual ground. Interpretation is secondary to the pragmatic concern for a gospel shared by catholic Christians everywhere. Yet the fourfold gospel requires interpretation like any other canonical text. Arguably, an interpretation is only truly canonical when its attention to one of the four is such as to evoke echoes in the other three, and where the differences that come into view are seen as promising rather than threatening.

CHAPTER 11

Image, Symbol, Liturgy

Towards the end of the second century, Irenaeus sought to promote the fourfold canonical collection by appealing to the "four living creatures" of Revelation 4.6-7, one like a lion (John), the second like a calf (Luke), the third with a human face (Matthew), the fourth like a flying eagle (Mark).[1] From the period of the Enlightenment onwards, these identifications have regularly been criticized for their arbitrariness. Lessing, for one, is dismissive:

> That absurd argument of Irenaeus betrays sufficiently clearly that it was only in his own time that people began to regard just *four* gospels — neither more nor less — as valid.[2]

In itself, the historical point is entirely correct. More significant is the implied connection between belatedness (*"only"* in Irenaeus's time) and absurdity or arbitrariness. It is assumed that truth inevitably decays with the passing of time and that it can be recovered only by pursuing it all the way back to its "source," its moment of origin — in Lessing's case, an *Urevangelium,* ancestor of the Q hypothesis. The historical point is set within a specific evaluative framework. As a result, another equally significant historical point is lost to sight: the fact that the four-gospel collection has maintained a communally normative status, *in* and not *in spite of* the

---

1. Irenaeus, *Adv. Haer.* iii.11.8.

2. §52 of the posthumous "Theses aus der Kirchengeschichte" (*LWB,* 8.626): "Jene ungereimtere [i.e. Ursache von der gevierten Anzahl der Evangelisten] des Irenäus verrät genugsam, dass man erst zu des Irenäus Zeiten angefangen hat, gerade nur *vier,* nicht mehr und nicht weniger, Evangelisten gelten zu lassen" (italics original).

differences affirmed by Irenaeus though problematized by Lessing.[3] Irenaeus does not merely align four putatively canonical texts with a convenient scriptural quartet. Rather, he sees the four living creatures as an effective parable of the fourfold gospel because, in and with their common orientation towards Christ, they are so strikingly different from one another.

Irenaeus's correspondences are subjected to rival revisions. The lion, linked to John by Irenaeus, is reassigned to Matthew by Augustine and to Mark by Jerome. Augustine and Jerome agree against Irenaeus in allocating the eagle to John rather than to Mark. Jerome retains the equation of Matthew and the human figure, while Augustine thinks this figure more appropriate to Mark. Only the identification of the calf or ox with Luke remains intact, and even this is lost in a pseudo-Athanasian text that assigns the human to Matthew and the eagle to John (as in Jerome) but proposes a calf-like Mark and a leonine Luke.[4] The evidence is usefully tabulated by H. B. Swete, who points out that "while in three out of the four distributions St. Matthew is the Man, St. Luke the Calf, and St. John the Eagle, to St. Mark each of the symbols is assigned in turn."[5] These divergences are said to demonstrate that all such attempted equations are "arbitrary" and indeed "unfortunate."[6] Swete notes that it was Jerome's view that "impressed itself on mediaeval art, although it was based on grounds not more reasonable than those which led Irenaeus to the opposite conclusion."[7] Underlying this negative assessment of the traditional gospel symbolism is the familiar claim that the unreasonableness of tradition is exposed by the plain sense of the scriptural texts — in this case the texts of Revelation 4 and Ezekiel 1. It is certainly true that neither the seer John nor the prophet Ezekiel could have associated the four living creatures they beheld in their visions with four gospels. Yet the patristic authors all assume a hermeneutical distinction between literal-historical and allegorical modes of interpretation. In the allegorical mode, points are no longer read *out of* the scriptural text ("exegesis"), but nor does one merely read *into* it ("eisegesis"). Allegorical interpretation may often be understood pragmatically, as a way of *using* the biblical text to address a theological problem — here, the problem of the coexistence of four gospels in their similarity and difference. The patristic hermeneutic rightly recognizes that the

3. See Chapter 2 of the present work.

4. *Synopsis Scripturae Sacrae* (PG 28.432). This may simply be a garbled version of Jerome's scheme.

5. H. B. Swete, *The Gospel according to St. Mark* (London: Macmillan, 1920³), p. xxxix.

6. Swete, *St. Mark*, p. xxxviii; *The Apocalypse of St. John* (London: Macmillan, 1911³), p. 72.

7. Swete, *St. Mark*, p. xxxviii.

function of a scriptural text is not just to generate a literal sense that reproduces its latent meaning but also to provide tools that further the community's work of self-construction. Patristic theologians *use* the visionary texts
to think through the fourfoldness of the canonical gospel, and they do so because these texts provide them with striking images or parables of fourfold
difference within a common orientation towards Christ.

Asked to account for the fourfold gospel, patristic theologians provide a
brief narrative of the circumstances in which they believed it came into being. Matthew wrote in Hebrew; Mark wrote as the interpreter of Peter, Luke
as a disciple of Paul; John wrote last of all, with a special emphasis on
Christ's divinity as a counterweight to his predecessors' emphasis on the humanity. Yet these theologians do not deny that other gospels exist, and that
in some cases they may even predate the canonical ones. When Luke refers to
the "many" who "attempted" to compose a narrative of the saving events, he
is said to refer to gospels that *failed* to achieve what their authors rashly set
out to achieve. While these "apocryphal" gospels were certainly not written
by apostles, there is no reason why they should not have been written by followers of apostles, like Mark and Luke. In other words, the fourfoldness of
the canonical gospel is not defended by appeal to apostolicity or to priority.
The traditional narrative of gospel origins only serves to vindicate the fourfold gospel in conjunction with the appeal to the four living creatures
around the divine throne, and it is *their* patronage — not that of the most
excellent Theophilus and his counterparts — that bestows transcendent
heavenly authority on just four out of the many early Christian gospels.

The traditional symbolism is no more or less arbitrary than the fourfold
gospel itself. And the fourfold gospel is itself no more or less arbitrary than
any other feature of mainstream Christian communal life — the practice of
baptism, say, or the observance of Easter. These things are as they are, even
though they might in principle have been otherwise.

The parabolic articulation of the four-gospel collection is particularly
effective when it is made *visible*. In church mosaics and other media,
Jerome's version of the Irenaean scheme is extracted from specialized literature known only to a theologically educated elite and projected onto a public
space such as an arch or apse, in full view of the entire worshipping community. The extant mosaics do not simply translate Jerome's correspondences
from words into images. Rather, they serve to affirm the liturgical context
and rationale of the fourfold gospel. Indeed their primary theme is worship
as such, and the identifications with evangelists and their gospels are subordinate to that concern. The four living creatures of Revelation and Ezekiel

are more than mere symbols of the evangelists. They are the cherubim who initiate the unceasing praise of the triune God: "Holy, holy, holy, Lord God Almighty . . ." (Rv. 4.8). The earthly congregation participates in this heavenly worship, and it is within this overarching context that the four gospels find their *Sitz im Leben* and their natural habitat.

The visual arts are generally underexploited as a potential source for early Christian theology and exegesis. Yet the artworks in question give every indication of careful theological and exegetical planning by their designers. Images of Christ exalted among the cherubim represent a locus of reflection on the church's fourfold gospel that complements and transcends the literary sources.

On the Cherubim

The church of Santa Pudenziana (Rome) was rebuilt in the late fourth century, and the apse mosaic probably dates from the early fifth. (Images of this artwork and others discussed in this chapter may be viewed at gospelwriting .wordpress.com.)[8]◆ Parts of the mosaic were destroyed during alterations in 1588 and 1711, and the rest has been extensively restored.[9] Inscriptions, now lost, referred to the date of the church's foundation (398) and to the pontificate of Innocent I (402-17). The one genuinely ancient inscription to survive occurs near the centre of the composition, in a codex in the left hand of the enthroned Christ, held open towards the viewer and identifying him as the preserver or defender of the Pudentian church: DOMINUS | CONSER|VATOR || ECCLESIAE | PUDENTI|ANAE.[10] It has been suggested that this may refer to the church's survival of the devastation caused by Alaric's Goths in 410.[11] The

8. On the website, images are linked to footnote numbers. A ◆ after the footnote number in the text (as above) indicates that images are available (see notes 13, 19, 68, 81, 82, 83, 85, 94, 121).

9. For a convenient summary of the extent of the restorations, see Thomas F. Mathews, *The Clash of Gods: A Reinterpretation of Early Christian Art* (Princeton: Princeton University Press, 2003²), p. 208. Mathews too easily assumes that the four living creatures of this mosaic are intended to symbolize the evangelists.

10. Here and elsewhere, a vertical line indicates a line break, a double vertical line a page break.

11. See Fredric W. Schlatter, S.J., "The Text in the Mosaic of Santa Pudenziana," *VC* 43 (1989), pp. 155-65. Schlatter argues that "when the mosaicist of S. Pudenziana deliberately chose *Conservator* as the title of the seated figure, his choice involved the concept of gratitude to a higher power for deliverance from danger. The text, therefore, involves a proclamation of gratitude to God for having rescued the Titulus Pudentis from a threatened destruction" (p. 161).

ambiguous genitive construction seems to underlie the transformation of the original *titulus Pudentis*, named after Pudens, Paul's first Roman convert (cf. 2 Tm. 4.21), into a "church of St. Pudentiana," supposed daughter of Pudens and sister of St. Praxedes (to whom a nearby church is dedicated).[12] The legend of the two sisters may also owe something to the female figures in the mosaic who bestow martyrs' wreaths on Paul, to the left of Christ's throne, and Peter, to the right. The figures may originally have been allegorical representations of the churches of the Jews and the Gentiles, associated with Peter and Paul respectively, like the veiled female figures identified as ECLESIA EX CIR| CUMCISIONE and ECLESIA EX | GENTIBUS in the church of Santa Sabina (Rome), dating from just a few years later.[13◆] Further to the left and right are a total of eight more apostolic figures; the two outermost apostles must have disappeared entirely, along with original inscriptions and an image of the *Agnus Dei*. Christ sits enthroned among the twelve against the backdrop of an arcade with further buildings visible behind it. The location is identified as Jerusalem by the hill or mound of Calvary immediately behind the throne, on which stands a golden, jewel-encrusted Latin cross. This cross is the focus of the upper zone of the composition as the enthroned Christ is of the lower. Distributed around it, above the apostles and the city, are the four living creatures of Revelation 4 and Ezekiel 1, six-winged and set against a blue background with white and red clouds (cf. Ez. 1.4). The creatures are half-submerged in the cloudy sea with only the upper or front parts of their bodies visible. On the far left and right, the human figure and the eagle are seen in profile, with the human gesturing with bare arms towards the enthroned Christ below. On either side of the central cross are the figures of an anthropomorphized lion and of a calf in half-profile, looking to the viewer's right and left respectively. In this way the artist has attempted to represent the distribution of the creatures "around the throne" (Rv. 4.6). The question is whether the creatures are also

12. The shift can be seen in the remark in the *Liber Pontificalis* about restorations under Hadrian I (772-95): *immo et titulum Pudentis, id est ecclesiae Sanctae Pudentianae, in ruinis perventam noviter restaurit* (cited in Schlatter, "Text in the Mosaic," p. 156). The "Pudentian church" has become the "church of St. Pudentiana."

13. In S. Sabina the two figures are placed on either side of a mosaic inscription which dates the church to the time of Pope Celestinus I (422-32). A seventeenth-century drawing indicates that images of Peter and Paul were originally located directly above the two female figures, with Peter associated with the Jewish figure and Paul with the Gentile one (reproduced in Beat Brenk, *Die frühchristlichen Mosaiken in S. Maria Maggiore zu Rom* [Wiesbaden: Franz Steiner Verlag, 1975], Fig. 10). Online images of the surviving figures and inscription are available at gospelwriting .wordpress.com. The link between the S. Sabina and S. Pudenziana figures is, however, rejected by F. Schlatter ("The Two Women in the Mosaic of Santa Pudenziana," *JECS* 3 [1995], pp. 1-24; p. 4).

intended to represent the four evangelists. While it is generally assumed that they do so, and that this is therefore the earliest extant depiction of the evangelists' symbols, the creatures lack the accompanying red jewelled books that make the link explicit in a slightly later iconography.

The artist has drawn inspiration from both Revelation 4 and Ezekiel 1. His order is that of Ezekiel's vision of the chariot-throne:

> And the likeness of their faces: the face of a human and the face of a lion on the right of the four [ἐκ δεξιῶν τοῖς τέσσαρσιν] and the face of a calf to the left of the four and the face of an eagle to the four. (Ez. 1.10)

The preceding verses suggest that this ambiguous description relates to four identical creatures, each with a human face in front, an eagle face behind, and lion and calf faces to right and left. Yet, in the absence of explicit references to front and back, it is also possible to envisage a row of different faces, one for each creature, with the references to right and left relating not to each creature's head but to the group as a whole. This would account for the transformation in Revelation 4 of four identical four-faced creatures into four different creatures with one face each:

> And amidst the throne and around the throne [I saw] four living creatures, full of eyes before and behind, and the first living creature was like a lion, the second living creature like a calf, the third living creature having the face as of a human, and the fourth living creature like a flying eagle. And the four living creatures, each one of them having six wings, around and within are full of eyes, and day and night they never cease saying, "Holy, holy, holy is the Lord God the Almighty, who was and is and is to come." (Rv. 4.6b-8)

The double reference to multiple eyes may imply familiarity with the four-face reading of the Ezekiel passage; a feature of the chariot-throne's wheels is here transferred to the cherubim themselves (cf. Ez. 1.8; 10.12). Yet the later author chooses to emphasize the difference between the creatures rather than their shared hybrid nature — a crucial interpretative move in which he is followed by the mosaicist of S. Pudenziana. In the mosaic the order of Ezekiel 1.10 is preferred to the Johannine one, where the human is relegated from first to third place, and further allusion is made to this text in the distribution of two figures each to left and to right — although a sense of circularity "around the throne" is also maintained, so far as is possible within the half-hemisphere of the apse. The emergence of the creatures from a background of fiery cloud is suggested by Ezekiel 1.4, where the prophet at the river Chebar sees coming from the north "a great cloud . . . and brightness round about it and a flashing fire." On the other hand, the creatures' six wings derive from the later seer's appropriation of the Isaianic seraphim and *trisagion* (Rv. 4.8; Is. 6.2-3). Identified as cherubim (Ez. 10.15, 20), Ezekiel's creatures have four wings corresponding to their four faces (Ez. 1.6).[14]

The disparity between the two zones of the S. Pudenziana image is striking. Below, the enthroned Christ instructs his disciples within the temple precincts of an earthly Jerusalem.[15] The worshipper beholds here the source and legitimation of the instruction he or she receives from the apostles' living successors. Above, the four living creatures encircle the bejewelled cross which, though set on a hill, belongs to the same heavenly realm as they do — an interpretation confirmed by representations elsewhere of a transfigured cross set against a starry background.[16] There is continuity between heaven and earth in the winged human gesturing down towards the enthroned Christ. Yet the living creatures otherwise play no part in the earthly scene. Their place is in heaven not earth, and the heavenly cross in their midst signifies an exalted divine Christ who cannot be imaged but can only be worshipped. The creatures belong within the ranks of cherubim and seraphim who, in the words of the *Te Deum*, "continually do cry, Holy, holy, holy. . . ."[17] The worshipping congregation below participates in a heavenly liturgy.

The S. Pudenziana mosaic does not explicitly identify the four living creatures with evangelists or their gospels. When mosaic artists elsewhere as-

14. As G. K. Beale puts it: "In Rev. 4.8a descriptions of the Isaiah 6 seraphim are merged with those of the Ezekiel 1 cherubim, but . . . the primary Old Testament framework of a heavenly being guarding God's throne is still retained" (*John's Use of the Old Testament in Revelation*, JSNTSupp [Sheffield: Sheffield Academic Press, 1998], p. 72).

15. On the basis of Jerome's interpretation of Ezekiel, Schlatter argues that the enthroned figure in the S. Pudenziana mosaic is not Christ but God ("Interpreting the Mosaic of Santa Pudenziana," *VC* 46 [1992], pp. 276-95; pp. 280-82). But it is hardly likely that a youthful God the Father could be portrayed as instructing the twelve beneath the cross. For further development of Schlatter's purely literary interpretation of the mosaic, see also "A Mosaic Interpretation of Jerome, *In Hiezechielem*," *VC* 49 (1995), pp. 64-81.

16. Mausoleum of Galla Placidia, Ravenna; Archiepiscopal Chapel, Ravenna; S. Apollinare in Classe, Ravenna; Baptistery, Alberga; S. Maria della Croce, Casarenello. For details, see Christa Ihm, *Die Programme der christlichen Apsismalerei vom vierten Jahrhundert bis zur Mitte des achten Jahrhunderts* (Wiesbaden: Franz Steiner, 1960).

17. *Tibi Cherubim et Seraphim incessabili voce proclamant, Sanctus, Sanctus, Sanctus, Dominus Deus Sabaoth*. This fourth-century hymn alludes here to Rv. 4.8 (καὶ ἀνάπαυσιν οὐκ ἔχουσιν ἡμέρας καὶ νυκτὸς λέγοντες, ἅγιος ἅγιος ἅγιος κύριος ὁ θεὸς ὁ παντοκράτωρ), as well as to Is. 6.3 (καὶ ἐκέκραγον ἕτερος πρὸς τὸν ἕτερον λέγοντες, ἅγιος ἅγιος ἅγιος κύριος σαβαωθ).

sign books to the creatures, the identification with evangelists is a secondary feature grafted onto a traditional representation of the worship of heaven. That is in no way to diminish the significance of the secondary motif; rather, it is to identify the liturgical context that gives the evangelist motif its significance. It is precisely the absence of the motif from the S. Pudenziana image that makes this context clear.[18]

That the cherubim of Ezekiel and the Apocalypse are initially unrelated to the evangelists is also evident from their appearance in a panel on the doors of the church of S. Sabina.[19]◆ This carved depiction occurs in the context of alternating rows of shorter and taller images, four to each row (i.e. two to each door). Eighteen of these panels survive, although their original order is unknown. Most of the ten smaller panels are concerned with the events of Christ's passion (4x) and resurrection (3x). Otherwise there are representations of the magi, Christ with Peter and Paul, and the abduction of Habakkuk — snatched up by an angel so as to deliver a meal to Daniel in the lion's den in faraway Babylon (cf. Dn. 14.33-39 LXX). Of the eight tall panels, three are concerned with the life of Moses: the burning bush (divided horizontally into three scenes), the victory over Pharaoh at the Red Sea (two scenes), and the provision of manna, quails, and water in the wilderness (three scenes). Two panels depict scenes from the gospels: Zechariah's emergence from the temple after his angelic vision,[20] and the miracles of Lazarus raised, loaves multi-

---

18. If there is a secondary allusion to the evangelists in the S. Pudenziana image, it may be to the Irenaean version of the scheme rather than to Jerome's. In the prologue to his Luke commentary, Ambrose adopts Irenaeus's identifications but reorders them so that they conform to the sequence both of Ez. 1.10 (as in S. Pudenziana) and of Old Latin gospel books: Matthew = human, John = lion, Luke = calf, Mark = eagle (Ambrose, *Expositio Evangelii secundum Lucam*, ed. G. Schenkl, CSEL 32/4 [Vienna: Österreichische Akademie der Wissenschaften, 1902], prol., 8). On this see Theodor Zahn, *Forschungen zur Geschichte des neutestamentlichen Kanons und der altkirchlichen Literatur*, II (Erlangen: Deichert, 1883), pp. 259-60n, 266-67. Ambrose here enumerates the gospels without naming them, and Zahn argues convincingly that the descriptions of the second and fourth gospels suggest the equations John = lion and Mark = eagle rather than the reverse. The lion is associated with power, the eagle with resurrection. It is said of the second, lion-like evangelist: ". . . a potentiae coepit expressione divinae, quod ex rege rex, fortis ex forti, verus ex vero, vivida mortem virtute contemserit." For the opening assertion of divine power, cf. Jn. 1.1-3; for the life that overcomes death, cf. Jn. 1.4-5. Likewise the *ex*- formulations, reminiscent of the Nicene Creed *(deum verum de deo vero)*, strongly suggest a connection to the Johannine prologue rather than the Markan one. Of the fourth, eagle-like evangelist it is said: ". . . copiosius ceteris divinae miracula resurrectionis expressit." Zahn plausibly suggests a reference to Mk. 16.9-20, which provides "die vollständigste Aufzählung der Erscheinungen der Auferstandenen" (*Forschungen*, II, p. 260n).

19. Online images at gospelwriting.wordpress.com.

20. The scene corresponds closely to Lk. 1.21-22, when allowance is made for minor adjust-

plied, and water into wine. Three further panels are concerned with assumptions or ascensions into heaven (Elijah, Moses, Christ). It is in the last of these that the four living creatures make their appearance, although the interpretation of this and other key images is disputed. If the identifications suggested here are correct, it is possible to identify an overall theological design based on a series of parallels between Moses and Jesus and focused especially on the theme of ascension. The role of the four cherubim is to bear Jesus to heaven. There is as yet no connection with the evangelists.

The panel is divided into upper and lower zones. In the upper zone, Christ stands facing forward, his head raised and his right arm extended. From his left hand hangs an open scroll, on which the letters I Θ | X C | Y are displayed — an anagram of ἰχθύς — between the enlarged A and ω on either side of him. He and the lettering that identifies him are contained within the inner rim of a circle or wheel, linked to the outer rim by crisscross patterning broken only by a further small circle at the summit, directly above Christ's head. The whole construction alludes to the wheels of Ezekiel's vision, which rose up with the living creatures that bore them (cf. Ez. 1.15-21). Outside the wheel and in the top left corner of the panel an eagle's head is seen in profile, its two wings filling most of the available space between the circle and the corner of the frame; in the top right corner is a corresponding lion's head with wings. The winged human and the calf are located to the left and right of the lower part of the wheel. The four creatures' heads are close to the wheel but do not quite touch it; rather, it is enclosed and borne up by their wings, its upward motion indicated above all by Christ's raised head. He is in mid-flight, with the earth and the visible heavens far beneath him but with further realms to traverse before he takes his seat at the right hand of God. Thus the dome of the lower heavens rises to touch the lower edge of the wheel; the human and the calf occupy the spaces

---

ments to the perspective and time frame required in order to display the angel. The only problematic element is the cross on the temple roof, which may have been introduced so as to present the Jerusalem temple as precursor to the new Christian churches there. Since the angel has just announced the birth of John the Baptist as the new Elijah (cf. Lk. 1.17), the panel is linked thematically to the one depicting Elijah's heavenly ascent. E. Kantorowicz's attempt to read this panel as a christianized and eschatological rendering of an imperial *adventus* reflects an overvaluation of the significance of imperial imagery for early Christian art ("The 'King's Advent' and the Enigmatic Panels in the Doors of Santa Sabina," *ArtB* 26 [1944], pp. 207-31; pp. 221-23). R. Delbrueck goes still further in this direction, finding here a visit of the Eastern emperor Theodosius II (408-50) to a provincial town ("The Acclamation Scene on the Doors of Santa Sabina," *ArtB* 31 [1949], pp. 215-17; p. 216). For critique of the political hermeneutic of Kantorowicz and others, see Mathews, *Clash of Gods,* pp. 3-22.

created by the two opposing curves. Within the lower dome are the moon on the left and a blazing sun on the right; five stars make up the complement of seven "planets" beneath the sphere of the fixed stars. Below the heavenly bodies stand three human figures, a veiled woman (probably Mary) between two male disciples (Peter and Paul?). Mary cranes her neck as if to catch a last glimpse of her ascending son. The disciples on either side of her hold over her head a mysterious object, a circle or wheel enclosing a cross with its vertical arm extended upwards beyond the circumference. Mary's head is framed by this object and the outstretched arms of the disciples. Has it descended from the heavenly chariot? Is it a diminutive mirror-image of the wheel in which Christ ascends, with the cross representing Christ himself? If so, it symbolizes the angelic promise — and the disciples' grasp of it — that Christ will one day return as he departed (cf. Acts 1.10-11). Thus the gaze of the two lower cherubim is directed not towards the heavenly chariot they convey upward but downward towards its descending simulacrum, the pledge of the disciples' future hope. Although the cherubim are beyond the dome of heaven while the disciples still stand beneath it, downward and upward gaze converge on the cross-circle which speaks of Christ's return to his own. Motifs from Ezekiel and Acts combine: the role of the cherubim is not only to conduct Christ to his heavenly throne but also to communicate the good news of his glorious parousia to disciples left behind on earth.[21]

This panel alludes to the parousia, but its primary theme is the ascending rather than descending Christ. It has been argued that the parousia itself is here depicted, in spite of Jesus' uplifted eyes and the presence of disciples as witnesses; Jesus' ascension is said to have been depicted already in the preceding panel, i.e. in the third of the upper sequence of tall panels.[22] But this is very unlikely. In this panel the ascending figure is dragged awkwardly into heaven by two angels who lean over the celestial walls and grasp him firmly by his hands. He has been raised from a lying rather than an upright posture. To the right, outside the walls, a third angel gestures with his right hand towards the corpse-like figure. Below are two pairs of human figures, surrounded by the swirling clouds that envelop the whole scene. Each pair seems to represent the same individual at a different point in time — a presentational technique also employed in the burning bush panel, where two

---

21. A verbal message is also transformed into a symbol in the panel that depicts Moses at the burning bush, where Moses' commission takes the form of a scroll handed down from heaven.

22. This is the influential view of E. Kantorowicz, who identifies the descending object in the panel with the cherubim as "the sign of the Son of man" (Mt. 24.30), the precursor of the descending Christ ("Enigmatic Panels," pp. 223-28).

adjacent figures represent Moses protesting his inadequacy and his eventual acceptance of his commission. In the first pairing, the seated figure on the left views the ascension event with intense concern, arms outstretched and neck craned. The figure on the right is also seated, but cross-legged on the ground and with his hand supporting his head, meditating on what he has seen. Below, in the second pairing, the right-hand figure looks up with outstretched arms in a pose very like that of the figure diagonally opposite above, although with less clearly focused gaze. This is the second individual's response to a moment of vision. To the left the same individual is now standing, gesturing with his left hand and descending from the elevated place where the vision has occurred.

It is astonishing that this panel could ever have been seen as depicting the ascension of Jesus. Jesus' body should not be dragged into heaven as if it were a corpse. Renderings in other panels of the assumption of Elijah and the abduction of Habakkuk indicate the artist's interest in Old Testament anticipations of Jesus' ascension, and this panel too must relate to some scriptural precedent. One obvious candidate would be Enoch, of whom it is said (by angels) that "he was taken away from the sons of men, and we conducted him into the garden of Eden in majesty and honour" (*Jubilees* 4.23; cf. Gn. 5.24). A still stronger candidate is Moses. The lost *Assumption of Moses* is said to have narrated a dispute between Michael and Satan over possession of Moses' body, which Michael was sent to bury in the sight of Joshua and Caleb.[23] Michael would then be the angel outside the heavenly walls who points to Moses' corpse. In the apocryphal text Moses is simultaneously seen to be both buried and assumed into heaven; as Origen reports, there is here a double vision of a dead Moses and of a living Moses.[24] It is this duality that the artist conveys by way of the corpse-like posture and the entrance into heaven respectively. The fullest account of this two-sided event is given by Clement of Alexandria, who interprets it as an allegory of the true scriptural hermeneutic:

So it is appropriate that Joshua son of Nun saw Moses being taken up [Μωϋσέα ἀναλαμβανόμενον] in two forms: one with the angels, the other

---

23. Cf. Dt. 34.5-6; Jude 9; Origen, *De Principiis* iii.2.1. The lost *Assumption of Moses* is to be distinguished from the fragmentary work sometimes given that title but more appropriately known as the *Testament of Moses*. For patristic references to the lost work, see R. H. Charles, *The Assumption of Moses* (London: Adam & Charles Black, 1897), pp. 105-10.

24. In his commentary on Joshua (*Homiliae* ii.1, cited by Charles, *Assumption*, p. 108), Origen states that, according to the noncanonical text, *duo Moses videbantur, unus vivus in spiritu, alius mortuus in corpore*.

on the mountains being honourably buried [ἀξιούμενον] within their clefts. Joshua beheld this sight from below, being raised up in the Spirit, along with Caleb. Yet the two of them did not behold in the same way, but one of them descended immediately, as if bearing a great weight, while the other descended later and told of the glory he had seen, having more power of perception than the other on account of his greater purity. In my view, the story indicates that not all possess knowledge. For some view the body of the scriptures, its words and names, like the body of Moses, while others see through to the ideas and the realities signified by the names, wholly absorbed [πολυπραγμονεύοντες] with the Moses who is with the angels.[25]

The S. Sabina image corresponds remarkably closely to the scene as described by Clement. Moses' body is drawn into heaven by angels in the sight of Joshua (above) and Caleb (below), who have been with him during his last moments on the mountaintop; Caleb hurries downward, Joshua remains behind to reflect on the vision. Since the subject of this panel is the assumption of Moses and not the ascension of Jesus, the latter theme remains available for treatment on the neighbouring panel. Like the assumption of Elijah, dramatically rendered at the end of the fourth row of panels, and the abduction of Habakkuk directly above it, the assumption of Moses is a scriptural or quasi-scriptural precedent for the ascension of Jesus. In each of the three cases, angels are actively involved. A (nonscriptural) angel deftly removes the mantle from the ascending Elijah as Elisha clutches at it from below. Another equally agile angel seizes Habakkuk by the hair — although he is to be transported not to heaven but to Babylon. Jesus' ascension is both the fulfilment of these scriptural types and the goal towards which the scenes from his nativity, ministry, passion, and resurrection are directed. In spite of impressive parallels especially with the life of Moses, Jesus' life, death, resurrection, and ascension represent a unique case. Moses is lifted up to heaven by cloud and wind below and angels above; Elijah ascends in a chariot drawn by heavenly horses. But Jesus is raised far above the visible heavens in a wheel-like chariot-throne conveyed by the four cherubim. His superiority to his precursors is manifest. Yet it cannot be said that he transcends the Old Testament itself, for the manner of his ascension is more decisively shaped by Ezekiel's vision than by the narrative of Acts. As in Ezekiel and in contrast to Revelation, the role of the cherubim here is not to worship

25. Clement of Alexandria, *Strom.* vi.15.132.2-3.

but to provide transport. As in the apse image of S. Pudenziana, there is as yet no reference to the fourfold gospel.

In spite of the differences between the images from the two Roman basilicas, the underlying structural parallel should be noted. In both cases, a contrast between what takes place above and below is immediately visible. The cherubim occupy the upper zone, Jesus' followers the lower: the twelve apostles and two unidentified women at S. Pudenziana, and Peter, Mary, and Paul at S. Sabina. The two images include both a representation and a symbol of the enthroned Christ. At S. Sabina, Christ appears within the chariot-throne in the upper zone, while his followers receive the encircled cross as the token of his future return. Conversely, at S. Pudenziana Christ is seated on a gold, jewel-encrusted throne in the midst of his apostles, while the cross that rises behind his throne signifies his heavenly enthronement among the cherubim. The fact that image and symbol change places is less significant than the common representation of earthly and heavenly zones, within which Christ is associated with his followers below and the cherubim above.

This bipartite structure is again in the literary evidence of an object allegedly donated by Constantine for the adornment of the *Basilica Constantiana*, San Giovanni in Laterano. The object is described in the *Liber Pontificalis* as a *fastigium*, perhaps referring to a *ciborium* or altar canopy.[26] Dating from the pontificate of Sylvester I (314-35), the *fastigium* is said to have been destroyed by Alaric's Goths and replaced by the emperor Valentinian III during the pontificate of Sixtus III (432-40). It incorporated silver statues of Christ seated among his apostles on one side, facing the nave and therefore visible to the congregation, and corresponding statues of Christ enthroned among four angels on the other, facing the apse and visible only to bishop and priests. This two-part design may represent not only Jesus' earthly life and subsequent exaltation but also, more abstractly, his humanity and his divinity.[27] The angels were equipped with spears, not books,

---

26. "Basilicam Constantianam, ubi posuit ista dona: fasti<g>ium argenteum battutilem, qui habet in fronte Salvatorem sedentem in sella . . . , et XII apostolos . . . , cum coronas argento purissimo; item in tergo respiciens in absida Salvatorem sedentem in throno . . . , et angelos IIII ex argento . . . , cum gemmis alabandenis in oculos, tenentes astas" (L. Duchesne [ed.], *Liber Pontificalis* [Paris: E. de Boccard, 1955], 1.172; references to height and weight omitted). For English translations of this sixth- or seventh-century work, see Louise Ropes Loomis, *The Book of the Popes, I. To the Pontificate of Gregory I* (New York: Columbia University Press, 1916); Raymond Davis, *The Book of Pontiffs (Liber Pontificalis to AD 715)* (Liverpool: Liverpool University Press, 1989).

27. So B. Brenk, *The Apse, the Image, and the Icon: An Historical Perspective of the Apse as a Space for Images* (Wiesbaden: Reichert, 2010), pp. 51-52; see also Figs. 12, 57, 58. The historicity of

and have no connection whatever to the evangelists; they are apparently en-visaged as a heavenly bodyguard. Yet the fact that there are four of them, two on either side of the enthroned Christ, suggests that these are still the cheru-bim but in anthropomorphic rather than theriomorphic guise. Later paral-lels suggest that the two schemes are interchangeable, and that the heavenly throne may be upheld and encircled either by the four living creatures of Ezekiel and Revelation (as at S. Pudenziana and S. Sabina), or by four winged angels bearing a human appearance.[28] Where books are assigned to the four living creatures, the theriomorphic and anthropomorphic schemes are differentiated and may even be combined;[29] yet the very fact of the com-bination confirms their original equivalence.

Further confirmation of this equivalence may be seen in the representa-tion of the *Agnus Dei* with pairs of doves facing it on either side, in the apse mosaic in the narthex of the baptistery of S. Giovanni in Laterano, dated to c. 440.[30] These unobtrusive and naturalistic figures are located in the sum-mit of the apse, standing on a semicircular rim that divides the upper zone from the acanthus design below. The rim imitates a marble egg-and-dart cornice, an appropriate setting for the birds that stand in profile along its upper edge, if not for the lamb, facing forward in their midst. Each figure is enclosed within the arc of a parabola with floral patterning, a substitute for the missing nimbus. Below the ends of the arcs six jewelled crosses hang as if suspended from the rim, overlapping with the upper scrolls of the acanthus rising from below and representing the point of contact between heaven and earth. Above the doves and lamb is a conch-like canopy. At the base of the design, beneath the green flowery meadow from which the acanthus grows, twelve stars distributed along a blue strip represent the twelve apostles. This horizontal line is connected to the lamb above by the vertical central shaft of the acanthus. While a lamb will normally represent Christ, the dove symbol

the statues described in the *Liber Pontificalis* has been questioned, in view of lack of evidence for iconic representation in the churches of the Constantinian era (so Robert Grigg, "Constantine the Great and the Cult without Images," *Viator* 8 [1977], pp. 1-32). Even if unhistorical, the description in the *Liber Pontificalis* would still attest a plausible representational programme.

28. The theriomorphic scheme is also exemplified in the vault of the Mausoleum of Galla Placidia (Ravenna) and in the baptistery of Naples Cathedral; the anthropomorphic, in S. Apollinare Nuovo (Ravenna, apse end of north wall), S. Vitale (Ravenna, choir vault), Chapel of S. Zeno (S. Prassede, Rome, vault).

29. Chapel of the Archiepiscopal Palace (Ravenna, vault); S. Cosmo e Damiano and S. Prassede (both Rome, apse arch).

30. See Brenk, *Apse*, Col. Fig. 11-12. Brenk sees here "an important aniconic answer to the sil-ver statues of the *fastigium* in the Lateran church" (p. 25).

is used more flexibly. Doves perched on the rim of a fountain and perhaps drinking from it can represent individuals submitting to baptism.[31] Twelve doves surrounding a Chi-Rho symbol,[32] or distributed along the horizontal and vertical arms of a cross,[33] obviously represent the twelve apostles. Four doves surrounding a lamb can only refer to the cherubim. Here too, as at S. Pudenziana and S. Sabina, the cherubim are associated with the exalted Christ in the upper zone of an image, with apostles or apostle-symbols below. The use of the dove image confirms that the cherubim, like the exalted Christ, can be variously represented, and that neither theriomorphic nor anthropomorphic images were intended to bear a naively literal sense. If the cherubim lead the heavenly worship of the divine and exalted Christ, the theriomorphic images underline their transcendent otherness while the anthropomorphic ones indicate the commonality of heavenly and earthly worshippers. As doves too, the cherubim are worshippers of Christ the lamb, whom they encircle and towards whom they turn. In contrast to the majestic yet alien figures in the S. Pudenziana mosaic, the message here is that there is nothing to fear from the exalted Christ or his heavenly attendants.

At much the same time as these images from the first half of the fifth century, the four cherubim acquire books and are henceforth rarely depicted without them. They become the heavenly patrons of the four evangelists. Yet they do not cease to be cherubim, the four living creatures who encircle the throne of Christ with their song of praise. The new images do not *replace* the cherubim with mere "symbols of the evangelists," rather they represent the comprehensive liturgical context within which the fourfold gospel has its being.

Jerome in Ravenna

As these images from Roman churches demonstrate, the link between the cherubim and the gospels is secondary, grafted onto a prior tradition in which the cherubim are associated not with the gospels but with the exalted Christ. Yet the linkage was already well-known in Christian literary circles, especially in Rome and the West. Given the likely overlap between such cir-

---

31. Mausoleum of Galla Placidia (Ravenna), where the image recurs four times between preaching apostles in the surfaces below the vault.

32. Brenk, *Apse,* Col. Fig. 13 (Alberga, baptistery).

33. S. Clemente (Rome, apse).

cles and those who commissioned the decoration of the new basilicas, it is only to be expected that the literary assimilation of the cherubim to the fourfold gospel should in due course exert its influence over the developing tradition of artistic representation. This confluence of literary and artistic traditions creates a range of new possibilities for conceptualizing and visualizing the fourfold gospel.

Irenaeus's linkage between the cherubim and the gospels was further developed by Victorinus of Petovium (d. 304) in his commentary on Revelation.[34] Arriving at the seer's account of the divine throne, the living creatures and the elders in Revelation 4, Victorinus discovers here a set of symbols referring either to the judgement or to scripture. His text follows the majority reading in omitting any reference to the occupant of the throne: what John saw was "a throne placed in heaven, and upon the throne seated like the appearance of jasper and carnelian, and a rainbow around the throne like the appearance of an emerald" (Rv. 4.2b-3). In spite of the word "seated," what was visible upon the throne was something like two precious stones, one of which Victorinus believes to be blue, the other red. The stones on the divine throne thus represent the two judgements, one by water, which is past, the other by fire, which is to come. Although the rainbow assures Noah and his descendants that there will be no further inundation, a judgement of fire remains. Salvation is at hand, however: the crystal sea before the throne represents baptism, the precious divine gift bestowed during the time of repentance that precedes the judgement. Further help in preparing for the judgement is provided by the holy scriptures, symbolized by the four living creatures and the twenty-four elders (Rv. 4.4, 6b-8):

> The four are gospels: the first (he says) like a lion, the second like a calf, the third like a man, the fourth like a flying eagle, each having six wings and with eyes round about, both within and without, and (he continues) they do not cease to say, "Holy, holy, holy, Lord God almighty!" The

34. Victorinus of Petovium, *Commentarii in Apocalypsim Iohannis*, in *Victorini Episcopi Petavionensis Opera*, ed. J. Haussleiter, CSEL 49 (Vienna: F. Tempsky; Leipzig: G. Freytag, 1916); *Victorin de Poetovio. Sur l'Apocalypse et autres écrits*, ed. Martine Dulaey, SC (Paris: du Cerf, 1997). According to Jerome, Victorinus also composed commentaries on Old Testament books (Genesis, Exodus, Leviticus, Isaiah, Ezekiel, Habakkuk, Ecclesiastes, and the Song of Songs), as well as a work against heresies; he died a martyr's death (*De Vir. Ill.* 74). Jerome is critical of his Latin style, however (*Letters* lviii.10; lxx.5). English translations of relevant excerpts from Victorinus's commentary are found in *Ancient Christian Commentary on Scripture, New Testament XII: Revelation*, ed. William C. Weinrich (Downers Grove, IL: IVP, 2005), pp. 58-68.

twenty-four elders are the twenty-four books of the prophets and the law, relating the testimonies of the judgement. They are also the twenty-four fathers, twelve apostles and twelve patriarchs.[35]

In spite of the songs of praise that continue to issue forth, it seems that the divine throne is now surrounded not by animate beings but by books — although Victorinus immediately adds that the elders represent not only the law and the prophets but also the apostles and patriarchs. His major interest is in the four living creatures, however, and here his interpretation is drawn directly from Irenaeus. The first living creature resembles a lion and signifies the Gospel of John, leonine in the boldness with which it proclaims the preexistent divinity of Christ. When John taught that "the Word was God," he "cried out like a lion roaring" *(tanquam leo fremens exclamavit),* and that is why his proclamation as a whole is signified by the lion-like face of the first living creature. The other three gospels emphasize the humanity rather than the divinity. The contrast is especially clear in the case of Matthew, whose gospel opens by tracing Jesus' human origins back through Joseph and Mary to David and Abraham. Thus Matthew is identified with the third living creature, which bore a human likeness. The second living creature is the calf and signifies Luke, whose narrative opens as the priest Zechariah ministers in the temple. The fourth living creature, the eagle in flight, is appropriate to Mark, who opens with the prophetic utterance of Isaiah. The sequence *lion-human-calf-eagle* corresponds to *John-Matthew-Luke-Mark.*

While this pairing of evangelists with their symbols is drawn from Irenaeus,[36] Victorinus has his own contribution to the development of this imagery. His contrast between divinity and humanity has necessitated a modification of the scriptural sequence, with the Matthean human promoted above the Lukan calf; this broad contrast will later be taken up by Augustine, although on the basis of a different set of identifications.[37] Victorinus has also noticed another scriptural foursome, surprisingly overlooked by Irenaeus: the four gospels proceed from one mouth, "like the river in paradise, from one source dividing into four heads."[38] Ingeniously, he points out that the

---

35. Victorinus, *In Apoc.* 4.3.

36. Irenaeus, *Adv. Haer.* iii.11.8.

37. Augustine, *De Cons. Evang.* i.2.3–6.9. On this see Chapter 1, above.

38. Victorinus, *In Apoc.* 4.4; cf. Gn. 2.10-14. This interpretation of the four rivers occurred earlier in Hippolytus, *In Danielem* i.17: "Christ, himself being the river, is preached in the whole world through the fourfold Gospel" (cited in C. E. Hill, *Who Chose the Gospels? Probing the Great Gospel Conspiracy* [Oxford: Oxford University Press, 2010], p. 44). On Hippolytus's commentary,

four six-winged creatures possess a total of twenty-four wings, corresponding to the twenty-four elders, i.e. the books of the law and the prophets. We
learn from this that, "as an animal cannot fly unless it has wings, so too the
announcement of the new covenant lacks credibility without the previously
announced testimonies of the old covenant, by which it is lifted up from the
earth and flies."[39] If the four living creatures (the gospels) are deprived of the
wings that represent their dependence on the elders (the scriptures), their exalted position will be unsustainable and they will fall Icarus-like from heaven
to earth. This is just what happens when certain heretics dispense with the
Old Testament scriptures while continuing to use the gospels. The eagle in
flight is representative of all the other winged creatures. Although it is appro-
priated to Mark in view of the Isaiah citation that opens this gospel, the inter-
dependence of gospel and scripture is equally important in the other gospels.

Jerome produced a new edition of Victorinus's commentary (c. 398) in
response to a correspondent, Anatolius, who had sent a copy with a request
for an evaluation.[40] The comments on Revelation 20–21 are rewritten in order
to eliminate millennialist traits, and Jerome also takes the opportunity to re-
consider Victorinus's identification of the four living creatures. The revised
sequence *lion-human-calf-eagle* is maintained, and Victorinus's remarks
about the Matthean human and the Lukan calf are allowed to stand with only
minor stylistic modifications. John and Mark change places, however: Mark
acquires the lion as his patron, John the eagle. According to Victorinus,

> Mark opens thus: "The beginning of the gospel of Jesus Christ, as it is
> written in Isaiah." He starts from the flying spirit [*advolante spiritu*], and
> so he has the image of the flying eagle.

In his version of this passage, Jerome makes two additions and one substitution:

> Mark <the Evangelist> opening thus, "The beginning of the gospel of Jesus
> Christ, as it is written in Isaiah <the prophet, The voice of one crying in
> the wilderness [*vox clamantis in deserto*]">, has the image <of the lion>.[41]

---

preserved in Old Slavonic and in extensive Greek fragments, see Charles Kannengieser, *Handbook
of Patristic Exegesis: The Bible in Ancient Christianity* (Leiden and Boston: Brill, 2006), pp. 530-31.

39. Victorinus, *In Apoc.* 4.5.

40. Jerome's revision of the commentary is printed alongside Victorinus's original in the
CSEL edition. There is an English translation of the Jerome version in ANF 7, pp. 344-60.

41. Jerome/Victorinus, *In Apoc.* 4.4.

The switch from the flying eagle to the lion involves a corresponding shift from the theme of prophecy as such, associated with the Holy Spirit and so, loosely, with wings and flight, to the content of that prophecy, the voice in the desert. Jerome's Markan lion derives his roar from Victorinus's Johannine one. According to Victorinus,

> The living creature like a lion is the Gospel according to John, because, after all the evangelists had preached Christ as made human, he preached him as God before he came down and took flesh, saying: "The Word was God." And because he cried out like a roaring lion [*tamquam leo fremens exclamavit*], his proclamation bears the lion's face.[42]

Jerome replaces this with the following: "John the Evangelist, taking wing like an eagle soaring into the heights, discourses of the Word of God."[43] Detached from John, Victorinus's reference to the lion's roar proves useful in establishing the new connection with Mark. The first, lion-like living creature now designates not John but Mark, and the voice of one crying in the wilderness *(vox clamantis in deserto)* is equated with the voice of the lion roaring in the desert *(vox leonis in heremo rugientis)*.[44] Victorinus's Johannine *leo fremens* is the source of Jerome's Markan *leo rugiens*. Irenaeus and Augustine underline the regal character of their respective Johannine and Matthean lions, but do not require them to roar.[45] At the very point where Jerome diverges from Victorinus's version of the scheme, he remains dependent on it.[46]

In the original scheme, Irenaeus draws from Revelation 4.7 the sequence *lion-calf-human-eagle*, which, he claims, corresponds to *John-Luke-Matthew-Mark*. This is at odds with Irenaeus's account of the historical order, in which

---

42. Victorinus, *In Apoc.* 4.4.

43. Jerome/Victorinus, *In Apoc.* 4.4.

44. Jerome/Victorinus, *In Apoc.* 4.4.

45. Irenaeus, *Adv. Haer.* iii.11.8; Augustine, *De Cons. Evang.* i.6.9, with a reference to "the lion of the tribe of Judah" (Rv. 5.5). Ambrose's lion is associated with strength and kingship, and is again probably identified with John (*In Luc.* Prol. 8). According to Epiphanius, however, it is the Markan Jesus who is a "lion king"; Jer. 27.44 LXX (50.44) is cited in the form, ὅτι κύριος ἀναβήσεται ὥσπερ λέων ἐξ Ἰορδάνου (*De Mens.* 35; the retroversion from the Syriac is from Zahn, *Forschungen*, II, p. 258n). Here the scriptural text is presumably linked with Jesus' baptism and the descent of the messianic Spirit (cf. Mk. 1.9-10).

46. The equations themselves (human = Mt, lion = Mk, calf = Lk, eagle = Jn) may derive from Epiphanius (*De Mens.* 35). In Jerome's work these equations are first attested in his *C. Iovin.* i.26.

Matthew wrote first in Hebrew, to be followed by the nonapostolic Mark and Luke and finally by John.[47] In Victorinus the calf and the human change places, so that the sequence *lion-human-calf-eagle* corresponds to *John-Matthew-Luke-Mark*. In Jerome's revision of Victorinus it is John and Mark who change places; the resulting sequence is *Mark-Matthew-Luke-John*, which approximates more closely both to the historical order and to the (Greek) canonical order that Jerome's translation seeks to establish in the West. A precise correspondence between historical and canonical order is achieved by deriving the scheme not from Revelation 4.7 but from Ezekiel 1.10, where the human face is mentioned first: *human-lion-calf-eagle* = *Matthew-Mark-Luke-John*. The simple mapping of the canonical order onto one of the two prophetic texts may account in part for the success of Jerome's identifications. While neither Victorinus nor Jerome as his editor mentions Ezekiel in the context of the Revelation commentary, the Ezekiel passage is cited as the primary source of the identifications in the preface to Jerome's commentary on Matthew, evidently written in the immediate aftermath of Jerome's work on Victorinus. Here he (1) differentiates canonical from noncanonical gospels, (2) recounts their circumstances of origin, and (3) links them to Ezekiel's cherubim. The preface concludes with an apologia for the perceived inadequacy of the commentary that follows; mention is made of persistent illness and an unreasonably tight deadline imposed by the dedicatee. Following the lead of Origen before him, Jerome chooses to preface this hastily composed commentary with introductory remarks not about Matthew alone but about the fourfold gospel as a whole.

(1) The preface opens with a contrast derived from Origen's homilies on Luke between the many spurious gospels and the provision the Lord has made for his church:

> That there are many who have written gospels is attested by the Evangelist Luke, who states: "Since many have attempted to compose a narrative of the things fulfilled among us, as those handed them down to us who from the beginning beheld the Word and ministered to him [*qui . . . ipsi viderunt sermonem et ministraverunt ei*] . . ." And texts persisting into the present time show that what was produced by a variety of authors became the starting-point for a variety of heresies — for example, those that are "according to" the Egyptians, or Thomas, or Matthias, or Bartholomew, or "of" the Twelve Apostles or Basilides or Apelles, and others

47. Irenaeus, *Adv. Haer.* iii.1.1.

too numerous to mention. All that is necessary at present is to state that there were some who, lacking the Spirit or grace of God, attempted to compose a narrative rather than setting down the historical truth [*historiae texere veritatem*]. To such people the prophetic word may properly be applied: "Woe to those who prophesy from their own heart, who walk according to their own spirit, who say, Thus says the Lord, when the Lord has not sent them." Of these the Saviour too speaks in the Gospel of John: "All who came before me are thieves and robbers" — that is, who "came" rather than being "sent." For he says, "They came and I did not send them." In those who "came" is presumption and rashness; in those who were "sent," obedience and service. But the church — founded upon a rock by the word of the Lord, whom "the King brought into his bedchamber," and to whom "he put forth his hand through the aperture" of a hidden channel, "like a roe or a young stag," pouring out four rivers as in Paradise — possesses four corners and rings through which is conveyed as it were the Ark of the Covenant that contains in solid wood the Law of the Lord.[48]

Following Origen, Jerome understands the Lukan preface to refer to the uninspired gospels that some continue to read alongside the canonical four, and finds an analogy in the scriptural conflict between true and false prophecy.[49] Apart from the reference to Apelles, Jerome's examples of noncanonical gospels are exactly the same as Origen's, suggesting that he may not have been acquainted with them at first hand. Neither author is concerned at the implication that noncanonical gospels may predate canonical ones. It is divine inspiration that differentiates the two types of gospel literature, not relative dating. According to Origen, the authors of the noncanonical gospels "attempted" to write gospels, whereas Matthew, Mark, Luke, and John "wrote through the Holy Spirit." Jerome similarly differentiates between gospel-writers who "came," writing on their own initiative, and those who were "sent." In a profusion of erotic imagery from the Song of Songs and Genesis, Jerome now sets the gospels within the context of Christ's love for his church. The four gospels are nothing less than the intimate communication of the divine lover with his beloved, who opens the door that separates

48. Text in Aland, pp. 546-47; PL 26.16-18; *Hieronymus, Commentariorum in Matheum libri IV*, ed. D. Hurst and M. Adriaen, CCSL 77 (Turnhout: Brepols, 1969), pp. 1-2. Scriptural citations are from Lk. 1.1-2; Ez. 13.3, 6; Jn. 10.8; Sg. 1.4; 2.9; 5.4.

49. Compare Jerome's amplified translation of Origen's remarks on Lk. 1.1, *Hom. in Luc.*, GCS, pp. 3-5.

them so that they may be one. Their source is the river that watered the Garden of Eden, which passed through a hidden underground channel and issued in the four great rivers that encircle the world (cf. Gn. 2.10-14).[50] To drink from these rivers is to experience communion with the Beloved. In a simpler image, the gospels resemble the four golden rings attached to the corners of the ark of the covenant so that it could be carried on poles and accompany the people of God on their pilgrimage (cf. Ex. 25.12).

(2) Matthew, also known as Levi, wrote his gospel in Hebrew, "mainly for those of the Jews who had believed in Jesus and were vainly observing the shadow of the law when the truth of the gospel had come."[51] Mark, disciple of Peter and bishop of Alexandria, never saw the Lord, "but what he had heard his master preaching he narrated in faith in what had occurred rather than in sequence."[52] Luke, a doctor from Antioch and disciple of Paul, also wrote what he had heard from others rather than seen for himself. In response to the rise of various heresies, John was moved "to write more profoundly about the divinity of the Saviour and, as I may say, to break through to the Word of God himself with a boldness not so much presumptuous as felicitous."[53] This is all conventional gospel preface material along the lines first established by Papias and Irenaeus.

(3) There follows an abbreviated version of the rewritten material from Victorinus, with several verbal overlaps (italicized) but with the sequence adjusted to correspond to Ezekiel 1 rather than Revelation 4:

That these four gospels were long before predicted is proved by the Book of Ezekiel, where his first vision is described as follows: "And in the midst as if the likeness of four living creatures, and their appearance was the face of a man and the face of a lion and the face of a calf and the face of an eagle." The first face, that of a man, signifies Matthew, who as if *of a man* began by writing, "The book of the genealogy of Jesus Christ, son of David, son of Abraham." The second signifies Mark, *in whom is heard the voice of a lion roaring in the desert*: "The voice of one crying in the wilderness, Pre-

---

50. For the underground channel or "aperture of a hidden descent" *(foramen descensionis occultae)*, see Philo, *Quaestiones et Solutiones in Genesin* i.12. Aware that the sources of the Tigris and Euphrates are in the mountains of Armenia and that no Paradise is to be found there, Philo hypothesizes an underground river flowing from a more distant Eden and giving rise to rivers throughout the world.

51. PL 26.18; CCSL 77, p. 2.

52. PL 26.18; CCSL 77, p. 2.

53. PL 26.19; CCSL 77, pp. 2-3.

pare the way of the Lord, make straight his paths." The third, the face of the calf, prefigures Luke, who begins with Zechariah the priest. The fourth is *John the Evangelist, who, taking wing like an eagle soaring into the heights, discourses of the Word of God.*[54]

Here the Ezekiel order of the faces corresponds to the historical order *Matthew-Mark-Luke-John*, familiar from gospel prefaces from Irenaeus onwards. Other relevant Ezekiel passages are identified before Jerome turns to the Apocalypse for further confirmation:

The points that follow produce the same sense: "their legs were straight," "their feet winged," "and wherever the spirit went, they went and did not turn," "and their backs were full of eyes," and "wheels in wheels," and "to each four faces." So too the Apocalypse of John, after speaking of the twenty-four elders who, holding harps and bowls, worship the Lamb of God, refers to lightning, and thunder, and seven spirits moving about, and a sea of glass, and four living creatures full of eyes, saying: "The first animal like a lion, and the second like a calf, and the third like a man, and the fourth like a flying eagle," and a little later he continues, "they were full of eyes and took no rest day or night, saying: Holy, holy, holy, Lord God Almighty, who was and who is and who is to come." All these things show clearly that just four gospels are to be received, and that all the apocryphal ones are the dirges of dead heretics rather than the songs of living ecclesiastics.[55]

Some years later, writing his commentary on Ezekiel in the aftermath of the fall of Rome in 410, Jerome returns once again to the topic of the four-fold gospel, referring his reader back to the definitive statement of his position in the preface to the Matthew commentary. Further details in the Ezekiel text provoke further applications to the gospels. It is said of the cherubim that "their wings were joined one to another" (Ez. 1.9). Similarly,

the gospels are joined and belong together, and flying over the whole world they dash hither and thither. Their flight does not come to an end, nor are they anywhere overcome and forced to withdraw, but they always move on towards the limits [*ad ulteriora*].[56]

54. PL 26.19; CCSL 77, p. 3. Citations are from Ez. 1.5a + 10; Mt. 1.1; Mk. 1.3.
55. PL 26.19-20; CCSL 77, pp. 3-4. Citations are from Ez. 1.7a, 8(?), 12bc, 18, 16c, 6a; Rv. 5.8; 4.5-8.
56. PL 25.24; *Commentariorum in Hiezechielem libri XIV*, ed. F. Glorie, CCSL 75 (Turnhout: Brepols, 1964), pp. 14-15.

In Ezekiel 1.10, the human and leonine faces are said to be located on the right side, with the ox *(bos)* or calf *(vitulus)* on the left and the eagle above *(desuper)*.[57] In translating Ezekiel 1.10, Jerome has rightly noted that the Hebrew *šôr* refers to an "ox," a mature adult animal rather than a "calf" as in the LXX, where μόσχος is selected in preference to βοῦς. The "calf" must be retained alongside the ox, however, in order to preserve the link with Revelation 4.7. This distribution of the faces may be applied to the gospels. Matthew the human and Mark the lion are on the right, with one of them beginning with the birth of Christ and the other with the voice of the prophet thundering *(tonantis)* in the desert. Luke the calf or ox is on the left because the priesthood represented by Zechariah is shortly to come to an end. Above them all is the Johannine eagle with its insight into the Son's eternal generation from the Father. Thus the distribution of the faces corresponds to the character of the respective gospel openings.

From the midst of the living creatures fire and lightning shone forth (Ez. 1.13): "For if you strike the gospels against each other, in the midst of the letter and of common history [*in medio litterae vilisque historiae*] you will detect signs [*sacramenta*] of the Holy Spirit."[58] Fire and light are generated at precisely those points where the gospels clash with one another. The whole body of the living creatures was full of eyes (Ez. 1.18), teaching us that "there is nothing in the gospels that does not shine and illuminate the world with its splendour, so that even what seems small and mean is radiant with the majesty of the Holy Spirit."[59]

Jerome's identifications of the four living creatures of Ezekiel and Revelation make surprisingly little impact on the biblical commentators of the following generations. Of the Western commentators on Revelation, Caesarius of Arles makes a general identification of the four living creatures in the midst of the throne with the four evangelists in the midst of the church, but proceeds to suggest that the lion symbolizes the church's courage, the calf the passion of Christ, the human figure the church's humility, and the eagle the heavenly mysteries.[60] Cassiodorus is similarly noncommittal about the specific identities of the living creatures.[61] Primasius of Hadrametum appeals to Augustine in aligning Matthew with the lion, Mark

57. PL 25.24; CCSL 75, p. 15.
58. PL 25.26; CCSL 75, p. 19.
59. PL 25.28; CCSL 75, pp. 20-21.
60. PL 35.2422-23. For a useful bibliographical essay on early Revelation commentaries, see Francis X. Gumerlock, "Patristic Commentaries on Revelation," *Kerux* 23 (2008), pp. 3-13.
61. PL 70.1407.

with the human.[62] So too does Bede, although he is aware of other possibilities.[63] In the East, Andrew of Caesarea remains loyal to Irenaeus, with his Johannine lion and Markan eagle,[64] whereas some centuries later Dionysius Bar Salibi finds the Augustinian scheme more persuasive.[65]

These literary interpretations of the four living creatures diverge from the artistic ones. Within a few years, mosaic images begin to appear that reflect Jerome's version of the scheme rather than Augustine's.

As we have seen, the four living creatures are the cherubim, and — in visual rather than literary contexts — they are never simply *equated* with evangelists or books although they may come to be *associated* with them. The association is clear where the theriomorphic cherubim are displayed in the upper zone of an arch with a book between their hands, paws, hooves, or claws. Yet identification with a *particular* book is not explicit even here. The book held between the hooves of the ox or calf is presumably the Gospel of Luke, but the book remains closed and no title appears on the cover. There is indeed one early image where book titles are provided, in the so-called Mausoleum of Galla Placidia in Ravenna (*c.* 430), but here the books are located on the shelves of a cupboard, at several removes from the living creatures in the starry vault overhead. The question is whether a linkage between living creatures and books is nevertheless present here, and, if it is, whether Jerome's identifications are in view.

The Mausoleum is a small cruciform building originally attached to the narthex of the church of S. Croce.[66] It is named after Galla Placidia (*c.* 392-450), daughter of Theodosius I, mother of the Western emperor Valentinian III (419-55), regent of the Western empire (425-37), and a zealous builder and restorer of churches in Ravenna (S. Croce, S. Giovanni Evangelista), Rome (S. Paulo fuori le Mura), and Jerusalem (Holy Sepulchre).[67] Mosaic work covers most of the interior of the Mausoleum, and the main images occur on three levels.[68]◆

---

62. PL 68.817.

63. PL 93.144.

64. PG 106.257.

65. J. Sedláček, *Dionysius Bar Salibi, In Apocalypsim, Actus et Epistulas Catholicas*, I, 20 (Latin), 6.11-20 = II, 101 (Syriac), 9.3-16.

66. While Galla Placidia herself was buried in Rome, the mausoleum may have been intended for her infant son (so Gillian Mackie, "The Mausoleum of Galla Placidia: A Possible Occupant," *Byzantion* 65 [1995], pp. 396-404).

67. See Stewart Oost, *Galla Placidia: A Biographical Essay* (Chicago and London: University of Chicago Press, 1968); Hagith Sivan, *Galla Placidia: The Last Roman Empress* (Oxford: Oxford University Press, 2011).

68. Online images at gospelwriting.wordpress.com. A comprehensive collection of black-

In the dome a golden Latin cross at the centre is surrounded by concentric rings of stars, with the four living creatures or cherubim located in the pendentives at the edge of the starry field. The creatures have two outstretched wings, and each is half-submerged in a sea of white and red cloud streaks. They are distributed in pairs, with the lion and the ox facing one another on the north side of the dome, opposite the entrance, and the human and the eagle facing one another on the south side, above the entrance. This distribution in pairs around a central cross recalls the apse mosaic of S. Pudenziana where, however, the pairs follow the sequence of Ezekiel 1.10 (human-lion, ox-eagle), and where the creatures have six wings rather than two, in line with Revelation 4.8. In both cases, the image as a whole represents the enthroned Christ surrounded by the praises of the cherubim (cf. Rv. 4.6), and not simply by "symbols" of Matthew, Mark, Luke, and John, or of their gospels.[69] This is confirmed by an inscription above the doors of the church to which the Mausoleum was originally attached, addressed to "Christ, Word of the Father, peace of the whole world."[70] The inscription refers to the four rivers of paradise, depicted on the doors below, but also to the "winged witnesses" who "stand around you uttering their thrice-repeated 'Sanctus' and 'Amen,' whom your right hand will rule" (cf. Rv. 4.8; 5.14). This is most likely a reference to the dome mosaic of the Mausoleum, just a few yards to the right. Once again the focus is on the heavenly worship of the exalted Christ, although the linkage between the four living creatures and the four rivers of paradise may imply a secondary reference to the evangelists.

Below the dome, on the four sides of the central tower, are lunettes in which pairs of apostles are seen preaching beneath a conch-like canopy, one on either side of a central window above an image of birds approaching a fountain or standing on its rim and drinking. In all there are eight images of apostles rather than twelve; four additional apostolic figures are to be found

---

and-white images is provided in F. W. Deichmann, *Frühchristliche Bauten und Mosaiken von Ravenna* (Baden-Baden: Bruno Grimm, 1958), Figs. 1-31.

    69. This reductionistic interpretation of these images seems to be unquestioned — appearing, for example, in Deichmann, *Bauten und Mosaiken*, Figs. 22-25, and in guidebooks and postcards available at the site.

    70. *Liber Pontificalis Ecclesiae Ravennatis*, PL 106.557; Eng. trans. Deborah Mauskopf Deliyannis, *The Book of Pontiffs of the Church of Ravenna* (Washington, D.C.: Catholic University of America Press, 2004), p. 150. The relevant part of the inscription runs: "Christe, Patris verbum, cuncti concordia mundi, Qui ut finem nescis, sic quoque principium, Te circumstant dicentes ter 'sanctus' et 'amen' aligeri testes, quos tua dextra reget, Te coram fluvii currunt per secula fusi Tigris et Eufrates, Fison et ipse Geon . . ."

within the barrel vaulting of the east and west arms of the building. The artistic programme has been constrained by the central windows, which allow full-length images to left and right but only a much smaller image beneath. Similar constraints are evident in the lunettes beneath the vaulting. In the west and east arms, pairs of deer approach a pool, located beneath a window.[71] Only above the door is there no window within the lunette, which depicts the Good Shepherd with his sheep.

Opposite the entrance, the lunette in the north arm is particularly striking. On the left stands an open cupboard in which books identified as MARCUS and LUCAS are visible on an upper shelf, with MATTEUS and IOANN|ES below. At the centre, beneath another window, is a gridiron, a bedstead-like metal frame with legs and wheels beneath which a fire blazes. On the right a young bearded man strides towards the gridiron, face turned toward the viewer, with an open book in his left hand and a cross-shaped staff over his right shoulder. He is clearly heading for martyrdom. What is less clear is how the cupboard with the books relates to the gridiron, the fire, and the would-be martyr. As Gillian Mackie has emphasized, correctly identifying the martyr is the key to the composition as a whole.[72]

The instrument of torture is generally thought to identify the prospective martyr as St. Lawrence.[73] While St. Lawrence could explain the gridiron, however, he cannot so easily account for the open book-cupboard and the gospel-books on its shelves. It is not clear whether the iconographical tradition that associates St. Lawrence with the gridiron is already established at this early date.[74] In a mosaic image in the church of S. Lorenzo in Agro

71. An allusion to Ps. 41.2 (42.1), "Quemadmodum desiderat cervus ad fontes aquarum, sic desiderat anima mea ad te, Deus." According to Augustine, the passage is traditionally taken to refer to catechumens longing to be baptized: "Unde et solemniter cantatur hic psalmus, ut ita desiderent fontem remissionis peccatorum, *quemadmodum desiderat cervus ad fontes aquarum.* Sit hoc, habeatque locum intellectus iste in Ecclesia et veracem et solemnem" *(Enarrationes in Psalmos, ad loc.).*

72. G. Mackie, "New Light on the So-Called Saint Lawrence Panel at the Mausoleum of Galla Placidia, Ravenna," *Gesta* 26 (1990), pp. 54-60. The analysis that follows is indebted to Mackie's article.

73. Prior to Mackie's article, this identification was widely though not universally assumed; see G. Bovini, *Ravenna: Art and History* (Ravenna: Longo, n.d.), p. 14, for some alternatives.

74. A lead medallion in the Vatican Museum (fourth century?) shows a seated judge and a naked figure stretched out on a gridiron with flames below, torturers at either end, and a young woman praying behind (see Mackie, "New Light," p. 57 [Fig. 2]). The figure on the gridiron can hardly be Lawrence, however, as Mackie assumes (p. 55). The tortured martyr appears to be female and is surely to be identified with the figure at prayer, above whom a martyr's wreath descends from heaven. The inscription is addressed to a female martyr: SUCCESSIA VIVAS.

Verano (Rome, late sixth century), the saint is named as SCS LAURENTIUS and is further identified by way of an open codex displayed in his left hand, where the words of Psalm 111.9 (112.9) are applied to himself: DIS|PER|SIT|| DEDIT|PAU|PERI|BUS. Lawrence is remembered for the manner of his life, not just for his death. While an accompanying inscription refers to his endurance of fire, there is no mention of a gridiron.[75] References to the means of death are not obligatory in early mosaic images of martyrs.[76]

A more plausible identification has been proposed by Mackie, who argues that the martyr is actually Vincentius of Saragossa, who suffered during the Diocletian persecution in 304 after refusing to surrender the church's copies of the scriptures.[77] St. Vincent is one of fourteen Spanish or Roman martyrs whose heroic faithfulness is celebrated by Prudentius in his *Liber Peristephanon*. In the passage that follows, his interrogator gives him a chance to save his own life by yielding up the scriptures to the fire:

Si tanta callum pectoris	"If such obstinacy hardens
praedurat obstinatio,	your unfeeling breast,
puluinar ut nostrum manu	so that our sacred pillow by hand
abomineris tangere,	you abhor to touch,
saltim latentes paginas	At least the hidden pages
librosque opertos detege,	and concealed books disclose,
quo secta prauum seminans,	so that the teaching that sows depravity,
iustis cremetur ignibus.	may be consumed in just fires."[78]

If this is the background to the image in the Mausoleum, the fire in the centre represents a threat not only to the martyr on the right but also to the gospelbooks in the open cupboard on the left. This threat is averted, as Vincent takes the opportunity to threaten his interrogator with a still worse fiery fate:

75. "Martyrium flammis olim levvita subisti/Iure tuis templis lux beneranda redit." "Martyrdom with flames you a priest once endured./Justly does venerable light return to your temple."

76. In Roman churches dedicated to martyrs, no instrument of torture or death is depicted in the apse mosaics of the churches or chapels dedicated to the martyrs Cosmas and Damian (seventh century), Venantius (seventh century), Prassede (ninth century), or Cecilia (ninth century). St. Agnes, however, stands between two small fires with a sword lying beneath her feet (seventh century).

77. Mackie, "New Light," pp. 57-58.

78. Prudentius, *Peristephanon*, v.177-84; ed. H. J. Thomson, LCL (London: Heinemann; Cambridge, Mass.: Harvard University Press, 1953), vol. 2. The translation here is my own.

His martyr auditis ait:	Hearing these things the martyr said:
quem tu, maligne, mysticis	"That fire with which you, wicked one,
minitaris ignem litteris,	threaten the mystic writings,
flagrabis ipse hoc iustius.	you yourself will justly burn in it.
Romfea nam caelestium	"For the sword of heaven
uindex erit uoluminum	will be protector of the books,
tanti ueneni interpretem	the tongue of such poison the interpreter
linguam perurens fulmine.	destroying with flame."[79]

The image of the open book-cupboard indicates that the precious gospel-books have indeed been preserved by heavenly powers from those once determined to erase all trace of them from the face of the earth. Vincent's own fate is sealed, of course:

His persecutor saucius	At these things the wounded persecutor
pallet, rubescit, aestuat	grows pale, turns red,
insana torquens lumina	whirling mad torches,
spumasque frendens egerit.	and foams and gnashes his teeth.
Tum deinde cunctatus diu	Then, after long delay,
decernit: extrema omnium	he decides: "Let the most extreme tortures
igni, grabato et lamminis	be applied, with fire,
exerceatur quaestio.	bed and plates."
Haec ille sese ad munera	To these gifts
gradu citato proripit	he hastens with rapid step
ipsosque pernix gaudio	and made swift by joy
poenae ministros praeuenit.	outpaces the torturers themselves.[80]

The "bed" and the fire are both represented in the Mausoleum image, and so too is the saint's arrival at the place of suffering in advance of his tormenters. The image as a whole is intended to remind the viewer that the four gospels and their message of salvation have been preserved for future generations by the heroic defiance of the martyrs.

The four gospels in the open book-cupboard are also linked to the four

79. Prudentius, *Peristephanon*, v.185-92.
80. Prudentius, *Peristephanon*, v.201-12.

cherubim in the heavenly vault. As we have seen, the cherubim are depicted theriomorphically and in facing pairs, with the lion and the calf on the north side of the vault and the human and the eagle on the south side. The gospel-books are similarly arranged in pairs, with Mark and Luke on the top shelf of the cupboard and Matthew and John on the bottom. The pairings differentiate gospels with apostolic authors from those written by *apostolici,* disciples of apostles. If the iconographical programme is following Jerome's scheme, the correspondences are exact: Mark and Luke are associated with the lion and the calf, Matthew and John with the human and the eagle. The cherubim are still cherubim, exalted heavenly beings who worship the enthroned Christ; they are not reduced to "symbols of the evangelists." Yet they acquire here an explicit connection with specific gospels. Jerome's scheme has made the transition from specialized theological literature into public art as it is incorporated into representation of the heavenly liturgy. In this context, the cherubim may be seen as heavenly patrons and defenders of the gospels, wielding the "sword of heaven" of which Vincent spoke so as to ensure their preservation.

In the Mausoleum of Galla Placidia, the association between the cherubim and the gospel-books is clear only to the viewer with prior knowledge of it. There is no visible connection between the cherubim in the starry vault and the books in the open cupboard. In the late-fifth-century mosaics of the Archiepiscopal Chapel in Ravenna, the connection is made visible as the gospel-books are elevated into the vault, where they are clasped by their theriomorphic heavenly patrons.[81]♦ The four living creatures are situated between four anthropomorphic counterparts who stand on patches of green ground in the pendentives of the small central dome, upholding a medallion with a christogram in which an *Iota* superimposed on a *Chi* represents both Jesus Christ and his cross. The anthropomorphized cherubim look directly down at the viewer, tall winged figures with arms aloft, spanning the gulf between earth and heaven. The theriomorphized figures are seen in profile, their lower parts hidden in red, white, and blue cloud streaks. The two sets of figures are set on a background of gold, representing the glory of the heavenly world. Like the Mausoleum, the Chapel is cross-shaped, and its four

81. The Chapel is situated on the first floor of a building that now houses the present Archiepiscopal Museum. According to Gillian Mackie, it is the one remaining example of a "clergyhouse oratory" (*Early Christian Chapels in the West: Decoration, Function, and Patronage* [Toronto: University of Toronto Press, 2003], p. 104). Online images of the mosaics at gospelwriting .wordpress.com. See also Bovini, *Art and History,* Figs. 88-90; Deichmann, *Bauten und Mosaiken,* Figs. 214-45.

short arms are separated from the dome by arches beneath which are located busts of Christ, the apostles, and male and female martyrs — seven for each arch, with the image of Christ or the I-X christogram at the apex. Like the four anthropomorphized angels and in contrast to the bearded disciples on either side, the Christ figures are androgynous in appearance.

The human figure with its gospel-book is located opposite the apex of the apse arch, with the eagle in the equivalent position on the right. The two are turned towards each other, although separated by one of the four angels. Opposite the human figure is the lion, with the calf to the left. These face away from each other, in contrast to the design in the Mausoleum; the calf follows the human figure, the lion the eagle. In the Mausoleum, the apostolic and nonapostolic gospels are distinguished from one another, both on the shelves of the cupboard and in the distribution of the cherubim in the vault. Assuming that the designer of the Chapel image has Jerome's identifications in view, the image represents the *subordination* of nonapostolic to apostolic gospels. Luke's angelic patron is seen following Matthew's while Mark's follows John's. Thus the human figure and the eagle are provided with a nimbus, but not the calf or lion. There are, then, three pairings implied here, one of equals and two of unequals: Matthew and John, Matthew and Luke, John and Mark. The books themselves are very similar in appearance. They are held sideways to the viewer, with a red cover decorated with jewels, spine uppermost, and a red tie across the edge of the closed pages. These heavenly books are not about to be read. Yet they remain real, physical books. Their association with the cherubim does not empty the book-cupboard of the Galla Placidia Mausoleum of its contents, nor does it deprive them of their human authors, identified in that image as Marcus and Lucas, Matteus and Ioannes.

It is these human authors who are portrayed within the extraordinarily intricate mosaic programme of the church of San Vitale (Ravenna), in four matching images high on the right and left walls of the choir. Here there is no assumption of the books into heaven, for the four living creatures have themselves descended to earth and preside over scenes in which the individual evangelists are completing the composition of their gospels. Matthew and Luke are located nearest the apse, to the right and left respectively, with Mark and John nearest the triumphal arch that leads into the choir, on the other side of elaborate internal windows.[82]◆ On each side the paired evange-

---

82. Online images at gospelwriting.wordpress.com. See also Deichmann, *Bauten und Mosaiken*, Figs. 312-13, 332-35; G. Malafarina, *La Basilica di San Vitale e il Mausoleo di Galla Placidia a Ravenna* (Modena: Panini, 2008).

lists — Matthew and Mark, Luke and John — are turned towards each other, although the gaze of each is directed upwards and there is no communication between them.

All four evangelists are depicted as seated alone within a mountainous and rocky landscape. Beneath their feet flow streams with wading birds, water plants, and in one case a frog. The streams are the four rivers of paradise, a reference to the apse mosaic where the rivers flow from a rock above which a youthful androgynous Christ is seated on a blue globe. A small, single-legged table with an inkwell and writing implements is set before three evangelists; Luke has to make do without. Matthew and Luke have an open basket containing scrolls on the ground by their feet, suggesting that they have been checking scriptural references as they write. The evangelists all hold open books. Mark and Luke have completed theirs, and display the title pages to the viewer: SEC|VN|DVM||MAR|CUM, and SECV|NDV|M||LV|CAM. John's title pages are also visible, but inverted, facing the evangelist as though he has only just finished writing: SEC|VNDV[M]||IOHA|NNEM. Only Matthew continues to write, and is apparently doing so in Hebrew although only the letter *šîn* can readily be identified. Diagonally above him is a winged human figure, hand outstretched, communicating encouragement or inspiration. The other three living creatures are depicted naturalistically on rocks behind and above their respective evangelists. They are impressive, powerful, potentially threatening figures, but otherwise they betray no sign of their heavenly origin. Each stands out starkly against its background, turquoise in the case of the golden-yellow lion and the black and grey eagle, green in the case of the white ox. The evangelists seem unaware of their presence behind and above them. They are intended purely for the viewer, who can learn Jerome's identifications directly from them without needing to know them in advance.

These portraits of evangelists in conjunction with their "symbols" have a future, but it is mainly within Western illuminated gospels rather than public art within churches. From at least the sixth century onward, evangelists' portraits are a recurrent feature of illuminated *Tetraevangelia*, codices containing all four gospels.[83] The portrait normally occupies the full page

83. Online images of mainly Western examples at gospelwriting.wordpress.com. Sixth-century evangelist portraits occur in the Syriac Rabbula Gospels, where images of Matthew and John occur within the canon tables (Folio 9b); the Rossano Gospels, where Mark writes his gospel against an Alexandrian backdrop; and the St. Augustine or Canterbury Gospels, where Luke is portrayed as seated with a winged calf above his head. Four portraits of evangelists, flanking John the Baptist and without identifying symbols, are to be found in the lower front ivory panels of the

preceding the *Incipit* of a gospel, and is thus part of a set of four distinct but related images. The evangelist is typically seated on a stool or chair and set against an architectural background.[84] He often seems to be in the open air, so that a canopy has had to be provided. While other human figures are generally absent, the context is unmistakably and reassuringly urban. An inkwell and other implements are placed on a single- or four-legged desk, though the book itself is normally held in the evangelist's lap. Western portraits usually avail themselves of Jerome's version of the symbolism, with the appropriate winged creature located above the evangelist's head. In contrast, Eastern portraits may provide the name of the individual evangelist, but the symbols are generally absent. Rare exceptions seem to betray both Western influence and an uncertainty about how these symbols are to be used. In the portrait of John in the Russian *Ostromir Gospel,* dating from the mid–eleventh century, the evangelist is seen writing his gospel on the left with furniture and equipment to the right.[85]◆ In a separate image, forward and at the centre, the evangelist stands with face turned upward and hands outstretched to receive the text of his gospel, held between the claws of an eagle descending from heaven. The artist imagines that the role of the living creatures is to convey the original of the inspired writing from its heavenly source — a view that also determines his portrayals of Luke and Mark later in the volume. Above the upper edge of the frame a lion prowls, his head turned to view the transaction below. The artist has adopted the Western, Jerome-inspired version of the symbolism, but is also aware of the earlier Irenaean version in which John is associated not with the eagle but with the lion. Unsure which version to select, he includes both. Western evangelist portraits betray no such uncertainty. While the symbols are not always included and traces of the alternative versions may still be found, Jerome's identifications generally prevail.

Chair of Maximianus in the Archiepiscopal Museum, Ravenna; see M. Baracchini, *Le Collezione del Museo Arcivescovile di Ravenna* (Ravenna: Opera di Religione della Diocesi di Ravenna, 2011), pp. 70-84.

84. This architectural background to evangelists' portraits may date back to the fourth century; see Caroline J. Downing, "Wall Paintings from the Baptistery at Stobi, Macedonia, and Early Depictions of Christ and the Evangelists," *Dumbarton Oaks Papers* 52 (1998), pp. 259-80.

85. On this manuscript, see Elina Gertsman, "All Roads Lead to Rus: Western Influences on the Eleventh- to Twelfth-Century Manuscript Illumination of Kievan Russia," *Comitatus* 31 (2000), pp. 39-55, esp. pp. 45-48. According to Gertsman, "Byzantine illuminated gospels never represent the evangelist's symbol along with the saint himself. . . . On the other hand, this feature is the standard type found in Carolingian, Ottonian, and Insular manuscripts" (p. 46). Online images at gospelwriting.wordpress.com.

The San Vitale evangelist portraits are an early example of this distinctive Western iconography, in which the four living cherubim are detached from their role within the heavenly liturgy and converted into symbols differentiating one evangelist from another. The mountainous setting contrasts with the more usual backdrop of civic architecture, suggesting that the evangelists have had to withdraw to the wilderness in order to fulfil their commission. Similar scenery appears in the images of Moses at the Burning Bush and at Sinai, directly beneath the portraits of Matthew and Luke; yet, beneath Mark and John, Isaiah and Jeremiah are set against a background of city walls. A civic context for the composition of the gospels would have been entirely possible, and would have avoided the apparent anomaly of writing in the wilderness. It is the three nonhuman creatures, naturalistically portrayed, who have evoked this wilderness setting — and not only the lion and the eagle, for this ox too is untamed. A mythical, winged lion or ox can perhaps be accommodated within a comfortable urban context, but not a real one. These images represent the otherness of the gospels and the world they render.

Four other features of these images confirm the link with Jerome. First, the ox is clearly the mature adult animal of the Masoretic text and the Vulgate rather than the Septuagintal calf. Its thickset neck and muscular body differentiate it from the delicate winged calves of the Mausoleum and the Archiepiscopal Chapel.

Second, the Matthean human and the Markan lion are located on the right and the Lukan ox on the left, in line with Jerome's interpretation of Ezekiel 1.10 *(facies hominis et facies leonis a dextris . . . , facies autem bovis a sinistris . . .)*. In S. Vitale the eagle is also on the left. In his commentary Jerome placed it "above" the others, emending the problematic Ezekiel text *(facies aquilae ipsorum quattuor)* by inserting *desuper.*[86] Yet the emendation is absent from Jerome's Vulgate translation. Without the *desuper,* it is open to a reader to conclude that the eagle is located on the left together with the ox.

Third, the Markan lion is roaring. Its teeth are apart, its tongue is visible, and unlike the other images it stares out directly at the viewer. This is Jerome's *leo in eremo rugiens,* an apt symbol of the gospel that opens with the prophetic voice crying out in the wilderness.

Fourth, and more generally, Jerome is closely associated with the ascetic life of the desert. In S. Vitale the evangelists have been reimagined as ascetic

---

86. PL 25.24; CCSL 75, p. 15.

saints who have rejected the corrupt life of the city and chosen the purity of the wilderness. As the streams, the reeds, and the wading birds indicate, this harsh landscape is the place where paradise is or might be regained.

Imaging the One Christ

The four living creatures may be depicted in a dome vault, the architectural equivalent of heaven, encircling either a symbol of the enthroned Christ[87] or an actual likeness.[88] They may be located in the upper register of an apse,[89] in a door panel,[90] in the west wall above the windows,[91] or in matching lunettes.[92] The living creatures may be depicted with jewelled gospel-books,[93] but elsewhere their association with the gospels is at best secondary. The situation only changes when, descending from heaven to earth, the living creatures appear in naturalistic form within evangelist portraits. Yet their natural habitat is heaven rather than earth, and their liturgical role there is an indication of how the secondary association with the gospels is to be understood.

In spite of the diversity of these early images, a distinctively Roman tradition of representing the four living creatures can be traced back to the church of Santa Maria Maggiore, where the elaborate mosaic programme on the triumphal arch is dated to the pontificate of Sixtus III (432-40).[94◆] Here images relating to the nativity are distributed over the upper three zones. In the first zone the annunciations to Mary and to Joseph are depicted on the left, with the presentation in the temple and the warning to flee to Egypt on the right. Between them, at the apex of the arch, Peter and Paul stand on either side of an empty throne (a *hetoimasia*) with a superimposed cross. Both throne and cross are bejewelled, and the lower edge of the cross's horizontal arm touches the top edge of the chair-back so that at a distance the two ob-

---

87. Ravenna: Galla Placidia Mausoleum, Archiepiscopal Chapel; Naples Cathedral, baptistery. For details of images listed here, see the comprehensive survey in Ihm, *Programme*.

88. Salonica: Hosios David (Brenk, *Apse*, Col. Fig. 37).

89. Rome: S. Pudenziana, S. Giovanni in Laterano baptistery narthex; Bawit: Monastery of St Apollo.

90. Rome: S. Sabina.

91. Rome: S. Sabina, originally (Brenk, *Maria Maggiore*, Fig. 10).

92. Capua Vetere: Cappella S. Matrona.

93. Ravenna: Archiepiscopal Chapel; Salonica: Hosios David.

94. Online images at gospelwriting.wordpress.com.

jects are barely distinguishable. The throne is held within a medallion of concentric white, turquoise, and blue circles, approximating to the "rainbow around the throne with the appearance of an emerald" (Rv. 4.3). Behind the apostles and on either side of each of them the four winged creatures are seen in profile, with only the upper half of their bodies visible, borne along by red streaks of cloud. The calf and the human approach the throne from the left, the lion and the eagle from the right. They are evidently silent; the lion's jaws are closed. They bear not books but wreaths, representing their praise of the Lamb: "Worthy art thou to take the scroll and to open its seals . . ." (Rv. 5.8-9). The scroll with seven seals has been placed on the footstool or *suppedaneum* in front of the throne, directly below the jewelled cross that represents the slain and enthroned Lamb. Thus the unfolding drama of Revelation 4–5 is compressed into a single image. If the twenty-four elders are identified with the apostles and patriarchs, then Peter and Paul may represent them here. Alternatively, the elders with their golden crowns may be represented by the four living creatures with their wreaths. Peter and Paul appear to be preaching, book in hand. Their left and right feet respectively are concealed behind an inscription on a blue background, on which the lower edge of the throne-medallion rests: XYSTVS EPISCOPVS PLEBI DEI. As Bishop to the People of God, Xystus or Sixtus embodies the ministry established by Peter and Paul.

The four living creatures are said to be "around the throne" (Rv. 4.6). In the broad symmetrical space of the Galla Placidia dome they can be located in the pendentives, separated by wide tracts of starry space from the golden cross-throne at the centre. In the more confined space of the summit of an arch, their positioning "around the throne" is represented by placing two of them on either side of it, all facing towards it. As a result, they now appear in sequence: *calf-human-lion-eagle*. Since the sequence is interrupted in the middle by the throne, however, it is also possible to interpret it as two pairs converging on the throne from opposite directions: *calf-human, lion-eagle*. One might then differentiate an inner pair *(human-lion)* from an outer *(calf-eagle)*. The question of priority might also be raised. Is there any prioritizing of the first figure, reading from left to right, or of the pair closest to the throne? Where the figures appear with books, the sequence *eagle-human-lion-calf,* reading from left to right, would represent a prioritizing of John over Matthew, Mark, and Luke (assuming it to be Jerome's version of the scheme that is followed).[95] On the other hand, the sequence, *lion-*

---

95. Ravenna: S. Apollinare in Classe.

human, eagle-calf would represent a prioritizing of the gospels with apostolic authors (Matthew and John) over those written by followers of apostles (Mark and Luke).[96] Rather than reading from left to right, one would now read from the centre outward. On Jerome's scheme, the sequence *calf-human-lion-eagle* would represent *Luke-Matthew-Mark-John.*[97] Luke would then have been promoted from third to first place, with the rest of the conventional sequence being left intact. If we follow Irenaeus, Victorinus, and Ambrose,[98] the sequence corresponds to *Luke-Matthew, John-Mark,* with priority accorded to apostolic authors nearest the central throne. It is notable that the earlier version agrees with Jerome's about the identification of the two figures to the left of the throne, the Lukan calf and the Matthean human; there is disagreement only about the figures to the right. The lion and the eagle may represent either John and Mark, or Mark and John.[99]

Since the only books in the S. Maria Maggiore image are held by the apostles Peter and Paul rather than by the four living creatures, it is not initially clear that any association with the gospels is intended here at all. Yet the sequence follows neither Revelation *(lion-calf-human-eagle)* nor Ezekiel (*human-lion-calf-eagle,* as at S. Pudenziana), and an explanation must be sought for the nonscriptural presentation. There are strong contextual indications here that the calf and the human figure are intended to represent Luke and Matthew. In the composite images on either side of the central Revelation-inspired tableau, a Lukan scene (the annunciation, the presentation) is given priority over a related Matthean one (Joseph's dreams). The symbolic *Luke-Matthew* sequence at the summit of the arch is matched by a *Luke-Matthew* narrative sequence both to the left and the right.

In the annunciation scene Mary is seated on a dais, dressed in an embroidered golden garment with white sleeves. To the left of her is a small building with a tiled roof and an arch supported by pillars to which latticed

96. Rome: SS. Cosma e Damiano (on which see below), S. Prassede, S. Clemente.

97. Rome: S. Maria Maggiore, S. Paolo fuori le Mura (see below), S. Venanzio (Lateran baptistery).

98. See note 18.

99. The continuing availability of the Irenaean scheme to Western artists is demonstrated by the Book of Durrow, a seventh-century insular gospel book which may have been produced in Northumbria or Iona. Here full-page evangelists' symbols accompany the incipit of Matthew (human figure, folio 21v), Mark (eagle, folio 84v), Luke (calf, folio 124v), and John (lion, folio 191v). In addition, folio 2r places the symbols within the four spaces created by the horizontal and vertical bars of a cross, in the order (clockwise from top left) *human-eagle-calf-lion.* On this see Martin Werner, "The Four Symbols Page in the Book of Durrow" (*Gesta* 8 [1969], pp. 3-17), although Werner underplays the Irenaean influence here.

doors are attached. The building is presumably her home, although it may also be a shrine. Mary's head is uncovered, and her dark hair is cut or tied short above her face and neck. She is a young but mature woman; she wears a tiara, and white pearls are placed over her forehead and ears.[100] She has drawn scarlet material from a tall basket to the left of the dais, and she now holds this over her lap as she stares out slightly to the viewer's right. Her features are controlled but not impassive, hinting at the overwhelming emotion of the momentous announcement she is in process of receiving. Above her and to the right an angel is seen with arm outstretched and in horizontal flight, suggestive of speed and thus the urgency and importance of his mission. To his and Mary's left a dove descends at a steep angle. There are also two angels standing to the left of Mary, with two more to her right; in seamless continuity with this grouping, yet another angel turns towards Joseph and marks the transition to the second part of this composite scene. Leaving Joseph's angel out of account for the moment, there are no fewer than five angelic figures in the annunciation to Mary, one in flight and two to either side of her.

These angelic figures are generally taken to represent five distinct angels, although there is little or nothing in their appearance to differentiate them from one another. In his detailed study of the S. Maria Maggiore mosaics, Beat Brenk finds a possible scriptural background for this unusual iconography in Hebrews 1.6: "When he brings the firstborn into the world, he says, 'Let all the angels of God worship him.'"[101] In the absence of other evidence for an importation of supplementary angels into the Lukan narrative, this seems highly unlikely.[102] In the mosaic, these figures are not worshipping but speaking with Mary. It is far more likely that they represent a *sequence* corresponding to the key moments in the Lukan annunciation story, thus depicting a single angel at five successive points. The sequence begins with the angel in flight, approaching Mary as she sits weaving. This is the angel Gabriel, "sent from God to a city of Galilee called Nazareth, to a virgin betrothed to a man named Joseph . . ." (Lk. 1.26-27). Of the four angelic figures standing on either side of Mary, the two outermost ones depict Gabriel's

---

100. See the excellent black-and-white image in Brenk, *Maria Maggiore*, Fig. 46.

101. Brenk, *Maria Maggiore*, p. 12.

102. S. Spain rightly points out that a plurality of angels makes no sense in the context of an annunciation ("'The Promised Blessing': The Iconography of the Mosaics of S. Maria Maggiore," *ArtB* 61 [1979], pp. 518-40; p. 538). However, her claim that the image originally depicted appearances of three angels first to Abraham and then to Sarah is no more plausible than the interpretation she rejects.

greeting and his farewell, and the two inner ones represent the two parts of his message, concerned respectively with her child's transcendent destiny and her conception through the Holy Spirit. Gabriel greets Mary with the words "Hail, favoured one, the Lord is with you" (Lk. 1.28). The corresponding angelic figure is turned towards Mary, his right hand raised in a gesture of blessing. This first figure encroaches onto the second; there is space between them only from the shoulders upwards and the ankles downwards. The second figure looks away from Mary to the left of the viewer, just as the message he is delivering turns away from the immediate situation towards a future in which her child will be called the son of the Most High and will inherit the throne of his father David (Lk. 1.30-33). The division between the angelic figures represents the moment between the greeting and the first part of the message, when Mary's initial shock is registered (Lk. 1.29). To Mary's right, the third figure gestures towards her womb while looking upwards towards the descending dove. Mary has asked, "How shall these things be . . . ?" (Lk. 1.34), and the angel now tells her that "the Holy Spirit will come upon you and the power of the Most High will overshadow you . . ." (Lk. 1.35). After Mary's acceptance of her vocation ("Behold, the handmaid of the Lord . . ."), it is said that "the angel departed from her" (Lk. 1.38). Thus the fourth angelic figure turns away from her with a gesture of farewell. The four figures therefore represent each of the four stages of the encounter, marked off from one another by three references to Mary's response. Unlike the angel, Mary is depicted only once, and all three elements in her response — the initial shock, the question "how . . . ?," the acceptance — are therefore combined in her expression. Rather than importing redundant angels from elsewhere in the New Testament, this image corresponds exactly to the sequential unfolding of the Lukan narrative.

To the right of the departing angel, yet another angelic figure addresses Joseph. There are, then, three angelic figures to the right of Mary, although only the first two relate directly to her. Nevertheless the three form a closely related group in which the first is turned towards Mary and the descending dove, the second is turning away, while the third is turned towards Joseph. This seamless transition from Mary to Joseph is also a transition from Luke's narrative to Matthew's. Joseph's angelic encounter occurs as he stands outside his house, his right hand raised and gesturing back towards himself, his left hand clutching a stick-like object. Joseph's house is of similar design to Mary's, although considerably larger as it will later have to accommodate the entire Holy Family. This standing Joseph contrasts with the recumbent figure at the opposite end of this sequence, in the top right corner of the triumphal arch, where he is depicted as asleep on a couch as he is warned by an angel in a dream to flee with his family to Egypt (cf. Mt. 2.13). Here on the left side of the arch, the standing rather than recumbent Joseph matches the figure of Mary, who, though seated, is actually at a slightly higher level than he is. Mary and Joseph are separated and connected by the three angelic figures who execute the turn from one to the other. Here we view not a sleeping figure but the angelic encounter that formed the content of his dream (cf. Mt. 1.20). Joseph's expression betrays the anxiety caused by his betrothed's apparent unfaithfulness, whereas the angel reassures him by communicating the true significance of her pregnancy. Joseph and Mary are turned inwards towards the centre of the image, highlighting both the sequential continuity between the two angelic announcements and the close parallel between them. Yet there is no doubt that Mary rather than Joseph is the figure at the heart of this drama. She is surrounded by five angelic images and the descending dove, so that every stage in the unfolding encounter is represented; Joseph's announcement can be represented much more simply. Since he is a Matthean figure whereas Mary is Lukan, the image as a whole represents a prioritizing of Luke over Matthew in terms of both chronology and significance. The announcement to Mary takes place before the announcement to Joseph, and it is in the first that the momentous significance of what is to take place is more fully disclosed. Yet the Matthean depiction of Joseph's perspective on events is taken seriously, even though his destiny is to play a supporting role to Mary. Though unequal in significance, the two announcements are parallel and can be represented within a single composite image. Lukan priority over Matthew, Matthean supplementation of Luke's narrative: these hermeneutical assumptions are also reflected in the prioritizing of the calf over the human figure in the throne-scene at the centre of the S. Maria Maggiore arch.

Brenk finds the source of the annunciation scene not in the canonical gospels but in the so-called *Infancy Gospel of Matthew* (= *IGMt*), or *pseudo-Matthew*.[103] While his rejection of direct Lukan influence is clearly mistaken, Brenk is right to draw attention to this noncanonical infancy gospel. He cites it, however, in the version published by Tischendorf in 1853, where it is presented as "The Book of the Birth of the Blessed Mary and the Infancy of the

---

103. Brenk, *Maria Maggiore*, pp. 11-13. For brief introductions to this text, see J. K. Elliott (ed.), *The Apocryphal New Testament* (Oxford: Clarendon Press, 1999²), pp. 84-87; H.-J. Klauck, *The Apocryphal Gospels: An Introduction*, Eng. trans. (London & New York: T. & T. Clark, 2003), pp. 78-80. Critical edition by Jan Gijsel (ed.), *Libri de Nativitate Mariae: Pseudo-Matthaei Evangelium Textus et Commentarius*, CCSA (Turnhout: Brepols, 1997).

Saviour, Written in Hebrew by the Blessed Evangelist Matthew, and Translated into Latin by the Blessed Presbyter Jerome."[104] In this form, the text opens with pseudonymous letters to and from Jerome, followed by an account of the life of Mary up to the birth of Jesus (*IGMt* 1-14) drawn from the *Protevangelium of James (= PJas)*. The *Protevangelium* itself concludes with the visit of the magi and Herod's murderous rage, directed here against the infant John the Baptist and leading to the death of his father Zechariah (*PJas* 21.1–24.4; cf. Mt. 23.35 = Lk. 11.51). In *IGMt* this ending is replaced with a cycle of stories about the Holy Family on the journey into Egypt (*IGMt* 18-24). Most manuscripts of *IGMt* end here, although Tischendorf's edition follows a fifteenth-century manuscript (Paris, 1652) which includes a further cycle of stories about Jesus' childhood derived from the *Infancy Gospel of Thomas* (*IGMt* 26-34, 37-39, 41).[105] These chapters did not originally belong to *IGMt*, however, and the introductory letters too are secondary: the attribution of the translation to Jerome and the original to Matthew replaced an earlier attribution to James.[106] This Latin text should be seen as a free paraphrase and rewriting of the much older Greek *PJas*.[107] *IGMt* is probably to be identified with the *Evangelium nomine Iacobi minoris* proscribed by the so-called "Gelasian decree," which indicates that a Latin work under this title was known in Italy in the sixth century.[108] An apocryphal work *sub nomine Iacobi minoris* is also mentioned disapprovingly in a letter from Pope Innocent I (401-17).[109] "James the Less," also known as James son of Alphaeus, was identified by Jerome with James the Lord's "brother" or cousin,[110] the supposed author of *PJas*. Jerome himself knows and rejects several traditions

---

104. Constantinus Tischendorf, *Evangelia Apocrypha* (Leipzig: Avenarius & Mendelssohn, 1853), pp. xxv-xxxiv, 50-105.

105. Tischendorf's longer version of this text is the basis of the English translations (or summaries) in ANF VIII, pp. 368-83; M. R. James, *The Apocryphal New Testament* (Oxford: Clarendon Press, 1924), pp. 70-79; and Elliott, *Apocryphal New Testament*, pp. 84-99.

106. The original prologue claimed James as author, and is preserved in one group of manuscripts; the new attribution to Matthew and Jerome may have occurred in response to its rejection as a gospel authored by "James the Less" (so Gijsel, *Pseudo-Matthaei Evangelium*, pp. 83-88). The original prologue was derived from the conclusion of *PJas*, and states: "Ego Iacobus filius Ioseph conversans in timore dei perscripsi omnia quae oculis meis ipse vidi fieri in tempore nativitatis sanctae Mariae sive salvatoris . . ." (Gijsel, p. 277).

107. Gijsel, *Pseudo-Matthaei Evangelium*, pp. 48-59.

108. The possibility is raised by É. de Strycker, *La forme la plus ancienne du Protévangile de Jacques* (Brussels: Société des Bollandistes, 1961), p. 43n.

109. Cited in Tischendorf, *Evangelia Apocrypha*, pp. xxv-xxvi.

110. Jerome, *Adversus Helvedium* 13-15 (PL 23.183-206). This text dates from 383.

common to *PJas* and *IGMt* (Joseph's sons by a former marriage, the role of the midwife at Jesus' birth)[111] and one unique to *PJas* (the murder of Zechariah).[112] Although subject to a chorus of disapproval, from Jerome to Innocent to the Gelasian decree, these traditions were in principle available to the S. Maria Maggiore artist. Overt use of noncanonical texts might seem surprising in a church closely linked to the Lateran, the papal residence, and in images commissioned by the pope himself.[113] Yet it cannot be ruled out.

Elaborating the account in *PJas*, the narrator of *IGMt* tells how Joseph received Mary into his care (*IGMt* 8.2-5; cf. *PJas* 9.1-2). In a procedure inspired by the story of Aaron's rod (Nm. 17), Joseph and other eligible males each leave a rod in the Holy of Holies. Joseph's rod is shorter than the others and is initially overlooked in view of his advanced age, but when he receives it back a dove comes forth from it, identifying him as Mary's future guardian. Joseph protests that he is an old man whereas Mary is younger than his grandchildren, but he acquiesces when the high priest reminds him of the fate of those who opposed the will of God in Korah's rebellion (Nm. 16). In the annunciation image at S. Maria Maggiore, Joseph holds the rod with his left hand while he is addressed by the angel. The rod represents his divine commission as Mary's protector, and this motif is clearly drawn from the noncanonical tradition.[114] On the other hand, this Joseph is a young man — in contrast to the much older figure in the presentation scene on the other side of the arch, but in keeping with two further representations in the arch's second register below. There are no children in view, and certainly no grandchildren. The separate houses show that he and Mary are not yet cohabiting, as they would be if the artist were following extracanonical rather than canonical sources. The rod motif is no more than an incidental detail within this rendering of the canonical Matthean text.

In *IGMt* 8.5, Mary is allowed five female companions to accompany her into Joseph's home, where they will together weave the various parts of the temple veil. Receiving the materials from the high priest, they draw lots to determine who is to be responsible for which part of it. When the purple material fell to Mary, her companions taunt her as "queen of virgins" but become frightened and ask her pardon when informed by an angel that their

---

111. Jerome, *In Mattheum*, at Mt. 12.46-50 (CCSL 77, pp. 100-101); *Adversus Helvedium* 10.

112. Jerome, *In Mattheum*, at Mt. 23.35 (CCSL 77, pp. 219-21).

113. On the relationship of S. Maria Maggiore to the Lateran, see Richard Krautheimer, *Three Christian Capitals: Topography and Politics* (Berkeley, Los Angeles, and London: University of California Press, 1983), pp. 115-21.

114. So Brenk, *Maria Maggiore*, p. 14.

words are prophetic. On the next day, the angel of the Lord appears to Mary as she fills her pitcher from a fountain, promising that her womb would be the habitation of the Lord who is to be the light of the world (*IGMt* 9.1). On the third day,

> while she was working the purple material with her fingers [*dum operaretur purpuram digitis suis*], there entered a youth of indescribable beauty. When Mary saw him she was frightened and began to tremble. He said to her, "Do not fear, Mary, for you have found grace with God. Behold, you shall conceive in your womb and bear a king who will rule not only on earth but also in heaven, and he will reign for ever and ever." (*IGMt* 9.1)

In *PJas* the entire annunciation scene takes place at the fountain or well (11.1-3), with references to Mary weaving preceding and following it (cf. 10.2; 12.1). In *IGMt* the annunciation takes place in two stages, the first at the fountain and the second while she is weaving.

According to Brenk, the S. Maria Maggiore image illustrates four motifs drawn from this text: Mary's royal attire, her weaving the purple material, the angel's entrance, and Mary's fear.[115] As we have seen, however, the five angelic figures in this image correspond exactly to the sequence of Luke's narrative. The descending dove is also Lukan; the Holy Spirit is not mentioned in either *IGMt* or *PJas*. In a church built in honour of the Virgin, her royal attire does not need any specific textual basis. Only in the case of her weaving is dependence on *IGMt* undeniable. The artist has selected this traditional but extracanonical motif to indicate that Mary is occupied with her ordinary daily work at the moment of the annunciation. His primary Lukan source says nothing about what Mary is doing at the time: whether she is standing or seated, praying or carrying out household chores like weaving or fetching water. Unlike the narrative, the image must depict her in a specific posture and engaged in a specific activity, the more so since this single image must encompass the entire sequence from the moment before the angel's arrival until his departure. In this context, the weaving motif represents an interpretation of the Lukan narrative and not an intrusive element from an alien text. Neither the weaving nor the rod motif represents an attempt to ascribe quasi-canonical status to a text other than Luke and Matthew. The claim that "the annunciation scene is represented on the basis not of the gos-

---

115. Brenk, *Maria Maggiore*, pp. 11-12.

pels but of the text of pseudo-Matthew" can only be regarded as an aberration.[116] Such a claim is historically improbable and overlooks the artist's profound interpretative engagement with the canonical texts.

The prioritizing of the calf and the human figure in the central throne scene represents a moment of hermeneutical reflection on the seamless Lukan and Matthean sequence in the image of the two angelic encounters. A similar sequential treatment of Lukan and Matthean narrative occurs to the right of the throne scene, where the presentation in the temple leads directly into the dream in which Joseph is warned to flee to Egypt. Further scenes from the canonical infancy narratives appear in the second and third registers of the arch,[117] although there is also one anomalous image where a basis in either canonical or noncanonical literature is hard to find.[118]

In early Christian churches an arch is usually created by the insertion of an apse into the end wall. An "apsidal" arch of this kind is also a *frame* that contains the mosaic composition of the apse. That is no longer the case at S. Maria Maggiore, where a transept was added and a new apse constructed that features a thirteenth-century image of the coronation of the Virgin. Thus an apsidal arch became a "triumphal" arch, and its mosaic programme became a freestanding composition. Its original function was different, however. As Richard Krautheimer noted seventy years ago,

> the entire nave, including the triumphal arch and the two aisles, forms one structural unit and is considerably earlier in date than the present transept and apse. . . . Excavations and observations made in 1932 give definite proof that the nave originally terminated in an apse, which projected immediately from the triumphal arch. . . . In 1932 its remains were exca-

---

116. Brenk, *Maria Maggiore*, p. 11: "Die Verkündigungsszene ist nicht nach dem Bericht der Evangelien, sondern nach dem Text des Pseudo-Matthäus dargestellt." The claim is repeated in a recent publication (Brenk, *Apse*, p. 72).

117. In the second register on the left, the Matthean magi bring their gifts to the enthroned Christ child, while behind the throne Lukan angels sing their hymn, two looking heavenward, the other two earthward: *Gloria in excelsis Deo, et in terra pax hominibus bonae voluntatis* (Lk. 2.14). In the third register, Herod confers with priests and magi on the right, and, in a harrowing image, prepares for the slaughter of the innocents on the left.

118. While there are loose connections between the right-hand image of the second register and the story of the Holy Family's arrival in Egypt in *IGMt* 22-24, the differences are at least as striking as the similarities. There is no trace of the fallen idols; the child is not held in Mary's arms; and it is difficult to see an Egyptian priest in the prophet-like figure in the delegation that meets the Holy Family and its angelic retinue. As Brenk notes: "Dass in dieser Szene Pseudo-Matthäus illustriert worden ist, lässt sich nicht beweisen" (*Maria Maggiore*, p. 29).

vated: it is a perfect semicircular apse, the diameter of which corresponds exactly to the span of the triumphal arch.[119]

Early apse images generally take the form of static tableaux with smaller or larger groups of named figures — apostles, martyrs, donors, angels — arranged symmetrically to the left and right of Christ. In the orginal apse image of S. Maria Maggiore the centre of the design was probably occupied by Christ and Mary herself.[120] She may perhaps have held the Christ child on her lap, which could explain why this well-established imagery is avoided in the scene with the magi on the arch. Mary's presence at the centre of the apse design would enhance and particularize the image's christological emphasis, rather than detracting from it. At this time the idea that Mary and Christ might be rival objects of devotion would have been inconceivable.

A christological focus is fundamental to most apse images, which depict the one who is himself the visible image of the invisible God (cf. Col. 1.15). In an apse mosaic from S. Michele in Affricisco (Ravenna, now in Berlin), Christ stands between the archangels Michael and Gabriel with a cross-staff in one hand and an open book in the other that contains two citations from the Gospel of John, one on each page: QUI VI | DIT ME | VIDIT ET | PATREM and EGO ET | PATER | UNUM | SUMUS.[121]◆ Whoever has seen Christ has also seen the Father (Jn. 14.9), for he and the Father are one (Jn. 10.30). In the Johannine context, seeing Jesus is the prerogative of his disciples; others must believe without seeing, on the basis of the apostolic word alone (cf. Jn. 20.29; 17.20). In the artistic rendering, *Qui vidit me* addresses the worshipper as a viewer, speaking self-referentially of the visible image of the Christ who himself makes the invisible Father indirectly visible.[122] The scriptural prohibition of the image is reinterpreted: the prohibition applies

---

119. Richard Krautheimer, "Recent Publications on S. Maria Maggiore in Rome," *AJA* 46 (1942), pp. 373-79; pp. 373, 375.

120. On this lost image see James Snyder, "The Mosaic in Santa Maria Nova and the Original Apse Decoration of Santa Maria Maggiore," in *Hortus Imaginum: Essays in Western Art*, ed. Robert Enggass and Marilyn Stokstad (Lawrence: University Press of Kansas, 1974), pp. 1-10.

121. See Ihm, *Programme*, pp. 161-63. An online image is available at gospelwriting.wordpress .com.

122. J.-M. Spieser cites a comparable inscription from a mid-fourth-century apse image of the enthroned Christ with Peter and Paul from the Catacomb of Domitilla: *Qui filius diceris et pater inveneris*, "If you acknowledge the Son you will have found the Father" ("The Representation of Christ in the Apses of Early Christian Churches," *Gesta* 37 [1998], pp. 63-73; p. 69). Spieser suggests that "the inscription could be used as a motto for all of the pictures with which we are concerned."

to the invisible Father, but it cannot apply to the Son if he is truly the Father's visible image. Images are prohibited in order to clear the way for the appearance of the incarnate Son as the true image of God, and there can be no objection in principle to the reenactment of that visibility through the artistic image.[123] The apse image of Christ makes the object of worship visible to worshippers, although only in the indirection of the passage from the Father to Christ and from Christ to his image, together with the return movement from visibility back to invisibility. The nonidentity of the invisible and the visible is indicated by the adverbial *et* of the Old Latin version of John 14.9, present also in the S. Michele text: to see Christ is *also* to see the Father. It is not that Christ and the Father are simply synonyms representing one person rather than two, as in modalist christologies. In John 14.9 the adverbial *et* preserves the distinction, just as the conjunctional *et* does in John 10.30. "I *and* the Father are one"; the *unum* does not entail the erasure of the *et*.[124] On the other hand, the oneness excludes the Arian assumption that the Father is essentially unknowable and inscrutable, that Christ is fundamentally unlike him, and that a likeness of Christ will merely reproduce his creaturely unlikeness to the divine. While the artistic image cannot claim to be *homoousios* with Christ as Christ is with the Father, it does possess an ontological basis in the actuality of the divine becoming-visible.[125]

These apse representations of Christ may present him in the company of his mother Mary, his apostles (primarily Peter and Paul), martyrs, and donors (normally bishops). On the arch above, Christ may be enthroned among the cherubim, his unrepresentable being signified by an empty throne or a golden cross. In the apse below, the incarnate Christ keeps hu-

---

123. As Sr. Charles Murray has persuasively argued, there is little if any convincing evidence for patristic disapproval of the visual arts as such ("Art and the Early Church," *JTS*, n.s., 28 [1977], pp. 304-45).

124. For a critiques of modalist interpretations of just these texts, see Tertullian, *Adversus Praxean* 20-24; Hippolytus, *Contra Haeresin Noeti* 7.

125. Spieser suggests that some apse representations of Christ serve to distance him from the worshipper, notably where he is depicted as seated on a globe as in S. Vitale, Ravenna ("Representation of Christ," p. 70). In the earlier period Christ is realistically portrayed: "[I]n an image like that of the apse of Santa Pudenziana, nothing in the picture breaks the feeling of continuity with the real space of the church." In contrast, at S. Vitale "it is no longer possible to see [Christ] seated in a space that could be perceived as a continuation of the space in which the believer is standing." Yet the S. Vitale Christ appears in the company not only of angels but also of a local martyr and a recent bishop. The more fundamental difference is between the incarnate Christ depicted in the apse and the symbolic representations of the divine, heavenly Christ at the apex of an arch or vault.

man company. Worshippers are expected to identify especially with the martyrs, who may be male or female, young or old, leaders or led, but who are elevated from ordinariness to celebrity status by their extraordinary and exemplary endurance. The apse represents the earthly church in a state of idealized holiness, with Christ in its midst. The link with the worshipping community is made explicit when the donor is represented bearing a model of the very building in which worship takes place. Worship takes place on earth under the overarching heavenly worship of the cherubim, and Christ is no less present to the one realm than to the other.[126]

The equation of apse and arch with earth and heaven applies especially to the upper, continuous zone of the arch where it is higher than the apse. It is most clearly evident in a group of mainly Roman church mosaics apparently influenced by the S. Maria Maggiore programme; elsewhere the relationship of apse to arch may take various forms. In this group of images, a problem comes to light — one that the mosaicist shares with the theologian, especially the theologian of the fifth century. What is the relationship between the incarnate Christ who keeps company with us and the divine Christ worshipped by cherubim and seraphim? How is that relationship to be represented visually or conceptually? The cherubim themselves can be represented either theriomorphically or anthropomorphically, but their exalted status is such that in neither case are they depicted as they truly are. All the more is this true of the divine Christ, the object of their worship. While the incarnate Christ can be depicted as one of us, the divine Christ is represented symbolically by the empty throne or the golden cross. How far is the Christ below really the same as the Christ above? Is the incarnate form of the Logos proper to him, or does the Logos remain transcendent over the assumed humanity, extraneous to it and unaffected by it?

These are precisely the questions evoked by Nestorius's insistence that the divine Logos is to be sharply distinguished from the human being that was assumed. According to Nestorius, bishop of Constantinople from 428

126. These features may be variously seen in a number of Roman apse mosaics of the fifth to ninth centuries: S. Cecilia in Trastevere, SS. Cosma e Damiano, S. Marco in Pallacine, S. Prassede, S. Pudenziana, S. Teodoro, S. Venanzio. In S. Agnese fuori le mura, the young martyr herself occupies the central position of the apse mosaic. In S. Stefano Rotondo, Christ is represented by a small medallion above a large cross planted in the ground between two martyrs. In S. Maria in Domnica, the only one of these churches not dedicated to a martyr, the apse depicts an enthroned Madonna and child surrounded by crowds of angels. In addition to the fuller information provided by Ihm, *Programme,* useful descriptions of these images are provided by William Warner Bishop, "Roman Church Mosaics of the First Nine Centuries," *AJA* 10 (1906), pp. 251-81.

until his deposition at the Council of Ephesus in 431, the divine Logos indwells the human Jesus yet the humanity is in no sense divinized. The Virgin Mary may be acknowledged as the mother of Emmanuel, God-with-us, in the sense that she is the mother of the human being in and through whom God the Logos keeps company with us. But she cannot be said to be *Theotokos,* the God-bearer or Mother of God. Within the one Christ the two natures remain distinct and are neither mingled nor changed. It is supposed that this distinction runs like an invisible thread through the gospel narratives, where certain statements are to be applied only to Christ's human nature while others refer exclusively to the indwelling divine Logos. The human Jesus is ignorant of the day or hour of the parousia whereas the divine Logos knows all things; the human Jesus weeps at the grave of Lazarus, who is raised from the dead by the power of the creative Logos; the human Jesus suffers whereas the Logos remains impassible. As there are two distinct natures in Christ, so the gospel narrative oscillates between two distinct protagonists. The divine Logos worshipped by angels is intimately *connected* to the human Jesus but is by no means to be *identified* with him. The assumed humanity is to be worshipped not in itself but only by virtue of its connection with deity.[127]

The S. Maria Maggiore mosaic programme dates from the years immediately following the Council of Ephesus at which this theology was rejected. An initial decision against Nestorius and in favour of his opponent, Cyril of Alexandria, was taken by Pope Celestine after correspondence with both. From a Roman standpoint the role of the Council was simply to enforce Celestine's decision, a point to which the *Acts* of the Council constantly refer. Responsibility for the basilica of S. Maria Maggiore is claimed by Celestine's successor Sixtus (432-40), who inherits his predecessor's claim to universal jurisdiction. In a mosaic inscription at S. Sabina, Celestine is described as the occupant of the apostolic throne who, "first among bishops, shone forth throughout the whole world" *(primus in toto fulgeret episcopus orbe).* On the S. Maria Maggiore arch Sixtus describes himself as bishop not to the people of Rome but to the whole people of God: *Xystus Episcopus Plebi Dei.* This mosaic programme is addressed to the worldwide church, and articulates the anti-Nestorian convictions that in Jesus God and humanity are truly one and that scrupulous distinctions between what is proper to each of his "na-

---

127. My summary loosely paraphrases a set of twelve Nestorian anathemas, for which see NPNF XIV, pp. 206-17. On the controversy see Frances M. Young, *From Nicaea to Chalcedon: A Guide to the Literature and Its Background* (London: SCM Press, 1983), pp. 213-89.

tures" are inadmissible. In a sermon preached in Ephesus Nestorius is reported to have said, "I do not confess a two- or three-month-old God."[128] The mosaic images seem to reassert the christology Nestorius rejected. In lines that may have referred to the lost apse mosaic, Sixtus addresses Mary as follows:[129]

> Virgo Maria tibi Xystus nova tecta dicavi
> Digna salutifero munera ventre tuo
> Tu Genitrix ignara viri te denique feta
> Visceribus salvis edita nostra salus.
> Ecce tui testes uteri tibi praemia portant
> Sub pedisque iacet passio cuique sua
> Ferrum, flamma, ferae, fluvius saevumque venenum
> Tot tamen has mortes una corona manet.

> Virgin Mary, to you have I Sixtus consecrated this new building,
> A worthy tribute to your salvation-bearing womb,
> You the Mother who knew not a man and yet are fruitful,
> From your healthful inward parts bringing forth our salvation.
> See, the witnesses of your womb bring you their trophies,
> Under their feet lies each one's suffering,
> Iron, flame, beasts, river, and cruel poison,
> Yet while the deaths are many there remains a single crown.

The image to which this referred must have depicted the Virgin, perhaps enthroned with the Christ child, with martyrs and the means of their deaths represented beneath their feet.[130] From a Nestorian perspective, Sixtus's language is in dubious taste. Our salvation originates not in Mary's *viscera* but in God, through the divine Logos who indwelt the human born to Mary. How can it be proper to describe martyrs who suffered for their confession of the divine Christ as witnesses of Mary's *uterus*? Yet the potentially offen-

---

128. Cited in a letter from delegates at the Council to Celestine (NPNF XIV, p. 238), and by Socrates, *Historia Ecclesiastica* vii.34 (NPNF II, p. 172). It is notable that Socrates' account of the Council and its antecedents is critical of both Nestorius and Cyril and does not mention Celestine (vii.29-34).

129. Cited in Brenk, *Maria Maggiore*, p. 2.

130. The inscription was recorded in the sixteenth century, and may refer either to an image on the entrance wall of the church or to the apse mosaic itself (see Snyder, "Original Apse Decoration," pp. 4-5).

sive language intends a crucial christological point about the Word become flesh, which is that flesh derived from flesh is integral to the being of the eternal and incarnate Word. He "does not abhor the Virgin's womb." On the contrary, it was precisely there that he began to "dwell among us," acquiring from it the human existence for which he was eternally predestined and which will forever identify him as who he is. In this theology, Mary serves as the guarantor of an incarnation that is not simply a loose conjunction of heavenly and earthly existences that can never be truly one. The martyrs bring their trophies to the fellow human who guarantees the full cohumanity of the divine Christ.

These christological convictions also make sense of the arch, the throne, and the four living creatures.[131] The throne and the living creatures represent the divine Christ, eternally worshipped by the cherubim, in contrast to the human figure depicted with his mother in the lost images of the apse or entrance wall. The question is how far this duality of divine and human is subsumed into unity. And the answer is that the unity is absolute and essential. The four cherubim who eternally worship the divine Christ are now associated with the four gospels that recount the human story he assumed. The association is not made explicit by depictions of books, but it is clearly implied by the *calf-human* sequence to the left of the throne, corresponding to the *Luke-Matthew* sequence of the images to the left and right of the upper zone of the arch. There is no space above these images for a purely divine Christ who transcends his own human story. As for the *lion-eagle* sequence to the right of the throne, this may correspond to a *Mark-John* or a *John-Mark* sequence, depending on whether the mosaicist is following Jerome or Irenaeus-Victorinus. Given the clear identifications of Luke and Matthew on the left, the uncertainty hardly matters. Mark and John (or John and Mark) are depicted here in a movement from right to left, towards the central throne, and thus in the opposite direction to the left-to-right flow of the infancy narrative. The obvious explanation is that these gospels lack the infancy narratives with which Luke and Matthew open, beginning their versions of the incarnate Word's human story with the testimony of John the Baptist. Given the Johannine connection, we may see in the counter-movement from right to left an emphasis on the divinity of Christ. Yet this orientation towards the divinity is not at odds with the left-to-right orientation towards the humanity. The movement and the countermovement do

---

131. On this see Joane Deane Sieger, "Visual Theology as Metaphor: Leo the Great's Sermons on the Incarnation and the Arch Mosaics at S. Maria Maggiore," *Gesta* 26 (1987), pp. 83-91.

not simply pass each other by; they converge on the bejewelled throne where the superimposed cross signifies Christ's absolute identification with the human story that begins with his nativity and culminates in his suffering.

In its context within both the larger mosaic programme and the christological debate, the image of the heavenly throne and the cherubim is a visual expression of the unity of the incarnate divine Word, as attested by the four gospels with which the cherubim are now associated. The one who is eternally worshipped in heaven is the same as the one who kept company with us on earth and is therefore worshipped here too.

Seven Theses on Jesus and the Canonical Gospel

THESIS I. The early church's reception of the figure of Jesus is a dynamic inter-pretative process attested above all in its diverse gospel literature.

While early Christian gospels can be considered synchronically and individually as stable, self-contained objects, they may also be viewed diachronically and collectively as moments within a single though complex interpretative process. Gospels are interconnected, with later ones always directly or indirectly dependent on their predecessors, and this dependence may be expressed in a variety of ways: word-for-word copying, minor interpretative clarifications, stylistic improvements, changes of sequence, insertion of new narrative material to fill perceived gaps, and so on. Both minor and major changes may represent ideological reactions against a precursor text, yet the later text will remain dependent on the earlier even as it opposes it. This manifold dependence of each new gospel on its predecessors is a precondition of its freedom to present traditional material in novel forms, combinations, or contexts, and so to contribute to the ongoing process of interpreting Jesus' significance to his later followers. It is initially unclear whether a single rendering of the gospel or a determinate number of them will come to be normative for the Christian community as a whole, or whether different gospels will continue to function in different locations without any overarching canonical norm. Such a norm was neither self-evidently necessary nor historically inevitable, at least until the later second century. What is earlier evident is simply the proliferation of gospel literature, and this is not just the product of individual authorial initiatives but also an expression of a momentum inherent in the tradition itself. It is this interconnectedness, proliferation, and momentum that are intended in the expression "gospel writing."

Each new gospel (or new version of an old one) represents a movement forward that is also intended as a movement back to Jesus himself. The interpretative activity that occurs in and through gospel writing is always focused on this single unique datum, and this is no less true of the later gospel than of the earlier. If, from some perspectives, the link back to Jesus seems to weaken as historical distance increases, that is not at all the view of gospel-writers and users themselves. Like modern literature on the so-called "historical Jesus," each new gospel promises its readers a fresh encounter with Jesus as he really was, in certain aspects at least of his manifold being. That every gospel is actually an interpretation reflecting a particular authorial stance in relation to Jesus, the contemporary context, and prior works in the same genre, is evident not so much from the individual text as from their plurality. This perspectival nature of gospel writing is registered in the shift in usage from εὐαγγέλιον to εὐαγγέλιον κατά . . . Yet interpretation continues to be oriented towards Jesus himself. It represents not a substitution of a particular evangelist's Jesus for the reality of the historical figure, but a distinctive perspective on that flesh-and-blood reality. If certain historical criteria suggest that major elements in an evangelist's portrait of Jesus are "unhistorical" and devoid of substance, a wider and more diverse range of historical criteria might considerably complicate such a judgement. Is the relation between the "historical" and the "unhistorical" one of pure opposition, like black and white or good and evil? Or might the unhistorical communicate aspects of a perceived reality beyond the reach of "normal" historical discourse, just as metaphor can communicate truth precisely because of its evident literal untruth?

Gospel writing does not come to a halt with the completion of a "fourth gospel" conveniently dated to the very end of the first century, to be resumed after an interval of several decades by those who perversely take it upon themselves to write merely apocryphal gospels.[1] Such a construction reflects the older Protestant distinction between an "apostolic" age of original purity and a "subapostolic" age of marked decline, with the death of the aged apostle John as the moment of transition from the one to the other. There is no reason to suppose that the Gospel of John was actually the "fourth" gospel at all, and that all gospels subsequently excluded from the canonical collection originated later than their more favoured counterparts. Nor is there any rea-

---

1. As Dieter Lührmann has emphasized, gospels *become* "canonical" or "apocryphal" (*Die apokryph gewordenen Evangelien: Studien zu Neuen Texten und zu Neuen Fragen*, NovTSupp [Leiden: Brill, 2004], p. 2). If so, they are initially just "early Christian gospels."

son to question the competence or good faith of those who compiled gospels later deemed noncanonical, as though they wrote in wilful defiance of an already established canonical limit. In composing a fifth, eighth, or tenth rendering of the gospel, neither the Egerton evangelist nor Luke has any conception of the dividing line that will shortly consign one gospel to near oblivion while preserving the other within an unanticipated intertextual context.

THESIS II. *Jesus is known only through the mediation of his own reception. There is no access to the singular, uninterpreted reality of a "historical Jesus" behind the reception process.*

Divergent responses to Jesus belong to his story from the beginning. Some who encounter him are hostile, denouncing him as a blasphemer or alleging that he is in league with Beelzebul (Mk. 2.7; 3.22). Others are more impressed, seeing in him a restored John the Baptist or Elijah or some other prophet (Mk. 8.28). For others still, he is the Christ (Mk. 8.29). While this last view is also the one to which the evangelist wishes to lead the reader, it still represents one among several interpretative options. Jesus is not transparent to his own messiahship or divine sonship. Indeed, the passing moment of transparency is granted only to his three closest disciples (Mk. 9.2-8), and is not itself the occasion for any confession of faith; Peter's confession is unprompted by the heavenly radiance and the divine voice, which confirm it rather than compelling it. Thus the free acknowledgement of Jesus as the Christ is integral to his narrated career as the Christ. He is who he is only in the event of his own reception as such. Reception is not a secondary occurrence that responds to the completed event of Jesus' life by arbitrarily converting the historical figure into a semimythical Christ of faith. Reception is original rather than secondary: there can be no giving without a corresponding receiving, and both together constitute the completed event in which Jesus acts out his calling. In consequence, no prior space is available for Jesus to enact a reality exclusively his own, recoverable by stripping away everything that may be attributed to the early church. There is nothing in early gospel literature that may *not* be attributed to the early church, however "authentic" it may be; for the story that is told speaks of *a gift received* rather than an object abstracted from this communicative context and accessible as it is in itself.

Perhaps the historical Jesus appeared on the scene as proclaimer of "the kingdom of God," an imminent eschatological reality already anticipated in his exorcisms, healings, and concern for the marginalized? If that is who he really was, the gospel story of his way to Jerusalem, suffering, and resurrection can be set aside as reflecting later convictions of the church, rather than belonging to that original moment in which Jesus was free to be himself. Yet it is only possible to make such a claim because the evangelist Mark has chosen to present Jesus' initial preaching as the announcement of the imminent kingdom of God: "The time is fulfilled, and the kingdom of God is at hand; repent, and believe in the gospel" (Mk. 1.15). This summary statement is wholly the evangelist's work; it does not even purport to represent *ipsissima verba* of Jesus. The content of the proclamation is largely unspecified, and, although the expression "kingdom of God" is fairly frequent in Jesus' later sayings (Mk. 4.11, 26, 30; 9.1; 10.14, 23-25; 14.25), it is nowhere else presented as the core and heart of his teaching. That it has become this in modern research is an extrapolation from Mark 1.15 itself, dependent on precisely the interpretative activity it seeks to overcome in its quest for an uninterpreted, singular, and transparent historical object.

The sought-after object is essentially the same whether one follows Johannes Weiss in highlighting the proclamation of the kingdom of God or Albert Schweitzer in setting the proclamation in the context of Jesus' entire career, and that career in the context of current Jewish eschatological expectations.[2] The Schweitzerian trajectory has the merit of taking seriously the gospel's orientation towards Jesus' death in Jerusalem, and of attempting to make historical sense of it. Here too, however, what is sought and supposedly found is a singular, uninterpreted or self-interpreting existence: immediate access to Jesus as he was in and for himself, before he became something else for others. In a more theoretically informed perspective, it is no longer possible to abstract Jesus from his own reception and to present him in the trappings of some preferred historical identity. If one claims to speak "as a historian" in doing so, defending the cause of "real history" against the imaginings of theology or hermeneutical theory, one perpetuates the naive reductionism endemic to the historical Jesus project and conceals the true nature of the historical problem.[3]

---

2. J. Weiss, *Jesus' Proclamation of the Kingdom of God* (1892[1]), Eng. trans. (London: SCM Press, 1971). The assumption that "the kingdom of God" is the key to Jesus' preaching and ministry is also maintained by those for whom it is a present reality rather than a future one (e.g. C. H. Dodd, *The Parables of the Kingdom* [London: James Nisbet, 1936[2]]; J. D. Crossan, *The Historical Jesus: The Life of a Mediterranean Jewish Peasant* [Edinburgh: T. & T. Clark, 1991]).

3. As defined by N. T. Wright, the "Third Quest" of the historical Jesus follows Schweitzer "in placing Jesus within apocalyptic Jewish eschatology," and represents "a real attempt to do history

THESIS III. The early reception of Jesus is marked by the interaction of the oral and the textual.

Jesus speaks, but neither he nor his disciples write. The only writers he encounters are "scribes" who are often hostile to him and whom he condemns as "hypocrites." Yet, like the scribes' writing, Jesus' speech is grounded in the textuality of scripture. In Luke, Jesus' first public utterance consists in a long citation from Isaiah (Lk. 4.18-19). The Jesus of *GEger* states that "Moses wrote about me to our fathers" (*P. Köln* 255v). The Matthean evangelist is a "scribe trained for the kingdom of heaven," who "brings out of his treasure what is new and what is old" in juxtaposing the events of Jesus' life with corresponding passages from scripture (cf. Mt. 13.52). For Mark, "the beginning of the gospel of Jesus Christ" dovetails with what is "written in Isaiah the prophet" (Mk. 1.1-2). Among the earliest gospels only *GTh* appears to sever the link with the scriptures, contrasting the living Jesus with the twenty-four dead prophets in Israel (*GTh* 52). Even here, deadness is not associated with writing as such: the only scribe in this text is "Didymus Judas Thomas" himself, whose writing perpetuates Jesus' sayings with their life-giving properties (*GTh, Prol.,* 1). Elsewhere Jesus' speech and activity are set against the backdrop of "the holy writings."

It is often claimed that communication within the first-century Greco-Roman world was overwhelmingly oral, that only an elite minority were able to engage with written texts, and that prior to Mark traditions about Jesus were handed down through exclusively oral media. Such claims are entirely misleading. The Qumran finds confirm the significance of authoritative texts for first-century Jewish culture. Evidence from Oxyrhynchus in the southeastern corner of the Roman Empire and Vindolanda in the far northwest demonstrates that people of diverse occupations and social classes had constant recourse to writing in their business or personal dealings with one

---

seriously" in its emphasis on the first-century Jewish context (*Jesus and the Victory of God* [London: SPCK, 1996], p. 84). Here, "the serious historian of Jesus" (p. 87) advances "serious historical hypotheses" (p. 88) which in this case — as in Schweitzer's — have to do primarily with Jesus' own "Aims and Beliefs" (pp. 475-653), and hardly at all with his reception by others. This Jesus was "conscious of a vocation," which was "to enact, symbolically, the return of YHWH to Zion," thus taking upon himself the role that, "according to scripture, YHWH had reserved for himself" (p. 653). As windows onto the historical Jesus, the synoptic gospels themselves are barely visible here. Even their differences reflect the likelihood that Jesus "said the same or similar things in many places at many times" (p. 51), rather than attesting an ongoing process of interpretation and reinterpretation.

another. The hypothesis that Jesus' words were gathered together into Sayings Collections from a very early date is plausible *prima facie* and is confirmed by the recovery of a later work in this genre *(GTh)* and by the evidence of texts such as *1 Clement* and *2 Clement*. Written collections of controversy- or miracle-stories may also have developed at an early date — as, perhaps, in the case of the pre-Johannine Signs Source. Groupings of related material within extant gospels may likewise derive from such early collections. There is, then, no basis for the current tendency to privilege the oral over the textual, viewing textuality as a rigid constraint imposed on primitive oral freedom. The phenomenon of rewriting (Matthew's of Mark, Luke's of Matthew and Mark, John's of *GEger*) indicates that textuality is both constrained and free, and that the constraint actually enables the freedom. Similarly, oral freedom cannot have operated without constraints stemming from the communal recollection of Jesus.[4]

Orality and textuality must have interacted from an early date, in the Jesus tradition just as in the ministry of Paul. Thus texts are reoralized as they are read liturgically and/or used as the basis for preaching and teaching. Gospel texts are intended for oral performance; the dependence of one text on another may in some cases be mediated through a "secondary orality." Even where a direct literary relationship exists, the later text's reinterpretation of the earlier may reflect a performative freedom stemming from the oral tradition. Nor does free oral communication come to an end even with the construction of the normative fourfold gospel. Normativization channels the performance of reoralization through prescribed texts, but here too constraint is a precondition of interpretive freedom.

THESIS IV. Differentiation between canonical and noncanonical gospels is not based on identifiable criteria inherent to the texts.

The major controversy evoked by noncanonical gospels concerns their relation to the canonical ones. Is the noncanonical secondary and dependent on the canonical, or is it primary and independent? Put differently: does the fourfold canonical gospel reflect an absolute historical priority of the texts it incorporates, so that the noncanonical is to be defined by its belatedness?

---

4. Free rewriting is no less possible than free retelling — a point that is missed when rewriting is reduced to "literary editing," leaving oral transmission as the preferred explanation whenever Matthew or Luke exercises a relative freedom in relation to Mark (see J. D. G. Dunn, *Jesus Remembered* [Grand Rapids: Eerdmans, 2003], pp. 210-54).

But neither belatedness nor dependence will do as a criterion for differentiation. If *GPet* is belated in relation to Matthew, so too is John in relation to Mark (on the conventional datings). There is no reason why an interval of several decades should be compatible with canonical status in one case but not in the other. So too with dependence. *GPet* is selectively dependent on Matthew and Mark, but that is also true of Luke. If *GTh* proves to be sometimes dependent on Luke and often on Matthew, that would only confirm its status as a fourth synoptic gospel.

The older assumption that canonical gospels are apostolic whereas noncanonical ones are not has proved equally untenable. Gospels or gospel-like texts are assigned to Matthew and John but also to Peter, James, Thomas, Judas, Mary, and the Twelve collectively. If indirectly authored texts are included, there is also a Pauline gospel (Luke) and a further Petrine one (Mark). It is true that named authors are ascribed to originally anonymous canonical texts by tradition, whereas noncanonical texts may make explicit authorship claims. Yet the distinction is not absolute. In its final form the Gospel of John makes a strong claim to individual authorship even though "the disciple whom Jesus loved" who is said to have written it (Jn. 21.24) is never identified by name. Noncanonical gospels identified by reference to their supposed original audiences were presumably anonymous *(GHeb, GEgy)*.

Canonical gospels are often supposed to be characterized by their essential historicity, whereas noncanonical ones are "apocryphal" in the sense that their contents are largely or entirely fictive. That the infant Jesus did not really convert clay models into real birds is uncontroversial, at least among non-Muslims.[5] Yet, as Origen already recognized, the plural form of the canonical gospel itself poses fundamental questions about historicity as conventionally understood. If the project of gospel harmonization eventually proves unworkable, then Tatian, Augustine, and their later successors were operating with the wrong conception of "gospel truth." Conversely, if presynoptic and/or pre-Johannine material is preserved in texts such as *GTh* and *GEger,* then positive judgements about the historicity of some noncanonical material are possible in principle.[6]

The canonical gospels all present an account of Jesus' ministry that begins with the baptism of John and culminates in his suffering, death, and

5. See Sura 5.110 of the Qur'an, where, however, the bird is singular; also, *Infancy Gospel of Thomas* 2.1-5.

6. Thus Robert L. Webb argues that a healing story from *GEger* may be set alongside Mk. 1.40-45 as "independent traditions" of "a historical event within the ministry of Jesus" ("Jesus Heals a Leper: Mark 1.40-45 and *Egerton Gospel* 35-47," *JSHJ* 4 [2006], pp. 177-202; p. 201).

resurrection. Other gospels focus on specific elements such as Jesus' nativity *(PJas)*, his final revelations *(GMary)*, or his sayings *(GTh)*. Yet canonical gospels are also concerned with the nativity (Mt. 1–2; Lk. 1–2), final revelations (Jn. 13–17), and sayings (Mt. 5–7). It is likely that *GPet* was a work of similar scope to the canonical four, and the same may also be true of *GEger*, extant fragments of which seem to anticipate a passion narrative. Given the lack of clear criteria for differentiating these not-yet-canonical and not-yet-noncanonical texts, an account of gospel origins that confines itself to the canonical literature — even as it constructs its implausible "Q" document — is no longer tenable.

The fact that internal grounds for the canonical/noncanonical distinction cannot be identified does not mean that they did not exist. It means that we have only limited access to the complex, shifting network of decisions about the textual embodiment of the gospel and to the reasoning underlying it. Individuals or communities who decided what gospel literature would and should be read will no doubt have had reasons for their preferences, and some of these reasons may well have had to do with content rather than external factors such as availability, familiarity, or patronage. It is characteristic of other canons too — literary or musical ones, for example — that the reasoning that produced them remains elusive even as their authority seems self-evident. Those who accept that authority are free to propose their own justifications for the canonical decisions they inherit.

THESIS V. The definition of "canonical status" presupposes both an ongoing production of gospel literature and divergent communal usage.

The "Gospel according to Mark" claims to be "the Gospel of Jesus Christ," which, unlike the more familiar later title, does not appear to allow for any further ventures of gospel writing. Whatever may have been intended in Mark 1.1, however, the gospel is written not once but repeatedly. There is no reason for the repetition to cease with the completion of a fourth gospel — even if we suppose that that gospel corresponds to John. In the absence of a canonical boundary or limit, gospel writing proliferates, with each new text drawing from, adding to, or reacting against its predecessors.

Gospel production implies gospel reception, and this will have been a matter not just for individual Christians but above all for Christian communities. While some churches may have used four gospels by the mid–second century, others appear to have used fewer (Rome) or more (Alexandria, Asia). It is likely that usage was diverse. Even where four gospels were used, one or more of them might have been regarded as peripheral (Mark or John) rather than possessing formally equal standing with Matthew or Luke. Usage presupposes circulation: some gospels circulate widely and rapidly, others more narrowly and slowly. The more widely and rapidly a gospel circulates, the higher its chances of inclusion if and when collective decisions are taken about normativity.

As defined by Irenaeus, the canonical collection is a proposed ecumenical consensus about the contents of "the gospel."[7] While grounded in the realities of prior usage, the fourfold gospel is underdetermined by them. Differences of usage might have lasted indefinitely, along with differences in the Old Testament canon; or a proposal might have been made to grant authoritative status to Matthew and Luke while allowing a subordinate position to other gospel literature. Indeed such speculations are unnecessary, for real alternatives were still available at the end of the second century: Tatian's harmony, or Marcionite preference for Luke, or the use of the *Gospel of Peter* in Sardis and Rhossus. While the fourfold gospel was not a historically inevitable and necessary development, however, it must have had a basis in widespread though not universal usage. The Irenaean claim that there are precisely four authentic gospels could hardly have been so widely adopted if these texts were not already well-known in a variety of locations. Conversely, it is unlikely that gospels excluded from the four were equally well-known, as Irenaeus shows no sign of wishing to dislodge any gospel that was already widely recognized. Irenaeus is an innovator in *articulating* the fourfold gospel, but he did not create it out of nothing.

The primary context and precondition of the fourfold gospel is thus the perceived need to harmonize communal usage. The distinction between the canonical and the noncanonical arises not from differences between the texts themselves but from their circulation and currency in wider or narrower spheres of the early Christian world. As the evidence of Clement of Alexandria indicates, the distinction reflects a dawning awareness that some gospels are almost universally known and acknowledged within the wider Christian community, whereas others are known only within more limited circles. In particular, a gospel must break through the barrier that divides East from West. The Gospel of John eventually succeeds in this, assisted by

---

7. There is little to suggest that it was "interactions with heretical forms of Christianity" such as Marcion's that "forced the issue of the canon," as Bart Ehrman argues (*Lost Christianities: The Battles for Scripture and the Faiths We Never Knew* [New York & Oxford: Oxford University Press, 2003], p. 238). The proto-orthodox characteristically debate the *interpretation* of texts with heretics, rather than their selection.

the advocacy of Irenaeus and Hippolytus. In contrast, the *Gospel of Peter* fails to make the transition, although known to Justin in Rome as well as to Melito in Sardis, Serapion in Antioch, and Origen in Caesarea. In the aftermath of the canonical definition it may seem self-evident that the "right" decision was made, whatever the contingent circumstances that led to it. But the rightness of the decision can be perceived only *a posteriori* from within a context already shaped by that decision. If Gaius of Rome had won the anti-Johannine argument, and if Serapion and others had aggressively promoted the cause of the *Gospel of Peter,* then that gospel might have prevailed over both the Gospel of John and the only indirectly Petrine Gospel of Mark. John and Mark would then have disappeared from sight, their memory preserved only in disparaging remarks by Eusebius. At a later date, post-Enlightenment biblical scholarship would have initiated an intense debate over the genuineness of the canonical *Gospel of Peter;* conservative scholarship would have fiercely resisted critical arguments for its pseudonymity. If, later still, fragments of a noncanonical "Johannine" gospel emerged from the sands of Egypt, they would have been consigned without hesitation to the category of the apocryphal. Appeal would be made to gnosticizing tendencies in its opening and dependence on the canonical Peter in its conclusion; and such arguments would no doubt have carried the day, disputed only by a minority of wilfully provocative critics.

That the actual canonical decision was shaped by contingencies need not make it "arbitrary," if that term is intended to undermine its legitimacy. It is hard to conceive of grounds on which a religious community's decision about its own sacred literature could be rejected as arbitrary and illegitimate from a standpoint external to that community. There is no reason to disallow the insider's appeal to the providential leading of the Holy Spirit, operating through a reception process now characterized as *discernment* — the art practised by the "experienced money changers" to whom Origen appeals in this connection. We should assume that these money changers know their own business. A customer who complains that their differentiation of genuine from counterfeit coinage is "arbitrary" is likely to leave them unmoved.

THESIS VI. Early gospel literature is retrospectively divided by the formalizing of canonical and noncanonical status. It is therefore necessary to differentiate pre- and postcanonical stages in the reception of this literature.

At the precanonical stage all gospels are interrelated, and their relationships do not necessarily prefigure their eventual position on one side or the other of the canonical boundary. It is not the case that the interrelatedness of the canonical four is of a different order to the looser relationships that obtain among excluded gospels. The impression that this is so is an illusion created by the division between a determinate collection of four texts and the open-ended "apocryphal" category, in which any number of texts can be accommodated.[8] If the canonical collection seems more coherent than the apocryphal one, that is because like is not being compared with like. If we take "early Christian gospels" as our primary category, it becomes clear that connections across the later canonical/noncanonical boundary are many and various, and that the boundary has retrospectively divided texts that initially belong to the same genre or subgenre. The "original context" of a not-yet-canonical gospel is the field of early gospel literature as a whole.

In consequence of the subsequent canonical division, the entity known as "the four gospels" emerges from among an indefinite number of broadly similar texts, and intertextual links are severed with those newly redefined as noncanonical. Absolute primacy is attributed to "the four gospels," which are henceforth *the* gospels just as their authors are *the* evangelists. That is all well and good: canon construction of one kind or another occurs routinely in the most diverse contexts, since canons are widely found to be useful in proposing what people will most profitably hear, read, perform, admire, study, debate, or otherwise engage with. Yet it is a mistake to suppose that any canon is given in advance, apart from a reception process in which readers make contingent and collective decisions about what will continue to be read and what will not. In historical perspective, a canonical context is always secondary — without detriment to its normative primacy.

A consensus gradually takes shape that gospels attributed to Matthew, Mark, Luke, and John are to be read alongside one another and that no other gospel is permitted to share in their intertextual conversation.[9] Within this

---

8. Thus for Martin Hengel, the term "apocryphal" can cover all gospel literature produced "from the first decades of the second century up to the Middle Ages" (*The Four Gospels and the One Gospel of Jesus Christ,* Eng. trans. [London: SCM Press, 2000], pp. 59-60). Incidentally, Hengel dates Matthew to "around 90-100" and John to "probably not too long after AD 100" (p. 105), which suggests that these texts may be chronologically closer to early apocryphal gospels than to Mark, dated "around AD 70" (p. 78).

9. As Jens Schröter puts this point: "Die Vierevangeliensammlung diente also nicht nur der Unterscheidung von anerkannten und verworfenen oder umstrittenen Evangelien, sondern implizierte zugleich, dass die vier anerkannten Evangelien als sich gegenseitig ergänzend gelesen und nicht gegeneinander ausgespielt werden sollten" ("Die apokryphen Evangelien und die Entstehung des neutestamentlichen Kanons," in *Jesus in apokryphen Evangelienüberlieferungen,* ed. J. Frey and J. Schröter, WUNT [Tübingen: Mohr-Siebeck, 2010], pp. 31-60; p. 54).

new context, the meaning and significance of each individual text are recon-figured.[10] If any gospel asserts or implies its own superiority over others, that claim is disallowed. While an intracanonical fault line between the syn-optics and John is acknowledged, that difference is understood in terms of theological complementarity: the synoptics underline Jesus' humanity, John his divinity, and yet the divinity is not alien to the synoptics nor the human-ity to John. And so the collection serves to articulate a "two natures" doc-trine at some distance from the christological emphases of its individual components. The event in which the divinity and humanity become one is attested in the textual union between the Johannine prologue and the Lukan annunciation. We do not learn from John alone that the Word became flesh in the moment of Jesus' conception, or from Luke alone that what took flesh in Mary's womb was the Word who was with God in the beginning. In the limitless semantic possibilities it opens up, the fourfold gospel is more than and other than the sum of its parts. It is itself a new text, the culmination and goal of all earlier gospel writing.

The fourfold retelling of Jesus' story complicates the relationship be-tween that story and empirical historical reality. Within its new fourfold context, the individual gospel's claim to retrace the exact course of historical events proves hard to sustain: when one gospel tells how Jesus performed a certain action as he approached Jericho, its claim is thrown into question when another gospel states that he performed this action on leaving Jericho. Innumerable small-scale divergences such as this together constitute the ir-reducible difference that establishes the gospels' plurality; without them there would not be four gospels but four copies of a single gospel. An indi-rect relationship to empirical occurrence and sequence is therefore integral to the fourfold canonical narrative. Like metaphor, narrative can further the communication of elusive truth precisely as its literal-historical sense is sus-pended; the event of the Word made flesh cannot be adequately communi-cated by conventional historical method. Yet plurality is also a feature of normal historiography, however much an individual historian may strive to monopolize his or her subject matter. The glossing of εὐαγγέλιον as εὐαγγέλιον κατά . . . acknowledges the perspectival nature of all history writing.

Where gospel difference is seen as a problem or weakness that calls for elaborate harmonization procedures or critical unmasking, the root cause is

10. Cf. Brevard S. Childs, *The New Testament as Canon: An Introduction* (London: SCM Press, 1984), pp. 143-209.

a dissatisfaction with canonical pluralism as such and a determination to reduce it to singularity. But that is to overlook the hermeneutical significance of the canon itself, which strives to integrate the voice of the individual witness into an encompassing polyphony. As an ancient tradition suggests in word and image, this evangelical polyphony echoes the song of the four living creatures around the divine throne.

THESIS VII. A *"canonical perspective"* models a convergence of historical, theological, and hermeneutical discourses, rejecting the assumption that these are necessarily opposed to one another.

It is a conviction deeply held by many biblical scholars that the only legitimate scholarly approach to the texts is the one they like to label "purely historical" or "nonconfessional." By this is meant (1) that the primary context of interpretation must be a text's circumstances of origin, understood both narrowly (in connection with authorial intentions or editorial practices) and broadly (in relation to cultural presuppositions, literary antecedents, or political developments); and (2) that questions of "contemporary" or "theological" significance are potentially corrosive of historical and exegetical inquiry and should be set aside or deferred to another occasion. These interpretative imperatives often express legitimate concerns. The assertion that there are and should be distinctively *scholarly* interpretative genres, not to be confused with devotional or homiletic or popularizing ones, ought not to be controversial. Neither should it be controversial to claim that understanding of texts is generally enhanced by a broader knowledge of their contexts of origin.

Crucially, however, the appeal for a purely historical, nonconfessional approach *also* serves rhetorically to eliminate dissent from a certain status quo, not by engaging dissenting positions on their own terms but by ruling them out *a priori*.[11] Thus, proposing a "canonical perspective" on early

---

11. John Barton rightly argues that the extent of modern biblical scholarship's commitment to history is often exaggerated, and that "biblical criticism" is to be preferred to "historical-critical method" as a characterization of the discipline in its most authentic forms (*The Nature of Biblical Criticism* [Louisville: WJK, 2007], pp. 31-68). Yet Barton's biblical criticism remains locked in the old struggle against canonical and theological modes of interpretation (pp. 137-86), aligning itself with those who aspire "to escape the hand of ecclesiastical and religious authority" (p. 185) in spite of its claim to have evaded the "religious/antireligious dichotomy" (p. 186). Why not speak simply of "biblical scholarship" and acknowledge that methodological and ideological differences are inevitable, here as in other humanities disciplines?

Christian gospel literature immediately exposes one to the charge that the resulting historical and exegetical positions are all somehow motivated, determined, and so invalidated by an "underlying theological agenda." And that means (so it will be said) that the engagement here with the precanonical phase of gospel writing is merely a circuitous route to a predetermined conclusion, the (re)establishment of the fourfold canonical gospel: a blatantly theological construct. To engage with issues of potential theological relevance is to deviate from the purely historical norm, whose purity must be preserved by vigilant policing of the boundary between history and theology. In consequence, there comes into being on the other side of the boundary a kind of mirror-image of this antitheological history, a theology or "theological interpretation" that announces its unconcern for all things historical. According to the essentialist mind-set evident on both sides of the boundary, history and theology are mutually and necessarily antagonistic.

Which history is in view here, and *which* theology? There is no single practice of history, differentiated only by the varying degrees of "purity" with which it succeeds in conforming itself to the historical being of its object. There is no single theology, characterized perhaps by a blind allegiance to unfounded confessional statements. And there is therefore no necessary antagonism between the two discourses. If anything is antagonistic to history broadly conceived, it is the truncated account of gospel origins which pays minute attention to processes of composition yet ignores reception, the very means by which four gospels acquire their ongoing theological *and* historical significance.[12] The fourfold gospel is not an imaginary object held together by sheer theological wishful thinking. Unlike Q, it actually and indisputably exists. While it remains subject to various challenges, not least through the ongoing production of supplementary gospel literature, its outlines and contours are more sharply defined than almost any other body of canonical texts. (Where else is canonical status so closely associated with a specific number?) It is within this enduring canonical structure that "the" four gospels enter the purview not only of the theologian but also of historians of art, literature, and music. The fourfold gospel is a potential interdisciplinary meeting place in a way that a reconstructed Q could never be, even if that hypothesis were to be placed on secure foundations. It should therefore

---

12. "Because history is about effects and consequences as much as it is about causes and conditions, an account of its impact and aftermath is indeed an integral part of all good historiography: causes and effects often help interpret each other" (Markus Bockmuehl, *Seeing the Word: Refocusing New Testament Study* [Grand Rapids: Baker, 2006], p. 168).

be an object of study in its own right, especially for the exegete who is also a theologian or the theologian who is also an exegete.[13]

The theologian in question is in the first instance a practitioner of a historical theology, one who is attentive to long-term consequences of communal decisions about belief and practice and who can make such decisions credible as *live options* concerning matters of real substance. Prerequisite for such a role is not so much the theologian's personal "faith perspective" or confessional allegiance as the capacity — however derived — to imagine oneself within such a perspective or allegiance, and to present the decision in question not as inherently and unassailably normative but as a proposal to which it *has* seemed and *might still* seem appropriate to ascribe normative authority. On this somewhat minimalist account of a possible theological practice, there is no place for the familiar rhetorical contrast between the theologian's enclosed faith perspective and the secular historian's fearless pursuit of inconvenient truth. One need be no less a historian for being a theologian, and no less a theologian for being a historian.[14] Conversely, an untheological historical practice might highlight the intellectual and cultural gulf between then and now, or present a decision about a specific issue — the fourfold gospel, for example — as masking an abstract power struggle in which an emergent proto-orthodox hierarchy finally succeeded in marginalizing its ideological opponents. A meaningful conversation between the two accounts would have to take place on shared historical terrain, rather than trading futile allegations about "presuppositions."

The point at issue may also be expressed in a broader hermeneutical idiom. Canonical status changes the artefacts to which it is accorded. It is

---

13. There is no reason to fear that a canonical perspective along the present lines would "mak[e] the Bible into an intellectual ghetto separated from all other truth . . ." (James Barr, *Holy Scripture: Canon, Authority, Criticism* [Oxford: Clarendon Press, 1983], p. 168). This canonical perspective does *not* declare that precanonical "sources, stages, and editions . . . are basically irrelevant" (p. 77), or foster "a strong zealotic legalism of the final text" (p. 92), or betray an "antipathy to historical criticism" (p. 133) or an "inability to accept that its guidance might be modified or complemented by any other method or approach" (p. 146); nor is it "likely to have a strong proconservative effect" (p. 148), nor will it refuse to "judge that one portion of scripture is more central or more essential than any other" (p. 149).

14. The present attempt to *coordinate* historical, theological, and hermeneutical orientations is pragmatically motivated by the specific concern to outline a canonical perspective on the fourfold gospel, and implies no necessary criticism of work in which history and hermeneutics are *subordinated* to theology (see Murray Rae, *History and Hermeneutics* [London and New York: T. & T. Clark, 2005]). The difference between more or less explicit theology is a matter of genre and occasion.

underdetermined by the largely unknown decisions that give rise to it, and yet it establishes social and institutional contexts that can foster and shape a reception process of indefinite duration. This is no more or less true of the four-gospel collection (and of the New Testament as a whole) than of the tragedies of Shakespeare or the symphonies of Beethoven. Canonical artefacts maintain a double existence, retaining the traces of their time and place of origin yet simultaneously the objects of a selection process that transports them to ever more distant times and places where their ascribed value is confirmed by repeated performance.

Given the institutional power they legitimate, canons *may* be perceived as oppressive rather than enabling, a problematic legacy rather than precious cultural and spiritual capital. In Western societies of the twenty-first century, there is no canon that can compel assent or place itself beyond critique. Yet critique itself is not obligatory. Canonical objects can still be engaged as they are, in their dual existence, in such a way that their enduring claim can be re-presented as a live option — a potential disclosure of reality that *might* and *may* be identified as truth.

Bibliography

Primary Sources

Ambrose. *Expositio Evangelii secundum Lucam,* ed. G. Schenkl, CSEL 32/4. Vienna: Österreichische Akademie der Wissenschaften, 1902.

Apostolic Fathers. Ed. Bart D. Ehrman, 2 vols., LCL. Cambridge, Mass.: Harvard University Press, 2003.

Augustine. *De Civitate Dei, Libri I-X,* ed. B. Dombart and A. Kalb, CCSL 47. Turnhout: Brepols, 1955.

————. *De Consensu Evangelistarum,* ed. F. Weihrich, CSEL 43. Vienna: Österreichische Akademie der Wissenschaften, 1904.

————. *Harmony of the Evangelists.* Eng. trans. in NPNF, first series, vol. 6. Repr. Grand Rapids: Eerdmans, 1991.

————. *Retractations.* Eng. trans. in FC. Washington, D.C.: Catholic University of America Press, 1968.

Bell, H. Idris, and Skeat, T. C. *Fragments of an Unknown Gospel.* London: British Museum, 1935.

Bernhard, A. *Other Early Christian Gospels: A Critical Edition of the Surviving Greek Manuscripts.* London & New York: T. & T. Clark, 2007.

Biblia Sacra iuxta Vulgatam Versionem. Ed. R. Gryson. Stuttgart: Deutsche Bibelgesellschaft, 1994⁴.

Brooke, A. E. *The Commentary of Origen on S. John's Gospel,* 2 vols. Cambridge: Cambridge University Press, 1896.

Charles, R. H. (ed.). *The Assumption of Moses.* London: Adam & Charles Black, 1897.

Chronicon Paschale. Ed. L. Dindorf. Bonn: E. Weber, 1832.

Chrysostom. *Homilies on Matthew,* Eng. trans. NPNF, first series, vol. 10. Repr. Grand Rapids: Eerdmans, 1991.

Clemens Alexandrinus. Ed. O. Stählin, L. Früchtel, and U. Treu, 4 vols., GCS. Berlin: Akademie-Verlag 1960-80³.

Clement of Alexandria Stromateis I-III. Trans. John Ferguson, FC. Washington, D.C.: Catholic University of America Press, 1991.

620

Bibliography

Codex Fuldensis. Ed. E. Ranke. Marburg & Leipzig: N. G. Elwert, 1868.

Davis, Raymond (ed.). *The Book of Pontiffs (Liber Pontificalis to AD 715)*. Liverpool: Liverpool University Press, 1989.

Deliyannis, Deborah Mauskopf. *The Book of Pontiffs of the Church of Ravenna*. Washington, D.C.: Catholic University of America Press, 2004.

Diatessaron de Tatien. Ed. A.-S. Marmardji. Beyrouth: Imprimerie Catholique, 1935.

Diels, H., and W. Kranz. *Die Fragmente der Vorsokratiker*, vol. 1. Berlin: Weidmann, 1960^9.

Dionysius Bar Salibi, In Apocalypsim, Actus et Epistulas Catholicas. Ed. J. Sedláček, CSCO 60 (I, 20 [Latin] = II, 101 [Syriac]). Leuven: Peeters, 1909-10.

Ehrman, Bart D., and Zlatko Pleše. *The Apocryphal Gospels: Texts and Translations*. New York & Oxford: Oxford University Press, 2011.

Eichhorn, J. G. *Einleitung in das Neue Testament*, Erster Band. Leipzig: Weidmann, 1820^2.

Elliott, J. K. (ed.). *The Apocryphal New Testament*. Oxford: Clarendon Press, 1999^2.

Éphrem de Nisibe, Commentaire de l'Évangile concordant ou Diatessaron: traduit du syriaque et de l'arménien. Ed. L. Leloir. Paris: du Cerf, 1966.

Epiphanius, Ancoratus und Panarion. Ed. K. Holl and H. Lietzmann, 3 vols., GCS. Hinrichs: Leipzig, 1915-33.

Epiphanius' Treatise on Weights and Measures: The Syriac Version. Ed. James Elmer Dean. Chicago: University of Chicago Press, 1935.

Eusebius Werke, Die Kirchengeschichte. Ed. E. Schwartz and Theodor Mommsen, 3 vols., GCS. Leipzig: J. C. Hinrichs'sche Buchhandlung, 1903-9.

Gijsel, Jan (ed.). *Libri de Nativitate Mariae: Pseudo-Matthaei Evangelium Textus et Commentarius*, CCSA. Turnhout: Brepols, 1997.

Gotthold Ephraim Lessing, Werke, Vol. 7: *Theologiekritische Schriften I-II*. Ed. H. Göbel. Munich: Carl Hanser Verlag, 1976.

Gotthold Ephraim Lessing, Werke, Vol. 8: *Theologiekritische Schriften III/Philosophische Schriften*. Ed. H. Göbel. Munich: Carl Hanser Verlag, 1979.

Gotthold Ephraim Lessings Sämtliche Schriften. Ed. K. Lachmann and F. Muncker. Leipzig: G. V. Göschen'sche Verlagshandlung, 1886-1924.

Gotthold Ephraim Lessing Werke und Briefe. Vol. 8, ed. Arno Schilson. Frankfurt am Main: Deutscher Klassiker Verlag, 1989.

Grenfell, B. P., and A. S. Hunt. *New Sayings of Jesus and Fragment of a Lost Gospel*. London: Egypt Exploration Fund, 1904.

—————. *Sayings of Our Lord from an Early Greek Papyrus*. London: Egypt Exploration Fund, 1897.

Griesbach, Jakob. *Commentatio qua Marci Evangelium totum e Matthaei et Lucae commentariis decerptum esse monstratur* (1789-90^1, 1794^2; repr. with Eng. trans. in J. J. *Griesbach*, ed. B. Orchard and T. Langstaff, pp. 74-135).

—————. *Synopsis Evangeliorum Matthei, Marci et Lucae: Textum Graecum ad fidem codicum versionum et patrum emendavit et lectionis varietatem adiecit . . . .* Halae: apud Io. Iac. Curt., 1776^1 (. . . *cum iis Joannis pericopis quae historiam passionis et resurrectionis Jesu Christi complectuntur*, 1797^2; . . . *cum iis Joannis pericopis quae omnino cum caeterorum evangelistarum narrationibus conferendae sunt*, 1809^3).

Gronewald, M. "255. Unbekanntes Evangelium oder Evangelienharmonie (Fragment aus dem 'Evangelium Egerton')." *Kölner Papyri (P. Köln)* 6, Abhandlungen der Rheinisch-Westfälischen Akademie der Wissenschaften, PapyCol VII. Opladen: Westdeutscher Verlag, 1987, pp. 136-44.

Hermann Samuel Reimarus: Apologie oder Schutzschrift für die vernünftigen Verehrer Gottes. Ed. Gerhard Alexander, 2 vols. Frankfurt am Main: Insel Verlag, 1971.

Herodian of Antioch's History of the Roman Empire from the Death of Marcus Aurelius to the Accession of Gordian III. Ed. Edward C. Echols. Berkeley and Los Angeles: University of California Press, 1961.

Hieronymus, Commentarii in epistulam Pauli apostoli ad Galatas. Ed. F. Bucchi, CCSL 77A. Turnhout: Brepols, 2006.

Hieronymus, Commentariorum in Hiezechielem libri XIV. Ed. F. Glorie, CCSL 75. Turnhout: Brepols, 1964.

Hieronymus, Commentariorum in Matheum libri IV. Ed. D. Hurst and M. Adriaen, CCSL 77. Turnhout: Brepols, 1969.

Hieronymus, Dialogus adversus Pelagianos. Ed. C. Moreschini, CCSL 80. Turnhout: Brepols, 1990.

Iustini Martyris Apologiae pro Christianis, Dialogus cum Tryphone. Ed. M. Marcovich. Berlin & New York: De Gruyter, 2005.

James, M. R. *The Apocryphal New Testament.* Oxford: Clarendon Press, 1924.

Kenyon, Frederick G. *The Chester Beatty Biblical Papyri.* London: Walker, 1933-58.

Kraus, Thomas J., and Tobias Nicklas. *Das Petrusevangelium und die Petrusapokalypse: Die griechischen Fragmente mit deutscher und englischer Übersetzung.* Berlin & New York: De Gruyter, 2004.

Lamy, Bernard. *Commentarius in Concordiam Evangelicam et Apparatus Chronologicus et Geographicus cum Praefatione in qua demonstratur veritas Evangelii.* Paris, 1699.

Leclerc, Jean. *Harmonia Evangelica, cui subjecta est Historia Christi ex Quatuor Evangeliis concinnata.* Amsterdam, 1699.

Lessing: Philosophical and Theological Writings. Ed. H. B. Nisbet. Cambridge: Cambridge University Press, 2005.

Lessing's Theological Writings. Eng. trans. Henry Chadwick. London: A. & C. Black, 1957.

Liber Pontificalis. Vol. 1, ed. L. Duchesne. Paris: E. de Boccard, 1955.

Loomis, Louise Ropes (ed.). *The Book of the Popes, I: To the Pontificate of Gregory I.* New York: Columbia University Press, 1916.

Lührmann, Dieter. *Fragmente apokryph gewordener Evangelien in griechischer und lateinischer Sprache.* Marburg: Elwert, 2000.

———. *Die apokryph gewordenen Evangelien: Studien zu Neuen Texten und zu Neuen Fragen.* NovTSupp. Leiden: Brill, 2004.

MacKnight, James. *Harmony of the Four Gospels, in Which the Natural Order of Each Is Preserved,* 2 vols. London, 1756[1]; 1809[4].

Melito of Sardis, On Pascha, and Fragments. Ed. S. G. Hall. Oxford: Clarendon Press, 1979.

Nag Hammadi and Manichean Studies. Gen. ed. J. M. Robinson and H. J. Klimkeit, vol. XXXIII, ed. Michael Waldstein and Frederik Wisse. Leiden: Brill, 1995.

Bibliography

Nag Hammadi Library in English, The. Ed. James M. Robinson. Leiden: Brill, 1984^2.

Nag Hammadi Studies. Gen. ed. Martin Krause, James M. Robinson, and Frederik Wisse, vols. XX-XXI, ed. Bentley Layton, 2 vols. Leiden: Brill, 1989.

Nestle-Aland. *Novum Testamentum Graece.* Stuttgart: Deutsche Bibelgesellschaft, 1993^{27}.

Origen, Commentary on the Gospel according to John. Ed. Ronald E. Heine, 2 vols., FC. Washington, D.C.: Catholic University of America Press, 1989-93.

Origen, Commentary on the Gospel of John. ANF 10. Repr. Grand Rapids: Eerdmans, 1974, pp. 297-408 (Books 1-10).

Origen, Homilies on Luke. Eng. trans. FC 94. Washington, D.C.: Catholic University of America Press, 1996.

Origen, Homilies on Numbers. Ed. Thomas P. Scheck, ACT. Downers Grove, IL: IVP Academic, 2009.

Origenes, Der Johanneskommentar. Ed. E. Preuschen, GCS. Leipzig: J. C. Hinrichs, 1903.

Origenes, Homilien zu Lukas in der Übersetzung des Hieronymus und die griechischen Reste der Homilien und des Lukas-Kommentars. Ed. Max Rauer, GCS. Berlin: Akademie-Verlag, 1959^2.

Origenes, Homilien zum Hexateuch in Rufins Übersetzung (Die Homilien zu Numeri, Josua, und Judices). Ed. W. A. Baehrens, GCS. Leipzig: J. C. Hinrichs, 1921.

Prudentius, Peristephanon. Ed. H. J. Thomson, LCL. London: Heinemann; Cambridge, Mass.: Harvard University Press, 1953.

Reimarus Fragments. Ed. Charles H. Talbert. London: SCM Press, 1971.

Saint Éphrem, Commentaire de l'Évangile concordant, version arménienne. Ed. L. Leloir. Louvain: Peeters, 1953-54.

Saint Éphrem, Commentaire de l'Évangile concordant, texte syriaque. Ed. L. Leloir. Dublin: Hoddaes Figgis, 1963.

Schaff, Philip. *Creeds of Christendom,* 3 vols. Repr. Grand Rapids: Baker, 1977.

Schleiermacher, F. D. E. *A Critical Study on the Gospel of Luke* (1817, Eng. tr. 1825). Repr. Lewiston/Queenston/Lampeter: Edwin Mellen, ed. Terrence E. Tice, 1993.

————. "Ueber die Zeugnisse des Papias von unsern beiden ersten Evangelien," *Theologische Studien und Kritiken* (1832), pp. 735-68.

Schneemelcher, W. (ed.). *Neutestamentlichen Apokryphen.* Tübingen: Mohr-Siebeck, 1990^6 (Eng. trans. *New Testament Apocrypha,* 2 vols., Cambridge: James Clarke; Louisville: WJK, 1991-92).

Selected Translations of Clement and Origen with Introductions and Notes. Ed. J. E. L. Oulton and H. Chadwick, Library of Christian Classics. Philadelphia: Westminster Press, 1954.

Semler, Johann Salomo. *Beantwortung der Fragmente eines Ungennanten insbesondere vom Zwecke Jesu und seiner Jünger.* Halle: Verlag des Erziehungsinstituts, 1779.

Synopsis Quattuor Evangeliorum. Ed. K. Aland. Stuttgart: Württembergische Bibelanstalt Stuttgart, 1967^4.

Tatian. *Diatessaron,* Eng. trans. ANF 10. Repr. Grand Rapids: Eerdmans, 1974.

Tatiani Evangeliorum Harmoniae Arabice. Ed. A. Ciasca. Rome: Bibliographia Polyglotta, 1888.

Tertullien, Traité de la prescription contre les hérétiques. Ed. R. Refoulé, SC. Paris: Éditions du Cerf, 1957.

Tischendorf, Constantinus. *Evangelia Apocrypha.* Leipzig: Avenarius & Mendelssohn, 1853.

Victorin de Poetovio. Sur l'Apocalypse et autres écrits. Ed. Martine Dulaey, SC. Paris: du Cerf, 1997.

Victorini Episcopi Petavionensis Opera. Ed. J. Haussleiter, CSEL 49. Vienna: F. Tempsky; Leipzig: G. Freytag, 1916.

Weisse, Christian Hermann. *Die evangelische Geschichte kritisch und philosophisch bearbeitet,* 2 vols. Leipzig: Breitkopf und Härtel, 1838.

Williams, Frank (trans.). *The Panarion of Epiphanius of Salamis, Books I-III,* 2 vols. Leiden: Brill, 1987-94.

Woolston, Thomas. *Six Discourses on the Miracles of Our Saviour, And Defences of His Discourses.* London, 1727-30; repr. New York & London: Garland, 1979.

Secondary Sources

Alexander, Loveday. "Ancient Book Production," in *The Gospels for All Christians,* ed. R. Bauckham. Grand Rapids: Eerdmans, 1998, pp. 71-105.

⸻. *The Preface to Luke's Gospel,* SNTSMS. Cambridge: Cambridge University Press, 1993.

Allison, Dale C. *Constructing Jesus: Memory, Imagination, and History.* Grand Rapids: Baker, 2010.

⸻. "The Eye Is the Lamp of the Body (Matthew 6.22-23 = Luke 11.33-36)," *NTS* 33 (1987), pp. 61-83.

Altaner, Bertold. "Augustinus und Irenäus," in his *Kleine patristische Schriften,* ed. G. Glockmann. Berlin: Academie Verlag, 1967.

Asgeirsson, Jon M. A., April DeConick, and Risto Uro (eds.). *Thomasine Traditions in Antiquity: The Social and Cultural World of the Gospel of Thomas.* Leiden & Boston: Brill, 2006.

Ashton, John. *Studying John: Approaches to the Fourth Gospel.* Oxford: Clarendon Press, 1994.

⸻. *Understanding the Fourth Gospel.* Oxford: Clarendon Press, 1991.

Assmann, Jan. "Form as a Mnemonic Device: Cultural Texts and Cultural Memory," in *Performing the Gospel: Orality, Memory, and Mark,* ed. Richard A. Horsley, Jonathan A. Draper, and John Miles Foley. Minneapolis: Fortress, 2006, pp. 67-82.

Asso, Cecilia. "Erasmus redivivus. Alcune osservazioni sulla filologia neotestamentaria di Jean Le Clerc," in *Vico nella storia della filologia,* ed. Silvia Caianiello and Amadeu Viana. Naples: Guida, 2004, pp. 79-115.

Attridge, Harold. *Hebrews,* Hermeneia. Philadelphia: Fortress, 1989.

⸻. "Thematic Development and Source Elaboration in John 7:1-36," *CBQ* 42 (1980), pp. 160-70.

Auwers, J.-M., and H. J. de Jonge (eds.). *The Biblical Canons,* BEThL 163. Leiden: Peeters, 2003.

Baarda, Tjitze. *Essays on the Diatessaron.* Kampen: Kok Pharos, 1994.

Badger, G. P. *The Nestorians and Their Rituals,* 2 vols. London: John Masters, 1852.

Baracchini, M. *Le Collezione del Museo Arcivescovile di Ravenna.* Ravenna: Opera di Religione della Diocesi di Ravenna, 2011.

Barr, James. *Holy Scripture: Canon, Authority, Criticism.* Oxford: Clarendon Press, 1983.

Barrett, C. K. *The Gospel according to St. John.* London: SPCK, 1978².

Barton, John. *The Nature of Biblical Criticism.* Louisville: WJK, 2007.

Bauckham, Richard. *Jesus and the Eyewitnesses: The Gospels as Eyewitness Testimony.* Grand Rapids: Eerdmans, 2006.

—————. "The Parable of the Vine: Rediscovering a Lost Parable of Jesus," *NTS* 33 (1987), pp. 84-101.

————— (ed.). *The Gospels for All Christians: Rethinking the Gospel Audiences.* Grand Rapids: Eerdmans, 1998.

Bauer, Walter. *Das Johannesevangelium,* HNT. Mohr-Siebeck, 1925².

Baum, A. D. "Papias, der Vorzug der *Viva Vox* und die Evangelienschriften," *NTS* 44 (1998), pp. 144-51.

—————. "Papias als Kommentator evangelischer Aussprüche Jesu: Erwägungen zur Art seines Werkes," *NovT* 38 (1996), pp. 257-76.

Beale, G. K. *John's Use of the Old Testament in Revelation,* JSNTSupp. Sheffield: Sheffield Academic Press, 1998.

Beaton, Richard C. "How Matthew Writes," in *The Written Gospel,* ed. Markus Bockmuehl and Donald A. Hagner. Cambridge: Cambridge University Press, 2005, pp. 116-34.

Bell, H. Idris. "The Gospel Fragments P. Egerton 2," *HTR* 42 (1949), pp. 53-64.

—————. "Recent Discoveries of Biblical Papyri: An Inaugural Lecture Delivered before the University of Oxford on 18 November 1936." Oxford: Oxford University Press, 1936.

Belle, G. van (ed.). *The Death of Jesus in the Fourth Gospel,* BEThL. Leuven: Leuven University Press, 2007.

Bellinzoni, A. J. *The Sayings of Jesus in the Writings of Justin Martyr.* Leiden: Brill, 1967.

Bernard, J. H. *A Critical and Exegetical Commentary on the Gospel according to St. John,* 2 vols., ICC. Edinburgh: T. & T. Clark, 1928.

Bienert, W. A. "Ἀναγωγή im *Johannes-Kommentar* des Origenes," in *Origeniana Sexta: Origène et la Bible/Origen and the Bible,* ed. G. Dorival and A. Le Boulluec, BEThL 118. Leuven: Peeters, 1995, pp. 419-28.

Bishop, William Warner. "Roman Church Mosaics of the First Nine Centuries," *AJA* 10 (1906), pp. 251-81.

Black, C. Clifton. *Mark: Images of an Apostolic Interpreter.* Edinburgh: T. & T. Clark, 2001.

Bludau, August. *Die ersten Gegner der Johannesschriften.* Freiburg: Herder, 1925.

Bockmuehl, Markus. *Seeing the Word: Refocusing New Testament Study.* Grand Rapids: Baker, 2006.

Bockmuehl, Markus, and Donald A. Hagner (eds.). *The Written Gospel.* Cambridge: Cambridge University Press, 2005.

Bollacher, Martin. *Lessing, Vernunft und Geschichte: Untersuchungen zum Problem religiöser Aufklärung in den Spätschriften.* Tübingen: Niemeyer, 1978.

Bovini, G. *Ravenna: Art and History.* Ravenna: Longo, n.d.

Bovon, François. *Das Evangelium nach Lukas (Lk.9,51–14,35),* EKKNT. Neukirchen-Vluyn: Benziger Verlag, 1996.

————. *Luke 1: A Commentary on the Gospel of Luke 1:1–9.50,* Eng. trans., Hermeneia. Minneapolis: Fortress, 2002.

Brenk, Beat. *The Apse, the Image, and the Icon: An Historical Perspective of the Apse as a Space for Images.* Wiesbaden: Reichert, 2010.

————. *Die frühchristlichen Mosaiken in S. Maria Maggiore zu Rom.* Wiesbaden: Franz Steiner Verlag, 1975.

Brent, Allen. *Hippolytus and the Roman Church in the Third Century: Communities in Tension before the Emergence of a Monarch-Bishop.* Leiden: Brill, 1995.

Brooks, James A. "Clement of Alexandria as a Witness to the Development of the New Testament Canon," *SecC* 9 (1992), pp. 41-55.

Brown, Raymond E. *The Birth of the Messiah: A Commentary on the Infancy Narratives in the Gospels of Matthew and Luke.* New York: Doubleday, 1993².

————. *The Death of the Messiah: A Commentary on the Passion Narrative in the Four Gospels,* 2 vols. New York: Doubleday, 1999.

————. *The Gospel according to John,* 2 vols., AB. New York: Doubleday, 1966.

————. "The Gospel of Thomas and St. John's Gospel," *NTS* 9 (1962-63), pp. 155-77.

Bultmann, Christoph, and Friedrich Vollhardt (eds.). *Lessings Religionsphilosophie im Kontext: Hamburger Fragmente und Wolfenbütteler Axiomata.* Berlin & New York: De Gruyter, 2011.

Bultmann, Rudolf. *Die Geschichte der synoptischen Tradition.* Göttingen: Vandenhoeck & Ruprecht, 1967⁷ (Eng. trans. *History of the Synoptic Tradition,* Oxford: Blackwell, 1963).

————. *The Gospel of John: A Commentary.* Eng. trans. Oxford: Blackwell, 1971.

Burkitt, F. C. *The Old Latin and the Itala.* Cambridge: Cambridge University Press, 1896.

Burridge, Richard. *Imitating Jesus: An Inclusive Approach to New Testament Ethics.* Grand Rapids: Eerdmans, 2007.

Burton, E. de W. *A Critical and Exegetical Commentary on the Letter to the Galatians,* ICC. Edinburgh: T. & T. Clark, 1921.

Byrskog, Samuel. *Story as History — History as Story: The Gospel Tradition in the Context of Ancient Oral History,* WUNT. Tübingen: Mohr-Siebeck, 2000 (repr. Leiden: Brill, 2002).

Caird, George B. *Saint Luke,* PNTC. Harmondsworth: Penguin, 1963.

Cameron, R. *Sayings Traditions in the Apocryphon of James.* Philadelphia: Fortress, 1984.

———— (ed.). *The Other Gospels: Non-Canonical Gospel Texts.* Guildford: Lutterworth Press, 1983.

Campbell, Douglas A. *The Quest for Paul's Gospel: A Suggested Strategy.* London & New York: T. & T. Clark International, 2005.

Campenhausen, Hans von. *The Formation of the Christian Bible,* Eng. trans. Philadelphia: Augsburg Fortress, 1972.

Carlson, Stephen C. "Clement of Alexandria on the 'Order' of the Gospels," *NTS* 47 (2001), pp. 118-25.

Catchpole, David. *The Quest for Q.* Edinburgh: T. & T. Clark, 1993.

Chadwick, H. "Ego Berengarius," *JTS*, n.s., 40 (1989), pp. 414-45.

Childs, Brevard S. *The New Testament as Canon: An Introduction.* London: SCM Press, 1984.

Cornell, Richard. "'I and the Father Are One': Scriptural Interpretation and Trinitarian Construction in the Monarchian Debate." Ph.D. diss., University of Aberdeen, 2010.

Cosaert, Carl P. *The Text of the Gospels in Clement of Alexandria.* Atlanta: SBL, 2008.

Crossan, John Dominic. *The Birth of Christianity.* New York: HarperCollins, 1998.

————. *The Cross That Spoke: The Origins of the Passion Narrative.* New York: Harper & Row, 1988.

————. *Four Other Gospels: Shadows on the Contours of Canon.* New York: Harper & Row, 1985.

————. *The Historical Jesus: The Life of a Mediterranean Jewish Peasant.* Edinburgh: T. & T. Clark, 1991.

————. *In Parables: The Challenge of the Historical Jesus.* New York: Harper & Row, 1973.

Cullmann, Oscar. *The Christology of the New Testament,* Eng. trans. London: SCM Press, 1959.

Culpepper, R. A. *Anatomy of the Fourth Gospel: A Study in Literary Design.* Philadelphia: Fortress, 1983.

Dahl, N. A. "The Crucified Messiah," in his *Jesus the Christ: The Historical Origins of Christological Doctrine,* ed. Donald H. Juel. Minneapolis: Fortress, 1991, pp. 27-47.

Daniels, Jon B. "The Egerton Gospel: Its Place in Early Christianity." Unpublished diss., Claremont Graduate School, 1989; University Microfilms International, Ann Arbor, 1990.

Davies, Stevan L. *The Gospel of Thomas and Christian Wisdom.* California: Bardic Press, 2005^2.

Davies, W. D., and Allison, D. C. *A Critical and Exegetical Commentary on the Gospel according to St. Matthew,* 3 vols., ICC. Edinburgh: T. & T. Clark, 1988-97.

DeConick, April D. *The Original Gospel of Thomas in Translation.* London & New York: T. & T. Clark, 2007.

————. *Recovering the Original Gospel of Thomas: A History of the Gospel and Its Growth.* London & New York: T. & T. Clark International, 2005.

————. *Seek to See Him: Ascent and Vision Mysticism in the Gospel of Thomas,* VCSupp. Leiden: Brill, 1996.

————. *Voices of the Mystics: Early Christian Discourse in the Gospels of John and Thomas and Other Ancient Christian Literature,* JSNTSupp. Sheffield: Sheffield Academic Press, 2001.

Deichmann, F. W. *Frühchristliche Bauten und Mosaiken von Ravenna.* Baden-Baden: Bruno Grimm, 1958.

Delbrueck, R. "The Acclamation Scene on the Doors of Santa Sabina," *ArtB* 31 (1949), pp. 215-17.

Delling, G. "Johann Jakob Griesbach. Seine Zeit, sein Leben, sein Werk," *ThZ* 33 (1977), pp. 81-99.

Denaux, Adelbert (ed.). *John and the Synoptics*, BEThL. Leiden: Leiden University Press, 1992.

Derrida, Jacques. *Dissemination*, Eng. trans. Chicago: University of Chicago Press, 1981.

————. *Margins of Philosophy*, Eng. trans. Chicago: University of Chicago Press, 1982.

————. *Of Grammatology*, Eng. trans. Baltimore & London: Johns Hopkins University Press, 1976.

Dibelius, Martin. *Botschaft und Geschichte: Gesammelte Aufsätze I*. Tübingen: Mohr-Siebeck, 1953.

————. *Die Formgeschichte des Evangeliums*. Tübingen: Mohr-Siebeck, 1959³ (Eng. trans. *From Tradition to Gospel*, London: Nicholson & Watson, 1934).

Dively Lauro, Elizabeth Ann. *The Soul and Spirit of Scripture within Origen's Exegesis*. Atlanta: JBL, 2005.

Dodd, C. H. *Historical Tradition in the Fourth Gospel*. Cambridge: Cambridge University Press, 1963.

————. *The Interpretation of the Fourth Gospel*. Cambridge: Cambridge University Press, 1953.

————. "A New Gospel," in his *New Testament Studies*. Manchester: Manchester University Press, 1953, pp. 12-52.

————. *The Parables of the Kingdom*. London: James Nisbet, 1936².

Donaldson, T. L. *Jesus on the Mountain: A Study in Matthean Theology*, JSNTSupp. Sheffield: JSOT Press, 1985.

Dorrival, Gilles, and Alain Le Boulluec. *Origeniana Sexta: Origène et la Bible/Origen and the Bible: Actes du Colloquium Origenianum Sextum Chantilly, 30 août–3 septembre 1993*, BEThL 118. Leuven: Peeters, 1995.

Downing, Caroline J. "Wall Paintings from the Baptistery at Stobi, Macedonia, and Early Depictions of Christ and the Evangelists," *Dumbarton Oaks Papers* 52 (1998), pp. 259-80.

Dunderberg, Ismo. *The Beloved Disciple in Conflict? Revisiting the Gospels of John and Thomas*. Oxford: Oxford University Press, 2006.

————. "The School of Valentinus," in *A Companion to Second-Century Christian "Heretics*," ed. Antti Marjanen and Petri Luomanen. Leiden: Brill, 2005, pp. 64-99.

Dungan, David. "Augustine and the Augustinian Hypothesis," in *New Synoptic Studies: The Cambridge Gospel Conference and Beyond*, ed. W. R. Farmer. Macon, GA: Mercer University Press, 1983, pp. 37-64.

————. *Constantine's Bible: Politics and the Making of the New Testament*. London: SCM Press, 2006.

————. "Theory of Synopsis Construction," *Bib* 61 (1980), pp. 305-29.

Dunn, J. D. G. *Jesus Remembered*. Grand Rapids: Eerdmans, 2003.

Edwards, Mark. *Catholicity and Heresy in the Early Church*. Farnham: Ashgate, 2009.

Ehrman, Bart. *Lost Christianities: The Battles for Scripture and the Faiths We Never Knew*. New York & Oxford: Oxford University Press, 2003.

Ennulat, A. *Die "Minor Agreements": Untersuchung zu einer offenen Frage des synoptischen Problems*, WUNT. Tübingen: Mohr-Siebeck, 1994.

Erlemann, K. "Papyrus Egerton 2: 'Missing Link' zwischen Synoptischer und Johanneischer Tradition," *NTS* 42 (1996), pp. 12-34.

Evans, C. F. *Saint Luke.* London: SCM Press; Philadelphia: Trinity Press International, 1990.

Farkasfalvy, Denis. "The Presbyter's Witness on the Order of the Gospels as Reported by Clement of Alexandria," *CBQ* 54 (1992), pp. 260-70.

Farmer, W. R. "The Two-Gospel Hypothesis: The Statement of the Hypothesis," in *The Interrelations of the Gospels,* ed. David L. Dungan. Leuven: Leuven University Press, 1990, pp. 125-56.

Farrer, A. M. "On Dispensing with Q," in *Studies in the Gospels: Essays in Memory of R. H. Lightfoot,* ed. D. E. Nineham. Oxford: Blackwell, 1955, pp. 55-88.

Farrow, Douglas, "St. Irenaeus of Lyons: The Church and the World," *Pro Ecclesia* 4 (1995), pp. 333-55.

Fieger, Michael. *Das Thomasevangelium: Einleitung, Kommentar, Systematik.* Münster: Aschendorff, 1991.

Fitzmyer, Joseph A. *The Gospel according to Luke: A New Translation with Introduction and Commentary,* 2 vols., AB. New York: Doubleday, 1981-85.

Fleddermann, H. T. "Mark's Use of Q: The Beelzebul Controversy and the Cross Saying," in *Jesus, Mark, and Q: The Teaching of Jesus and Its Earliest Records,* ed. Michael Labahn and Andreas Schmidt, JSNTSupp. Sheffield: Sheffield Academic Press, 2001, pp. 17-33.

―――. *Q: A Reconstruction and Commentary.* Leuven: Peeters, 2005.

Fortna, Robert T. *The Fourth Gospel and Its Predecessor: From Narrative Source to Present Gospel,* SNTW. Edinburgh: T. & T. Clark, 1988.

Foster, Paul. "Are There Any Early Fragments of the So-Called *Gospel of Peter?*" *NTS* 52 (2006), pp. 1-28.

―――. "The Epistles of Ignatius of Antioch and the Writings That Later Formed the New Testament," in *The Reception of the New Testament in the Apostolic Fathers,* ed. Andrew Gregory and Christopher Tuckett. Oxford: Oxford University Press, 2006, pp. 159-86.

―――. *The Gospel of Peter: Introduction, Critical Edition, and Commentary.* Leiden & Boston: Brill, 2010.

Frey, Jörg. "Die Lilien und das Gewand: *EvThom* 36 und 37 als Paradigma für das Verhältnis des *Thomasevangeliums* zur synoptischen Überlieferung," in *Das Thomasevangelium: Entstehung — Rezeption — Theologie,* ed. J. Frey, E. Popkes, and J. Schröter, BZNW. Berlin & New York: De Gruyter, 2008.

Frey, J., and J. Schröter (eds.). *Jesus in apokryphen Evangelienüberlieferungen,* WUNT. Tübingen: Mohr-Siebeck, 2010.

Frey, J., E. Popkes, and J. Schröter (eds.). *Das Thomasevangelium: Entstehung — Rezeption — Theologie,* BZNW. Berlin & New York: De Gruyter, 2008.

Fuller, R. H. "Christmas, Epiphany, and the Johannine Prologue," in *Spirit and Light: Essays in Historical Theology,* ed. M. L. Engle and W. B. Green. New York: Seabury Press, 1976, pp. 63-73.

Gamble, Harry Y. *The New Testament Canon: Its Making and Meaning.* Philadelphia: Fortress, 1985.

Gathercole, Simon J. *The Composition of the Gospel of Thomas: Original Language and Influences*, SNTSMS. Cambridge: Cambridge University Press, 2012.

———. "Torah, Life, and Salvation: Leviticus 18:5 in Early Judaism and the New Testament," in *From Prophecy to Testament: The Function of the Old Testament in the New*, ed. C. A. Evans and J. A. Sanders. Peabody, MA: Hendrickson, 2004, pp. 131-50.

Gertsman, Elina. "All Roads Lead to Rus: Western Influences on the Eleventh- to Twelfth-Century Manuscript Illumination of Kievan Russia," *Comitatus* 31 (2000), pp. 39-55.

Goodacre, Mark. "*Beyond the Q Impasse* or Down a Blind Alley?" *JSNT* 76 (1999), pp. 33-52.

———. *The Case against Q: Studies in Markan Priority and the Synoptic Problem*. Harrisburg, PA: TPI, 2002.

———. "Fatigue in the Synoptics," *NTS* 44 (1998), pp. 45-58.

———. *Goulder and the Gospels: An Examination of a New Paradigm*, JSNTSupp. Sheffield: Sheffield Academic Press, 1996.

———. "A Monopoly on Markan Priority? Fallacies at the Heart of Q," *SBL Seminar Papers* 2000. Atlanta: SBL, 2000, pp. 538-622.

———. "On Choosing and Using Appropriate Analogies: A Response to F. Gerald Downing," *JSNT* 26 (2003), pp. 237-40.

———. "When Is a Text Not a Text? The Quasi-Text-Critical Approach of the International Q Project," in *Questioning Q*, ed. M. Goodacre and N. Perrin. London: SPCK, 2004; Downers Grove, IL: IVP, 2005, pp. 115-26.

———. "A World without Q," in *Questioning Q*, ed. M. Goodacre and N. Perrin. London: SPCK, 2004; Downers Grove, IL: IVP, 2005, pp. 174-79.

Goodacre, M., and N. Perrin (eds.). *Questioning Q*. London: SPCK, 2004; Downers Grove, IL: IVP, 2005.

Goulder, Michael. "Is Q a Juggernaut?" *JBL* 115 (1996), pp. 667-81.

———. *Luke: A New Paradigm*, 2 vols., JSNTSupp. Sheffield: Sheffield Academic Press, 1989.

———. "Two Significant Minor Agreements (Mat. 4:13 Par.; Mat. 26:67-68 Par.)," *NovT* 45 (2003), pp. 365-73.

Grant, Robert M., with David Noel Freedman. *The Secret Sayings of Jesus according to the Gospel of Thomas*. London & Glasgow: Collins, 1960.

Greeven, H. "The Gospel Synopsis from 1776 to the Present Day," in *J. J. Griesbach: Synoptic and Text-Critical Studies, 1776-1976*, ed. B. Orchard and T. Longstaff, SNTSMS. Cambridge: Cambridge University Press, 1978, pp. 22-49.

Gregory, Andrew. "*1 Clement* and the Writings That Later Formed the New Testament," in *The Reception of the New Testament in the Apostolic Fathers*, ed. A. Gregory and C. Tuckett. Oxford: Oxford University Press, 2005, pp. 129-57.

Gregory, Andrew, and Christopher Tuckett. "*2 Clement* and the Writings That Later Formed the New Testament," in *The Reception of the New Testament in the Apostolic Fathers*, ed. A. Gregory and C. Tuckett. Oxford: Oxford University Press, 2005, pp. 251-92.

————— (eds.). *The Reception of the New Testament in the Apostolic Fathers.* Oxford: Oxford University Press, 2005.

Grigg, Robert. "Constantine the Great and the Cult without Images," *Viator* 8 (1977), pp. 1-32.

Groetsch, Ulrich. "The Miraculous Crossing of the Red Sea: What Lessing and His Opponents during the Fragmentenstreit Did Not See," in *Lessings Religionsphilosophie im Kontext: Hamburger Fragmente und Wolfenbütteler Axiomata*, ed. C. Bultmann and F. Vollhardt. Berlin & New York: De Gruyter, 2011, pp. 181-99.

Gumerlock, Francis X. "Patristic Commentaries on Revelation," *Kerux* 23 (2008), pp. 3-13.

Gwynn, J. "Hippolytus and His 'Heads against Gaius,'" *Hermathena* 6 (1888), pp. 397-418.

Hahneman, Geoffrey M. *The Muratorian Fragment and the Development of the Canon.* Oxford: Clarendon Press, 1992.

Harnack, Adolf von. *Das Neue Testament um das Jahr 200: Theodor Zahn's Geschichte des Neutestamentlichen Kanons.* Freiburg i.B.: J. C. B. Mohr, 1889.

—————. *Sprüche und Reden Jesu: Die zweite Quelle des Matthäus und Lukas.* Leipzig: J. C. Hinrichs, 1907 (Eng. trans. *The Sayings of Jesus: The Second Source of St. Matthew and St. Luke,* London: Williams & Norgate; New York: Putnam, 1908).

—————. *What Is Christianity?* Eng. trans. London: Williams & Norgate; New York: Putnam, 1904³.

Harvey, A. E. *Jesus and the Constraints of History.* London: Duckworth, 1982.

Hawkins, Sir John. *Horae Synopticae: Contributions to the Study of the Synoptic Problem.* Oxford: Clarendon Press, 1909².

Head, Peter M. *Christology and the Synoptic Problem: An Argument for Markan Priority,* SNTSMS. Cambridge: Cambridge University Press, 1997.

—————. "On the Christology of the Gospel of Peter," *VC* 46 (1992), pp. 209-24.

Heckel, Theo K. *Vom Evangelium des Markus zum viergestaltigen Evangelium,* WUNT. Tübingen: Mohr-Siebeck, 1999.

Heine, Ronald E. "Can the Catena Fragments of Origen's Commentary on John Be Trusted?" *VC* 40 (1986), pp. 118-34.

—————. "The Role of the Gospel of John in the Montanist Controversy," *SecC* 6 (1987), pp. 1-19.

Hengel, Martin. *The Four Gospels and the One Gospel of Jesus Christ,* Eng. trans. London: SCM Press, 2000.

—————. *The Johannine Question,* Eng. trans. London: SCM Press, 1989.

—————. *Studies in the Gospel of Mark,* Eng. trans. London: SCM Press, 1985.

Hieke, Thomas, "Methoden und Möglichkeiten griechischer Synopsen zu den ersten drei Evangelien," in *"Wenn drei das gleiche sagen": Studien zu den ersten drei Evangelien,* ed. Stefan H. Brandenburger and Thomas Hieke. Münster, Hamburg, and London: LIT Verlag, 1998, pp. 1-36.

—————. "Das Petrusevangelium vom Alten Testament her gelesen: Gewinnbringende Lektüre eines nicht-kanonischen Textes vom christlichen Kanon her," in *Das Evangelium nach Petrus: Text, Kontexte, Intertexte,* ed. Thomas J. Kraus and Tobias Nicklas. Berlin & New York: De Gruyter, 2007, pp. 91-115.

Hill, Charles E. *The Johannine Corpus in the Early Church.* Oxford: Oxford University Press, 2004.

———. *Who Chose the Gospels? Probing the Great Gospel Conspiracy.* Oxford: Oxford University Press, 2010.

Hirsch, Emanuel. *Geschichte der neuern evangelischen Theologie im Zusammenhang mit den allgemeinen Bewegungen des europäischen Denkens,* 5 vols. Gütersloh: G. Mohn, 1949-54.

Hoek, Annewies van den. "Divergent Gospel Traditions in Clement of Alexandria and Other Authors of the Second Century," *Apocrypha* 7 (1996), pp. 43-62.

Holsinger-Friesen, Thomas. *Irenaeus and Genesis: A Study of Competition in Early Christian Hermeneutics,* JTISupp. Winona Lake, IN: Eisenbrauns, 2009.

Horsley, Richard A., Jonathan A. Draper, and John Miles Foley (eds.). *Performing the Gospel: Orality, Memory, and Mark.* Minneapolis: Fortress, 2006.

Hoskyns, E. C., and F. N. Davey. *The Fourth Gospel,* 2 vols. London: Faber, 1940.

Howard, W. F. *The Fourth Gospel in Recent Criticism and Interpretation.* London: Epworth Press, 1931.

Hübner, R. M. "Melito von Sardes und Noët von Smyrna," in *Oecumenica et Patristica,* ed. D. Papandreou, W. A. Bienert, and K. Schäferdiek. Stuttgart: Kohlhammer, 1989, pp. 219-40.

Hurtado, Larry. *The Earliest Christian Artifacts: Manuscripts and Christian Origins.* Grand Rapids: Eerdmans, 2006.

Ihm, Christa. *Die Programme der christlichen Apsismalerei vom vierten Jahrhundert bis zur Mitte des achten Jahrhunderts.* Wiesbaden: Franz Steiner, 1960.

Jeremias, Joachim. *New Testament Theology,* Eng. trans. London: SCM, 1971.

Johnson, Luke Timothy. *The Gospel of Luke,* Sacra Pagina. Collegeville, MN: Liturgical Press, 1991.

———. *The Real Jesus: The Misguided Quest for the Historical Jesus and the Truth of the Traditional Gospels.* San Francisco: HarperCollins, 1997.

Jonge, H. J. de. "Augustine on the Interrelations of the Gospels," in *The Four Gospels (FS Frans Neirynck),* vol. 3, ed. F. Van Segbroeck. Louvain: Louvain University Press/ Peeters, 1992, pp. 2409-17.

Kannengieser, Charles. *Handbook of Patristic Exegesis: The Bible in Ancient Christianity.* Leiden and Boston: Brill, 2006.

Kantorowicz, E. "The 'King's Advent' and the Enigmatic Panels in the Doors of Santa Sabina," *ArtB* 26 (1944), pp. 207-31.

Karmann, Thomas. "Die Paschahomilie des Melito von Sardes und das Petrusevangelium," in *Das Evangelium nach Petrus: Text, Kontexte, Intertexte,* ed. Thomas J. Kraus and Tobias Nicklas. Berlin & New York: De Gruyter, 2007, pp. 215-35.

Käsemann, Ernst. *Essays on New Testament Themes,* Eng. trans., SBT. London: SCM Press, 1964.

Kelber, Werner H. "In the Beginning Were the Words: The Apotheosis and Narrative Displacement of the Logos," *JAAR* 58 (1990), pp. 69-98.

———. *The Oral and the Written Gospel: The Hermeneutics of Speaking and Writing in the Synoptic Tradition, Mark, Paul, and Q.* Philadelphia: Fortress, 1983[1], 1997[2].

————. "The Oral-Scribal-Memorial Arts of Communication in Early Christianity," in *Jesus, the Voice, and the Text: Beyond the Oral and the Written Gospel,* ed. Tom Thatcher. Waco, TX: Baylor University Press, 2008, pp. 235-62.

———— (ed.). *The Passion in Mark: Studies on Mark 14–16.* Philadelphia: Fortress, 1976.

Kelber, Werner H., and Tom Thatcher. "'It's Not Easy to Take a Fresh Approach': Reflections on *The Oral and the Written Gospel,*" in *Jesus, the Voice, and the Text: Beyond the Oral and the Written Gospel,* ed. Tom Thatcher. Waco, TX: Baylor University Press, 2008, pp. 27-43.

Kelhofer, James A. "'Gospel' as a Literary Title in Early Christianity and the Question of What Is (and Is Not) a 'Gospel' in Canons of Scholarly Literature," in *Jesus in apokryphen Evangelienüberlieferungen,* ed. J. Frey and J. Schröter, WUNT. Tübingen: Mohr-Siebeck, 2010, pp. 399-422.

Kierkegaard, S. *Concluding Unscientific Postscript* [1846], Eng. trans. Princeton: Princeton University Press, 1941.

King, Karen. *The Secret Revelation of John.* Cambridge, MA: Harvard University Press, 2006.

————. *What Is Gnosticism?* Cambridge, MA: Harvard University Press, 2003.

Klauck, H.-J. *The Apocryphal Gospels: An Introduction,* Eng. trans. London & New York: T. & T. Clark, 2003.

Kloppenborg, John. *Excavating Q: The History and Setting of the Sayings Gospel.* Minneapolis: Fortress, 2000.

————. *The Formation of Q: Trajectories in Ancient Wisdom Traditions.* Philadelphia: Fortress, 1987.

————. "On Dispensing with Q? Goodacre on the Relation of Luke to Matthew," *NTS* 48 (2003), pp. 210-36.

————. *Q Parallels Synopsis, Critical Notes and Concordance.* Sonoma, CA: Polebridge, 1988.

————. *Q the Earliest Gospel: An Introduction to the Original Stories and Sayings of Jesus.* Louisville: WJK, 2008.

————. "Variation in the Reproduction of the Double Tradition and an Oral Q?" *ETL* 83 (2007), pp. 49-79.

Koester, Helmut. *Ancient Christian Gospels: Their History and Development.* Philadelphia: Trinity Press International; London: SCM Press, 1990.

————. *From Jesus to the Gospels: Interpreting the New Testament in Its Context.* Minneapolis: Fortress, 2007.

————. *Synoptische Überlieferung bei den Apostolischen Vätern.* Berlin: Akademie-Verlag, 1957.

Körtner, U. H. J. *Papias von Hierapolis,* FRLANT. Göttingen: Vandenhoeck & Ruprecht, 1983.

Kraus, Thomas J., and Tobias Nicklas (eds.). *Das Evangelium nach Petrus: Text, Kontexte, Intertexte.* Berlin & New York: De Gruyter, 2007.

Kraus, Thomas J., Michael J. Kruger, and Tobias Nicklas. *Gospel Fragments,* Oxford Early Christian Gospel Texts. Oxford: Oxford University Press, 2009.

Krautheimer, Richard. "Recent Publications on S. Maria Maggiore in Rome," *AJA* 46 (1942), pp. 373-79.

————. *Three Christian Capitals: Topography and Politics.* Berkeley, Los Angeles, and London: University of California Press, 1983.

Kröger, W. *Das Publikum als Richter: Lessing und die "kleineren Respondenten" im Fragmentenstreit,* Wolfenbütteler Forschungen 5. Nendeln/Liechtenstein: KTO Press, 1979.

Kuhn, Heinz-Wolfgang. *Ältere Sammlungen im Markusevangelium.* Göttingen: Vandenhoeck & Ruprecht, 1971.

Kümmel, W. G. *Introduction to the New Testament,* Eng. trans. London: SCM Press, 1975.

Kürzinger, J. "Das Papiaszeugnis und die Erstgestalt des Matthäusevangeliums," *BZ* 4 (1960), pp. 19-38.

————. "Irenäus und sein Zeugnis zur Sprache des Matthäusevangeliums," *NTS* 10 (1963-64), pp. 108-15.

Kysar, Robert. "Anti-Semitism and the Gospel of John," in *Anti-Semitism and Early Christianity: Issues of Polemic and Faith,* ed. Craig A. Evans and Donald A. Hagner. Minneapolis: Fortress, 1993, pp. 113-27.

Labahn, Michael. *Jesus als Lebensspender: Untersuchungen zu einer Geschichte der johanneischen Tradition anhand ihrer Wundergeschichten,* BZNW. Berlin & New York: De Gruyter, 1999.

Labahn, Michael, and Andreas Schmidt (eds.). *Jesus, Mark, and Q: The Teaching of Jesus and Its Earliest Records,* JSNTSupp. Sheffield: Sheffield Academic Press, 2001.

Lambrecht, Jan. "Die Logia-Quellen von Markus 13," *Bib* 47 (1966), pp. 321-60.

————. "John the Baptist and Jesus in Mark 1.1-15: Markan Redaction of Q?" *NTS* 38 (1992), pp. 357-84.

Lasserre, Guy. *Les synopses: élaboration et usage.* Rome: Pontifical Biblical Institute, 1996.

Lemcio, Eugene E. *The Past of Jesus in the Gospels,* SNTSMS. Cambridge: Cambridge University Press, 1991.

Leonhardt-Balzer, Jutta. "On the Redactional and Theological Relationship between the *Gospel of Thomas* and the *Apocryphon of John,*" in *Das Thomasevangelium: Entstehung — Rezeption — Theologie,* ed. J. Frey, E. E. Popkes, and J. Schröter, BZNW. Berlin & New York: De Gruyter, 2008, pp. 251-71.

Leppin, Volker. "Ein mittelalterlicher Fund für das aktuelle Gespräch. Lessings *Berengarius Turonensis,*" in *Lessings Religionsphilosophie im Kontext: Hamburger Fragmente und Wolfenbütteler Axiomata,* ed. Christoph Bultmann and Friedrich Vollhardt. Berlin & New York: De Gruyter, 2011, pp. 88-10.

Lieu, Judith M. *Neither Jew nor Greek? Constructing Early Christianity.* London & New York: T. & T. Clark, 2002.

Lightfoot, J. B. *The Apostolic Fathers, Part I: S. Clement of Rome,* 2 vols. London: Macmillan, 1885.

Lightfoot, R. H. *St. John's Gospel: A Commentary.* Oxford: Clarendon Press, 1956.

Lincicum, David. *Paul and the Early Jewish Encounter with Deuteronomy,* WUNT. Tübingen: Mohr-Siebeck, 2010.

Lindbeck, George A. *The Nature of Doctrine: Religion and Theology in a Postliberal Age.* London: SPCK, 1984.

Bibliography

Lindemann, A. "Die Logienquelle Q: Fragen an eine gut begründete Hypothese," in *The Sayings Source Q and the Historical Jesus,* ed. A. Lindemann. Leuven: Leuven University Press, 2001, pp. 3-26.

———— (ed.). *The Sayings Source Q and the Historical Jesus.* Leuven: Leuven University Press, 2001.

Logan, Alastair H. B. *The Gnostics: Identifying an Early Christian Cult.* London: T. & T. Clark, 2006.

————. *Gnostic Truth and Christian Heresy: A Study in the History of Gnosticism.* Edinburgh: T. & T. Clark, 1996.

Lohmeyer, Ernst. *Galiläa und Jerusalem.* Göttingen: Vandenhoeck & Ruprecht, 1936.

Löhr, Winrich A. *Basilides und seine Schule,* WUNT. Tübingen: Mohr-Siebeck, 1996.

Loisy, A. *Le Quatrième Évangile.* Paris: Picard, 1903.

Loofs, F. *Theophilus von Antiochien adversus Marcionem und die anderen theologischen Quellen bei Irenaeus,* TU. Leipzig: J. C. Hinrichs, 1930.

Louth, Andrew. "The Date of Eusebius' *Historia Ecclesiastica*," *JTS* 41 (1990), pp. 111-23.

Lowe, Malcolm. "Who Were the ΙΟΥΔΑΙΟΙ?" *NovT* 18 (1976), pp. 101-30.

Lubac, Henri de. *Histoire et esprit: L'Intelligence de l'Écriture d'après Origène.* Paris: Éditions Montaigne, 1950 (Eng. trans. *History and Spirit: The Understanding of Scripture according to Origen,* San Francisco: Ignatius Press, 2007).

Lührmann, Dieter. *Die apokryph gewordenen Evangelien: Studien zum neuen Texten und zu neuen Fragen.* Leiden & Boston: Brill, 2003.

Lundsteen, A. C. *Hermann Samuel Reimarus und die Anfänge der Leben-Jesu-Forschung.* Copenhagen: O. C. Olsen, 1939.

Luomanen, P. "The Jewish-Christian Gospels and the *Gospel of Thomas*," in *Das Thomasevangelium: Entstehung — Rezeption — Theologie,* ed. J. Frey, E. Popkes, and J. Schröter, BZNW. Berlin & New York: De Gruyter, 2008, pp. 119-53.

Luttikhuizen, Gerard P. "The Creation of Man and Woman in *The Secret Book of John,*" in *The Creation of Man and Woman: Interpretations of the Biblical Narratives in Jewish and Christian Traditions,* ed. G. P. Luttikhuizen. Leiden: Brill, 2000.

Luz, Ulrich. *Matthew 1–7: A Commentary,* Hermeneia. Minneapolis: Augsburg Fortress, 1989.

Mackie, Gillian. *Early Christian Chapels in the West: Decoration, Function, and Patronage.* Toronto: University of Toronto Press, 2003.

————. "The Mausoleum of Galla Placidia: A Possible Occupant," *Byzantion* 65 (1995), pp. 396-404.

————. "New Light on the So-Called Saint Lawrence Panel at the Mausoleum of Galla Placidia, Ravenna," *Gesta* 26 (1990), pp. 54-60.

Marcus, Joel. "Crucifixion as Parodic Exaltation," *JBL* 125 (2006), pp. 73-87.

————. *Mark: A New Translation with Introduction and Commentary,* 2 vols., AYB. New Haven & London: Yale University Press, 2000-2009.

Marjanen, Antti. "Is Thomas a Gnostic Gospel?" in *Thomas at the Crossroads: Essays on the Gospel of Thomas,* ed. R. Uro, SNTW. Edinburgh: T. & T. Clark, 1998, pp. 107-39.

Marjanen, Antti, and Petri Luomanen (eds.). *A Companion to Second-Century Christian "Heretics."* Leiden: Brill, 2005.

Markschies, Christoph. *Origenes und sein Erbe: Gesammelte Studien*, TU. Berlin & New York: De Gruyter, 2007.

―――. *Valentinus Gnosticus? Untersuchungen zur valentinianischen Gnosis mit einem Kommentar zu den Fragmenten Valentins*, WUNT. Tübingen: Mohr-Siebeck, 1992.

Marshall, I. Howard. *The Gospel of Luke: A Commentary on the Greek Text*, NIGTC. Exeter: Paternoster, 1978.

Martyn, J. L. *History and Theology in the Fourth Gospel*. New York: Harper & Row, 1968[1].

Marxsen, W. *Introduction to the New Testament*, Eng. trans. Philadelphia: Fortress, 1968.

―――. *Mark the Evangelist: Studies on the Redaction History of the Gospel*, Eng. trans. Nashville: Abingdon Press, 1969.

Mathews, Thomas F. *The Clash of Gods: A Reinterpretation of Early Christian Art.* Princeton: Princeton University Press, 2003[2].

Matson, Mark A. "Luke's Rewriting of the Sermon on the Mount," in *Questioning Q*, ed. M. Goodacre and N. Perrin. London: SPCK, 2004; Downers Grove, IL: IVP, 2005, pp. 43-70.

Mayeda, G. *Das Leben-Jesu-Fragment Papyrus Egerton 2 und seine Stellung in der urchristlichen Literaturgeschichte*. Bern: P. Haupt, 1946.

McCant, Jerry W. "The Gospel of Peter: Docetism Reconsidered," *NTS* 30 (1984), pp. 258-73.

McGuckin, J. A. "Structural Design and Apologetic Intent in Origen's *Commentary on John*," in *Origeniana Sexta: Origène et la Bible/Origen and the Bible*, ed. G. Dorival and A. Le Boulluec, BEThL 118. Leuven: Peeters, 1995, pp. 441-57.

McNicol, Allan J., with David L. Dungan and David B. Peabody (eds.). *Beyond the Q Impasse — Luke's Use of Matthew: A Demonstration by the Research Team of the International Institute for Gospel Studies*. Valley Forge, PA: Trinity Press International, 1996.

Meeks, Wayne. "Hypomnemata from an Untamed Sceptic: A Response to George Kennedy," in *The Relationships between the Gospels: An Interdisciplinary Dialogue*, ed. William O. Walker. San Antonio: Trinity University Press, 1978, pp. 157-72.

Meier, John P. *A Marginal Jew: Rethinking the Historical Jesus*, vol. 1. New York: Doubleday, 1991.

Merkel, H. *Die Pluralität der Evangelien als theologisches und exegetisches Problem in der Alten Kirche*. Bern: Lang, 1978.

―――. "Die Überlieferung der Alten Kirche über das Verhältnis der Evangelien," in *The Interrelations of the Gospels*, ed. David L. Dungan. Leuven: Leuven University Press, 1990, pp. 566-90.

―――. *Die Widersprüche zwischen den Evangelien: Ihre polemische und apologetische Behandlung in der Alten Kirche bis zu Augustin*, WUNT. Tübingen: Mohr-Siebeck, 1971.

Metzger, Bruce M. *The Canon of the New Testament: Its Origin, Development, and Significance.* Oxford: Clarendon Press, 1987.

Michalson, G. E. "Lessing, Kierkegaard, and the 'Ugly Ditch': A Reexamination," *JR* 59 (1979), pp. 324-34.

————. *Lessing's "Ugly Ditch": A Study of Theology and History.* University Park: Pennsylvania State University Press, 1986.

Milgrom, Jacob. *Leviticus 23–27*, AB. New York: Doubleday, 2000.

Minnen, Peter van. "The Akhmîm *Gospel of Peter*," in *Das Evangelium nach Petrus: Text, Kontexte, Intertexte,* ed. Thomas J. Kraus and Tobias Nicklas. Berlin & New York: De Gruyter, 2007, pp. 53-60.

Mitchell, Margaret. "Patristic Counter-Evidence to the Claim That 'The Gospels Were Written for All Christians,'" *NTS* 51 (2005), pp. 36-79.

Moberly, R. W. L. "Theological Interpretation, Presuppositions, and the Role of the Church: Bultmann and Augustine Revisited," *JTI* 5 (2011-12), pp. 1-22.

Molland, E. *The Conception of the Gospel in the Alexandrian Theology.* Oslo: Jacob Dybwad, 1938.

Monaci Castagno, A. "Origene e Ambrogio: L'indipendenza dell' intellettuale e le pretese del patronato," in *Origeniana Octava,* ed. L. Perrone, BEThL. Leuven: Peeters, 2004, pp. 165-93.

Moreland, M. "*Thomas* 52 as Critique of Early Christian Hermeneutics," in *Thomasine Traditions in Antiquity: The Social and Cultural World of the Gospel of Thomas,* ed. Jon M. A. Asgeirsson, April D. DeConick, and Risto Uro. Leiden & Boston: Brill, 2006, pp. 75-91.

Murray, Sr. Charles. "Art and the Early Church," *JTS,* n.s., 28 (1977), pp. 304-45.

Nautin, Pierre. *Origène: sa vie et son oeuvre.* Paris: Beauchesne, 1977.

Neirynck, Frans. "Matthew 4:23–5:2 and the Matthean Composition of 4:23–11:1," in *The Interrelations of the Gospels,* ed. David L. Dungan. Leuven: Leuven University Press, 1990, pp. 23-46.

————. "Papyrus Egerton 2 and the Healing of the Leper," in his *Evangelica 2: Collected Essays, 1982-1991,* BEThL 99. Leuven: Peeters, 1991, pp. 773-83.

————. *Q-Synopsis: The Double Tradition Passages in Greek.* Leuven: Leuven University Press, 1995².

Nicklas, T. "The 'Unknown Gospel' on *P. Egerton* 2," in *Gospel Fragments,* ed. Thomas J. Kraus, Michael J. Kruger, and Tobias Nicklas, Oxford Early Christian Gospel Texts. Oxford: Oxford University Press, 2009.

Nienhuis, David R. *Not by Paul Alone: The Formation of the Catholic Epistle Collection and the Christian Canon.* Waco, TX: Baylor University Press, 2007.

Nisbet, Hugh Barr. *Lessing: Eine Biographie.* Munich: C. H. Beck, 2008.

Norelli, Enrico. "Le Papyrus *Egerton* 2 et sa localisation dans la tradition sur Jésus," in *Jésus de Nazareth: Nouvelles approches d'une enigme,* ed. D. Marguerat. Geneva: Labor et Fides, 1998, pp. 397-435.

Norris, Richard A. "Irenaeus of Lyons," in *The Cambridge History of Early Christian Literature,* ed. Frances Young, Lewis Ayres, and Andrew Louth. Cambridge: Cambridge University Press, 2004, pp. 45-52.

Oost, Stewart. *Galla Placidia: A Biographical Essay.* Chicago and London: University of Chicago Press, 1968.

Orchard, Bernard. "Are All Gospel Synopses Biased?" *ThZ* 34 (1978), pp. 149-62.

Orchard, Bernard, and Thomas R. W. Longstaff (eds.). *J. J. Griesbach: Synoptic and*

Text-Critical Studies, 1776-1976, SNTSMS. Cambridge: Cambridge University Press, 1978.

Pagels, Elaine. *Beyond Belief: The Secret Gospel of Thomas.* New York: Random House, 2003.

———. "Irenaeus, the 'Canon of Truth,' and the *Gospel of John*: 'Making a Difference' through Hermeneutics and Ritual," *VC* 56 (2002), pp. 339-71.

Pearson, Birger A. *Gnosticism and Christianity in Roman and Coptic Egypt.* New York & London: T. & T. Clark International, 2004.

Penna, Angelo. "Il 'De Consensu Evangelistarum' ed i 'canoni eusebiani,'" *Bib* 36 (1955), pp. 1-19.

Perkins, P. "Irenaeus and the Gnostics: Rhetoric and Composition in *Adversus Haereses* Book One," *VC* 30 (1976), pp. 193-200.

Perrin, Nicholas. *Thomas, the Other Gospel.* London: SPCK, 2007.

———. *Thomas and Tatian: The Relationship between the Gospel of Thomas and the Diatessaron.* Atlanta: SBL, 2002.

Perrin, Norman. *The New Testament: An Introduction.* New York: Harcourt Brace Jovanovich, 1982².

Petersen, William L. *Tatian's Diatessaron: Its Creation, Dissemination, Significance, and History in Scholarship*, VCSupp. Leiden: Brill, 1994.

———. "Textual Evidence of Tatian's Dependence on Justin's ΑΠΟΜΝΗΜΟΝΕΥ-ΜΑΤΑ," *NTS* 36 (1990), pp. 512-34.

Peterson, Silke. "Die Evangelienüberschriften und die Entstehung des neutestament-lichen Kanons," *ZNW* 97 (2006), pp. 250-74.

Pilhofer, P. "Justin und das Petrusevangelium," *ZNW* 81 (1990), pp. 60-78.

Piper, Ronald A. "The Characterisation of Pilate and the Death of Jesus in the Fourth Gospel," in *The Death of Jesus in the Fourth Gospel*, ed. G. van Belle, BEThL. Leuven: Leuven University Press, 2007, pp. 121-62.

Pitassi, Maria Cristina. *Entre croire et savoir: Le problème de la méthode critique chez Jean Le Clerc.* Leiden: Brill, 1987.

Polag, Athanasius. *Fragmente Q: Textheft zur Logienquelle.* Neukirchen-Vluyn: Neukirchener Verlag, 1979.

Popkes, Enno. "The Image Character of Human Existence: GThom 83 and GThom 84 as Core Texts of the Anthropology of the *Gospel of Thomas*," in *Das Thomas-evangelium: Entstehung — Rezeption — Theologie*, ed. J. Frey, E. Popkes, and J. Schröter, BZNW. Berlin & New York: De Gruyter, 2008, pp. 416-34.

———. *Das Menschenbild des Thomasevangeliums: Studien zu seiner religionsgeschicht-lichen und theologischen Einordnung*, WUNT. Tübingen: Mohr-Siebeck, 2007.

Pryor, John W. "Papyrus Egerton and the Fourth Gospel," *ABR* 37 (1989), pp. 1-13.

Quispel, G. "'The Gospel of Thomas' and the 'Gospel of the Hebrews,'" *NTS* 12 (1965-66), pp. 371-82.

———. *Makarius, das Thomasevangelium und das Lied von der Perle*, NovTSupp. Leiden: Brill, 1967.

———. "Some Remarks on the Gospel of Thomas," *NTS* 5 (1958-59), pp. 276-90.

Rae, Murray. *History and Hermeneutics.* London and New York: T. & T. Clark, 2005.

Reicke, B. "Griesbach's Answer to the Synoptic Question," in *J. J. Griesbach*, ed. B. Orchard and T. Langstaff, SNTSMS. Cambridge: Cambridge University Press, 1978, pp. 50-67.

―――. "Synoptic Problem," in *Dictionary of Biblical Interpretation,* ed. John Hayes. Nashville: Abingdon Press, 1999, vol. 2, pp. 517-24.

Reinhartz, Adele. "The Johannine Community and Its Neighbors: A Reappraisal," in *What Is John? Volume II: Literary and Social Readings of the Fourth Gospel,* ed. Fernando F. Segovia, SBLSS. Atlanta: Scholars Press, 1998, pp. 111-38.

Rendel Harris, J. "Presbyter Gaius and the Fourth Gospel," in his *Hermas in Arcadia and Other Essays.* Cambridge: Cambridge University Press, 1896, pp. 43-57.

Reventlow, H. Graf von. "Das Arsenal der Bibelkritik des Reimarus: Die Auslegung der Bibel, insbesondere des Alten Testaments, bei den englischen Deisten," in *Hermann Samuel Reimarus (1694-1768): Ein "bekannter Unbekannter" der Aufklärung in Hamburg,* Joachim Jungius Gesellschaft der Wissenschaften. Hamburg & Göttingen: Vandenhoeck & Ruprecht, 1973, pp. 44-65.

Rhoads, David, and Donald Michie. *Mark as Story: An Introduction to the Narrative of a Gospel.* Philadelphia: Fortress, 1982.

Robinson, James M. "The Critical Edition of Q and the Study of Jesus," in *The Sayings Source Q and the Historical Jesus,* ed. A. Lindemann. Leuven: Leuven University Press, 2001, pp. 27-52.

―――. "History of Q Research," in *The Critical Edition of Q,* ed. James M. Robinson, Paul Hoffmann, John S. Kloppenborg. Minneapolis: Fortress, 2000, pp. xx-lxxi.

―――. *The Sayings Gospel Q: Collected Essays.* Leuven: Leuven University Press, 2005.

Robinson, James M., Paul Hoffmann, and John S. Kloppenborg (eds.). *The Critical Edition of Q.* Minneapolis: Fortress, 2000.

Robinson, T. H. "The Authorship of the *Muratorian Canon,*" *The Expositor 7* (1906), pp. 481-95.

Ruwet, J., S.J. "Clement d'Alexandrie: Canon des écritures et apocryphes," *Bib* 29 (1948), pp. 77-99, 240-68, 391-408.

Sabbe, Maurits. "The Trial of Jesus before Pilate in John and Its Relation to the Synoptic Gospels," in *John and the Synoptics,* ed. Adelbert Denaux, BEThL. Leiden: Leiden University Press, 1992, pp. 341-85.

Sanday, William. *The Criticism of the Fourth Gospel.* Oxford: Clarendon Press, 1905.

Sanders, E. P., and Margaret Davies. *Studying the Synoptic Gospels.* London: SCM Press, 1989.

Schaberg, Jane. *The Illegitimacy of Jesus: A Feminist Theological Interpretation of the Infancy Narratives.* Sheffield: Sheffield Academic Press, 1995.

Schenck, W. *Synopse zur Redenquelle der Evangelien.* Düsseldorf: Patmos Verlag, 1978.

Schenke, Gesa. "Das Erscheinen Jesu vor den Jüngern und der ungläubige Thomas: Johannes 20, 19-31," in *Coptica-Gnostica-Manichaica: Mélanges offerts à Wolf-Peter Funk,* ed. Louis Painchaud and Paul-Hubert Poirier. Louvain: Peeters; Quebec: Les Presses de L'Université Laval, 2006, pp. 893-904.

Schenke, H.-M. *Das Matthäus-Evangelium im mittelägyptischen Dialekt des Koptischen (Codex Schøyen),* Coptic Papyri in the Schøyen Collection I. Oslo: Hermes Publishing, 2001.

―――. "The Phenomenon and Significance of Gnostic Sethianism," in *The Rediscov-*

ery of Gnosticism: Proceedings of the International Conference at Yale, New Haven, Connecticut, March 28-31, 1978, vol. 2, *Sethian Gnosticism,* ed. B. Layton. Leiden: Brill, 1981, pp. 588-616.

Schlatter, Fredric W., S.J. "Interpreting the Mosaic of Santa Pudenziana," *VC* 46 (1992), pp. 276-95.

――――. "A Mosaic Interpretation of Jerome, *In Hiezechielem,*" *VC* 49 (1995), pp. 64-81.

――――. "The Text in the Mosaic of Santa Pudenziana," *VC* 43 (1989), pp. 155-65.

――――. "The Two Women in the Mosaic of Santa Pudenziana," *JECS* 3 (1995), pp. 1-24.

Schmidt-Biggemann, W. *Hermann Samuel Reimarus: Handschriften Verzeichnis und Bibliographie.* Göttingen: Vandenhoeck & Ruprecht, 1979.

Schnackenburg, R. *The Gospel according to John,* 3 vols., Eng. trans. London: Burns & Oates, 1968-82.

Schneider, Gerhard. "The Political Charge against Jesus (Luke 23:2)," in *Jesus and the Politics of His Day,* ed. E. Bammel and C. F. D. Moule. Cambridge: Cambridge University Press, 1984, pp. 403-14.

Schrage, W. *Das Verhältnis des Thomas-Evangeliums zur synoptischen Tradition und zu den koptischen Evangelienübersetzungen.* Berlin: Töpelmann, 1964.

Schröter, Jens. "Die apokryphen Evangelien und die Entstehung des neutestamentlichen Kanons," in *Jesus in apokryphen Evangelienüberlieferungen,* ed. J. Frey and J. Schröter, WUNT. Tübingen: Mohr-Siebeck, 2010, pp. 31-60.

――――. *Erinnerung an Jesu Worte: Studien zur Rezeption der Logienüberlieferung in Markus, Q und Thomas,* WMANT. Neukirchen-Vluyn: Neukirchener Verlag, 1997.

――――. "Die Frage nach dem historischen Jesus und der Charakter historischer Erkenntnis," in *The Sayings Source Q and the Historical Jesus,* ed. A. Lindemann. Leuven: Leuven University Press, 2001, pp. 207-54.

Schweitzer, Albert. *Aus meinem Leben und Denken.* Leipzig: Felix Meiner, 1931.

――――. *Geschichte der Leben-Jesu-Forschung.* Tübingen: Mohr-Siebeck, 1913² (Eng. trans. *The Quest of the Historical Jesus: First Complete Edition,* London: SCM Press, 2000).

――――. *The Quest of the Historical Jesus: A Critical Study of Its Progress from Reimarus to Wrede,* trans. W. Montgomery. London: A. & C. Black, 1910¹ (German original, *Von Reimarus zu Wrede: Eine Geschichte der Leben-Jesu-Forschung,* Tübingen: J. C. B. Mohr [Paul Siebeck], 1906¹).

Sieger, Joanne Deane. "Visual Theology as Metaphor: Leo the Great's Sermons on the Incarnation and the Arch Mosaics at S. Maria Maggiore," *Gesta* 26 (1987), pp. 83-91.

Sivan, Hagith. *Galla Placidia: The Last Roman Empress.* Oxford: Oxford University Press, 2011.

Smith, Joseph D. "Gaius and the Controversy over the Johannine Literature." Ph.D. diss., Yale University, 1979.

Snyder, James. "The Mosaic in Santa Maria Nova and the Original Apse Decoration of Santa Maria Maggiore," in *Hortus Imaginum: Essays in Western Art,* ed. Robert Enggass and Marilyn Stokstad. Lawrence: University Press of Kansas, 1974, pp. 1-10.

Souter, A. *The Text and Canon of the New Testament.* New York: Scribner, 1913.

Bibliography

Spain, S. "'The Promised Blessing': The Iconography of the Mosaics of S. Maria Maggiore," *ArtB* 61 (1979), pp. 518-40.

Spalding, Almut. *Elise Reimarus (1735-1805), the Muse of Hamburg: A Woman of the German Enlightenment.* Würzburg: Königshausen & Neumann, 2005.

Spieser, J.-M. "The Representation of Christ in the Apses of Early Christian Churches," *Gesta* 37 (1998), pp. 63-73.

Sprinkle, Preston M. *Law and Life: The Interpretation of Leviticus 18:5 in Early Judaism and in Paul,* WUNT. Tübingen: Mohr-Siebeck, 2008.

Stanton, Graham N. *The Gospels and Jesus.* Oxford: Oxford University Press, 1989.

Steiger, Lothar. "Die 'gymnastische' Wahrheitfrage: Lessing und Goeze," *EvTh* 43 (1983), pp. 430-45.

Stibbe, Mark. "The Elusive Christ: A New Reading of the Fourth Gospel," *JSNT* 44 (1991), pp. 19-38.

Strauss, David Friedrich. *Hermann Samuel Reimarus und seine Schutzschrift für die vernünftigen Verehrer Gottes.* 1862; repr. Hildesheim: Georg Olms Verlag, 1991.

Strecker, G. "Eine Evangelienharmonie bei Justin und Pseudoklemens?" *NTS* 24 (1977-78), pp. 297-316.

——— (ed.). *Minor Agreements: Symposion Göttingen 1991.* Göttingen: Vandenhoeck & Ruprecht, 1993.

Streeter, B. H. *The Four Gospels.* New York: Macmillan, 1925,

———. "St. Mark's Knowledge and Use of Q," in *Oxford Studies in the Synoptic Problem,* ed. W. Sanday. Oxford: Clarendon Press, 1911, pp. 165-83.

Strycker, É. de. *La forme la plus ancienne du Protévangile de Jacques.* Brussels: Société des Bollandistes, 1961.

Sundberg, Albert C. "Canon Muratori: A Fourth Century List," *HTR* 66 (1973), pp. 1-41.

Swanson, Reuben J. (ed.). *New Testament Greek Manuscripts: Variant Readings Arranged in Horizontal Lines against Codex Vaticanus: Acts.* Sheffield: Sheffield Academic Press; Pasadena, CA: William Carey International University Press, 1998.

———. *New Testament Greek Manuscripts: Variant Readings Arranged in Horizontal Lines against Codex Vaticanus: John.* Sheffield: Sheffield Academic Press; Pasadena, CA: William Carey International University Press, 1995.

———. *New Testament Greek Manuscripts: Variant Readings Arranged in Horizontal Lines against Codex Vaticanus: Luke.* Sheffield: Sheffield Academic Press; Pasadena, CA: William Carey International University Press, 1995.

———. *New Testament Greek Manuscripts: Variant Readings Arranged in Horizontal Lines against Codex Vaticanus: Mark.* Sheffield: Sheffield Academic Press; Pasadena, CA: William Carey International University Press, 1995.

———. *New Testament Greek Manuscripts: Variant Readings Arranged in Horizontal Lines against Codex Vaticanus: Matthew.* Sheffield: Sheffield Academic Press; Pasadena, CA: William Carey International University Press, 1995.

Swete, H. B. *The Apocalypse of St. John.* London: Macmillan, 1911³.

———. *The Gospel according to St. Mark.* London: Macmillan, 1920³.

Talbert, Charles H. *Reading Luke: A Literary and Theological Commentary on the Third Gospel.* New York: Crossroad, 1982.

Tannehill, Robert C. *The Narrative Unity of Luke-Acts: A Literary Interpretation. Volume 1: The Gospel according to Luke*. Philadelphia: Fortress, 1986.

Telford, W. R. *Writing on the Gospel of Mark*. Blandford Forum: Deo Publishing, 2009

Thatcher, Tom. "Reflections on *The Oral and the Written Gospel*," in *Jesus, the Voice, and the Text: Beyond the Oral and the Written Gospel*, ed. T. Thatcher. Waco, TX: Baylor University Press, 2008.

Theissen, Gerd. "Historical Scepticism and the Criteria of Jesus Research, or, My Attempt to Leap across Lessing's Yawning Gulf," *SJT* 49 (1996), pp. 147-76.

Thornton, C.-J. "Justin und das Markusevangelium," *ZNW* 84 (1993), pp. 93-110.

Tillich, Paul. *Systematic Theology 2: Existence and the Christ*. Chicago: University of Chicago Press, 1957.

Trevett, Christine. *Montanism: Gender, Authority, and the New Prophecy*. Cambridge: Cambridge University Press, 1996.

Trobisch, David. *The First Edition of the New Testament*. Oxford: Oxford University Press, 2000, pp. 38-43.

Tuckett, Christopher. *Q and the History of Early Christianity*. Edinburgh: T. & T. Clark, 1996.

———. *The Revival of the Griesbach Hypothesis: An Analysis and Appraisal*, SNTSMS. Cambridge: Cambridge University Press, 1983.

Uro, Risto. *Thomas: Seeking the Historical Context of the Gospel of Thomas*. London & New York: T. & T. Clark, 2003.

———. "*Thomas* and Oral Gospel Tradition," in *Thomas at the Crossroads: Essays on the Gospel of Thomas*, ed. R. Uro, SNTW. Edinburgh: T. & T. Clark, 1998, pp. 8-32.

——— (ed.). *Thomas at the Crossroads: Essays on the Gospel of Thomas*, SNTW. Edinburgh: T. & T. Clark, 1998.

Vaganay, L. *L'Évangile de Pierre*. Paris: Librairie Lecoffre, 1930.

Valantasis, Richard. *The Gospel of Thomas*. London & New York: Routledge, 1997.

Verheyden, Joseph. "The Canon Muratori: A Matter of Dispute," in *The Biblical Canons*, ed. J.-M. Auwers and H. J. de Jonge, BEThL 163. Leiden: Peeters, 2003, pp. 487-556.

Vogels, Heinrich Joseph. *St Augustins Schrift De Consensu Evangelistarum unter vornehmlicher Berücksichtigung ihrer harmonistischen Anschauungen*. Freiburg i.B.: Herdersche Verlagshandlung, 1908.

Voigt, Christopher. *Der englische Deismus in Deutschland. Eine Studie zur Rezeption english-deistischer Literatur in deutschen Zeitschriften und Kompendien des 18. Jahrhundert*, BHT. Tübingen: Mohr-Siebeck, 2003.

Wahlde, Urban von. "The Terms for Religious Authorities in the Fourth Gospel: A Key to Literary Strata?" *JBL* 98 (1979), pp. 231-53.

Watson, Francis. "Beyond Suspicion: On the Authorship of the Mar Saba Letter and the Secret Gospel of Mark," *JTS*, n.s., 61 (2010), pp. 128-70.

———. "Eschatology and the Twentieth Century: On the Reception of Schweitzer in English," in *Eschatologie/Eschatology: The Sixth Durham-Tübingen Research Symposium: Eschatology in Old Testament, Ancient Judaism, and Early Christianity*, ed. H.-J. Eckstein, C. Landmesser, and H. Lichtenberger. Tübingen: Mohr-Siebeck, 2011, pp. 331-47.

————. "The Fourfold Gospel," in *The Cambridge Companion to the Gospels*, ed. Stephen C. Barton. Cambridge: Cambridge University Press, 2006, pp. 34-52.

————. " 'I Received from the Lord . . .': Paul, Jesus and the Last Supper," in *Jesus and Paul Reconnected*, ed. Todd D. Still. Grand Rapids: Eerdmans, 2007, pp. 103-24.

————. "Is John's Christology Adoptionist?" in *The Glory of Christ in the New Testament: Studies in Christology in Memory of George Bradford Caird*, ed. L. D. Hurst and N. T. Wright. Oxford: Clarendon Press, 1987, pp. 113-24.

————. *Paul, Judaism, and the Gentiles: Beyond the New Perspective.* Grand Rapids: Eerdmans, 2007².

————. *Paul and the Hermeneutics of Faith.* London & New York: T. & T. Clark International, 2004.

————. "Paul the Reader: An Authorial Apologia," *JSNT* 28 (2006), pp. 363-73.

————. "Q as Hypothesis: A Study in Methodology," *NTS* 55 (2009), pp. 397-415.

————. *Text, Church, and World: Biblical Interpretation in Theological Perspective.* Edinburgh: T. & T. Clark; Grand Rapids: Eerdmans, 1994.

————. *Text and Truth: Redefining Biblical Theology.* Edinburgh: T. & T. Clark; Grand Rapids: Eerdmans, 1997.

Webb, Robert L. "Jesus Heals a Leper: Mark 1.40-45 and *Egerton Gospel* 35-47," *JSHJ* 4 (2006), pp. 177-202.

Webster, John. *Holy Scripture: A Dogmatic Sketch.* Cambridge: Cambridge University Press, 2003.

Weinrich, William C. *Ancient Christian Commentary on Scripture, New Testament XII: Revelation.* Downers Grove, IL: IVP, 2005.

Weiss, Herold. "The Sabbath in the Fourth Gospel," *JBL* 110 (1991), pp. 311-21.

Weiss, Johannes. *Die Predigt Jesu vom Reiche Gottes.* Göttingen: Vandenhoeck & Ruprecht, 1892 (Eng. trans. *Jesus' Proclamation of the Kingdom of God* [1892¹], ed. R. H. Hiers and D. L. Holland, London: SCM Press, 1971).

Wellhausen, Julius. *Einleitung in die ersten drei Evangelien.* Berlin: Georg Reimer, 1911² (repr. in J. Wellhausen, *Evangelienkommentare*, Berlin: De Gruyter, 1987, pp. 1-176).

————. *Das Evangelium Marci Übersetzt und Erklärt,* Berlin: Georg Reimer, 1909² (repr. in J. Wellhausen, *Evangelienkommentare*, Berlin: De Gruyter, 1987, pp. 321-457).

Werner, Martin. "The Four Symbols Page in the Book of Durrow," *Gesta* 8 (1969), pp. 3-17.

Wernle, Paul. *Die Synoptische Frage.* Tübingen: J. C. B. Mohr, 1899.

Westcott, B. F. *The Gospel according to St. John.* London: John Murray, 1887.

Williams, Michael A. *Rethinking "Gnosticism": An Argument for Dismantling a Dubious Category.* Princeton: Princeton University Press, 1996.

Wisse, F. "The Nag Hammadi Library and the Heresiologists," *VC* 25 (1971), pp. 205-23.

Wolff, C. *Der erste Brief des Paulus an die Korinther,* ThHKNT 7/II. Berlin: Evangelische Verlagsanstalt, 1982.

Wright, N. T. *Jesus and the Victory of God.* London: SPCK, 1996.

Yashikata, Toshimasa. *Lessing's Philosophy of Religion and the German Enlightenment.* Oxford: Oxford University Press, 2002.

Young, Francis M. *From Nicaea to Chalcedon: A Guide to the Literature and Its Background.* London: SCM Press, 1983.

Zahn, Theodor. *Einleitung in das Neue Testament,* vol. 2. Leipzig: Deichert, 1899.

———. *Forschungen zur Geschichte des neutestamentlichen Kanons und der altkirchlichen Literatur,* II. Erlangen: Deichert, 1883.

Index of Patristic Authors

Index of Modern Authors

Alexander, Loveday, 122n.13, 170n.26
Allison, D. C., 88n.99, 126n.27, 134n.42,
  150n.74, 161n.7, 163n.15, 167n.22,
  189n.45, 207n.83, 373n.60, 374n.64
Altaner, Berthold, 24n.40
Annet, Peter, 75n.54
Ashton, John, 289n.2, 327, 328n.86
Assmann, Jan, 353n.24
Asso, Cecilia, 44n.83
Attrige, Harold, 336n.98, 529n.57
d'Auzoles à la Peyre, Jacobus, 53n.109

Baarda, Tjitze, 430n.70
Badger, G. P., 481n.125
Baracchini, M., 585n.83
Barr, James, 618n.13
Barrett, C. K., 294n.25, 317n.67, 333n.94,
  362n.47, 391n.92, 526n.49
Barton, John, 616n.11
Bauckham, Richard, 121n.9, 122n.13,
  124n.18, 126n.25, 128n.31, 230n.45,
  281n.185, 349-50, 351n.17, 416n.23,
  445n.141, 463n.43, 464n.48, 470n.74
Bauer, Walter, 526n.49, 543n.95
Baum, A. D., 126n.26, 273n.173
Beale, G. K., 559n.14
Beaton, Richard C., 457n.19
Bell, H. Idris, 290-93, 301n.36, 305n.44,
  306n.46, 307n.48, 310n.54, 316n.63, 321

Bellinzoni, A. J., 263n.139, 264n.144,
  474n.98
Bernard, J. H., 336n.98, 391n.91
Bienert, W. A., 527n.52
Bishop, William Warner, 599n.126
Black, C. Clifton, 16n.9
Bludau, August, 477n.114, 480n.124,
  488n.151
Bockmuehl, Markus, 617n.12
Bollacher, Martin, 63n.2, 68n.23
Bovini, G., 579n.73, 582n.81
Bovon, François, 143n.61, 189n.44,
  195n.57, 203n.76
Brenk, Beat, 557n.13, 565n.27, 566n.30,
  567n.32, 587n.88, 587n.91, 590, 592,
  594n.113, 595, 596n.116, 596n.118,
  601n.129
Brent, Allen, 477n.114, 480n.121, 481n.126,
  482n.128, 486n.141, 489n.156
Brooks, James E., 430n.74
Brown, Raymond, 132-33, 142n.58,
  294n.25, 357n.31, 374n.63, 376n.67,
  405n.110, 526-27
Bultmann, Rudolf, 147n.68, 275n.175,
  276n.177, 280n.183, 336n.98, 344n.1,
  344n.2, 345n.2, 346n.5, 351, 372n.56,
  374n.62, 391n.92, 403n.108, 464n.47
Burkitt, F. C., 18n.14
Burridge, Richard, 206n.82

647

Index of Subjects

Index of Scripture and Other Ancient Texts